A 21ST CENTURY
ETHICAL TOOLBOX

ANTHONY WESTON

THIRD EDITION

New York   Oxford
OXFORD UNIVERSITY PRESS

Oxford University Press, Inc., publishes works that further Oxford University's
objective of excellence in research, scholarship, and education.

Oxford   New York
Auckland   Cape Town   Dar es Salaam   Hong Kong   Karachi
Kuala Lumpur   Madrid   Melbourne   Mexico City   Nairobi
New Delhi   Shanghai   Taipei   Toronto

With offices in
Argentina   Austria   Brazil   Chile   Czech Republic   France   Greece
Guatemala   Hungary   Italy   Japan   Poland   Portugal   Singapore
South Korea   Switzerland   Thailand   Turkey   Ukraine   Vietnam

Copyright © 2013, 2008, and 2001 by Oxford University Press.

For titles covered by Section 112 of the US Higher Education
Opportunity Act, please visit www.oup.com/us/he for the latest
information about pricing and alternate formats.

Published by Oxford University Press.
198 Madison Avenue, New York, New York 10016
www.oup.com

Oxford is a registered trademark of Oxford University Press.

All rights reserved. No part of this publication may be reproduced,
stored in a retrieval system, or transmitted, in any form or by any means,
electronic, mechanical, photocopying, recording, or otherwise,
without the prior permission of Oxford University Press.

Library of Congress Cataloging-in-Publication Data

Weston, Anthony, 1954–
    A 21st century ethical toolbox / Anthony Weston.—3rd ed.
        p. cm.
    Includes bibliographical references.
    ISBN 978-0-19-975881-4
    1. Ethics.   2. Applied ethics.   I. Title.   II. Title: Twenty-first century ethical toolbox.
    BJ1012.W447 2013
    170—dc23   2012039477

Printing number: 9 8 7 6 5 4 3 2

Printed in the United States of America
on acid-free paper

CONTENTS

PREFACE

A 21ˢᵗ Century Ethical Toolbox is a textbook for a college ethics or applied ethics course with applications in any course that ventures into practical ethical issues. Its most basic aim is to enable its users to make a more constructive difference, in both word and deed, in problematic ethical situations. To do so requires, as you will see, a wide range of skills. We all need those skills, and we need them all—daily, it seems, we need them more—in the life of community and state, in raising families and on the job, as well as across the range of practical ethical work, from the law, the ministry, and community service to medicine, the service professions, teaching at all levels, and just plain good citizenship.

In service of that aim, you will find here a wide range of topics, from a careful survey of moral values to tools for critical, creative, and constructive thinking, moral vision, making a real difference, and finally the future of ethics itself. You will also encounter a wide range of writers, from ancient Greek and Chinese philosophers to contemporary college students, famous novelists, cranks, prophets, Nobel Peace Prize winners, unsung community activists, architects, some provocative contemporary philosophers, and others too. Good company. I hope you find this book a rewarding, inspiring, and consistently useful resource—a good toolbox indeed.

Dozens of introductory ethics textbooks are available. Mostly they distinguish themselves in subtle ways: a slightly different selection of theories here, a little more history or a more multicultural perspective there. Each approach is important and useful. For better or worse, though, this text differs from the others in bigger and bolder ways.

First, every theme introduced here is directly in service of an improved ethical intelligence and through it of an engaged and enabled moral practice. Other skills often lovingly inculcated in ethics courses, such as theory building and argumentative skills, do come up, but only in the way that music theory might come up in a piano course. We're really here, as it were, to make music.

Second, a far wider range of skills are offered in this book than in traditional ethics texts. Problem-solving creativity may be as crucial to ethical intelligence as responsiveness to values and the analytical and critical skills usually featured in ethics courses. Finding the facts, taking care with the shape of our very speech itself, moral vision and imagination, learning how to "break out of the box" that reduces so many ethical problems to dilemmas between two sharply opposed and supposedly exhaustive options—all have their place here.

Contentious issues are likewise approached with a reconstructive intent. The familiar controversies are here—abortion, animals, sex, environment, social justice—as well as some that will be less familiar. But the familiar points of disagreement are not the main focus—certainly not the only focus—of attention. Moral theories are not deployed as argumentative or combative frameworks, and issuing definitive moral judgments is not the aim. About the various contending arguments we instead shift the questions we ask. Rather than trying to figure out which side is right, we ask what *each* side is right *about*. Then we may be able to find some common ground, or at least some creative ways to shift the problem toward matters that we can do something about—together.

Finally, the working hypothesis of this book is that it is actually possible to make progress on the ethical issues of the day. Thinking clearly about those issues is a good start, for sure, but we can ask for much more than that. We can also make progress on deeper levels: seeing farther into the issue; understanding each other better; and devising new, mutually agreeable ways forward, while strengthening and enlivening the ethical community that enables us to take up any issue constructively together in the first place. Welcome to the good work.

TEACHING WITH THIS BOOK

Ethics so conceived readily lends itself to interactive teaching. In fact it *requires* interactive teaching. It requires constant in-class practice. There is no other way to learn it. This book therefore differs from most other ethics texts in pedagogical terms too. It insistently invites, and consistently supports, an active and engaged pedagogy.

Toolbox had its start in ever-growing sets of readings designed to free up my own classes' time for practice. My aim was to collect most of the necessary introductions and discussions and put them in material that could be assigned prior to class and for the most part could be understood by students on their own. At the same time, my focus on teaching constructive ethical skills pushed and continues to push me into regions and topics not usually visited by ethical philosophers: creative problem solving in ethics, for example, and, more recently, moral vision and imagination. Throughout, my aim is to do the usual work of lecture in the book instead, leaving actual class meetings for the class to work.

This text therefore invites a wide range of experiential and "applied" activities for an ethics class. Some of these are in-class activities: structured dialogues and workshops, simulations, surveys, idea-generating challenges. Exercises at the end of each chapter, along with more ambitious challenges to "Use Your Tools" between every other chapter, introduce some of these activities. My Appendix, "The Toolbox in the Classroom," offers more detail and some further suggestions. A second Appendix, by Sharon Hartline of Radford University, frames the pedagogical possibilities in terms of emerging paradigms of experiential education.

Many of these activities in turn aim beyond the classroom. My classes have sponsored workshops on conflict mediation and creativity, co-framed beds with the guests at local shelters for the homeless and mediated closer long-term collaboration between the shelters and our college, conducted a "Council of All Beings" for the college community to extend our discussion of environmental ethics, created websites to help local teens think and act responsibly in sexual explorations, and launched an initiative to partner with a local high school to overcome socioeconomic isolation on both sides. In recent years I have structured my course directly around student-designed ethical change projects, using this book as a conceptual and practical support structure and scaffolding for the process. All of this flows naturally from the *Toolbox*. More, again, in "Notes for Teachers."

CHANGES IN THE THIRD EDITION

Between first and second editions this book was so overhauled as to be almost a new book. I do hope users of the first edition were able to adjust without too much difficulty–and of course, I hope that you appreciated the changes. The second edition was a much better developed text, in my view. I learned a great deal from helpful feedback on the first, and tried to take full account of it.

For this third edition I am grateful again for a great deal of helpful feedback. However, things have settled down quite a bit. Those of you who are regular users will be relieved to hear, I hope, that that although there are changes throughout, they are on a much smaller scale.

A number of users suggested a somewhat streamlined outline, especially so that classes can move more quickly into the Moral Theory section. Agreeing with this, I have relocated the second edition's chapter on "Dialogue" to Part III, where it fits better anyway, as several reviewers pointed out, so it now takes the place of the "Communicative Ethics" chapter formerly in Part III, with many of that chapter's themes interpolated into it. I have pared down and melded the service learning material into a variety of other places in the text. The first part of the book is therefore down from five to only three chapters.

Although there are two fewer chapters, though, the book is not shorter. Instead, many chapters are slightly expanded, with more readings or text or exercises. Most notably, this third edition also offers a new feature: nine new extended exercises, called *Using Your Tools,* one for every two chapters, each carrying the themes of the two preceding chapters (and to some extent all the preceding parts of the book) farther and more thoroughly into practice. A few of these re-position selected exercises from earlier editions' individual chapters, but for the most part they introduce new themes, sometimes also with new and especially provocative readings as well. They are optional—though good reading (like the chapter exercises) in any case. You'll note that some draw on prominent philosophers such as John Rawls and Peter Singer. Others prompt engaged community work. The first aims to directly provoke some energetic moral thinking to motivate us to avoid "ethics-avoidance disorders."

Apart from these larger changes, there are some tweaks throughout: references and sources updated, naturally; some new or recast issues introduced in place of old ones; some rearrangement of articles; some new readings in place of old ones that proved less effective than I'd hoped. Exercises are now numbered for ease of reference. By popular request, I have also recast Part IV somewhat more as a survey of ethics' various practical challenges, somewhat less directly as an exhortation to get out there and do something. Still, that wouldn't be a bad idea, and one central offering of Part IV is some resources and encouragement to do so.

RETURN OF THANKS

Thirty years of teaching in a wide variety of settings leaves me with many debts both large and small. First among these is my debt to my students, who have always taught me much and who lately, especially, have answered the challenge to take ethics into action—again and again—with a range of projects I could never have anticipated but that always open up novel and inspiring prospects. Their feedback on the text along the way has also improved it immeasurably.

Among colleagues, I am continuously grateful to my collaborators in the Elon University Department of Philosophy—Nim Batchelor, Ann Cahill, Martin Fowler, Yoram Lubling, Stephen Bloch-Schulman, and John Sullivan—where for some years we have been moving, each in our own interlacing ways, toward a practical ethics in something like the sense laid out here. Other colleagues, far and near and recent and past, have inspired various commissions and omissions: Beth Raps, Amy Halberstadt, Peter Williams, Elsebet Jegstrup, Tom Birch, Betty Morgan, J. Christian Wilson, Bob Jickling, Eva Feder Kittay, Joe Cole, Mike Simon, Richard McBride, and Patrick Hill, as well as a host of others, including my children, Anna Ruth and Molly, even in ways unbeknownst to them. A deep bow to you all.

Some of the users of earlier editions have also become treasured colleagues and contributors to later ones. Among my colleagues, Professors Fowler and Sullivan again contribute writing to this new edition. Professor Batchelor joins them this time around. Professor Hartline, long ago my student, again offers an energetic and useful Appendix. Professor Vance Ricks of Guilford College contributes a discussion to Chapter 9 based on a running dialogue we have had for years about the places where critical thinking intersects with and informs ethics. As a reviewer in preparation for the second edition, Professor Spoma Jovanovic of the University of North Carolina at Greensboro showed me how much further the book could go in the direction of communicative ethics; in this third edition she contributes a major reading on that theme to the relocated "Dialogue" chapter. My student, maggie castor, Elon class of 2012, who encountered this book first as a textbook for her own introductory class in ethics taught by Professor Fowler, became my research assistant for this third edition in the Summer of 2011, and helped find and fit into the book a number of the new readings. She also contributes a provocative set of thoughts and discussion questions to the first "Using Your Tools" exercise.

I am also enormously grateful to many other users of the first and second editions of this book, along with my little book *A Practical Companion to Ethics* (Oxford University Press, 4th edition, 2011), whose enthusiasm and encouragement have emboldened me to undertake this third edition of "the big book." People across the United States and Canada are using this book to approach ethics in a new key, and increasingly in institution-wide general studies programs concerned with moral citizenship and "ethics across the curriculum" as well. I have heard from many and even met some of you. I am honored, and I hope this new edition, tailored with some of your needs in mind, will be even more helpful. Please continue to be in touch.

At Oxford University Press, Robert B. Miller patiently nurtured the first incarnation of this project through its slow coalescence and allowed it to come to completion in its own good time. Both times since he has repeated the feat, generally under conditions of more resistance and alarm from my end. I could not ask for a more consistently responsive, supportive and politic editor. Publisher's reviewers for the first edition were David Boersema, Richard L. Lipke, Verna Gehring, Patricia Murphy, and Jack Green Musselman. Reviewers in preparation for the second edition, along with Professor Jovanovic, included Ralph Acampora, Greta Bauer, Deborah Hawkins, and Stevens Wandmacher. My colleagues Professors Sullivan and Cahill also read significant parts of the manuscript for the second edition and offered helpful feedback and encouragement. Beth Raps was my utterly reliable and savvy assistant in every aspect of the preparation of that edition.

Reviewers for the third edition were Russell DiSilvestro, California State University–Sacramento; Douglas Drabkin, Fort Hays State University; Steven M. Duncan, Bellevue College; Jeremy Garrett, California State University–Sacramento; Paul F. Jeffries, Ripon College; Keith Korcz, University of Louisiana at Lafayette; Karla Pierce, Florida State College–Jacksonville; Davis Sweet, Middlesex Community College and Massachusetts Bay Community College; and Kathryn Valdivia, University of San Diego. My daughter Molly, a budding writer herself, lent her sharp eye to the final copy-editing. I would like to add that for all three editions, but most notably this most recent one, almost all of the reviewers went well above and beyond the usual level of reviewing to offer exceptionally detailed and useful critiques and suggestions. I have not been able to take account of all of them (any author will recognize the amusing bind that arises when different reviewers sometimes recommend diametrically opposite changes; and there are others that would simply change the book into something quite different, though perhaps just as good or better an idea) but I was honored by all of them, and hope that all of you who worked so carefully through the earlier edition will recognize the fruits of your labors in the book you now hold in your hands.

Needless to say, the commissions and omissions that remain—some of them even, scandalously, repeated—are to be charged to me alone. As always, feedback of all sorts is very welcome. May the circle continue to widen.

Anthony Weston
Durham, North Carolina
June, 2012

I

EMBRACING ETHICS

CHAPTER 1

Re–Introducing Ethics

Ethics is already familiar in many ways. You are not entering a foreign country. Indeed, if ethics really were so unfamiliar, you would not be likely to be around to read this book, nor I to write it.

Yet you are about to enter into the *study* of ethics, a project that will ask of you some new learning and may well be surprising, demanding, and, yes, difficult on many levels. (Indeed, let's hope it is—what's the point of just rehearsing what you already know?) It may not show you a foreign country, but this book will invite you into a richer understanding of your own "country," so to speak—really, *our* own country—that will fascinate you at times (I hope), complicate things, and ultimately invite you to take responsibility (or, more responsibility) for some of it yourself.

This opening chapter, then, is not so much an introduction to ethics as it is a *re*–introduction: a look at the familiar in a new and deeper way. We must both be specific and explicit about what we mean by "ethics" itself, and then outline the learning that lies ahead.

WHAT IS ETHICS?

In stores today you can find household products made by a company called "Seventh Generation." The name comes from an idea attributed to Native Americans: that in making decisions we must consider not only the effects of those decisions on people now, but also the effects for seven generations into the future. Therefore, "Seventh Generation"—the company—designs everything, from the actual products to their containers and business practices, for the least environmental impact and the greatest sustainability in the long run.

Thinking in such a long-term way is a useful standard for environmental ethics, to which we'll return later in this book. Here at the beginning, though, we can look at it in a broader way. We can find in it some useful clues to the nature of ethics itself.

The first and most basic clue is this: *ethics asks us to pay attention to something beyond ourselves.* The whole point of thinking about the future in this way is to consider not just ourselves but also others: our children and their children; society generally; maybe even the natural world in its own right. All of them are affected by big choices, such as how we understand and sustain "liberty and justice for all," say, but also even by small and seemingly irrelevant things like what kind of dish detergent we use and what we do with the bottle afterward.

Ethical attention needn't only focus on the future, either. Here and now, it also matters both how we seek justice and what we do with discarded containers—and sometimes these are the very same issue, for example when affluent countries ship off their wastes, including toxics, to poorer countries to burden their peoples and natural systems alike. As we recognize a widening circle of effects, ethics suggests, at least, that we recognize a widening circle of responsibilities.

ETHICS FROM THE INSIDE

Now consider the "seven generations" idea from another angle. Especially in traditional cultures where women began bearing children in their teens, it would have been common for a young person to know their parents' parents' parents—their great-grandparents, who might even still be in their vigorous fifties or sixties. In the very same way, at the other end of life, they themselves would have been likely to know their own great-grandchildren: three generations in the other direction. Add all of this together, counting a person's own generation in between, and your view could encompass . . . seven generations.

That is, we also stand in the *middle* of the generations. One of the most powerful imperatives in Native American culture is to "Remember who you are!" We are individuals, no doubt, but we are also children and grandchildren and great-grandchildren of particular known people, and likewise may be parents and grandparents and great-grandparents of particular though as yet unknown people who will inherit this earth after our stewardship.

In just the same way, we typically stand in the middle of ethics. This is a second clue to the nature of ethics as such. On the whole, we work from inside of it. Again, ethics is not like a foreign country. For one thing, we ourselves are products of the same kind of care-taking that ethics asks of us in turn. After all, we are here because our parents bore and raised us; because others bore and raised *them*; because whole multitudes of people raised food and created cities and struggled over systems of governance and inquired into the workings of the natural world and of the heart. We have seen all of this already, and are, at least in some ways, part of it already too.

This too is not just a point about the past. Here and now, parents—yours, for example, and possibly you yourself as well—give of themselves to sustain the safety and love of a family for children and partners. If you are a college student, a multitude of others, from parents and grateful former alumni to dedicated faculty and a variety of taxpayers, are covering much of the cost of your education. They're "paying it forward" in the hopes that you will pay it forward too, eventually, in turn. Out in the public world, think of the legions of strangers, every day, who take care to drive carefully, treat you and each other decently, and just do their jobs, whatever they are, honestly and well, sustaining and maybe even improving the world. As do we, ourselves (I hope).

TAKING CARE

Two clues, then. Ethics asks us to pay attention to something beyond ourselves, and in many ways both we and others do so already. Can we now, like good philosophers, make of these clues a general definition of ethics? That is, can we say what ethics *is*, at its essential core, and what it is that distinguishes ethics from other kinds of action or thinking?

The first clue gives us part of a definition already. To make it more exact, let's start by stipulating that to think or act ethically is to *take care for the basic needs and legitimate expectations of others as well as our own*. We can then use both clues to help elaborate both "basic needs and legitimate expectations" and the idea of "taking care."

Consider "taking care" first. We can distinguish three different and relevant ways in which we "take care."

(1) We take care for something, in an initial, first-step sense, when we *look into* or investigate it. When we or someone else is in need, for example, ethics would have us ask how weighty or basic a need it is, and who, if anyone, can legitimately be expected to meet or respond to it. In the same way, an exploration or inquiry is ethical when you pay attention to the effects (of all sorts) that your actions or non-actions may have on the needs and expectations of others (possibly also of all sorts), or ask just who or what exactly "counts," *whose* needs and expectations are relevant, anyway.

These questions might be answered in various ways—many different ethical norms may be considered—but the questions themselves are already ethical. We're paying attention, or "taking care," just to ask them.

(2) In a second sense, we "take care" for something when we are *conscientious* about it: that is, when we're "careful" of it. In part, then, ethical thinking and action, in the broadest sense, is an attempt to acknowledge the others around and next to us, which is certainly one basic legitimate expectation. Everyday decency, acknowledging others who have cared or "paid forward" for us, respecting others' rights, following the rules (as in, for example, good sportsmanship) . . . these (and others) are forms of careful action in this sense, reflecting and sustaining an understanding of ourselves as one among others—in the middle of things.

(3) In a third sense, we take care for something when we act to *sustain and further it.* To act ethically, in this case, again very broadly speaking, is to actually try to meet some of the basic needs and legitimate expectations of others as well as ourselves: to sustain or nurture others, as well as ourselves, materially or spiritually or both. It might be as simple as trying to be a good steward of the Earth or taking your extra produce or clothes to the local homeless shelter; or building homes with Habitat for Humanity, which serves specific people and families, who are often building right alongside you. It might be as extreme as the Russian botanists who starved themselves to death during the siege of Leningrad in World War Two rather than eat the abundant food all around them, which happened to be the world's last reserves for hundreds of berry species. Those species, saved at such cost, are now regenerated and spread around the world.

Or think of Peter Benchley, author of *Jaws*, who was so chagrined by the anti-shark hysteria that his book created that he devoted the rest of his life and fortune to shark conservation and ocean protection. Not just for future human generations, either—also for the *sharks*. He felt as though he'd incurred an ethical debt to them as well.

It is a question within ethics just what those needs and expectations are or how far and in what ways you or I are obliged to try to meet them. The basic point, though, is that ethics at least requires that the needs and expectations of others have *some* role in what we do and how we decide about it—that is, that we "take care" in some sense.

NEEDS AND EXPECTATIONS

The other essential terms in this definition are "basic needs" and "legitimate expectations." We'll find that ethics offers a variety of perspectives on these. As a rough beginning, we can say that *basic needs* include things like food, clothing, and shelter; more broadly, sustenance. Health. Education. Community and a chance to participate. Freedom. A voice.

These are the goods that all of us need to survive and to have some chance to flourish. I don't mean, though, that people are obliged to simply give these things to anyone in need. That is one possible ethics, but not the only one. Ethics in general, again, just requires us to pay attention to them—not to live as an island, unaware or unconcerned, blind to anyone else. Ethics calls us to recognize that others have needs and expectations as well as ourselves, regardless of how exactly we go on to respond to them, if we do.

I also don't mean that this list of basic needs is final or fixed. Debating exactly what our basic needs *are* is one more debate within ethics. Our conception of morally relevant basic needs itself has shifted over time. Medicine, for example, wasn't considered a basic need until quite modern times, which was the first time it became especially effective. (Or put it this way: health was always a basic need, but until modern times there were few effective ways in which others might be obliged to help when health failed.) Other needs may now be on their way toward recognition as "basic," for better or worse: a clean environment, for one. Human diversity within ecological diversity, perhaps.

We all have legitimate expectations to be treated with respect and as equals. Some legitimate expectations are rights: to "life, liberty, and the pursuit of happiness"; to be able to speak our minds or worship (or not) as we please; and so on. But rights are only one aspect or expression of legitimate expectations; other legitimate expectations take other forms. We legitimately expect each other to act responsibly, to keep promises, and so on. There are a variety of views within ethics about how to think about legitimate expectations (starting with: what makes some expectations "legitimate"?), once again a debate to which we will come in due time.

A FEW OTHER THINGS

There is, finally, that term "others." Ethical thinking and action take care for the basic needs and legitimate expectations of *others* as well as our own.

Who is this? Other people, yes: that is now a given (though historically, as some of our readings will note, this was not always the case: all too often ethics has been limited to one's own class or gender or city . . .). These days, "others" may also include (some?) other animals and the natural world too. Even sharks, maybe. Exactly what other "others" ethics may include is one more foundational question in ethics. Often, indeed, it is ethical questions at the "edges"—such as, today, questions about other animals—from which we learn the most about ethics at its core. These are the most challenging questions, as well, to ethical "business as usual." It seems that a certain open-endedness is a key to ethics as well.

Again, note that our own selves are included too. Ethics takes care for the basic needs and legitimate expectations of others *and also our own.* Ethics according to this definition is not opposed to the self. Quite the contrary: our own needs and expectations are built into the definition. Our own needs get a voice as well as others'. The essential thing, though, is that our own needs cannot be the whole story. Ethics connects us to a larger world. The self doesn't vanish—it just awakens to itself as, yes, one among others.

Here is one other note about terms. The term "moral" is typically used in much the same sense as "ethical," but there can be a difference of shading. Sometimes a "moral" person is a little more like a person who just reliably does what's right, while an "ethical" person is a little more like someone who thinks twice about it, or is more engaged with issues where values are in flux or at odds. Some philosophers use the word "moral" to describe the values we actually hold—the word "moral" traces back to the Latin "mores," meaning manners or customs—whereas by "ethics" they mean the *study* of morals, or more broadly the deliberate process of thinking our morals through, of systematizing and criticizing and possibly even revising our moral values, as well as more consciously embracing them.

I will respect these shadings in this book, but without making much more of them. From now on, for example, typically I will speak of moral *values* but ethical *issues* or *debates* or *problems*. Again, though, nothing serious hangs on this usage. Some authors, even some reprinted in this book, use the terms interchangeably without making such a distinction. In the end there is still one subject, our vital subject: taking care for the basic needs and legitimate expectations of others as well as our own.

ETHICS AS A LEARNING EXPERIENCE

It should already be clear that ethics, so conceived, invites and requires a variety of kinds of learning and skills. We could list four of these that together make it clear that ethics is definitely a *learning experience*.

SYSTEMATIC THINKING

Philosophy in general might be defined as the study of how things hang together in the broadest sense—that, at least, is how the 20th-century pragmatist philosopher Wilfred Sellars put it. Sellars' definition certainly applies in ethics: part of the philosopher's work in ethics is to try to figure out which of our moral values are the most basic and whether there is a common and single core to all of ethics—in short, whether and how moral values "hang together." Studying ethics is, in part, learning something of the history and general outline of this *systematic* thinking.

Consider: we hold a lot of moral values. Fairness, equality, respect, and responsibility; reducing pain and suffering; "life, liberty, and the pursuit of happiness"; humility, benevolence, keeping your promises; honesty, responsibility, community, dignity . . . and that is only a barest beginning of a list. A natural question is: how can we discern the forest—a bigger and hopefully clearer picture, more order and less confusion—amidst all these trees?

Many of our moral values are related to fairness, equality, and justice. Perhaps we could find some elegant and clear way of drawing them together, some relatively simple criterion or bottom line? Or again, many moral values have to do with personal virtues, like honesty, humility, and self-possession. Maybe there is some relatively clear and focused human ideal that connects these different virtues—that gives them each a logical place in a single, unified picture. We would understand all the virtues better if we could paint that bigger picture with confidence and clarity.

You begin to see the hope: that we might discover that many of our moral values actually "hang together" in basic ways. There may be deep connections among moral values that can bring some order to the confusion that may strike us at first. In this book, in particular, we will explore how moral values may be systematized into families, introducing one of the main projects of philosophical ethics. This is probably the most traditional form of "ethics as a learning experience": we will explore a bit of the history of ethics and what philosophers call ethical *theory*.

CRITICAL THINKING

Ethics also requires us, remember, to "take care" in the sense of *investigation*. The study of ethics requires us to *look into* the questions that underlie and define many ethical issues. For example, is "restorative justice"—reconciliation rather than retribution—possible? How much do animals suffer in laboratories and slaughterhouses? What demonstrable dangers, if any, does gay marriage pose to the familiar heterosexual sort? Who actually is on welfare? Do homeless people tend to be drug addicts—or is it that drug addicts tend to be homeless?

"Investigation" in this sense is primarily factual. Actual evidence is available, though it can be complex and uncertain at times. We need to do more than simply assert what we think is obvious or seek out a few facts that seem to support what we already think. The real challenge is to find out more, to understand better, even if we have to change what we think as a result. You can find some answers—but it takes looking, and being open to learning and even possibly changing your view.

Learning about other cultures' practices may provoke critical thinking as well. In Australia many couples live together in so-called "de facto" marriages—a legally recognized category. They do about as well as the more official kind. You can get marijuana legally in the Netherlands and the result is not a disaster. There are some societies that will not tolerate leaving even a single person homeless. Abortion, one of America's most divisive, painful, and seemingly fundamental social conflicts over the past thirty years, is barely an issue in many other countries (though now we're exporting it), and historically was not much of an issue even here. Can we learn anything from all this? Well, sure . . . and we can systematically seek to find out more.

Here's another thing: when we explore some of the ways in which moral values hang together, we also may well find ourselves provoked to rethink some of our judgments that might not fit so well, or that come into conflict with one another. This too is a form of critical thinking.

Later in this chapter, for example, we will look at two readings about the human relation to animals. Both aim to place the eating of animals in a larger context, to take a larger perspective—but they are very different perspectives. One reading links it to the moral blindness and injustice that is all too familiar in the treatment of black slaves and the sexual oppression of women. The other sees eating (and hunting) animals as a form of communion with the land, and with wildness. This raises questions. Can we reconcile these perspectives?

If not, does one take precedence? How do these perspectives relate to other ethical values and perspectives we hold? (For example, is hunting "pro-life"? Should "life" only mean *human* life? Why or why not?)

We'll return to all of this, of course. It's a big part of the work that lies ahead. The point for now is just that ethics does not leave you alone. Putting together a consistent and well-founded set of ethical judgments is hard work. Once again: there is more learning and thinking to do.

CREATIVE PROBLEM SOLVING

Here's a challenge to consider.

> A child in second grade underwent chemotherapy for leukemia. When she returned to school, she wore a scarf to hide the fact that she had lost all her hair. But some of the children pulled it off, and in their nervousness laughed and made fun of her. The child was mortified and that afternoon begged her parents not to make her go back to school. Her parents tried to encourage her, saying, "The other children will get used to it, and anyway your hair will soon grow in again."

Suppose you are the teacher. This is your class. Rights and wrongs are pretty clear in this case, don't you think? You need to defend the afflicted child. You can defend her with more or less skill—maybe by angrily lecturing the class about not hurting her feelings, maybe by telling a parable that makes the point more deftly—but the fact is (so it seems) that you need to read the riot act. This is a time when even young children must take some responsibility to avoid causing hurt. Even second grade is not too early to learn the lesson.

Still, you can predict what the effects will be. A few children will get it, maybe. More are just going to "really feel sorry" for the poor kid, making both her and themselves terribly self-conscious. Others will retreat into sullenness. A few will put on a show of care but keep on taunting her behind your back, maybe even with sharper (because hidden) twists of the knife. And she herself will be even more embarrassed and hurt.

Is there any other way? Are there alternative ways to approach the whole situation so that the class begins to learn the right kind of sensitivity and care but does not end up feeling strained or stuck? Think about it. Really, what would *you* do?

> The next morning, when their teacher walked into class, all the children were sitting in their seats, some still tittering about the girl who had no hair, while she shrank into her chair. "Good morning, children," the teacher said, smiling warmly in her familiar way of greeting them. She took off her coat and scarf. Her head was completely bald.

After that, a rash of children begged their parents to let them cut their hair. And whenever a child came to class with short hair, newly bobbed, all the children laughed merrily, not out of fear but out of the joy of the game. And everybody's hair grew back at the same time.

How wonderful—and how ethical! This teacher did something transformative and memorable, and far more powerful than a lecture would have been. By shaving her own head, she invited the children into an entirely new way of relating to the child with no hair. She showed them that there is something to do besides gape at her or feel sorry for her. The bald child was no longer a problem or an object of pity, but a playmate with options, just like she was before. Maybe even better. The possibility of a whole new kind of solidarity (not to mention fun) opens up.

What a creative teacher! Would that all our teachers were like her—would that we were like her ourselves. And in all seriousness: why not? Another kind of ethical learning, not so familiar as systematic and critical skills but arguably just as important, is creative thinking. It turns out to be a genuinely learnable skill, as well. (Don't even *think* of saying, "You can't learn creativity." How do you know until you've tried?) What if even the most seemingly "stuck" situations have totally unexpected possibilities, ways out or beyond that are far outside the range of options we usually consider? What kinds of skills and vision does it take to begin to discover them?

DIALOGUE AND RESPONSIVENESS

Finally, ethics is a learning experience because it invites and requires us to develop our skills at both dialogue and responsiveness to others *in practice*.

It's sad and certainly ironic that we have such trouble talking or debating respectfully and productively about ethical disagreements. Nonetheless, notoriously, we do. Abortion, affirmative action, animal rights, assisted suicide. . . .: that's just the A's, and already we have four totally polarized issues on which even otherwise perfectly lovely and reasonable people apparently cannot manage to begin to talk decently to each other. Ironically, it seems that in ethics itself we have great difficulty being ethical: that is, actually listening to one another and honoring our relationship as we work together toward constructive solutions.

Still, as we'll see, these are learnable skills too. Sometimes it doesn't even take two to tango—one is enough. So why not *you*?

Responsiveness also takes some learning. It is not just a matter of feeling sympathy for others, though of course that is a fine start (and also is a skill that improves with practice). As well, it means knowing how to get involved and make a difference: how to make yourself an ethical change-maker and how to join change-making communities.

Many people feel unable to make a difference in a world as complex and fast-changing as ours. Young people, especially, like students, may feel this way. "What can *I* do?" The answer, actually, is: quite a lot. It's just that putting ethics into action in this way takes a little more attention to method and opportunities than we are usually offered. It turns out that there are many ways to do so, some of them not just equally available to young people and students but *more* available to you. Some attention to these will complete your ethical toolbox—anyway, for now!

REPORT FROM MY STUDENTS

I ask my students what they've learned about ethics in the last few years. Only a few say that very little has changed for them. More say that not so much has changed yet, but they're looking forward to it. Most say that they *have* changed, ethically, sometimes in ways they could never have predicted. They travel, for fun maybe, but come back with whole new ideas about life. They learn about some new subject and have to change their ways. They have a friend or a family member who has an accident or a challenged child, and suddenly they have both more sympathy for others and more passion for the moment. Some learn the hard way to see people beyond labels and categories: race categories, sexual orientation, politics. The phrase, "They're people just like me" keeps coming up—something we know (we know the words, anyway) and yet, often, don't quite "know" well enough. This too must actually be learned, perhaps again and again, and not just by young people.

It turns out that the story of ethics itself is continuously unfolding. The idea of rights, for example, which most of us take for granted, is a piece of ethical theory that was literally revolutionary in the 18th century. On July 4 we shoot off fireworks and celebrate the Declaration of Independence as if it were the most natural and obvious thing. But it was a radical document in its time—after all, it started a revolution—and even now we struggle to realize the full promise of "all [people] are created equal."

My students, like you, see new ethical perspectives arising. Instead of Declarations of Independence we are now beginning to see Declarations of *Inter*dependence: the insistence that humans are deeply dependent on the rest of the biosphere for health, wealth, and, indeed, our very survival—and that it would therefore be a good idea to treat nature with more respect. "Environmental ethics" itself is a coming field. Forty years ago whales were being slaughtered all over the high seas, and no one recycled anything. Young people now can listen to whale songs on CD, whale hunting is banned (though some still goes on), and recycling bins are everywhere. What's next?

Other unheard-of issues will be coming up, such as an entire range of thorny and unprecedented questions about cloning and genetic engineering.

Old issues will come up in new forms, such as questions about privacy rights in an age preoccupied with security. In personal and professional life, "just getting by" by current standards is soon likely to be nowhere near enough. Ethical norms for managers and CEOs are changing so fast that some of yesterday's accepted behavior is already becoming grounds for dismissal, or even jail. New ideals are arising—for work, for the place of older people in a new world, for diversity and tolerance and also for the reaffirmation of certain traditional values. My students, like you, want to be ready. An ethical toolbox should help!

READING

"Am I Blue?"

ALICE WALKER

MANY WRITERS, NOVELISTS, and storytellers have weighed in on ethical matters. Some have even started moral revolutions. Harriet Beecher Stowe's *Uncle Tom's Cabin*—the best-selling novel of the 19th Century—inspired the anti slavery movement. Aldo Leopold's *Sand County Almanac* jump-started modern environmental ethics. In general, stories and essays can be powerful ways to bring basic needs and legitimate expectations into view, even—maybe especially—where we've had trouble seeing them before.

The novelist and activist Alice Walker is best known as the author of *The Color Purple*, but she has penned other fine novels too, as well as numerous books of reflective and autobiographical essays. Here a well-known essay in which she struggles with several ethical issues: with the fate of a horse who has become a distant sort of friend, with her commitment to fighting oppression of all sorts, and ultimately, in the very last lines, with diet as an ethical issue. They come together in unexpected and uneasy ways—and she doesn't flinch.

These are all deeply important issues, and there is much to be learned from her even if you disagree. My suggestion is to just read the essay, at least the first time through, without being

"Am I Blue?" From *Living by the Word: Selected Writings* 1973–1987, © 1986 by Alice Walker, reprinted by permission of Harcourt, Inc.

very concerned to work out your reactions as you go. Then we will think together about the ethical issues and perceptions it raises—after which you may want to read it again.

---

*"Ain't these tears in these eyes tellin' you?"**

For about three years my companion and I rented a small house in the country that stood on the edge of a large meadow that appeared to run from the end of our deck straight into the mountains. The mountains, however, were quite far away, and between us and them there was, in fact, a town. It was one of the many pleasant aspects of the house that you never really were aware of this.

It was a house of many windows, low, wide, nearly floor to ceiling in the living room, which faced the meadow, and it was from one of these that I first saw our closest neighbor, a large white horse, cropping grass, flipping its mane, and ambling about—not over the entire meadow, which stretched well out of sight of the house, but over the five or so fenced-in acres that were next to the twenty-odd that we had rented. I soon learned that the horse, whose name was Blue, belonged to a man who lived in another town, but was boarded by our neighbors next door. Occasionally, one of the children, usually a stocky teen-ager, but sometimes a much younger girl or boy, could be seen riding Blue. They would appear in the meadow, climb up on his back, ride furiously for ten or fifteen minutes, then get off, slap Blue on the flanks, and not be seen again for a month or more.

There were many apple trees in our yard, and one by the fence that Blue could almost reach. We were soon in the habit of feeding him apples, which he relished, especially because by the middle of summer the meadow grasses—so green and succulent since January—had dried out from lack of rain, and Blue stumbled about munching the dried stalks half-heartedly. Sometimes he would stand very still just by the apple tree, and when one of us came out he would whinny, snort loudly, or stamp the ground. This meant, of course: I want an apple.

It was quite wonderful to pick a few apples, or collect those that had fallen to the ground overnight, and patiently hold them, one by one, up to his large, toothy mouth. I remained as thrilled as a child by his flexible dark lips, huge, cubelike teeth that crunched the apples, core and all, with such finality, and his high, broad-breasted

---

* © 1929 Warner Bros., Inc. (renewed). By Grant Clarke and Harry Akst. All rights reserved. Used by permission.

enormity; beside which, I felt small indeed. When I was a child, I used to ride horses, and was especially friendly with one named Nan until the day I was riding and my brother deliberately spooked her and I was thrown, head first, against the trunk of a tree. When I came to, I was in bed and my mother was bending worriedly over me; we silently agreed that perhaps horseback riding was not the safest sport for me. Since then I have walked, and prefer walking to horseback riding—but I had forgotten the depth of feeling one could see in horses' eyes.

I was therefore unprepared for the expression in Blue's. Blue was lonely. Blue was horribly lonely and bored. I was not shocked that this should be the case; five acres to tramp by yourself, endlessly, even in the most beautiful of meadows—and his was—cannot provide many interesting events, and once rainy season turned to dry that was about it. No, I was shocked that I had forgotten that human animals and nonhuman animals can communicate quite well; if we are brought up around animals as children we take this for granted. By the time we are adults we no longer remember. However, the animals have not changed. They are in fact *completed* creations (at least they seem to be, so much more than we) who are not likely *to* change; it is their nature to express themselves. What else are they going to express? And they do. And, generally speaking, they are ignored.

After giving Blue the apples, I would wander back to the house, aware that he was observing me. Were more apples not forthcoming then? Was that to be his sole entertainment for the day? My partner's small son had decided he wanted to learn how to piece a quilt; we worked in silence on our respective squares as I thought . . . .

Well, about slavery: about white children, who were raised by black people, who knew their first all-accepting love from black women, and then, when they were twelve or so, were told they must "forget" the deep levels of communication between themselves and "mammy" that they knew. Later they would be able to relate quite calmly, "My old mammy was sold to another good family." "My old mammy was ———— ————." Fill in the blank. Many more years later a white woman would say: "I can't understand these Negroes, these blacks. What do they want? They're so different from us."

And about the Indians, considered to be "like animals" by the "settlers" (a very benign euphemism for what they actually were), who did not understand their description as a compliment.

And about the thousands of American men who marry Japanese, Korean, Filipina, and other non-English-speaking women and of how happy they report they are, *"blissfully,"* until their brides learn to speak English, at which point the marriages tend to fall apart. What then did the men see, when they looked into the eyes of the women they married, before they could speak English? Apparently only their own reflections.

I thought of society's impatience with the young. "Why are they playing the music so loud?" Perhaps the children have listened to much of the music of oppressed people their parents danced to before they were born, with its passionate but soft cries for acceptance and love, and they have wondered why their parents failed to hear.

I do not know how long Blue had inhabited his five beautiful, boring acres before we moved into our house; a year after we had arrived—and had also traveled to other valleys, other cities, other worlds—he was still there.

But then, in our second year at the house, something happened in Blue's life. One morning, looking out the window at the fog that lay like a ribbon over the meadow, I saw another horse, a brown one, at the other end of Blue's field. Blue appeared to be afraid of it, and for several days made no attempt to go near. We went away for a week. When we returned, Blue had decided to make friends and the two horses ambled or galloped along together, and Blue did not come nearly as often to the fence underneath the apple tree.

When he did, bringing his new friend with him, there was a different look in his eyes. A look of independence, of self-possession, of inalienable *horse*ness. His friend eventually became pregnant. For months and months there was, it seemed to me, a mutual feeling between me and the horses of justice, of peace. I fed apples to them both. The look in Blue's eyes was one of unabashed "this is *it*ness."

It did not, however, last forever. One day, after a visit to the city, I went out to give Blue some apples. He stood waiting, or so I thought, though not beneath the tree. When I shook the tree and jumped back from the shower of apples, he made no move. I carried some over to him. He managed to half-crunch one. The rest he let fall to the ground. I dreaded looking into his eyes—because I had of course noticed that Brown, his partner, had gone—but I did look. If I had been born into slavery, and my partner had been sold or killed, my eyes would have looked like that. The children next door explained that Blue's partner had been "put with him" (the same expression that old people used, I had noticed, when speaking of an ancestor during slavery who had been impregnated by her owner) so that they could mate and she conceive. Since that was accomplished, she had been taken back by her owner, who lived somewhere else.

Will she be back? I asked.

They didn't know.

Blue was like a crazed person. Blue *was*, to me, a crazed person. He galloped furiously, as if he were being ridden, around and around his five beautiful acres. He whinnied until he couldn't. He tore at the ground with his hooves. He butted himself against his single shade tree. He looked always and always toward the road down which his partner had gone. And then, occasionally, when he came up for apples, or I took apples to him, he looked at me. It was a look so piercing, so full of grief, a look so *human*, I almost laughed (I felt too sad to cry) to think there are people who do not know that animals suffer. People like me who have forgotten, and daily forget, all that animals try to tell us. "Everything you do to us will happen to you; we are your teachers, as you are ours. We are one lesson" is essentially it, I think. There are those who never once have even considered animals' rights: those who have been taught that animals actually want to be used and abused by us, as small children "love" to be frightened, or women "love" to be mutilated and raped. . . . They are the great-grandchildren of those who honestly thought, because someone taught them this: "Women can't think," and "niggers can't faint." But most disturbing of all, in Blue's large brown eyes was a new look, more painful than the look of despair: the look of disgust with human beings, with life; the look of hatred. And it was odd what the look of hatred did. It gave him, for the first time, the look of a beast. And what that meant was that he had put up a barrier within to protect himself from further violence; all the apples in the world wouldn't change that fact.

And so Blue remained, a beautiful part of our landscape, very peaceful to look at from the window, white against the grass. Once a friend came to visit and said, looking out on the soothing view: "And it *would* have to be a *white* horse; the very image of freedom." And I thought, yes, the animals are forced to become for us merely "images" of what they once so beautifully expressed. And we are used to drinking milk from containers showing "contented" cows, whose real lives we want to hear nothing about, eating eggs and drumsticks from "happy" hens, and munching hamburgers advertised by bulls of integrity who seem to command their fate.

As we talked of freedom and justice one day for all, we sat down to steaks. I am eating misery, I thought, as I took the first bite. And spit it out.

ETHICAL OPENINGS IN "AM I BLUE?"

What are the chief moral values that Alice Walker invokes in this essay? How does she speak to basic needs and legitimate expectations? What does she—and what does Blue, through her—tell us about ethics? Whether we agree with her or not is not the question right now: let us simply try to understand her essay as an ethical expression.

Some values are named in the essay. Justice, in particular, is invoked explicitly: "There was a different look in his eyes. A look of independence, of self-possession, of inalienable horseness. . . . For months and months there was a feeling of justice, of peace." Like any creature, Blue has basic needs and expectations, and for these few months, they are met. "Justice" is that sense of things being right, the world being rightly ordered. He's able to truly be what he is.

But Blue is a horse, of course, not a human, and so we may wonder whether ethics, strictly speaking, even applies. Some people think that only human needs and expectations are relevant to ethics. Walker is clearly out to argue the opposite. All the way through the essay, she draws parallels between the suffering of animals and the suffering of oppressed humans. We're invited to see the owners' treatment of Blue—and, by extension, it seems, much human treatment of all animals—as another kind of oppression. And overcoming oppression and reducing suffering are understood to be key moral values, though not stated explicitly.

Look at the title again, for example. Am *I* Blue? Or more exactly, what would happen if we saw ourselves in the fate and treatment of this horse? What would change? What would *have* to change?

Walker also draws parallels between our denials of the suffering of animals and our denials of the suffering of oppressed humans. And so something else is going on beneath her explicit appeal to justice and the implicit appeal to reduce suffering: it's an appeal to all of us to pay attention to the sufferings of others, especially those others whose suffering we have learned to deny (or perhaps, worse, *need* to deny in order to go on living as we do, eating meat, for example). We need to take more care at least to look.

Another moral value here, then, is something like sympathy—real, compassionate attention, especially to those so oppressed and stereotyped that we usually give ourselves excuses not to notice. We need to commit ourselves to no longer "ignore" what animals, or any suffering beings, really express. You could also call it honesty—with ourselves—about what is really happening. Walker puts it very personally. Chilled by the sense that Blue has retreated from her, that he has taken on a "disgust" with human beings, we sense that she pulls away too, but still with the hope that we may find ways of being able to look into animals' eyes (if not Blue's, then some animals, sometime) without shame, without a sense of having failed them. With a kind of sympathy that has made a difference. The ideal is that someday we may be able to come into the larger-than-human world with a sense of mutuality and, again, peace.

Sympathizing can be tricky. Sometimes we respond to the sufferings of others by imagining how we would feel if we were them—which is laudable as far as it goes, but also has the danger of imagining that the other (person or creature) is really just like us. It doesn't allow for *difference*. That disturb-ing story about American men who marry non-English-speaking wives, for instance. The very possibility that they might have something of their own to communicate is often denied. Too often we see only our own reflections in those we subordinate and oppress. I think this is why Walker is careful to acknowledge Blue in what she calls his "inalienable *horse*ness" and "his high, broad-breasted enormity." He's a horse, not a human, but that does not somehow disqualify him from ethical consideration: rather, it qualifies him in his own horsey way.

And so Walker ends with the decision not to eat meat. Indeed she has made herself a major advocate for animal-rights causes and meat-free diets. It is interesting to compare her approach with the usual arguments for vegetarianism. Her argument is certainly not from "animal rights," for example, which is a general, formal, or detached way of arguing—though certainly important and challenging as well. Walker works on a more per-sonal and sympathetic level. Ultimately, for her, it is a question of how we can live with other animals and other humans, rather than exploiting them and denying any connection: so it is truly a question of mutuality and community.

It's important to acknowledge, finally, that you or I might have responded differently. After all, there's no direct connection between how Blue was treated and the production of steaks. But Walker's essay follows a much big-ger track. By compelling us to see Blue as a real, feeling being, she raises both the question of animals in general and the question of our own moral defen-siveness in an unforgettable way. It is now, unavoidably, one of the ethical questions of the times. If this brief exploration of "Am I Blue?" has done its work, you can begin to see why.

READING

From Bloodties: Nature, Culture, and the Hunt

TED KERASOTE

NATURALIST AND AUTHOR TED KERASOTE is another writer struggling with the question of the human relation to animals. Kerasote wrote *Bloodties* to explore hunting in many varied forms, from aboriginal hunters in Greenland to globe-trotting trophy hunters, but he ends back at home, with his own hunting

From Ted Kerasote, *Bloodties* (Kodansha International, 1994), pp. 232–236, 240, 245–247.

practice. He's as reflectively autobiographical, and seriously ethical, as Walker. He even holds many of the same values—but he
ends up in a very different place.

Read Kerasote's thoughts in the same spirit that you read
Walker's. (I will leave the further analysis to you and your
classmates.) What specific moral values does Kerasote invoke?
How do they compare with Walker's? Certain values he makes
explicit: reducing pain, for instance; responsibility (in hunting,
specifically, but also in thinking through our impact on the
Earth in general); respect for life. Ask yourself how he shows
these values, but ask yourself too if there isn't something still
deeper in his commitment to hunting, harder to express but
vital to his practice. Notice how lovingly he speaks of his high
Wyoming home country, "still singing of glaciers and big mammals." Like Walker, he too ends by writing of sympathy, but
does he mean the same thing by it?

Slowly, she angles away from me. In a few more steps she will
be gone from sight and down the steep north slope. In the many
miles walked this fall, among all the elk I've seen, she has become
the possible elk—the elk approached with care, the elk close to
home, the elk seen far enough into the season so that soon the
season will be over . . . the elk whom the morning, the snow, and
the elk themselves have allowed me to approach. Only the asking
remains.

"Mother elk," I say. "Please stop." I speak the words in my
mind, sending them through the trees and into her sleek brown
head. She crosses an opening in the forest, and there, for no reason
I can understand, she pauses, her shoulder and flank visible.

It is a clear shot, though not a perfect one—I have to stand at
full height to make it. But I know I can make it and I say, "Thank-
you. I am sorry." Still I hesitate, for though I can lose myself in the
hunting, I have never been able to stop thinking about its results—
that I forget it's *this* elk rather than *that* elk who is about to die; that
it's *this* creature whom I'm about to take from the world rather than
some number in an equation proving the merits of wild-food harvesting over being a supermarket vegetarian; that this being before
me—who sees, who smells, who *knows*—will no longer be among
us, so that I may go on living. And I don't know how to escape this
incongruous pain out of which we grow, this unresolvable unfair-
ness, other than saying that I would rather be caught in this lovely
tragedy with those whom I love, whom the ground beneath my feet
has created alongside me, than with those far away, whose deaths I
cannot own. Not that I think all this. I know it in my hesitation.

Still she stands, strangely immobile. I raise the rifle, and still she stands, and still I wait, for there have been times that I have come to this final moment, and through the air the animal's spirit has flown into my heart, sending me its pride and defiance, or its beseeching, frightened voice, saying, "I am not for you." And I have watched them walk away. She sweeps her eye across the forest and begins to graze down the north slope, exposing her flank for one more instant, and allowing me to decide. I listen, hearing the air thrum with the ambivalence of our joining, about which I can only say, once again, "I am sorry." As she disappears from sight, I fire behind her left shoulder, the sound of the shot muffled by the forest.

Then she's gone, and the woods are alive with the sound of hooves and branches crashing. I run forward, seeing a dozen cows and an enormous six-point bull stream from the pines and climb into the upper meadow, full of aspen. They pause and look back at me, but I can't see the elk I fired at. For one instant I think of shooting another cow as they stand and stare—the easiest shot imaginable. But I know I hit the animal I shot at.

As I start forward, the elk wheel and run up through the white trees, their tan rumps bobbing. Then they disappear into the next stand of conifers. In a few more steps I see an elk lying in the swale below me, her legs tucked under her, her head erect. She jumps up and moves off at an ungainly trot. I fire, and miss, and she disappears behind a small knob of pines that juts into the aspen.

I climb over several fallen trees and find her lying not thirty feet away, her head turned over her left shoulder, great brown eyes utterly calm. My heart tears apart. . . .

She kicks several more times, gasps once, and lies still, a great, reddish-brown creature, her rear legs straight, her front ones tucked under her. There isn't a speck of blood anywhere. . . .

It takes about an hour to skin her, and as she passes under my hands I note what she is as food—the layer of white fat on her hips, which is good for frying pancakes and for mixing into pemmican; the steaks decreasing in tenderness from the loins to her rump; the burger, jerky, kabob, and sausage. I smile because I can feel saliva lubricating my mouth. Going in the other direction, I smell what she has been—her hair smells of pine, her meat of grass, her fat like the undersides of rocks.

Then I saw her into quarters, the hardest job, and warmest. I'm down to my shirt as the sun begins to shine into our snowy north-facing dell, and the temperature feels as if it finally goes above zero. I hang her two hindquarters in a nearby aspen that has been tilted over by the wind. I also hang her shoulders there, and put each side of her rib cage on a downed aspen. Then I fold the hide and place it alongside the rib cage. The liver and heart I bury in the snow so the Canadian jays, already pecking at the fat around her intestines, will leave them alone.

I wash my hands with snow, have another cup of tea, then I take her hooves and place them on a nearby rise that looks north across the valley. I place her head on top of her legs. Her eyes have sunken a bit forward and are no longer wide and glistening. Sometimes I have used the head, boiling off its meat and eating the tongue. Today I don't. Kneeling by her hooves and head, I stroke her long brown hair and say a few more words. . . .

Bullfighting, cockfighting, dogfighting . . . shooting live pigeons and prairie dogs for "sport" and money . . . dropping cosmetics into rabbits' eyes so humans can have nonirritating and frivolous products . . . keeping calves in stalls for tender veal, and chickens in crowded, filthy boxes to increase production . . . wounding elk through carelessness—all of these examples, and thousands of others whose common denominator is disrespect, seemed to me to be gratuitous forms of pain that are best removed from the world. Different from them is the instrumental pain caused by the honest biological clamor of our guts' wanting to be fed and which seems irreducible.

Once, in an attempt to outwit this pain, I became a vegetarian, and stayed one for quite a while. But when I inquired about the lives lost on a mechanized farm, I realized what costs we pay at the supermarket. One Oregon farmer told me that half the cottontail rabbits went into his combine when he cut a wheat field, that virtually all of the small mammals, ground birds, and reptiles were killed when he harvested windrow crops like rye and sugar beets, and that when the leaves were stripped from bush beans all the mice and the snakes who were living among them were destroyed as well. Perhaps he exaggerated; certainly he hadn't taken a census of his fields' small-animal populations. Nonetheless, from boyhood, he had seen many animals being killed as he made America's food. Because most of these animals have been seen as expendable, or not seen at all, few scientific studies have been done measuring agriculture's effects on their populations. Those that have been done demonstrate that agricultural lands often act as "ecological traps," attracting birds, for instance, who begin their nesting only to have machinery pass over the land, destroying their nests and often the birds themselves. This is particularly true in the case of alfalfa, grown to feed livestock, but it also happens in corn, soybean, and spring wheat fields. When one factors in the lives lost to pesticides, the toll is enormous. . . .

. . . And as one biologist told me, when you find dead birds, you're only finding what's been "hit over the head with a baseball bat." You don't see, except after several years, the decline in reproduction among these bird populations, which these pesticides also cause. Raised on a farm in Iowa, he went on to say that current agricultural practices, particularly combining, left the earth a "biological desert." Our fields might be brimming over with wheat and corn and soybeans, but unless we began to leave habitat for wildlife—stubble, hedgerows, and ditches—we were going to find ourselves in an austerely quiet world, as silent as the silent spring about which Rachel Carson warned . . . unless one counted the growl of tractors as song.

Such data, scanty as it is, addresses only the lives lost on the farm itself. When our produce is transported along the interstate highway system, birds . . . deer . . . skunks . . . raccoons all get flattened. Who hasn't witnessed the carnage? And this doesn't even begin to count the animals lost to the development of the oil fields themselves, the transportation of petroleum across tundra, mountain ranges, and the oceans, and in the wars fought over that oil. In short, being a supermarket vegetarian didn't take me out of the web in which animals are constantly dying to feed humans, it merely put their deaths over the horizon, making them, in the bloodless jargon of cost-accounting, externalities.

When I looked into that web, so full of pain, I came to see that my killing an elk each year did less harm, expressed in animal lives who I believe count equally, than importing the same amount of vegetable food to my bioregion. That didn't ease my conscience; but it did make the choices clearer. . . .

. . . I'm attached to these cold places, still singing of glaciers and big mammals, and in my bones I know that farming has abandoned a connection to them, a relationship of provision by uncultivated land, and concern for that land by its inhabitants, that seems clearest while hunting well. I decided to go back to hunting because it attaches me to this place and the animals I love, asking me to own what each of us ought to own in some personal way—the pain that runs the world. And hunting elk in particular because they are the loved totem of my home . . . because this home makes them and leaves them free . . . and because eating them does nothing to increase the aggregate pain of the world. In fact, by attaching me lovingly here, the relationship between elk and me decreases it.

All of this I have known most keenly walking in this forest, with the wind in my face, and pine in my nostrils, and snow under my boots. None of which means that someone else, trying the same experiment, would have reached a similar conclusion about how to treat animals. In the end, I think you have to *listen,* and if you can't *listen* to the quiet sadness of this world, a lifetime of roaming the outdoors, or thinking in libraries, is not going to tell you that the country is you and you are it, and when you cause it to suffer needlessly then you have broken a cord of sympathy, which is a much more demanding tie to nature than any system of ethics.

FOR REVIEW

1. What is ethics?
2. Explain the text's interpretations of the "seven generations" idea and its relevance to ethics.
3. What are the three senses in which ethics "takes care"?
4. What are "basic needs"?
5. What are "legitimate expectations"?
6. What is an example of systematic thinking in ethics?
7. Why is critical thinking a key skill in ethics?
8. How can creative thinking serve ethics?
9. Why, in the end, does Alice Walker put down her fork? What does this have to do with ethics?
10. Why, in the end, does Ted Kerasote hunt? What does *this* have to do with ethics?

EXERCISES AND NOTES

1.1 FOR REFLECTION

What experiences and expectations do you bring to the study of ethics? What did you expect when you signed up for this course or first cracked the covers of this book? Having read this chapter, do you think you are going to find ethics challenging and inviting in ways you didn't expect? What hopes, and also fears, do you bring to this new study?

Think about events in your life that were occasions for ethical learning. What did you learn? What made that learning possible? How specifically do you think you have changed, ethically speaking? How do you expect to change in the future? Look for biographies or autobiographies of people you admire (and maybe some of people you don't) and pay attention to the ways in which they learned and changed, ethically speaking—and to what made learning and change possible for them. Or interview some people you know or could contact, asking the same questions: What have been major ethical changes in your life? Why did those changes happen? Were they hard? Why? How do you feel about them now that you look back at them? What advice do you have for younger people looking ahead to such changes in their own lives?

1.2 LIMBERING UP

Here are some provocative questions—just to think about, for now, as we begin a broad and open-ended engagement with ethics, and also specifically to open class discussion or for reflective writing projects. They're not invitations to pass judgment: take them in an exploratory spirit instead.

- What specifically do you think would a "seven generations" view might change? Or, to put it another way: what are we doing right now that cannot be sustained for at least seven generations? How would the world look if we stopped doing those things? That is, what are the alternatives? (Try to be imaginative here. Don't just imagine the world without certain unsustainable practices. Consider what an inventive world might do *instead*.)

- Imagine a dialogue between Alice Walker and Ted Kerasote on the subject of killing and eating animals. What do you think they would say to each other? Remember, these are thoughtful and reflective authors who are struggling with these issues—not ideologues who have some fixed and insistent position and "argue" just by broadcasting and repeating it. (That is, imagine a *real* dialogue. There is more on dialogue in chapter 11 of this book, if you want a quick reminder of what dialogue can be.)

  Here's a further question: what would *you* say if you were a third voice in that dialogue—with the same kind of care and reflectiveness? Where do you think such a dialogue could or should end up, ideally?

- What if people lived forever? Would that be wonderful? Awful? How would we adjust? Totally switch identities every few hundred years? (Would you want to be the same person forever?) Would some people want out? What about you? What might be some of the effects on ethics as we know it?

- What if men got pregnant rather than (or in addition to) women? Would we think about sexual relations differently? What about abortion? What do you think Gloria Steinem meant when she said "If men got pregnant, abortion would be a sacrament"? (Is this an uneasy subject? Why?)

- Could a computer have rights? What kind of computer would it take? What kind of rights?

- One person, on reading the story of the teacher who shaved her head, wrote "Ethics is the development of solidarity." What do you think? What unexplored opportunities for solidarity lie right around us right now?

- Take some painful and unproductive contemporary ethical debates— abortion is one but certainly not the only possible example—and deliberately and creatively look for some alternative possible approaches, off the scale of "pro" or "con." Look for alternative approaches *now*: are there organizations working on reconciliation, for instance, or alternative ways of framing the problem so that it doesn't come up in so destructive a way? How is abortion, for example, dealt with in societies that do not have the polarized kind of abortion debate we have? (Again: this is *not* an invitation to recap the usual abortion debate. Instead, can you think of any other, very different ethical approaches?)

- What if there were a cheap, legal, "up" hallucinogenic drug with no side effects? What ethical objections would remain?

- Try designing a company (or if you're really ambitious, a whole economic or political system) without knowing what your own status will be within it. If you don't know whether you'll be the janitor or the CEO, a movie star or heiress, or a bag lady, how will you set up your company's decision-making processes, or your society's way of taking care of the needy? How does your answer "without knowing" differ from your answer when you do know? Which way of asking the question is more ethical, do you suppose? Why?

- What if the world developed an international reconstruction and peace-keeping force? What kinds of skills would such a "force" call for? Who would join? (Think afresh here: it wouldn't have to be, perhaps should not be, the youngest and most able-bodied.) How would it work? How would the peace-makers and peace-keepers be trained?

- If you could use genetic engineering to totally remake human beings, how would you do it? Don't stop with everyday stylistic improvements, like adding gills so we can breathe underwater and such. How about creating people without the capacity, say, for certain kinds of violence or fanaticism? How would you do that? Would there be losses as well as gains?

NOTES

For more on the "seven generations" idea, see Oren Lyons (Chief of the Onondaga Nation), "An Iroquois Perspective," in Christopher Vecsey and Robert W. Venables, editors, *American Indian Environments: Ecological Issues in Native American History* (NY: Syracuse University Press, 1994), pp. 173–174. The Constitution, or "Great Binding Law," of the Iroquois Nations is online at http://www.indigenouspeople.net/iroqcon.htm; see section 28.

For a good first sense of the range of ethics and an introduction to a wide range of philosophical resources in ethics, check out the "Ethics Updates" website at http://ethics.sandiego.edu/ and EthicsWeb Canada at http://www. ethicsweb.ca/resources/.

A few contrasts to other definitions of ethics might be useful here. For example, a fairly standard philosophical definition of ethics is Aristotle's definition of ethics as "the science of conduct," an approach mirrored and elaborated in this definition from the *Internet Encyclopedia of Philosophy* (http://www.iep.utm.edu/ethics/, retrieved 5/28/12):

> The field of ethics (or moral philosophy) involves systematizing, defending, and recommending concepts of right and wrong behavior.

This kind of definition captures much of what philosophical ethics, in particular, aims to do. It is fair enough as far as it goes. However, in my view, it does not go far enough. For one thing, there are many "concepts of right and wrong behavior" that are not necessarily ethical: religious concepts of ritual correctness, for example, or competitive or other notions, like the "right" move in a chess game or the courtroom. The task in defining ethics is, in part, to distinguish *ethically* right and wrong behavior from these other sorts. That, I argue, takes reference to a more substantive goal: in the case of ethics, something broadly to do with basic needs and legitimate expectations. So, these need to be part of the definition itself.

It may be responded that ethics has to do with "right and wrong" *simpliciter*—without being relative to specific situations or contexts: with values that are mandatory, in some sense, and that override all other values in cases of conflict. My view, however, is that moral values have much more complex and often less "overriding" relations with other values so that any such special status claimed for ethics is one ethical (or, as philosophers may say, meta-ethical) position among others, and does not belong in the definition of ethics itself. There it would be (as philosophers would also say) question-begging: it presupposes what in fact needs to be established.

Of course, there are other definitions of ethics too, such as George Bernard Shaw's, one of whose characters declares in *The Doctor's Dilemma* that "Morality consists in suspecting other people of not being legally married." Shaw's not completely serious, of course, but he's more serious than you might think: certainly there can be an element of obsessiveness and resentment and, yes, sometimes, stuffiness about sex in particular, not far beneath the surface.

We should keep all of this in mind as a pitfall to be avoided. On the whole, though, I hope you'll find in this toolbox a balance between the kinds of thinking that invite us to recast familiar problems and rethink ethical values on the one hand, and on the other, the recognition that certain basic values may after all really be, well, basic. Probably even so we'll end up erring on the side of not being stuffy enough. You'll just have to see what you think!

CHAPTER 2

Ethics-Avoidance Disorders

Ethics can be inviting, intriguing, and expansive. For just the same reasons, though, it can also be challenging, difficult, even painful. Sometimes we may even have to change our minds!

For these reasons, there is always also the temptation to avoid and resist ethics too. In fact, some people regularly invest huge amounts of energy in avoiding and resisting it. Others stumble into the common pitfalls without meaning to, so common and familiar are some of those traps. Before moving full-scale into ethics, in any case, we need to survey some of the common pitfalls in ethics and equip ourselves with a few good countermeasures.

FLYING BY INSTINCT

The easiest way to avoid ethical thinking is simply not to think at all. Go with the flow, fly by instinct, follow your feelings. It may mean taking the path of least resistance, or simply doing what's easy or familiar or popular or profitable without a second thought.

Feeling is part of the story—of course. Care, concern, and passion are part of what make ethics so engaging and so compelling. Even instinct plays a role. Sometimes feelings and instincts alert us to moral problems that we might otherwise paper over with excuses. Feelings like these can even start moral revolutions. The arguments come later.

Still, we must also examine and temper our feelings, even the strongest feelings. Take prejudice. To be prejudiced may be to have a strong negative feeling about someone because they are of a different ethnicity or gender or age or social class from yourself. If ethics were just a matter of feelings, then there would be nothing to say against such prejudices. It would be perfectly moral to discriminate against people you don't like.

Feeling may say yes. Ethics says no. Ethics instead asks us to challenge these very feelings. "Prejudice" literally means "prejudgment": it is one way of not really paying attention. But we *need* to pay attention. We need to ask why we feel as we do, whether our beliefs and feelings are true or fair, how we would feel in the other person's shoes, and so on. In short, we need to ask whether our feelings are *justified*—and when not, what alternative feelings might be.

Instincts and feelings may also oversimplify complex situations. We want things to feel clear-cut even when they are not, and so we may persuade ourselves that they really are. Mindful thinking, by contrast, is more patient. Where things are really unclear, in particular, feeling may even have to wait. Premature clarity is worse than confusion. We may have to live with some questions a long time before we can decide how we ought to feel about them.

Our feelings are also easily manipulated. For instance, it is easy to be swayed either way by "loaded language," language that plays upon our emotional reactions. Define abortion as "baby-killing" and you create a negative feeling that closes the case against abortion before it really can even be opened. On the other hand, if you describe abortion as no more than "minor surgery," you suggest that it is both unintrusive and even healthy. Either way, we are led into a prepackaged emotional commitment without ever thinking it through. Habit and conformity take over.

Mindful thinking, by contrast, is more complex and open-ended. It is in this spirit that ethics approaches controversial issues of the day, like abortion or professional ethics or assisted suicide. We do want to honor life, for instance. But we don't necessarily think that life should be prolonged under all circumstances, either. Should people be allowed to request medical help in dying, then? Or would this violate the spirit of medicine itself? Could assisted suicide be allowed sometimes and not others? Why? How do you decide? Questions like these cannot be adequately answered by consulting your preexisting feelings. There are too many different possibilities, too many different opinions and prejudices (on all sides) that need to be sorted out carefully. Think, think, think!

OFFHAND SELF-JUSTIFICATION

Apart from not thinking at all, the next easiest ethics-avoidance strategy is to think as little as possible. Imagine, for example, that I offer some view in a moral discussion. I endorse assisted suicide, maybe. Someone challenges me. My natural first reaction may be to defend whatever it was I just said— even if the challenge is exactly on target. It's a kind of ethical laziness, an automatic excuse-making or defensiveness, or what we sometimes call "rationalizing." I will call it *offhand self-justification*.

I may not even get to the point of asking if the challenge actually is on target. Indeed, that's the idea. I'd rather not. Self-defense is all that counts. I try to paper over my uncertainties (or insecurities, or half-knowledge, or wishful thinking) by grabbing for some excuse—and any excuse will do. "It's

OK to cheat the phone company, because . . . because, well, everyone else does it too . . . because the phone company cheats *you* . . . because. . . . "

Asked for your reasons, you should give them. There is nothing wrong with trying to defend yourself. The problem lies with the offhand or automatic spirit (or, more accurately, spiritlessness) of the defense. Once again, it becomes an excuse for not really *thinking*.

S: Of course the death penalty deters murders. It's a proven fact that murder rates are lower in states with the death penalty.

A: I'm not so sure about that. My understanding is that most states with the death penalty have higher murder rates.

S: Well, you can prove anything with numbers.

S initially appeals to "numbers"—comparative murder rates—to support her position. Challenged, though, she does not reconsider her position or explore other possibilities. She just dismisses any studies that disagree with what she believes—and in the process manages to dismiss the very "numbers" she herself just cited. But she doesn't even notice. You can tell that in the next discussion she'll be right back citing the same "proven fact" again.

RESISTING OFFHAND SELF-JUSTIFICATION

There are no surefire ways to avoid rationalizing. It takes a kind of self-confidence, honesty, and maturity that develop slowly, and even then we seldom escape the temptation entirely. Sometimes it's hard even to recognize an offhand self-justification when it is right in front of our eyes. Yet there are some useful strategies for overcoming the urge.

Remind yourself how self-defeating it is. Making excuses only allows us to go on with some questionable behavior until we get into even worse trouble. It may even be worse than merely hanging on to one unintelligent opinion. When we rationalize, we saddle ourselves with more and more unintelligent opinions—new ones invented, off the top of the head, to patch up the holes in the old ones. But the new ones are likely to be full (or fuller) of holes too. It's not a winning game.

Watch yourself. Step a little more slowly the next time you find yourself casting about for some excuse to put questions to rest. Ask instead whether you really are justified in the first place.

Watch for that telltale anger or irritation at being challenged. We often find ourselves becoming irritated or angry when our especially precious excuses are too persistently or effectively challenged by someone else. But, of course, we get angry at the person challenging us, rather than considering that we might be at fault for offering an offhand excuse in the first place.

Anger at someone else keeps us from having to be angry at ourselves. Better take the irritation as a warning sign.

Avoid the automatic counterattack. Again, watch yourself. Listening to someone else, are you trying to understand, or just waiting for them to stop so that you can give your comeback? Are you trying to win, or to learn? Watch your voice tone: are you conveying ridicule, irritation? Take a time-out if you need it. Give yourself some space to think.

"EVERYONE IS SELFISH"

Here is an especially tempting kind of offhand self-justification that needs a special look of its own. It is the assertion that "everyone is selfish"—sometimes even taken to the point of arguing that there is no other way anyone could possibly be, a view usually called "psychological egoism." It's certainly an easy way out of ethics: if everyone is really selfish anyway, you have no reason not to be selfish yourself, right? Indeed, you can't help it!

We Are Social Animals

Actually, though, very few people past infancy are *that* wrapped up in themselves. We're social animals—and in almost any life with others there's also awareness and responsiveness to others. An athlete sets a new record and all of us, watching, are thrilled too. A kid gets lost in the airport and right away a dozen strangers are ready to help. Think of parents' love for children. Teachers, scientists, soldiers, artists—our lives become compelling and meaningful only when we give them over to something greater than ourselves.

Not that the self doesn't count at all. We do not have to go so far as self-sacrifice—although very often people do: think again of parents, or teachers, or soldiers. For basic ethics it's enough that others' needs register as well as our own. Of course, most people are *somewhat* self-concerned—it's just that the self is nowhere near the whole story.

"Sure," says the egoist, "but if I give myself to science or art, or feel compelled to help the lost kid in the airport, it's because I *want* to. And doing what I want is certainly following my self-interest."

But it all depends on how you want it. If you want to discover a cure for cancer just because it would make you famous, then it's just a selfish want. Most people, though, would actually want to discover a cure for cancer at least in part because it would alleviate a lot of suffering. And that's enough to get us well beyond egoism. Same for the kid in the airport. You want to help the kid because the kid needs help. It's only a kind of extremism to try to reduce everything to some variety of self-interest. We are actually much more interesting creatures than that.

Egoism as a Self-Fulfilling Prophecy

Egoism can sometimes drive others *into* a cynical kind of selfishness. If everyone around you is acting selfishly, you may feel driven to do the same out of discouragement, hurt, or sheer self-protection. If all of your soccer teammates hog the ball, so will you, probably. If all of your business competitors are solely driven by the bottom line (you think), you will be tempted too.

Here, as in offhand self-justification, egoism is made an *excuse*—in this case, for convenient kinds of selfishness. It allows people to justify their own egoism to themselves as well as to others. It is an invitation to mutual mistrust and cynicism. Selfishness becomes a sort of self-fulfilling prophecy, but not because it is somehow "natural." Rather, normal ethical relations have failed.

The point is that this is not how things usually go. In soccer, for example, no team of ball-hogs is going very far. Some basic lessons about teamwork have been forgotten. In business as well, most of the time, businesses answer to other values too: some community responsibility, some care for employees and customers. (It's just that we tend to hear about the flagrant violations.)

Anthropologists do offer (a few) examples of whole societies of seemingly totally selfish people. If you look at those societies closely, though, you will see that they are on the brink of extinction, living in desperate straits. The lesson here too is *not* that "Deep down everyone is really selfish," but exactly the opposite: that it takes almost total social collapse to bring us to actual, full-scale egoism. And oftentimes not even that is enough.

The Truth in Egoism

Any view as persistent as egoism must have something going for it. So we also need to ask: what's the *truth* in egoism? I think there are several.

There are times in your life when you are naturally and appropriately more self-oriented than at other times. Young people going to college, for one example, may find themselves with fairly few attachments and somewhat unsure of their direction. At such times, a turn inward—a preoccupation for awhile with yourself—is natural and probably healthy. It's dramatically limited (I've been suggesting) as a full-time way of life, but it can be sensible in the short run.

Besides, selves are often fragile. Sometimes (it's true) we are *too* tuned to the needs and expectations of others. Sometimes we need to give ourselves the support and attention we need to recover a sense of who we are and what we want. This is probably much more common than the opposite—the self that claims too much and needs to be put in its place. Here too a little bit of self-preoccupation is again a good idea.

More common than any kind of egoism, I think, are other reasons we fail to take account of the needs and expectations of others. The real concern of moralists should be *inattention*. Habit, for one thing, and the inability to listen. Or maybe the unwillingness to listen, as in offhand self-justification. Or the unwillingness to acknowledge sheer *difference*—this would be "self-centeredness," not in the sense of pursuing only one's own interests but in the sense of taking one's self to be the only kind of self there can be. You can't even begin to cross the gap between self and the other if you don't think there is a gap in the first place.

So, of course, ethics sometimes has an uphill fight. There are parts of ourselves that resist. It just may not be so useful to think of those parts as "selfish." To say it again: we're more complex and interesting than that!

DOGMATISM

We all know people who are so committed to their ethical beliefs that they cannot see any other side and cannot defend their own beliefs beyond simply asserting and reasserting them. This is dogmatism. They may appear to listen (or not), but they *will not* change their minds. Name "their" issue (or perhaps *any* issue), and they know the answer already.

To be clear: being committed to a certain set of values—living up to them, or trying to, and sticking up for them when we can—is a fine thing. And there are certain basic moral values to which we are and *should be* deeply and unshakably committed. Dogmatism is a problem because some people go much further. They make no distinction between the basic "givens" of our moral life and everyday moral opinions that are not at all so clear-cut. Every one of their value judgments, to them, has the same status as the Ten Commandments.

Dogmatists tend to disagree about the actual issues—which in fact is a bit ironic. Dogmatists do agree, though, that careful and open-ended thinking about ethical issues is not necessary. After all, if you already know the answer, there is no need to think about it. If you need to argue for your position, you admit that it needs defending, which is to say that people can legitimately have doubts. But that can't be true: you already know that your position is the only right one. Therefore, any reasoned argument for your position is unnecessary. And any reasoned argument *against* your position is obviously absurd. So, why listen?

Dogmatism, then, is a form of ethics-avoidance too. No more thinking is going on here than when we offhandedly justify ourselves with whatever reasons come along. Dogmatists may have their reasons better organized, and may happily debate them with you all afternoon, but they are not really *thinking* about those reasons, only repeating them—louder and louder, probably.

AVOIDING DOGMATISM

Ethics, once again, paints a different picture. Despite the stereotypes, the point of ethics is generally not to moralize or to dictate what is to be done. The real point of ethics is to offer some tools, and some possible directions, for thinking about difficult matters, recognizing from the start—as the very rationale for ethics, in fact—that the world is seldom so simple or clear-cut. Struggle and uncertainty *are* part of ethics, as they are part of life.

So we need to think carefully if we are to act ethically. In fact, thinking carefully about ethical issues—avoiding dogmatism—is *itself* a moral act. Thinking carefully *is* (part of) acting ethically. Philosopher Joshua Halberstam puts it well:

> We need an "ethics of belief" that places value on the way we arrive at our opinions. A healthy ethics of belief requires that our judgments be based on sound evidence. Opinionated people have a weak ethics of belief. They make no distinction between a legitimate opinion and an arbitrary opinion; all that matters is that they have an opinion. The problem with opinionated people is that they don't take their own views seriously enough! When we do take our opinions seriously, humility follows.

Here are some strategies for avoiding dogmatism.

Whenever you find yourself insisting too strongly on some view of your own, try to stop yourself and really listen to the "other side." Imagine that you're an anthropologist or psychologist studying other people's views. Just consider what they're saying without immediately thinking of your responses to it. What sort of world do these people live in? How does it hang together? How can it seem like the simple and obvious truth to them, just as yours does to you? Later on you can kick in your own views and compare them. First just give yourself a little space to listen.

Another useful strategy is to seek out *arguments* for the other side(s). One way that dogmatic views ensure themselves long lives is by systematically avoiding the other side's arguments. Only the other side's *conclusions* are registered. This person is for (or against) capital punishment, let's say, and that's all a dogmatist needs to know. He doesn't ask *why*: he's not interested. Looking at the *reasons* for other and opposed positions both helps you understand the positions better and may begin to introduce some more complex thinking. It's amazing but true: people don't just disagree with us out of sheer perversity or ignorance! Again this is an "obvious" thing that sometimes we don't really quite know well enough.

It pays to adjust our language as well. Instead of categorical statements of dogmatic opinions, especially bumpersticker style slogans ("Meat Is Murder"; "It's Adam and Eve, Not Adam and Steve," etc.), try to speak in a way that is less categorical and final. Very few reasonable ethical positions can be shoehorned into a bumpersticker or slogan, clever as they might be—in fact, you might avoid any view that *could* be shoehorned into a bumpersticker for just that reason—and besides, this way of putting things polarizes views and makes the other side seem stupid and misled. Don't call names either ("You animal-rights fanatics . . . "; "You Bible-thumpers . . . "). Avoid the easy labels ("liberal," "right-wing," etc.).

Sometimes language leads the mind. Speaking in an open-ended way may help you begin to *think* in an open-ended way as well. Certainly it will create quite different conversations. Typically one dogmatic statement just provokes an equal and opposite dogmatic statement. Speak differently and not only your mind but your discussions may open up differently, and more constructively too! (This book will have a lot more to say about language in chapter 11.)

Halberstam again:

> Don't elevate your every whim into a conviction. Having an opinion is one thing, delivering the Ten Commandments is something else. Intellectual honesty demands that unless you're a bona fide expert in the field, a hint of tentativeness should accompany all your views and decisions. Indeed, a hint of uncertainty is appropriate even if you *are* an authority. Here's a simple device to ensure that you have the proper humility when offering your opinion: When you speak, imagine that an expert is sitting right across from you. Now offer that opinion.

RELATIVISM

"It's all relative," we sometimes say. What's right for you may not be right for me. Mind your own business. Don't criticize. Any moral opinion is as good as the next. This attitude is a form of *relativism.*

Relativism begins with the simple observation that different individuals and societies sometimes have different moral values. Maybe I think speeding is OK. You think speeders ought to have their licenses revoked. Some societies actually execute them! Or again, some societies tolerate homeless populations running into the millions, while in others the very idea of allowing even one person to be homeless, whatever the cause, would be shameful, unthinkable. Some societies condemn sex between unmarried young people; others approve and even encourage it.

Relativists go on to wonder if any single standard can be "right." And we should acknowledge right away that this can be a good question. At the very least, it's mind-opening to look at other points of view, and ethical matters are complex enough that no one point of view is likely to have a monopoly on the truth anyway. Besides, sometimes we need to assert our right to do as we please, even if others think we are making a big mistake. This is one of relativism's chief uses in practice: making a space for us to figure things out for ourselves.

OFFHAND SELF-JUSTIFICATION AGAIN

But relativists typically go much further—and here relativism becomes a "disorder." From our differences about ethical questions they may conclude that there is no legitimate basis for arguing about them at all. It's all just opinion, they say, and one opinion is as good as another. But here, though relativism may appear to be the very model of open-mindedness, it actually has just the opposite effect. It begins to close our minds instead.

U: I support the death penalty. I believe that it saves lives because it makes murderers think twice before killing someone. As the Bible says, "An eye for an eye, a tooth for a tooth."

V: I don't agree.

U: Why?

V: I just don't. That's my opinion, and it's as good as yours!

Maybe that's a little blatant, but you get the idea. Here relativism slides right into offhand self-justification. V treats it like a magic key to escape any kind of thinking whatsoever. She cannot even be bothered to offer any reasons, let alone engage U's.

In fact, all opinions on this and most ethical subjects require further thinking. Are U's arguments good ones? What values stand on the other side? What are V's reasons *against* the death penalty? Is the death penalty really a deterrent? Doesn't the Bible also tell us not to kill?

The key point here may be a bit surprising to people who have grown used to using "relativism" as another form, in effect, of offhand self-justification (and to their teachers too, maybe). To say it again: even if moral values vary all over the map, there is no way out of some good hard thinking.

The very contrast of values is a great occasion for thinking, for one thing. When we look at other societies' or people's values, we may find ourselves asking if our own values are really the best ones: usually a useful question, even if we end up deciding that they are the best, at least for us.

MINDING OUR OWN BUSINESS

There is another practical problem with relativism—again, *even if* values really do differ, maybe even fundamentally.

Ethics often concerns matters that affect us all. Take pollution. If the air is polluted, it doesn't merely affect the polluters. If we spend money on pollution cleanup and prevention, on the other hand, we can't spend that money on other things, perhaps better things, maybe again for all of us. For some people it could be a life-or-death matter, however we decide. The same goes for issues like fair trade, professional ethics, other animals, and many others. None of these are just our "own" business. Other people's lives and health and possibilities are at stake too. These matters—basic ethical issues—are *everyone's* business.

The relativist's stock phrase, "Mind your own business," is therefore an antisocial response. It not only avoids thinking on the relativist's part, it also refuses to acknowledge that on issues like these, however much we differ, we still need to work out some way of going on together.

D: I oppose legal abortion.

E: Why don't you just mind your own business? Like the slogan says, if you're against abortion, then don't have one!

But there is more to it than this. If some of us practice abortion and some do not, the result is a society in which abortion is practiced. The rest of us have to stand for it, at least insofar as we have to stand aside. Likewise, if some of us pollute and some don't, the result is pollution for everyone. In such matters, we cannot act as though everyone can simply do as they please without anyone else being affected.

Some philosophers argue that this is the very *point* of ethics: to help us arrive at certain standards that we all are to live by when all of us are affected by each other's behavior. Some philosophers even start from this point to build a theory of ethics. On this view, ethics is precisely for those cases where "Mind your own business!" doesn't work as an approach to a problem. Instead, we need to work things out together. Keep an open mind; stay in touch and keep talking.

Relativism actually isn't a bad beginning: it does remind us that there are others, probably with different views, with whom we have to work things out. But then we need to go and do it!

RELATIVISM: PHILOSOPHICAL QUESTIONS

This chapter concentrates on practical objections to ethical relativism. Even if most of relativism's claims are true, I argue, we can and must actually *think*, long and hard, about ethical issues. The tools in your ethical toolbox are no less vital.

Relativism is also much argued over among philosophers. In this box I want to explore some of these further objections and arguments over relativism—briefly—to give you a sense both of how philosophers argue and of how complex some seemingly obvious things really are. Here are a number of loosely linked questions and challenges to think about.

Is the Diversity of Values Overrated?

Ethical relativism is based upon the claim that moral values differ in fundamental ways among different people and cultures. This is called *descriptive* ethical relativism: it is an empirical claim about the world.

Empirical claims need testing. So what's the evidence? How much *real* disagreement is there about moral values? That is, do we really disagree "all the way down," so to speak, or might apparently different moral values flow instead from different factual beliefs about the world?

Eskimo (Inuit) bands were discovered by early European explorers to sometimes leave their old people out in the cold of winter to die. This was contrasted to the European attitude, which was supposed to be one of respect and care for the old (though in fact it was a fair bit spottier than that). The explorers, anyway, were scandalized. It looked like a clear difference of values.

Later explorers, however, discovered several more things. One was that these bands often lived at the margins between survival and starvation during the winter and had to move quickly in the spring to find food. Very old people could not keep up. Leaving them behind was a matter of social survival—a choice that we too might make in the same circumstances.

Another discovery was that the Eskimo believe in an afterlife—and believe that people enter the afterlife in the same condition they leave this one. So allowing or even encouraging the old to die once their usefulness was past was not evidence of heartlessness or disrespect for life—quite the opposite. Again, if we (really, truly) shared their belief, we presumably would do the same.

In this case, then, what seemed to be a disagreement about values turned out to be a disagreement about certain facts. So how real are other alleged disagreements about moral values? Do we really differ that much? Is descriptive ethical relativism true? Can you think of contemporary ethical disagreements that might dissolve under scrutiny, like the Eskimo case might? Can you think of some that wouldn't?

Why Should Diversity Be the Last Word?

No doubt there are at least *some* serious disagreements about moral values themselves. But what exactly does this prove? Is disagreement the last word?

After all, we could take our disagreements as *starting points*—something to think about and learn from—rather than end points. The fact that some people are racists, for example, doesn't prove that racism is only wrong *for us*. It only proves that people have some learning to do. Now people are disagreeing about global warming. Perhaps the same thing can be said: if and when we really look at the evidence, will we really conclude that we have no obligation to take global warming seriously?

So perhaps the real question is, how much disagreement about moral values would remain after all of this thinking and learning? Is it so obvious that we would still disagree in such fundamental ways, about values themselves? Again, a little humility and investigation—and indeed, some real ethical argument—would be a much better idea.

What Does the Diversity of Values Imply?

Now suppose that descriptive ethical relativism *is* true. That is, suppose we really do differ, and differ sharply, about moral values, and would continue to differ even after careful criticism and argument. What then? What follows, if anything, about moral values or ethical arguments? That is, what follows about relativism in what philosophers call the *prescriptive* sense?

Does it follow, in particular, that there is no single "right" answer to ethical questions? Not necessarily. Sheer difference, by itself, does not prove that no one single standard is "right." Maybe all sides but one are *wrong*. People disagree about all kinds of issues (Is the Earth flat? Does vitamin C prevent colds?), but we don't suppose there is no truth of the matter in those cases. Is there something special about value judgments that makes them different from "facts" in this way? Maybe, but if you think so, see if you can explain what it is. Spell out the argument.

One note of caution. It may actually be true that there is no one single "right" answer to (many) ethical questions—but not for relativistic reasons. Maybe there is no one single "right" answer because most ethical situations are so *complex* that a variety of different but equally good responses are possible. This would not mean that any answer is as good as the next (there are still plenty of *wrong* answers) or that critical thinking is somehow pointless in ethics. Quite the opposite: once again, it would call for more flexible and subtle thinking still.

Does the Diversity of Values Make a Practical Difference?

Now suppose that prescriptive ethical relativism *is* true. That is, suppose there is no arguably "right" answer to ethical questions, and maybe even that any answer is in some sense as good as the next. What exactly would this imply?

Suppose the "cultural" relativist is right that you and I cannot argue with, say, cannibals about cannibalism. Well, how often do you argue with cannibals? Mostly we argue with people who share our terms. I have never argued with a cannibal, not even once, but I argued constantly with my own children, whose eating habits also left something to be desired. And I *could* argue with them—they were growing into *our* culture and had some learning to do.

On the other hand, sometimes we *are* asked to make ethical judgments across cultural lines, as when American corporations were pressured to (and mostly did) pull out of South Africa to protest apartheid. Was that a valid action, in your view? What would the relativist say about it? What do you think of the relativist's response?

The Truth in Relativism

Finally, for those who reject relativism, what do you think relativism is nonetheless *right* about?

The complexity of many situations, making it hard to say that there is one single right answer? That's a useful reminder: it encourages some moral humility.

The need for some ethical space, even to make our own mistakes? A good point also: ethical demands can sometimes be very confining, especially when dogmatic moralists get going on them. Relativism is a way of at least winning a little space to think for yourself. Just don't think that you therefore have to defend "relativism" in the sense we have been exploring. Again, it may not be relativism at all, really: more like the *complexity* of real ethical issues. "Relativism" here just stands for a freer spirit, more flexibility in ethics, a reminder that the truth is not so easy to come by.

Relativism also can amount to an insistence that we need to look at things from others' points of view. Our own view is *not* the only view around; we have much to learn from others, as they may from us, and in any case we have to work out some way of going on together. Again, relativism tempers dogmatism . . . but still, we'd be better off without either.

█ FOR REVIEW

1. What is an "ethics-avoidance disorder"?
2. Why not fly by instinct?
3. Illustrate "offhand self-justification."

4. What is wrong with offhand self-justification?

5. "Everyone is really just out for themselves." How is this true? How is it not true?

6. Illustrate dogmatism, using yourself as an example if you can.

7. What are some concrete strategies for avoiding dogmatism?

8. When does relativism "slide into offhand self-justification"?

9. Why does the text accuse relativism of being antisocial?

10. What are some philosophical difficulties with relativism?

EXERCISES AND NOTES

2.1 SELF-REFLECTIONS

We have noted some of the ways in which people avoid ethical thinking—often without even noticing or admitting that that is what is happening. So now consider yourself. What do you get dogmatic about? What do you rationalize about? What do you get defensive about? What do you have trouble hearing? Why? (Explore that *why* question—understanding yourself better is often the key to change.)

Give yourself some credit too. What are you *good* at hearing? On what topics are you truly open-minded? Where do you *embrace* ethical thinking? And why is this?

Admitting to a degree of ethics-avoidance does not mean that you instantly have to change. Perhaps you will never be able to change completely. The point is instead to mark out the areas that need special attention—places where you need to watch yourself, and where others need to be both more sensitive and maybe more insistent.

2.2 HEARING THE "OTHER SIDE"

Name some ethical positions that you find especially hard to take seriously. Do this before reading on.

Now, as an exercise in opening the mind a little, your task is to write or state these positions in as neutral a way as possible. You don't have to be effusive, and don't try to be extremely positive—usually it is easier to be overly positive than to state a view carefully. Just try to state each position in a reasonable way, not loaded or satirical but simply straight. You may have to do a little research to get them right. In class, ask a classmate who holds those moral views to help you out.

Consider also the *reasons* that are typically used to support these views. What are those reasons? What are the best reasons according to *you*—the reasons that would persuade you if any reasons could? Again, don't argue with the positions. Just look for the strongest defense of each position you can find.

You don't have to agree with these positions, of course—after all, you picked them because you not only disagree with them but also find them hard to take seriously. The point is to try to understand them, and in general to try to get a little distance from your own reactions, to create a little more space for open-mindedness.

This exercise works best if you avoid the hottest issues that we have all heard debated too many times already, such as abortion. People seem to have heard the two main positions on abortion enough that it is too easy to rattle them off. On other issues, it takes more care and work—and that is really the point.

2.3 A DIALOGUE

Ethics-avoidance disorders are partly conversational or argumentative moves: they occur in dialogue, in the back-and-forth of conversation or argument. Sometimes they are also subtle.

A class of mine recently found itself in a discussion about gay marriage. It was the day after newspapers reported that the federal district judge who invalidated California's Proposition 8 in early 2010 was himself in a long-term relationship with another man. (Proposition 8 was an attempt to ban gay marriage in California: the judge ruled it unconstitutional.) Below is an exchange from part of that discussion. Carefully consider this exchange. Consider where (and why) you think ethics-avoidance strategies are "disordering" the participants' thinking. You might also try rewriting the dialogue, or writing your own, to avoid the pitfalls you point out.

F: I can see why people think this situation is scandalous. That judge had a direct interest in the outcome: he might get to marry his partner. He should have taken himself off the case!

G: I wouldn't assume that all gay people necessarily want to marry their partners.

F: How do you know? Are you gay?

H: Would you take a female judge off a sex-discrimination case? How about taking an Italian judge off a case against the Mafia?

I: Not to get into stereotypes or anything.

G: It would make more sense to take a *male* judge off the sex-discrimination case, actually. Men are the ones who might feel threatened by it, and therefore less able to be impartial.

J: Yeah, that's a good point. Why are you assuming that it would be more objective to have a straight person decide this case? A straight person would be a better judge of whether marriage should be a privilege reserved just for straight people? Really?

I: Get a monk or something, somebody who is not going to marry anyone at all.

J: No, he couldn't be objective either. Maybe he'd just ban marriage entirely. There's no objectivity on this question.

K: That's just what I've always said: whatever you do, somebody will complain about discrimination.

H: So what? Maybe Mister Somebody's just wrong.

L: I don't see what the big deal is, really. Everybody I know is just "live and let live" about gay marriage.

F: A majority of Californians aren't, apparently.

L: The media just riled up all the Bible-thumpers. They're all for freedom and against any kind of regulation, except when they don't like what other people do in bed.

H: The trend is against them, anyway. Quite a few states now allow gay marriage. I predict that in ten years it will be a non-issue.

NOTES

I know: it's not entirely fair to label dogmatism, relativism, and so on as "disorders," at least on the model of "attention deficit disorder" and other cognitive disorders that can be long-standing physiological conditions. Ethics-avoidance is a matter of habit and choice. But the label also makes a point. These are actually *disorders,* patterns of behavior that are not good for you or anyone else and that can be identified and corrected. I've tried to show how.

Joshua Halberstam's book *Everyday Ethics* (Penguin, 1993) is an interesting and opinionated complement to this one. He is cited here from pp. 155 and 156.

Rationalizing may be one of the deepest of all pitfalls in ethics (and probably in life generally). For some psychological background, including some fascinating and unsettling experiments, see David Myers, *Social Psychology* (McGraw-Hill, 10th edition, 2009), chapters 2–4. For a useful overview of self-deception, see chapter 6 of Mike Martin's *Everyday Morality* (Wadsworth Publishing Company, 2006).

For a more traditional discussion of relativism, see James Rachels, *The Elements of Moral Philosophy* (McGraw-Hill, 6th edition, 2010), chapter 2.

I deal with relativism from a different angle in my *Toward Better Problems* (Temple University Press, 1992), chapter 7. Ethical thinkers who have tried to derive a substantive ethics precisely from the need to go on together in the face of diverse values include John Rawls, in *A Theory of Justice* (Harvard University Press, 1971), sections 3 and 20–26, and David Gauthier, in *Morals by Agreement* (Clarendon Press, 1986).

For a discussion of pluralism and relativism in ethics, ethical egoism, and related questions, go to the "Ethics Updates" website at http://ethics.sandiego .edu and look under "Ethical Theory."

USING YOUR TOOLS #1
"IS FOOD THE NEW SEX?"

This is the first of nine sections in this book, inserted between every other chapter, called "Using Your Tools." UYTs, for short (just say "yoot"). The aim of the UYTs in general is to offer some additional exercises and activities that are somewhat longer and more ambitious than those in the individual chapters. This first UYT, for example, speaks to the themes of both chapters 1 and 2 and should make for a provocative exploration and class discussion (I hope) after you have worked through the first two chapters. Even if you do not undertake it as a class discussion project, you should find the reading provocative and the questions that follow it useful to carry on your own thinking.

The opposite of ethics-avoidance is something like this: *enthusiasm* for ethical thinking, even seeking out questions and issues to explore, on your own and with others. Enjoyment—yes, believe it or not, enjoyment—of that process, and a desire to share it with others. Ethical thinking is difficult, sometimes painful, sometimes it requires us to seriously rethink our ways—this is all true. But ethical thinking is also inviting, intriguing, and potentially transformative. Perhaps already you have a taste for that side of ethics as well . . . but I would like to be sure. My aim with this first UYT, then, is to put before you a question that you might find enjoyable, inviting, maybe even irresistible in this way. The best way to overcome ethics-avoidance is to make ethical thinking actually tempting!

Here, then, is a recent article comparing the evolution of our attitudes toward food and toward sex. It is a provocative, sweeping comparison between our views on two ethical subjects that matter to us greatly—but that are not usually compared in this way. The author of this article, Mary Eberstadt, also has a very definite position, at least on the sex question, and (as the saying goes) has an axe to grind. You may or may not agree with her. Either way, though, I suspect you will find this article engaging, and that is the real aim. The issues are of course serious, but that doesn't mean that thinking about them must necessarily be ponderous and over-moralized. These subjects themselves may invite another attitude or mode of engagement. See what you think.

READING

"Is Food the New Sex?"

MARY EBERSTADT

MARY EBERSTADT is an author and a research fellow at Stanford University's Hoover Institution. She writes extensively on culture and politics from a conservative point of view. She has

served as an editor and consulting editor for journals such as
Policy Review, the Hoover Institution's bimonthly journal, and
The National Interest. In 1984–85 she was a special assistant
to Jeane J. Kirkpatrick, President Reagan's Ambassador to the
United Nations. This essay is abridged (by AW) from a longer
article that you can find on the Web at http://www.hoover.org
/publications/policy-review/article/5542.

Of all the truly seismic shifts transforming daily life today—deeper than our
financial fissures, wider even than our most obvious political and cultural
divides—one of the most important is also among the least remarked. That is
the chasm in attitude that separates almost all of us living in the West today
from almost all of our ancestors, over two things without which human beings
cannot exist: food and sex.

The question before us today is not whether the two appetites are closely connected. About that much, philosophers and other commentators have been
agreed for a very long time. Ordinary language itself verifies how similarly the
two appetites are experienced, with many of the same words crossing over to
describe what is desirable and undesirable in each case. In fact, we sometimes
have trouble even talking about food without metaphorically invoking sex, and
vice versa. In a hundred entangled ways, judging by either language or literature, the human mind juggles sex and food almost interchangeably at times.
And why not? Both desires can make people do things they otherwise would
not; and both are experienced at different times by most men and women as
the most powerful of all human drives.

One more critical link between the appetites for sex and food is this: Both,
if pursued without regard to consequence, can prove ruinous not only to
oneself, but also to other people, and even to society itself. No doubt for
that reason, both appetites have historically been subject in all civilizations
to rules both formal and informal. Thus the potentially destructive forces of
sex—disease, disorder, sexual aggression, sexual jealousy, and what used to
be called "home-wrecking"—have been ameliorated in every recorded society
by legal, social, and religious conventions, primarily stigma and punishment.
Similarly, all societies have developed rules and rituals governing food in
part to avoid the destructiveness of free-for-alls over scarce necessities. And
while food rules may not always have been as stringent as sex rules, they have
nevertheless been stringent as needed. Such is the meaning, for example, of
being hanged for stealing a loaf of bread in the marketplace, or keel-hauled for
plundering rations on a ship.

These disciplines imposed historically on access to food and sex now raise
a question that has not come up before, probably because it was not even
possible to imagine it until the lifetimes of the people reading this: What happens when, for the first time in history—at least in theory, and at least in the
advanced nations—adult human beings are more or less free to have all the
sex and food they want?

This question opens the door to a real paradox. For given how closely
connected the two appetites appear to be, it would be natural to expect

that people would do the same kinds of things with both appetites—that they would pursue both with equal ardor when finally allowed to do so, for example, or with equal abandon for consequence; or conversely, with similar degrees of discipline in the consumption of each.

In fact, though, evidence from the advanced West suggests that nearly the opposite seems to be true. The answer appears to be that when many people are faced with these possibilities for the very first time, they end up doing very different things—things we might signal by shorthand as mindful eating and mindless sex. This essay is both an exploration of that curious dynamic, and a speculation about what is driving it.

AS MUCH AS YOU WANT

Up until just about now, the prime brakes on sex outside of marriage have been several: fear of pregnancy, fear of social stigma and punishment, and fear of disease. The Pill and its cousins have substantially undermined the first two strictures, at least in theory, while modern medicine has largely erased the third. Even HIV/AIDS, only a decade ago a stunning exception to the brand new rule that one could apparently have any kind of sex at all without serious consequence, is now regarded as a "manageable" disease in the affluent West, even as it continues to kill millions of less fortunate patients elsewhere.

As for food, here too one technological revolution after another explains the extraordinary change in its availability: pesticides, mechanized farming, economical transportation, genetic manipulation of food stocks, and other advances. As a result, almost everyone in the Western world is now able to buy sustenance of all kinds, for very little money, and in quantities unimaginable until the lifetimes of the people reading this.

One result of this change in food fortune, of course, is the unprecedented "disease of civilization" known as obesity, with its corollary ills. Nevertheless, the commonplace fact of obesity in today's West itself testifies to the point that access to food has expanded exponentially for just about everyone. So does the statistical fact that obesity is most prevalent in the lowest social classes and least exhibited in the highest.

And just as technology has made sex and food more accessible for a great many people, important extra-technological influences on both pursuits— particularly longstanding religious strictures—have meanwhile diminished in a way that has made both appetites even easier to indulge. The opprobrium reserved for gluttony, for example, seems to have little immediate force now, even among believers. On the rare occasions when one even sees the word, it is almost always used in a metaphorical, secular sense.

Similarly, and far more consequential, the longstanding religious prohibitions in every major creed against extramarital sex have rather famously loosed their holds over the contemporary mind. Of particular significance, perhaps, has been the movement of many Protestant denominations away from the sexual morality agreed upon by the previous millennia of Christendom. The Anglican abandonment in 1930 of the longstanding prohibition against artificial contraception is a special case in point, undermining as it subsequently did for many believers the very idea that any church could tell people what to do with their bodies, ever again. Whether they defended their traditional teachings or abandoned them, however, all Western Christian churches in the past century have found themselves increasingly belea-guered over issues of sex, and commensurately less influential over all but a fraction of the most traditionally minded parishioners.

Of course this waning of the traditional restraints on the pursuit of sex and food is only part of the story; any number of non-religious forces today also act as contemporary brakes on both. In the case of food, for example, these would include factors like personal vanity, say, or health concerns, or preoc-cupation with the morality of what is consumed (about which more below). Similarly, to acknowledge that sex is more accessible than ever before is not to say that it is always and everywhere available. Many people who do not think they will go to hell for premarital sex or adultery, for example, find brakes on their desires for other reasons: fear of disease, fear of hurting children or other loved ones, fear of disrupting one's career, fear of financial setbacks in the form of divorce and child support, and so on.

Even men and women who do want all the food or sex they can get their hands on face obstacles of other kinds in their pursuit. Though many people really can afford to eat more or less around the clock, for example, home eco-nomics will still put the brakes on; it's not as if everyone can afford pheasant under glass day and night. The same is true of sex, which likewise imposes its own unwritten yet practical constraints. Older and less attractive people simply cannot command the sexual marketplace as the younger and more attractive can (which is why the promises of erasing time and age are such a booming business in a post-liberation age). So do time and age still circum-scribe the pursuit of sex, even as churches and other conventional enforcers increasingly do not.

Still and all, the initial point stands: As consumers of both sex and food, today's people in the advanced societies are freer to pursue and consume both than almost all the human beings who came before us; and our culture has evolved in interesting ways to exhibit both those trends.

BROCCOLI, PORNOGRAPHY, AND KANT

To begin to see just how recent and dramatic this change is, let us imagine some broad features of the world seen through two different sets of eyes: a hypothetical 30-year-old housewife from 1958 named Betty, and her hypotheti-cal granddaughter Jennifer, of the same age, today.

Begin with a tour of Betty's kitchen. Much of what she makes comes from jars and cans. Much of it is also heavy on substances that people of our time are told to minimize—dairy products, red meat, refined sugars and flours—because of compelling research about nutrition that occurred after Betty's time. Betty's freezer is filled with meat every four months by a visiting com-pany that specializes in volume, and on most nights she thaws a piece of this and accompanies it with food from one or two jars. If there is anything "fresh" on the plate, it is likely a potato. Interestingly, and rudimentary to our contemporary eyes though it may be, Betty's food is served with what for us would appear to be high ceremony, i.e., at a set table with family members present.

As it happens, there is little that Betty herself, who is adventurous by the standards of her day, will not eat; the going slogan she learned as a child is about cleaning your plate, and not doing so is still considered bad form. Aside from that notion though, which is a holdover to scarcer times, Betty is much like any other American home cook in 1958. She likes making some things and not others, even as she prefers eating some things to others—and there, in personal aesthetics, does the matter end for her. It's not that Betty lacks opinions about food. It's just that the ones she has are limited to what she does and does not personally like to make and eat.

Now imagine one possible counterpart to Betty today, her 30-year-old grand-daughter Jennifer. Jennifer has almost no cans or jars in her cupboard. She has no children or husband or live-in boyfriend either, which is why her kitchen table on most nights features a laptop and goes unset. Yet interestingly enough, despite the lack of ceremony at the table, Jennifer pays far more attention to food, and feels far more strongly in her convictions about it, than anyone she knows from Betty's time.

Wavering in and out of vegetarianism, Jennifer is adamantly opposed to eating red meat or endangered fish. She is also opposed to industrialized breeding, genetically enhanced fruits and vegetables, and to pesticides and other artificial agents. She tries to minimize her dairy intake and cooks tofu as much as possible. She also buys "organic" in the belief that it is better both for her and for the animals raised in that way, even though the products are markedly more expensive than those from the local grocery store. Her diet is heavy in all the ways that Betty's was light: with fresh vegetables and fruits in particular. Jennifer has nothing but ice in her freezer, soymilk and various other items her grandmother wouldn't have recognized in the refrigerator, and on the counter stands a vegetable juicer she feels she "ought" to use more.

Most important of all, however, is the difference in moral attitude separating Betty and Jennifer on the matter of food. Jennifer feels that there is a right and wrong about these options that transcends her exercise of choice as a consumer. She does not exactly condemn those who believe otherwise, but she doesn't understand why they do, either.

And she certainly thinks the world would be a better place if more people evaluated their food choices as she does. She even proselytizes on occasion when she can. In short, with regard to food, Jennifer falls within Immanuel Kant's definition of the Categorical Imperative: She acts according to a set of maxims that she wills at the same time to be universal law.

Betty, on the other hand, would be baffled by the idea of dragooning such moral abstractions into the service of food. This is partly because, as a child of her time, she was impressed—as Jennifer is not—about what happens when food is scarce (Betty's parents told her often about their memories of the Great Depression; and many of the older men of her time had vivid memories of deprivation in wartime). Even without such personal links to food scarcity, though, it makes no sense to Betty that people would feel as strongly as her granddaughter does about something as simple as deciding just what goes into one's mouth. That is because Betty feels, as Jennifer obviously does not, that opinions about food are simply "de gustibus," a matter of individual taste—and only that.

This clear difference in opinion leads to an intriguing juxtaposition. Just as Betty and Jennifer have radically different approaches to food, so do they to matters of sex. For Betty, the ground rules of her time—which she both participates in and substantially agrees with—are clear: Just about every exercise of sex outside marriage is subject to social (if not always private) opprobrium. Wavering in and out of established religion herself, Betty nevertheless clearly adheres to a traditional Judeo-Christian sexual ethic. Thus, for example, Mr. Jones next door "ran off" with another woman, leaving his wife and children behind; Susie in the town nearby got pregnant and wasn't allowed back in school; Uncle Bill is rumored to have contracted gonorrhea; and so on. None of these breaches of the going sexual ethic is considered by Betty to be a good thing, let alone a celebrated thing. They are not even considered to be neutral things. In fact, they are all considered by her to be wrong.

Most important of all, Betty feels that sex, unlike food, is not "de gustibus." She believes to the contrary that there is a right and wrong about these choices that transcends any individual act. She further believes that the world would be a better place, and individual people better off, if others believed as she does. She even proselytizes such on occasion when given the chance.

In short, as Jennifer does with food, Betty in the matter of sex fulfills the requirements for Kant's Categorical Imperative.

Jennifer's approach to sex is just about 180 degrees different. She too disapproves of the father next door who left his wife and children for a younger woman; she does not want to be cheated on herself, or to have those she cares about cheated on either. These ground-zero stipulations, aside, however, she is otherwise laissez-faire on just about every other aspect of nonmarital sex. She believes that living together before marriage is not only morally neutral but actually better than not having such a "trial run." Pregnant unwed Susie in the next town doesn't elicit a thought one way or the other from her, and neither does Uncle Bill's gonorrhea, which is of course a trivial medical matter between him and his doctor.

Jennifer, unlike Betty, thinks that falling in love creates its own demands and generally trumps other considerations—unless perhaps children are involved (and sometimes, on a case-by-case basis, then too). A consistent thinker in this respect, she also accepts the consequences of her libertarian convictions about sex. She is pro-abortion, pro-gay marriage, indifferent to ethical questions about stem cell research and other technological manipulations of nature (as she is not, ironically, when it comes to food), and agnostic on the question of whether any particular parental arrangements seem best for children. She has even been known to watch pornography with her boyfriend, at his coaxing, in part to show just how very laissez-faire she is.

Most important, once again, is the difference in moral attitude between the two women on this subject of sex. Betty feels that there is a right and wrong about sexual choices that transcends any individual act, and Jennifer—exceptions noted—does not. It's not that Jennifer lacks for opinions about sex, any more than Betty does about food. It's just that, for the most part, they are limited to what she personally does and doesn't like.

Thus far, what the imaginary examples of Betty and Jennifer have established is this: Their personal moral relationships toward food and toward sex are just about perfectly reversed. Betty does care about nutrition and food, but it doesn't occur to her to extend her opinions to a moral judgment—i.e., to believe that other people ought to do as she does in the matter of food, and that they are wrong if they don't. In fact, she thinks such an extension would be wrong in a different way; it would be impolite, needlessly judgmental, simply not done. Jennifer, similarly, does care to some limited degree about what other people do about sex; but it seldom occurs to her to extend her opinions to a moral judgment. In fact, she thinks such an extension would be wrong in a different way—because it would be impolite, needlessly judgmental, simply not done.

On the other hand, Jennifer is genuinely certain that her opinions about food are not only nutritionally correct, but also, in some deep, meaningful sense, morally correct—i.e., she feels that others ought to do something like what she does. And Betty, on the other hand, feels exactly the same way about what she calls sexual morality.

As noted, this desire to extend their personal opinions in two different areas to an "ought" that they think should be somehow binding—binding, that is, to the idea that others should do the same—is the definition of the Kantian imperative. Once again, note: Betty's Kantian imperative concerns sex not food, and Jennifer's concerns food not sex. In just over 50 years, in other words—not for everyone, of course, but for a great many people, and for an especially large portion of sophisticated people—the moral poles of sex and food have been reversed. Betty thinks food is a matter of taste, whereas sex is governed by universal moral law of some kind; and Jennifer thinks exactly the reverse. [. . .]

RESPECTING SOME HAZARDS, IGNORING OTHERS

If it is true that food is the new sex, however, where does that leave sex? This brings us to the paradox already hinted at. As the consumption of food not only literally but also figuratively has become progressively more discriminate and thoughtful, at least in theory (if rather obviously not always in practice), the consumption of sex in various forms appears to have become the opposite for a great many people: i.e., progressively more indiscriminate and unthinking.

Several proofs could be offered for such a claim, beginning with any number of statistical studies. Both men and women are far less likely to be sexually inexperienced on their weddings now (if indeed they marry) than they were just a few decades ago. They are also more likely to be experienced in all kinds of ways, including in the use of pornography. Like the example of Jennifer, moreover, their general thoughts about sex become more laissez-faire the further down the age demographic one goes.

Consider as further proof of the dumbing-down of sex the coarseness of popular entertainment, say through a popular advice column on left-leaning *Slate* magazine called "Dear Prudence" that concerns "manners and morals." Practically every subject line is window onto a world of cheap, indiscriminate sex, where the only ground rule is apparently that no sexual urge shall ever be discouraged unless it manifestly hurts others—meaning literally. "Should I destroy the erotic video my husband and I have made?" "My boyfriend's kinky fetish might doom our relationship." "My husband wants me to abort, and I don't." "How do I tell my daughter she's the result of a sexual assault?" "A friend confessed to a fling with my now-dead husband." And so on. The mindful vegetarian slogan, "you are what you eat," has no counterpart in the popular culture today when it comes to sex.

The third and probably most important feature of sex in our time testifying to the ubiquity of appetites fulfilled and indulged indiscriminately is the staggering level of consumption of Internet pornography. As Ross Douthat recently summarized in an essay for *The Atlantic*, provocatively titled "Is Pornography Adultery?":

> Over the past three decades, the VCR, on-demand cable service, and the Internet have completely overhauled the ways in which people interact with porn. Innovation has piled on innovation, making modern pornography a more immediate, visceral, and personalized experience. Nothing in the long history of erotica compares with the way millions of Americans experience porn today, and our moral intuitions are struggling to catch up.

Statistics too, or at least preliminary ones, bear out just how consequential this erotic novelty is becoming. Pornography is the single most viewed subject online, by men anyway; it is increasingly a significant factor in divorce cases; and it is resulting in any number of cottage industries, from the fields of therapy to law to academia, as society's leading cultural institutions strive to measure and cope with its impact.[1]

This junk sex shares all the defining features of junk food. It is produced and consumed by people who do not know one another. It is disdained by those who believe they have access to more authentic experience or "healthier" options. Internet pornography is further widely said—right now, in its relatively early years—to be harmless, much as few people thought little of the ills to come through convenient prepared food when it first appeared; and evidence is also beginning to emerge about compulsive pornography consumption, as it did slowly but surely in the case of compulsive packaged food consumption, that this laissez-faire judgment is wrong.[2]

This brings us to another similarity between junk sex and junk food: People are furtive about both, and many feel guilty about their pursuit and indulgence of each. And those who consume large amounts of both are also typically self-deceptive too: that is, they underestimate just how much they do it and deny its ill effects on the rest of their lives. In sum, to compare junk food to junk sex is to realize that they have become virtually interchangeable vices—even if many people who do not put "sex" in the category of vice will readily do so with food.

At this point, the impatient reader will interject that something else—something understandable and anodyne—is driving the increasing attention to food in our day: namely, the fact that we have learned much more than humans used to know about the importance of a proper diet to health and longevity. And this is surely a point borne out by the facts, too. One attraction of macrobiotics, for example, is its promise to reduce the risks of cancer. The fall in cholesterol that attends a true vegan or vegetarian diet is another example. Manifestly, one reason that people today are so much more discriminating about food is that decades of recent research have taught us that diet has more potent effects than Betty and her friends understood and can be bad for you or good for you in ways not enumerated before.

All that is true, but then the question is this: Why aren't more people doing the same with sex?

For here we come to the most fascinating turn of all. One cannot answer the question by arguing that there is no such empirical news about indiscriminately pursued sex and how it can be good or bad for you; to the contrary, there is, and lots of it. After all, several decades of empirical research—which also did not exist before—have demonstrated that the sexual revolution, too, has had consequences, and that many of them have redounded to the detriment of a sexually liberationist ethic.

Married, monogamous people are more likely to be happy. They live longer. These effects are particularly evident for men. Divorced men in particular and conversely face health risks—including heightened drug use and alcoholism—that married men do not. Married men also work more and save more, and married households not surprisingly trump other households in income. Divorce, by contrast, is often a financial catastrophe for a family, particularly the women and children in it. So is illegitimacy typically a financial disaster.

By any number of measures, moreover, nontraditional sexual morality—and the fallout from it—is detrimental to the well-being of one specifically vulnerable subset: children. Children from broken homes are at risk for all kinds of behavioral, psychological, educational, and other problems that children from intact homes are not. Children from fatherless homes are far more likely to end up in prison than are those who grew up with both biological parents. Girls growing up without a biological father are far more likely to suffer physical or sexual abuse. Girls and boys, numerous sources also show, are adversely affected by family breakup into adulthood and have higher risks than children from intact homes of repeating the pattern of breakup themselves.

This recital touches only the periphery of the empirical record now being assembled about the costs of laissez-faire sex to American society—a record made all the more interesting by the fact that it could not have been foreseen back when sexual liberationism seemed merely synonymous with the removal of some seemingly inexplicable old stigmas. Today, however, two generations of social science replete with studies, surveys, and regression analyses galore stand between the Moynihan Report and what we know now, and the overall weight of its findings is clear. The sexual revolution—meaning the widespread extension of sex outside of marriage and frequently outside commitment of any kind—has had negative effects on many people, chiefly the most vulnerable; and it has also had clear financial costs to society at large. And this is true not only in the obvious ways, like the spread of AIDS and other STDs, but also in other ways affecting human well-being, beginning but not ending with those enumerated above.

The question raised by this record is not why some people changed their habits and ideas when faced with compelling new facts about food and quality of life. It is rather why more people have not done the same about sex. [. . .]

NOTES

1. For a general discussion, see Pamela Paul, *Pornified: How Pornography is Transforming Our Lives, Our Relationships, and Our Families* (Times Books, 2005).
2. For clinical accounts of the evidence of harm, see, for example, Ana J. Bridges, "Pornography's Effects on Interpersonal Relationships," and Jill C. Manning, "The Impact of Pornography on Women," papers presented at a conference on "The Social Costs of Pornography," Princeton University (December 2008). For further information and for pre-consultation drafts of these papers, see http://www.winst.org/family_marriage_and_democracy/social_costs_of_pornography/consultation2008.php (accessed January 7, 2008). The papers also include an interesting econometric assessment of what is spent to avoid or recover from pornography addiction: Kirk Doran, "The Economics of Pornography."

READING

"Food and Sex Reconsidered"

MAGGIE CASTOR

MAGGIE CASTOR was a Philosophy major at Elon University, Class of 2012. After reading Mary Eberstadt's essay, she was provoked to write the following set of thoughts and discussion prompts especially for this exercise.

So you've just finished reading Mary Eberstadt's piece on food and sex. I hope you're feeling challenged. Eberstadt has invited us to think critically about two aspects of our lives that are ever-present, requiring various choices and decisions to be made.

Yet, we probably don't think of our food and sex habits in a moral or ethical context nearly as much as we think of food and sex themselves. So, how were you challenged? Maybe you were challenged because you've never thought so much about the ethical implications of food or sex. Or, you could be challenged as to how Eberstadt (or anyone) could make the claims she did. (Do we really have a "laissez-faire" attitude toward sex, for example? And does the article's main analogy really hold?) Possibly, you ended up wondering why Eberstadt even wrote the article in the first place. (For example, everyone knows you should only buy grass-fed beef. Or do they?)

I propose that we thank Mary Eberstadt for the challenge she poses by challenging her in return. In doing so you'll be practicing critically engaging with arguments, as well as thinking more deeply about ethics and some vital daily topics.

To get started, I'll adopt Eberstadt's use of hypothetical narratives. The narratives I have created intentionally contrast with and question the narratives of Betty and Jennifer. By no means do I mean these narratives to be comprehensive—in fact, you'll end up creating your own narratives too.

ARNOLD

First, meet Arnold, a single father of three. A chef at a local restaurant, Arnold recognizes the importance of well-rounded meals and attempts to create healthy diets for his children. However, finances are tight, and he is unable to provide the ideal diet for the family. The children receive reduced-price lunch at school, but Arnold is convinced the "chicken nugget" meals his children are served do more harm than good for their bodies.

Yet, the reduced-price lunch program is the most viable option for the family right now. Arnold is also able to offset the cost of food for the family by receiving one free meal for every work shift. For other meals, Arnold shops at bulk grocery stores. Not always being able to afford fresh ingredients, Arnold often uses pre-packaged meals filled with preservatives. Arnold has worked into his budget, however, the ability to cook dinner twice a week with fresh, home-made ingredients. In three months, Arnold knows he will receive a raise and already has plans to begin making meals from scratch three days a week.

KC

Now let's meet KC. Throughout her teenage years KC's home environment could best be described as hostile. Her parents' marriage began to disintegrate after her father began taking night classes at a local college. Her father began developing new interests, became unsatisfied with his construction career, and wanted to pursue a PhD to become a psychiatrist. While neither of KC's parents had malicious intentions, their increasingly divergent interests no longer made them compatible. Her father especially felt as if his marriage prevented him from personal growth.

However, KC's parents were convinced they would be doing the best thing for their children to stay together. KC on the other hand felt this decision created an unloving environment for her and her siblings. It was not until after her youngest brother left for culinary school that her parents separated.

This experience troubled KC's notion of intimate relationships. KC had always envisioned a partnership supporting her and her partner's growth, as well as their growth together. For years KC stayed away from intimate relationships because she found friendship a much better model for cultivating growth than her parents' marriage. Eventually, KC realized she could model intimate relationships based on the positive features of friendships. She began engaging in polyamorous, or open, relationships.

Departing monogamy, KC began having multiple intimate partners, recognizing—like her friendships—different partners fulfilled different needs and desires. Along with this new model of relationships came an increased value of communication, enabling her to be more attuned to her partner(s) needs and goals in order to grow as a person. KC's fear of getting restricted in a stagnant, inhibiting relationship gradually disappeared.

A FULLER PICTURE

Arnold and his family never have to skip a meal, so it cannot be denied they have access to food. So far, Arnold's narrative and concern with health and quality supports Eberstadt's claims about the accessibility of food. However, because Arnold believes some of the food quality he has to serve his children may actually be harmful to their bodies, Arnold's narrative evokes further questions somewhat obscured in Eberstadt's narrative.

"Access" is not somehow given and total. We must also be concerned about what kind of food people are able to *afford*. In a world in which grocery costs are often significantly higher for poorer and inner-city populations—when groceries are easily accessible at all—and food quality and healthiness are significantly lower at the same time, to speak of "access" pure and simple is misleading. If Arnold's concerns regarding the affordability of quality food are just, then his narrative no longer fits well with Eberstadt's argument. (On the other hand, how does Arnold's case relate to people who can afford quality food while choosing to eat, say, fast food constantly?)

Still other concerns arise beyond affordability and quality. For farmers, for example, the question of food is framed by their work, the *production* of food. Part of the ethic of food, especially for the new breed of small, organic growers, is the ability to produce it oneself. "Locavores" add an ecological critique: it is simply not sustainable to make ourselves ever more dependent on foodstuffs that have to be shipped from hundreds or thousands of miles away. Here the question of "access" takes on another flavor still. Ultimately, say the locavores, the only *truly* accessible food is from right next door, and possibly grown partly oneself. (And who knows what other kinds of questions various narratives could inspire?!)

In addition, we can inquire about the analogy between food and sex that Eberstadt emphasizes. Arnold is concerned with healthful or quality food. Likewise, healthful sexual decisions or quality sexual experiences *do* matter to many people when evaluating the ethical implications of sex. As evidence for what she alleges is our "laissez-faire" attitude toward sex, Eberstadt brandishes a "popular advice column on left-leaning *Slate* magazine"—curious already for the guilt-by-association suggested by the gratuitous adjective "left-leaning," but in any case hardly any real evidence for the sexual mores of a whole generation—my generation. Like most conservatives (to return the gratuity), Eberstadt has no ear at all for irony.

And what about the farmer's concern with production? Does this break down the parallel between food and sex? Or could it enhance the analogy by requiring we *produce our own meaning* in regards to sexual experiences other than society's dominant narratives? Could we relate this meaning production to KC's narrative?

In fact, let's return to KC, and also remember Betty's narrative. If we were to consider KC and Betty's narratives together, although strikingly different, we may see that they both reveal some similar desires. For example, Betty condemned Mr. Jones, her neighbor. He was considered a home wrecker when he ran off with a woman other than his wife. Yet, KC found her home was wrecked when her parents kept an unhealthy relationship together.

Here, the production of meaning in regard to sexual experiences is highlighted and influenced by different contexts. Betty has incorporated dominant societal narratives into her analysis of her personal experiences, whereas, it could be said, KC's personal experiences caused her to abandon society's dominant narrative.

On the one hand, KC and Betty are similar in their desire to foster loving and supportive families. On the other hand, they attempt to create these families in ways that conflict with one another's narratives. KC's polyamory is a newly visible sexual ethic, also, interestingly, called "responsible non-monogamy." Do you think Betty could "get" polyamory, even if she herself were not attracted to it? Why not? I am not persuaded KC and Betty must be doomed to be enemies. A discussion of values might enable them to reach at least a friendly understanding.

But then what would happen with someone who held different values altogether? How would KC and Betty interact with someone's who's narrative rejected family values entirely, for example, and cultivated solely friendship? What would sexual practices look like in a world that rejected family values and cultivated the value of friendship? Once again, I suggest, whatever they would end up looking like, it would hardly be the sheer "dumbing-down of sex," which is all Eberstadt seems to be able to see. I would have said it is more like the opposite.

Let's push our narratives and Eberstadt's arguments just a little further. Imagining that sexual practices arose out of the cultivation of family or friendship values, what would the *food* parallel look like? Would it mean our food choices would be dependent on the ability to foster familial ties? Perhaps this would mean that one would feel responsible for keeping one's family fed. Or, perhaps, this would mean that one would feel responsible for keeping one's family fed and healthy.

In short, the more we interact with Eberstadt's narratives and mine, the more different possibilities arise for potential moral implications for food and sex practices. By introducing the narratives of Arnold and KC, we can investigate different angles or approaches to Eberstadt's arguments. This is only the beginning, however. Now you have the opportunity to explore even more possibilities through the exercises below.

CHALLENGES

1. Expanding on the work we've already begun, return to Eberstadt's argument and articulate how she might respond to Arnold's narrative and its ethical implications. Would she—should she—welcome the complexities this kind of story brings? Are food and sex morals really as simple as Eberstadt portrays them? Include in your response a discussion of the implications of Arnold's narrative for Eberstadt's parallels between food and sex.

2. Create your own narrative regarding the ethics of food. What are the key values regarding food for you? After identifying your "food values" in general, identify the ways in which you (may) moralize food. Compare and contrast your narrative with Jennifer's narrative. Are they compatible? How would the two narratives engage with one another? If you had a conversation with Jennifer, how might it go?

3. Can you articulate ways that Betty and KC have similar moral values, even though they reach those values differently? Are there aspects of their perspectives that are or seem irreconcilable? How specifically might Betty and KC's sexual morals coexist (even, happily?) with one another?

4. For Eberstadt, it seems that KC's sexual practices would have to fall under a "laissez-faire"—or anything goes—model. How do you think KC would respond to this description of her sexual ethics? Again, aren't things possibly much more complex? Respond by creating a dialogue between Eberstadt and KC. Include at least one point of agreement and one point of disagreement, as well as how one perspective is altered as a result of the conversation. Be aware of, and address specifically, the points in their conversation that are to be left up to personal choice versus those subject to social regulation, as well as the ethical reasons for these different forms of regulation.

CHAPTER 3

Ethics and Religion

We look next to those large regions where ethics and religion overlap. Despite how it may sometimes seem when we are in the midst of certain heated public debates, religious ethics fits readily into the picture that the last two chapters have been painting. All ethics, whether it be divinely inspired or empirically based, is in more or less the same boat when it comes to real-life practice: serious and constant thinking is required. And serious and constant thinking is in fact the *norm,* even at the very heart of religious ethics.

AN APPROACH TO RELIGIOUS ETHICS

RELIGIOUS ETHICS AS A LEARNING EXPERIENCE

Most religions take moral values very seriously. Religious texts advance explicit statements of values, such as the Ten Commandments for Jews and Christians and the Eightfold Path for Buddhists. Religions also provide moral training—for many people the only formal moral training we ever get. And they offer moral support communities, backed by long and honored histories of ethical thinking and moral engagement.

Religions also understand moral values as *complex.* Medieval Christianity developed elaborate methods for moral decision making based on analogies to settled cases (casuistry). Muslim ethical thinking has the additional complication of politics, since Islam does not separate church and state. Judaism offers volume upon volume of intricate rabbinical discussion of all kinds of moral issues in light of Torah.

All of these religions are also changing and adapting. Of course they work from their existing bodies of doctrine, interpretation, and experience. But experience keeps changing. In America in the 1960s, the big challenge was civil rights. Most established religions entered the decade with a poor record of speaking up against segregation. They rose to the challenge to do better. Then came the Vietnam War; then the rise of multiculturalism; now, especially after 9/11, new challenges and imperatives of inter-faith understanding.

Another example: most religious texts say little or nothing about ecology or climate change, but now all of the major religions are working out their own forms of environmentalism. Religious leaders of our time, from the Dalai Lama to Pope John Paul II to Eastern Orthodoxy's Bartholomew I, have spoken for nature in the strongest terms. Bartholomew, mincing no words, condemns environmental degradation as a sin. Varied spokespeople for less centralized religions such as Judaism, Protestantism, and Islam have done the same. There is even an Evangelical Environmental Network (also in league with Jewish and Catholic environmental groups in the National Religious Partnership for the Environment) that affirms "Creation Care" as a moral imperative. Individual churches here at home embrace environmental responsibility and are cleaning up their own acts, trying to go greener and even asking questions like "What Would Jesus Drive?"

Of course, this is not a question that Jesus himself asked. He never drove anything except maybe a donkey (and perhaps still wouldn't). Neither Moses nor Buddha nor Mohammed nor Lao Tsu talked about sustainable energy or "Creation Care" or any such thing as sins against the environment. Yet this is what their legacies now seem, to many of their followers, to ask of us. Christian and Jewish eco-theologians take issue, for example, with the traditional reading of Genesis as a basis for "subduing" and exploiting the Earth: the real implication, they argue, is more like stewardship. As the Quakers say, truth is continually revealed. Religious ethics continues to change and grow.

DIVERSITY IN RELIGIOUS ETHICS

Just like nonreligious ethical and philosophical systems, religious views of ethics also vary—often fundamentally. And variation goes all the way down. The world's great religions vary, in fact dramatically, and so do their denominations, and so do specific congregations within denominations. Even individual religious persons may find themselves, in their own thinking, pulled in different directions.

Despite how people sometimes talk then, there is really no such thing as "the" Christian view of gay marriage or capitalism or preemptive war, any more than there is any one Jewish or Buddhist (or atheist) view either. There are *many* Christian views, as there are many views in general. Meanwhile Christians are also in dialogue with a variety of other religions—which are just as varied and diverse within themselves—and with a variety of secular points of view as well. Episcopalians and Methodists and Jews contend with each other over gay marriage. Some affirm it, some condemn it, some are trying to find a middle way. Some radicals hold that the Quran (Koran) sanctions terror; most Muslim religious authorities hold the opposite.

Once again, all of this thinking and rethinking, this challenging and moral back-and-forth, is the *norm*. In fact, we should *welcome* it as part of the interest and depth of ethics. In any case, welcome or not, the key response to any religious dogmatist, as against any other kind of dogmatist, is that there are people with at least as much intelligence and good faith who hold opposite views, based as thoroughly and conscientiously on *their* experience and training as our own dogmatists' views are on theirs. The only option is open-ended discussion.

Regardless of whether or not we are Catholic or agree with the pope, for example, we ought to respect the Catholic Church for speaking so insistently in favor of "life"—and remember that in this they not only oppose abortion and contraception, but also question multinational capitalism and try to defend local communities and "good livelihood." Defending "life," they say, also means defending the poor, resisting wars, and speaking for the larger living Earth. It's a challenge to just about everyone. And, yes, it is controversial: critics point out that the same insistence also contributes to the global population explosion, which is a concern for everyone who wants to defend the *rest* of life on the planet, as well as the lives of present populations. Some argue as well that the Church greatly overemphasizes the "life" of fetuses as opposed to other forms of "life" to follow. We may not agree about these issues, but—again—it is essential to *think* about them, and indeed also to "defend life" in some form, however much we disagree about how.

FINDING SHAREABLE TERMS

How do we proceed when religion seems to divide us on ethical matters? The answer is more or less the same as when we are morally divided for any other reason. As chapter 2 suggested, part of the very point of ethics is to help us find ways to think and act together when we do have basic disagreements but must still work out some shared values to live by. The main way we do so is by finding shareable terms and arguments.

You, or some tight group of which you are a member, may be totally persuaded of a particular moral position already. Appeals to a specific Bible, or specific interpretation of a Bible, may help guide those who share that Bible or that interpretation. Still, when the task is to persuade others—all of us, in the broader and more diverse moral community that includes differently religious people as well as nonreligious people—then the appeal must be to mutually agreeable starting points. This is true whether your own tight group is religious or based on something else. In any case, what's required are not pronouncements but arguments: you need to give reasons that address listeners in their own terms, and to acknowledge and speak to counterarguments as well.

While many non-Catholics admire the pope, for example, we are unlikely to take his word on family planning or the economy just because it is his word. (Strikingly enough, many Catholics don't either.) Just like the rest of us, he has to persuade. In fact, the longtime and enormously influential Pope John Paul II was so effective for just this reason. He reached across many differences not by appealing to his official religious authority but by thoughtful argument and by example. In Communist countries he spoke for freedom and individual dignity—hardly just Catholic ideas, or just Christian ideas, or just religious ones. In the West, he spoke of respect for life and against our obsessions with material things. Again, common values, even if we don't always live up to them. Some of his proclamations were (and remain) controversial even among Catholics, but he was still in certain ways "the world's conscience." His biographer called him "a pope for the world, not just the Church."

This book should help find "shareable terms." We will learn to identify the values at stake in ethical issues, both shared and not shared, and will develop a variety of tools to help us address those values and issues more clearheadedly, collaboratively, and creatively. You will see, I hope, that there are ways to enter the ethical discussion not just from a Catholic or Muslim (or, for that matter, agnostic or atheist) point of view, but instead as people united by certain basic values that we are aiming to understand and put into practice together, drawing on our traditions as complementary ways of understanding those values, for sure, but meanwhile also valuing our disagreements as invitations to more learning. (Yes, there really is hope!)

NELSON MANDELA AND DESMOND TUTU

Nelson Mandela's remarkable life carried him from his birth into one of the leading families of the Xhosa people to the resistance movement against South African apartheid as one of the founders of the African National Congress (ANC); twenty-seven years imprisonment, some of it in solitary confinement; and then release and election as the first president of post-apartheid South Africa. Through it all he carried himself with a kind of saintliness that made him one of the most striking moral exemplars of recent times. Without rancor, without racial hatred, he and South African Anglican Archbishop Desmond Tutu were able to guide a hatefully divided society into majority rule without the massive bloodshed everyone expected and feared. His own life story showed a whole nation how to transcend the bitterness of past oppression.

Mandela is also a resolutely secular person. His values were shaped by a wide mix of factors, starting with Xhosa heritage and coming in time to encompass moral traditions from around the world. The ANC was influenced by the revolutionary ideas of English nonconformists and Jewish immigrants and by South Africa's Indian community (both Hindu and Muslim) with its Gandhian traditions (Gandhi himself lived and worked in South Africa for twenty years). Over a quarter century of imprisonment, Mandela and his fellow prisoners, from all over the religious and revolutionary spectrum, debated politics in the mineshafts, staged Sophocles and Shakespeare, read Xhosa poets and the atheist and pacifist Bertrand Russell, and on and on. You begin to see why in the end no single religious or ethical orientation was enough for them, and thus what forged the ANC's distinctive vision of a multicultural and multireligious society, bound together by a common goal and based on that "common ground" that Mandela describes as "greater and more enduring than the differences that divide."

The South African regime, throughout those long years, smeared the ANC as "godless" while appealing to the Bible to justify apartheid. Yet Mandela, characteristically, continues to speak appreciatively of religion. Religious schools educated him, for one thing—the apartheid regime had no interest in educating blacks. And more:

> In a South African jail under apartheid, you can see a cruelty of human beings to others in a naked form. But it was religious institutions, Hindus, Moslems, leaders of the Jewish faith, Christians, it was them who gave us the hope that one day, we would come out, we would return. And in prison, the religious institutions raised funds for our children, who were arrested in thousands and thrown into jail, and many of them one day left prison at a high level of education, because of this support we got from religious institutions. And that is why we so respect religious institutions. And we try as much as we can to read the literature, which outlines the fundamental principles of human behaviour . . . like the [Bhagavad Gita], the Qur'an, the Bible, and other important religious documents.

Notice again: Mandela is not embracing any one of these religions. He appreciates them all. "Hope" is not sectarian. At times he himself uses religious language—for sometimes, surely, only the language of the sacred will do—but he does not feel the need to take it literally.

Yet here alongside him stands his great colleague Desmond Tutu, who does. Tutu's lifelong struggle against apartheid was from his pulpits, and the result is a stunning "Truth and Reconciliation" movement both in South Africa—facing apartheid in order to move ahead together—and in the wider world.

Two very different life paths, then, but common values still: one direction and one heart. Mandela and Tutu *together* moved people of all stripes—religious and secular, Anglican and Buddhist and Catholic, political leaders and CEOs as well as ordinary folks—to action. An example both inspiring and instructive!

LET THE STORIES BE STORIES

All of the world's great religious traditions offer a rich bounty of stories. Many of them are moral stories, and naturally we look to them for moral guidance—which is why we so often speak of "the moral of the story." Those stories that are part of a religion's Bible often claim a special authority that makes their interpretation both essential and, well, contentious.

The stories are often fascinating and deep. Whole generations of devout people have immersed themselves in them. But again: precisely because our religious stories are so often rich, poetic, and complex, they seldom yield clear, specific guidance in specific situations—certainly not in the problematic situations that really concern us. They are contentious because they are ambiguous, and thus they invite (surprise!) more *thinking*.

Consider this parable from the Sufi master Yusuf of Andalusia:

> Nuri Bey was a respected and reflective Albanian, who had married a wife much younger than himself. One evening when he had returned home earlier than usual, a faithful servant came to him and said: "Your wife, our mistress, is acting suspiciously. She is in her apartments with a huge chest, large enough to hold a man, which belonged to your grandmother. It should contain only a few ancient embroideries. I believe that there may now be much more in it. She will not allow me, your oldest retainer, to look inside."
>
> Nuri went to his wife's room, and found her sitting disconsolately beside the massive wooden box. "Will you show me what is in the chest?" he asked.
>
> "Because of the suspicion of a servant, or because you do not trust me?"
>
> "Would it not be easier just to open it, without thinking about the undertones?" asked Nuri.
>
> "I do not think it possible."
>
> "Where is the key?"
>
> She held it up. "Dismiss the servant and I will give it to you."
>
> The servant was dismissed. The woman handed over the key and herself withdrew, obviously troubled in mind.
>
> Nuri Bey thought for a long time. Then he called four gardeners from his estate. Together they carried the chest by night unopened to a distant part of the grounds, and buried it. The matter was never referred to again.

Sufis have been teaching with this story for eight hundred years. But exactly what lesson does it teach? You might take some time to figure out how *you* would interpret it—and see how your interpretation compares with others.

Is Nuri Bey's act a wise one? Does the story mean to suggest that it is? He doesn't push the point—he doesn't open the chest—but he apparently doesn't entirely trust his wife either. Or in burying the chest is his idea to also bury mistrust—is he still trying to avoid the "undertones"? Would his wife agree that he succeeded at this? Is the "moral" therefore that certain matters between husband and wife shouldn't be pushed?

And—after all—what was in the box? Is it obvious that his wife is hiding a lover? This is probably what we think at first, but could it be something else—a present, maybe, that she is not prepared to give him yet? Some other kind of magical possibility that his jealousy "buries" for them? Notice that for *her* the issue is trust. "Because of the suspicion of a servant," she asks, "or because you do not trust me?" She "herself withdrew, obviously troubled in mind"—but not in denial or defiance.

The Sufis themselves, by the way, value such stories precisely because they *are* complex and unclear in this way. The whole point is to explore their hidden and deeper meanings and symbolism. To insist that they mean one and only one thing misses the very point—so they would say. How many other stories are like that?

THE SIN OF SODOM?

Here's another religious story—this one a little closer to home. When some Christians insist that the Bible condemns homosexuality, a common scriptural reference is to the story of the destruction of Sodom.

> The two angels came to Sodom in the evening; and Lot was sitting in the gate of Sodom. When Lot saw them, he rose to meet them . . . and said, "My lords, turn aside, I pray you, to your servant's house, and spend the night, and wash your feet; then you may rise up early and go on your way." . . . He urged them strongly; so they turned aside to him and entered his house; and he made them a feast, and baked unleavened bread, and they ate.
>
> But before they lay down, the men of the city, the men of Sodom, both young and old, all the people to the last man, surrounded the house, and they called to Lot, "Where are the men who came to you tonight? Bring them out to us, that we may know [i.e, rape] them." Lot went out of the door to the men, shut the door after him, and said, "I beg you, my brothers, do not act so wickedly. . . . Do nothing to these men, for they have come under the shelter of my roof. Behold, I have two daughters who have not known man; let me bring them out to you, and do to them as you please; only do nothing to these men, for they have come under the shelter of my roof." But [the crowd] said, "Stand back!" . . . Then they pressed hard against Lot, and drew near to break the door. But [the angels] put forth their hands and drew Lot into the house to them, and shut the door. And they struck with blindness the men who were at the door of the house, so that they wearied themselves groping for the door. (Genesis 19:1–11)

God destroys the city the next day, after helping Lot and his family to flee.

So what *is* the true sin of Sodom? Some insist that it is homosexuality. And it's true that homosexual acts (of a sort) are threatened in the story. Other verses can be cited in support of this reading as well. Nonetheless, the insistence that *the* sin *must* be homosexuality—that no other reading is even possible, and no other possible sin matters—misses the depth of the story itself.

An ancient reading is that the true crimes of Sodom are its shocking level of violence and its extreme disrespect for strangers. That's certainly in the story too—in fact, one might have thought, a lot more central to it. Traditional Jewish readings stressed Sodom's extreme inhospitality. As the prophet Ezekiel put it, "Behold, this was the guilt of . . . Sodom: she and her daughters had pride, surfeit of food, and prosperous ease, but did not aid the poor and needy" (Ezekiel 16:49). On this view, the story is really a call to social justice.

Moderns might suppose that if anything is specifically condemned in this story, it is rape. After all, rape is what the crowd had on their minds. It turns out that gang rape was a common practice of the times for humiliating enemies. So maybe *that* is the true sin of Sodom—the readiness to sexualize humiliation?

But we can't stop there either. Lot, who is presented as the only decent man in Sodom, actually offers the crowd his own daughters in the place of his guests. The angels prevent these rapes too from happening. But God still saves Lot from the destruction of the rest of the city. Does not Lot's treatment of his own daughters offend God? Is the shelter of his roof for strangers more important than the shelter of his home for his own children? We are reminded that this story was written at a time when some values were very different than they are now: when, for one thing, women were regarded only as a father or husband's property, for him to dispose of as he saw fit. And it therefore becomes hard to take the story, whatever exactly it condemns or doesn't condemn, as the ethical last word.

In any case, again, the main point can hardly be said to be *clear*. You begin to see why, for some religious traditions, exploring the interpretation of such stories is the core of the worship service itself. Christians inherit long traditions of debate and disagreement about Scripture, and Judaism's second most sacred text, the Talmud, is essentially a history of (loving!) disputation about the Torah.

Reading the stories in this way is, once again, a shareable approach—a kind of common ground. It's the opposite of trying to squeeze a single moral out of them, which barely is to read them as *stories* at all. Let us approach them, together, as the complex, many-layered narratives that they are.

THINKING FOR YOURSELF

The Bible is not all stories, of course. Sometimes God explicitly commands certain acts and condemns others. Here too, though, for better or worse, it turns out that things are complicated. Here too is a large element of interpretation and choice. Ethical thinking remains essential!

THE NEED FOR INTERPRETATION

"Thou shalt not kill" seems the clearest of the Ten Commandments. But almost all Christians and Jews eat other animals, which requires killing on a massive scale. Many Christians and Jews support capital punishment. Most fight in wars. Some also believe that suicide may be permissible too.

The Torah reads, "Thou shalt not *murder*." This seems a little more reasonable: it is at least arguable that killing in war or in the electric chair is not murder (though it is also arguable that it is), and the notion of murder is implicitly limited to other humans (though it is arguable that it shouldn't be). Once we get into alternative translations, however, we return quickly to the question of alternative interpretations. After all, the word in the traditional Christian phrasing—both in the King James Bible and the Revised Standard Version—is "kill," so if you take it literally, at least in English, that should be the end of the matter.

Also, to say "Thou shalt not murder" is not helpful as a practical guide. In effect it says: "Don't kill unjustly." But when is killing unjust? Is capital punishment, for example, "murder"? You may have views about the answers to these questions, but they aren't given in the commandment "Thou shalt not murder." One way or the other we are back to, well, interpretation.

Or again: we are commanded to honor the Sabbath. But when is the Sabbath? Even this simplest of questions is unclear. Jews celebrate Sabbath from Friday sunset until Saturday sunset. Early Christians followed Jewish practice, only gradually shifting the observance to Sundays (dishearteningly, to distinguish themselves from Jews). Some Christians still celebrate Sabbath on Saturdays (the "Seventh-Day Adventists"). Is there a "right" answer? Not, it seems, in the text. . . .

WE STILL DECIDE

There are also a large number of explicit commandments that almost no one takes seriously and almost all of us feel free to ignore. Not too many people even "Honor the Sabbath" any more, come to think of it—whenever we think it is. Here are a few more dramatic examples from Leviticus:

11:7: "You shall not eat the swine; it is unclean to you."

11:11–12: "Everything in the waters that has not fins and scales is an abomination to you. Of their flesh you shall not eat, and their carcasses you shall have in abomination."

19:9–10: "When you reap the harvest of your land, you shall not reap your field to its very border . . . and you shall not strip your vineland bare, neither shall you gather the fallen grapes of your vineyard; you shall leave them for the poor and the sojourner."

19:19: "There shall not come upon you a garment of cloth made of two kinds of stuff."

19:27: "You shall not round off the hair on your temples or mar the edges of your beard."

A few people actually do follow (some of) these commandments: some Orthodox Jews, some Amish orders. But almost all other Christians feel free to disregard them entirely. Even confronted with explicit commandments, then, and commandments put in the strongest terms too (Leviticus's punishment for "abomination" is usually stoning), we still feel entirely free to go our own way—if, for example, we think that some of these commands are just "historical relics," as I hear many people say, like dietary restrictions that once made sense but no longer are necessary.

The point is not that we are hypocritical. The point is that we can and must decide for ourselves—understanding, for example, that regardless of what the text literally says, it comes from a historical place very unlike our own, and is also the product of contentious translations and interpretations and therefore may apply differently to our time, or not apply at all. Even if we decide to follow its commands, that is still a *decision*—our decision.

This is not just an abstract point. Here is another passage from the same part of Leviticus:

> 20:13: "If a man lies with a man as with a woman, it is an abomination."

This commandment is regularly cited by people who claim (as they put it) that "God hates homosexuality." But these very same people, like most of the rest of us, disregard most of the rest of Leviticus. Down where I live, certain churches even hold pig roasts at rallies where speakers rail against homosexuality and other modern sins. If you take the text literally, though, it seems that God hates pig eating just as much as He hates (male) homosexuality. (Leviticus says nothing at all about female homosexuality.) And if you *don't* take the text literally, as seems plausible enough in the case of pig eating, you can hardly claim that you have no choice but to take it literally in cases where it happens to accord with your preexisting convictions. In neither case is an explicit commandment really the end of the story.

People who continue reading Exodus after the Ten Commandments are often disturbed to discover that in the very next chapter the Bible seems to condone slavery:

> When you buy a Hebrew slave, he shall serve six years, and in the seventh he shall go out free, for nothing. If he comes in single, he shall go out single; if he comes in married, his wife shall go out with him. . . . [But] when a man sells his daughter as a slave, she shall not go out as the male slaves do. . . . When a man strikes his slave, male or female, with a rod and the slave dies under his hand, he shall be punished. But if the slave survives a day or two, he is not to be punished; for the slave is his money. (Exodus 21:2–3, 7, 20–21)

These passages were used by American slaveholders during the struggle over abolition to show that God approved of slavery. Now, with slavery gone and its evil recognized, the rationalization is transparent. Yet the words are there. Literally, the text does not say that slavery is wrong. Literally, it condones slavery under pretty broad conditions.

We can appreciate the writers of Exodus for what they tried to do: adapt a living ethical tradition to the needs of the time. No doubt these rules promised at least some small improvement over slavery as it had been practiced. They began to give (some) slaves (some) rights. But now of course times have changed—drastically. We still have a living tradition (again, *many* living traditions) but three thousand years have changed everything. We need to rethink and adapt the tradition just as the prophets and lawgivers of biblical times did. And that may mean—as clearly it does mean in the case of these words about slavery—that we need to go beyond their words to the *spirit* of their acts and of our shared tradition, as full of ambiguity and uncertainty as that is too. Again there is no refuge in the text—no alternative but to decide for ourselves.

A BIBLICAL IDEAL

On the angels' way to Sodom, they visit the patriarch Abraham in his desert tent. As they leave, they declare God's intention to destroy Sodom if the rumors about it are true. Abraham is troubled by this. He cannot see the justice of killing the innocent along with the wicked. So Abraham, says the Bible, "went before the Lord." He actually took it upon himself to question God!

> Abraham drew near and said: "Wilt thou indeed destroy the righteous with the wicked? Suppose there are fifty righteous within the city; wilt thou then destroy the place and not spare it for the fifty righteous who are in it? Far be it from thee to do such a thing, to slay the righteous with the wicked, so that the righteous fare as the wicked! Far be that from thee! Shall not the Judge of all the Earth do right?"
>
> And the Lord said, "If I find at Sodom fifty righteous in the city, I will spare the whole place for their sake." Abraham answered, "Behold, I have taken upon myself to speak to the Lord, I who am but dust and ashes. Suppose five of the fifty righteous are lacking. Wilt thou destroy the whole city for lack of five?" And He said, "I will not destroy it if I find forty-five there." Again he spoke to him, and said, "Suppose forty are found there." He answered, "For the sake of forty I will not do it." Then he said, "Oh let not the Lord be angry, and I will speak. Suppose thirty are found there." He answered, "I will not do it, if I find thirty there." He said, "Behold, I have taken upon myself to speak to the Lord. Suppose twenty are found there." He answered, "For the sake of twenty I will not destroy it."
>
> Then [Abraham] said, "Oh let not the Lord be angry, and I will speak again but this once. Suppose ten are found there." The Lord answered, "For the sake of ten I will not destroy it." And the Lord went his way, when he had

finished speaking to Abraham; and Abraham returned to his place. (Genesis 18: 23–33)

What is the Bible telling us here? Surely not that we should simply do what we're told and accept whatever authority—even the highest religious authority of all—decides to do. Quite the contrary. Abraham, the revered forefather, did not simply obey. He would not accept injustice even when God Himself proposed to do it. Abraham went to God—Abraham who knows himself to be, in comparison, "but dust and ashes"—and complained. He questioned, he challenged. "Shall not the Judge of all the Earth do right?"

Abraham thought for himself. Moreover, he was honored for doing so. God listened and answered. Indeed Lot himself was saved, the Bible says later, because God was "mindful of Abraham."

Mustn't we do the same? Of course I don't mean that we must never listen to others. Listening to good advice and thinking about new perspectives are crucial. Religious texts too have long been sources of great inspiration and stimulation. Use them. Speak the shared language; retell the stories. Still, in the end, it is up to *us* to interpret, ponder, and decide what they mean. So the next time someone acts as though it is yours only to obey the commands of God (according to their interpretation), or yours only to obey some other authority—remember Abraham!

A LAST WORD FROM THE WISE

Some people may find it hard to reconcile such a message with the experience of tight-knit religious communities in which the leaders fervently believe that they speak for God Himself and therefore *do* expect obedience. Critical thinking may be explicitly forbidden, and even when it is tolerated, it is seldom understood or encouraged. Not only is it hard to buck such insistent and accepted authority, it can also be hard to question leaders whom you rightly respect and may even love.

Still, though—one last time—there is a deep wisdom in what ethics asks. We can see this best by looking to the wisest of the wise. We have spoken of Nelson Mandela and Archbishop Tutu; I also think of Gandhi, the Sufi poet Rumi, the original philosopher Socrates, just to name a few. Many others will be cited and discussed in later chapters. These are great people. And they don't avoid ethical issues—often they wade right in. They may advise us. They may attempt to persuade us, as may any respected and loved moral leader.

But here is the crucial thing: none of these people would claim to speak for God or demand that you put their judgment in place of your own. On the contrary, they are acutely aware of their own limits as well as the limits of others. They recognize that even with the best of intentions, they are still creatures of their time and place, and therefore *even they* will hear the voice of God (or however they might describe their moral perceptions) through the filters of partial understanding, or the residues of local prejudice, or the lack of the full range of human experience. So they lead by inspiring *more* thinking—not less.

God came to Elijah alone in the cave at Mt. Horeb. There, the Bible says, God spoke in a "still small voice" (1 Kings 19:12)—a phrase that can also be translated as "gentle breeze," "soft whisper," "hardly a sound." A hiss, a rustle. There is a vital caution here. Hearing that voice can be a very tricky thing— and in any case it comes to each of us, very quietly, on our own. You begin to see why Quakers and many others, both religious and secular, have put their livelihoods and even their lives on the line for freedom of conscience. Protestant Christianity itself began with the insistence that everyone should be able to read and interpret the Scriptures for themselves. Thinking for yourself is not somehow irreligious—it is at the very core not only of the ethical but also of the religious experience.

READING

"Making Peace with the Sword Verse"

JAMAL RAHMAN

ABRAHAM BECAME UNEASY when the killing of innocents seemed to be ordered by God Himself. So might we. (What about the children of Sodom? The fewer than ten innocent men? The women? Nor is Sodom by any means the only such occasion.) Some Christians may be aware that the Bible once was regularly cited in support of slavery; many know that it contains many other rules and commandments that seem at best quaint and at worst unloving, intolerant, even barbaric. Certainly Christianity's critics are aware of these things, however seldom they are talked about in Christian circles, and some bring them up regularly and hold them against Christianity and the whole Christian world.

This chapter has argued, in response, that *interpretation* is necessary, that religious ethical traditions are living and complex traditions, carrying forward much that is good and indeed vital, but also, quite likely, much that is problematic and even, by present lights, unethical; much that may be mis-interpreted, pulled out of context; distorted by our wish to avoid thinking for ourselves or admitting that things are not really so obvious or nailed down. All of this, again, is what makes religious thinking so potent, so hard, and yet also so interesting.

In the reading that follows, a Muslim addresses the same sort of problem in the Quran. Just like the Bible, the Quran at points also seems unloving, intolerant, even barbaric. Islam's critics also bring up some of those passages regularly, especially in the wake of the increased tensions between the Christian/ secular and Muslim worlds in the last decade. But Islam, like Christianity and Judaism, also has an interpretive tradition that addresses these issues—once again a form of thinking for one-self, and even, as Imam Jamal Rahman argues here, required by the faith itself. Interestingly, and very much in character, Rah-man also hints at a similar process (and a similar need for it) in Hindu thinking in turn.

Rahman is one of three Seattle-area religious leaders who reached out to one another in the wake of the attacks of Septem-ber 11th, 2001, to create what eventually became the "Interfaith Amigos." The three of them—Jewish rabbi, Christian minis-ter, Muslim imam—now travel and speak widely, their website says, to "explore an inclusive spirituality to promote healing that expresses as concrete environmental, social, and political action." Rahman is also the cofounder and Muslim Sufi Min-ister at Interfaith Community Church in Seattle and adjunct faculty member at Seattle University. This article appeared orig-inally in *Yes!* Magazine.

The sacred texts of all religions contain many verses of exquisite beauty and wisdom that fully satisfy the universal longings of the human heart. But it is equally true that all our texts also contain painful and awkward verses that do not enrich the human spirit or support universal values. To those who may be offended by this second statement because they believe their scriptures are the inspired and irreproachable words of God, spiritual teachers explain that scriptures might be divine, but the human conscious-ness with which we approach our scriptures is less than perfect. In the wise words of Mahatma Gandhi, "God reveals His truth to instruments that are imperfect."

FACING THE DIFFICULT VERSES

For purposes of healing the wounds between people of faith, and understanding the scriptures that inform our beliefs and practices, it is helpful to acknowledge and embrace the difficult verses in our holy scriptures and spend time with them. Rather than avoiding them or going through mental gymnastics to justify them, we should consider them an invitation to allow a higher light from within to shine on them. As the Prophet Muhammad said, we need to move from "knowledge of the tongue" to "knowledge of the heart."

This is a large part of the work that my Interfaith Amigos and I have been doing in the years since 9/11. Within the goodwill and safety of our trusted friendship, we are able to address the difficult passages in our scriptures and expand our understanding by bringing to bear the "knowledge of the heart" that has been developing steadily in the years of our friendship. The willingness to bare our vulnerabilities and share our feelings honestly about our own awkward verses and also about verses in each others' scriptures that give us pain has greatly fostered authenticity in our relationships with ourselves, with each other, and with the sacred texts that we hold so dear.

For me as a Muslim, the Quran offers insights and wisdom for this endeavor. "Of knowledge We have given you but a little," says the Holy Book (17:85), and every verse has many levels of meaning and "none understands except those who possess the inner heart" (3:7). Paradoxes exist, says the Quran, because, "Of everything We have created opposites so that you might know that only God is One" (51:49). When all else fails, the Quran also offers two ardent prayers: "O my Sustainer! Open for me my heart! (20:25), and "O my Sustainer, increase me in knowledge!" (20:114).

SO WHAT ABOUT THE SWORD VERSES?

Among the most problematic verses in the Quran are the so-called "sword verses" exemplified by the verse commonly summarized as "Kill the unbeliever." Sadly and tragically, this verse has been quoted countless times both by Islamic extremists in support of terrorism against the "ungodly" West and by misinformed Christians as proof that Islam was spread at the point of a sword. But neither side is correct in its understanding of this verse.

In the first place, the verse is seriously limited and defined by its historical context. This 7th-century revelation came at a time when the Islamic community in Arabia was a tiny embryonic group in Medina under constant attack by the Quraiysh tribe and their allies in Mecca, who were overwhelmingly superior in arms and numbers. In the second place, the verse is even more seriously qualified by its textual context. Some of the qualifications appear in Chapter 2. The verse immediately preceding the sword verse says, "Fight in the way of God with those who fight you, but begin not hostilities. Lo! Allah loveth not aggressors" (2:190), while the verses immediately following it say, "but if they cease, God is Oft-forgiving, most Merciful

. . . let there be no hostility . . . and know that God is with those who restrain themselves" (2:192–4).

Thus the verses that surround the sword verse soften its sharp edges. The verse refers to defensive fighting and if the attacker inclines to peace, the Muslim must cease fighting. However, even if I factor in those qualifications, I have to acknowledge that it is extremely uncomfortable and confusing to read "Kill the unbeliever" as a divine revelation. Why would the All-Merciful and All-Powerful God, who has infused every human with divine breath and holds every human heart between divine fingers, instruct anyone to kill? Why would the "Light of the Heavens and Earth" advise a Muslim engaged in battle against his attackers to "smite them at their necks" (47:4)? Some of my co-religionists may call me naive and unrealistic and refer me to other verses in the Quran, but when presented with such a puzzlement, I take refuge in Rumi's utterance: "Sell your cleverness and buy bewilderment." What else can one do with a verse like this?

A general principle of Quranic interpretation is that if a verse does not seem to support the overall message of the Quran or reflect God's divine attributes, we have to dig deeper to achieve a more enlightened understanding. So in addition to establishing the contextual limits on this particular revelation—allowing one to kill only in self-defense—it is critical to emphasize that this verse is not about a divine permission to kill non-believers simply because of their non-belief or to gain power or control. Such an interpretation would place the verse in direct conflict with the spirit and content of the universal verses in the Quran.

In an abundance of verses celebrating pluralism and diversity, the Quran explains that God could easily have made all of humanity "one single people" but instead, by divine design, chose to establish diversity so that you might "vie, then, with one another other in doing good works!"(5:48) and "get to know one another" (49:13). The Holy Book emphatically says, "Let there be no compulsion in religion" (2:256) and makes it clear that the passage to heaven depends not on gender or religion but essentially on doing "righteous deeds" (4:124 and 5:69). Except when in mortal danger at the hands of an enemy, Muslims are commanded to repel evil with something which is better so that an enemy becomes a bosom friend (41:34).

A METAPHORICAL UNDERSTANDING

In a continuing attempt to advance my understanding of this difficult sword verse, I have discussed it with both scholars and students. Some of the scholars, who happen to be Hindus who are fully conversant with the Quran, believe that the revelation in question is about God's exhortation to humanity to be courageous and take action in the face of unavoidable attack by others. Indeed, this line of thought is consistent with another revelation in the Quran: "For if God had not enabled people to defend themselves against one another, monasteries and churches and synagogues and mosques—in which God's name is abundantly extolled—would surely have been destroyed" (22:40).

Reinforcing the need for courage when under attack, the scholars pointed to an epic conversation in the Bhagavat Gita between Krishna and the mortal Prince Arjuna on the eve of engaging in the battle of Kurukshetra. Viewing the multitude of soldiers on the opposing side, the prince hesitates and laments to Krishna about spilling the blood of "cousins." Krishna berates the mortal for using false piety to cover up his fear and lack of courage and tells him that without action, the cosmos would fall out of order. Then, Krishna utters the immortal words, "If any man thinks he slays, and another thinks he is slain, neither knows the way of truth. The Eternal in man cannot kill; the Eternal in man cannot die."

The students, who were young Muslims in high school, suggested that the verse should be interpreted metaphorically. After all, they pointed out, the Quran clearly states that some verses are literal and some are metaphorical (3:7) but it doesn't say which ones are which! To these young, creative minds, the sword verse is about slaying the idols of arrogance and ignorance within ourselves.

And finally, I consulted my old friend, the 13th-century sage Rumi, who reminded me that any interpretation depends on our level of consciousness and our intention, on what we hope to learn. "A bee and wasp drink from the same flower," says Rumi. "One produces nectar and the other, a sting." When I'm troubled by the way the sword verse could be interpreted, I remember that the way of Islam is to produce nectar.

FOR REVIEW

1. What are some examples of change and growth in religious ethics?
2. How does the text argue that there is no such thing as "the" Christian view on controversial ethical matters?
3. What are "shareable terms"?

4. How might Pope John Paul II's broad appeal illustrate the possibilities of shareable terms?

5. What might we learn from Nelson Mandela and Desmond Tutu's collaboration?

6. What are two possible interpretations of the story of Nuri Bey?

7. What are two possible interpretations of the story of the destruction of Sodom?

8. How does the text argue that "we still decide" even when explicit commandments tell us what to do?

9. How does Abraham argue with God, and what might be the moral of that story?

10. What are two possible interpretations of the Quran's "Sword Verse"?

EXERCISES AND NOTES

3.1 CARRY ON

Is there a distinctive way that you approach ethical questions that traces back to your religious background? If so, what is it? If you are religious, explore the ethics of your religion more fully. Ask your religious guides or leaders for some guidance—and ask to explore a variety of views within your own tradition.

Next, explore ethics in religious frameworks other than your own. Talk to people from other traditions. Take a course in comparative religions. And read. Learn how other people see things. Is there a distinctive way that they approach ethical questions that traces back to their religious background? If so, what is it? You don't have to give up your own beliefs to do so, of course, but you will certainly come back to them with greater understanding.

3.2 READ THE OLD STORIES

What Christians call the Old Testament is shared, in one way or the other, with Jews and also in part with Muslims. Those stories also are morally complex—and therefore fascinating. They still repay study and thinking, regardless of exactly what you believe.

Abraham, the chosen forefather of the forefathers, raises the knife over one son and exiles the other, mirroring the immensely painful divide of closely related Semitic peoples to this day. Since he was willing to argue with God over the fate of Sodom, why did he not, only a decade or so later, argue with

God over the fate of his very own sons? And why would God ask him to sacrifice Isaac or exile Ishmael in the first place? (Don't just say "to put him to the test." There is more depth in the story. Why would God need or want to put Abraham to the test? And why this particular test?) Were these (and others) good acts? Did God think so? How could we tell?

Consider the Cain and Abel story in Genesis 4:1–16: the story of the first murder in history, mythologically speaking. Why does God reject Cain's offering and accept Abel's, thus setting off Cain's anger and the murder—a fairly foreseeable result? What does Cain mean when he asks, "Am I my brother's keeper?" Is the moral of the story that he *is* (that we *are*) his/our brothers' (one another's) keepers? If so, or in any case, why doesn't God say so—why doesn't God answer him? Isn't Cain partly suggesting that *God* ought to be Abel's "keeper"—that God also bears some responsibility for what happened? Does God dodge the question?

In the New Testament, Jesus' disciples constantly complain that his parables are confusing and ambiguous. (And don't you think it's interesting that the Bible reports this?) Each has been interpreted in many ways—put to many uses. Might they be more than a little like the story of Nuri Bey?

Could it be—could it just possibly be—that what Jesus meant to teach us with these stories is not an exact moral lesson or rule but something more like a sense for the subtlety of things, maybe the mysterious ways of God Himself?

Some intriguing parables and sayings of Jesus can be found in Matthew 6:25–33, Matthew 20:1–16, Luke 19:12–26, and Luke 9:23–27, just for a few of many examples.

A variant: Look carefully at the ethical arguments of religious leaders. For example, why do the popes oppose birth control? Read Pope Paul VI's *Humanae Vitae* and other relevant papal encyclicals (most papal encyclicals are available directly from the United States Catholic Conference Publishing Service at www.nccbuscc.org) and find out. It's *not* because the embryo or fetus is a human being—in many cases, there's no fertilization at all. So why *is* it? Once you figure out the argument (it *is* an argument, not a mere pronouncement) ask yourself whether the values to which Pope Paul appeals are specific to Catholicism or more general. You may not necessarily agree, but there's often a lot to be learned anyway.

Another remarkable encyclical is John Paul II's "Laborem Exercens" (1981). John Paul's marriage of Christian humanism and Marxist influences here produces a widely applicable and eloquent plea for work and workplaces that befit human beings, and therefore a sharp critique of what John Paul calls the "economism" of both capitalism and communism. John Paul II also made himself an eloquent and persistent advocate of the Third World debt relief and income redistribution. Here too a pope entered the contemporary discussion in a way that was far broader and more powerful than a merely sectarian pronouncement.

Finally, consider moral stories from other religions and their sacred texts. Read the Quran. Read Zen stories in collections such as *Zen Flesh, Zen Bones*, compiled by Paul Reps and Nyogen Senzaki (Shambhala, 1994); and explore African stories, such as Mohammed Naseehu Ali, *The Prophet of Zongo Street* (Amistad, 2006); and Sufi stories, in lovely collections such as Idries Shah's *Tales of the Dervishes* (Penguin, 1993), and others.

3.3 ABORTION AND THE BIBLE

Nowhere does the Bible discuss abortion explicitly, but related themes do come up, and Christian pro-life advocates regularly cite certain passages that suggest that a fetus has human standing in the eyes of God. For example, there is a stirring passage in Psalms 139:

> For thou didst form my inward parts; thou didst knit me together in my mother's womb. . . . My frame was not hidden from Thee, when I was being made in secret, intricately wrought in the depths of the earth. Thy eyes beheld my unformed substance, in thy book were written, every one of them, the days that were formed for me.

If God cares for us even in the womb, then, pro-life advocates conclude, there must be an "us" to care for: we must already exist as persons in God's eyes.

However, others have questioned this reading of the passage, pointing out that it is more poetic than anything else (the Psalms are hardly meant literally) and is more concerned with creation in general than with the point at which life begins (indeed, the last two lines seem to suggest that God knows and cares for us even before we are in the womb, but it's hardly plausible that we are fully human even *before* conception).

Christian pro-choice advocates, meanwhile, cite other passages that seem to suggest that abortion might be acceptable. One is in Exodus 21:

> When men strive together, and hurt a woman with child, so that there is a miscarriage, and yet no harm follows, the one who hurt her shall be fined, according as the woman's husband lays upon him; and he shall pay as the judges determine.

The penalty for murder is death (e.g., in verse 12 of the same chapter: "Who strikes a man so that he dies shall be put to death"), so pro-choice Christians argue that the Bible can hardly consider causing the death of a fetus (miscarriage) to be murder if only a fine is specified as punishment.

On the other hand, the phrase "and no harm follows" is puzzling. Isn't there necessarily harm to the fetus? From this pro-life advocates have taken heart, arguing that the passage is, well, ambiguous. The Hebrew phrase translated in the Revised Standard Version (given here) as "so that there is a miscarriage" *might* also be translated as "so that her child comes out" (apparently there is no ancient Hebrew word specifically for miscarriage), which *might* be read as meaning that birth occurs prematurely but with no (other?) harm to the baby—in which case the passage could have just the opposite meaning. The Greek version has still other ambiguities.

Here are some other places where the Christian Bible touches (or has been interpreted as touching) on the question of the status of fetal human life: Job 3 and 10, Ecclesiastes 4 and 6, Jeremiah 1, Luke 1. Read them (all), and read them in context (that is, read the whole chapters, even when only a few verses are usually cited; also, read all of Psalm 139 and Exodus 21, cited earlier). Then ask what you can conclude about what the Bible thinks of the status of fetal human life. Does a clear picture emerge from these chapters taken together? Does a clear picture emerge from any of them taken separately? Explain your answers. (Good luck!)

3.4 CAN GOD DEFINE THE GOOD?

Here's an old philosophical paradox for you—something to think about. Are good things good because God says they are, or does God say they are good because they are good?

One view is: what's good is good because God says so. God's commanding something *defines* it as good. This view is called the *Divine Command Theory*.

The Divine Command Theory seems simple, straightforward, and—if you believe in God—pretty natural. That it leaves atheists and the nonreligious out in the cold is a problem, though: it would be odd to say that they had no moral values at all just because God doesn't come into the picture, even though they may take as much care for others' basic needs and/or legitimate expectations as the rest of us. And there certainly will be problems when the commands of God are unclear or the commands of one religion's God conflict with those of another's. But there is also an intriguing problem with this theory, quite different, first pointed out nearly 2,500 years ago by the Greek philosopher Socrates.

If God's commands alone define the good, then God's commands begin to seem arbitrary. Suppose that instead of commanding us not to kill, God had commanded us to kill. Thou *shalt* kill. According to the Divine Command Theory, then, killing would be good and refraining from killing would be bad.

But this can't be right. Killing really is wrong whether God says so or not. And in fact we do have reservations and second thoughts at some of the points in the Bible where God's own ethics actually seem, well, a little questionable. If the Divine Command Theory were true, Abraham's question—"Shall not the Judge of all the Earth do right?"—could not even be asked.

There's a related problem too. If the Divine Command Theory is true, it makes no sense to say "God is good." Whatever He commands is—well, whatever He commands. If His commands *define* the good, then there is no point admiring Him for His goodness. (This is also why we can't respond by arguing that God never *would* command killing. Why not? *Whatever* He commanded, whatever He did, would be good—by definition.) But this seems, in a sense, to cheapen God. It ought to mean something (and God ought to want it to mean something) to say "God is good."

We could conclude that God says certain things are good because they *are* good. Then, however, we consider the good to be independent of God. To say "God is good" is in a certain sense to judge God. God's commands are not the end of the story: we must still decide whether or not God (or rather, God's many and varied interpreters) is right. In the abstract this may sound like some kind of heresy, but as I've just been arguing, we actually do it all the time, for example, when we disregard commandments that we consider outdated. What do *you* think?

NOTES

Peggy Morgan and Clive Lawton's *Ethical Issues in Six Religious Traditions* (Edinburgh University Press, 2007) offers a thorough and evenhanded overview of each of the great religious traditions' basic approach. On current issues in religion and ethics, see the website of the PBS series "Religion and Ethics Newsweekly," http://www.pbs.org/wnet/religionandethics/. On philosophical issues between ethics and religion, the "Ethics Updates" website offers extensive resources at http://ethics.sandiego.edu/theories/Religion/index.asp.

For a survey of today's religions' turn to environmentalism, see Roger Gottlieb, *A Greener Faith: Religious Environmentalism and Our Planet's Future* (Oxford, 2006). On Mandela and Tutu, see Mandela's autobiography, *Long Walk to Freedom* (Back Bay Books, 1995) and Michael Battle's *Reconciliation: The Ubuntu Theology of Desmond Tutu* (Pilgrim Press, 1997). For Mandela's multicultural and secular formation, along with his words cited here (part of a 1999 speech to the Parliament of the World's Religions in Capetown), see Anders Hallengren, "Nelson Mandela and the Rainbow of Culture," http://www.nobelprize.org/nobel_prizes/peace/laureates/1993/mandela-article.html, accessed 9/20/11. Walter Sinott-Armstrong's lively little book *Morality Without God?* (Oxford University Press, 2009) addresses believers who can't imagine how a nonreligious ethics is possible.

"The Ancient Coffer of Nuri Bey" comes from Idries Shah, *Tales of the Dervishes* (Penguin, 1970). Citations from the Revised Standard Version of the Bible are given in the text. On the Genesis passage cited in the text, remember that in Biblical Hebrew, "to know" means to have sexual intercourse. (Compare Genesis 4:1: "And Adam knew Eve his wife, and she conceived and bore

Cain.") The classic historical source on the Sodom story, as well as on evolving Christian attitudes toward homosexuality generally, is John Boswell's *Christianity, Social Tolerance, and Hemosexuality* (University of Chicago Press, 1980).

On arguing with God, see also Exodus 32:1–15, where Moses dissuades God from destroying Israel after the incident of the Golden Calf. Here Moses argues with God almost as with an equal. And the Bible explicitly says that, as a result, God "repented of the evil which He thought to do to His people." I am grateful to my colleague J. Christian Wilson for help with biblical references and translation issues.

For the original of the argument sketched in the section on "Can God Define the Good?" see Plato's *Euthyphro*, available in many editions as well as in complete collections of Plato's work. For a rigorous contemporary discussion of the problem, see James Rachels, *The Elements of Moral Philosophy* (McGraw-Hill, many editions), chapter 4.

Jamal Rahman's discussion of the Sword Verse was written for *Yes! Magazine* and appears on the *Yes!* blogsite at http://www.yesmagazine.org/blogs/interfaith-amigos/making-peace-with-the-sword-verse. As of 9/20/11 there was a fascinating discussion thread following this article, raising many of the issues discussed in this chapter, including replies by Rahman as well.

II

MORAL VALUES

CHAPTER 4

Taking Values Seriously

Part II of this book offers a survey of moral values and the most prominent and useful frameworks that philosophers and others have developed to systematize and apply them. Chapter 4 begins that survey with an exploration of the nature of values generally, an introduction of the main families into which moral values fall, and some guidelines for how to be more attentive to moral values when they arise, in all their concreteness and diversity, in real situations.

VARIETIES OF VALUES

We hold many values. There is fairness, trustworthiness, the well-being of others and the world. We also value good neighbors, good music, good humor, daily exercise, children and parents, old friends and new, and many other things that are not moral values (not *im*moral values, simply *non*moral values). Truth, cleanliness, good sportsmanship, wilderness; life, liberty, and the pursuit of happiness; random kindness and senseless acts of beauty; the thrill of victory and sometimes even the agony of defeat—all of these are "values" in the broad sense.

Or rather, all of these are *examples* of values in a broad sense. They are all things that we value. But they do not tell us what values themselves *are*. A philosopher will ask: what do they all have in common that makes them all examples of "values"? We need a working definition of "value" in general.

Try this: our values are *those things we care about, that matter to us; those goals and ideals we aspire to and measure ourselves or others or our society by*. When I say that I value playing fair or staying healthy, then I mean (at least) that I am interested in these things, that I care about them, and probably that I do specific things to promote or safeguard them—certainly that I *would* under the right circumstances.

Notice that this definition does not say anything about where values ultimately come from or how they might be prioritized or evaluated or theorized. All of that comes later. Right now we just need a standard for classification. Notice also that nearly anything could be included. "Bad" or questionable or conflicting values count too. We value having a lot of stuff, driving fast, and lording it over others too. Maybe we shouldn't, but sometimes we do. Pirates value their loot; addicts value their drugs; misers obsess over their money. Without all of this confusion and conflict, life would be a lot less interesting.

We may classify values in general into a variety of types. *Aesthetic* values have to do with art, beauty, and attractiveness. *Scientific* values have to do with knowledge, truth, experiment, and so on. *Economic* values have to do with production, efficiency, and market prices. *Instrumental* values have to do with the means to our ends: the effectiveness of technologies, the usefulness of our tools. There are other types too.

Moral values, then, are a kind of value distinct from those just listed, a subset of values generally. You know the examples: fairness, equality, respect, and responsibility; reducing pain and suffering; "life, liberty, and the pursuit of happiness"; humility, benevolence, keeping your promises. From chapter **1** you also have a definition: ethics concerns *those values that give voice to the basic needs and legitimate expectations of others as well as our own.* These values connect us to a larger world ("the needs of others as well as ourselves") and introduce the question of what others are entitled to ask from us and what we are entitled to ask from ourselves ("legitimate expectations").

When you turn to specific ethical questions and debates then, keep this definition in mind. To spell out the values involved, ask what needs and legitimate expectations—both your own and others'—are at stake here? For what needs and legitimate expectations are the parties to this debate trying to speak?

Some ethical debates will be new to you, and answering these questions will take some research or exploration—listening carefully to the different sides, asking around. For other debates we can fill in the blanks more easily—we've heard the contending positions already, or can easily figure them out. The point of our definition of moral values, in any case, is to give us the right blanks to fill in. It gives us the right questions to ask.

FAMILIES OF MORAL VALUES

So, we have distinguished moral values—the subject matter of ethics—from other kinds of values. The next step is to recognize that moral values themselves come in different types. Here too there is diversity—indeed a fascinating complexity.

In particular, certain types of moral values are linked together, sometimes loosely and sometimes tightly, around certain key ideas or central values. They fall into *families.*

Much of the rest of Part II of this book will be a guide to these families of moral values. Most will be somewhat familiar already, I am sure, and they will grow on you! Here at the beginning, though, I want to just outline them by way of introduction. On pages 90–91 you will find an outline of four families of moral values, each identified by its main focus or center. Please read and compare the four summaries before reading on in the text.

UNDERSTANDING ETHICAL DEBATES

These four families of values give us a useful way to begin to organize the field of moral values and to sort out ethical issues and debates. To begin to get a feel for them, let us look briefly at the different families of moral values in action in a particular issue.

In 2005, my state, North Carolina, instituted a state lottery. We were slower than many states to do so, and even when we did it was a bitterly fought-over measure, brought up again and again, finally to get through the State Senate on a dramatic tie vote broken by the Lieutenant Governor. It remains debated today. Though many people have trouble imagining why a state lottery would be controversial at all, in fact many of the reasons— actually on both sides—are ethical in character, and as we may see, of several different sorts.

The chief argument for the lottery is that the state can raise more money for essential services, especially the schools. Tax funds are limited by people's unwillingness to support the taxes, but more money is needed from somewhere. This is an argument from social benefits, then—our second family of moral values. A lottery will enhance the schools, it's argued, and in the long run make society better off. Until the Governor (the same person who as Lieutenant Governor broke the tie back in 2005) started raiding the Lottery Fund for other purposes, the state lottery was actually called the Education Lottery (and it still is in some places).

Social benefits? Critics were more apt to see harms. For one thing, poorer communities, whose schools benefit the most from state-distributed lottery money, are also the communities that in fact spend the most on lottery tickets. It would be much more efficient, say the critics, for people simply to give the money to the schools (or use it to help their kids succeed there) rather than gambling it away and having the schools get a fraction back. In short, there may not be a *net* benefit—maybe even a net loss. It's a question that must be settled, with careful looks at the facts and the actual benefits, or lack of benefits, of lotteries elsewhere.

This, again, is an argument within the Ethics of Happiness: broadly speaking, it is about social benefits, just taking the other side. Not surprisingly, though, there are other arguments too, and different families of values also in play.

The third family—the Ethics of Virtue—for example. A lottery is, after all, a form of gambling. But gambling is a *vice*, isn't it? What's more, it associates

PERSONS

The Ethics of the Person affirms that *persons* are special, precious, and have a dignity that demands respect. No one is to be reduced to a mere means to others' ends. Social relations require fairness, justice, and equality. Human and civil rights are essential too: they secure the space in which each person is recognized and can flourish. We explore the values of persons in chapter 5.

HAPPINESS

The Ethics of Happiness challenges us to achieve the greatest balance of happiness (well-being, satisfaction, pleasure) over suffering. Include in the great calculation the happiness of others as well as oneself, and we find ourselves looking to achieve the greatest balance of happiness over suffering in society as a whole. Ethical thinking in this family of values is quantitative and economic, concerned with trade-offs and the distribution of goods, maximizing tangible social benefits. We explore this family of values in chapter 6.

all too easily with other vices, such as laziness, greed, and a weak sense of the value of work. It is more morally appropriate to work for an honest living. Quite apart from its financial benefits, then, we need to worry about what sort of people the lottery will make us and what kind of character the lottery will build. The more you prize the virtues, the less appealing you may find the answer.

Just by making the distinction between the Ethics of Happiness (social benefit) and the Ethics of Virtue then, you get a first hint of how we can get a more detailed map of ethical debates—debates that may otherwise seem just a hodgepodge of values. Different *types* of moral values are at stake. Non-moral values are also involved—economic and political considerations, for example—but even within ethics, clarifying the issue (let alone trying to resolve it) requires carefully sorting out the types of values involved.

We can also use the families of moral values to inquire after values that may not emerge or be recognized right away in ethical discussions. That is, you can always ask, of whatever is under discussion, how we might think about it from the point of view of a family of values not yet heard from. This is another important function of our distinction between different families of moral values.

VIRTUE

The Ethics of Virtue encompasses those moral values concerned with *character*: with traits like self-discipline, responsibility, honesty, charity, loyalty, devotion. Christendom's great virtues are faith, hope, charity, prudence, justice, temperance, and fortitude. In the Eastern traditions, other virtues come to the fore: tranquillity, non-attachment, compassion, truthful speech and thought, "right livelihood," and nonviolence. We explore these and many other virtues in chapter 7.

RELATIONSHIP

The Ethics of Relationship encompasses those moral values concerned with our connections to others, from families to larger human communities. We are social beings as well as individuals: we grow up in families, take on traditions and heritages, and live within and depend upon human and also ecological communities. Recognizing how deeply our many communities make us who we are calls forth not only gratefulness but also a responsibility to care for and participate in them. We explore these values in chapter 8.

For example, in regard to the lottery, we've heard a little from the second and third families of values, but we might ask after the first. What might an Ethics of the Person say about a state lottery?

Maybe it approves. Some argue that taxes should be kept minimal because it is unjust, or a violation of rights, to take away people's money to spend on purposes they might not choose themselves. People have the right to gamble their money away, this argument goes, but the state has no right to tax away any more money than absolutely necessary for purposes of its own choosing. Respect for persons requires us to accept the choices people make, regardless of whether we'd make them ourselves, simply because they are those people's choices—choices that are their right alone to make, anyway up to the point that they infringe other peoples' equal rights, which does not seem to be the case here.

Consider, finally, the Ethics of Relationship. Here the perspective is rather different. We may look in particular at the relationship between individuals and the state—a specific moral community too. A subtle but striking argument is that the lottery is morally offensive because it encourages false hopes in 99.99 percent of the ticket buyers. A true community should be giving people *real* hope, say the critics, not tempting them (us) with false hopes.

We're not going to settle this question here. Once again, the idea is simply that before we can get very far toward settling ethical debates like these, we need to be able to see more clearly the different sorts of moral values at stake. First steps first! Already you can see, just from the discussion in the last few paragraphs, that we have both a clearer map of the debate and a sense of some of its less developed but quite real possibilities.

TWO OTHER QUESTIONS

Is one family of values somehow more basic, more comprehensive, or even more *right* than the others? Many moralists and philosophers have thought so. Certainly some types of values apply better in some situations than others, and some values may matter more to some people than others. Maybe certain values even matter more than the others in general. Respecting persons, some people say, is more important—if it comes to a pinch—than achieving the greatest good of the greatest number. Some philosophers, on the other hand, try to show that all moral values can really be reduced to (or, they might say, fitted into) one system. For example, some argue that respecting persons, properly understood, really *reduces* to achieving the greatest good of the greatest number.

We will consider these kinds of claims in due course. For now, however, let us stick to values as they actually show up in our lives—which is to say, at least on the surface, in more than one flavor and type of family. Even the theorists and moralists who ultimately want to simplify or theorize them need to start with values as they actually show up in our experience. Let us start there too.

Another question is: Do all moral values have a family? *Most* do, yes. But a few don't, or anyway may not — and there is not necessarily any reason they must. At least at this point in our inquiry, the families of values are simply a means of classifying them, and it would not be surprising, given all their complexity and change, that not every value fits.

A few moral values, on the other hand, may fit into more than one family. Justice, for example, shows up in two—under the values of the person and as a virtue—though in somewhat different senses. You could argue that virtues like loyalty and sensitivity also fit in the relationship family.

Still, on the whole, these four families of values give us a useful way to begin to organize the field of moral values and to sort out ethical issues and debates. Keep these questions in mind—we'll come back to them—but for now, let's put the families of values into our ethical toolbox and look ahead.

ATTENDING TO VALUES

Suppose now that you are looking at a specific ethical issue and trying to discern the different values involved. You want to figure out the main values, not overlooking anything big, and to articulate each of them, at least a little. You want to *understand* the ethical discussion of this issue, in short, just as we began to understand the debate over the lottery just above. This means, in general, *paying careful attention* to the moral values that arise in it: listening carefully to what people say, making connections to widely understood moral values, even picking up on hints and things unsaid. It takes work. Here are some guidelines for paying attention to values in this way.

WELCOME DIVERSITY

We hold a lot of moral values, and they aren't shy about showing up all the time. In the first place, then, welcome diversity.

You've seen some of the diversity already, just considering the four families of moral values and beginning to look at one case in point. You can do the same at every turn. Just read the newspaper, for example. A photo today shows a line of Amish buggies stretching along a country road—a funeral procession for a buggy driver killed by a drunk driver in a car. An all too familiar story, made more poignant still because the accident we imagine is also a collision—literally—of two radically different cultures. A life of sobriety and devotion (I will underline the values named) cut short too soon. We also remember how much trust we place in each other on the roads: how can people better live up to it?

We learn from another article, meanwhile, that the Texas State Senate is about to approve a bill that "would make people under age 21 who climb behind a wheel after drinking subject to losing their licenses for four to six months—even if there is only a trace of alcohol on their breaths." "Zero tolerance," the sponsor calls it. If we expect responsibility in drivers, he says, we have to get (very) tough.

The federal minimum wage is being raised for the first time in many years. It's a matter of basic fairness, advocates say. Incomes at the top end have gone off into the stratosphere: how can we justify leaving behind other people, at the low end of the wage scale, who are also working hard, supporting themselves and their families, and contributing to society? They should be able at least to get by, to be able to raise their children in dignity. Many of those struggling to get by on minimum-wage jobs are single mothers whose only fallback is welfare or homelessness. Meeting even their basic needs—survival and some degree of independence—requires action.

Opponents worry about losing the social benefits of lower wages, such as more jobs, and about fairness again, this time to employers at the margins. Would raising the minimum wage push some of them out of business? Might it therefore actually reduce the number of jobs available?

Environmental issues are all over the news. Climate is changing: we are worried about the future of the earth and the well-being of our children as well as justice to future generations. We are beginning to rethink our practices and to consider new questions about <u>sustainability</u>: how can we live so as to pass on the Earth in as good (or better) shape as we found it? As we begin to comprehend the possibility that we may have altered the very Earth, seemingly so immense and for so long taken for granted, we find that ethics now reaches into the biosphere. What does good "<u>biospheric citizenship</u>" require?

So: there are three issues, broadly speaking—and already a baker's dozen or so values, across all four families (really? check it out), including some overlaps (fairness comes up more than once, for instance). Many more could be found in each issue too. And that's just a start. Each debate also has its own context—from political and environmental issues to personal responsibility and the nature of the "simple life"—or sometimes several at once. Doing the best by the most people, for instance (as in: what are the overall social effects of raising the minimum wage?). Old ways versus new ways. The place of the Earth, as the setting for all of our other values, in ethics itself. And others as well.

LOOK IN DEPTH

Many different values also come up *within* each issue, quite apart from other issues. Call this *depth*.

That Amish funeral again. Most obviously, what's at stake is drunk driving: once again, a severe form of social irresponsibility. Think of what it means to take the wheel of a machine that can maim and kill when you are not fully aware and capable. Even worse is when you are just a beginning driver: hence the Texas response.

The Texas response, however, raises questions too. Other concerns come up. If a "trace of alcohol" is enough to revoke someone's license, how little is a "trace"? If an officer smells anything, is that enough? Is a blip on a Breathalyzer enough? What about people whose prescription drugs might have a trace of alcohol? My students, barely 21 themselves, worry that the proposed law gives police officers an unsettling amount of discretion.

Fairness comes up. Is it fair only to target minors in this way? Isn't drunk driving an irresponsible act regardless of the driver's age? Or is the idea that minors are more dangerous at the wheel with *any* alcohol because they are inexperienced drivers? Or is the idea that if minors have been drinking at all, they've already violated the law and therefore deserve even stricter punishment? The article doesn't say. In that case, is a four- to six-month revocation strict *enough*?

There is still more. This photo would not have appeared in the paper had the victim not been Amish. The Amish won the legal right to drive buggies on the roads only after a hard-fought struggle in many states and over many years. Why? They don't care for the conveniences that the rest of us take for granted. Why not? Modern "conveniences," they say, corrupt the simplicity of our relation to each other, the Earth, and God. Without them, the Amish have created and sustained tight-knit, mutually supportive communities and farms that are the finest in their areas. Lately some environmentalists have begun to champion Amish methods on ecological grounds. A world of Amish people, for one thing, would certainly not be threatening the climate!

So there is much to think about here. Can we reclaim some of the virtues the Amish represent without giving up on the 21st century? If not, what does that say about how things are with us? If so, why aren't we doing it?

Notice again: all of this complexity arises from thinking about just one photograph—and still, we have just scratched the surface. Ethical issues like these have histories, and they represent the intersection or manifestation of many different concerns and struggles, many of them still unfolding. When you are exploring an ethical issue then, don't just mention one or two main concerns and move on. Take some time with them—and give yourself some time to take. Look in depth.

BE FAIR

Spelling out some of the values at stake in these cases may be hard, especially when you disagree with them. Buggy drivers, or drunk drivers, may make you impatient, and you may not want to consider the moral dangers of "zero tolerance" or burning a lot of fossil fuels. People who always complain about helping the poor, or tobacco company representatives who still won't admit that smoking causes cancer, may just annoy you. And maybe you've already heard too much about global warming.

But your first job is not to decide what you think. Suspend judgment until later. Here is another place that we often turn more dogmatic than we should. It's wiser to remind ourselves again that we don't know everything there is to know. Remember chapter 2! In particular, if we dismiss some moral values without any kind of exploration or careful attention, we might never know what kinds of depth we missed. To look at a buggy driver as a mere curiosity, or as a hazard that ought to keep out of your way, misses a lot that is intriguing and maybe even enriching. So *be fair* to those who come at ethical issues from other angles and places. Don't rush to judge. Ask what these people are about instead. What are their goals and ideals? What matters to them? What are their needs and expectations? How do they invite us to rethink our own?

At least try to see matters from others' points of view. You're not being asked to decide who is right and who is wrong, or which way we finally ought to choose. The task here is just to figure out the values involved. And that means on all sides. Not just filtered through a moral position you've already taken. Put your own position aside for a moment. Listen first; decide later.

CLARIFY!

Moral values often show up in forms that are not fully spelled out or clear. Part of our job in unpacking ethical issues then, is to do some of the explaining and clarifying ourselves. We may need to make some distinctions.

Molly [4 years old]: Ruthie got to use the big markers, and I only got to use the plain ones.

Me: Yup. [to myself: Uh-oh.]

Molly: That's not fair!

Me: Why not?

Molly: Because I should get to use the big ones if Ruthie does!

Me: But the big markers are not washable and you're not quite old enough to remember to keep them off your clothes and the table. As soon as you can keep them just on the paper, you can use them too.

Molly: I can! I can! [sniffle]

Me: Oh, Molly, that's what you said yesterday, and I let you use them, but you ended up with a big orange splot on your shirt. A nonwashable splot!

Is it fair that Molly cannot use the big markers? If so, it is because fairness is not as simple as it looks on its face—because fairness cannot necessarily be measured by immediate equality of results. It's complicated. Fairness asks us to allow each child all that she is capable of, consistent with other needs and limits, including fairness to the parents who have to try to wash markers off clothes or tables, or buy new ones.

It's not so easy to spell out in a way that a 4-year-old can understand. In fact, just for that reason, some other approach to the problem sometimes may be needed, may even be more fair. Getting bigger washable markers, for example. The point is that this is how it goes, in real-life practice. Pay attention and take seriously the demand for clarification and distinctions.

In fact, fairness is a passion with all of us. Is it fair, for example, to set up a system of preferences for one group over another, even if it only comes into play when qualifications are otherwise equal and/or does not compel any particular choice? Some people argue that it is; others argue that it cannot be. It's the same sort of issue. Would some distinctions help? Can you know until you've tried?

GIVE EMOTION ITS DUE

One last clip from the newspaper. Developers and environmentalists clash over new building along a river that serves as many downstream communities' water supply and feeds major shellfish banks in the sounds off the coast. The river is already stressed by runoff from farms and lawn fertilizers, sewage treatment plants, and so on, though for just that reason the impact of any single new development by itself is not that great.

The civil engineer who works for the developer and presented the case to the City Planning Commission has this to say about his environmentalist counterparts: "We're doing this from a fact standpoint, and they [the environmentalists] are doing this from an emotional standpoint." *We* have facts, he says; *they're* just "emotional." His suggestion, of course, is that they should not be taken seriously. Emotion is supposed to be inappropriate when ethical or political matters come up.

It's not. Being emotional can be entirely appropriate. In fact, it's necessary. Remember, values themselves are things we *care* about. Care is an emotion. It's not *only* an emotion—it rests on facts, perspectives on the world, histories and personal choices, and many other things—but the emotional side, the caring side, is essential as well.

The developers "care" too, of course. They too have values. They want to build houses and roads and malls, creating more choices and ease, and making money while doing it. They're a little annoyed in this case too, if you read between the lines, because they have to work under many more restrictions than they used to and still are being criticized for not doing enough. The suggestion is that this isn't quite fair—and that is a feeling, in part, too.

What *would* be inappropriate is "pure" emotion: having no facts at all, *just* a "feeling." But clearly this is not true of either side in this debate. The environmentalists in this case have at least as many facts as the developers: facts about the overall state of the river, about alternative uses of the site in question, and so on. Perhaps the developers, sensing they have the Planning Commission on their side, can afford to speak with the appearance of dispassion, while the environmentalists sound more upset or desperate. But this has nothing to do with who has facts and who doesn't—it has to do with who is being heard.

In short: moral values are partly emotional, just as they are partly fact based. All moral values, on both (all) sides. Moral emotions are parts of our thinking, parts of our very selves, and by including them we keep ourselves more intact, less fragmented, better able to integrate our selves as well as our values. How many unethical results of ethical deliberation come because we disconnect from our decision making emotionally, because we unhook deliberation from caring? Do not therefore become maudlin or hysterical; but also do not pretend to be dispassionate and accuse the other side of being uninformed or "emotional." Both are unhelpful extremes. Just speak carefully, listen sympathetically, and try to give all of the relevant values a voice that is measured, but strong.

READING

"XYLO"

RAYNA RAPP

"XYLO" is about a particularly painful abortion choice.

The minute the abortion issue is mentioned, alas, some people assume that they've heard it all already—and it's true, we've heard the same few things many, many times—or that the "other side" (whichever it is) has nothing worthwhile listening to anyway.

That is, however, exactly why I chose to put this reading here. It challenges us to pay close attention to moral values even in a case where we may think there's nothing more to hear, or we fervently wish not to hear it. "XYLO" is in fact a deep and suggestive story in certain ways. I promise it will reward your careful attention.

I first encountered this story in a collection of stories intended to illustrate "how varied, complex, and personal are the factors surrounding reproductive choice, and . . . the suffering that results when choice is denied." (The book was Angela Bonavoglia, ed., *The Choices We Made*, Random House, 1991.) If you are single-mindedly looking to classify it as pro-life or pro-choice, you'd probably conclude from the last phrase that this story has a pro-choice "moral." But it would be wiser to suspend judgment on that question and pay more attention to the first phrase: *"how varied, complex, and personal are the factors surrounding reproductive choice."* Again, try reading the story just for that. Note both the overwhelming importance of *life* to Rayna Rapp, and her partner and her parents too, and their conviction, nonetheless, that choice—abortion in this case—is necessary too. How is this possible? Note too all of the ways in which social factors beyond their control—especially the lack of "decent humane attention and services for other-than-fully-abled children and adults"—also seem to compel that choice.

Of course, one can argue with this too. Still, for purposes of paying attention, just try to listen carefully. You do not have to agree, or even worry about whether you agree or not.

Your results may be surprising. Share them with each other in a discussion format that encourages careful listening: there are some suggestions in chapter **11**. Is it just possible that this story, tragic as it is, helps to show us a way *out*—beyond the current opposition of "life" versus "choice"?

Rayna Rapp, "XYLO." Reproduced by permission of Rayna Rapp.

Mike called the fetus XYLO, XY for its unknown sex, LO for the love we were pouring into it. Day by day we fantasized about who this growing cluster of cells might become. Day by day, we followed the growth process in the myriad books that surround modern pregnancy for the over-thirty-five baby boomlet. Both busy with engrossing work and political commitments, we welcomed this potential child with excitement, fantasy and the ratonality of scientific knowledge. As a Women's Movement activist, I had decided opinions about treating pregnancy as a normal, not a diseased condition, and we were fortunate to find a health-care team—obstetrican, midwives, genetic counseling—who shared that view.

The early months of the pregnancy passed in a blur of exhaustion and nausea. Preoccupied with my own feeling, I lived in a perpetual underwater, slow-motion version of my prior life. As one friend put it, I was already operating on fetal time, tied to unfamiliar regimen of enforced naps, loss of energy, and rigid eating. Knowing the research on nutrition, on hormones, and on miscarriage rates among older pregnant women, I did whatever I could to stay comfortable.

I was thirty-six when XYLO was conceived, and like many of my peers, I chose to have amniocentesis, a prenatal test for birth defects such as Down syndrome, Tay-Sachs disease, and sickle-cell anemia. Both Mike and I knew about prenatal diagnosis from our friends' experiences, and from reading about it. Each year, many thousands of American women choose amniocentesis to detect birth defects. The procedure is performed between the sixteenth and twentieth weeks of pregnancy. Most obstetricians, mine included, send their pregnant patients directly to the genetic division of a hospital where counseling is provided, and the laboratory technicians are specially trained. Analysis of amniotic fluid requires complex laboratory work, and can cost between five hundred dollars and two thousand dollars.

It was fear of Down syndrome that sent us to seek prenatal diagnosis of XYLO. Down syndrome produces a characteristic physical appearance—short, stocky size, large tongue, puffy upward-slanting eyes with skin folds in the inner corners—and is a major cause of mental retardation, worldwide. People with Down syndrome are quite likely to have weak cardiovascular systems, respiratory problems, and run a greater risk of developing childhood leukemia. While the majority of Down syndrome infants used to die very young, a combination of antibiotics and infant surgery enables modern medicine to keep them alive. And programs of childhood physical-mental stimulation may facilitate their assimilation. Some parents also opt for cosmetic surgery—an expensive and potentially risky procedure. Down syndrome is caused by an extra chromosome, at the twenty-first pair of chromosomes, as geneticists label them. And while the diagnosis of Down spells mental retardation and physical vulnerability, no geneticist can tell you how seriously affected your particular fetus will be. There is no cure for Down syndrome. A pregnant woman whose fetus is diagnosed as having the extra chromosome can either prepare to raise a mentally retarded and physically vulnerable child, or decide to abort it.

On the February morning Mike and I arrived at a local medical center for genetic counseling, in my nineteenth week of pregnancy, Nancy Z., our counselor, took a detailed pedigree (or family tree) from each of us, to discover any rare diseases or birth defects for which we could be tested. She then gave us an excellent genetics lesson, explained the amniocentesis procedure and the risks, both of the test and of discovering a serious genetic defect. One third of one percent of pregnancies miscarry due to amniocentesis. Most women feel fine after the test, but some (perhaps 10 percent) experience uterine cramping or contractions. Overall, about 98 percent of the women who go for amniocentesis will be told that no fetal defects or anomalies have been found.

After counseling, we descended to the testing area, where an all-female team of radiologist, obstetrician, nurses, and staff assistants performed the tap. In skilled hands, and with the use of sonogram equipment, the tap is a rapid procedure. I spent perhaps five minutes on the table, belly attached to sonar electrodes. Mike holding my feet for encouragement. The radiologist snapped Polaroid pictures of XYLO, and we had our first "baby album"—gray blotches of a head and spine of our baby-in-waiting. She located the placenta, which enabled the obstetrician to successfully draw a small, clear sample of amniotic fluid (less than one eighth of a cup). The tap felt like a crampier version of drawing blood—not particularly painful or traumatic. We marched the fluid back to the genetic lab where it would be cultured, and went home.

The waiting period for amniocentesis results is a long one, and I was very anxious. Cells must be cultured, then analyzed, a process that takes two to four weeks. We wait, caught between the late date at which amniocentesis can be performed (usually sixteen to twenty weeks); the moment of quickening, when the woman feels the fetus move (roughly eighteen to twenty weeks); and the legal limits of abortion (very few of which are performed after twenty-four weeks in the United States). Those of my friends who have had amniocentesis report terrible fantasies, dreams, and crying fits, and I was no exception: I dreamed in lurid detail of my return to the lab, of awful damage. I woke up frantic, sobbing, to face the nagging fear that is focused in the waiting period after amniocentesis.

For the 98 percent of women whose amniotic fluid reveals no anomaly, reassurance arrives by phone, or more likely, by mail, confirming a negative test. When Nancy called me twelve days after the tap, I began to scream as soon as I recognized her voice; in her office, I knew only positive results (very negative results, from a potential parent's point of view) are reported by phone. The image of myself, alone, screaming into a white plastic telephone is indelible. Although it only took twenty minutes to locate Mike and bring him and a close friend to my side, time is suspended in my memory. I replay the call, and my screams echo for indefinite periods. We learned, after contacting our midwives and obstetrician, that a diagnosis of a male fetus with Down syndrome had been made. Our fantasies for XYLO, our five months' fetus, were completely shattered.

Mike and I had discussed what we would do if amniocentesis revealed a serious genetic condition long before the test. For us, the diagnosis of Down syndrome was reason to choose abortion. Our thinking was clear, if abstract, long before the question became reality. We were eager to have a child, and prepared to change our lives to make emotional, social, and economic resources available. But the realities of raising a child who could never grow to independence would call forth more than we could muster, unless one or both of us gave up our work, our political commitments, our social existence beyond the household. And despite a shared commitment to coparenting, we both understood that in this society, that one was likely to be the mother. When I thought about myself, I knew that in such a situation, I would transform myself to become the kind of twenty-four-hour-a-day advocate such a child would require. I'd do the best and most loving job I could, and I'd undoubtedly become an activist in support of the needs of disabled children.

But other stark realities confronted us: to keep a Down syndrome child alive through potentially lethal health problems is an act of love with weighty consequences. As we ourselves age, to whom would we leave the person XYLO would become? Neither Mike nor I have any living kin who are likely to be young enough, or close enough, to take on this burden after our deaths. In a society where the state provides virtually no decent, humane services for the mentally retarded, how could we take responsibility for the future of our dependent Down syndrome child? In good conscience, we couldn't choose to raise a child who would become a ward of the state. The health care, schools, various therapies that Down syndrome children require are inadequately available, and horrendously expensive in America; no single family should have to shoulder all the burdens that a decent health and social policy may someday extend to physically and mentally disabled people. In the meantime, while struggling for such a society, we did not choose to bring a child into this world who could never grow up to care for himself.

Most women who've opted for amniocentesis are prepared to face the question of abortion, and many of us *do* choose it, after a diagnosis of serious disability is made. Perhaps 95 percent of Down syndrome pregnancies are terminated after test results are known. Reports on other diseases and conditions are harder to find, but in one study, the diagnosis of spina bifida led to abortion about 90 percent of the time.

In shock and grief, I learned from my obstetrician that two kinds of late second-trimester abortions were available. Most common are the "installation procedures"—saline solution or urea is injected into the uterus to kill the fetus, and drugs are sometimes used to bring on labor. The woman then goes through labor to deliver the fetus. The second kind of midtrimester abortion, and the one I choose, is a D&E—dilation and evacuation. This procedure demands more active intervention from a doctor, who vacuums out the amniotic fluid, and then removes the fetus. The D&E requires some intense, upsetting work for the medical team, but it's over in about twenty minutes, without putting the woman through labor. Both forms of late abortion entail some physical risk, and the psychological pain is enormous. Deciding to end the life of a fetus you've wanted and carried for most of five months is no easy matter. The number of relatively late second-trimester abortions performed for genetic reasons is very small. It seems an almost inconsequential number, unless you happen to be one of them.

Making the medical arrangements, going back for counseling, the pretests, and finally, the abortion, was the most difficult period of my adult life. I was then twenty-one weeks pregnant, and had been proudly carrying my expanding belly. Telling everyone—friends, family, students, colleagues, neighbors—seemed an endless nightmare. But it also allowed us to rely on their love and support during this terrible time. Friends streamed in from all over to teach my classes; I have scores of letters expressing concern; the phone never stopped ringing for weeks. Our community was invaluable, reminding us that our lives were rich and filled with love despite this loss. A few weeks afterward, I spoke with another woman who'd gone through selective abortion (as this experience is antiseptically called in medical jargon). She'd returned to work immediately, her terrible abortion experience unspoken. Colleagues assumed she'd had a late miscarriage, and didn't speak about it. Her isolation only underlined my appreciation of the support I'd received.

My parents flew a thousand miles to sit guard over my hospital bed, answer telephones, shop, and cook. Filled with sorrow for the loss of their first grandchild, my mother told me of a conversation she'd had with my father. Despite their grief, they were deeply grateful for the test. After all, she reasoned, we were too young and active to be devastated like this; if the child had been born, she and my dad would have taken him to raise in their older years, so we could get on with raising other children. I can only respond with deep love and gratitude for the wellspring of compassion behind that conversation. But surely, no single woman, mother or grandmother, no single family, nuclear or extended, should have to bear all the burdens that raising a seriously disabled child entails. It points out, once again, the importance of providing decent, humane attention and services for other-than-fully-abled children and adults.

And, of course, parents of disabled children are quick to point out that the lives they've nurtured have been worth living. I honor their hard work and commitments, as well as their love, and I think that part of "informed consent" to amniocentesis and selective abortion should include information about parents' groups of Down syndrome children, and social services available to them, not just the individual, medical diagnosis of the problem. And even people who feel they could never choose a late abortion may nonetheless want amniocentesis so they'll have a few extra months to prepare themselves, other family members, friends, and special resources for the birth of a child with special, complex needs.

Recovering from the abortion took a long time. Friends, family, coworkers, students did everything they could to ease me through the experience. Even so, I yearned to talk with someone who'd "been there." Over the next few months, I used my personal and medical networks to locate and talk with a handful of other women who'd opted for selective abortions. In each case, I was the first person they'd ever met with a similar experience. The isolation of this decision and its consequences is intense. Only when women (and concerned men) speak of the experience of selective abortion as a tragic but chosen fetal death can we as a community offer the support, sort out the ethics, and give the compassionate attention that such a loss entails.

For two weeks, Mike and I breathed as one person. His distress, loss, and concern were never one whit less than my own. But we were sometimes upset and angered by the unconscious attitudes toward his loss. He was expected to "cope," while I was nurtured through my "need." We've struggled for male responsibility in birth control, sexual mutuality, childbirth, and child-rearing, and I think we need to acknowledge that those men who do engage in such transformed practices have mourning rights during a pregnancy loss, as well.

Nonetheless, our experiences *were* different, and I'm compelled to recognize the material reality of my experience. Because it happened in my body, a woman's body, I recovered much more slowly than Mike did. By whatever mysterious process, he was able to damp back the pain, and throw himself back into work after several weeks. For me, it took months. As long as I had the fourteen pounds of pregnancy weight to lose, as long as my aching breasts, filled with milk, couldn't squeeze into bras, as long as my tummy muscles protruded, I was confronted with the physical reality of being post-pregnant, without a child. Mike's support seemed inadequate; I was still in deep mourning while he seemed distant and cured. Only much later, when I began doing research on amniocentesis, did I find one study of the stresses and strains of selective abortion. In a small sample of couples, a high percentage separated or divorced following this experience. Of course, the same holds true after couples face a child's disablement, or child death. Still, I had no idea that deep mourning for a fetus could be so disorienting. Abortion after prenatal diagnosis has been kept a medical and private experience, so there is no common fund of knowledge or support to alert us as individuals, as couples, as families, as friends, to the aftermath our "freedom of choice" entails.

Which is why I've pierced my private pain to raise this issue. As feminists, we need to speak from our seemingly private experience toward a social and political agenda. I'm suggesting we lift the veil of privacy and professionalism to explore issues of health care, abortion, and the right to choose death, as well as life, for our genetically disabled fetuses. If XYLO's story, a true story, has helped to make this a compelling issue for more than one couple, then his five short months of fetal life will have been a great gift.

FOR REVIEW

1. What are values?
2. What makes a family of moral values?
3. What four families of moral values are distinguished in this chapter?
4. How—roughly—are the four families distinct?
5. Apply one moral value from each of the four families to the question of a state lottery.

6. What are this chapter's general guidelines for drawing out the moral values at stake in an issue?

7. Explain: "Look in depth."

8. Explain: "Give emotion its due."

9. What are two moral values invoked by Rayna Rapp in "XYLO"?

10. Why, in the end, does Rapp choose abortion?

EXERCISES AND NOTES

4.1 FOR REFLECTION

What values are most important to you? Not just moral values, first of all, but *any* values. What is it that you care most deeply about? Love? Money? Satisfying and productive work? One or two things, or a great many? Things easily described in a few words, or things that take a long story or two to explain?

Now turn to *moral* values. What moral values are most important to you? Respect? The greatest happiness (your own *and* others')? Keeping your word? Care and community? Fairness? Are there one or two things, or a great many? Things easily described in a few words, or things that take a long story or two to explain? Are most of your key values in one specific family? Which one, and why?

Think of a time when you felt proud of yourself. What were you proud of having done (or not done) or of being (or not being)? Then think of some time when you felt angry at yourself. What were you angry about? Why? What values are called upon when you make these judgments? How many of these are moral values?

4.2 ISSUES

Here are some issues to explore with an eye for the values in play—and other relevant values that perhaps *ought* to be in play!

- What moral values (if any) are involved in driving (besides not driving drunk)? Does ethics have anything to say about following speed limits, keeping your insurance up to date, keeping the car well-maintained, and so on? (Clearly there are values involved; the question is whether you consider them *moral* values, and why or why not.) What about radar detectors? Moral, nonmoral, immoral? Why? What families of values are involved?

- What moral obligations do you have toward your parents? Why? Are they (and if so *why* are they) different from the moral obligations your parents have toward you? If there is a difference, is the difference fair? Or does the value of fairness just not apply here?

- Ease of life today may impose immense costs on the future. When we waste scarce natural resources and litter the earth with nonbiodegradable but cheap items, our descendants bear the burdens of compensation and cleanup. When we alter the climate, we impose unknown but possibly immense costs on the future too. William McDonough calls this "intergenerational remote tyranny" (more from him in chapter 18). What kinds of moral values is he invoking? What others are relevant?

- Population policy: what kinds of moral values are at stake as we think about having children and about religious or political policies that affect family choices and reproduction rates, at home or abroad?

- Many businesses now have codes of ethics. What kinds of moral values would, or should, such a code include? Also: could there be a debate about this? That is, might it be that a business code of ethics should only concern certain kinds of moral values and not others? Must business serve the social good, for example, or should businesspeople be judged only by their personal virtuousness?

- Rights of accused (and convicted) criminals (to fair trials, against cruel and unusual punishments, etc.) versus the social good (*what* good[s], exactly?) that might be achieved by rapid trials, limited appeals, and cheap jails. What families of moral values are most directly invoked here? Are there other moral values also in play?

- Some of us expect that U.S. presidents will be sterling personal role models. Others ask: isn't it enough if they do what they can to improve the quality of life, the economy, world politics, and so on? What values, again, are invoked here? Do the same expectations apply to other leaders, for example, corporate CEOs, movie stars, athletes? Why or why not? What moral values shape these expectations?

- Should academic honor codes require students to turn in fellow students who cheated on an exam? What families of values have something to say about this? What do they say?

- How should the government respond to the demands of dispossessed Indian tribes for some kind of compensation or return of ancient ancestral lands? Is this an *ethical* issue? What kinds of options can be morally considered? How does this issue relate to the question of reparations for slavery?

4.3 READING VALUES STATEMENTS AND STORIES

Look at the mission statements of a variety of organizations: local business, big corporations, nonprofit organizations, groups like Amnesty International or the Sierra Club or the National Rifle Association (NRA) or the American

Civil Liberties Union (ACLU). Nearly all of these can be found on the Web: the research is easy. Be sure to pick some you dislike as well as some you like.

Once again, spell out the moral values involved. What kinds of values tend to show up? Typically in what families? Many of these organizations we only know through a few media stereotypes, or perhaps because they are very visible on one or two controversial issues. Don't assume that you already know who and what they are and that you don't need to look carefully at what they themselves say they are. Every organization on this list will surprise you if you look closely enough.

Look at your own college or university catalog. The first pages usually offer some larger sense of the institution's mission, often in moral terms. Again, what kinds of values tend to show up? Typically in what families? Would it be the same for educational institutions of other sorts—like military academies, Zen monasteries, museums, auto-mechanic training schools? Find out.

Political speeches and party platforms are a good place to look as well. (Full texts can sometimes be found in newspapers like *The New York Times,* or on the Web.) Don't forget the United Nations—look at its founding documents, like the UN Declaration of Human Rights. Look at the speeches of ambassadors from places you don't like. For those with a historical bent, look to the great documents and speeches of American history. Look at the encyclicals of the popes.

If your interests run in a more literary direction, look at popular stories in the same way. Children's stories, for example. They often clearly promote moral values and in fact invite us to spell them out as we interpret the story— as we find the "moral." Useful collections are William Bennett's *The Book of Virtues* (Simon and Schuster, 1993) and his follow-up *The Moral Compass* (Simon and Schuster, 1995).

NOTES

Many disciplines study values (in general). The aim may be to classify values, to relate them to each other and to other factors, or sometimes to begin to systematically evaluate them as well. For a useful survey of social-scientific approaches to the question of the nature of values, as well as a survey of typologies and developmental theories of value, see Richard Kilby, *The Study of Human Values* (University Press of America, 1993). A stimulating and accessible look at values that goes back to the very beginning (how do we know values are even *real?*) is Howard Richards, *Life on a Small Planet: A Philosophy of Value* (Philosophical Library, 1966). For the classic introduction to the philosophical theory of values, see Risieri Frondizi, *What Is Value?* (Open Court Library of Philosophy, 1963). Classic but more difficult sources are John Dewey, *Theory of Valuation* (University of Chicago Press, 1939) and G. H. von Wright, *The Varieties of Goodness* (Humanities Press, 1963).

USING YOUR TOOLS #2
VALUES ON THE EDGE

Edward Abbey was an American nature writer, backcountry hiker, and militant defender of wilderness whose writings include the classic *Desert Solitaire* as well as the controversial novel *The Monkeywrench Gang*, which allegedly inspired some infamous environmental sabotage in the 1980s and 90s. In this selection from his book *The Journey Home*, Abbey is trying to explain why he loves the desert—why he values it and why you and I should too.

You might expect a nice poetic rhapsody to the loveliness of the desert, making us think of cactus-and-sunset pictures in Sierra Club calendars or travel magazines. But this is not what Abbey says—just the opposite. First he details the desert's horrors, then he tells you how to prepare to hike there if you're crazy enough to go in the first place (not that *he* ever prepares at all), then he reminds you to disrupt any mining or hunting or road-building activities you happen to run across, and finally he tells a story about an ancient arrow pointing at nothingness. What are we to make of this?

Yet he *is*, after all, explaining why he loves the desert. He is calling on certain values. This is your challenge: see if you can figure out what they are. What *is* he saying about the arrow pointing at nothingness, for example? What kinds of values is he so proudly appealing to here?

Having spelled out some of Abbey's values, you can then ask the other question that naturally arises in chapter 4: are the values to which he appeals—and that you have just carefully spelled out—*moral* values? Can love for the other-than-human—even *inhuman*—also be moral, be *ethical*? Why or why not?

Don't overlook the irony in this piece. That too calls for some careful interpretation. The long list of desert horrors comes right after Abbey tells us that he loved the desert "at first sight." Somehow the horrors make the desert *loveable*—how? And why does he tell us to pull up survey stakes, take out billboards, etc., etc.? Isn't that illegal?

READING

"The Great American Desert"

EDWARD ABBEY

In my case it was love at first sight. This desert, all deserts, any desert. No matter where my head and feet may go, my heart and my entrails stay behind,

"The Great American Desert," from *The Journey Home* by Edward Abbey, © 1977 by Edward Abbey. Used by permission of Dutton, a division of Penguin Putnam, Inc.

here on the clean, true, comfortable rock, under the black sun of God's for-
saken country. When I take on my next incarnation, my bones will remain
bleaching nicely in a stone gulch under the rim of some faraway plateau, way
out there in the back of beyond. An unrequited and excessive love, inhuman
no doubt but painful anyhow, especially when I see my desert under attack.
"The one death I cannot bear," said the Sonoran-Arizonan poet Richard Shel-
ton. The kind of love that makes a man selfish, possessive, irritable. If you're
thinking of a visit, my natural reaction is like a rattlesnake's—to warn you off.
What I want to say goes something like this.

Survival Hint #1: Stay out of there. Don't go. Stay home and read a good
book, this one for example. The Great American Desert is an awful place.
People get hurt, get sick, get lost out there. Even if you survive, which is not
certain, you will have a miserable time. The desert is for movies and God-
intoxicated mystics, not for family recreation.

Let me enumerate the hazards. First the Walapai tiger, also known as conenose
kissing bug. *Triatoma protracta* is a true bug, black as sin, and it flies through
the night quiet as an assassin. It does not attack directly like a mosquito or
deerfly, but alights at a discreet distance, undetected, and creeps upon you,
its hairy little feet making not the slightest noise. The kissing bug is fond of
warmth and like Dracula requires mammalian blood for sustenance. When it
reaches you the bug crawls onto your skin so gently, so softly that unless your
senses are hyperacute you feel nothing. Selecting a tender point, the bug slips
its conical proboscis into your flesh, injecting a poisonous anesthetic. If you
are asleep you will feel nothing. If you happen to be awake you may notice the
faintest of pinpricks, hardly more than a brief ticklish sensation, which you will
probably disregard. But the bug is already at work. Having numbed the nerves
near the point of entry the bug proceeds (with a sigh of satisfaction, no doubt)
to withdraw blood. When its belly is filled, it pulls out, backs off, and waddles
away, so drunk and gorged it cannot fly.

At about this time the victim awakes, scratching at a furious itch. If you recognize the symptoms at once, you can sometimes find the bug in your vicinity
and destroy it. But revenge will be your only satisfaction. Your night is ruined.
If you are of average sensitivity to a kissing bug's poison, your entire body
breaks out in hives, skin aflame from head to toe. Some people become seriously ill, in many cases requring hospitalization. Others recover fully after five
or six hours except for a hard and itchy swelling, which may endure for a week.

After the kissing bug, you should beware of rattlesnakes; we have half a
dozen species, all offensive and dangerous, plus centipedes, millipedes,
tarantulas, black widows, brown recluses, Gila monsters, the deadly poisonous coral snakes, and giant hairy desert scorpions. Plus an immense variety
and near-infinite number of ants, midges, gnats, blood-sucking flies, and
blood-guzzling mosquitoes. (You might think the desert would be spared
at least mosquitoes? Not so. Peer in any water hole by day: swarming with
mosquito larvae. Venture out on a summer's eve: The air vibrates with their
mournful keening.) Finally, where the desert meets the sea, as on the coasts
of Sonora and Baja California, we have the usual assortment of obnoxious
marine life: sandflies, ghost crabs, stingrays, electric jellyfish, spiny sea
urchins, man-eating sharks, and other creatures so distasteful one prefers
not even to name them.

It has been said, and truly, that everything in the desert either stings, stabs, stinks, or sticks. You will find the flora here as venomous, hooked, barbed, thorny, prickly, needled, saw-toothed, hairy, stickered, mean, bitter, sharp, wiry, and fierce as the animals. Something about the desert inclines all living things to harshness and acerbity. The soft evolve out. Except for sleek and oily growths like the poison ivy—oh yes, indeed—that flourish in sinister profusion on the dank walls about the quicksand down in those corridors of gloom and labyrinthine monotony that men call canyons.

We come now to the third major hazard, which is sunshine. Too much of a good thing can be fatal. Sunstroke, heatstroke, and dehydration are common misfortunes in the bright American Southwest. If you can avoid the insects, reptiles, and arachnids, the cactus and the ivy, the smog of the southwestern cities, and the lung fungus of the desert valleys (carried by dust in the air), you cannot escape the desert sun. Too much exposure to it eventually causes, quite literally, not merely sunburn but skin cancer.

Much sun, little rain also means an arid climate. Compared with the high humidity of more hospitable regions, the dry heat of the desert seems at first not terribly uncomfortable—sometimes even pleasant. But that sensation of comfort is false, a deception, and therefore all the more dangerous, for it induces overexertion and an insufficient consumption of water, even when water is available. This leads to various internal complications, some immediate—sunstroke, for example—and some not apparent until much later. Mild but prolonged dehydration, continued over a span of months or years, leads to the crystallization of mineral solutions in the urinary tract, that is, to what urologists call urinary calculi or kidney stones. A disability common in all the world's arid regions. . . .

Up north in the Great Basin Desert, on the Plateau Province, in the canyon country, your heart will break, seeing the strip mines open up and the power plants rise where only cowboys and Indians and J. Wesley Powell ever roamed before.

Nevertheless, all is not lost; much remains, and I welcome the prospect of an army of lug-soled hiker's boots on the desert trails. To save what wilderness is left in the American Southwest—and in the American Southwest only the wilderness is worth saving—we are going to need all the recruits we can get. All the hands, heads, bodies, time, money, effort we can find. Presumably—and the Sierra Club, the Wilderness Society, the Friends of the Earth, the Audubon Society, the Defenders of Wildlife operate on this theory—those who learn to love what is spare, rough, wild, undeveloped, and unbroken will be willing to fight for it, will help resist the strip miners, highway builders, land developers, weapons testers, power producers, tree chainers, clear cutters, oil drillers, dam beavers, subdividers—the list goes on and on—before that zinc-hearted, termite-brained, squint-eyed, near-sighted, greedy crew succeeds in completely californicating what still survives of the Great American Desert.

So much for the Good Cause. Now what about desert hiking itself, you may ask. I'm glad you asked that question. I firmly believe that one should never—I repeat *never*—go out into that formidable wasteland of cactus, heat, serpents, rock, scrub, and thorn without careful planning, thorough and cautious preparation, and complete—never mind the expense!—*complete* equipment. My motto is: Be Prepared.

That is my belief and that is my motto. My practice, however, is a little different. I tend to go off in a more or less random direction myself, half-baked, half-assed, half-cocked, and half-ripped. Why? Well, because I have an idolent and melancholy nature and don't care to be bothered getting all those *things* together—all that bloody *gear*—maps, light, inspirational poetry, water, food— and because anyhow I approach nature with a certain surly ill-will, daring Her to make trouble. Later . . . I may wish I had packed that something extra: matches perhaps, to mention one useful item, or maybe a spoon to eat my gruel with. . . .

A few tips on desert etiquette:

1. Carry a cooking stove, if you must cook. Do not burn desert wood, which is rare and beautiful and required ages for its creation (an ironwood tree lives for over 1,000 years and juniper almost as long).

2. If you must, out of need, build a fire, then for God's sake allow it to burn itself out before you leave—do not bury it, as Boy Scouts and Campfire Girls do, under a heap of mud or sand. Scatter the ashes; replace any rocks you may have used in constructing a fireplace; do all you can to obliterate the evidence that you camped here. (The Search & Rescue Team may be looking for you.)

3. Do not bury garbage—the wildlife will only dig it up again. Burn what will burn and pack out the rest. The same goes for toilet paper. Don't bury it, *burn it*.

4. Do not bathe in desert pools, natural tanks, *tinajas*, potholes. Drink what water you need, take what you need, and leave the rest for the next hiker and more important for the bees, birds, and animals—bighorn sheep, coyotes, lions, foxes, badgers, deer, wild pigs, wild horses—whose *lives* depend on that water.

5. Always remove and destroy survey stakes, flagging, advertising signboards, mining claim markers, animal traps, poisoned bait, seismic exploration geophones, and other such artifacts of industrialism. The men who put those things there are up to no good and it is our duty to confound them. Keep America Beautiful. Grow a Beard. Take a Bath. Burn a Billboard.

Anyway—why go into the desert? Really, why do it? That sun, roaring at you all day long. The fetid, tepid, vapid little water holes slowly evaporating under a scum of grease, full of cannibal beetles, spotted toads, horsehair worms, liver flukes, and down at the bottom, inevitably, the pale cadaver of a ten-inch centipede. Those pink rattlesnakes down in The Canyon, those diamondback monsters thick as a truck driver's wrist that lurk in shady places along the trail, those unpleasant solpugids and unnecessary Jersualem crickets that scurry on dirty claws across your face at night. Why? The rain that comes down like lead shot and wrecks the trail, those sudden rockfalls of obscure origin that crash like thunder ten feet behind you in the heart of a dead-still afternoon. The ubiquitous buzzard, so patient—but only so patient. . . . The ragweed, the tumbleweed, the Jimson weed, the snakeweed. The scorpion in your shoe at dawn. The dreary wind that blows all spring, the psychedelic Joshua trees waving their arms at you on moonlight nights. Sand in the soup de jour. Halazone tablets in your canteen. The barren hills that always go up, which is bad, or down, which is worse. Those canyons like catacombs with quicksand lapping at your crotch. Hollow, mummified horses with forelegs casually crossed, dead for ten years, leaning against the corner of a barbed-wire fence. Packhorses at night, iron-shod, clattering over the slickrock through your camp. The last tin of tuna, two flat tires, not enough water and a forty-mile trek to Tule Well. An osprey on a cardón cactus, snatching the head off a living fish— always the best part first. The hawk sailing by at 200 feet, a squirming snake in its talons. Salt in the drinking water. Salt, selenium, arsenic, radon and radium in the water, in the gravel, in your bones. Water so hard it bends light, drills holes in rock and chokes up your radiator. Why go there? Those places with the hardcase names: Starvation Creek, Poverty Knoll, Hungry Valley, Bitter Springs, Last Chance Canyon, Dungeon Canyon, Whipsaw Flat, Dead Horse Point, Scorpion Flat, Dead Man Draw, Stinking Spring, Camino del Diablo, Jornado del Muerto . . . Death Valley.

Well then, why indeed go walking into the desert, that grim ground, that bleak and lonesome land where, as Genghis Khan said of India, "the heat is bad and the water makes men sick"?

Why the desert, when you could be strolling along the golden beaches of California? Camping by a stream of pure Rocky Mountain spring water in colorful Colorado? Loafing through a laurel slick in the misty hills of North Carolina? Or getting your head mashed in the greasy alley behind the Elysium Bar and Grill in Hoboken, New Jersey? Why the desert, given a world of such splendor and variety?

A friend and I took a walk around the base of a mountain up beyond Coconino County, Arizona. This was a mountain we'd been planning to circumambulate for years. Finally we put on our walking shoes and did it. About halfway around this mountain, on the third or fourth day, we paused for a while—two days—by the side of a stream, which the Navajos call Nasja because of the amber color of the water. (Caused perhaps by juniper roots—the water seems safe enough to drink.) On our second day there I walked down the stream, alone, to look at the canyon beyond. I entered the canyon and followed it for half the afternoon, for three or four miles, maybe, until it became a gorge so deep, narrow and dark, full of water and the inevitable quagmires of quicksand, that I turned around and looked for a way out. A route other than the way I'd come, which was crooked and uncomfortable and buried—I wanted to see what was up on top of this world. I found a sort of chimney flue on the east wall, which looked plausible, and sweated and cursed my way up through that until I reached a point where I could walk upright, like a human being. Another 300 feet of scrambling brought me to the rim of the canyon. No one, I felt certain, had ever before departed Nasja Canyon by that route.

But someone had. Near the summit I found an arrow sign, three feet long, formed of stones and pointing off into the north toward those same old purple vistas, so grand, immense, and mysterious, of more canyons, more mesas and plateaus, more mountains, more cloud-dappled sun-spangled leagues of desert sand and desert rock, under the same old wide and aching sky.

The arrow pointed into the north. But what was it pointing *at*? I looked at the sign closely and saw that those dark, desert-varnished stones had been in place for a long, long time; they rested in compacted dust. They must have been there for a century at least. I followed the direction indicated and came promptly to the rim of another canyon and a drop-off straight down of a good 500 feet. Not that way, surely. Across this canyon was nothing of any unusual interest that I could see—only the familiar sun-blasted sandstone, a few scrubby clumps of blackbrush and prickly pear, a few acres of nothing where only a lizard could graze, surrounded by a few square miles of more nothingness interesting chiefly to horned toads. I returned to the arrow and checked again, this time with field glasses, looking away for as far as my aided eyes could see toward the north, for ten, twenty, forty miles into the distance. I studied the scene with care, looking for an ancient Indian ruin, a significant cairn, perhaps an abandonded mine, a hidden treasure of some inconceivable wealth, the mother of all mother lodes. . . .

But there was nothing out there. Nothing at all. Nothing but the desert. Nothing but the silent world.

   That's why.

The Ethics of the Person

In the last chapter we outlined the family of person-centered values like this:

PERSONS

The Ethics of the Person affirms that persons are special, precious, and have a dignity that demands respect. No one is to be reduced to a mere means to others' ends. Social relations require fairness, justice, and equality. Human and civil rights are essential too: they secure the space in which each person is recognized and can flourish.

Let us now explore the Ethics of the Person in more detail.

VALUING PERSONS

Values ultimately arise from our experience. We may try to speak for them abstractly or theoretically, so much so that sometimes we may lose the connection back to the basics that motivated them in the first place. Still, we can always ask, of any such value, where it comes from: how it traces back to concrete experience. A good place to start, then, is with the kinds of experiences that bring *persons* to our attention, and in an insistently ethical light, it turns out, from the beginning.

I am sure that there are times in your life when some other individual suddenly stands out of the background of friends or co-workers or even strangers on the street, out of routine everyday experience, and you are brought up short with a realization: here is a unique spark, another self or soul, fascinating and endless in its complexity and depth. Falling in love can be like that, sometimes, but it can also happen on the sidewalk and with people you don't know and will never see again. Even a brief encounter with another person can be complete in itself, and it may change the way we experience not just him or her but people in general.

One of my students wrote about meeting a homeless woman in New York's Pennsylvania Station.

> I was waiting for a friend, but she was late and I was all alone and scared. A woman who was selling spin tops outside the station saw me and came over to me. She asked my name and I told her and she said her name was Mona Lisa. We ended up talking for an hour and a half. . . . She told me all about her life and how she ended up in the streets of New York. All for love . . .

A country kid, alone and frightened on a first visit to New York, approached by a kind of person she had never known face to face, who she knew only as a stereotype—*the homeless*—repeated a thousand times over on television and in the papers: still this student found herself able to see her and respond to her as a person, as "Mona Lisa" did in return.

Responding in this way is not at all the same as just being nice. To be "nice" would have been to buy a spin top and back away: to stay on the level of habit and stereotyped response. This student did something entirely different. She responded to something unique and unexpected in this stranger, and some very basic recognition and affirmation then passed between them. We don't even know whether "Mona Lisa's" story is true, but the interesting thing is that it doesn't exactly matter, either. The point is that her story, embellished or entirely made up as it might have been, is a reflection of a personality, and it is the unexpected and unlikely emergence of *that*, out of fear and stereotype, that was the great learning for my student.

We also know what it's like when others do not treat us as "persons" in this sense. Cheery salespeople greet you on the phone like an old friend but hang up in mid sentence when they realize that they are not going to make a sale. How do you feel? What was *missed*? Sexual exploitation—realizing that you are only a body for someone else, only a means to someone else's momentary pleasure—is far more deeply chilling. We say, "You're just treating me like an object." Cases in which people are completely reduced to "things" are among the greatest of evils. The Nazi concentration camps were meant to dehumanize: it is no surprise that they were the first step to mass slaughter.

The key ethical recognition is that none of us are really just "objects" that can be related to as if we are just things, easily reduced to someone else's stereotype or "use." Philosophers put it like this: we are *subjects* (as opposed to "objects"), centers of our own experience and thinking, our own hopes and fears and dreams, choices large and small. And, crucially, we recognize also that others are just like us—and just as precious—in the same way.

ETHICAL PHILOSOPHIES OF "THE OTHER"

Some philosophers have worked out their ethical perspectives by trying to carefully describe and more deeply understand experiences like these. We may briefly consider two of the most influential: Martin Buber (1898–1965) and Emmanuel Levinas (1906–1995).

Buber, an Austrian and Israeli philosopher and theologian, was especially concerned to recover and defend the recognition of persons in a time when he saw depersonalization increasing dramatically. In his most famous book *I and Thou*, originally written in 1923, Buber tried to go back to absolute basics and to carefully describe the encounter with persons in this sense— with the *Other*, as he put it: as unique and self-determining beings.

Too often, Buber says, we "go over the surface of the world" and just "pile up information" without really going to the depths of anything. When we confront a "Thou" or a "You," however, we are pulled up short. The Other we are encountering "is no longer He or She, limited by other Hes or Shes, a dot in the world grid of space and time, nor . . . a loose bundle of named qualities. Neighborless and seamless, he fills the firmament. Not as if there were nothing else but he, but everything lives in his light." Buber says that this kind of encounter as if it strikes us with a "flash," like lightning. The "You" or "Thou" is unpredictable, spontaneous, deep. Our "I"—the other half of the "I/Thou" relationship—is transformed too: we no longer stand apart but are wholly engaged with the other person. "Relation is reciprocity."

And it is, naturally, deeply ethical. To see others in this way is to treasure them—certainly not to stand in their way or impose anything upon them, but much more too: to recognize a profound kind of value, both in the other person and in the encounter itself. We stand in awe and respond with respect. Buber goes on to conceive our relation to God in similar relational terms.

True, it's not really as though the only way to experience persons is in this electrifying, one-on-one kind of way, totally distinct from everyday habitual experience. Most of the time, as Buber admits, we relate to other people both as subjects and objects, and in other ways besides (as parts of "Wes," for example). Still, by returning to basics and exalting one compelling way in which the world of persons opens up to us, Buber reminds us of a core ethical experience, even if not the only one. In fact we have an "innate longing for relation," he says, traceable even in the attentions of babies and in animistic worldviews. We want the whole world to be alive to the I/Thou relation.

Levinas was a French philosopher whose ethical thinking was shaped both by Buber's work and by his experiences in the brutal environments of war and as a captured Jewish French soldier in a Nazi prisoner-of-war camp. He looks specifically at the experience of another's *face*. Like Buber, Levinas is concerned that we not glance over the face too fast, as if everything there is to know about the person were somehow on the surface, just pieces of "objective information" (that is, having to do with the self as object), to be defined or pinned down. Instead, Levinas stresses the unplumbable depth of a person, which may be seen through the face but not, as it were, *on* the face. The Face is an opening, as he puts it, to "infinity." When we really see a person as a person, Levinas says, we don't even notice the person's features, like their eye color—a very interesting fact, wouldn't you say? What we do "see" is their spontaneity, their "inexhaustibility"—that is, that they can't be pinned down or objectified.

And then, Levinas concludes, we also can't do violence to them. The Other also demands infinite respect. Of course Levinas cannot deny that people actually do violence to one another all the time. His suggestion is that when we do, though, we either have not really seen the other's face at all (which is often literally true: think of how readily we can do things to people at a distance that we could never do if they were right in front of us and looking us in the eye) or do it in "uneasy awareness" of what an evil we are doing. We see their faces but deny our own response.

Dialogue is another way that others' "infinity" opens up to us. Here too, as in the face literally, there is spontaneity, something more and unknown, always just now emerging. Indeed, Levinas says that the "face" names both the actual face and also the tendency for the Other, in whatever way, to "exceed the idea of him in me." "The face refuses to be contained." "The other overflows absolutely every idea I can have of him."

Levinas insists that ethics always comes first. We don't "pile up information," as Buber puts it, about the world or about others, and then, later, somewhere down the road, get an ethics. No: ethics shapes how we relate to the world from the very start. Knowledge is only possible through love, he says. "Knowledge of love" works before "love of knowledge." The only way we can really know anything about the other person is to see them in this "infinite" way.

THE IMAGE OF GOD

Another way that philosophers and theologians have understood the experience and value of persons is more religious. In the Judeo-Christian view, Creation is an act of free and gracious love that produces a world that at its heart must be beautiful and good, like God himself. Persons too must partake in this sort of innocent and original goodness. But humans are usually also pictured as a more distinctive part of Creation. Jews and Christians make much of the passage at Genesis 1:26–27 where God declares that He has made humans "in his own image": "Then God said, 'Let us make man in our image, in our likeness . . .' So God created man in his own image, in the image of God he created him."

Human persons are therefore pictured as uniquely and directly partaking in God's own nature. We too can comprehend the world rationally and with full self-consciousness; we too are free beings, able to deliberate and choose for ourselves; we too can create worlds and re-create even ourselves; and as a result we too can act morally and think ethically, consciously identifying values and bringing them into reality. In Psalms 8:4–5, the Psalmist writes

> What is man, that you think of him?
> What is the son of man, that you care for him?
> For you have made him a little lower than God,
> and crowned him with glory and honor.

The moral upshot is that in loving God we are also called to love other humans—and ourselves—as reflections of God. The traits that make us persons—self-consciousness, creative freedom, morality itself—are the ways in which we mirror God, and consequently are of supreme value. They define an ethic both of self-actualization and of a profound respect for other humans. Not that it's easy: the very freedom that makes us Godlike persons also gives us the possibility of deliberately falling away, turning from God and also from the reflection of God in one another and even ourselves. Correspondingly, though, striving to live in accord with the "image of God" in one's life can be seen as a quest for one's essential self.

Of course there are differences. Jews and Christians often picture God as a Father and speak of persons as all being equal and precious as "children of God." Muslims understand God (Allah) as more distinct and unique—though Allah nonetheless has seemingly human characteristics, such as compassion, mercy, wisdom, and goodness. Muslims also do not think of Allah as having children: instead we're related to God as his creatures and as servants (in an affirmative sense, that is, not as slaves but as free service-givers).

Yet the idea that persons are special, sacred, morally central "subjects," even of infinite value, is emphatically shared. Commenting on the killing of Abel by his brother Cain, the Quran tells us that "Anyone who saves one life, it is as if he has saved the whole of mankind, and anyone who has killed another person (except in lieu of murder or mischief on earth), it is as if he has killed the whole of mankind" (5:32). There is a kind if "infinity" too: somehow a single self can be a moral microcosm of the whole world. There is a very similar teaching in the Jewish Mishnah: "Anyone who destroys a single person, the Torah accounts it to him as if he has destroyed a whole world. And anyone who maintains a single person, the Torah accounts it to him as if he maintained a whole world" (*Sanhedrin* 4:5).

A whole ethics then follows—in parallel ways across the great traditions. There is a shared prohibition against murder: "Thou shalt not kill." The preciousness of persons must be maintained in all things: so there are shared prohibitions of theft, dishonesty, unprovoked war, callousness to the sufferings of others as well. We are enjoined to help reduce suffering, to care for those who need help. "Love your neighbor as yourself"—for you are equally beloved creatures of God.

All of this is idealistic, of course. In practice, as we also know, people in all the great traditions (and not just the religious ones) are capable of huge moral blind spots, selective and self-serving interpretations, and, alas, ongoing hatefulness. Christianity has been harsh in its treatments of heretics and unbelievers and has been deeply mistrusted in the Muslim world since the Crusades. The historical parts of the Old Testament are all too often records of wars and slaughters. The quote from the Quran above comes, ironically enough, in the midst of a violent harangue against Jews and Christians. In modern times too, as we know all too well, mistrust and hatred continue. Yet it is at least somewhat reassuring that at the hearts of all of these religions—the point toward which all but the harshest feel the pull and which many of the most intent never leave—is still the message of love and respect for one another, premised, once again, on the profound value of the person. We are left with the ongoing challenge to better live up to it.

READING

"Le Chambon"

PHILIP HALLIE

PHILIP HALLIE was an American philosopher (1922–1994) who explored the dark sides of human nature to better understand the ways in which ethics nonetheless can move us "From Cruelty to Goodness," as he puts it in the title of the essay from which this excerpt is taken.

In the course of this search, as Hallie tells us here, he discovered the story of the French village of Le Chambon-sur-Lignon, whose inhabitants managed to save 6,000 Jewish people from the Nazis during World War II, despite the savagely anti-Semitic German occupation and the presence of an SS division nearby. Notice, though, that Hallie is not telling us this story as a historian, though it is certainly based upon history. His interest is in the *ethics*: in how such acts were not only possible but seemed totally natural—indeed, as if there were no other alternatives—to the people who did them, even though it was at great risk to their own lives and over the course of many years.

The opposite of cruelty, Hallie came to see, is not merely the absence of cruelty but the presence of something positive, which he calls *hospitality*. Hospitality is a complete and unreserved recognition and "welcome" to the Other. Strikingly, Buber also uses the term "welcome," in much the same sense: we not only recognize something of value in other persons but open heartedly embrace them, as if (again) there were no other way.

Hallie's story gives us one very concrete sense then, of what it means to value persons. It is not just a matter of externals—rescuing imperiled innocents—though of course that is the outcome, and from a practical point of view, we might think, the main point. Hallie and his respondents are careful to distinguish Le Chambon's kind of welcome from the rescue activities of the Swiss, which had the same external outcome—refugees' lives were saved—but had, they say, a very different heart. Just as crucial for ethics is, once again, the experience: the very distinctive kind of response to Others that Le Chambon's rescue expressed and from which it flowed.

Pay attention also to the role of religious understandings in the story. One central figure, Hallie says, was Le Chambon's Huguenot minister with his activist ethic of non-violence. The Huguenots' literalist faith was important too, as was their own history of persecution, to the point that the very paths by which they shepherded Jewish children over the French Alps to safety in Switzerland were the same paths, remembered literally for centuries, that their own ancestors used to flee the pogroms of the French Catholics. A history of persecution can sensitize you to the persecution of others—though sometimes it can also have the opposite effect.

But there is more still. The people of Le Chambon managed to see, even in the midst of universal killing and war, that "every human being was just as precious as God Himself." Notice the spectacular generosity of the Huguenot minister, at least, who in the midst of all the horror still understood the rescue not only as saving the Jews but also saving the *Germans*—their would-be murderers. And the unforgettable scene in which a Jewish mother, desperately begging for eggs for her children at the risk of utter betrayal—being Jewish was virtually a death sentence in occupied Europe—is instead embraced with joy by an ordinary farm-woman as one of the Chosen People. *Welcome* indeed!

Finally, consider Hallie's response to the letter he received from a writer in Massachusetts, discussed near the end of his essay. What is the role of "abstraction" in "blinding people to individuals"? What does this have to do with the values of persons?

If cruelty is one of the main evils of human history, why is the opposite of cruelty not one of the key goods of human history? Freedom from the cruel relationship, either by escaping it or by redressing the imbalance of power, was not essential to what western philosophers and theologians have thought of as goodness. Escape is a negative affair. Goodness has something positive in it, something triumphantly affirmative.

Hoping for a hint of goodness in the very center of evil, I started looking closely at the so-called "medical experiments" of the Nazis upon children, usually Jewish and Gypsy children, in the death camps. Here were the weakest of the weak. Not only were they despised minorities, but they were, as individuals, still in their nonage. They were dependents. Here the power imbalance between the cruel experimenters and their victims was at its greatest. But instead of seeing light or finding insight by going down into this hell, into the deepest depth of cruelty, I found myself unwillingly becoming part of the world I was studying. I found myself either yearning to be viciously cruel to the victimizers of the children, or I found myself feeling compassion for the children, feeling their despair and pain as they looked up at the men and women in white coats cutting off their fingertips one at a time, or breaking their slender bones, or wounding their internal organs. Either I became a would-be victimizer or one more Jewish victim, and in either case I was not achieving insight, only misery, like so many other students of the Holocaust. And when I was trying to be "objective" about my studies, when I was succeeding at being indifferent to both the victimizers and the victims of these cruel relationships, I became cold; I became another monster who could look upon the maiming of a child with an indifferent eye.

To relieve this unending suffering, from time to time I would turn to the literature of the French resistance to the Nazis. I had been trained by the U.S. Army to understand it. The resistance was a way of trying to redress the power imbalance between Hitler's Fortress Europe and Hitler's victims, and so I saw it as an enemy of cruelty. Still, its methods were often cruel like the methods of most power struggles, and I had little hope of finding goodness here. We soldiers violated the negative ethic forbidding killing in order, we thought, to follow the positive ethic of being our brothers' keepers.

And then one gray April afternoon I found a brief article on the French village of Le Chambon-sur-Lignon. I shall not analyze here the tears of amazement and gladness and release from despair—in short, of joy—that I shed when I first read that story. Tears themselves interest me greatly—but not the tears of melancholy hindsight and existential despair; rather the tears of awe you experience when the realization of an ideal suddenly appears before your very eyes or thunders inside your mind; these tears interest me.

And one of the reasons I wept at first reading about Le Chambon in those brief, inaccurate pages was that at last I had discovered an embodiment of goodness in opposition to cruelty. I had discovered in the flesh and blood of history, in people with definite names in a definite place at a definite time in the nightmare of history, what no classical or religious ethicist could deny was goodness.

The French Protestant village of Le Chambon, located in the Cévennes Mountains of southeastern France, and with a population of about 3,500, saved the lives of about 6,000 people, most of them Jewish children whose parents had been murdered in the killing camps of central Europe. Under a national government which was not only collaborating with the Nazi conquerors of France but frequently trying to outdo the Germans in anti-Semitism in order to please their conquerors, and later under the day-to-day threat of destruction by the German Armed SS, they started to save children in the winter of 1940, the winter after the fall of France, and they continued to do so until the war in France was over. They sheltered the refugees in their own homes and in various houses they established especially for them; and they took many of them across the terrible mountains to neutral Geneva, Switzerland, in the teeth of French and German police and military power. The people of Le Chambon are poor, and the Huguenot faith to which they belong is a diminishing faith in Catholic and atheist France; but their spiritual power, their capacity to act in unison against the victimizers who surrounded them, was immense, and more than a match for the military power of those victimizers.

But for me as an ethicist the heart of the matter was not only their special power. What interested me was that they obeyed *both* the negative and the positive injunctions of ethics; they were good not only in the sense of trying to be their brothers' keepers, protecting the victim, "defending the fatherless," to use the language of Isaiah; they were also good in the sense that they obeyed the negative injunctions against killing and betraying. While those around them—including myself—were murdering in order, presumably, to help mankind in some way or other, they murdered nobody, and betrayed not a single child in those long and dangerous four years. For me as an ethicist they were the embodiment of unambiguous goodness.

But for me as a student of cruelty they were something more: they were an embodiment of the opposite of cruelty. And so, somehow, at last, I had found goodness in opposition to cruelty. In studying their story, and in telling it in *Lest Innocent Blood Be Shed*, I learned that the opposite of cruelty is not simply freedom from the cruel relationship; it is *hospitality*. It lies not only in something negative, an absence of cruelty or of imbalance; it lies in unsentimental, efficacious love. The opposite of the cruelties of the camps was not the liberation of the camps, the cleaning out of the barracks and the cessation of the horrors. All of this was the *end* of the cruelty relationship, not the opposite of that relationship. And it was not even the end of it, because the victims would never forget and would remain in agony as long as they remembered their humiliation and suffering. No, the opposite of cruelty was not the liberation of the camps, not freedom; it was the hospitality of the people of Le Chambon, and of very few others during the Holocaust. The opposite of cruelty was the kind of goodness that happened in Le Chambon.

Let me explain the difference between liberation and hospitality by telling you about a letter I received a year ago from a woman who had been saved by the people of Le Chambon when she was a young girl. She wrote:

> Never was there a question that the Chambonnais would not share all they had with us, meager as it was. One Chambonnais once told me that even if there was less, they still would want more for us.

And she goes on:

> It was indeed a very different attitude from the one in Switzerland, which while saving us also resented us so much.
>
> If today we are not bitter people like most survivors it can only be due to the fact that we met people like the people of Le Chambon, who showed to us simply that life can be different, that there are people who care, that people can live together and even risk their own lives for their fellow man.

The Swiss liberated refugees and removed them from the cruel relationship; the people of Le Chambon did more. They taught them that goodness could conquer cruelty, that loving hospitality could remove them from the cruel relationship. And they taught me this, too.

It is important to emphasize that cruelty is not simply an episodic, momentary matter, especially institutional cruelty like that of Nazism or slavery. Not only does it persist while it is being exerted upon the weak; *it can persist in the survivors* after they have escaped the power relationship. The survivors torture themselves, continue to suffer, continue to maim their own lives long after the actual torture is finished. The self-hatred and rage of the blacks and the despair of the native Americans and the

Jews who have suffered under institutional crushing and maiming are continuations of original cruelties. And these continuations exist because only a superficial liberation from torture has occurred. The sword has stopped falling on their flesh in the old obvious ways, but the wounds still bleed. I am not saying that the village of Le Chambon healed these wounds—they go too deep. What I am saying is that the people I have talked to who were once children in Le Chambon have more hope for their species and more respect for themselves as human beings than most other survivors I have met. The enduring hospitality they met in Le Chambon helped them find realistic hope in a world of persisting cruelty.

What was the nature of this hospitality that saved and deeply changed so many lives? It is hard to summarize briefly what the Chambonnais did, and above all how they did it. The morning after a new refugee family came to town they would find on their front door a wreath with "*Bienvenue!*" "Welcome!" painted on a piece of cardboard attached to the wreath. Nobody knew who had brought the wreath; in effect, the whole town had brought it.

It was mainly the women of Le Chambon who gave so much more than shelter to these, the most hated enemies of the Nazis. There was Madame Barraud, a tiny Alsatian, who cared for the refugee boys in her house with all the love such a tiny body could hold, and who cared for the way they felt day and night. And there were others.

But there was one person without whom Le Chambon could not have become the safest place in Europe for Jews: the Huguenot minister of the village, André Trocmé. Trocmé was a passionately religious man. He was massive, more than six feet tall, blonde, with a quick temper. Once long after the war, while he was lecturing on the main project of his life, the promotion of the idea of nonviolence in international relations, one of the members of his audience started to whisper a few words to his neighbor. Trocmé let this go on for a few moments, then interrupted his speech, walked up to the astonished whisperer, raised his massive arm, pointed toward the door, and yelled, "Out! Out! Get out!" And the lecture was on nonviolence.

The center of his thought was the belief that God showed how important man was by becoming Himself a human being, and by becoming a particular sort of human being who was the embodiment of sacrificially generous love. For Trocmé, every human being was like Jesus, had God in him or her, and was just as precious as God Himself. And when Trocmé with the help of the Quakers and others organized his village into the most efficient rescue machine in Europe, he did so not only to save the Jews, but also to save the Nazis and their collaborators. He wanted to keep them from blackening their souls with more evil—he wanted to save them, the victimizers, from evil.

One of the reasons he was successful was that the Huguenots had been themselves persecuted for hundreds of years by the kings of France, and they knew what persecution was. In fact, when the people of Le Chambon took Jewish children and whole families across the mountains of southeastern France into neutral Switzerland, they often followed pathways that had been taken by Huguenots in their flight from the Dragoons of the French kings.

A particular incident from the story of Le Chambon during the Nazi occupation of France will explain succinctly why he was successful in making the village a village of refuge. But before I relate the story, I must point out that the people of the village did not think of themselves as "successful," let alone as "good." From their point of view, they did not do anything that required elaborate explanation. When I asked them why they helped these dangerous guests, they invariably answered, "What do you mean, 'Why'? Where else could they go? How could you turn them away? What is so special about being ready to help (*prête à servir*)? There was nothing else to do." And some of them laughed in amazement when I told them that I thought they were "good people." They saw no alternative to their actions and to the way they acted, and therefore they saw what they did as necessary, not something to be picked out for praise. Helping these guests was for them as natural as breathing or eating—one does not think of alternatives to these functions; they did not think of alternatives to sheltering people who were endangering not only the lives of their hosts but the lives of all the people of the village.

And now the story. One afternoon a refugee woman knocked on the door of a farmhouse outside the village. The farmers around the village proper were Protestants like most of the others in Le Chambon, but with one difference: they were mostly "Darbystes," followers of a strange Scot named Darby, who taught their ancestors in the nineteenth century to believe every word of the Bible, and indeed, who had them memorize the Bible. They were literal fundamentalists. The farm-woman opened the door to the refugee and invited her into the kitchen where it was warm. Standing in the middle of the floor the refugee, in heavily accented French, asked for eggs for her children. In those days of very short supplies, people with children often went to the farmers in the "gray market" (neither black nor exactly legal) to get necessary food. This was early in 1941, and the farmers were not yet accustomed to the refugees. The farm-woman looked into the eyes of the shawled refugee and asked, "Are you Jewish?" The woman started to tremble, but she could not lie, even though that question was usually the beginning of the end of life for Jews in Hitler's Fortress Europe. She answered, "Yes."

The woman ran from the kitchen to the staircase nearby, and while the refugee trembled with terror in the kitchen, she called up the stairs, "Husband, children, come down, come down! We have in our house at this very moment a representative of the Chosen People!"

Not all the Protestants in Le Chambon were Darbyste fundamentalists; but almost all were convinced that people are the children of God, and are as precious as God Himself. Their leaders were Huguenot preachers and their following of the negative and positive commandments of the Bible came in part from their personal generosity and courage, but also in part from the depths of their religious conviction that we are all children of God, and we must take care of each other lovingly. This combined with the ancient and deep historical ties between the Huguenots and the Jews of France and their own centuries of persecution by the Dragoons and Kings of France helped make them what they were, "always ready to help," as the Chambonnais saying goes.

A CHOICE OF PERSPECTIVES

We have come a long way from cruelty to the people of Le Chambon, just as I have come a long way in my research from concrete evil to concrete goodness. Let me conclude with a point that has been alternately hinted at and stressed in the course of this essay.

A few months after *Lest Innocent Blood Be Shed* was published I received a letter from Massachusetts that opened as follows:

> I have read your book, and I believe that you mushy-minded moralists should be awakened to the facts. Nothing happened in Le Chambon, nothing of any importance whatsoever.
>
> The Holocaust, dear Professor, was like a geological event, like an earthquake. No person could start it; no person could change it; and no person could end it. And no small group of persons could do so either. It was the armies and the nations that performed actions that counted. Individuals did nothing. You sentimentalists have got to learn that the great masses and big political ideas make the difference. Your people and the people they saved simply do not exist . . .

Now between this position and mine there is an abyss that no amount of shouted arguments or facts can cross. And so I shall not answer this letter with a tightly organized reply. I shall answer it only by telling you that one of the reasons institutional cruelty exists and persists is that people believe that individuals can do nothing, that only vast ideologies and armies can act meaningfully. Every act of institutional cruelty—Nazism, slavery, and all the others—lives not with people in the concrete, but with abstractions that blind people to individuals. Himmler's speech to the SS leadership in 1943 is full of phrases like "exterminating a bacillus," and "The Jewish people will be exterminated." And in that speech he attacks any German who believes in "his decent Jew." Institutional cruelty, like other misleading approaches to ethics, blinds us to the victim's point of view; and when we are blind to that point of view we can countenance and perpetrate cruelty with impunity.

I have told you that I cannot and will not try to refute the letter from Massachusetts. I shall only summarize the point of view of this essay with another story.

I was lecturing a few months ago in Minneapolis, and when I finished talking about the Holocaust and the village of Le Chambon, a woman stood up and asked me if the village of Le Chambon was in the Department of Haute-Loire, the high sources of the Loire River. Obviously she was French, with her accent; and all French people know that there are many villages called "Le Chambon" in France, just as any American knows that there are many "Main Streets" in the United States. I said that Le Chambon was indeed in the HauteLoire.

She said, "Then you have been speaking about the village that saved all three of my children. I want to thank you for writing this book, not only because the story will now be permanent, but also because I shall be able to talk about those terrible days with Americans now, for they will understand those days better than they have. You see, you Americans, though you sometimes cross the oceans, live on an island here as far as war is concerned . . ."

Then she asked to come up and say one sentence. There was not a sound, not even breathing, to be heard in the room. She came to the front of the room and said, "The Holocaust was storm, lightning, thunder, wind, rain, yes. And Le Chambon was the rainbow."

Only from her perspective can you understand the cruelty and the goodness I have been talking about, not from the point of view of the gentleman from Massachusetts. You must choose which perspective is best, and your choice will have much to do with your feelings about the preciousness of life, and not only the preciousness of other people's lives. If the lives of others are precious to you, your life will become more precious to you.

KANT'S CATEGORICAL IMPERATIVE

The Prussian philosopher Immanuel Kant (1724–1804), a central figure in the development of modern philosophy in all of its main branches, understood and defended the value of persons in a distinctive and highly influential way.

Kant begins with the claim that persons are not just means but "ends in themselves." You know the language of "means." A means is a way of getting something: a car is a means of getting around, money is a means of buying what we want or need to live. An "end," by contrast, is valued at least in part for its own sake—it is not just one more link in a chain of means, but a place where the chain comes to an end.

To some degree, we inevitably are "means" to each other. A waiter is partly our means of getting food; a parent is partly a means of support. But the claim is that we get the world wrong—we mistake reality itself—if we begin to take other people (or ourselves) *just* as means in this sense. Another person is not just a way to get something for ourselves, whether it be something trivial or something vital, such as ongoing pleasure or company. We are all *also* centers of our own experience and thinking and choice. We are also ends in ourselves!

THE CATEGORICAL IMPERATIVE

Means-thinking is situational and dependent. It recommends things to us "hypothetically": *if* we want such and such, *then* we should choose something else which is a means to it. But ethics, says Kant, applies "categorically." It is not dependent on something else but calls to us simply by virtue of our ability to think of it in the first place. No *ifs*. Thus Kant seeks what he calls the "Categorical Imperative": a basic obligation that applies to us regardless of our other goals or situation.

Kant proposes four forms of what he thinks is one basic Categorical Imperative. The most approachable form he puts explicitly in terms of ends and means:

> *Always act so as to treat humanity, whether in yourself or in another, as an end and never merely as a means.*

Kant is careful here. He is not saying that we should never treat others as means at all. Again, the truth is that we must. Even Buber, the apostle of I/Thou relations, allows that sometimes and in some ways we do have to treat other people at least in part as "Its" or objects. The point for both Kant and Buber is that we must *also* always keep alive a fuller and more complete sense of others as more-than-Its, more-than-means.

SELF AS ONE AMONG OTHERS

So how do we justify placing this kind of value on persons? Levinas and Buber appeal to direct experience. The religious traditions base their appeals on revelation. By contrast, most philosophy is committed to making *arguments*. The aim is to *show*—that is, by a chain of reasoning—that persons have the sort of ultimate value being claimed for them. It is here that Kant makes his distinctive contribution.

The essence of ethics, according to Kant, is to live according to the moral law. It is not merely to act in accord with "inclination" (to be ethical because it pleases us, even if it does in fact deeply please us) or even to act in opposition to inclination (because we would still be in the orbit of inclination, still obsessed with desire, though now for the purpose of putting it down). No: to be ethical is to do what is right just because it is right. It is of the essence of ethics to be impersonal, impartial—not to depend on passing, personal feeling.

But it is no merely political or legal "law" that Kant has in mind. "Law" for Kant means a universal principle that all rational minds could hold themselves to in the situation in question. That is, the idea of "law" leads us to the ideal of universality, and thus to the recognition that, even though I may be deciding for myself, to decide *ethically* means to decide as one rational mind among others, as if setting the law for all. Anyone else in the same situation should do the same thing.

Another form of Kant's Categorical Imperative therefore reads:

Act only according to that maxim whereby you can at the same time will that it become a universal law.

By "maxim" he means, roughly, the rule you propose to yourself when trying to decide what to do. This form of the Categorical Imperative thus is a test to see whether the rule you have in mind can be ethical: the test is whether you could consistently will it to be a rule that everyone follows.

Should I lie, for example, to get myself out of an embarrassing or sticky situation? No, says Kant. I could not will it to be a universal law that *everyone* should lie to get out of a sticky situation, for then no such lie would work. On the contrary: by wanting my lie to work, I am implicitly willing that others *not* lie in the same situation, so that the general expectation of truthfulness will be maintained, that is, so that my lie will succeed. I am only making an exception for myself.

And that is the place at which everything goes wrong. For there is no basis for taking myself to be somehow different or more special than other people in a way that could justify my flaunting a rule that I expect everyone else to follow. No: again, others are centers of experience and choice as real as we know ourselves to be. Others are persons too! Recognize that, says Kant, and a recognition of equal dignity and equal standing necessarily follows—thus the second form of the Imperative.

A profound sense of equality follows—and also, in a way, a sense of wonder. The first impulse is one of standing aside, of letting the other person *be*—in the sense of "letting them alone," and also, more fundamentally perhaps, in the sense of pure appreciation. Let them *be*! The essence of personhood again shines through.

READING

From Grounding for the Metaphysics of Morals

IMMANUEL KANT

Now I say: man and generally any rational being exists as an end in himself, not merely as a means to be arbitrarily used by this or that will, but in all his actions, whether they concern himself or other rational beings, must be always regarded at the same time as an end.

. . . Beings whose existence depends not on our will but on nature's, have nevertheless, if they are irrational beings, only a relative value as means, and are therefore called things. Rational beings, on the contrary, are called persons, because their very nature points them out as ends in themselves, that is as something which must not be used merely as means, and so far therefore restricts freedom of action (and is an object of respect). These, therefore, are not merely subjective ends whose existence has a worth for us as an effect of our action, but objective ends, that is, things whose existence is an end in itself; an end moreover for which no other can be substituted, which they should subserve merely as means, for otherwise nothing whatever would possess absolute worth; but if all worth were conditioned and therefore contingent, then there would be no supreme practical principle of reason whatever.

If then there is a supreme practical principle or, in respect of the human will, a categorical imperative, it must be one which, being drawn from the conception of that which is necessarily an

http://www.gutenberg.org/cache/epub/5682/pg5682.html
accessed 10/2/12, n.p.

end for everyone because it is an end in itself, constitutes an objective principle of will, and can therefore serve as a universal practical law. The foundation of this principle is: rational nature exists as an end in itself. Man necessarily conceives his own existence as being so; so far then this is a subjective principle of human actions. But every other rational being regards its existence similarly, just on the same rational principle that holds for me: so that it is at the same time an objective principle, from which as a supreme practical law all laws of the will must be capable of being deduced. Accordingly the practical imperative will be as follows: So act as to treat humanity, whether in thine own person or in that of any other, in every case as an end withal, never as means only.

[Declaring that we must now see whether such a "practical imperative" can be put into action, Kant considers a range of examples. One of these is the case of the lie in the sticky situation, discussed in the text. Kant considers it in terms of both forms of the Categorical Imperative. Here it is in terms of the "end in itself" form. —AW]

He who is thinking of making a lying promise to others will see at once that he would be using another man merely as a means, without the latter containing at the same time the end in himself. For he whom I propose by such a promise to use for my own purposes cannot possibly assent to my mode of acting towards him and, therefore, cannot himself contain the end of this action. This violation of the principle of humanity in other men is more obvious if we take in examples of attacks on the freedom and property of others. For then it is clear that he who transgresses the rights of men intends to use the person of others merely as a means, without considering that as rational beings they ought always to be esteemed also as ends, that is, as beings who must be capable of containing in themselves the end of the very same action.

[Here is the same case considered in terms of the "universal law" form of the Categorical Imperative. —AW]

A [person] finds himself forced by necessity to borrow money. He knows that he will not be able to repay it, but sees also that nothing will be lent to him unless he promises stoutly to repay it in a definite time. He desires to make this promise, but he has still so much conscience as to ask himself: "Is it not unlawful and inconsistent with duty to get out of a difficulty in this way?" Suppose however that he resolves to do so: then the maxim of his action would be expressed thus: "When I think myself in want of money, I will borrow money and promise to repay it, although I know that I never can do so." Now this principle of self-love or of one's own advantage may perhaps be consistent with my whole future welfare; but the question now is, "Is it right?" I change then the suggestion of self-love into a universal law, and state the question thus: "How would it be if my maxim were a universal law?" Then I see at once that it could never hold as a universal law of nature, but would necessarily contradict itself. For supposing it to be a universal law that everyone when he thinks himself in a difficulty should be able to promise whatever he pleases, with the purpose of not keeping his promise, the promise itself would become impossible, as well as the end that one might have in view in it, since no one would consider that anything was promised to him, but would ridicule all such statements as vain pretences. . . .

If now we attend to ourselves on occasion of any transgression of duty, we shall find that we in fact do not will that our maxim should be a universal law, for that is impossible for us; on the contrary, we will that the opposite should remain a universal law, only we assume the liberty of making an exception in our own favour or (just for this time only) in favour of our inclination. Consequently if we considered all cases from one and the same point of view, namely, that of reason, we should find a contradiction in our own will, namely, that a certain principle should be objectively necessary as a universal law, and yet subjectively should not be universal, but admit of exceptions. . . . Now, although this cannot be justified in our own impartial judgement, yet it proves that we do really recognise the validity of the categorical imperative and (with all respect for it) only allow ourselves a few exceptions, which we think unimportant and forced from us.

RIGHTS, EQUALITY, JUSTICE

RIGHTS AND PERSONS

Jefferson's "Declaration of Independence" famously announces that

> We hold these truths to be self-evident, that all men are created equal, that they are endowed by their Creator with certain unalienable Rights, that among these are Life, Liberty and the pursuit of Happiness.—That to secure these rights, Governments are instituted among Men, deriving their just powers from the consent of the governed . . .

On this view, human beings have certain moral claims—rights—so basic they can't be taken away (hence, "unalienable"). And they are rooted, once again, in personhood.

Rights create the necessary space for persons to become what they are. The first section of this chapter, remember, argues that in truth "we are *subjects* (as opposed to 'objects'), centers of our own experience and thinking, hopes and fears and dreams, choices large and small." Jewish and Christian traditions, again, picture the person as a model of God: rational, self-aware, creative, and free. The term "person" itself originates in Greek drama, where the *personae* were individual parts in the drama, as opposed to the impersonal, non-individual characters who spoke together in the Chorus. But without life and liberty, obviously, it is pretty hard to act rationally or creatively, or to take your own individual path.

Of course there are many different interpretations of rights. Human life is sacred, the religious traditions say, and taking life is therefore wrong: a right to life immediately follows. Catholic moral theology would go on to say that the right to life implies the moral requirement to protect and support those whose life is endangered—especially the poor and dispossessed and disempowered (notice again that this goes a lot further than fetuses). Others more concerned with liberty would argue that even basic rights like the right to life are only "negative" rights: that is, they only prohibit people doing certain things but do not demand that they *do* other things. The right to life, on this view, only prohibits killing. We're not required to feed and shelter the needy too. Likewise, libertarians are fond of pointing out that Jefferson does not speak of a right to happiness: he only speaks of the right to *pursue* happiness. Success is not guaranteed—and presumably could not be, without constraining a lot of other people's liberty.

EQUALITY

We are all equally persons. Therefore, it seems to follow that all persons are, in some basic sense, morally equal. "All men are created equal" is the very first of Jefferson's "self-evident truths." Of course we know that he wasn't thinking quite as broadly as we would today about who counts as "men." Still, there was a built-in widening tendency in this "self-evident truth," and it continues to inspire many groups' struggles for moral and political recognition.

What does equality require? Not that every person should be treated exactly the same or have exactly the same things or life prospects—that is only a caricature. "Equality" in the civil rights struggle, for example, meant certain very specific and very basic things: the right to vote, the equal protection of the law, an end to second-rate schools and segregated facilities. In employment and education it might mean equal *opportunity*—not being closed out because of some prejudice or irrelevant factor. It's not as though everyone should have the same job, but everyone should have a fair chance, based on qualifications alone, at the good ones.

Economic equality gets trickier. Certainly it could require taking some corrective actions when economic disparities get too great. Economists track the ratios between the highest-paid members of corporations and the average worker: in America, currently the best-paid get about 230 times what the average (note: by no means the worst-paid) get—and the ratio is increasing. It's a fair question whether any person's contribution is really 230 times more valuable than another's, when both are giving their best energies to the enterprise, and each has, at least roughly, the same needs. We need to ask (and can debate about, of course, but surely need to *ask*) how this kind of arrangement could truly respect persons—all individuals who are after all equally precious from a moral point of view.

JUSTICE

Justice seems to be a more complex idea than equality. For one thing, it is a little less tempting to think that justice necessarily requires literally equal outcomes. Again, maybe it's more that everyone has an equal *chance,* an equal opportunity. Or that, however things end up, our way of getting there was at least *fair.*

This last idea—that a just arrangement is one that is the outcome of a fair process—emerged into philosophical attention in the late 20th century with the work of the philosopher John Rawls. Rawls asks us to imagine a group of people gathered to choose the principles under which they will live together. These people are a little unusual, however, because they don't yet know who they are, so to speak. Rawls argues that a fair set of principles would be principles that people would choose prior to knowing how the principles would affect them—when they have to imagine possibly being *anyone* in the society that will eventually result. After all, if being an "end in yourself" has nothing to do with your particular accomplishments (or lack thereof) or family or willpower or anything else—that is, with "who we are" in the usual sense—then it would be helpful to put these things aside, at least in imagination, while trying to think about ethical principles. At the most basic moral level, we are all just persons!

If you see some shades of Kant here, you're right. Rawls agrees with Kant that ethics asks us to take a sort of universal point of view. Rawls's innovation was to give us a specific and decidable way to visualize such a point of view.

You might think in such a situation that people would opt for complete equality. Rawls agrees that this would indeed be so when one person's having more of something—say, political liberty—would mean an equivalent loss for someone else. Equality is the best we can do. Thus one principle of justice is what he calls the *Equal Liberty Principle.*

However, there are some goods—chiefly economic goods—that work in a different way. Here, one person's gain does not necessarily mean someone else's loss. Sometimes everyone can have more—although not necessarily equally. In this case, still under what Rawls calls the "veil of ignorance" (that is, not yet knowing who we are), we will aim, Rawls says, to make sure that any inequalities that arise bring the least well-off persons as far up as any arrangement can. This is what Rawls calls the *Difference Principle*. It is a second and far more subtle principle of justice.

Careful argument and evidence may be required to decide. One could argue, for example, that large ratios between the best-paid and the average-paid in corporations serve the good of everyone because large benefits at the top serve as incentives to attract the most talented executives, ultimately making everyone in the enterprise better off. But it's an empirical question. How much incentive is really necessary? The top-to-average ratio is only about 10 to 1 in Japan—it would be considered dishonourable for it to go much higher— and no one could argue that Japan isn't competitive.

Also, by Rawls's principles, it's not enough that inequalities merely improve the lot of the least well-off: they have to improve it more than any other workable arrangement. We may have to get quite creative!

You see once again that vital and intriguing questions arise—and questions we will not settle here. They are, however, the natural and logical questions once we enter the discussion of what the ethical value of *persons* actually implies—and that, as you now see, is a discussion for all of us.

READING

From The United Nations Universal Declaration of Human Rights

THE UNITED NATIONS was formed in the wake of the disasters of World War II to try to establish a more stable and cooperative world order and to facilitate dialogue in place of war among nations. Today all internationally recognized sovereign states (192 total) belong to the UN (except Vatican City, which has observer status). Its agencies are active in many causes around the world, including the World Health Organization (WHO), the UN Children's Fund (UNICEF), and the UN High Commission on Refugees, as well as the main deliberative bodies, the General Assembly and Security Council, which are also engaged with security issues and with mitigating conflicts around the globe.

A Universal Declaration of Human Rights was adopted by the UN General Assembly in 1948, one of the earliest and most significant acts of that body, becoming one of the fundamental constitutive documents of the UN. Technically its aim was to clarify certain key terms—"fundamental freedoms" and "human rights"—in the UN Charter. Ethically and politically, however, the aim was much larger: to spell out and advance the cause of those freedoms and rights in an uncertain world that needed them affirmed in a succinct, ambitious, and universal way. The hope of Eleanor Roosevelt and its other authors was that the Declaration might have the same influence on the world as the American Declaration of Independence, and later our Bill of Rights, had within the United States. In that it seems to have at least partly succeeded. The UN Declaration of Human Rights has helped to shape (and sometimes is directly cited in) most national constitutions written since 1948, as well as many international laws and treaties. According to The *Guinness Book of Records,* the Universal Declaration of Human Rights is the most translated document in the world.

PREAMBLE

Whereas recognition of the inherent dignity and of the equal and inalienable rights of all members of the human family is the foundation of freedom, justice and peace in the world,

Whereas disregard and contempt for human rights have resulted in barbarous acts which have outraged the conscience of mankind, and the advent of a world in which human beings shall enjoy freedom of speech and belief and freedom from fear and want has been proclaimed as the highest aspiration of the common people,

Whereas it is essential, if man is not to be compelled to have recourse, as a last resort, to rebellion against tyranny and oppression, that human rights should be protected by the rule of law . . .,

Whereas the peoples of the United Nations have in the Charter reaffirmed their faith in fundamental human rights, in the dignity and worth of the human person and in the equal rights of men and women and have determined to promote social progress and better standards of life in larger freedom . . .,

Whereas a common understanding of these rights and freedoms is of the greatest importance for the full realization of this pledge,

Now, Therefore THE GENERAL ASSEMBLY proclaims THIS UNIVERSAL DECLARATION OF HUMAN RIGHTS as a common standard of achievement for all peoples and all nations, to the end that every individual and every organ of society, keeping this Declaration constantly in mind, shall strive by teaching and education to promote respect for these rights and freedoms and by progressive measures, national and international, to secure their universal and effective recognition and observance, both among the peoples of Member States themselves and among the peoples of territories under their jurisdiction.

Article 1. All human beings are born free and equal in dignity and rights. They are endowed with reason and conscience and should act towards one another in a spirit of brotherhood.

Article 2. Everyone is entitled to all the rights and freedoms set forth in this Declaration, without distinction of any kind, such as race, colour, sex, language, religion, political or other opinion, national or social origin, property, birth or other status . . .

Article 3. Everyone has the right to life, liberty and security of person.

Article 4. No one shall be held in slavery or servitude; slavery and the slave trade shall be prohibited in all their forms.

Article 5. No one shall be subjected to torture or to cruel, inhuman or degrading treatment or punishment.

Article 6. Everyone has the right to recognition everywhere as a person before the law.

Article 7. All are equal before the law and are entitled without any discrimination to equal protection of the law. All are entitled to equal protection against any discrimination in violation of this Declaration and against any incitement to such discrimination.

Article 8. Everyone has the right to an effective remedy by the competent national tribunals for acts violating the fundamental rights granted him by the constitution or by law.

Article 9. No one shall be subjected to arbitrary arrest, detention or exile.

Article 10. Everyone is entitled in full equality to a fair and public hearing by an independent and impartial tribunal, in the determination of his rights and obligations and of any criminal charge against him.

Article 11. Everyone charged with a penal offence has the right to be presumed innocent until proved guilty according to law in a public trial at which he has had all the guarantees necessary for his defence . . .

Article 12. No one shall be subjected to arbitrary interference with his privacy, family, home or correspondence, nor to attacks upon his honour and reputation. Everyone has the right to the protection of the law against such interference or attacks.

Article 13. Everyone has the right to freedom of movement and residence within the borders of each state. Everyone has the right to leave any country, including his own, and to return to his country.

Article 14. Everyone has the right to seek and to enjoy in other countries asylum from persecution . . .

Article 16. Men and women of full age, without any limitation due to race, nationality or religion, have the right to marry and to found a family. They are entitled to equal rights as to marriage, during marriage and at its dissolution. Marriage shall be entered into only with the free and full consent of the intending spouses. The family is the natural and fundamental group unit of society and is entitled to protection by society and the State.

Article 17. Everyone has the right to own property alone as well as in association with others. No one shall be arbitrarily deprived of his property.

Article 18. Everyone has the right to freedom of thought, conscience and religion; this right includes freedom to change his religion or belief, and freedom, either alone or in community with others and in public or private, to manifest his religion or belief in teaching, practice, worship and observance.

Article 19. Everyone has the right to freedom of opinion and expression; this right includes freedom to hold opinions without interference and to seek, receive and impart information and ideas through any media and regardless of frontiers.

Article 20. Everyone has the right to freedom of peaceful assembly and association. No one may be compelled to belong to an association.

Article 21. Everyone has the right to take part in the government of his country, directly or through freely chosen representatives. Everyone has the right of equal access to public service in his country. The will of the people shall be the basis of the authority of government; this will shall be expressed in periodic and genuine elections which shall be by universal and equal suffrage and shall be held by secret vote or by equivalent free voting procedures.

Article 22. Everyone, as a member of society, has the right to social security and is entitled to realization, through national effort and international co-operation and in accordance with the organization and resources of each State, of the economic, social and cultural rights indispensable for his dignity and the free development of his personality.

Article 23. Everyone has the right to work, to free choice of employment, to just and favorable conditions of work and to protection against unemployment. Everyone, without any discrimination, has the right to equal pay for equal work. Everyone who works has the right to just and favorable remuneration ensuring for himself and his family an existence worthy of human dignity, and supplemented, if necessary, by other means of social protection. Everyone has the right to form and to join trade unions for the protection of his interests.

Article 24. Everyone has the right to rest and leisure, including reasonable limitation of working hours and periodic holidays with pay.

Article 25. Everyone has the right to a standard of living adequate for the health and well-being of himself and of his family, including food, clothing, housing and medical care and necessary social services, and the right to security in the event of unemployment, sickness, disability, widowhood, old age or other lack of livelihood in circumstances beyond his control. Motherhood and childhood are entitled to special care and assistance. All children, whether born in or out of wedlock, shall enjoy the same social protection.

Article 26. Everyone has the right to education. Education shall be free, at least in the elementary and fundamental stages. . . . Elementary education shall be compulsory.

Article 27. Everyone has the right freely to participate in the cultural life of the community, to enjoy the arts and to share in scientific advancement and its benefits . . .

Article 29. Everyone has duties to the community in which alone the free and full development of his personality is possible. In the exercise of his rights and freedoms, everyone shall be subject only to such limitations as are determined by law solely for the purpose of securing due recognition and respect for the rights and freedoms of others and of meeting the just requirements of morality, public order and the general welfare in a democratic society . . .

FOR REVIEW

1. Why is treating someone as a person not the same as being nice to them?
2. How do Buber and Levinas's understanding of Others relate to the value of persons?
3. What is a religious understanding of the preciousness of persons?
4. What does Philip Hallie mean by "hospitality"? How does it relate to the value of persons?

5. What is Immanuel Kant's Categorical Imperative?

6. Why shouldn't we lie to get ourselves out of sticky situations, according to Kant?

7. How do rights relate to personhood?

8. How does equality relate to personhood?

9. How does justice relate to personhood?

10. What is the United Nations Universal Declaration of Human Rights?

EXERCISES AND NOTES

5.1 FOR DISCUSSION

Can you identify times in your own experience when other persons emerged in the radical, stop-everything kind of way that Buber and Levinas describe? Correspondingly, when do you live mostly in the "I/It" world? What do you think of the balance between the two in your own life?

Likewise, when have you experienced "hospitality" in Hallie's sense? And when have you offered it? Or put it in Kantian terms, where and how do we tend to treat others as "ends," and where and how mainly (or entirely?) as "means"? How about how you yourself are treated? When and by whom are you treated in each way? Why?

Why do you think it is sometimes so hard to see other people as persons? Is it something inherent in us, selfishness for example? Is it our language, all too often reducing people to objects to be derided or exploited? Is it our stereotypes? Notice also that when people are reduced to objects in one way or another, the reductions can easily become self-fulfilling prophecies. One of the chief excuses for the enslavement of blacks in America, for example, was that black people were naturally "ignorant and depraved." But one of the prime effects of slavery was that the slaves were often *made* ignorant and depraved. Slavery wore down and degraded the slave; then this very degradation was blamed on the slaves themselves (it was said to be "their nature"), thus justifying more slavery and still more degradation. Call this *self-validating reduction*. Can you see similar processes at work today?

5.2 CONTESTED RIGHTS

The United Nations Universal Declaration of Human Rights carries the word "universal" in its very title. Yet its universality has been challenged by some critics, raising the question of how universal any ethics might be.

On the one hand, the Declaration has been praised by many people from across the world spectrum. Pope John Paul II notably called it "one of the highest expressions of the human conscience of our time." Around the world, much as its authors hoped, the Declaration is constantly invoked in defense of the rights of unjustly persecuted prisoners (for example, political opponents of various regimes), indigenous peoples (there is also a separate, further UN Declaration on the Rights of Indigenous peoples), missionaries and other religious practitioners, journalists and reporters, and many others who are made to suffer for actions that, officially, their governments are committed to respecting under the Declaration. As with the American Bill of Rights, their actual application is a matter of continuous struggle. One could argue that this is already a major success.

Yet the Declaration has been criticized by others in a variety of serious ways. That it is so closely modeled on the American Bill of Rights, in both content and intention, is itself an indication that it may be less culturally neutral than we'd like to think. Islamists have pointed out, for example, that it presupposes an American-style separation of religion and state, whereas at least on some understandings, the proper Islamic state is a theocracy in which freedom of religion (Article 18), along with certain related claims such as the equality of the sexes (Articles 16 and 26 and others), do not fully apply. Iran's representative to the United Nations once described the UN Declaration as "a secular understanding of the Judeo-Christian tradition." It seems a fair description, but he did not mean it very positively. Islamic countries have adopted their own version, the Cairo Declaration of Human Rights in Islam, worth a look at http://www1.umn.edu/humanrts/instree/cairodeclaration.html, which Western organizations such as the International Humanist and Ethical Union have criticized, in turn, as unacceptably limiting the rights of non-Muslims and women.

The Declaration also has its critics within the Western philosophical and political tradition. For example, libertarians argue that so-called "positive" rights, such as the claimed right to a job (Article 23) and to adequate food, clothing, and medical care (Article 25), seem to require the infringement of the rights of others who must fulfill these claims, or pay for them. Article 26 also comes in for criticism for making elementary education compulsory. Did it perhaps already strike you as a little paradoxical for a declaration of rights to insist on anything as *compulsory*? Or is it more that this is a defense of children—that is, that the ones who really need to be compelled are the parents, who otherwise may not choose to send their children to school—or actively oppose schooling, especially for girls, for example in a number of traditional societies.

You see that these are difficult matters. What do you think? Can rights—or more broadly, the values of the person—be specified in some way that is truly universal? And if not, what should give: the idea of a fundamental and universal ethics, in the name of greater tolerance and diversity, or the less liberal and universal values, in the name of recognizing basic transcultural ethical values, even if change will be difficult and wrenching for some people and cultures? How would you begin to resolve such questions?

5.3 DRAWING LINES

We speak easily of "human rights," thinking that in so doing we are being liberal, inclusive, and even radical. Certainly even today there are places where human rights are not recognized, at least in the ways we think they should be. Maybe so. But in so doing we also emphatically close off moral consideration at the species boundary. We think: humans have rights, non-humans don't. And this may not really be liberal or inclusive at all.

At the very least, it is arbitrary, according to some philosophers, to limit personhood or rights to humans simply on the basis of species. That biological category must be connected with *ethically relevant* traits in order to make an argument: it cannot be just a matter of how we are pleased to talk about ourselves. On the one hand, then, we may at least wonder whether a biological human couldn't lose human rights, or indeed personhood itself, under certain conditions. What do we mean when we say of a person in an irreversible coma that they have become (not to mince words here) a "vegetable"? A vegetable is a living form, but not capable of the self-awareness and choice essential to personhood. If such people continue to have rights anyway, what kind or degree of rights might they be (life, for example, or maybe more like the right to die with dignity)? Is this because once they were persons, rather than because in some way they still are?

Parallel questions arise at the other end of life. Fetuses have few or none of the capacities we have been identifying as essential to personhood. They are human, we might say, but not yet human *beings*. Do they have human rights because they are potential persons, then? Or perhaps do they not yet have such rights, after all, or have them only partially?

Such line-drawing questions become especially pointed when we ask the same about other animals. Surely some other animals are as self-aware and free as many humans (say, humans in reduced states; but then again, apparently some animals are perceptually much sharper than even normally functioning humans). So if those humans are persons and have rights, why not those animals?

Animal rights advocates have at least succeeded in showing that a system of rights that includes animal rights is not impossible or incoherent or even necessarily cumbersome. Even partial rights for animals, or subordinate-but-still-serious rights, are entirely imaginable. We might not even want to think that personhood is all-or-nothing. Maybe the question of "marginal" humans and other animals should make us think seriously about partial persons, or a variety of ways to be somewhat a person.

The same sorts of questions arise for views like Buber or Levinas's. Buber, in *I and Thou*, often writes about relationships with animals and even trees, though officially he seems to be saying that they are not persons (while insisting that there can be other-than-human persons, for example, God). Levinas writes evocatively of the roots of ethics literally in the Face of the Other. But animals have faces too, don't they? (Or at least most do: is there a morally relevant distinction here?) Though both Buber and Levinas were insistent that ethics does not extend to other animals, more recent philosophers in their tradition haven't been so sure.

A related question: In Alice Walker's "Am I Blue?," the reading in chapter 1, do you think that Walker is recognizing Blue as a person? Is this crucial to her ethical response to him?

Levinas writes about a dog who strayed into the Nazi concentration camp where he and his fellow prisoners were daily being treated as less than human, as dirt. Yet every morning the dog greeted them with wagging tail as they were being marched out to work. Every night he barked excitedly for their return. The *dog* at least treated them like human beings—as persons. In a wrenching phrase, Levinas calls that dog "the last Kantian in Nazi Germany." Can we sometimes learn ethics from other animals, then? And if so, how could they not also count ethically?

NOTES

Martin Buber's *I and Thou*, translated by Walter Kaufmann (Scribner's, 1970), is cited from pp. 69–72 and 59. Emmanuel Levinas's major work is *Totality and Infinity* (Duquesne University Press, 1969) and is cited from p. 50. A good introduction to Levinas's philosophy is *Ethics and Infinity*, translated by Richard Cohen and published in 1985 by Duquesne University Press. See also Alphonso Lingis, *The Community of Those Who Have Nothing in Common* (Indiana University Press, 1994).

Philip Hallie's essay is based on his best-known book, *Lest Innocent Blood Be Shed* (Harper, 1994). The Hastings Report by the Hastings Center. Copyright 1981. Reproduced with permission of Hastings Center in the format republished in a textbook via Copyright Clearance Center.

For a systematic look at respect for persons, see R. S. Downie and Elizabeth Telfer, *Respect for Persons* (Schocken, 1970). A classic theory of the right, much less formal than Kant's, is W. D. Ross's *The Foundations of Ethics* (Oxford University Press, 1939). For background reading on Kantian ethics, start with Onora O'Neill, "A Simplified Account of Kant's Ethics," in Tom Regan, ed., *Matters of Life and Death* (McGraw-Hill, 1986) and also reprinted elsewhere. For an exceptionally vigorous introduction to philosophical theories about rights, see Lawrence Becker, "Individual Rights," and Hugo Bedeau's essay, "International Human Rights," both in Tom Regan and Don Vandeveer, eds.,

And Justice for All: New Introductory Essays in Philosophy and Public Policy (Rowman and Allenheld, 1982).

For data on CEO-versus-average-worker compensation, see Lawrence Mishel, "CEO pay 231 times greater than the average worker" and Lawrence Mishel and Natalie Sabadish "Methodology for measuring CEO compensation and the ratio of CEO-to worker compensation" at http://www.epi.org/publications, accessed 6/27/12.

John Rawls's classic work on justice is *A Theory of Justice* (Belknap Press, Harvard, 1971). Michael Walzer, in *Spheres of Justice: A Defense of Pluralism and Equality* (Basic Books, 1990), argues that there is no single criterion for the just distribution of all goods: each has its own meaning and appropriate criteria, and a "fair" society is simply one that keeps inequalities in one "sphere" from spilling over into others. Robert Nozick, in *Anarchy, State, and Utopia* (Basic Books, 1977), argues for a libertarian, lasseiz-faire view of justice based on strong individual rights. For a useful survey of this very large discussion and literature, see the "Ethics Updates" website at http://ethics.sandiego.edu/theories/Justice/index.asp. There is also a detailed and helpful page under "Animal Rights."

CHAPTER 6

The Ethics of Happiness

Chapter 4 outlined the family of happiness-centered values like this:

H A P P I N E S S

The Ethics of Happiness challenges us to achieve the greatest balance of happiness (well-being, satisfaction, pleasure) over suffering. Include in the great calculation the happiness of others as well as oneself, and we find ourselves looking to achieve the greatest balance of happiness over suffering in society as a whole. Ethical thinking in this family of values is quantitative and economic, concerned with trade-offs and the distribution of goods, maximizing tangible social benefits.

Let us now explore the Ethics of Happiness in more detail.

HAPPINESS

A great deal of what we do is obviously not for its own sake but for the sake of something else. We go to the dentist, for instance, even though it's nobody's idea of a fun afternoon, to keep our teeth in shape. We fight the rush hour traffic to get home or to work, the pool or the grocery store.

Even these goals in turn don't seem "final," though. We don't really keep our teeth in shape for its own sake (come on, flossing?). And getting to work or the pool or the store—what's the point?

We know why: we want good jobs, healthy teeth and bodies, and some level of physical comfort and ease. But again, why do we want *these* things? These may not exactly be final goals either. But then, what is?

The natural answer is unsurprising, everyday, even "obvious" to many people. Our ultimate goal, we say, is to be happy. Happiness is the "final end" of human action. That is why we want everything else that we seek.

This is a strong claim—stronger than it might seem at first. It is actually a rough psychological theory: a systematic account of human motivation. More than anything else, we are saying, people seek happiness—and, correspondingly, in the end, what we try to avoid is unhappiness: pain and suffering. In terms of values, we value happiness as a basic and inclusive goal, and everything else is valued insofar as it serves happiness. What we disvalue, we disvalue in the end because it impedes or counteracts happiness.

THE QUESTION OF PLEASURE

We must be careful, however, to clarify the relation of this claim about happiness to the more specific and perhaps familiar claim that the final end of human action is specifically *pleasure*.

"Pleasure" usually suggests a more immediate kind of satisfaction or gratification, most often of the senses. It seems fairly clear, though, that people do all sorts of things that are not for the sake of pleasure in this sense. Almost every great endeavor, in art or politics or science or even family raising, let alone exploratory or military, tends to decrease, not increase, the net pleasure (in a strict sense, anyway) of the people who undertake them. Moreover, for this and other reasons the moral tradition tends to suspect that the pursuit of pleasure makes us grasping and self-centered. The gratification of the senses is important, obviously, but it is much less than the whole story.

Philosophers who nonetheless advocate a pleasure-based ethics therefore typically broaden their notion of "pleasure" in the direction of what we have been calling "happiness." There is no reason that all pleasures must be intense, they say, or just sensual, or that more such pleasures should be our primary goal. Though popularly the term "hedonist" tends to suggest a self-seeking and shallow person, notably preoccupied with sex and maybe a few other sensual gratifications, the ancient philosophical hedonists had (mostly.) a bigger picture in mind. The Epicureans, for example (a Greek school of philosophy of the 3rd century BCE—not a kind of gourmet), actually recommended only the most modest pleasures. Epicurus himself, the founder and namesake, virtually advocated asceticism. The best way to be happy, he said, was to live a simple life and reduce pains as much as possible. We're not built to take too much intensity. For a sustainable life of pleasures—not blazing out too quickly and spending the rest of our lives unhappily regretting it—something fairly quiet is best.

Even when intense pleasure is sought and celebrated, there is not necessarily anything crude or shallow about it. The popular notion of hedonism, it might be argued, actually sells pleasure short. We get crude when we reduce sex, say, to nothing but the immediate release of tension. But if you get "crude" in this way, you also miss most of the pleasure itself. Sex involves the many pleasures of companionship and mutual appreciation, of touching and simple physical togetherness, of gracefulness and humor and spiritual connection too. The needs it can fulfill are not just passing and physical but go to the very core of our beings. That is the source of its deepest pleasures, and there is nothing crude or shallow about that.

If we are careful, then, we can continue to use the word "pleasure," in a broad sense, for the positive kinds of experience we picture as a basic, ultimately good thing, and the goal for which we seek most other things along the way. Or "happiness," if you prefer. That such a goal exists is the main thing, and, as we'll soon see, the starting point for a modern ethical philosophy.

READING

From Flow: The Psychology of Optimal Experience

MIHALY CSIKSZENTMIHALYI

IT IS TEMPTING to think of happiness as a static state of mind. The senses are being agreeably stimulated, no pain or distraction intrudes . . . we're feeling good. Psychological understandings, though, suggest that this is far too simple a picture. In fact, people can have all sorts of agreeable sense stimulation and still be desperately unhappy. Conversely, we can be in a great deal of pain or under stress and still be having the time of our lives. Happiness is not so simple.

Lionel Barrymore, of all people, once said that "Happiness is not a station you arrive at—it is the train you are riding on." There is a clue here. In his well-known work *Flow: The Psychology of Optimal Experience,* the American psychologist Mihaly Csikszentmihalyi argues that Barrymore is exactly right. Happiness lies in the flow of experience itself.

Indeed, Csikszentmihalyi uses the very term *flow* for "the state in which people are so involved in an activity that nothing else seems to matter; the experience itself is so enjoyable that people will do it . . . for the sheer sake of doing it." We must be confronting a task, he says, that we have a chance of completing and that has clear goals and immediate feedback. We concentrate on it with "an effortless involvement that removes from awareness the worries and frustrations of everyday life." Concern for the self disappears, and even our sense of time is altered: "hours can seem like minutes," yet at other times mere minutes seem endless. "The combination of all of these ele-

Pp. 1–4 from *Flow: The Psychology of Optimal Experience* by Mihaly Czikszentmihalyi. © 1990 by Mihaly Czikszentmihalyi. Reprinted by permission of HarperCollins Publishers.

ments causes a sense of deep enjoyment that is so rewarding
people feel that expending a great deal of energy is worthwhile
simply to be able to feel it." *That's* happiness!

Twenty-three hundred years ago Aristotle concluded that, more
than anything else, men and women seek happiness. While happiness itself is sought for its own sake, every other goal—health,
beauty, money, or power—is valued only because we expect that it
will make us happy. Much has changed since Aristotle's time. Our
understanding of the worlds of stars and of atoms has expanded
beyond belief. The gods of the Greeks were like helpless children
compared to humankind today and the powers we now wield. And
yet on this most important issue very little has changed in the intervening centuries. We do not understand what happiness is any better than Aristotle did, and as for learning how to attain that blessed
condition, one could argue that we have made no progress at all.

Despite the fact that we are now healthier and grow to be older,
despite the fact that even the least affluent among us are surrounded
by material luxuries undreamed of even a few decades ago (there
were few bathrooms in the palace of the Sun King, chairs were rare
even in the richest medieval houses, and no Roman emperor could
turn on a TV set when he was bored), and regardless of all the stupen-
dous scientific knowledge we can summon at will, people often end
up feeling that their lives have been wasted, that instead of being filled with happiness their years were spent in anxiety and boredom.

Is this because it is the destiny of mankind to remain unfulfilled,
each person always wanting more than he or she can have? Or is the
pervasive malaise that often sours even our most precious moments
the result of our seeking happiness in the wrong places? My intent
is to use some of the tools of modern psychology to explore this very
ancient question: When do people feel most happy? If we can begin
to find an answer to it, perhaps we shall eventually be able to order
life so that happiness will play a larger part in it.

Twenty-five years before I began to write these lines, I made
a discovery that took all the intervening time for me to realize I
had made. To call it a "discovery" is perhaps misleading, for people
have been aware of it since the dawn of time. Yet the word is appropriate, because even though my finding itself was well known, it
had not been described or theoretically explained by the relevant
branch of scholarship, which in this case happens to be psychology. So I spent the next quarter-century investigating this elusive
phenomenon.

What I "discovered" was that happiness is not something that
happens. It is not the result of good fortune or random chance. It

is not something that money can buy or power command. It does not depend on outside events, but, rather, on how we interpret them. Happiness, in fact, is a condition that must be prepared for, cultivated, and defended privately by each person. People who learn to control *inner experience* will be able to determine the quality of their lives, which is as close as any of us can come to being happy.

Yet we cannot reach happiness by consciously searching for it. "Ask yourself whether you are happy," said J. S. Mill, "and you cease to be so." It is by being fully involved with every detail of our lives, whether good or bad, that we find happiness, not by trying to look for it directly. Viktor Frankl, the Austrian psychologist, summarized it beautifully in the preface to his book *Man's Search for Meaning:* "Don't aim at success—the more you aim at it and make it a target, the more you are going to miss it. For success, like happiness, cannot be pursued; it must ensue . . . as the unintended side-effect of one's personal dedication to a course greater than oneself."

So how can we reach this elusive goal that cannot be attained by a direct route? My studies of the past quarter-century have convinced me that there is a way. It is a circuitous path that begins with achieving control over the contents of our consciousness.

Our perceptions about our lives are the outcome of many forces that shape experience, each having an impact on whether we feel good or bad. Most of these forces are outside our control. There is not much we can do about our looks, our temperament, or our constitution. We cannot decide—at least so far—how tall we will grow, how smart we will get. We can choose neither parents nor time of birth, and it is not in your power or mine to decide whether there will be a war or a depression. The instructions contained in our genes, the pull of gravity, the pollen in the air, the historical period into which we are born—these and innumerable other conditions determine what we see, how we feel, what we do. It is not surprising that we should believe that our fate is primarily ordained by outside agencies.

Yet we have all experienced times when, instead of being buffeted by anonymous forces, we do feel in control of our actions, masters of our own fate. On the rare occasions that it happens, we feel a sense of exhilaration, a deep sense of enjoyment that is long cherished and that becomes a landmark in memory for what life should be like.

This is what we mean by *optimal experience.* It is what the sailor holding a tight course feels when the wind whips through her hair, when the boat lunges through the waves like a colt—sails, hull, wind, and sea humming a harmony that vibrates in the sailor's veins. It is what a painter feels when the colors on the canvas begin to set up a magnetic tension with each other, and a new *thing*, a living form, takes shape in front of the astonished creator. Or it is the feeling a father has when his child for the first time responds to his smile. Such events do not occur only when the external conditions are favorable, however: people who have survived concentration camps or who have lived through near-fatal physical dangers often recall that in the midst of their ordeal they experienced extraordinarily rich epiphanies in response to such simple events as hearing the song of a bird in the forest, completing a hard task, or sharing a crust of bread with a friend.

Contrary to what we usually believe, moments like these, the best moments in our lives, are not the passive, receptive, relaxing times—although such experiences can also be enjoyable, if we have worked hard to attain them. The best moments usually occur when a person's body or mind is stretched to its limits in a voluntary effort to accomplish something difficult and worthwhile. Optimal experience is thus something that we *make* happen. For a child, it could be placing with trembling fingers the last block on a tower she has built, higher than any she has built so far; for a swimmer, it could be trying to beat his own record; for a violinist, mastering an intricate musical passage. For each person there are thousands of opportunities, challenges to expand ourselves.

Such experiences are not necessarily pleasant at the time they occur. The swimmer's muscles might have ached during his most memorable race, his lungs might have felt like exploding, and he might have been dizzy with fatigue—yet these could have been the best moments of his life. Getting control of life is never easy, and sometimes it can be definitely painful. But in the long run optimal experiences add up to a sense of mastery—or perhaps better, a sense of *participation* in determining the content of life—that comes as close to what is usually meant by happiness as anything else we can conceivably imagine.

UTILITARIANISM

Happiness is certainly *one* of our basic values. An entire family of values centers on such positive states of mind or flow: satisfaction, welfare, the relief of pain and suffering, and "pleasures" in many senses. These are good and worthy goals, as long as they don't turn too shallow or self-centered. What we have here, so far, is an appealingly relaxed and inclusive family of values, like going home to a soft chair after spending a little too long in church with the person-centered in-laws.

The Ethics of Happiness, however, goes much further. In the hands of certain philosophers, the rather relaxed and rough-and-ready concern with happiness, as we have so far been sketching it, becomes something much more far-reaching: it actually becomes a theory of ethics. Indeed, it can become so systematic that the result, the theory or family of theories known as "utilitarian," pretty much defines what an ethical theory as such is now expected to look like and the questions it is expected to answer.

THE ARGUMENT BEGINS

Three basic steps, each of them arguably very plausible, lead us from our basic claims about happiness to a utilitarian ethical theory.

One step we have practically made already. We have said that happiness is one of the main ultimate aims of human action. In truth, though, isn't it *the* ultimate aim of human action? Don't we want *everything* else, in the end, for the sake of the happiness it brings or the suffering it avoids?

Remember that we are not defining "pleasure" or "happiness" in any crude or narrow sense. We are speaking generally of positive experiences, of positive states of mind, of flow. What else could we want but that? Happiness in this sense, then, is the "final end" of human action.

A second step also seems natural. If something is a good thing, more of it is pretty clearly better. Thus, in general, we should act in such a way as to produce the *most* happiness. Maximize happiness; minimize pain and suffering.

The claim is that this is just what any rational person already does. You may have to do some careful thinking, and even restrain yourself at times—giving up some short-term pleasure, for example, for longer-term gains. Maximizing happiness over a *life* does not mean that we will be happy every moment of that life.

Our strategy for happiness, in short, must become calculating. Even suffering can sometimes actually be a good thing in the long run. It may be painful to work hard, for instance, but we do it for the extra-pleasurable rewards that status or more money bring. You sweat in the sauna, uncomfortably, for the unmatchable rush of pleasure that comes when you leap into the cold water afterward. The trick is to work in just enough adversity to maximize flow, or at least pleasure, later, without overdoing the pain. No point in sweating too long or working too hard or flossing more than you have to. But when a little pain now increases your net happiness in the long run, it's worth it.

THE STEP INTO ETHICS

One step remains. This step may also seem hardly more than a clarification of what we've been saying already, a more careful look at the nature of pleasure—but it turns out to make a dramatic claim.

The argument so far, strictly speaking, has been about our own individual happiness. But ethics, remember, asks us to take care for others as well as ourselves. One reason that many ethical thinkers have mistrusted hedonism, indeed, is that it seems all too easy for a concern with one's own pleasure or happiness to remain self-centered and even careless of others.

Utilitarians, however, argue that happiness itself, properly understood, is social. Our concern with happiness does not stop at the boundaries of our own selves but *must* grow to encompass others. For one thing, quite simply, it is hard to be happy all alone. Our lives take on their emotional tone from the people around us. Moreover, we naturally seek the well-being of others close to us—spouses, children, parents, friends, lovers, students and teachers, those we work for and those who work for us. Anyone who knows love knows this simple fact. Often we also care for those who are distant, those whose plight or whose successes engage our sympathies or inspire us.

These are psychological, empirical claims: our own happiness is in fact bound up with the happiness of others. Beside them, some philosophers propose a more conceptual argument as well. We are beginning with the idea that happiness is the ultimate good thing. This claim in turn is based on a general claim about human beings (and perhaps some non-human beings as well). It's not just about me. From an ethical point of view, then, I cannot say that someone else's happiness is of no concern to me simply because I'm me, so to speak, and they're them. (Notice there's more than a shade of Kant here.) The conclusion is that happiness as such is a morally good thing, wherever it occurs—and it is good in the same way and to the same extent.

We are left, in short, with a commitment to the happiness of others beyond the self. And if happiness alone is the good, and if more of it is better and the most the best, then we have a commitment to achieve the *most* happiness we can in *society as a whole*. We have arrived at utilitarianism.

FOUNDERS

Two English thinkers advanced utilitarianism as a modern theory of ethics: Jeremy Bentham (1748–1832) and John Stuart Mill (1806–1873.)

Bentham started out as a social critic, concerned for more enlightened legislation, and was a lifelong opponent of the severe British penal codes of his time. It was Bentham who popularized the most famous version of utilitarianism: the formula of the *greatest good of the greatest number*. He called it the "Principle of Utility" in ethics—the formula that economists put as "Maximize Utility"—from which the term "utilitarianism" comes. (Technically modern utilitarians are a bit more careful: the greatest *good* is the goal, for sure, but it might not be of the greatest *number*—a question to which we'll return.)

"Good" for Bentham emphatically meant *pleasure*. Moreover, he thought pleasures could readily be quantified, and he tried to devise criteria for weighing pleasures directly against each other. Bentham actually imagined that we could one day solve ethical problems by sitting down with a calculator, figuring up the amounts of pleasure on either side!

Mill inherited the utilitarian project from Bentham and from his own father, James Mill. He gave it his own characteristic twists and developments, but on the key points he is one with them:

> Pleasure, and freedom from pain, are the only things desirable as ends; all desirable things . . . are desirable either for the pleasure inherent in themselves, or as means to the promotion of pleasure and the prevention of pain. . . . Actions are right in proportion as they tend to promote happiness; wrong as they tend to produce the reverse of happiness.

And Mill insists that such an ethic appeals directly to our social nature.

> The deeply rooted conception which every individual even now has of himself as a social being, tends to make him feel it one of his natural wants that there should be harmony between his feelings and those of his fellow creatures. . . . This feeling in most individuals is much inferior in strength to their selfish feelings, and is often wanting altogether. But to those who have it, it possesses all the characters of a natural feeling. It does not present itself to their minds as a superstition of education, or a law despotically imposed by the power of society. . . . This conviction is the ultimate sanction of the greatest happiness morality.

UTILITARIANISM IN PRACTICE: ECONOMIC THINKING

Solving ethical problems by quantifying pleasures turns out to be trickier than Bentham thought. For one thing, pleasure seems to be too subjective to measure in any accurate way, even when we are comparing our own pleasures with one another, certainly when we are trying to compare different people's. Happiness is probably even less quantifiable. Utilitarianism in practice has therefore moved toward a more economic way of thinking, looking at a more external (not so psychological) calculus of costs and benefits, and the more neutral and seemingly objective language of "utilities."

The logic, though, stays the same. When there are multiple choices with different utilities, or when utilities conflict, we should always pick the greatest one. Should you finish your degree now, say, even under financial and emotional hardship, or let it go and make things easier? Each choice has its specific benefits and its costs, and many can be at least partly quantified. In theory, the utilitarian answer is clear: choose a way that achieves the greatest net benefit—the highest total benefits over costs.

Social questions are to be decided the same way. We debate about assisted suicide, for example: about whether doctors should be allowed or expected to help people die if they so choose. Utilitarians would decide the question by looking at the effects on society as a whole. If assisted suicide would promote social utility, all told, then it should be allowed. If it doesn't, it shouldn't. What else (they would ask) could be relevant?

This looks like an empirical question. Maybe we can actually resolve it. The benefits of assisted suicide seem very concrete: relief of suffering—for dying people, who are often in great physical pain and sometimes emotional pain too, unable to secure relief by themselves, and also for their families, who may suffer greatly too, emotionally and financially, when dying is prolonged and hard. The costs, by contrast, are much more indefinite and speculative, and do not necessarily have any effect on happiness. Some people may feel pressured into choosing assisted suicide, for example, and we might come somehow to "devalue life." Put in the balance with the clear benefits, though, many utilitarians tend to think that these sorts of costs—such as they are—will be outweighed.

Sometimes utilitarians call on economics directly. Suppose that the question is whether to build a dam that will generate electricity and provide irrigation and recreation but will also cost money, displace families or towns, and flood valuable land. How do we decide? Naturally, say utilitarians, we try to quantify the various benefits and costs. How much social utility will be gained from the dam? How much will be lost?

As far as possible, economists calculate the answers in dollars. What will the dam cost? How much money will it take to compensate people who have to move? What is the monetary value of the land that will be lost? All of these costs must be weighed against the monetary value of the electricity produced, the dollar gain in food production due to irrigation, added income from recreation, and so on—as well as the net benefits that could be gained from doing something else with the same resources. More sophisticated calculations factor in the long-run probability of these benefits continuing (maybe high but less than 100 percent) and consider the costs when the dam's useful life is over (dams eventually silt up and become useless). In the end, though, once again, the aim is still to answer a simple question: which choice has the highest net benefits?

Utilitarianism, then, draws attention squarely back to what is actually good or bad for people—to specific consequences for utilities, and behind them for what we suppose to be happiness—rather than to the sometimes abstract rules that too often (say utilitarians) are supposed to define what's ethical. In this utilitarianism regards itself as no more than systematized common sense. *Do what has the best effects*—surely no one could disagree with so obvious a maxim!

READING

From Utilitarianism

JOHN STUART MILL

The creed which accepts as the foundation of morals, Utility, or the Greatest Happiness Principle, holds that actions are right in proportion as they tend to promote happiness, wrong as they tend to produce the reverse of happiness. By happiness is intended pleasure, and the absence of pain; by unhappiness, pain, and the privation of pleasure. To give a clear view of the moral standard set up by the theory, much more requires to be said; in particular, what things it includes in the ideas of pain and pleasure; and to what extent this is left an open question. But these supplementary explanations do not affect the theory of life on which this theory of morality is grounded—namely, that pleasure, and freedom from pain, are the only things desirable as ends; and that all desirable things (which are as numerous in the utilitarian as in any other scheme) are desirable either for the pleasure inherent in themselves, or as means to the promotion of pleasure and the prevention of pain . . .

The ultimate end, with reference to and for the sake of which all other things are desirable (whether we are considering our own good or that of other people), is an existence exempt as far as possible from pain, and as rich as possible in enjoyments, both in point of quantity and quality; the test of quality, and the rule for measuring it against quantity, being the preference felt by those who in their opportunities of experience, to which must be added their habits of self-consciousness and self-observation, are best furnished with the means of comparison. This, being, according to the utilitarian opinion, the end of human action, is necessarily also the standard of morality; which may accordingly be defined, the rules and precepts for human conduct, by the observance of which an existence such as has been described might be, to the greatest extent possible, secured to all mankind; and not to them only, but, so far as the nature of things admits, to the whole sentient creation.

. . . When it is positively asserted to be impossible that human life should be happy, the assertion, if not something like a verbal quibble, is at least an exaggeration. If by happiness be meant a continuity of highly pleasurable excitement, it is evident enough that this is impossible. A state of exalted pleasure lasts only moments, or in some cases, and with some intermissions, hours or days, and is the occasional brilliant flash of enjoyment, not its permanent and steady flame. Of this the philosophers who have taught that happiness is the end [goal] of life were as fully aware as those who taunt them. The happiness which they meant was not a life of rapture; but moments of such, in an existence made up of few and transitory pains, many and various pleasures, with a decided predominance of the active over the passive, and having

From John Stuart Mill, *Utilitarianism*, chapter 2 (available in many editions, including online; I draw on http://etext.library.adelaide.edu. au/m/mill/john_stuart/m645u/).

as the foundation of the whole, not to expect more from life than it is capable of bestowing. A life thus composed, to those who have been fortunate enough to obtain it, has always appeared worthy of the name of happiness. And such an existence is even now the lot of many, during some considerable portion of their lives. The present wretched education, and wretched social arrangements, are the only real hindrance to its being attainable by almost all.

The objectors perhaps may doubt whether human beings, if taught to consider happiness as the end of life, would be satisfied with such a moderate share of it. But great numbers of mankind have been satisfied with much less. The main constituents of a satisfied life appear to be two, either of which by itself is often found sufficient for the purpose: tranquillity, and excitement. With much tranquillity, many find that they can be content with very little pleasure: with much excitement, many can reconcile themselves to a considerable quantity of pain. There is assuredly no inherent impossibility in enabling even the mass of mankind to unite both; since the two are so far from being incompatible that they are in natural alliance, the prolongation of either being a preparation for, and exciting a wish for, the other . . . When people who are tolerably fortunate in their outward lot do not find in life sufficient enjoyment to make it valuable to them, the cause generally is, caring for nobody but themselves. To those who have neither public nor private affections, the excitements of life are much curtailed, and in any case dwindle in value as the time approaches when all selfish interests must be terminated by death: while those who leave after them objects of personal affection, and especially those who have also cultivated a fellow-feeling with the collective interests of mankind, retain as lively an interest in life on the eve of death as in the vigour of youth and health. Next to selfishness, the principal cause which makes life unsatisfactory is want of mental cultivation. A cultivated mind—I do not mean that of a philosopher, but any mind to which the fountains of knowledge have been opened, and which has been taught, in any tolerable degree, to exercise its faculties—finds sources of inexhaustible interest in all that surrounds it; in the objects of nature, the achievements of art, the imaginations of poetry, the incidents of history, the ways of mankind, past and present, and their prospects in the future . . .

The deeply rooted conception which every individual even now has of himself as a social being, tends to make him feel it one of his natural wants that there should be harmony between his feelings and aims and those of his fellow creatures. If differences of opinion and of mental culture make it impossible for him to share many of their actual feelings—perhaps make him denounce and defy those feelings—he still needs to be conscious that his real aim and theirs do not conflict; that he is not opposing himself to what they really wish for, namely their own good, but is, on the contrary, promoting it. This feeling in most individuals is much inferior in strength to their selfish feelings, and is often wanting altogether. But to those who have it, it possesses all the characters of a natural feeling. It does not present itself to their minds as a superstition of education, or a law despotically imposed by the power of society, but as an attribute which it would not be well for them to be without. This conviction is the ultimate sanction of the greatest happiness morality. This it is which makes any mind, of well-developed feelings, work with, and not against, the outward motives to care for others, afforded by what I have called the external sanctions; and when those sanctions are wanting, or act in an opposite direction, constitutes in itself a powerful internal binding force, in proportion to the sensitiveness and thoughtfulness of the character; since few but those whose mind is a moral blank, could bear to lay out their course of life on the plan of paying no regard to others except so far as their own private interest compels.

READING

"The Harm That Good Men Do"

BERTRAND RUSSELL

BERTRAND RUSSELL (1872–1970) was a 20th-century English philosopher who made his philosophical name working in logic and mathematics but who contributed to nearly every area of philosophy, including ethics, over his long life. He also was famous—or infamous—for regularly changing his mind. This essay, written during his utilitarian period, nicely counterpoints Mill's earnestness by setting out utilitarianism in an ironic and rhetorical fashion.

Notice that Russell appears to be attacking Bentham here, at least until he turns "serious" about halfway through, but in fact he is entirely on Bentham's side.

Reproduced by permission of Taylor & Francis Books UK. © by The Bertrand Russell Peace Foundation Ltd.

Russell's account of "respectable" or "traditional" morality may seem quaint and dated in some ways, even acknowledging that he's not exactly putting it sympathetically. Few moralists are so preoccupied with "bad language," or smoking, or going to church anymore. On the other hand, though, the underlying logic of the anti-utilitarian position on preventing venereal disease, as he lays it out, is exactly the same as the logic used today by some opponents of sex education and birth control. Society has moved toward a more utilitarian perspective since Russell wrote this essay, but by no means has everyone gone all the way.

A hundred years ago there lived a philosopher named Jeremy Bentham, who was universally recognized to be a very wicked man. I remember to this day the first time that I came across his name when I was a boy. It was in a statement by the Rev. Sydney Smith to the effect that Bentham thought people ought to make soup of their dead grandmothers. This practice appeared to me as undesirable from a culinary as from a moral point of view, and I therefore conceived a bad opinion of Bentham. Long afterwards, I discovered that the statement was one of those reckless lies in which respectable people are wont to indulge in the interests of virtue. I also discovered what was the really serious charge against him. It was no less than this: that he defined a "good" man as a man who does good. This definition, as the reader will perceive at once if he is right-minded, is subversive of all true morality. How much more exalted is the attitude of Kant, who lays it down that a kind action is not virtuous if it springs from affection for the beneficiary, but only if it is inspired by the moral law, which is, of course, just as likely to inspire unkind actions. We know that the exercise of virtue should be its own reward, and it seems to follow that the enduring of it on the part of the patient should be its own punishment. Kant, therefore, is a more sublime moralist than Bentham, and has the suffrage of all those who tell us that they love virtue for its own sake.

It is true that Bentham fulfilled his own definition of a good man: he did much good. The forty middle years of the nineteenth century in England were years of incredibly rapid progress, materially, intellectually, and morally. At the beginning of the period comes the Reform Act, which made Parliament representative of the middle-class, not, as before, of the aristocracy. This Act was the most difficult of the steps towards democracy in England, and was quickly followed by other important reforms, such as the abolition of slavery in Jamaica. At the beginning of the period the penalty for petty theft was death by hanging; very soon the death penalty was confined to those who were guilty of murder or high treason. The

Corn Laws, which made food so dear as to cause atrocious proverty, were abolished in 1846. Compulsory education was introduced in 1870. It is the fashion to decry the Victorians, but I wish our age had half as good a record as theirs. This, however, is beside the point. My point is that a very large proportion of the progress during those years must be attributed to the influence of Bentham. There can be no doubt that nine-tenths of the people living in England in the latter part of last century were happier than they would have been if he had never lived. So shallow was his philosophy that he would have regarded this as a vindication of his activities. We, in our more enlightened age, can see that such a view is preposterous; but it may fortify us to review the grounds for rejecting a grovelling utilitarianism such as that of Bentham.

We all know what we mean by a "good" man. The ideally good man does not drink or smoke, avoids bad language, converses in the presence of men only exactly as he would if there were ladies present, attends church regularly, and holds the correct opinions on all subjects. He has a wholesome horror of wrongdoing, and realizes that it is our painful duty to castigate Sin. He has a still greater horror of wrong thinking, and considers it the business of the authorities to safeguard the young against those who question the wisdom of the views generally accepted by middle-aged successful citizens. Apart from his professional duties, at which he is assiduous, he spends much time in good works: he may encourage patriotism and military training; he may promote industry, sobriety, and virtue among wage-earners and their children by seeing to it that failures in these respects receive due punishment; he may be a trustee of a university and prevent an ill-judged respect for learning from allowing the employment of professors with subversive ideas. Above all, of course, his "morals," in the narrow sense, must be irreproachable.

It may be doubted whether a "good" man, in the above sense, does, on the average, any more good than a "bad" man. I mean by a "bad" man the contrary of what we have been describing. A "bad" man is one who is known to smoke and to drink occasionally, and even to say a bad word when someone treads on his toe. His conversation is not always such as could be printed, and he sometimes spends fine Sundays out-of-doors instead of at church. Some of his opinions are subversive; for instance, he may think that if you desire peace you should prepare for peace, not for war. Toward wrongdoing he takes a scientific attitude such as he would take towards his motor-car if it misbehaved; he argues that sermons and prison will no more cure vice than mend a broken tire. In the matter of wrong thinking he is even more perverse. He maintains that what is called "wrong thinking" is simply thinking, and what is called "right thinking" is repeating words like a parrot; this gives him a sympathy with all sorts of undesirable cranks. His activities outside his working hours may consist merely in enjoyment, or, worse still, in stirring up discontent with preventable evils which do not interfere with the comfort of the men in power. And it is even possible that in the matter of "morals" he may not conceal his lapses as carefully as a truly virtuous man would do, defending himself by the perverse contention that it is better to be honest than to pretend to set a good example. A man who fails in any or several of these respects will be thought ill of by the average respectable citizen, and will not be allowed to hold any position conferring authority, such as that of a judge, a magistrate, or a schoolmaster. Such positions are open only to "good" men. . . .

Consider, again, such a matter as venereal disease: it is known that this can be almost entirely prevented by suitable precautions taken in advance, but owing to the activities of good men this knowledge is disseminated as little as possible, and all kinds of obstacles are placed in the way of its utilization. Consequently sin still secures its "natural" punishment, and the children are still punished for the sins of the fathers, in accordance with Biblical precept. How dreadful it would be if this were otherwise, for, if sin were no longer punished, there might be people so abandoned as to pretend that it was no longer sin, and if the punishment did not fall also upon the innocent, it would not seem so dreadful. How grateful we ought to be, therefore, to those good men who ensure that the stern laws of retribution decreed by Nature during our days of ignorance can still be made to operate in spite of the impious knowledge rashly acquired by scientists. All right-thinking people know that a bad act is bad quite regardless of the question whether it causes any suffering or not, but since men are not all capable of being guided by the pure moral law, it is highly desirable that suffering should follow from sin in order to secure virtue. Men must be kept in ignorance of all ways of escaping the penalties which were incurred by sinful actions in pre-scientific ages. I shudder when I think how much we should all know about the preservation of mental and physical health if it were not for the protection against this dangerous knowledge which our good men so kindly provide.

To speak seriously: the standards of "goodness" which are generally recognized by public opinion are not those which are calculated to make the world a happier place. This is due to a variety of causes, of which the chief is tradition, and the next most powerful is the unjust power of dominant classes. Primitive morality seems to have developed out of the notion of taboo; that is to say, it was originally purely superstitious, and forbade certain perfectly harmless acts (such as eating out of the chief's dish) on the supposed ground that they produced disaster by magical means. In this way there came to be prohibitions, which continued to have authority over people's feelings when the supposed reasons for them were forgotten. A considerable part of current morals is still of this sort: certain kinds of conduct produce emotions of horror, quite regardless of the question whether they have bad effects or not. In many cases the conduct which inspires horror is in fact harmful; if this were not the case, the need for a revision of our moral standards would be more generally recognized. Murder, for example, can obviously not be tolerated in a civilized society; yet the origin of the prohibition of murder is purely superstitious. It was thought that the murdered man's blood (or, later, his ghost) demanded vengeance, and might punish not only the guilty man, but any one who showed him kindness. The superstitious character of the prohibition of murder is shown by the fact that it was possible to be purified from blood-guiltiness by certain ritual ceremonies, which were apparently designed, originally, to disguise the murderer so that the ghost would not recognize him. This, at least, is the theory of Sir J. G. Frazer. When we speak of repentance as "washing out" guilt we are using a metaphor derived from the fact that long ago actual washing was used to remove blood-stains. Such notions as "guilt" and "sin" have an emotional background connected with this source in remote antiquity. Even in the case of murder a rational ethic will view the matter differently: it will be concerned with prevention and cure, as in the case of illness, rather than with guilt, punishment, and expiation.

Our current ethic is a curious mixture of superstition and rationalism. Murder is an ancient crime, and we view it through a mist of age-long horror. Forgery is a modern crime, and we view it rationally. We punish forgers, but we do not feel them strange beings set apart, as we do murderers. And we still think in social practice, whatever we may hold in theory, that virtue consists in not doing rather than in doing. The man who abstains from certain acts labelled "sin" is a good man, even though he never does anything to further the welfare of others. This, of course, is not the attitude inculcated in the Gospels: "Love thy neighbour as thyself" is a positive precept. But in all Christian communities the man who obeys this precept is persecuted, suffering at least poverty, usually imprisonment, and sometimes death. The world is full of injustice, and those who profit by injustice are in a position to administer rewards and punishments. The rewards go to those who invent ingenious justifications for inequality, the punishments to those who try to remedy it. I do not know of any country where a man who has a genuine love for his neighbour can long avoid obloquy.

Those who defend traditional morality will sometimes admit that it is not perfect, but contend that any criticism will make all morality crumble. This will not be the case if the criticism is based upon something positive and constructive, but only if it is conducted with a view to nothing more than momentary pleasure. To return to Bentham: he advocated, as the basis of morals, "the greatest happiness of the greatest number." A man who acts upon this principle will have a much more arduous life than a man who merely obeys conventional precepts. He will necessarily make himself the champion of the oppressed, and so incur the enmity of the great. He will proclaim facts which the powers that be wish to conceal; he will deny falsehoods designed to alienate sympathy from those who need it. Such a mode of life does not lead to a collapse of genuine morality. Official morality has always been oppressive and negative: it has said "thou shalt not," and has not troubled to investigate the effect of activities not forbidden by the code. Against this kind of morality all the great mystics and religious teachers have protested in vain: their followers ignored their most explicit pronouncements. It seems unlikely, therefore, that any large-scale improvements will come through their methods.

More is to be hoped, I think, from the progress of reason and science. Gradually men will come to realize that a world whose institutions are based upon hatred and injustice is not the one most likely to produce happiness. . . . We need a morality based upon love of life, upon pleasure in growth and positive achievement, not upon repression and prohibition. A man should be regarded as "good" if he is happy, expansive, generous, and glad when others are happy; if so, a few peccadilloes should be regarded as of little importance.

CAN UTILITY BE THE SINGLE MEASURE OF VALUES?

The utilitarian theory of ethics is compelling in its way and surely must find some place in our moral thinking. However we theorize it, happiness and the means to happiness are among our prime values. Sometimes at least, we must calculate and weigh different benefits and costs, and different benefits and costs to different people, under conditions of scarcity. Hard choices are necessary, but there are rational ways to make them.

But there are also questions and problems, and some serious objections, once utilitarianism pushes beyond these modest claims. Here we must enter, at least a little, the debate over utilitarianism as an ethical theory.

UTILITY AS THE SINGLE MEASURE OF VALUES

One of the main motives for ethical theory is simplification: finding some sort of order and unity in what might seem to be a hodgepodge of different values, both for intellectual elegance and to make it easier to decide what to do in the end. From this point of view, even four families of values are three too many. Ideally—so theorists say—we need just one.

Utilitarians argue that ultimately all values reduce to benefits and costs. All ethical thinking, and all ethical conflict, they say, is really about one thing— what will truly achieve the greatest happiness of all, all things considered and in the long run. And so, utilitarians say, we are justified in *translating* all other values into benefit-and-cost terms—"cashing them out," so to speak. Happiness becomes utilitarianism's single measure for all moral thinking.

Think of assisted suicide again, or the dam-building example. In the last section we discussed these issues briefly from a utilitarian point of view. On the face of it, though, there are also nonutilitarian values involved. Issues of justice and rights, for example: justice to people whose land the dams might flood, say—maybe long time owners who have cherished this one place on Earth—or people's rights to choose to die, even if it doesn't serve the "greatest good."

But: couldn't these values be understood in terms of happiness, a calculus of benefits and costs? Certainly justice, say, promotes happiness much of the time. Indirectly, it also promotes social stability, which in turn leads to happiness. An unjust social order—unfair, unequal, arbitrary—would make a lot of people unhappy much of the time, and it would also be prone to resistance and overthrow, leading to even more uncertainty and unrest. It's not a picture that looks too satisfying.

Mill explicitly grounded justice on utility:

> Justice is a name for certain classes of moral rules which concern the essentials of human well-being more nearly, and are therefore of moral absolute obligation, than any other rules for the guidance of life. . . . [T]hey are the main element in determining the social feelings of mankind. It is their observance which alone preserves peace among human beings.

We should indeed promote justice, then, but not ultimately for its own sake. We should promote it because it helps maximize utility. It serves the social good.

Utilitarians would go on to argue that while justice is *usually* a good thing, it is not *always* a good thing. In fact, it is not a good thing if it irresolvably conflicts with social utility. In an emergency, for example, we sometimes cut corners—even violate some people's rights—for the sake of saving greater social goods. Mill again:

> [C]ases may occur in which some other social duty is so important as to overrule . . . the general maxims of justice. Thus, to save a life, it may not only be

allowable, but a duty, to steal or take by force the necessary food or medicine, or to kidnap and compel to officiate the only qualified medical practitioner.

So even stealing or kidnapping doctors might be morally acceptable, or even a duty, in a pinch! Strong stuff—but not necessarily implausible, and perfectly natural if you are a utilitarian. In a system where utility rules, every other value must eventually pass utility's muster.

Utilitarians would say the same of the virtues. No character trait, they argue, is simply good by itself. Rather, good traits are good because they promote utility. Take honesty, for example. It might seem that dishonesty often has major benefits. Little (or not so little) deceptions can keep you ahead of the crowd and out of trouble. But deception also has costs and dangers. It takes a lot of work. It's emotionally draining to have your guard up all the time. Besides, when the deceptions fail, as they often will, you may lose your friends. Thus, arguably, dishonesty is a bad idea, even on utilitarian grounds. It is not a matter of benefits to you being trumped by some more abstract kind of value, but simply of thinking more carefully about the tangible costs in the long run.

Some people think that no deception can ever be ethical and propose to tell the truth even to criminals who threaten you and to children too young to understand. But it is not at all clear that this kind of "hyper-truthfulness" has positive overall effects. Surely, at least in this case, most of us will say that here is where the value of honesty ends: when it really does have bad consequences, all things considered. Here, in short, the utilitarian "single measure" becomes the *judge* of other values. Those moral values that don't "cash out" in terms of utility are not really moral values after all.

DOES UTILITARIANISM GO TOO FAR?

As you might imagine, though, these utilitarian moves are controversial. Critics argue that while utility and utilitarian considerations are indeed important, they cannot be the whole story.

First of all, is it really true that justice, say, is only good so far as it serves social utility? Certainly our legal system doesn't think so. Everyone is entitled to a fair trial and to be presumed innocent, even though he or she may turn out to be guilty. It might be much more satisfying, not to mention cheaper, simply to put away a whole class of criminal suspects without any trial at all. Yet we will not stand for it. Ethically as well as legally, it is not *right*—not just, not fair, not respectful of persons.

Utilitarians do try to defend many important rights. Rights to free speech, liberty, and all the rest serve social utility. They maximize the general happiness—usually. When they don't, though, utilitarians can only conclude that there are no such rights. Mill, again, even endorses kidnapping doctors under some (extreme) circumstances. But what good is a utilitarian kind of "right," critics say, if the moment social needs conflict with them, utilitarianism no longer stands behind them? The whole point of rights is to stop this kind of thinking—taking a person as a mere means to some social good—dead in its tracks.

We may be no happier with utilitarianism's treatment of the virtues. Can pleasure (or "utility" in *any* guise) really be the ethical bottom line? Aren't some pleasures just wrong, however pleasurable they may be? And not wrong because they lead to greater displeasure somewhere down the line, but just plain *wrong*—wrong because we should not take pleasure from such things in the first place.

Mill vacillated on this point, speaking at times of "higher" and "lower" pleasures. "Higher" pleasures are supposed to be better—worthier of human beings. "It is better to be a human being dissatisfied than a pig satisfied; better to be Socrates dissatisfied than a fool satisfied." But it is not at all clear why. If pleasure alone is the good, how can one of two equally pleasurable pleasures still be "better"? It appears that Mill himself wants to introduce some nonutilitarian factors into the mix—a sensible move, for sure, but no credit to utilitarianism.

THE PROBLEM OF MEASUREMENT

If utility is to be the single measure of values, it must also, obviously, be a *measure* of values. It must offer a usable and concretely applicable way to think. Some critics of utilitarianism argue, however, that "happiness" and "utility" are such vague terms that we cannot really "measure" or "weigh" the relative utilities of different courses of action. Seldom am I even sure about what would make *me* happiest, for instance, let alone other people—or how to compare my happiness to theirs, or even my own specific happinesses to each other. Meanwhile, the ripple effects of even the simplest act are almost incalculable, all the more so if it affects large numbers of people.

Should I spend my vacation at the beach or helping build houses with Habitat for Humanity? I would probably enjoy the beach more, though I do like to build and to help out too. Building houses would help make the future occupants happier, though the houses will get built anyway, just about as well whether I am there or not. Is there any precise way to weigh a sharp and immediate pleasure for me—one person—against the smaller and less definite contribution I might make to the quite different and longer-term happiness of others? And even this is barely the beginning. If I go on the Habitat trip, someone else will not go: perhaps the trip would be better for them than for me? Or maybe *they* would up the total happiness more by going to the beach? (Or somewhere else?) Who are they, anyway? And how do I weigh in the possible benefits to others (my students, say, or my family) from my being somewhat better rested after the beach? What about my long-run contribution to beach erosion and the commercial overdevelopment of fragile coast ecologies?

Despite its appearance of hardheaded practicality then, utilitarianism may actually be useless, or worse, as a practical way to make decisions. What really happens in such cases, critics worry, is that utilitarian language lends itself too readily to offhand self-justification. Whatever I do, I can justify myself by pointing to the happiness I (might) produce or costs I (might) avoid. Just this accusation has been leveled against the monetary calculation of "costs" and "benefits," for example, as in the dam project. All the numbers look very rational and impartial and responsible, but underneath it's all really guess-work, say the critics, dressed up to justify whatever the decision maker is inclined to do anyway.

CONCLUSIONS

You can see that these are controversial matters. My proposed conclusion—itself debatable, of course!—is that utilitarianism is a limited tool. It system-atizes *some* of our moral values and can help resolve *some* conflicts of moral values, especially conflicts between fairly specific utilities. These are genuine and important uses.

Utilitarianism also has some edgy implications very much worth explor-ing, such as serious consideration for other animals, whose pains and suffer-ings are sometimes as great or greater than ours but who have traditionally been ignored in ethical thinking entirely. Some modern utilitarians campaign strongly for "animal liberation." Other implications may also be radical. Jer-emy Bentham, as I've mentioned, was best known as a prison and criminal law reformer, and one could argue, as Russell does, that we still have not learned his lessons. From a utilitarian point of view, the point of punish-ment is not to exact revenge or retribution somehow, but to serve the social good, which seems to suggest a more restorative and less punitive approach to crime than we continue to practice today.

Still, arguably, utilitarianism is not the whole story, or even close. There are many other moral values that need to be understood in their own rights, as we have tried to do with the values of the person and will continue in the next two chapters. Much as we might want everything simple and neat, the moral world may not cooperate. And perhaps we should even be glad of that.

FOR REVIEW

1. How could it be argued that pleasure or happiness is our ultimate goal?
2. What exactly *is* happiness, in the utilitarian view?

3. What is "flow"? How does it relate to happiness?

4. How does utilitarianism become an ethic?

5. Who were Jeremy Bentham and John Stuart Mill?

6. What is "the harm that good men do"?

7. How do utilitarians argue that utility is the single measure of all values?

8. Why do critics argue that there is no single measure of all values?

9. What are some important uses of utilitarian thinking, according to the text?

10. What are some important limits of utilitarian thinking, according to the text?

EXERCISES AND NOTES

6.1 IS HAPPINESS OUR FINAL GOAL?

Hedonists believe that pleasure or happiness is the chief and indeed only ultimate human end. How might they deal with people who pretty clearly seek
something other than happiness, or even seek things that are guaranteed to
produce *un*happiness: people who give their lives in battle, say, or willingly
undergo great suffering to achieve something magnificent or uncertain? You
could stretch and say that in some metaphysical or unusual sense they're
"happy," but this is not true, really, if they're in great pain, or never see the
fruits of their labors, or die in the pursuit. Yet these may still be morally admirable things to do.

Even without a moral mission we sometimes seek things that are guaranteed to produce unhappiness. Indeed, if you look around the world today, you
do not find that people in general are very happy. Wealthy countries seem to
be even less happy than poor ones. We are now spectacularly richer and more
technologically accomplished than anyone could even have dreamed for most of
human history, but at the same time suicide and depression are epidemic and
massive numbers of people need medication just to get through their day.

How can this be? Why do we so reliably produce our own unhappiness? Is
the answer that we really don't understand happiness? Or that we don't understand what we are doing? But how could *that* be? Happiness is supposed to be
our prime concern . . .

6.2 UTILITARIAN NIRVANA?

Suppose that it becomes possible to set up a grand virtual-reality "experience–
machine" that creates for you any kind of experience you choose. For the rest

of your life you could be plugged into a fantasy world, tailor-made to make you delirious with pleasure, riding the biggest surf in the world, or heroically saving the galaxy from evil invaders, or playing Rachmaninoff while conducting the New York Philharmonic from the keyboard, or whatever else your fantasy might be (filling in the blanks is a fun part). You'd never know that really you are just lying on a bed somewhere, kept alive by IV and a few doctors, your head wired to a monitor. *But what's the difference, if happiness is the only thing that counts?*

This is a famous philosophical thought experiment meant to challenge hedonistic utilitarianism. Like the questions just raised about unhappiness and the modern world, it is not merely hypothetical, either. Americans currently watch 250 billion hours of TV a year. (Yup! that's *250 billion*.) The average elementary-school child watches four hours a day. (And you?) Is this so very different? If this kind of experience-machine makes you uneasy, shouldn't TV make you uneasy too? If you say in either case that we ought not to be settling for such paltry substitutes for the real world, what kinds of moral values are you appealing to?

6.3 MORE QUESTIONS

Can utilitarianism take better account of justice and fairness? How? Should it try? What do you think of Mill's endorsement of kidnapping doctors? Are there any real-world analogues to this? How about torturing someone to extract information that might save a lot of lives?

On the utilitarian view, the pleasures of a sadist are not bad in themselves. No pleasure can be bad in itself, remember, since pleasure just *is* the good. Rather, as with everything else on the utilitarian view, the pleasures of the sadist are supposed to be bad because of their effects: more unhappiness for other people than the sadist gains for himself or herself. So, could sadistic pleasure be OK (in fact, be *good*) if no one else were harmed by it (for example, if it were only "virtual," with no likelihood of spilling over into actual harm to others)?

Or, what if a sadist had an enormous capacity for pleasure, so that his or her pleasures actually exceeded the suffering of all those who were harmed? Would sadism be a good thing then? Is this what utilitarianism implies? Ought we be able to criticize some pleasures or happinesses themselves?

A further problem, illustrated by this last case, is the problem hinted at in the text with Bentham's formula of the "Greatest good of the greatest number." Utilitarianism wants to promote the greatest net happiness in society as a whole, but it does not follow that this happiness must be equitably distributed, so that the "greatest good" could only come from happiness being as widely shared as possible (i.e., distributed to the "greatest number"). The greatest good might also come from making a few people *very* much happier while causing harm to the greater number, but just enough less harm in total that there is still a net gain overall. This would be troubling from the point of view of justice, to say the least.

The last exercise in Chapter 6 raised the question of animals in the context of the Ethics of the Person. How do you think utilitarianism might address the same question? Some hints: first, consider the question of who or what kind of beings utilitarian ethics applies to, and why. Then consider the question of animal pain and suffering, which of course is front and center in utilitarian ethics. (There is a relevant discussion of moral vegetarianism in chapter 16, by the way.) Finally, consider some implications and complications. If animals count, or some animals count, under utilitarianism, must they or should they count in the same way as humans? To the same extent? Why or why not?

NOTES

Bertrand Russell's essay "The Harm That Good Men Do" is excerpted from a longer piece of the same title in his book *Sceptical Essays* (Unwin Paperbacks, 1977), pp. 84–92. One note: Russell's remark about "good" men "preventing an ill-judged respect for learning from allowing the employment of professors with subversive ideas" is not just ironic: it refers to an incident in his own life. A world-renowned scholar by 1940, Russell was offered a professorship by the City College of New York only to have the offer rescinded after a massive, politically orchestrated outcry against him because he was something of a sexual freethinker for his time—supporting trial marriage, for example. Such things no longer happen, of course.

The Australian philosopher Peter Singer is today's most prominent utilitarian; you'll meet him momentarily in the "Using Your Tools" exercise to follow. A readable and provocative application of utilitarianism to a range of contemporary issues is his *Practical Ethics* (3rd edition, Cambridge University Press, 2011). On animals specifically, see also his *Animal Liberation* (many editions).

The "Ethics Updates" website has a wide range of links to utilitarian texts and other philosophical resources: go to http://ethics.sandiego.edu/theories and then to the "Utilitarianism" link. Dan Brock's essay "Utilitarianism," in Tom Regan and Don Vandeveer, eds., *And Justice for All: New Introductory Essays in Philosophy and Public Policy* (Rowman and Allenheld, 1982), is an excellent though dense guide to philosophical utilitarianism as well as some of the critical issues hinted at here. Classic is J. J. C. Smart and Bernard Williams's little book *Utilitarianism: For and Against* (Cambridge University Press, 1983.)

USING YOUR TOOLS #3
A UTILITARIAN APPROACH TO POVERTY

The Australian philosopher Peter Singer is today's best-known and most controversial utilitarian. His application of utilitarianism to the question of our relation to animals, in his book *Animal Liberation,* originally published in 1975, is considered one of the touchstones of the modern "animal rights" movement (though like all utilitarians, he does not argue for rights per se). He has also written widely and controversially on many bioethical topics.

Singer also brings utilitarianism to bear on the question of world poverty. In several academic essays and books, along with a widely read *New York Times Magazine* piece called "The Singer Solution to World Poverty," he argues that the solution is quite simple, though also, it seems, radical. It is for well-off people to give large portions of their income to provide for the basic needs of poor people around the world. Singer backs up this claim with a moral argument that is also extremely simple—but, it seems, irresistible.

Most of us in well-off countries spend large chunks of our incomes on things that we do not really need: regularly eating expensive restaurant food, for example, rather than perfectly nutritious but simple and inexpensive fare. For millions of people in the world, however—including millions of children, just to make the picture sharper—even a tiny fraction of that money could make the difference between life and death. Any plausible ethic, Singer would say, and certainly and obviously utilitarianism, must conclude that we should give as much as we can of our income to help alleviate world hunger and readily treated diseases that kill or disable millions of children a year in other parts of the world.

Singer is incontestably right about the data. Right now the average American family spends at least a third of its income on relatively indulgent things like eating out, buying new clothes or shoes, or even cars, just because the old ones have gone out of style, and taking vacations in distant and luxurious places, or driving to Disneyland or the Yellowstone in the summers. These things, necessary as they may get to seem to us, look like "needs" only to the affluent. Most of the world's population gets on quite well without them. Many would consider them unimaginable luxuries. Depending on what you count as necessities, the proportion of income spent on non-necessities could actually be considered much higher. It's clear in any case, though, that much of our income is spent on things not essential to the preservation of our lives and health.

Others, meantime, are in desperate need. According to Oxfam International (http://www.oxfamamerica.org/whatyoucando/donate, accessed 12/22/11), 840 million people go hungry each year. Over a billion people live on less than $1 a day. Twelve million people die each year just from a lack of water. Over 30,000 children under the age of five die *each day* due to hunger and other preventable causes.

For people in such straits, aid of even a few dollars might mean the difference between life and death. The simplest food would be enough—the sort of thing you'd never see in a fancy restaurant, unadorned and sparse perhaps, but sufficient for the revival of strength and work for a better day. Medicines—the simplest and cheapest of antibiotics or water purification, for example, which for pennies per child could eliminate the diarrhea that kills two million children in the developing world every year. Education—basic female literacy, for starters, at the cost of a few teachers and teaching materials, the single most significant factor in empowering women, reducing birth rates, and promoting economic growth in poor countries.

It is clear to utilitarians—and surely, not just to them—that this is a morally unjustifiable situation. The same money that keeps us stylish or entertained or expensively fed, often with little or no gain to our real well-being, could do vastly more good if given instead to charities that aid the poor in developing countries as well as here at home. No elaborate or exact scale is needed to see this. It's life or death on one hand, and only passing pleasure, at best, on the other hand—on ours. Therefore, we are morally obliged to give a large portion of our income to provide basic goods to people around the world who desperately need them.

THE CASE OF BOB'S BUGATTI

Singer draws on another utilitarian philosopher, Peter Unger, to lay out several analogies that help make the logic of the argument clear. One is the case of a man named Bob and his rare and precious old car. Imagine that Bob is almost ready to retire, and he has invested his entire savings in a very valuable antique car—a Bugatti. Unfortunately he has not been able to insure it, but he tends to it very carefully. He loves driving and caring for the Bugatti, and he also knows that he will always be able to sell the car in the future, should he need to, and live very well on the proceeds.

One day, however, when Bob is out for a drive,

> he parks the Bugatti near the end of a railway siding and goes for a walk up the track. As he does so, he sees that a runaway train, with no one aboard, is running down the railway track. Looking farther down the track, he sees the small figure of a child very likely to be killed by the runaway train. He can't stop the train and the child is too far away to warn of the danger, but he can throw a switch that will divert the train down the siding where his Bugatti is parked. Then nobody will be killed —but the train will destroy his Bugatti. Thinking of his joy in owning the car and the financial security it represents, Bob decides not to throw the switch. The child is killed. For many years to come, Bob enjoys owning his Bugatti and the financial security it represents.

So what do you think of Bob's action? What would you have done in his situation? Most of us, Singer suggests, would consider that what Bob did was wrong. Most of us would think we should throw the switch. To say this we need not deny in any way that there is a real loss to Bob—emotional as well as financial—in the destruction of his car. But between a car, however precious, and a child's life, there is no comparison. This is true even though the child's being on the track is no fault of Bob's—likely he does not know the kid at all—and even if he took great pains to park his car safely. Whether anyone is to be blamed is not the question.

Unger and Singer argue that we—you and I and most everyone living in affluent countries today—are in exactly the same situation in regard to people in desperate need elsewhere in the world. Not to help them—not to "throw the switch" by sending money we can readily spare—is in effect to abandon them to miserable but preventable fates. In *effect*: remember, like good utilitarians, we are talking about the *consequences* of action or inaction, not about intentions or blame or anything else the least bit morally fancy. The point is simply that we can make the world dramatically better for many other people at a comparatively minor cost to ourselves. Therefore, we should.

OBJECTIONS

It's not like we don't know, or couldn't readily figure out, where to send the money, should that be anyone's worry. I will even follow Singer and Unger's lead and give you some options right now. To "throw the switch," you can get out your credit card right now and go to https://secure.oxfamamerica.org/site/SPageServer?pagename=main_donate_go (for Oxfam; or call 1–800–77–OXFAM) or http://www.supportunicef.org/site/c.dvKUI9OWInJ6H/b.7677883/k.2C8F/Donate_now.htm (for UNICEF; or call 1–800–FOR–KIDS). Or look up your local soup kitchen or homeless shelter. One or two phone calls and you will have, alas, plenty of options. The problem cannot be that we just don't know what to do.

Other worries may come up. It may be objected, for example, that we don't know for sure that money donated to charitable organizations will actually end up feeding or helping people. This is a legitimate concern, for sure. But surely it doesn't justify doing or giving nothing at all. It is not hard to research the available options and find out which do the best by the intended recipients. Seriously: this is not a real obstacle for people who are very used to searching the Web to look into user feedback on competing products or to research political issues. If nothing else, just give to Oxfam or UNICEF, as noted, which are reliably among the best. Besides, even if there are some inefficiencies, at least some aid will get through. Which is way better than none at all.

Singer considers some other likely objections. It is true, for example, that every affluent person, including those far more affluent than you or me, has the same obligation (barring those situations where every dollar really is needed for basic survival). If everyone who has the same obligation contributed their fair (perhaps, proportional?) share, though, then your obligation and mine would probably be much lower. So why should we contribute more than our "fair shares"? Moreover, it could be argued that affluent people ought to contribute collectively through governmental aid, which is funded more equitably, at least in theory, through taxes.

The fact is, however, that other people, right now at least, are *not* stepping up to do their part. However unfortunate or unfair it might be, that is part of the scene too. There is still the question of how we—those of us who are trying to think about the situation morally and do the right thing—should respond to real needs that are not, for whatever reason, being met.

Suppose Bob were at the siding with a dozen other Bugatti owners, say—maybe they are holding a little Bugatti show in the railroad yard—and any of the others could also throw the switch and take out his or her car instead of Bob's. But none of them do. Is Bob thereby excused? Again, if you were Bob, what would you do? Of course it isn't fair, but why are we arguing about fairness at a time like this?

Certainly there is a good case for increasing foreign aid, too. Organized and sustained by governments, the aid could be more reliably and widely delivered, and the costs shared proportionally by all. That too, a utilitarian could argue, is an ethical imperative. At the moment, however, such foreign aid is miniscule compared to the need, and also (despite some persistent misconceptions) miniscule relative to the resources of affluent countries like the United States. The U.S. contribution to global food and health aid, for instance, does not even meet the very modest United Nations recommended target of 0.7 percent of Gross National Product. Currently our rate is 0.09 percent—a tiny 135th of our military budget—not even half of Japan's 0.22 percent or a tenth of Denmark's 0.97 percent.

Thus, just as we cannot count on other individuals, situated as we are, to do their parts, neither can we count on our government to step up to the task, at least as things stand today. Presumably the argument therefore also requires that we get involved politically to try to change American budget priority in the future. In the meantime, however, the need remains, as does our individual capacity to address it directly.

Singer does not deny that morality asks of us a sacrifice of sorts here. We all could live more luxuriously and conveniently if we spent that money on ourselves or our families. There are genuine pleasures we will have to forgo. The analogy to Bob and his Bugatti is carefully constructed: Bob too pays a price. But if the moral life can be tough, Singer says, that is just the way things are. We should be thankful that we somehow lucked into being on the giving end instead of on the needy end—since from the moral point of view it could just as easily have been the other way around.

Nor is anything particularly imposing really being asked of us—certainly nothing like the costs potential recipients are suffering now. A used car, kept longer, rather than a new one, will get us around just as well. Not dropping $50 or $100 for a restaurant meal will not kill us. Singer is not even requiring any particular percentage of "tithe." He himself now gives about one quarter of his income to famine-relief agencies, a level he says he hopes to increase still further, but the amount will vary with different people's situations. The question to all of us is how much we truly need, not how little we can get away with giving or whether some preset amount is enough. Singer reports that from the first time he saw appeals in the newspapers or on TV to help starving people, he wondered why people were asked to donate so very little. Why indeed.

EVALUATING THE ARGUMENT

To "Use Your Tools," as students of ethics and readers of this book, your first challenge is to make sure you understand Singer's argument. The case is not necessarily just utilitarian, but for our purposes you might concentrate on the utilitarian basics. (Part of the strength of Singer's argument, indeed, is that the very basics are all he thinks we need.) To be sure you have it right, write Singer's main argument over in your own words. Try to put it as clearly and simply as possible. You might even try it out on a few people to be sure you have succeeded—and take note of their reactions.

Once you have outlined and understood Singer's argument, your task is to analyze and evaluate it. What do you think are the likely objections to it? How do you think Singer would respond?

As you consider objections, keep in mind the families of values we have been reviewing. Some objections will likely be from a utilitarian point of view: that is, they will share Singer's starting point. Is it true, for example, that giving away substantial chunks of our income will have the strongly positive net benefits Singer projects? Why or why not?

Are they the best possible consequences achievable with that money? (If they aren't, according to you, what would be? Shouldn't we therefore give substantial amounts of money for *those* purposes, then?)

Or might the problems with Singer's argument (if there are such) trace back to utilitarianism itself? Traditionally it is the Ethics of the Person that stands most clearly in opposition to utilitarian thinking. Utilitarianism, as we've seen, makes a somewhat conditional defense of rights, for example. Perhaps we have *rights* to do with our income as we please, even if the consequences of not doing something else with it are very bad for some other people. What would it take to work out this response? (You might also check out the critical literature in response to Singer.)

On the other hand, is Singer denying this? He's not for *forcing* people to make such major donations, is he? Though there could be a question of taxes. . . .

Then again, maybe the Ethics of the Person could also make a case, even as strong a case as Singer's, for donating money to help save others' lives. Maybe those others are the ones with the really pressing or relevant rights. Or maybe it is not really a question of rights at all, but of respect for persons understood in a somewhat different way. Don't assume, anyway, that a case against utilitarianism disposes of Singer's challenge: it may recur from the point of view of other families of values as well.

Consider setting up a symposium or some other whole-class ways of bringing your thoughts to your classmates and working them through together. Remember that your task is still exploratory. You don't have to come up with some final and ironclad view about these questions. On the other hand, they are not just abstract, either. There are many ways to help others in need, right around us and right now, and it certainly would not hurt to make it part of your questioning, whatever you conclude, to ask how you might find at least some immediate and unobjectionable ways to do so, on whatever scale you think appropriate.

NOTE

For Singer's full argument, see his book *The Life You Can Save: Acting Now to End World Poverty* (Random House, 2009), and for more of his writings in general, see *http://www.utilitarian.net/singer/*). See also the FAQ page of his website. Full text of "The Singer Solution to World Poverty" can be found online at http://www.utilitarian.net/singer/by/19990905.htm.

CHAPTER 7

The Ethics of Virtue

Chapter 4 outlined the family of virtue-centered values like this:

VIRTUE

The Ethics of Virtue encompasses those moral values concerned with *character*: with traits like self-discipline, responsibility, honesty, charity, loyalty, devotion. Christendom's great virtues are faith, hope, charity, prudence, justice, temperance, and fortitude. In the Eastern traditions, other virtues come to the fore: tranquillity, non-attachment, compassion, truthful speech and thought, "right livelihood," and nonviolence.

Let us now explore the Ethics of Virtue in more detail.

AN ABUNDANCE OF VIRTUES

Character traits are specific and varied. The usual lists of moral virtues therefore tend to be long and lovingly detailed. For starters, here are eighty (!) or so:

acceptance, altruism, appreciation, autonomy, awareness, charity, chastity, cleanliness, compassion, continence (i.e., sexual self-discipline), cooperation, courage, courtesy, creativity, dependability, diligence, discipline, empathy, endurance, enthusiasm, fairness, faith, fidelity, foresight, forgiveness, fortitude, freedom, friendship, generosity, helpfulness, honesty, honor, hope, hospitality, humility, humor, idealism, imagination, independence, innocence, integrity, kindness, knowledge, love, loyalty, mercy, moderation, manners, modesty, nonviolence, nurturance, obedience, openness, optimism, patience, peacefulness, perseverance, piety, prudence, purpose, respect, social responsibility, restraint, sacrifice, self-awareness, self-discipline, self-esteem, self-reliance, sensitivity, sharing, sincerity, spirituality, sympathy, tact, temperance, tolerance, trustworthiness, truthfulness, understanding, wisdom . . .

Even this list is far from complete. On other lists you find lightheartedness, neighborliness, valor, liberality. My mother would insist that I add politeness. The familiar "work ethic" is primarily a system of virtues: hard work, frugality, persistence, self-reliance, thrift, industriousness, dependability. Eastern moralists stress tranquillity, nonattachment, compassion. People speak of still other virtues in specific contexts, in business or sports, for example. And the list changes over time, as societies evolve and understandings shift.

Any particular item on these lists may also be contested. Not every society affirms every single one of them as moral virtues or even as virtues at all. You yourself may have doubts about some of them. Still, they are all at least recognizable. Even when specific virtues conflict, as they sometimes do—obedience versus independence, empathy versus fairness, humor versus sensitivity—we do not feel the need to reject one or the other. It's just that another virtue is *balance*: finding good ways to keep them all in play.

CLASSIFICATIONS

Are some virtues more basic than others? The classical Greeks emphasized four basic virtues: temperance, prudence, courage, and justice. When Greek philosophy was Christianized, three "theological" virtues were added: faith, hope, and charity, getting us to medieval Catholicism's key seven: faith, hope, charity, prudence, justice, temperance, and fortitude.

Among moderns, Joseph Pieper categorizes Western virtues into three general categories: virtues of *self-control*, such as temperance and other forms of self-restraint and self-redirection; virtues of *self-efficacy*, such as persistence and courage; and virtues of *regard*, such as justice and fairness. William Bennett, former U.S. Secretary of Education and advocate of character education, lists ten key virtues, under which he argues many others fall: self-discipline, compassion, responsibility, friendship, work, courage, perseverance, honesty, loyalty, and faith.

Opposite the virtues stand the vices. Medieval Catholicism's Seven Deadly Sins are pride, wrath, envy, lust, gluttony, avarice, and sloth. Note these are not the exact reverses of the key virtues, though there are lists that emphasize parallels: temperance opposite gluttony, humility opposite pride, service opposite avarice. I have seen yet other traits listed as vices, more modern and secular: gracelessness, insensitivity, discontent, insatiability, willful ignorance or denial, crudeness, bad temper, even discouragement.

Christian moral tradition distinguishes two basic kinds of vice: those we owe to the body, such as lust, and those that are spiritual perversities, like blasphemy or pride, which are seen as false idolatries. False idolatries are supposed to be much worse than merely perverse instincts—although they too are sinful. Pride was supposed to be the worst of all. Essentially a kind of idolatry of the self, pride was thought to bring the worst evils into being.

DO WE NEED A THEORY OF THE VIRTUES?

Notice that we have moved from lists of virtues to questions about their inter-relationships and classifications. There are still other such questions, leading us to look for something like—yes—a *theory* of virtue.

One question is: is everything considered a virtue really so? After all, we have been looking not only at long lists of possible virtues, but at a conglomeration of virtues from many different historical times and social contexts. All manner of outdated customs, prejudices, even accidents, are probably implicated. Etymologically the term "virtue" itself comes from the Latin *vir*, meaning "man" and suggesting, originally, the supposedly manly warlike virtues like courage and martial valor. By the Middle Ages it most often referred to a woman's chastity: that is, sexual self-restraint. Especially on sexual and gender matters, the traditional Western virtue framework seems to be rife with double standards and dubious valuations. Critical reconsideration might be a good idea.

This leads to a deeper question: what *makes* something a virtue? In practice, we seem to be tempted simply to declare that certain things are virtues and then enthusiastically start listing them. There seems to be much less reflection on *why* some character trait is a virtue in the first place, that is, about what makes a virtue a virtue (and a vice a vice). How do we really tell which are which?

You know how utilitarians would answer. A character trait is a virtue, they'd say, if it makes people happier on the whole and in the long run—if it serves the greatest good of the greatest number.

There is surely something to this. It might even be true that, on the whole, virtue does promote happiness and vice causes misery. On the other hand, even if the virtues do make us happier and vices unhappier, that may not be the *reason* that they are virtues or vices. The virtues' advocates would say that the virtues are the kinds of character traits that we *ought* to seek and to sustain, maybe because they flow from something very deep in human nature, or because they meet certain legitimate expectations—perhaps of others, perhaps even of God's. If so, then the real relation between virtue and happiness may be the other way around: maybe the virtues make us happy because they are virtues, rather than being virtues because they make us happy.

Something more may be going on. We have a genuinely different set of values here. There may be more of a story to tell.

A GREEK VIEW OF VIRTUE ₊Western ＊

The most influential Western theory of the virtues comes from the Greek philosopher Aristotle (384–322 BCE).

Everything in the world, according to Aristotle, has a distinctive and essential function or activity. Trees grow in certain ways depending on their kinds; buildings are made for certain purposes; human artisans have their particular arts. And in Aristotle's view, this function or activity in turn determines admirable or "excellent" characteristics or traits—that is, virtues.

"For all things that have a function or activity," Aristotle writes, "the good and the 'well' [as in: doing a job well] is thought to reside in the function." Good carpenters, for example, are those who build sturdy and beautiful things. Therefore virtue in carpenters is an eye for proportion, skill with saw and plane, a feel for what a piece of wood can and cannot do, and so on.

Similarly, there must be a characteristic or set of characteristics that defines *our* essence—the human "function," as Aristotle also puts it:

> For just as for a flute player, a sculptor, or any artist, and, in general, for all things that have a function or activity, the good and the "well" is thought to reside in the function, so it would seem to be for man, if he has a function.

According to Aristotle, rational self-regulation is the characteristic activity and therefore "function" of humans. We are, in his famous definition, *rational animals*. What Aristotle means by "rational," though, is quite different from what Kant meant by the same word, 2,000 or so years later. For Aristotle, reason means the ability—the habits and the wisdom and the judgment—that enables us to bring a complex self into order as it unfolds. This vision of balanced self-actualization Aristotle even calls "happiness"—but notice that it is a rather different conception than the utilitarians'.

This essentially human function and activity in turn therefore determines morally admirable or "excellent" characteristics or traits for us—in short, moral virtues. For example, one key activity of practical reason is to find the "mean"—the appropriate middle—between extremes of emotion or action. In responding to danger we may feel either fear or confidence, leading to two opposite failings: either cowardice (too much fear, too little confidence) or foolhardiness (too much confidence, too little fear). We need to find the appropriate, rational middle—and this is the virtue, says Aristotle, of courage. The vices, on this view, are the *excesses* (too much) or the *defects* (too little): that is, going to the extreme—either extreme—rather than following the middle path of moderation.

Likewise, between excessive self-indulgence or profligacy on one hand and self-denial on the other lies the mean of temperance. Between the defect of miserliness and the excess of prodigality lies the mean or virtue Aristotle calls "liberality." Between vanity on the one hand and undue humility on the other lies the virtue he calls "high-mindness." Even a sense of humor is a virtue on this view—the mean between being foolish and being a bore.

READING

From Nicomachean Ethics

ARISTOTLE

If, then, there is some end of the things we do, which we desire for its own sake (everything else being desired for the sake of this), and if we do not choose everything for the sake of something else (for at that rate the process would go on to infinity, so that our desire would be empty and vain), clearly this must be the good and the chief good. Will not the knowledge of it, then, have a great influence on life? Shall we not, like archers who have a mark to aim at, be more likely to hit upon what is right? If so, we must try in outline at least to determine what it is, and of which of the sciences or capacities it is the object. . . .

Verbally there is very general agreement, for both the general run of men and people of superior refinement say that it is happiness, and identify living well and doing well with being happy, but with regard to what happiness is they differ, and the many do not give the same account as the wise. For the former think it is some plain and obvious thing, like pleasure, wealth, or honor; they differ, however, from one another—and often even the same man identifies it with different things, with health when he is ill, and wealth when he is poor, but, conscious of their ignorance, they admire those who proclaim some great ideal that is above their comprehension. . . .

Presumably, however, to say that happiness is the chief good seems a platitude, and a clearer account of what it is is still desired. This might perhaps be given, if we could first ascertain the function of man. For just as for a flute player, a sculptor, or any artist, and, in general, for all things that have a function or activity, the good and the "well" is thought to reside in the function, so would it seem to be for man, if he has a function. Have the carpenter, then, and the tanner certain functions or activities, and has man none? Is he born without a function? Or as eye, hand, foot, and in general each of the parts evidently has a function, may one lay it down that man similarly has a function apart from all these? What then can this be?

Life seems to be common even to plants, but we are seeking what is peculiar to man. Let us exclude, therefore, the life of nutrition and growth. Next there would be a life of perception, but it also seems to be common even to the horse, the ox, and every animal.

From Aristotle, *Nicomachean Ethics*, translated by W. D. Ross, Book I, 1097b23–1098a19.

There remains, then, an active life of the element that has a rational principle; of this, one part has such a principle in the sense of being obedient to one, the other in the sense of possessing one and exercising thought. And, as "life of the rational element" also has two meanings, we must state that life in the sense of activity is what we mean; for this seems to be the more proper sense of the term.

Now if the function of man is an activity of soul which follows or implies a rational principle, and if we say "a so-and-so" and "a good so-and-so" have a function which is the same in kind, for example, a lyre player and a good lyre player, and so without qualification in all cases, eminence in respect of goodness being added to the name of the function (for the function of a lyre player is to play the lyre, and that of a good lyre player is to do so well): if this is the case, [and we state the function of man to be a certain kind of life, and this to be an activity or actions of the soul implying a rational principle, and the function of a good man to be the good and noble performance of these, and if any action is well performed when it is performed in accordance with the appropriate excellence: if this is the case,] human good turns out to be activity of soul in accordance with virtue, and if there are more than one virtue, in accordance with the best and most complete.

But we must add "in a complete life." For one swallow does not make a summer, nor does one day; and so too one day, or a short time, does not make a man blessed and happy. . . .

We must . . . not only describe [moral] virtue as a state of character, but also say what sort of state it is. We may remark, then, that every virtue or excellence both brings into good condition the thing of which it is the excellence and makes the work of that thing be done well; e.g., the excellence of the eye makes both the eye and its work good; for it is by the excellence of the eye that we see well. Similarly the excellence of the horse makes a horse both good in itself and good at running and at carrying its rider and at awaiting the attack of the enemy.

Therefore, if this is true in every case, the virtue of man also will be the state of character which makes a man good and which makes him do his own work well . . .

If reason is divine, then, in comparison with man, the life according to it is divine in comparison with human life. But we must not follow those who advise us, being men, to think of human things, and, being mortal, of mortal things, but must, so far as we can, make ourselves immortal, and strain every nerve to live in accordance with the best thing in us; for even if it be small in bulk, much more does it in power and worth surpass everything. This would seem, too, to be each man himself, since it is the authoritative and better part of him. It would be strange, then, if he were to choose not the life of his self but that of something else. And what we said before will apply now; that which is proper to each thing is by nature best and most pleasant for each thing; for man, therefore, the life according to reason is best and pleasantest, since reason more than anything else *is* man. This life therefore is also the happiest.

AQUINAS ON THE VIRTUES

Aristotle deeply influenced medieval Christian thinkers such as Saint Thomas Aquinas (1224–1274). Aquinas borrowed Aristotle's "logic of virtue," so to speak—deriving virtue from our essential activity or function—but understood our essential activity or function in very different terms. In particular, reason is not an end in itself, for Aquinas, but instead a means to better knowing ourselves and God. Our ultimate purpose he supposes to be communion with God, as far as we can achieve it in this life.

Here we begin to see the underlying rationale for the Christian systems of virtue so prominent in the lists like the key, or "cardinal," virtues given earlier. It was Aquinas who added the "theological" virtues of faith, hope, and charity to the older Greek, or "natural," virtues like justice and temperance. Those Greek virtues were also expanded. Temperance, for example, came to include humility, patience, and chastity. All of them are now conceived as character traits essential to drawing and staying as close to God as we can in this life.

The Seven Deadly Sins, meanwhile, were those traits considered fatal to that same spiritual quest. Pride, lust, avarice, and all the rest: to fall into these pits was a sure way of allowing yourself to be pulled away from God, and thus to fail not only to meet God's legitimate expectations but also to fail as a human being: to fall away from our own deepest and most essential possibilities and nature.

PROFESSIONAL ETHICS
ARISTOTELIAN VIRTUE ETHICS IN PRACTICE

Aristotle speaks of carpenters and tanners, whose work defines their goals and therefore their virtues *as* carpenters or tanners. Likewise for teachers and doctors and athletes and (why not?) car mechanics and computer programmers and even fund-raisers. Each of these professions or activities we entrust with important things; each of them therefore has a moral dimension; and for each of them, just as by now you'd expect, their moral dimension is determined by their specific function or goal—just as Aristotle proposes. Teachers enable and inform; doctors heal; athletes must "play fair"; and so on.

Here virtue is determined by what contemporary philosopher Alasdair MacIntyre calls "practices." Medicine, teaching, and so on are practices, like many other organized, cooperative activities—politics, child-raising, even games. Each of these activities or disciplines has its own "internal goods"—

goals that define the practice itself, such as health and life for medicine, justice for the law, and so on. Thus, technically, on MacIntyre's view, a virtue is

> an acquired human quality the possession and exercise of which tends to enable us to achieve those goods which are internal to practices and the lack of which effectively prevents us from achieving any such goods.

Devotion to the truth, for example, enables lawyers to seek justice. Cool-headedness enables chess masters to concentrate. Liveliness and imagination make a good teacher.

Consider medicine in a little more detail. Doctors' famous oath traces back to Hippocrates, a Greek physician of the fifth century BCE. The core of the Hippocratic Oath reads

> I will apply dietetic measures for the benefit of the sick according to my ability and judgement; I will keep them from harm and injustice.
>
> I will neither give a deadly drug to anybody if asked for it, nor will I make a suggestion to this effect. . . . In purity and holiness I will guard my life and my art.
>
> Whatever houses I may visit, I will come for the benefit of the sick. . . . What I may see or hear in the course of the treatment . . . which on no account one must spread abroad, I will keep to myself. . . .

There are more modern medical codes of ethics too. The Hippocratic Oath does not deal with questions of truthfulness, for example, but the American Medical Association (AMA) Principles of Medical Ethics requires that "A physician shall uphold the standards of professionalism, be honest in all professional interactions" and even "strive to report physicians deficient in character or competence." The International Council of Nurses Ethical Code as well as the Constitution of the World Health Organization require "respect for life . . . unrestricted by considerations of nationality, race, creed, age, sex, politics, or social status."

Many codes also oblige the medical professional to try to improve the profession, including "establish[ing] and maintain[ing] equitable social and economic working conditions" (International Council of Nurses), as well as contributing to the community at large. The AMA again: "A physician shall recognize a responsibility to participate in activities contributing to the improvement of the community and the betterment of public health."

These codes make explicit the virtues of a good doctor or nurse—and they begin to show us how these virtues flow from what MacIntyre would call the "internal goods" of medicine considered as a "practice." Medicine serves health—it is practiced "for the benefit of the sick"—therefore medical professionals must put their patients' health above all other goals, including the professional's own enjoyments or income, and even sometimes personal safety. The doctor must above all "do no harm." A doctor also enters a person's life at moments of great vulnerability—sickness and death—and is therefore legitimately expected to show the utmost respect for the patient and all of his family and household, including confidentiality. "What I may see or hear in the course of the treatment . . . I will keep to myself."

The Hippocratic Oath clearly has some outdated parts. Would-be Hippocratic doctors also promised not to do surgery (in Greek times that was another profession's work) or have sex with household slaves. Other parts are currently in contest: Hippocratic doctors also swear not to give "abortive remedies" or, as we just saw, "deadly drugs." Still, the oath remains in use—it still speaks to us—because it identifies the key virtues of medicine against the background of medicine's *function,* or medicine as a *practice.* Aristotle's and MacIntyre's logic is still at work.

Once you understand professional codes of ethics in this way, you can outline the virtues for almost any profession. Teachers nurture the young, open minds, inform and enable: hence teachers must be supportive, must not indoctrinate, should be accurate and clear, and so on. Airline pilots must remain alert at all times and keep themselves well-trained and ready. Same for truck drivers. Accountants must be objective, avoid conflicts of interest, and report clearly and accurately.

Or consider journalism. The aim of journalism is to inform people and by so doing to help promote democratic decision making. Therefore telling the truth is crucial. An attempt to present both (all) sides of a dispute is crucial too, especially when most of the established powers stand on one side. Careful distinction between news and "advocacy" allows people to make up their own minds.

> Members of the Society of Professional Journalists believe that public enlightenment is the forerunner of justice and the foundation of democracy. The duty of the journalist is to further those ends by seeking truth and providing a fair and comprehensive account of events and issues. . . .
>
> Journalists should be honest, fair, and courageous in gathering, reporting, and interpreting information. . . .

Again all of these are quite literally *virtues;* and again the proposed list of virtues is inferred directly from the "internal goods" of the profession.

CHINESE VIEWS OF VIRTUE ✗Eastern✗

On the other side of Eurasia from ancient Greece, at about the same time, three great philosophical and ethical systems were taking shape. All of these systems concentrate on the virtues as well.

CONFUCIAN VIRTUE: PROPRIETY AND PIETY

For the Chinese sage Confucius (551–479 BCE), the greatest virtue is humanity (*jen* or *ren,* variously translated as humaneness, kindheartedness, or benevolence). Associated virtues are just or appropriate action, ritual propriety (and not just going through the motions but truly seeing to the heart of the ritual), wisdom, loyalty, faithfulness, trustworthiness, courtesy, magnanimity, good faith, diligence, and piety.

On the Confucian view, these are all legitimate expectations deriving from *relationship*. Our task is not so much to live up to our own inner nature, as Aristotle thought, as to live up to the requirements of the relationships within which we find ourselves. We stand among the generations, for example: we are children to our parents and at the same time parents to our own children. More generally, we find ourselves among a variety of relationships, all with their histories and rituals and depth, and therefore associated virtues. We are citizen and ruler: here the prime virtue is righteousness. We are sibling among siblings: here the prime virtue is order. We are friend among friends: the prime virtue here is faithfulness. These virtues make possible a harmonious society—very unlike the constantly warring and fractured Chinese society of Confucius's time—and likewise a harmonious society allows us to cultivate the virtues.

Confucius spent his middle life traveling throughout China trying to persuade various rulers to put his ideas into effect. Unsuccessful in his lifetime (he eventually gave up and went home), he nevertheless would have been happy to know that a version of his ideas eventually became the official Chinese system, literally for millennia. Virtue was the essential—and at times the only—requirement for serving the Chinese state. It was Confucius's radical idea that heredity is not enough: even a high-born man can be but a "small man" without virtue. Contrariwise, any person who cultivates virtue or "humaneness" can become truly noble and worthy to lead.

BUDDHISM AND TAOISM

Buddhism was founded in India by Siddhartha Gautama (most likely fifth century BCE), also called "the Buddha," meaning "the Enlightened One." Buddhism flourished in India, spread to China and Japan, and reached the ancient Western world—Greece—as well.

What we call "self," the Buddha taught, is an imagined entity, not any kind of permanence but only a flux. We are different today than we were yesterday or will be tomorrow. In fact, to be attached to a supposedly permanent "I" only leads to suffering because change and eventually death are inevitable. Really we are just a part of the ceaseless becoming of the whole universe—a beautiful thing, too, but a fact that calls for awareness, acceptance, and adjustment, not resistance or dramatic gestures.

Here we begin to glimpse a very different view of the virtues—different both from the self-actualizing virtues of Aristotle and the society-centered virtues of Confucius. In a Buddhist view, the key virtues are traits like tranquillity, nonattachment, compassion, truthful speech and thought, "right livelihood" (which means finding a way to live that does not increase your own or others' suffering), and nonviolence. These are all ways of living in appropriate relationship with the world as it really is and of freeing ourselves from "craving." Desire in the Buddhist view is not so much the having of desires as it is the desire having *us*. We are invited instead to try not only to free ourselves from craving but also to free others as well.

Free from craving, Buddhists say, we can rejoin the world on its own terms. "To forget the Self is to be enlightened by all things," the Japanese Zen master Dogen wrote, and "To be enlightened by all things is to remove the barrier between the Self and Other." But how do we know what the world's terms actually are? The answer, especially for Taoism, is to look at the workings of *nature*—not the human world, which is usually a distraction and often a hyperstimulation of craving, but the workings of winds and streams, mountains and forests.

A prominent analogy in the *Tao Te Ching* is the working of water. To be virtuous, in fact, is to be very much like water: to be infinitely flexible and responsive, "going with the flow," a life based on spontaneity, simplicity, tranquillity, unselfishness, and humility. It is not, however, *weak*. The *Tao Te Ching* notes that though nothing in the world is as soft and yielding as water, "yet nothing can better overcome the hard and the strong."

> According to the book of Chuang-tzu, an old man is seen by some followers of Confucius swimming in a raging torrent; suddenly, he disappears. The pupils of Confucius rush to save him, but the man reaches the bank entirely unaided. Asked how he had pulled off this remarkable feat of survival, the man replied that he had simply let himself go with the descending and ascending currents in the water. The true Taoist, in other words, moulds his senses, body and mind until they are at one with the currents of the world without.

Notice the "letting go" as well. We don't have to resist the world. In fact, we can't. Resistance will only get us drowned, at least metaphorically. Even fighting is not really a matter of meeting blow for blow, irresistible force meeting immoveable object. The wisdom of the martial arts: if someone is rushing at you to fight, don't rush back at them. Step aside and let them rush past, but maybe just change their direction a little as you do. "Tao abides in non-action. Yet nothing is left undone."

And the Tao itself? The *Tao Te Ching* opens with these words:

> The Tao that can be told
> is not the eternal Tao
> The name that can be named
> is not the eternal Name . . .

We sense, in short, a vast and all-encompassing reality, which at some level just is the whole world considered all together, but nothing that can be pinned down, labeled and dissected and analyzed. The Tao is not God; it is not personal, or even unchanging; and it is not to be worshiped. It is not graspable in language yet can be clear enough when we sit with a clear mind by a peaceful stream—or, just as well, enter a raging current. To be sure, life will offer us both.

READING

From the Tao Te Ching

LAO TSU

Translated by Stephen Mitchell

THE *TAO TE CHING* is the founding expression of Taoism and the second most translated book in the world. It was written, officially, by Lao Tsu in third or fourth century BCE China. But so little is known about Lao Tsu that it is not even clear whether such a person actually existed. One story is that a bridgekeeper asked the wanderer Lao Tsu to write a book containing his thoughts and beliefs, which he did—and then disappeared forever. Other stories, perhaps not inconsistent with this one, consider the author of the *Tao* a divine being.

Tao literally means "way" or "path." *Te* means "virtue," both in the sense of "personal character" and in the sense of "inner potency," as when we speak of the "healing virtue" of a drug. *Ching* originally meant "norm" but expanded to mean "scripture," "canon," or "classic." Thus, *Tao Te Ching* means something like: "The Scripture/Classic/Canon of the Way/Path and the Power/Virtue."

8

The supreme good is like water,
which nourishes all things without trying to.
It is content with the low places that people disdain.
Thus it is like the Tao.

In dwelling, live close to the ground.
In thinking, keep to the simple.
In conflict, be fair and generous.
In governing, don't try to control.

Numbers 8, 10, 16, 22, 23, 24, 49, 67 from *Tao Te Ching by Lao Tsu*. A new English Version, with foreword and notes by Stephen Mitchell. Translation © 1988 by Stephen Mitchell. Reprinted by permission of HarperCollins Publishers.

In work, do what you enjoy.
In family life, be completely present.

When you are content to be simply yourself
and don't compare or compete,
everybody will respect you.

10

Can you coax your mind from its wandering
and keep to the original oneness?
Can you let your body become
supple as a newborn child's?
Can you cleanse your inner vision
until you see nothing but the light?
Can you love people and lead them
without imposing your will?
Can you deal with the most vital matters
by letting events take their course?
Can you step back from your own mind
and thus understand all things?

Giving birth and nourishing,
having without possessing,
acting with no expectations,
leading and not trying to control:
this is the supreme virtue.

16

Empty your mind of all thoughts.
Let your heart be at peace.
Watch the turmoil of beings,
but contemplate their return.

Each separate being in the universe
returns to the common source.
Returning to the source is serenity.

If you don't realize the source,
you stumble in confusion and sorrow.
When you realize where you come from,
you naturally become tolerant,
disinterested, amused,

kindhearted as a grandmother,
dignified as a king.
Immersed in the wonder of the Tao,
you can deal with whatever life brings you,
and when death comes, you are ready.

22

If you want to become whole,
let yourself be partial.
If you want to become straight,
let yourself be crooked.
If you want to become full,
let yourself be empty.
If you want to be reborn,
let yourself die.
If you want to be given everything,
give everything up.

The Master, by residing in the Tao,
sets an example for all beings.
Because he doesn't display himself,
people can see his light.
Because he has nothing to prove,
people can trust his words.
Because he doesn't know who he is,
people recognize themselves in him.
Because he has no goal in mind,
everything he does succeeds.

When the ancient Masters said,
"If you want to be given everything,
give everything up,"
they weren't using empty phrases.
Only in being lived by the Tao can you be truly yourself.

23

Express yourself completely,
then keep quiet.
Be like the forces of nature:
when it blows, there is only wind;
when it rains, there is only rain;
when the clouds pass, the sun shines through.

If you open yourself to the Tao,
you are at one with the Tao
and you can embody it completely.
If you open yourself to insight,
you are at one with insight
and you can use it completely.
If you open yourself to loss,
you are at one with loss
and you can accept it completely.

Open yourself to the Tao,
then trust your natural responses;
and everything will fall into place.

24

He who stands on tiptoe
doesn't stand firm.
He who rushes ahead
doesn't go far.
He who tries to shine
dims his own light.
He who defines himself
can't know who he really is.
He who has power over others
can't empower himself.
He who clings to his work
will create nothing that endures.

If you want to accord with the Tao,
just do your job, then let go.

49

The Master . . . is good to people who are good.
She is also good to people who aren't good.
This is true goodness.

She trusts people who are trustworthy.
She also trusts people who aren't trustworthy.
This is true trust . . .

67

Some say that my teaching is nonsense.
Others call it lofty but impractical.

> But to those who have looked inside themselves,
> this nonsense makes perfect sense.
> And to those who put it into practice,
> this loftiness has roots that go deep.
>
> I have just three things to teach:
> simplicity, patience, compassion.
> These three are your greatest treasures.
> Simple in actions and in thoughts,
> you return to the source of being.
> Patient with both friends and enemies,
> you accord with the way things are.
> Compassionate toward yourself,
> you reconcile all beings in the world.

CULTIVATING VIRTUE

The Ethics of Virtue is concerned with character traits. But character traits do not just happen. They need to be consciously developed and sustained, both by the people whose character traits they are and by others around them: parents, teachers, role models, and the community at large. A little like plants, they need seeding and nurturing and regular attention in order to prosper. This is what is called the *cultivation* of the virtues.

HOW VIRTUE IS TAUGHT

To some extent the virtues can be taught directly. They can be identified, praised, and rewarded early on, by parents and later by schools and society. Discipline is a good example. Originally imposed from outside, it is gradually internalized to become, later, *self*-discipline. Not that this kind of parenting or teaching is easy—and obviously I am not talking about the kind of harshness that really serves the discipline*r* and not the learner—but surely it is also crucial.

Stories play an essential role too. William Bennett, former U.S. Secretary of Education and compiler of several large books of virtue stories, writes in the preface of one of them that

> what we choose to read to our children matters a great deal. Legends, folk-tales, sacred stories, biographies, and poems can introduce the youngest children to the virtues; they can clarify notions of right and wrong for young people; and they can serve as powerful reminders of [humanity's] best ideals all the way through adulthood. More than one great man or woman at a critical instant has recalled a simple fable, a familiar verse, a childhood hero.

Other virtues must come from the heart, of course—empathy, generosity, hospitality—but even here, early experience of these virtues in others may be a critical part of the learning. Or perhaps they are "innate," but even so, it's clear that people can *lose* them without the proper development and support.

For Confucius too, cultivating the virtues is a social project. Virtuous rulers and other role models, in particular, are crucial. Virtue is not something we discover for ourselves; it is *shown* to us, daily, in the actions of those most visible and most admired. Classic texts reinforce virtues; art and story celebrate them. In China, ultimately the entire society came to be built around the virtues of its officials. By 165 BCE, candidates for high public office began to be called for examination of their moral excellence by the emperor. More and more were examined until finally almost anyone who wished to become an official had to pass written examinations, and thus it went for centuries. In fact this Confucian system inspired the modern European civil service.

"It takes a village" then—maybe even a whole society—to nurture and sustain the virtues. Aristotle would invoke the city, or *polis.* Remember that "cities" for the Greeks were self-sufficient political entities, city-*states,* not parts of any larger nation. Governance was face-to-face, and everyone in the ruling class (landowning, free, male citizens, often also those who fought the city's wars) knew each other intimately. When you grow up and fight and decide alongside others in this way, visibly interdependent though distinctive personalities, everyone's virtues and vices are well known to all, and a man's training of his sons (and sometimes protégés) clearly reflects his own virtue—or lack of it. Everyone could tell. Conversely, some observers have argued that the decline of such face-to-face communities in modern societies underlies our (perceived) decline in virtue as well.

PRACTICE IS ESSENTIAL

In the individual moral life especially, *practice* is crucial to cultivating virtue. Think psychologically for a moment here. A character trait is (at least) a reliable disposition to act in certain ways in certain specific circumstances. Another term we could use is "habit." But habits need practicing. The simplest principle of psychology is that habits are established and grow stronger with repetition. So, to promote and engrain virtue in oneself, repetition is key. Honesty, hospitality, temperance, and all the rest—we don't come by these settled character traits simply by choice or commitment. We have to *be* honest, *be* hospitable, *practice* temperance—again and again and again.

Sometimes we are inclined to excuse our moral lapses by arguing that we couldn't help ourselves. "Circumstances made me do it!" And it may well be true that, faced with specific temptations with no settled habits of resistance or redirection, temptations are hard to resist. Too much liquor, the white lie or worse, the habit of denigrating others behind their backs, or much worse: all of these can come out all too easily. But here is the key point: the contrary power does not necessarily lie in a pure act of will at the moment of choice, as if each time we must "just say no" all over again. The power lies with the reconstruction of our habits. Make it a *habit* never to say something behind someone's back that you wouldn't say to their face, and each time it becomes easier. Moral character is an ongoing project.

READING

From Living Large

JOHN SULLIVAN

JOHN SULLIVAN is emeritus professor of philosophy at Elon University and a mentor and inspiration to me and many others. He works, as he puts it, "at the place where philosophy, psychology and spirituality—East and West—intersect and mutually enhance one another."

Sullivan's question in this selection is this: how to win ourselves some freedom of mind. Awareness is crucial. What Sullivan calls *response-ability* arises when we come to recognize that our ways of understanding and responding to events and experiences are themselves choices—and then *practice* making different and more conscious ones. Response-ability is both a key virtue in itself and also the means by which other virtues can be cultivated and deepened.

Confucius (Master K'ung) would say we have a *small-minded person-in-us* and a noble or *large-minded person-in-us*—both possibilities existing at any moment.[1] He would encourage us to remember our nobility and to live in large mind. He would remind us that this takes daily practice.

What is "practice" on this model? It is *to recognize when we are in small mind and to shift to large mind.* . . . In small mind, we tend to be partial in the double sense of being biased and of seeing less than the whole. In small mind, we are asleep in our life, on automatic pilot, "going through the motions" according to cultural

From *Living Large: Transformative Work at the Intersection of Ethics and Spirituality* (Tai Sophia Press, 2004), pp. 29–33 and 43–48. © 2004 by John Greenfelder Sullivan.

scripts. In small mind, we are enslaved and reactive in the sense that someone or something triggers us and we react immediately—with no space and no time between the incoming stimulus and the automatic response.

In large mind, we see more of the whole and live in a larger world. In large mind, we are more mindful, more wakeful, opening the senses and opening the heart. In large mind, we are freer, acting from a place beneath surface disturbance. In large mind, we are *response-able*—able to choose our response in a way that benefits the whole.

RECOGNIZING TWO LEVELS

Practice begins with recognizing when we are in small mind. To do this, we must distinguish two levels—a WHAT and a HOW. Call this the fundamental distinction for all inner work: the distinction between (a) *what is going on* and (b) *how I am relating to what is going on*.

(b) **How I Am Relating To**

        and

(a) **What Is Going On**   (What Is Going On)

Always there are two levels. Yet often we merge the two. "How we are relating" disappears from our awareness, as if how we are relating is the only possible way we could relate.

Victor Frankl was an Austrian psychiatrist and a Jew. During the time of the Holocaust, the Nazis sent him to the camps. While he was a prisoner under unimaginable conditions, Frankl discovered this fundamental distinction. His way of phrasing it was to distinguish "liberty" (on the first level) and "freedom" (on the second level). In the camps, Frankl had no liberty—he could not go and come as he wished. Yet Frankl discovered that he did have a bit of freedom—the freedom to choose how he would relate to his situation. This he came to call "the last human freedom." It was something his Nazi captors could not take from him.[2]

Consider liberty and freedom in our own lives. We may or may not have the power to change what is occurring. Hurricanes and floods, sicknesses and accidents may restrict our liberty. Yet we still have an important freedom—the capacity to recognize, and possibly alter, how we relate to what is occurring in our life.

Leadership consultant Stephen Covey uses the Frankl example to emphasize the first of his seven habits of highly successful people.³ "Be proactive," Covey says. "Develop the capacity to choose your response."

Covey speaks not of small and large mind but of reactivity and proactivity. The stimulus happens—someone makes a cutting remark. The response follows immediately—an angry retort. *Reactivity*. No freedom, no ability to choose your response. *Proactivity*, on the contrary, is another name for "response-ability." Proactivity is the ability to choose one's response. Being proactive is often confused with being nice. This misses the key distinction. At times, hard truths must be faced. Proactivity, in this instance, is the ability to choose what you will say, and when, and how. It may or may not be "nice."

Several years ago, my wife, Gregg, discovered she had breast cancer. At that moment, she had no choice about having cancer. Cancer was already present. But she did have a second level choice: how to relate to the cancer. First, she could choose her treatment. Second, during and after treatment, she could choose how she would live with this illness. She chose not to let cancer be her identity (not to be "Miss Cancer of the Year," she would say). And she chose not to die before she died. By cultivating *awareness,* she realized that she was at least *free to choose* **how** she would understand and respond to this event in her life. . . .

We humans are "meaning-creating, value-generating" beings. The odd thing is that generally we forget that *we* are labeling situations. We forget that *we* are generating the emotions we feel. It's as if we are wearing glasses and forgetting we are wearing them. We "see through" our stories and emotions. We do not see that the stories and emotions are produced by us.

Without awareness, I take my interpretation as the truth of the matter. I defend it as such. I am unaware that I have any choice about the story I am telling. I think: "That is just the way it is!"

Without awareness, I fail to see that, in the wake of the story, I am the one putting an emotional charge on the situation. It is as if situations arrived already wrapped in language and already charged with strong emotion. I simply think: "That's the way it is." Aren't I justified to be angry about it?

When the stakes are high or emotions are high, reactivity increases. Yet, even in these situations, with awareness, I can notice the key distinction: what is happening is one thing; how I interpret and respond is another. Victor Frankl could distinguish liberty and freedom even under horrendous conditions. My wife could distinguish between having cancer (no liberty here) and how she would

relate to having cancer (some freedom here). To notice this fundamental distinction does not come easily. We need practice.

TEACHING STORY 1: FIGHT OR KEY?

When my daughter Heather was very little, she thought that I existed
solely to play with her. In order to get my work done, I decide one
Sunday afternoon to go over to my office in Carlton Building on the
Elon campus. When I arrive, I find that the locks have been changed
and I cannot get to my office. Immediately the soap opera of my
mind scoops up the whole situation and I launch into high drama.
"That's just the way THEY are (THEY being the nasty, unfeeling
administration and WE being the hard-working, noble faculty). Just
the way they are—never thinking of faculty, acting without any con-
sultation, so insensitive as to not even bother telling us!"

I start to fume and get into a state. I try to call campus security,
with no results. Anger mounts. Finally, I spy the Vice President for
Academic Affairs coming out of a campus luncheon. I jump him
like a hungry lion. He produces a key and I get into the building.

Yet the soap opera of oppression continues to pop up when I'm
working, when I'm driving home, when I'm lying in bed. And of
course, I tell the tale on Monday. This, I am now ashamed to say,
continues for several days.

Finally, after days pass, I become conscious of a small voice
that cuts through the tattered tale of imagined abuse. The voice
says: *"John, do you want a fight or do you want a key?"*

Now part of me wants a fight. After all I am Irish. I share the
heritage of the Irish man who saw a fight and inquired: "Is this
a private fight or can anyone join in?" Yet the better part of me
answers: "Well—*[long pause]*—I guess I really want a key." I dial
Physical Plant and ask: "May I have a key to Carlton Building?"
"Sure," comes the reply, "it'll be ready in an hour." . . .

My emotions would have been very different that Sunday, if
the meaning I attached to my frustration had been different. Suppose, for instance, I had thought, "Oh, they've changed the locks.
The locksmiths must have worked overtime to do it when the few-
est people would be around to be inconvenienced—too bad I'm
one of the few!" From that understanding, my response might
have been a hearty laugh—and then I could have sought a key in
a completely different spirit. Or I could have worked under a tree.
Or I could have taken the whole event as a sign from the gods to
go home and take a nap, or take my family for a picnic. Any such
response flowing from a larger understanding would have caused

a good deal less suffering, both for me and for other people. My ranting was far from harmless!

That's not what I did, though. In the grip of my small-minded self, my understanding was small, my language followed. On the basis of my quick judgment, my response was anger, resentment, and condemnation. And I locked onto those feelings, I froze my interpretation and valuation together by saying, in effect, "That's just the way it is!"

"That's just the way it is!" or "That's just the way I am" is a hallmark of a small mind. Labels, emotions, stereotypes—these are part of the dynamic. Also, in small, ego-centered mind, I move very quickly to EITHER-OR (dualistic understanding and response—us vs. them; right vs. wrong, win vs. lose). In such a mindspace, true partnership cannot even be thought or spoken, let alone achieved. Alternatively, Confucius, by pointing out the large-minded-person-in-us, was laying the groundwork for partnership, for community.

TEACHING STORY 2: HARRIET'S CHILDHOOD

Some years ago, I was participating in a group. One of the other participants—I'll call her Harriet—was in her mid-sixties at the time. Her mother had been dead for some years. Here is Harriet's story:

"When I was a little girl, I lived in Texas with my mother. I never knew who my father was. My mother would be in and out of work. She kept sending me to my grandmother whenever she was 'laid off' from work. My grandmother would care for me. Then back to my mother and the same cycle."

On the basis of what she perceived was going on, Harriet installed a "story" about her mother. The story centered on Harriet's mother sending her away. Harriet came to believe that her mother did not want her, never loved her. Harriet's evidence? The fact that her mother kept sending her away—to stay with her grandmother. When did Harriet install this story? At age four or five perhaps. At any rate, quite early on.

Suppose that you were Harriet, the little girl, and you interpreted the situation as a sign that your mother never loved you. What thoughts and emotions might arise? Perhaps confusion, anger, resentment—all directed outward. Perhaps feelings of being unworthy, worthless, alone, unloved—all directed inward.

The interpretation and consequent emotional charge arose early and lasted long. Harriet and her mother were estranged for all of her mother's life. Even after her mother's death, Harriet's alienation continued.

In the group, people listened to Harriet, hearing the pain and suffering this story had caused and was causing still. Then the group members began to explore what life must have been like for Harriet's mother—a "single mother" before there was such a term. How was it in Texas at that time for a young woman with a young child—the woman poorly educated and without many skills? A woman who had to pick up what work she could. A woman working in situations where she was easily laid off. Harriet's mother did send Harriet away. And she also asked for her back. Again and again and again. Was Harriet's interpretation the only way of understanding the situation? Would an alternative interpretation open up alternate emotional responses? We who have an observer present can see how Harriet "languaged her life." We who have an observer present can understand the emotional charge that followed her interpretation. Harriet had no observer for this story. For her it was the truth of the matter—that was exactly how it was!

Through the group work we were doing, Harriet awoke to notice that this was not the only way to interpret and respond to the events. The events were in the past—"frozen in amber" as it were.[4] Harriet had no liberty to change the past but, with awareness, she did have the freedom to observe her story and the emotions arising with the story. She did, with awareness, have the freedom to shift her story. This she did. She came to see that perhaps her mother did love her after all. That her mother did the best she could for Harriet in difficult circumstances. Tears and grieving. Then regret: why did I not see this possibility while my mother was still alive? Regret and finally closure. To tell her mother certain things—even now. We do not quite have the words. Some kind of forgiveness— of Harriet for herself, for her mother, for the human condition we all share. How easy to see in others, how difficult to see in our own lives!

Being asleep in our lives can cause great unnecessary suffering. Great pain. Waking up can bring the capacity for compassion, forgiveness, and renewed hope.

NOTES

1. I am rendering the Confucian term "hsiao jen" as the small-minded person-in-us. I am rendering the Confucian term "chün-tzu" as the noble or large-minded person-in-us. This distinction can be seen in the Image section of the commentary on each hexagram in the *I Ching*, where Wilhelm translates the terms as "the superior man" and "the inferior man." See the *I Ching or Book of Changes*, trans. Richard Wilhelm, 3rd ed. (Princeton, N.J.: Princeton University Press, 1967). It is also a key distinction used by Confucius. See *The*

Analects (Lun Yu), trans. D.C. Lau (New York: Viking Penguin, 1979) where the distinction appears more than 50 times.

2. See Victor Frankl, *Man's Search for Meaning*, 3rd ed. (New York: Simon & Schuster, 1984).

3. See Stephen Covey, *The Seven Habits of Highly Effective People* (New York: Simon & Schuster Fireside Book, 1990), pp. 66–93. Covey acknowledges that the first habit must be joined to the second—"Begin with the End in View," and, in fact, that all the habits interlock.

4. The phrase is from Kurt Vonnegut.

FOR REVIEW

1. What (kind of thing) is a virtue?
2. What is a vice?
3. Why might we need a *theory* of the virtues?
4. What is Aristotle's theory of virtue?
5. How do professional codes of ethics determine what traits to put forward as virtues?
6. What is the Confucian view of virtue?
7. What is the Taoist view of virtue?
8. How does the *Tao Te Ching* invite us to live?
9. What are some ways that virtue can be taught?
10. What is "response-ability"? How can we cultivate it?

EXERCISES AND NOTES

7.1 INTERCONNECTIONS

In the Greek view, the virtues connect. Plato and Aristotle argued that the key virtues each depend on the others—to have one, you need all—and Plato in particular argued that virtue is a kind of knowledge, so that the lack of any virtue suggests the lack of the knowledge of virtue as such.

What do you think? Is it really true that the virtues are a package deal? If a person has one virtue, are they more likely to have others? Why or why not? Use some examples to help your investigation along.

Are the vices connected in the same way? Does every vice require the others to some extent? Do most? Could we then infer the presence of other vices in a person who has one? For example, take a mild vice like littering. Are litterers more likely to have other vices too? To be pushy drivers, or white liars, or . . .? Can you get any evidence to help answer this question?

Is it best to cultivate all the virtues? Though tradition would say so, not everyone agrees. The philosopher Friedrich Nietzsche thought that we could and should develop only a few, indeed maybe a few vices too: it makes us more interesting and possibly fertile personalities . . .

7.2 VIRTUES IN FLUX

Some virtues remain constant over time, even between us and the ancients and between East and West. Others shift. The Greeks of the Golden Age found themselves in the middle of a shift from the old Homeric warrior virtues to the new and very different virtues of the democratic citizen of a city-state. That tension between two sets of virtues is part of what provoked the rise of philosophy itself.

Or consider the work ethic. The work ethic was itself a relatively new set of virtues a few hundred years ago. It dominated the stage for a while. But now we are (perhaps!) moving beyond it to something new. Fifty or a hundred years ago, for example, no one would have used a term like "workaholic." Those character traits that we now think are a little obsessive would then have been widely admired. It's arguable that we are still obsessively overworked, and overwork ourselves, anyway, but—maybe partly for just this reason—the question of the work ethic is at least on the table.

Which virtues, in general, do you think stay constant, and which change? Why? Specifically, how do you think we will look back on the work ethic in yet another fifty or a hundred years? What will take its place? What in your view *should* take its place?

In November 1987, *Harper's Magazine* commissioned seven major advertising firms to produce ads promoting the Seven Deadly Sins: gluttony, envy, wrath, and all the rest. The results were disturbing—not so different, in some ways, from the ads we see every day. Have we turned even deadly sins into virtues? Is this a good idea?

7.3 THEORIZING VIRTUE

We've looked at several theories of the virtues. Would one of these theories be yours? Which—and why? Or perhaps you'd suggest some other and better theory?

MacIntyre argues that virtue theory is most plausible with regard to specific practices with clear "internal goods." Assuming this is true, how far do you think virtue theory can be generalized? Does human life as a whole have a clear and specific "internal good"? What is it? How can you establish this?

Utilitarians sometimes argue that virtue theory is radically incomplete if taken as an overall theory of ethics. We can say, with MacIntyre, that the "internal goods" of certain "practices" elevate those character traits that serve those goods. The utilitarians' question, though, would be, what makes those practices themselves good? We would not consider an effective concentration-camp guard to be a virtuous person—not good in the *ethical* sense—even though he or she served ably and well the "internal goods" of the concentration camp. No—we need some external standard, they conclude, by which to judge social practices as well. Utilitarians would argue that this standard can only be social utility. What do you think?

When roles with different "internal goods" conflict, how do we decide which takes priority? How I respond to a student's needs as a *teacher* may be very different than how I'd respond as a *friend*. If I can only respond in one way or the other, which should it be? Often the question of which role takes priority lies at the very core of the ethical issue in the first place. Can you make such a decision without sliding back into utilitarianism? How?

7.4 PRACTICING LARGE MIND

John Sullivan speaks of "small mind" and "large mind" as contrasting "ways of understanding and reacting to things" and calls our attention to two modes in which they can be seen at work: in the language we tend to use and in the emotional charge we experience.

Small-mindedness arises in speech when we say things like "I'm bad at X"—whatever X is. To shift to larger mind, Sullivan would have us rephrase the same description as "I am a beginner at X." He'd point out that this second phrasing gives us some space, some sense of possibility, that is decisively closed out in the first.

Small-mindedness arises in "emotional charge," he says, when we find ourselves blaming others, complaining about the state of things, and excusing and justifying ourselves and perhaps our inaction. We separate ourselves from the situation, interpret it in a fixed and often narrowly self-serving way, and contribute nothing to resolving it. Here Sullivan would have us ask instead how the same events or behavior might be interpreted in a more expansive way, what could be done about them, and where there might be room to move in the situation.

As a way of trying out these suggestions, observe your own ways of understanding and relating to things for a set period of, say, a week. It might help to keep notes. Then, if you have seen either of these modes of "small mind" emerging in your behavior, see if you can shift them toward larger mind. Can you tell a different story in a troubling but open-ended situation, for instance, as Harriet learned to do in Sullivan's example? When you are tempted by complaint or self-justification, can you find ways instead to express a sense of joint purpose and mutual appreciation? In general, Sullivan advises, try to "recognize 'story as story'—recognize when you take one point of view as the only point of view and get stuck there. Shift to another wider way of seeing and being, of speaking and emotionally responding."

It may be that your practice will first consist mostly of noticing what Sullivan calls "reactivity"—our tendency to fasten onto one story about things as if that is the one and only story that can be told. Later on, you might become more proactive. Try out some new attitudes in advance, rather than waiting to see what daily forms of small-mindedness need expanding. Can you make a practice of greeting everyone in a fresh way? How about decisively viewing problems as something to work out together, separate from the people involved, rather than seeing the other people themselves as the problem?

Resolve to try this practice for a time, and then step back and consider your results. What have you learned? Does Sullivan's analysis ring true? If so, what might you do about it?

NOTES

This chapter's opening list of virtues is selected from a still more extensive list at http://en.wikipedia.org/wiki/List_of_virtues, accessed 10/3/12. One striking feature of this list is that every single virtue listed has its own linked page. Follow up some of these links, or search around a little, and all manner of intriguing websites come up (check it out!). It is not always clear who is putting up these sites or what his or her agenda is. Some of them seem to be designed mainly to sell certain books or services. But the very diversity and appeal of this material is telling.

Joseph Pieper's study of the virtues is *The Four Cardinal Virtues* (University of Notre Dame Press, 1990). Interesting reading on historical changes in virtues is Maria Ossowska's book *Social Determinants of Moral Ideas* (University of Pennsylvania Press, 1970). On the work ethic, see Juliet Schor's now-classic book *The Overworked American* (Basic Books, 1993).

On Aristotle's ethics, a classic and accessible treatment is Henry Veatch, *Rational Man* (Indiana University Press, 1966). Aristotle's cited work is the *Nicomachean Ethics* (sometimes just titled *Ethics*). I use the W. D. Ross translation published by the Clarendon Press in 1908.

For Aquinas, see Anton Pegis, ed., *Introduction to St Thomas Aquinas* (Modern Library, 1948). Alasdair MacIntyre is quoted from *After Virtue* (University of Notre Dame Press, 1981), pp. 178 and 204. Full texts of the Hippocratic Oath and the AMA Principles of Medical Ethics can be found online, as can the

Society of Professional Journalists' code at http://www.spj.org/ethics. For general resources and a detailed guide to the extensive (Western) philosophical literature on the virtues, see "Aristotle and Virtue Ethics" at the "Ethics Updates" site, http://ethics.sandiego.edu/.

On Confucianism and the virtues, see Philip Ivanhoe, *Confucian Moral Self-Cultivation* (Hackett, 2000). For Taoism, start with the *Tao Te Ching* itself. Zen master Dogen is cited from Hee-jin Kim, *Eihei Dogen, Mystical Realist* (Wisdom Publications, 2004), p. 25. The story of the old man and the current shows up in many discussions of Taoism: this one I have from http://masterymagazine.com/issue/may-2012/article/qi-dao-testimonial1, accessed 10/3/12. The selections from the *Tao* reprinted here are from Stephen Mitchell's fine translation, online at   http://academic.brooklyn.cuny.edu/core9/phalsall/texts/taote-v3.html. For the translation of the title "Tao Te Ching," I draw on Alan Chan's entry "Laozi" in the Stanford Encyclopedia of Philosophy, online at http://plato.stanford .edu/entries/laozi/ and accessed 10/3/12.

William Bennett is cited from the preface to his collection *The Moral Compass* (Simon and Schuster, 1995), pp. 12–13.

CHAPTER 8

The Ethics of Relationship

Chapter 4 outlined the family of relationship-centered values like this:

R E L A T I O N S H I P

The Ethics of Relationship encompasses those moral values concerned with our connections to others, from families to larger human communities. We are social beings as well as individuals: we grow up in families, take on traditions and heritages, and live within and depend upon human and also ecological communities. Recognizing how deeply our (many) communities make us who we are calls forth not only gratefulness but also a responsibility to care for and participate in them.

We can now explore the Ethics of Relationship in more detail.

CARE ETHICS

At the very beginning someone bore us into this world. We will never again be so intimately connected to anyone as we are to our own mothers for the nine months of pregnancy. There's a song by Stan Rogers in which he sings of birth as the time "when communion is lost forever, when a heart first beats alone." It's a melancholy song. His larger point is that even though we later may become very invested in separateness, on some deep level we still remember and yearn for that primal "communion."

Mothers and others cared for us through all those years of babyhood and childhood. Without that care in our time of utter dependence, we simply wouldn't be here. Later, when we start becoming conscious of ourselves and our social relations and much of that early care for us is mostly lost to our memory, we also feel an urge to be separate. That's the developmental project of late childhood. Our culture also stresses independence—indeed we learn to practically identify it with personhood itself—and the result is that some people never recover a sense of how deeply we are bound up with others. Still, for most people, separateness is only a phase that doesn't last long. Friends come and go but soon some grow close and stick around. You fall in love. Teammates claim your care and concern. Co-workers do the same. Causes arise, and there are others with you in religious groups or building houses or fighting wars. You have children, maybe, yourself.

There is a dual point here. First, we are deeply, inescapably, and permanently in relationship with particular other people, and in a way that goes far beyond the relatively distant sort of relationships that seem to be the main models for the other types of moral values. Sure, we have moral and legal obligations to our children (and parents!) as well as to co-workers and fellow soldiers, and so on. But these obligations do not truly get to the core of the values at stake.

Second, relationships like these evoke deep *feelings*, and it is these feelings that ground deep values in turn. Sometimes it is the helpless love of a parent for a child. (A line from the writer Elizabeth Stone: "Having a child is to decide forever to have your heart go walking outside your body.") Sometimes it is the chosen love of a life partner; sometimes love of friends or care for long time fellow workers—but in any case, feeling is key.

You'll remember that Martin Buber and Emmanuel Levinas lay out "philosophies of encounter." People can emerge in certain extraordinary experiences as unique and precious others. Yet the suggestion here is that this is only one aspect of our relation to others. There is also an earthier way in which we come to care for and love some of those people close to us. It's extraordinary in its own way but at the same time totally ordinary too. Care does grow for those who care for us and for those with whom we work and act together. Everyday love is crucial to ethics too.

AN ETHICS THAT HONORS FEELINGS

The formal tradition in ethics, as so far sketched, does not speak much of love, or indeed of feeling in general. Kant even argued that feelings distort ethics. We need to act morally toward others out of a sense of duty and obligation, he argued, and not on the basis of feelings. After all, feelings can vary between people and for ourselves from moment to moment as well, but morality claims us "categorically," as Kant says: all of us, all the time. We should tell the truth, comfort the sick, speak up for the downtrodden, even if we don't especially feel care, let alone love, for them.

These are not the best arguments. For one thing, in terms of constancy, feelings often greatly outdo the intellectual convictions to which Kant appeals. Few things are as utterly unshakeable as parents' love for their children. Feelings certainly motivate a great deal of moral action.

It might be better to conclude that care and connection need develop-ment and cultivation, just like the virtues. Indeed, they *are* virtues. Certainly the practice of sustaining relationships has "internal goods," to use Alasdair MacIntyre's term. The virtues, in this view, will be those traits that sustain and deepen relationships, enable us to raise children well, keep love strong, and build comradeship and solidarity. Thus the psychologist Carol Gilligan describes an "Ethics of Care," rooted once again in a specific view of the (or *a*) world, this time "a world of relationships and psychological truths where an awareness of the connection between people gives rise to a recognition of a responsibility for one another, a perception of the need for response. Seen in this light, morality arises from a recognition of relationship." Believing in "the restorative activity of care," as Gilligan puts it, we come to

> see the actors in [moral] dilemma[s] arrayed not as opponents in a contest of rights but as members of a network of relationships on whose continuation they all depend. Consequently [the] solution to the dilemma[s] lies in activat-ing the network by communication, . . . strengthening rather than severing connections.

Key virtues thus include perceptiveness, imagination, and sensitivity; skill in responding and nurturing; patience and creativity; and acceptance. Moral-ity itself emerges, in the philosopher Margaret Walker's lovely words, as (in part) "a collection of perceptive, imaginative, appreciative, and expressive skills and capacities which put us and keep us in contact with the realities of ourselves and specific others."

CARE ETHICS AND MORAL DEVELOPMENT

Gilligan began her work with the moral development research of the psy-chologist Lawrence Kohlberg. Kohlberg had concluded that most children go through several markedly different stages of moral reasoning. They start, he thought, with obedience to authority figures such as parents or teachers. Self-interest then begins operating. At its middle stages, moral thinking becomes "conventional," meaning that children are oriented toward social approval, and later toward the law and responding to the obligations of duty. Kohl-berg's final stages of moral thinking are initially a kind of utilitarianism, an eye for the good of society as a whole. Those few who reach the height of eth-ical maturity then move to an ethics of universal principles.

Gilligan noticed some striking omissions in this research. For one thing, Kohlberg's interviewers initially talked only to boys—but he generalized his results to girls as well. When they did look at girls, the girls were judged by the boys' standards and tended to score lower in moral development. But what if they were actually developing *in a different way*? When Gilligan began using the same dilemmas with girls, she got very different results. As Eve Browning Cole puts it,

Gilligan's results . . . showed a pattern of moral reasoning among the women studied which diverged from [Kohlberg's] paradigm in several distinct ways. First, women reasoning their way through a moral dilemma tended to focus on the specific personal relationships within which the principal agents find themselves situated. They pondered . . . the nature and character of these relationships, tending to derive relevant ethical considerations from specific connectedness among persons. Second, they reasoned that relationships generate responsibilities and that these responsibilities might be quite specific within the relationship. . . . [T]here was thus an emphasis on . . . the concrete details of a moral situation, as opposed to its universalizable or general features, which figure so prominently in mainstream ethical discourse.

Gilligan pointed out that this approach—working within particular relationships and attending to the feelings that constitute them—is every bit as appropriate an ethics as the more familiar "male" model. Many times, surely, it is more appropriate. To construct a seemingly empirical theory of ethics built on devaluing this "different voice" is, for one thing, sexist. It is also just plain bad science. We need a more inclusive view.

Gilligan produced her own stage theory of moral development. On Gilligan's model too, moral thinking begins with selfishness. The "conventional" middle stage, however, is the opposite of selfishness: self-sacrifice. The more mature final stages find a balance between self and other, including the growing sense that self and other are intertwined—an ethics, once again, of relationship.

READING

From Caring

NEL NODDINGS

SINCE GILLIGAN'S groundbreaking book *In a Different Voice* (Harvard University Press, 1982), Care Ethics has become a major project of feminist philosophers and other thinkers intent on recovering ethics in a relational key. Nel Noddings is prominent among them. A teacher and philosopher of education now retired from Stanford University after a long and varied career—also the mother of ten children—she is the author, most influentially, of *Caring: A Feminine Approach to Ethics and Moral Education*, along with other books. This essay is a selection from the introduction.

From Nel Noddings, *Caring* (University of California Press, 1984), pp. 1–6.

Ethics, the philosophical study of morality, has concentrated for the most part on moral reasoning. Much current work, for example, focuses on the status of moral predicates and, in education, the dominant model presents a hierarchical picture of moral reasoning. This emphasis gives ethics a contemporary, mathematical appearance, but it also moves discussion beyond the sphere of actual human activity and the feeling that pervades such activity. Even though careful philosophers have recognized the difference between "pure" or logical reason and "practical" or moral reason, ethical argumentation has frequently proceeded as if it were governed by the logical necessity characteristic of geometry. It has concentrated on the establishment of principles and that which can be logically derived from them. One might say that ethics has been discussed largely in the language of the father: in principles and propositions, in terms such as justification, fairness, justice. The mother's voice has been silent. Human caring and the memory of caring and being cared for, which I shall argue form the foundation of ethical response, have not received attention except as outcomes of ethical behavior. . . .

The view to be expressed here is a feminine view. This does not imply that all women will accept it or that men will reject it; indeed, there is no reason why men should not embrace it. It is feminine in the deep classical sense—rooted in receptivity, relatedness, and responsiveness. It does not imply either that logic is to be discarded or that logic is alien to women. It represents an alternative to present views, one that begins with the moral attitude or longing for goodness and not with moral reasoning. It may indeed be the case that such an approach is more typical of women than of men, but this is an empirical question I shall not attempt to answer.

Women . . . enter the practical domain of moral action through a different door, so to speak. It is not the case, certainly, that women cannot arrange principles hierarchically and derive conclusions logically. It is more likely that we see this process as peripheral to, or even alien to, many problems of moral action. Faced with a hypothetical moral dilemma, women often ask for more information. We want to know more, I think, in order to form a picture more nearly resembling real moral situations. Ideally, we need to talk to the participants, to see their eyes and facial expressions, to receive what they are feeling. Moral decisions are, after all, made in real situations; they are qualitatively different from the solution of geometry problems. Women can and do give reasons for their acts, but the reasons often point to feelings, needs, impressions, and a sense of personal ideal rather than to universal principles and their application. We shall see that, as a result of this "odd" approach, women have often been judged inferior to men in the moral domain.

. . . [P]ractical ethics from the feminine view is very different from the utilitarian practical ethics of, say, Peter Singer. While both of us would treat animals kindly and sensitively, for example, we give very different reasons for our consideration. I must resist his charge that we are guilty of "speciesism" in our failure to accord rights to animals, because I shall locate the very wellspring of ethical behavior in human affective response. Throughout our discussion of ethicality we shall remain in touch with the affect that gives rise to it. This does not mean that our discussion will bog down in sentiment, but it is necessary to give appropriate attention and credit to the affective foundation of existence. Indeed, one who attempts to ignore or to climb above the human affect at the heart of ethicality may well be guilty of romantic rationalism. What is recommended in such a framework simply cannot be broadly applied in the actual world.

I shall begin with a discussion of caring. What does it mean to care and to be cared for? The analysis will occupy us at length, since relation will be taken as ontologically basic and the caring relation as ethically basic. For our purposes, "relation" may be thought of as a set of ordered pairs generated by some rule that describes the affect—or subjective experience—of the members.

Taking *relation* as ontologically basic simply means that we recognize human encounter and affective response as a basic fact of human existence. As we examine what it means to care and to be cared for, we shall see that both parties contribute to the relation; my caring must be somehow completed in the other if the relation is to be described as caring.

The focus of our attention will be upon how to meet the other morally. Ethical caring, the relation in which we do meet the other morally, will be described as arising out of natural caring—that relation in which we respond as one-caring out of love or natural inclination. The relation of natural caring will be identified as the human condition that we, consciously or unconsciously, perceive as "good." It is that condition toward which we long and strive, and it is our longing for caring—to be in that special relation—that provides the motivation for us to be moral. We want to be *moral* in order to remain in the caring relation and to enhance the ideal of ourselves as one-caring.

It is this ethical ideal, this realistic picture of ourselves as one-caring, that guides us as we strive to meet the other morally. Everything depends upon the nature and strength of this ideal, for we shall not have absolute principles to guide us. Indeed, I shall reject ethics of principle as ambiguous and unstable. Wherever there is a principle, there is implied its exception and, too often, principles function to separate us from each other. We may become dangerously self-righteous when we perceive ourselves as holding a precious principle not held by the other. The other may then be devalued and treated "differently." Our ethic of caring will not permit this to happen. We recognize that in fear, anger, or hatred we will treat the other differently, but this treatment is never conducted ethically. Hence, when we must use violence or strategies on the other, we are already diminished ethically. Our efforts must, then, be directed to the maintenance of conditions that will permit caring to flourish. Along with the rejection of principles and rules as the major guide to ethical behavior, I shall also reject the notion of universalizability. Many of those writing and thinking about ethics insist that any ethical judgment—by virtue of its *being* an ethical judgment—must be universalizable; that is, it must be the case that, if under conditions X you are required to do A, then under sufficiently similar conditions, I too am required to do A. I shall reject this emphatically. First, my attention is not on judgment and not on the particular acts we perform but on how we meet the other morally. Second, in recognition of the feminine approach to meeting the other morally—our insistence on caring for the other—I shall want to preserve the uniqueness of human encounters. Since so much depends on the subjective experience of those involved in ethical encounters, conditions are rarely "sufficiently similar" for me to declare that you must do what I must do. There is, however, a fundamental universality in our ethic, as there must be to escape relativism. The caring attitude, that attitude which expresses our earliest memories of being cared for and our growing store of memories of both caring and being cared for, is universally accessible. Since caring and the commitment to sustain it form the universal heart of the ethic, we must establish a convincing and comprehensive picture of caring at the outset.

Another outcome of our dependence on an ethical ideal is the emphasis upon moral education. Since we are dependent upon the strength and sensitivity of the ethical ideal—both our own and that of others—we must nurture that ideal in all of our educational encounters. I shall claim that we are dependent on each other even in the quest for personal goodness. How good *I* can be is partly a function of how *you*—the other—receive and respond to me. Whatever virtue I exercise is completed, fulfilled, in you. The primary aim of all education must be nurturance of the ethical ideal.

To accomplish the purposes set out above, I shall strike many contrasts between masculine and feminine approaches to ethics and education and, indeed, to living. These are not intended to divide men and women into opposing camps. They are meant, rather, to show how great the chasm is that already divides the masculine and feminine in each of us and to suggest that we enter a dialogue of genuine dialectical nature in order to achieve an ultimate transcendence of the masculine and feminine in moral matters.

An important difference between an ethic of caring and other ethics that give subjectivity its proper place is its foundation in relation. The philosopher who begins with a supremely free consciousness—an aloneness and emptiness at the heart of existence—identifies *anguish* as the basic human affect. But our view, rooted as it is in relation, identifies *joy* as a basic human affect. When I look at my child—even one of my grown children—and recognize the fundamental relation in which we are each defined, I often experience a deep and overwhelming joy. It is the recognition of and longing for relatedness that form the foundation of our ethic, and the joy that accompanies fulfillment of our caring enhances our commitment to the ethical ideal that sustains us as one-caring.

ETHICS AND COMMUNITY

A community is some linked set of others with whom we have some compelling commonality. Maybe we share interests or work; maybe we share political convictions; maybe we live in the same neighborhood or country. There are faith communities, sports communities, online communities, and all sorts of others. Each of us, in fact, belongs to many such communities. All of us belong to at least the largest and most inclusive ones.

Here, then, ethical relationship is with a *group* of others, and with the associated institutions, like churches or professions or organizations or forms of governance, all the way up to ethnic and other kinds of heritages. Some are voluntary. Take a certain job, move to a certain area, and you more or less automatically acquire a set of well-defined links to others. You may join political or religious organizations. You may also leave them. But other communities you are simply born into, and leaving is not an option: ethnic communities, for instance, or a religious heritage, even if you decide to give it up or change later, and of course the current global "community"—for as co-inhabitants of this fragile ecosphere we are also and inescapably linked with every other human on the planet.

Such communities literally make us who we are. The educator Janie Ward writes of African Americans:

Throughout our history, from plantation proverbs to freedom songs, we have grappled with questions about who we are as an African people and where we are headed. The moral lessons we've learned and passed on have had to be culturally specific, responsive to the effects of injustice that have circumscribed our lives, and respectful of the care, connectedness, and interdependence that assured our survival through the best and the worst of times.

Such relationships are "culturally specific," she says—distinct from (though surely overlapping with) the legacies of other peoples—but still, crucial to the identities of individual African Americans.

In fact, identity is *always* communal in essential ways. We cannot even imagine being without a specific history, without family or a civic community in a broader sense, or even without a place. For most of human history, people lived in groups and communities so small that everyone's name and personal history were known to almost everyone they might encounter. In modern times, most of us typically have much more anonymous encounters, but we still share communal identities such as ethnicity or politics, or even allegiances to certain soccer or hockey teams.

Even speaking a particular language is a form of community. A language is an automatic link with any other speaker of the same tongue. Halfway around the world, maybe, think of running into someone who speaks your language, when maybe you haven't heard it out of anyone else's mouth for months. A language is also a rather amazing link with everyone in the past— literally millions and millions of people—who made that tongue what it is today so that it could be passed on to you as such a supple and live cultural legacy. This kind of community is so basic as to often be invisible, but it is no less essential for all that.

IMPLICATIONS

Gratefulness follows, for starters. What precious and immense legacies we all inherit! Countless people over long stretches of time have helped make me what I am—what a gift.

Second, right away, in consequence, a commitment also follows to do our part to respect and sustain our communities and their core values. Ward, for example, speaks immediately and emphatically of the need to be "respectful of the care, connectedness, and interdependence that assured our survival through the best and the worst of times."

It's not that community values necessarily trump all others. Here, as in many places, some kind of balance is required. To take the example of African-American community ethics once again, listen to the words of Vanessa Siddle Walker and John R. Snarey in their book *Race-ing Moral Formation*:

[T]hose who follow African American ethics refuse to starkly dichotomize self and community. To care for the self is to care for the group, and to care for the group is to care for the self. . . . [This is a] moral legacy of the West African heritage of most African Americans. The successful realization of a balanced community-and-individual ethic produces the fruit of *uplift*—the enhancement of the community and the valuing of the individual's diverse gifts. . . . [T]he weakness that would result from a large imbalance is either *one-sided selfishness,* acting according to one's needs and interests without any balanced regard for the larger community; or *one-sided self-sacrifice,* the obliteration or denial of one's own interests, needs, or selfhood for the sake of "more worthy" community or cause.

Notice also the parallels to Gilligan's model of moral development here: again, on another level now, the struggle of moral maturation is to find a balanced way between and beyond both self-seeking and self-sacrifice. It also sounds rather like Aristotle's doctrine of the Mean!

Finally, beyond both gratefulness and respect, it is our challenge to *contribute* in turn to the communities that form and sustain us. Ethnic or religious heritages are ours to carry on. The work of a profession; sustaining, adjusting, or improving a form of government or a style of art; rebuilding a landscape or a place: all of these may call to us, and among them, somewhere, we will find our life's tasks.

Once again, it's not that the current or the most visible or insistent community values necessarily rule. One kind of contribution can even be loving resistance. If there are wrongs, it is our responsibility to right the wrongs. Still, this is *our* tradition, our country, our community. We are responsible for it even if we would rather sometimes walk away.

READING

From "The Moral Foundations of an African Culture"

KWASI WIREDU

COMMUNITY IS ALWAYS PARTICULAR. We are linked with *these* specific others in thus-and-such a way. Even in making the very general and introductory points just above, I have needed to draw on a specific relationship, in this case African-American ethnic identity. To carry the point further we must get still more

From Kwasi Wiredu, "The Moral Foundations of an African Culture," *Person and Community: Ghanaian Philosophical Studies* I (Center for Research in Values Philosophy, 1992), pp. 193–206.

specific. These passages by Kwasi Wiredu (b. 1931), a widely read contemporary Ghanaian philosopher who teaches in the United States, paint a rich picture of an ethical life deeply constituted by family and communal relations, in his own people, the Akan of West Africa. Wiredu both shows us an explicitly communal ethics from the inside, so to speak, and shows us a few of the deep historical and cultural roots of African-*American* ethical practice in turn.

Akan society is of a type in which the greatest value is attached to communal belonging. And the way in which a sense of communal belonging is fostered in the individual is through the concentrated stress on kinship identity. . . . Thus conceived, a human person is essentially the centre of a thick set of concentric circles of obligations and responsibilities matched by rights and privileges revolving round levels of relationships irradiating from the consanguinity of household kith and kin, through the "blood" ties of lineage and clan, to the wider circumference of human familyhood based on the common possession of the divine spark. . . .

. . . [T]he Akan philosophy of life . . . is made explicit in the maxim, *Onipa hia moa,* meaning, by way of first approximation, "A human being needs help." The intent of the maxim, however, is not just to observe a fact, but also to prescribe a line of conduct. The imperative here is carried by the word *hia,* which in this context also has a connotation of entitlement: a human being deserves, ought, to be helped.

This imperative is born of an acute sense of the essential dependency of the human condition. The idea of dependency may even be taken as a component of the Akan conception of a person. "A human being," says a noted Akan proverb, "is not a palm tree so as to be self-sufficient" (*Onipa nye abe na ne ho ahyia ne ho*). Indeed, at birth a human being is not only not self-sufficient but also radically self-insufficient, if one may be permitted the expression: he/she is totally dependent on others. In due course, through growth and acculturation, acquired skills and abilities will reduce this dependency but will never eliminate it completely. Self-reliance is, of course, understood and recommended by the Akans, but its very possibility is predicated upon this ineliminable residue of human dependency. Human beings, therefore, at all times, in one way or another, directly or indirectly, need the help of their kind.

One very standard situation in Akan life in which this truth was continually illustrated was in traditional agriculture. As hinted earlier, this was generally based on smallholdings worked by individual farmers and their households. In such a mode of production recurrent stages were easily foreseeable where the resources of any one farmer would be insufficient to accomplish a necessary task efficiently—be it the initial clearing of the ground or the scooping out of, say, cocoa beans from great heaps of pods. At such moments, all that was necessary was for one to send word to one's neighbours indicating the time, place, and the nature of the help needed. Very much as day follows night, the people would assemble at the right time at the indicated place with their own implements of work and together help get the job done speedily and with almost festive enthusiasm, in full and warranted conviction that when their turn came the same gesture would be returned in exactly the same spirit. Anybody who availed himself of the benefits of this system and yet dragged his feet when the call came from others was liable to be convicted, at the bar of public opinion, of such fathomless degeneracy as to be branded a social outcast. The type of mutual aid here discussed probably occurs in varying intensities in rural communities all over the world, but in traditional Akan society it was so much and so palpably a part of working experience that the Akans actually came to think of life (*obra*) as one continuous drama of mutual aid (*nnoboa*). *Obra ye nnoboa:* "Life is mutual aid," according to an Akan saying. . . .

. . . [K]inship support . . . is of the highest importance in the Akan communal set-up, for it is the basis of the sense of belonging which gives the individual much of his/her psychological stability (this, incidentally, is why a traveller bereft of it strikes the Akan so forcefully as a sad case). It is also, conversely, the basis of a good proportion of the obligations in terms of which the individual's moral standing is assessed. The smallest and most intimate Akan kinship unit is the matrilineal household. This includes a person's mother and his/her mother's children, his/her mother's sisters and brothers, the children of the mother's sisters, and, at the top, the grandmother. It is instructive to observe that the English words aunt and cousin fail to capture the depth of kinship feelings corresponding to the relations of mother's sister and mother's sister's children respectively, in spite of their mechanical correctness as translations. In the Akan language the words for mother and mother's children are the same as for mother's sister and mother's sister's children. Since the relationships noted already comprehend quite a sizeable community, especially if the grandmother concerned has been even averagely fertile, this guarantees that in a traditional setting an Akan child begins life with quite a large sense of belonging and a broad sweep of sympathies.

The next extension of the circle of the kinship relations just described brings us to the level of the lineage. Here the *basic unit* consists of a person's grandmother and her children and grandchildren, together with the grandmother's brothers and sisters and the children and grandchildren of her sisters. This unit quickly swells with the culturally legitimate addition of a grandmother's maternal "cousins" and their descendants. From the point of view of a person's civic existence, this is the most significant circle of relations, for it was through the head of the lineage that, in traditional times, a person had his/her political representation. The lineage, as can easily be imagined, is a quite considerable group of people, but it is small in comparison with the maximal limit of kinship grouping, which is the set of all the people descending from one woman. The latter is the clan. For a quick idea of magnitude, consider that the Akans, now numbering in the region of seven million, trace their collective ancestry to seven women. Patently, individual Akans will never know all their relatives, but they can rest assured that they have a million of them.

THE EXPANDING CIRCLE

Finally, we are invited also to recognize how deeply we are related to the rest of the Earth and Earth's creatures. Until now this chapter has spoken of "community" in a wholly human sense, and we've been acting like this is the most natural thing in the world. But in fact it is not natural at all. We are also inescapably linked with the Earth: with other living creatures and with the all-encompassing ecosphere. Recall our definition of community at the beginning of the last section: a community is some linked set of others with whom we have a compelling commonality. Many philosophers and others now hold that any ethics of relationship must recognize the *Earth* community as well.

We know that *egocentrism* is a spectacularly narrow-minded way of living. But what about our still-easy assumption that ethics goes only as far as the human—as if the entire world apart from us were simply a means to our ends, merely a collection of resources, morally irrelevant? Call this *anthropocentrism:* a kind of human-centeredness exactly parallel to self-centeredness. It's species-egoism, as it were. It's also a kind of blindness. As Gregory Bateson put it:

> When you narrow down . . . and act on the premise "What interests me is me, or my organization, or my species," you chop off consideration of other loops of the loop structure [that includes your loop]. You decide that you want to get rid of the by-products of human life and that Lake Erie will be a good place to put them. You forget that the . . . system called Lake Erie is a part of *your* wider . . . system—and that if Lake Erie is driven insane, its insanity is incorporated in the larger system of *your* thought and experience.

Contrariwise, to try to live in harmony with larger natural systems is not to serve narrow ends. "Sanity" means being in relation, indeed what Buddhists call "right relation"; it's sane, it's right, and it's *rich:* the natural world becomes more like a companion and less like a resource, or adversary, or merely stage scenery.

The Lakota people have a phrase used to open and close many ceremonies. It has been translated into English as "all my relations," and its point is to highlight the interrelatedness of all life on Earth—not only in the sense of global interdependency, but also in the specific sense that each species is a relative, a member of our family, quite genuinely and literally a *relation.* We're in *community* with them (too).

Animals, for instance. In chapter 1 you read Alice Walker's story of her relation to one animal—a relation that prompted her to rethink her (and our) relations with many other animals, as well as with oppressed groups and peoples. Animals surround us, work with us, sing in the trees all around us and swim in the same seas, romp through our dreams and stories and myths, and often enough through our houses and daily lives too. The ecologist Paul Shepard even wrote a book subtitled *How Animals Made Us Human.* Just as with our other relations, life in the community of other beings shapes our own identities as well.

And of course we are animals too! The whole point is that we have many of the same feelings, experiences, and needs as other creatures. Utilitarians argue that therefore animal suffering counts morally just as the same suffering in us would count; but here suffering is not the whole story, either. Just like suffering in any other of our relations, it is morally bad partly because these are our *kin.*

It's not just animals that "make us human." Truly, it's nature as a whole. This is, after all, the world in which humans evolved. Its climates shaped our skins, its terrains shaped our bodies, its sounds and sights and textures shaped our senses, its mysteries shaped our minds. And all of this shaping continues. The magician-philosopher David Abram writes beautifully of the Pacific Northwest:

> Oak, madrone, Douglas fir, red-tailed hawk, serpentine in the sandstone, a certain scale to the topography, drenching rains in the winter, fog off-shore in the summer, salmon surging in the streams—all of these together make up a particular state of mind, a place-specific intelligence shared by all the humans that dwell therein, but also by the coyotes yapping in those valleys, by the bobcats and the ferns and the spiders, by all beings who live and make their way in that zone. Each place its own psyche. Each sky its own blue.

This same sense of the depth of specific places, to the point that they shape our identities themselves, arises naturally when people have lived since time out of mind in a specific place (like Abram, I mean *really* specific: this mountain range, this valley, this stream, this village—also this burial ground, where my ancestors lie). I can't know my distant ancestors or descendants, anyway past the three generations or so each way, but I can know this place that we all share and that will nurture future generations as it has nurtured me and my ancestors (who are also all still here in spirit, merged back into the land perhaps). Thus the place itself moves into more central attention. You begin to see how care for people and care for the land can merge and finally become indistinguishable.

IMPLICATIONS

Again, gratefulness surely follows, for starters. Respect too, as toward those human communities that also nurture us. A commitment to attend to the world's needs and to respond. As the Swiss doctor and humanitarian Albert Schweitzer wrote

> The great fault of all ethics hitherto has been that they believed themselves to have to deal only with the relations of man to man. In reality, however, the question is what is his attitude to the world and all life that comes within his reach. A man is ethical only when life, as such, is sacred to him, and when he devotes himself helpfully to all life that is in need of help.

Schweitzer acknowledges human ethics too—as a special case of the larger *life* ethic. "The ethic of the relation of man to man is not something apart by itself; it is only a particular relation which results from the universal one."

These are in fact huge questions. Philosophers have been asking them seriously for several decades now, and only the barest outlines of answers are emerging. Some, like Schweitzer, want to extend ethics to all of life—not only to ourselves and all other animals, but also to trees and plants. Usually the argument is that all living things, even if not "aware," at least strive toward something, have a "good of their own," which can also be taken as a good by others.

This is still a new and challenging idea. Much of the Western tradition in ethics teaches that it is what makes us distinctive as humans that makes us special, and we have learned to identify our distinctiveness with a certain kind of consciousness. Yet even in this book so far we have also seen that there are counter-ideas even within our tradition: philosophers of "encounter," for example, like Martin Buber, who suggest that encounter goes well beyond the species boundary, and utilitarian philosophers who argue that suffering in any creature is morally bad and ought to be minimized. Meanwhile, indigenous peoples everywhere—a vastly older "tradition"—insist that humans belong to the larger world. They're ethically invested not in distinctiveness but in *belonging*.

Many do not even divide living from nonliving forms as insistently as we do. The Lakota, for example, consider everything "living" to some extent.

In any case, it may well be that rivers and mountains must also have a direct voice in our ethics: they too are "relations." Families of animals or plants—species—may also count in their own right.

For that matter, what about whole ecosystems, systems that include many different kinds of creatures and elements? Ecology is supposed to be a holistic science—surely moral value should attach to whole natural systems too, and not just to certain of their parts.

The ethical circle, in short, is expanding. Our survey of the Ethics of Relationship comes to rest, perhaps, with a maximally expansive understanding of relationship. And why not? "All our relations"!

READING

From "The Land Ethic"

ALDO LEOPOLD

ALDO LEOPOLD (1887–1948)—forester, educator, philosopher, farmer—is widely considered the father of the contemporary American environmental movement. In this famous essay from the end of his book *Sand County Almanac,* he arrives at an explicit environmental ethics.

Notice how Leopold roots human communities in the character of the land they inhabit. All relationships intertwine and are grounded in the largest ecological wholes. Note also, near the end, Leopold's famous criterion for right action: "A thing is right when it tends to preserve the integrity, stability, and beauty of the biotic community. It is wrong when it tends otherwise."

When god-like Odysseus returned from the wars in Troy, he hanged all on one rope a dozen slave-girls of his household whom he suspected of misbehavior during his absence. This hanging involved no question of propriety. The girls were property. The disposal of property was then, as now, a matter of expediency, not of right and wrong.

Concepts of right and wrong were not lacking from Odysseus' Greece: witness the fidelity of his wife through the long years before at last his black-prowed galleys clove the wine-dark seas for home. The ethical structure of that day covered wives, but had not

By permission of Oxford University Press.

yet been extended to human chattels. During the three thousand years which have since elapsed, ethical criteria have been extended to many fields of conduct, with corresponding shrinkages in those judged by expediency only.

THE ETHICAL SEQUENCE

This extension of ethics, so far studied only by philosophers, is actually a process in ecological evolution. Its sequences may be described in ecological as well as in philosophical terms. An ethic, ecologically, is a limitation on freedom of action in the struggle for existence. An ethic, philosophically, is a differentiation of social from anti-social conduct. These are two definitions of one thing. The thing has its origin in the tendency of interdependent individuals or groups to evolve modes of co-operation. The ecologist calls these symbioses. Politics and economics are advanced symbioses in which the original free-for-all competition has been replaced, in part, by co-operative mechanisms with an ethical content. . . .

The first ethics dealt with the relation between individuals; the Mosaic Decalogue is an example. Later accretions dealt with the relation between the individual and society. The Golden Rule tries to integrate the individual to society; democracy to integrate social organization to the individual.

There is as yet no ethic dealing with man's relation to land and to the animals and plants which grow upon it. Land, like Odysseus' slave-girls, is still property. The land-relation is still strictly economic, entailing privileges but not obligations.

The extension of ethics to this third element in human environment is, if I read the evidence correctly, an evolutionary possibility and an ecological necessity. It is the third step in a sequence. The first two have already been taken. Individual thinkers since the days of Ezekiel and Isaiah have asserted that the despoliation of land is not only inexpedient but wrong. Society, however, has not yet affirmed their belief. I regard the present conservation movement as the embryo of such an affirmation.

An ethic may be regarded as a mode of guidance for meeting ecological situations so new or intricate, or involving such deferred reactions, that the path of social expediency is not discernible to the average individual. Animal instincts are modes of guidance for the individual in meeting such situations. Ethics are possibly a kind of community instinct in-the-making.

THE COMMUNITY CONCEPT

All ethics so far evolved rest upon a single premise that the individual is a member of a community of interdependent parts. His instincts prompt him to compete for his place in that community, but his ethics prompt him also to co-operate (perhaps in order that there may be a place to compete for).

The land ethic simply enlarges the boundaries of the community to include soils, waters, plants, and animals, or collectively: the land.

This sounds simple: do we not already sing our love for and obligation to the land of the free and the home of the brave? Yes, but just what and whom do we love? Certainly not the soil, which we are sending helter-skelter down river. Certainly not the waters, which we assume have no function except to turn turbines, float barges, and carry off sewage. Certainly not the plants, of which we exterminate whole communities without batting an eye. Certainly not the animals, of which we have already extirpated many of the largest and most beautiful species. A land ethic of course cannot prevent the alteration, management, and use of these "resources," but it does affirm their right to continued existence, and, at least in spots, their continued existence in a natural state.

In short, a land ethic changes the role of Homo sapiens from conqueror of the land-community to plain member and citizen of it. It implies respect for his fellow-members, and also respect for the community as such.

In human history, we have learned (I hope) that the conqueror role is eventually self-defeating. Why? Because it is implicit in such a role that the conqueror knows, ex cathedra, just what makes the community clock tick, and just what and who is valuable, and what and who is worthless, in community life. It always turns out that he knows neither, and this is why his conquests eventually defeat themselves. . . .

That man is, in fact, only a member of a biotic team is shown by an ecological interpretation of history. Many historical events, hitherto explained solely in terms of human enterprise, were actually biotic, interactions between people and land. The characteristics of the land determined the facts quite as potently as the characteristics of the men who lived on it.

Consider, for example, the settlement of the Mississippi valley. In the years following the Revolution, three groups were contending for its control: the native Indian, the French and English traders, and the American settlers. Historians wonder what would have happened if the English at Detroit had thrown a little more weight into the Indian side of those tipsy scales which decided the out-come of the colonial migration into the cane-lands of Kentucky. It is time now to ponder the fact that the cane-lands, when subjected to the particular mixture of forces represented by the cow, plow, fire, and axe of the pioneer, became bluegrass. What if the plant succession inherent in this dark and bloody ground had, under the impact of these forces, given us some worthless sedge, shrub, or weed? Would Boone and Kenton have held out? Would there have been any overflow into Ohio, Indiana, Illinois, and Missouri? Any Louisiana Purchase? Any transcontinental union of new states? Any Civil War?

Kentucky was one sentence in the drama of history. We are commonly told what the human actors in this drama tried to do, but we are seldom told that their success, or the lack of it, hung in large degree on the reaction of particular soils to the impact of the particular forces exerted by their occupancy. In the case of Kentucky, we do not even know where the bluegrass came from—whether it is a native species, or a stowaway from Europe.

Contrast the cane-lands with what hindsight tells us about the Southwest, where the pioneers were equally brave, resourceful, and persevering. The impact of occupancy here brought no bluegrass, or other plant fitted to withstand the bumps and buffetings of hard use. This region, when grazed by livestock, reverted through a series of more and more worthless grasses, shrubs, and weeds to a condition of unstable equilibrium. Each recession of plant types bred erosion; each increment to erosion bred a further recession of plants. The result today is a progressive and mutual deterioration, not only of plants and soils, but of the animal community subsist-ing thereon. . . .

In short, the plant succession steered the course of history; the pioneer simply demonstrated, for good or ill, what successions inhered in the land. Is history taught in this spirit? It will be, once the concept of land as a community really penetrates our intellec-tual life.

THE LAND PYRAMID

. . . In the beginning, the pyramid of life was low and squat; the food chains short and simple. Evolution has added layer after layer, link after link. Man is one of thousands of accretions to the height and complexity of the pyramid. Science has given us many doubts, but it has given us at least one certainty: the trend of evolution is to elaborate and diversify the biota.

Land, then, is not merely soil; it is a fountain of energy flowing through a circuit of soils, plants, and animals. Food chains are the living channels which conduct energy upward; death and decay return it to the soil. The circuit is not closed; some energy is dissipated in decay, some is added by absorption from the air, some is stored in soils, peats, and long-lived forests; but it is a sustained circuit, like a slowly augmented revolving fund of life. There is always a net loss by downhill wash, but this is normally small and offset by the decay of rocks. It is deposited in the ocean and, in the course of geological time, raised to form new lands and new pyramids.

The velocity and character of the upward flow of energy depend on the complex structure of the plant and animal community, much as the upward flow of sap in a tree depends on its complex cellular organization. Without this complexity, normal circulation would presumably not occur. Structure means the characteristic numbers, as well as the characteristic kinds and functions, of the component species. This interdependence between the complex structure of the land and its smooth functioning as an energy unit is one of its basic attributes.

When a change occurs in one part of the circuit, many other parts must adjust themselves to it. Change does not necessarily obstruct or divert the flow of energy; evolution is a long series of self-induced changes, the net result of which has been to elaborate the flow mechanism and to lengthen the circuit. Evolutionary changes, however, are usually slow and local. Man's invention of tools has enabled him to make changes of unprecedented violence, rapidity, and scope. . . .

THE OUTLOOK

It is inconceivable to me that an ethical relation to land can exist without love, respect, and admiration for land, and a high regard for its value. By value, of course, I mean something far broader than mere economic value; I mean value in the philosophical sense. . . .

The "key-log" which must be moved to release the evolutionary process for an ethic is simply this: quit thinking about decent land-use as solely an economic problem. Examine each question in terms of what is ethically and esthetically right, as well as what is economically expedient. A thing is right when it tends to preserve the integrity, stability, and beauty of the biotic community. It is wrong when it tends otherwise.

It of course goes without saying that economic feasibility limits the tether of what can or cannot be done for land. It always has and it always will. The fallacy the economic determinists have tied around our collective neck, and which we now need to cast off, is the belief that economics determines all land use. This is simply not true. An innumerable host of actions and attitudes, comprising perhaps the bulk of all land relations, is determined by the land-users' tastes and predilections, rather than by his purse. The bulk of all land relations hinges on investments of time, forethought, skill, and faith rather than on investments of cash. As a land-user thinketh, so is he.

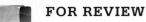

FOR REVIEW

1. What is Care Ethics?
2. Contrast Kohlberg and Gilligan's views of moral development.
3. According to Nel Noddings, what are some of the implications of an Ethics of Care?
4. What is a "community"?
5. What ethical difference does a community make?
6. How does kinship shape morality for the Akan people?
7. What is "anthropocentrism"?
8. What is the "expanding circle"?
9. What do the Lakota mean by "all my relations"?
10. What is Aldo Leopold's criterion for the ultimate standard of right and wrong?

EXERCISES AND NOTES

8.1 SELF-REFLECTIONS

Think about the communities that are most present in your own life. Family, a team or other group perhaps, maybe a religious community. Maybe something as simple as your dormitory, which for many students is the first real experience of community, at least with biologically unrelated people: the first time living so interdependently with a large number of people to whom there are responsibilities and with whom there is accountability as sharers of a common place. In dormitories, the entire residence hall may be affected by the actions of one member—what kind of ethics then follows?

Imagine being without any of these relationships. Can you picture it at all? Remember that it is not simply a matter of being a "loner," say, for loners still live in society, among other creatures, and so on (in fact to some degree they may consciously live *against* others, which paradoxically enough is a very strong form of relationship). Can you even begin to conceive yourself without a history, or a people, or a language? And again, if not, what follows?

Would you want to be a member of Akan society? Why or why not? Also, in what ways are our own societies more similar to the Akan than at first it may seem? And again, if there are specific ways in which you do think you'd like a community more like theirs, what are some ways within our own traditions to bring it about?

8.2 QUESTIONS—PRACTICAL AND PHILOSOPHICAL

Here are some more involved questions about different forms of the Ethics of Relationship.

Noddings calls Care Ethics a "feminine" approach and the "ethics of the mother." Hers is a gendered approach, in short, even though she is careful to say that care is available to men and fathers as well. (She's even willing to speak of appropriately caring men as "mothers," though it's hard for me to decide whether this truly transcends gender or does just the opposite.) But this is a matter of contention among many feminists. In work that followed the more widely known research featured in the text, Gilligan concluded that both Care Ethics and the more traditional "Justice Ethics" are represented by *both* males and females: that is, that a full ethical toolbox needs to recognize both sets of values (and more) and that both care and justice are capacities we *all* have and use. To the extent that women are more associated with the care approach— the empirical evidence is complex and unclear on this—it may be more due to social training and stereotype than, somehow, to "nature." You might want to consider this question in more depth.

How can one *criticize* relationships—specifically, how can one criticize them morally? Specifically, to take Care Ethics again, consider the all too common stories of women who stay with abusive spouses long after there is any hope of reform for him or even safety for her. Such loyalty, sometimes literally to the death, is certainly one way to honor relationships. It is, sometimes at least, a genuine testament to the power of relational care, though there are certainly also other, more coercive reasons why a woman might make this choice. Most of us, though, would probably say that this is going much too far. Certainly that it is not something that ethics could *require*. More than that, though, shouldn't ethics, sometimes at least, actually require the opposite: breaking the relationship? If so, can the reasons be found somehow in an ethic of care itself—perhaps in the imperative for a woman also to care for *herself*—or do they necessarily, or anyway more powerfully and appropriately, arise from one (or more) of the other families of moral values?

An Ethic of the Person, for example, might say that when women are thoroughly conditioned for loyalty to relationship, especially when men are not, they are systematically discriminated against. Justice calls for something quite different than an Ethics of Relationship. What do you think?

The Ethics of Relationship, so firmly and often compellingly grounded in families and communities, also has problems dealing with those who stand outside families and communities: the outsider or stranger. By definition, outsiders do not share the relationships that underlie the relations of care and connection that this chapter has been discussing (except of course when we are thinking of the whole Earth, where it's a crucial point, in fact, that there are no outsiders). In that case, though, it seems that the Ethics of Relationship has not much to say about them.

But this offends our moral sense. For Hallie's French villagers, for example, the Jewish refugees from the Nazis were strangers. Why not abandon them to their fate, then, especially when hospitality might well endanger the existing village community? What about homeless people, abandoned children, today's refugees from war or environmental disaster? Surely we owe them something, however "strange" they may be, or perhaps even precisely for that reason. It is not clear how the Ethics of Relationship could answer in any satisfactory way.

Give this problem some careful thought. How do you think someone might respond to it in defense of a relationship- or community-based ethics? Two hints might be:

1. Maybe this is just a point at which we have to acknowledge that the Ethics of Relationship is incomplete. We need the other families of moral values to help out. After all, arguably at least, none of the families of moral values are complete and self-sufficient. Each of them overlooks some things. Utilitarianism, for example, arguably overlooks individual rights, while a rights perspective sometimes gives too short shrift to utilities. Both may sometimes slight the virtues. Arguably, we need all of them. The outsider, it might be said, is just one place where the Ethics of Relationship doesn't go.

2. A second possible response is that real communities do, in fact, work out ways to include outsiders, to grant them *some* moral standing in the community, even if not equality. On this point you might find it useful to look at the chapter called "Membership" in Michael Walzer's book *Spheres of Justice* (Basic Books, 1983). Walzer is a moral philosopher in a school of thought sometimes called "communitarian"—a political analogue of the Ethics of Relationship. Real communities, he argues, have usually acknowledged the moral claims of strangers in their midst, depending in part on how they came to be there, in a variety of sometimes indirect and subtle ways. On the other

hand, the very preservation of the community generally requires that the community welcome strangers with some reservation, or grant them only partial or gradual membership. It is a difficult and certainly relevant problem: for example, Walzer discusses the question of "guest workers" in many Western European countries today. See what you think.

Finally, there are many difficult and intriguing philosophical questions about the ground and nature of environmental values. Aldo Leopold suggests that we think of ourselves as just "plain members and citizens" of the land community, and that this relationship is the basis of what he calls the "Land Ethic." To adapt a famous line attributed to Chief Seattle, the land doesn't belong to us, we belong to it. But consider these questions a little farther. In how strong a sense of a community can we say that the "land," in Leopold's sense of the biotic system, is in fact a "community"? Mightn't this stretch the term past some logical breaking point? In human communities, after all, part of the connection among the members is some sense of mutual obligation: a sense of reciprocity. It is harder to see that reciprocity holds in relation to the Land. Is this a problem?

Do we need, perhaps, a different story (instead, or also?) about the moral value of nature? Recall the reading from Edward Abbey—certainly a radical environmentalist voice—in "Using Your Tools" #2, for example, where it is not at all clear that the desert is a community of which humans are an integral part. For Abbey that may even be the *source* of (some of) its value. (And by the way, what did you decide about whether this value is a moral value or not?) Consider the possibility, then, that none of our families of moral values yet adequately articulates the values of nature. So do environmental values need their own, new family?

8.3 ISSUES REVISITED

Now that we have completed our survey of the main families of moral values, go back to the issues you first analyzed in Exercise 4.2 and analyze them again, using the understanding you have gained since then of the Ethics of the Person, Happiness, Virtue, and Relationship. Give yourself credit for seeing a lot more than you did the first time (I hope you do!). Similarly, you could go on to read Values Statements and Stories, as you did in Exercise 4.3, with your newer and fuller understanding in hand.

For a variation on this exercise, survey some other ethical issues of interest to you, or issues that show up in the current news, and do the same thing: articulate the moral values involved, using any or all of the four families of values we have surveyed. You might also go another step to ask if there are *other* values involved that may be overlooked in the news reports or in our usual understanding of "the" issue. Do this by deliberately looking at the issue from the point of view of families of values that haven't yet been, or aren't usually, mentioned. Are there certain families of values that tend to be overlooked when we think about certain types of issues? Why do you think this happens? Is it a problem?

8.4 FAMILY SPIRITS

Here is a final, quite different exercise looking back and comparing all four families of moral values.

Families—the flesh and blood kind—tend to have distinctive emotional characters or "family spirits." One family is outgoing, optimistic, argumentative, a little too cheerful sometimes. Another is very demanding, especially each individual of themselves, constantly striving for excellence in sports, say, or the arts. Yet a third might be reflective, appreciative, nature loving, a little too quiet sometimes. These are just a few of the dimensions on which families differ, of course.

Likewise, I would suggest, our families of moral values also have distinctive emotional characters or "family spirits." Some are more sociable, others more solitary. Some are more optimistic, some not so sure. Some, perhaps, are more willing to take and appreciate the world as it is, while others are more interested in changing it. Utilitarianism, for example, is a model of cheerfulness and engagement, always looking to make things a little more pleasant all around, a little impatient or edgy sometimes. You don't typically find Bertrand Russell's kind of irony or playfulness, for example, in any of the other families of values. It's probably also no accident that most of utilitarianism's most prominent advocates (Bentham and Mill, as well as Russell) were English, whereas Kant, and some of the "feel" of the Ethics of the Person at least as he sees it, was Prussian.

Now try to work out the emotional character, or "family spirit," of the other three families of values (and go farther with the Ethics of Happiness too). You might consider a variety of multimedia forms—not all necessarily verbal—in which to present your results. If the Ethics of Relationship were a dance number, what would it look like? If the Ethics of Person were a dinner party, what would be on the menu? Who's invited?

NOTES

Carol Gilligan is quoted from *In a Different Voice* (Harvard University Press, 1982, 1993), pp. 30–31. The quote in the text about Gilligan's findings is from Eve Browning Cole's *Philosophy and Feminist Criticism: An Introduction* (Paragon House, 1993), pp. 105–106. Against Kant's dismissal of the emotions, see Lawrence Blum, *Friendship, Altruism, and Morality* (Routledge, 1982). For a thorough and wide-ranging contemporary exposition of Care Ethics, see Virginia Held, *The Ethics of Care: Personal, Political, and Global* (Oxford, 2007). A useful survey of a variety of positions in Care Ethics is chapter 8, "Care-Focused Feminism," in Rosemarie Tong's *Feminist Thought: A More Comprehensive Introduction* (Westview, 2008).

Janie Ward is quoted from Gilligan and Ward, "Foreword," *Race-ing Moral Formation: African American Perspectives on Care and Justice* (Teacher's College Press, 2004), p. xi. Vanessa Siddle Walker and John R. Snarey are cited from the same book's "Introduction: Race Matters in Moral Formation," pp. 10–11, and "Conclusion: Primary Values and Developing Virtues of African American Ethics," pp. 136–137. In the same book, see also Walker's essay with Renarta Tompkins, "Caring in the Past: The Case of a Southern Segregated African American School," pp. 77–92. Classic in this area is Patricia Hill Collins, *Black Feminist Thought* (Routledge, revised 10th anniversary edition, 2000).

In the last section, the first quote is from Gregory Bateson, "Pathologies of Epistemology," in *Steps to an Ecology of Mind* (Chandler Publishing Company, 1972), p. 484. David Abram is cited from his book *The Spell of the Sensuous* (Pantheon, 1996), p. 262. Albert Schweitzer is cited from his *Out of My Life and Thought* (Holt, Rinehart and Winston, 1949), pp. 158–159. Aldo Leopold's essay "The Land Ethic" can be found at the very end of *A Sand County Almanac* (Oxford University Press, 1949, 1968)—the whole book is well worth the read. For a general "next step" into environmental ethics, see my collection *An Invitation to Environmental Philosophy* (Oxford University Press, 1999); don't overlook its extensive annotated bibliography, "Going On."

Many thanks to Beth Raps for the early conceptualization and drafts of parts of this chapter.

USING YOUR TOOLS #4
BUILDING A STUDENT
CODE OF ETHICS

The Ethics of Persons addresses persons as such, wherever and whoever we are. Utilitarianism addresses us simply as beings capable of pleasures and pains, perhaps even regardless of species. The Ethics of Virtue, however, locates moral values within specific social practices or even roles. The Ethics of Relationship locates them within relationships, most of which are again particular, like families or communities. Going more deeply into the Ethics of Virtue and the Ethics of Relationships therefore invites us to look at our practices and communities more specifically. That is the project of this "Using Your Tools" exercise.

Most readers of this book will be students in a college or university setting. That is, you already belong to a specific community: your institution, with its own unique and no doubt proud history, and its self-understanding in terms of a specific set of practices, centering around teaching and learning and possibly research: the generation and transmission of knowledge, the nurturing of wisdom, and service to larger communities. The project of this UYT is to explore the values, especially the moral values, that arise from this setting.

COMMUNITIES AND PRACTICES

Begin by exploring the ways that your college or university is a community. Physically, it brings large numbers of people together at times. Intellectually, the faculty may think of themselves as a community of scholars (especially in smaller institutions: look up the etymology of the word "college," for example) through which generations of students pass. From the point of view of a particular school, another image of community is the community of its alumi/ae—a community across time. (Every Commencement at my school, Elon University, the president welcomes the graduates into the community of alumni/ae. "You may leave Elon," he says, "but Elon is not leaving you.") From the point of view of the disciplines, the community of scholars is sometimes pictured as including all highly educated people in that field (the granting of a PhD, for example, by examination by a committee of established PhD-holders, is a rite of passage into an exclusive and demanding kind of community), and/or again may be pictured historically, linking today's scholars with an honored tradition that in the case of some fields, like philosophy, reaches back thousands of years.

Meantime, as a student at your school, you are also a member of a community of students. Physically, once again, students live and study together. On weekends and evenings, resident students pretty much *are* the school. You are invited to embrace and carry on the many and varied student-life traditions of your school, from certain rituals and allegiances to certain sports teams to a long-term loyalty to the school and to fellow graduates. And underneath all of the trappings, you share a common role, a fundamental practice. You are *students*, here for a specific purpose: to study and grow, to master both the general knowledge it has been deemed necessary for you to have to productively enter the larger community, and specific fields as you choose.

Now consider what moral values arise from these different images of community and shared practice. What are the "internal goods," to use MacIntyre's concept, of the practices of teaching and learning? What virtues are thereby defined for students? That is, what is it to be a *good student*, specifically in the moral sense that the Ethics of Virtue derives from shared practices, in the same way that a person may be a good auto mechanic or a good parent?

Again what values arise, as the Ethics of Relationship would have it, out of the many relations of trust and dependency that make up college or university communities? This, too, is a wide-ranging question. Consider values that address students' relationship to *each other*: in- and out-of-classroom demeanors that safeguard and/or enhance learning, for example. Part of my recent work for my own school has been on a committee setting out guidelines for Campus Technology use. The ethics of being a good student in this sense, we decided, include everything from taking care of the hardware, to avoiding email scams or even weak passwords that may lead to crashes or slowdowns in the university system, inconveniencing everyone, to not making or uploading video recordings of anyone without their knowledge and permission. Can you articulate the underlying community values that put all of these behaviors out of bounds? And what alternative behaviors *should* be expected or required (that is, can and should a student code of ethics tell us what *to* do and not just what *not* to do)?

Consider values that address students' relationship to *teachers*, to the faculty, from the respect due to their learning and devotion to classroom demeanor. What are teachers' obligations to students in turn? What are appropriate processes for dealing with problems that may arise in this relationship, especially when one side or the other is not holding up their end? Many schools have Judicial Boards or similar mechanisms to deal with the worst cases, but is a legal model appropriate for schools? Could other approachs serve learning better?

Consider values that address students' relationship to *knowledge*: academic honesty, for example. Once again, do the values at stake go deeper (deeper, in this case, than the usual disvalue of dishonesty) when we see them from the point of view of certain communities or relationships or practices? There are "good students" in the purely academic sense of doing well in the classroom and on tests—of mastering the subject. To what extent is this sense of "good" also moral? Does the moral sense also go farther? Can you be a good student in the moral sense and get low grades? Even flunk out? (Answer: yes . . . but how is this possible?)

Consider values that address students' relationship to the *institution*. For example, what are your obligations to your school simply because it is *your* school? When I take students abroad, I urge them to think of themselves as ambassadors for Elon University: that is, to think of themselves not just as individuals but also as taking the institution out into the world. It is different than going abroad on your own (and even then you may be seen, like it or not, as a representative of some country or ethnicity, at least).

Think of the generations of generosity that make your own education possible, on the part of previous graduates, teachers, local craftspeople, taxpayers, and many other supporters and donors of many kinds. What follows? Is it not now your responsibility to "pay it forward," just as they did? When Elon's president welcomes new graduates to the community of alumni/ae, he adds: you'll be hearing from us shortly. Meaning: you'll be getting requests for donations. The newly minted graduates laugh, but they get it too. The obligation is real. And they step up to it.

You may consider still other relationships that may give rise to moral expectations for students. Your relationship to your *parents*, for example, who may be supporting you financially, helping to make this experience possible. For that matter, what of your relationship to the generations before them, who are much less likely to have had this opportunity and might have only distantly dreamed of it for their descendants? Today, here you are. To what extent might you consider something like a seven-generation perspective even shere? Your ancestors (and descendants) bear you up, as you bear them up. What does this mean for students? Do other generations, past or future, have legitimate expectations to which you as a student should also respond?

OUTCOMES

Once you have explored all of this, I suggest that you try to put it together into a comprehensive Student Code of Ethics that might be one of your class's contributions to your school.

You could start by reviewing your school's Honor Code and/or any other ethical statements or Codes that your school may already have. Why do these Codes say what they say? Are they enough? What other kinds of ethical obligations do you think specifically apply to students? Why?

In my experience, most Student Codes of Ethics confine themselves to certain narrow and specific and mostly negative kinds of issues, like issues that arise about academic honesty (plagiarism) or dormitory living or substance abuse. And they mostly lay out sets of proscriptions—what *not* to do, a kind of legalistic boundary setting. You might aim to improve these sorts of Codes in two ways. First, can you make the Codes more than negative? Consider their deeper rationales. Are there not positive implications also, for being a *good* student? Can you spell out a persuasive and even inspiring ethical rationale for such rules, for example? (Not just that you should avoid some behaviour because it's illegal or disruptive, etc.) Why are there such rules? What ultimately are they serving? How do we have to understand ourselves to see that these rules make sense and apply to us? Use the Ethics of Virtue and of Relationship to make your case clear and persuasive to your fellow community members.

Such codes also tend, again in my experience, to be fairly narrowly defined. Typically they are first put forward by Residence Life offices or other administrative offices that tend to focus on judicial sorts of models and offences. But what about a general Student Code of Ethics that starts with the widest values—that takes us all the way back, again, to the fundamental practices and relationships that structure educational institutions as such? What would a Student Code of Ethics look like if it spoke first and foremost to them?

Talk to the relevant administrators and student leaders as you explore your school's existing Code and develop your own. Find ways to offer your new Code to your school's community for their consideration and discussion. What's the next step then?

III

SKILLS FOR
ETHICAL PRACTICE

CHAPTER 9

Critical Thinking

A diverse set of skills are key to effective ethical practice: these are what Part III of this book explores. You will also see that these skills themselves embody moral values. The very process of thinking and debating about ethical issues must be ethical itself: that is, the process and not merely (hopefully) the outcome need to take care for the needs and legitimate expectations of others as well as our own. Looking carefully into the facts at stake, listening carefully to each other and looking as much for areas of agreement and commonality as to the areas of difference, and all the rest of the skills we will practice in Part III, will make your practice both more effective and also more *ethical*.

FACTS AND SOURCES

Moral disagreements are much more than differences about values. Sometimes, indeed, we hardly differ about values at all. Many moral disagreements basically come down to the *facts*: facts about how to produce certain desired effects, for instance, or about what the causes of a current problem really are, or even just about simple and specific information that you could look up in 10 minutes on the Web or in the library.

On some issues even a few simple facts can change everything. A young chocolate-loving friend of mine was chagrined to learn that many chocolates are harvested by virtual slave laborers. Now she makes a point of eating only Fair Trade chocolate (and spreading the word: her efforts have led to my telling *you* about this issue, for example). Facts about environmental damage, facts about who is actually "on welfare" and what kind of support they get, facts about the recovery prospects of comatose patients on life support, or about the sweatshops that make collegiate T-shirts, or about the actual history of the institution of marriage: all of these facts may transform our understanding of an issue and our ethical views about it.

Since even a few facts can change everything, then it is part of our responsibility to *seek out* the facts—honestly and persistently. We need to do more than simply assert what we think is "obvious" or cherry-pick a few facts to support what we already think. The real challenge is to find out more, to understand better—even if our views, and our actions too, may have to change as a result.

WHAT IS AT STAKE?

The first step is to get clear yourself just what is at stake. Clarify the underlying factual questions in pressing moral issues. How much animal suffering does a non-meat diet alleviate? How many Americans are effectively without medical care because they have no insurance and can't afford to pay for it? Do children raised by same-sex couples grow up any more sexually confused than the average adolescent? When and where is "restorative justice"—reconciliation and greater understanding, rather than retribution—possible?

These questions are factual. That is, actual *evidence* is available. By now many children have been raised by same-sex couples, for instance. No one is entitled to make assumptions about them without actually checking them out. Or again, does the average mother on welfare have more kids than the average mother not on welfare? It's not that hard to find out.

Check out even those claims you think are obvious. If they're central to serious moral disagreements, then they're pretty likely *not* obvious to others. In any case, you need actual evidence. Don't just appeal to what "everybody knows." Case in point: though American fear of crime is at an all-time high, and everyone seems to "know" that crime is skyrocketing, in fact it isn't. What's really increased dramatically is crime *coverage* on TV. The specific stories are no doubt true, but overall they create a false impression. Think, think, think!

GETTING THE FACTS

Is it ethically better to drive more fuel-efficient cars? It depends in part on how fuel-efficient cars can get, and at what cost. My students were discussing this question one day when two of them began to argue very vocally about it. One argued that cars could easily be ten times more efficient than they are now. The other acknowledged that some hybrids now get two or three times the mileage of the average car but argued that these are specialty cars—expensive and hard to get—and that still higher efficiency is just wishful thinking.

Well, I said, why don't you find out? No point in having a debate as if this were just a contest for the firmest opinion or loudest voice. There are facts of the matter, there is actual data—go find out.

They did. The next class we had actual facts before us. The average U.S. car, it turns out, only gets around 22 miles per gallon (mpg) right now. This figure drops to around 20 when you include SUVs and vans. It also turns out that there are indeed cars, right now, that get over 100—adaptations of currently available hybrids, with a plug-in device for recharging the car batteries overnight from line current. The same vehicles *can* average over 200 mpg under the right conditions. On the other hand, the plug-in device is hard to get and expensive so far, and not marketed with the original cars, which also must be driven just right to get the highest possible mileage.

So both students were right in a sense. *Nearly* ten times better mileage (200+ mpg) is possible (at least going by the overall passenger fleet average of 22 mpg rather than the average for new cars, which is into the 30s), *but* right now at least, it is a stretch. Even more important, though, when these students came back with what they'd learned (I assigned it as a joint project), the issue itself was transformed. It was no longer a contest of off-the-cuff opinions competing to defeat each other. They were no longer even disagreeing, for one thing. And with a few facts on hand, the ensuing discussion was far more productive. As I write, the Obama Administration is floating the idea of roughly doubling the current federal CAFE (Corporate Average Fuel Economy) standard—to 56.2 mpg. Students began to see the possibility. They also asked good questions, like how it might be possible to make plug-in hybrids less costly and more widely available. What's likely to develop in the next few years? Carmakers wildly underestimated the demand for hybrids in the first place. Should we believe them now when they opine that most drivers won't be willing to plug in their cars at night? What if we took the opposite tack and tried to make plug-in cars more chic?

My two at-first-antagonistic students also found out a few other truly amazing facts that I can't resist adding, such as the worst fuel economy for any car, which is for some dragsters that consume the equivalent of 24 gallons per mile (that would be about .04 mpg). The absolutely best so far was the PAC-Car II, which really *is* an extremely specialized vehicle. This car got a staggering 12,660 mpg in the 2005 Eco-Marathon (no misprint: that's twelve thousand six hundred sixty). It does look like there is a little room for improvement, doesn't it?

INTERPRETING THE DATA

Some people defend the death penalty by arguing that it deters would-be murderers from committing murders. This is often said to be "obvious." But is it? How would you get *evidence* for or against a deterrence effect?

You could compare states with the death penalty to states without it. Or, you could compare U.S. murder rates when the death penalty was widely used to the murder rates when it was barred. These kinds of studies have been done. What do they say? You need to know before you can weigh in on this question.

One widely publicized study from the 1970s correlated the decline in capital punishment in the United States between 1933 and 1969 with a rise in murders and therefore concluded that the death penalty does indeed deter murderers. On the other hand, it's hard to know what to make of this. It seems far more likely that other huge social changes in the United States between 1933 and 1969 (that is, besides the decline in executions) better account for the increase in murder rates in that period.

Another remarkable statistic is that states with the death penalty on average have *higher* murder rates than states that don't. Is it possible that the death penalty actually encourages some would-be murderers? Or is the murder rate now higher in death penalty states for reasons unrelated to the death penalty? (Or perhaps such states have enacted the death penalty *because* the murder rate is felt to be unacceptably high?)

So this question, in turns out, can't be answered with an emphatic yes or no. But we nonetheless learn something very useful: that the actual effects of the death penalty are uncertain. It's just *not* obvious, either way. That's a fact too, and it makes a difference. For example, uncertainties about deterrence have pushed some defenders of the death penalty away from utilitarian arguments and toward arguments about justice. They have come to realize that their real reasons for favoring the death penalty do not depend on exactly what effects it may or may not have on murder rates. Contrariwise, the same uncertainties about deterrence have also prompted some utilitarians to come out against the death penalty. That is, they have come to realize that their real reasons for favoring the death penalty are much less solid than they thought, and now conclude that its costs probably outweigh its benefits.

You see, again: it is possible to think intelligently about such issues in the face of complex or surprising evidence. But it is *not* possible to think intelligently about such issues if we don't look for the evidence at all. So look for it!

WHICH FACTS ARE RELEVANT?

by VANCE RICKS

With some difficult moral issues, it is pretty clear what the underlying factual questions are, even if we may not know where to find answers to them. Some of the examples so far in this chapter are like that: moral debates about how to control pollution, or about the deterrent effects of capital punishment, are ones where we know—or can easily figure out—what the main related factual debates are.

With other difficult moral issues, it may not be so easy to see what the main underlying factual questions are. For example, what factual questions are relevant to a dispute about the moral permissibility of same-sex marriages? Or the opening of adoption files? Or assisted suicide? If you find yourself struggling to figure out what the main "relevant" facts are, keep some of these tips in mind.

1. *Read and listen widely.* Sometimes the best way to see what facts are relevant to a particular moral issue is by reading or listening to a variety of people who are discussing that issue. What are some of the facts that those people bring up? What are some of the facts about which they agree or disagree?

In the case of same-sex marriage, for example, there are many types of facts that people on all sides of the question consider relevant. Many of those facts fall into one or more of these interrelated categories:

a. Definitions: What does "marriage" mean? The definition of "marriage" is complicated by the fact that marriage can be a civil institution, a religious sacrament, or both. For example, it is possible for two (or more) people to be married as part of a religious ceremony, without having that marriage recognized by civil authorities. "Fundamentalist Mormon" churches allow polygynous (more than one wife) marriages, for instance, but no U.S. state currently recognizes polygynous unions as marriages. Most U.S. states currently have legal or constitutional provisions that restrict state-recognized marriages to those between one man and one woman. (A few of those states offer "covenant" marriages that require premarital counseling and that make a divorce harder to get.). On the other hand, some U.S. states legally recognize same-sex unions as marriage. And several states offer state-recognized "civil unions"—they are not called "marriages," but they confer many of the rights and responsibilities that are associated with the unions that *are* called "marriages."

The converse—civilly-sanctioned marriages that are not recognized by religious authorities—also occurs. The Roman Catholic Church forbids its members to divorce, and it considers a divorced person who remarries to be an adulterer. Along with many Protestant denominations it also does not recognize same-sex unions as marriages, even in states that do.

b. Histories: What is the history of marriage, as an ideal and in practice, in this society and in other societies? Is it true that most things called "marriages" throughout history have consisted of only one man and only one woman? Have most societies viewed marriage as an exclusive, lifelong partnership, between two people, for the raising of children? What sorts of restrictions—by age, race, blood ties, mental ability—have been (or continue to be) placed on those seeking to get married?

c. Contemporary Law and Society: What percentage of people in our society live in a companionate but non-marital relationship? What sorts of tangible benefits—tax exemptions, health insurance, inheritance rights, and so on—are granted to people in state-recognized marriages but not to people in other kinds of relationship?

d. Consequences of Change: What has happened to marriage rates among opposite-sex couples in places where (state-sanctioned) same-sex marriages are allowed? What has happened to divorce rates in those places?

2. *Approach the topic from the perspective of the different families of values.* Each family of values brings some features to the foreground and puts others into the background. The facts that are most relevant, from the perspective of someone holding one set of values, might not seem as relevant from the perspective of someone who is using a different "lens" of values.

Take capital punishment as an example. From a utilitarian point of view, the most relevant factual questions include: how do the violent crime rates in places without capital punishment compare to those with it? How much (in attorneys' fees, court costs, utilities, medical expenses) does capital punishment cost when compared to alternatives? How many people are actually sentenced to death, and for which crimes? How are executions actually carried out?

A virtue-centered ethics, by contrast, asks questions more like: what percentage of people convicted of serious crimes express remorse and offer to make amends? What psychological effects are reported by officials who conduct executions? What psychological effects are reported by the victims' loved ones when the criminal is executed—or when the criminal is imprisoned for life?

Likewise, a person-centered ethics might be most interested in how the courts have interpreted and balanced the rights of accused and convicted murderers, and whether sentencing guidelines require (or at least allow) consideration of impairments such as mental retardation, a childhood history of abuse, or psychological disturbances.

From the point of view of an ethics of relationship, finally, a vital question is: are there workable methods of punishment that also help restore community—that speak to the needs and possibilities of everyone involved?

3. *Be wary of "research by opinion poll."* When I ask my students which facts might be relevant to a given moral issue, often some reply that "what people's opinions are" is a relevant fact. And, they suggest, we can look for opinion polls or other statistical instruments to see what people's opinions actually are.

The question of people's opinions can indeed be approached as a question of fact. Polls (if well-conducted!) will give you some answers. And of course, as we consider whether to change or keep various social structures and institutions, or how to implement changes, it is important to take people's strongly held feelings and opinions into account. However, the real question is how well people's opinions are based upon the actual facts of the case. Mere opinion is not the end of the matter—only the beginning.

In other words, the real question is: What *should* we think? What information do people need—in particular, do *we* need—in order to have an *informed*

opinion? Asking around, listening to others, and using the different families of moral values to guide your factual inquiries are vital to that outcome.
This is a good point at which to reiterate central themes from Chapters 1 and
2 of this book: Careful, informed thinking is central to ethical deliberation
and action!

SOURCES

Go to the source when you can. A useful all-around source is the *Statistical
Abstract of the United States*. There are similar volumes for other countries.
Crime statistics and automotive fuel economies are all easily accessible public information. You may need to search for books or articles on the topic that
concerns you. Library catalogs and online databases have keyword-search systems: using them you can spotlight helpful sources very quickly. Ask for help
when you need it. That's what reference librarians are for!

Look for thorough and careful coverage of the issues in books or journal articles by well-informed people. Check to see who the authors are,
and where they get *their* information. What are their qualifications? Are
they relatively impartial? On global climate change, for example, neither
oil-industry publications nor environmental magazines are likely to survey
all the evidence or draw the most carefully considered conclusions. The
best sources are established scientific journals, whose articles are carefully
reviewed by other experts and where the norm is supposed to be scrupu-
lous neutrality. (They will mostly tell you that climate change is quite real,
though the causes and timetables are less clear.) Books published by academic presses are more reputable (more carefully and critically reviewed)
than books from presses that only publish books promoting a specific point
of view.

Cross-check sources, too, to see if other, independent sources agree. Are
the experts sharply divided, or pretty much in agreement? If they're pretty
much in agreement, theirs is the safe view to take. (At the very least, if you
propose to take a different view, you have some serious explaining to do.)
Where even the experts disagree, it is best to reserve judgment yourself too.
Don't jump in with two feet where truly informed people tread with care. See
if you can argue on some other grounds—or change your conclusions.

Watch the tone of your sources. Sources that make extreme or simplistic
claims, or spend most of their time attacking and demeaning the other side,
weaken their own claims. On most issues, reasonable disagreement is possible. Seek out sources that engage the arguments and evidence on the other
side responsibly and thoroughly.

THE WEB

Used carefully, the Web is a great resource—the world at your fingertips. Many sites are very informative—I cite them myself repeatedly in this book. However, other sites are pure fabrication. Academic libraries and even most public libraries have at least some checks on the reliability of the books and other materials they collect, but there are very few (in fact, usually, there are *absolutely no*) checks on Internet sites. Any site can announce all it wants that it is objective or unbiased, but that hardly makes it so.

Even the flimsiest opinion site can dress itself up to look professional. Without a critical eye then, the Web can seem just a mass of conflicting viewpoints and claims, and you are left adrift or misled. Sometimes the results can be lethal. I regularly run across hate sites disguised as "information," or deliberately misleading sites designed to snare unsuspecting and perhaps desperate people looking for the facts: sites on abortion, for example, that look sympathetic and objective but are actually designed to frighten pregnant young women away from even thinking about it. Sometimes these sites are downright lies, other times they merely cherry-pick their facts, which may be true enough, but they also leave aside others, so that they paint a false picture without telling an actual lie. You have to read carefully and critically.

Do not rely on the Internet alone then, unless you are dealing with an identifiable and independently reputable source—and don't rely on a website *at all* unless you have some idea of what its source is. Ask some questions of any site: who created this site? Why did they create it? What are their qualifications? What does it mean if they don't tell you? Again, cross-check sources, look for the most thorough and impartial sources you can, and never stop thinking!

INFERENCES

We make *inferences* when we move from certain facts to further conclusions. We may generalize from a few cases to many, or use a similar case to draw conclusions about a case that interests us, or notice the correlation of two events and conclude that one causes the other. Each kind of inference can be tricky.

GENERALIZATIONS

You or I will never know all sweatshop workers, or women in the army, or gay couples, or rich people or poor people, or drug users or businesspeople or environmental activists, and so on and on—yet we may need to draw conclusions about them if we are to form an intelligent opinion about certain moral issues. So we have to *generalize:* we take a small sample—limited data, a few examples—to stand for the whole.

But we may generalize well, or poorly. A good generalization:

1. Rests on *specific* and *clear* examples.

2. Rests on *many* examples.

3. Rests on *representative* examples—that is, not all from one possibly atypical sample—and offers enough *background information* to allow us to evaluate for ourselves how significant and representative the examples are.

We generalize, for example, about the conditions and nature of happiness. What does it take to be happy? There are striking examples of spectacularly rich people who have been spectacularly unhappy. Shall we therefore conclude that money cannot make you happy? (Or even, that it makes you unhappy?) People do:

> The misery of the rich is legendary. The late oil billionaire J. Paul Getty was notoriously unhappy and lonely for much of his life. Entrepreneur and socialite Howard Hughes became reclusive and paranoid, while multi-millionaire pop star George Michael revealed in a recent documentary how his wealth and fame had never made him happy. . . . The tales of many lottery winners are replete with envy, spite, and family break-up.

So that's it, eh? If you want to be happy, give away your money if you have any, and never enter lotteries. Well, slow down a little. . . . First it might be wise to ask how this argument fares on our criteria.

Requirement 1 asks for specific and clear examples. But the ones offered here are sketchy and anecdotal, almost one-liners. Those cited need more detail and support: citations (how do we find out whether the claims about these billionaires are true?), biographies, careful scientific surveys of lottery winners. None of that is offered here.

Requirement 2 asks for many examples—more than a few, at least if the class being generalized over is large. Here, conclusions are being suggested about all people—a pretty large group! More examples are needed than three rich people and a few lottery winners.

Requirement 3 is the key here, and helps justify requirement 2. Without a range of examples, we have no way of judging whether a few miserable rich people are representative or not. Surely there are *some* people who will be unhappy regardless of how much money they have—just as there are surely some who will be happy regardless. Or maybe something else, quite unrelated to money, leads to unhappiness in their case. The question remains whether *most* richer people tend to be happier. Maybe, maybe not—but a large number of examples, fairly detailed and as representative and varied as possible, rather than a few striking cases, are necessary before we can say anything with confidence.

This is a poor argument then, as it stands. But don't overgeneralize from that fact either. A failed generalization does not prove its opposite. This argument so far fails to prove that wealth makes you miserable, but its failure does *not* prove that wealth makes you happy. A failed generalization proves nothing at all. Until you can get more information, the question remains open.

COMPARISONS

Sometimes we make inferences by comparing one kind of situation with another seemingly similar situation about which more is known. A good comparison:

1. Cites as a comparison a *clear* case about which *true* claims are made.
2. Cites as a comparison a *relevantly similar* case. That is, the cases compared must be as similar as possible in ways that matter to the conclusion—though they can be very different in other, less relevant ways.

In the Netherlands, people are allowed to have small amounts of marijuana for personal use and "coffeehouses" sell small amounts openly for use on the premises. The results of this policy are reasonably positive. People therefore argue that legal marijuana should be manageable in America. This is an argument by comparison. Is it a good one?

To meet requirement 1 we need to know more about the Dutch policy and its results. Technically all drugs are illegal there, but in practice only harder drugs are prosecuted. The coffeehouse system is meant to make it difficult to buy large amounts. Documented marijuana use has increased significantly among Dutch young people, but hard drug use has actually declined. Dutch law still prohibits unsafe driving and public nuisances created by any intoxicant, legal or not: rates have not increased. Some political arguments continue—the current policy seems hypocritical to some, and the issue of supply has not been addressed (some argue that the Dutch state should grow its own marijuana so there are legal sources for the coffeehouses!)—but on the whole, it seems fair enough to conclude that the results are indeed "reasonably positive."

Requirement 2 requires a *relevantly similar* comparison. Can we infer that a social policy that works in the Netherlands will therefore also work in America? How similar are the two?

The Netherlands is a small, densely populated, homogeneous nation, whose people tend to be more socially minded than many Americans. These are major relevant differences. Drug abuse is therefore less likely (in fact, it turns out that the bulk of the customers in the coffeehouses are foreigners, including many American college students) and much harder to hide if it does occur. On the other hand, the Netherlands is a modern, developed, democratic state, like the United States, and it gives its citizens a wide range of freedoms. These are major relevant similarities.

This comparison, then, is only partly successful on the second requirement. It seems likely that the potential for abuse is higher in the United States (at least, the comparison doesn't persuade me that it isn't). On the other hand, the Dutch system does suggest that some creative forms of controlled availability could be workable here too as well. We could even take it as an incentive to do some creative thinking about other possible systems here. To that extent, the comparison is useful and revealing.

INFERRING CAUSE FROM CORRELATION

Happiness may not correlate with money, but it does correlate with things like good health, a loving marriage, and lots of friends. Therefore it might be concluded that good health, a loving marriage, and lots of friends *lead to* or *cause* happiness. This is an argument from correlation to cause.

A good argument from correlation to cause:

1. Cites *accurate* correlations.

2. *Explains* how the (proposed) cause leads to the (proposed) effect.

3. Argues that the proposed cause-effect relationship is the *best explanation* of the correlation.

To meet requirement 1, you'd need to consult social-scientific research for reliable statistics to show that married people, say, are more likely than unmarried people to report being happy.

The proposed cause-effect connection then needs to be spelled out—that is the point of requirement 2. How marriage is supposed to lead to happiness, psychologically, is pretty clear: having a spouse can be a pleasurable and supportive thing. Filling in such links is crucial: it's what turns a mere cooccurrence into a plausible *connection*.

Requirement 3, however, is still hard to meet. The problem is a general philosophical one: *any correlation can be explained in a variety of ways.*

A and B, let's say, are correlated. It could well be that A causes B. It could *also* be that B causes A (instead, or in addition), or that both A and B have a common cause, or that A and B are not causally related at all.

It is true that a strong correlate of happiness is marriage. The proposed conclusion is that marriage tends to cause happiness. But the evidence only really says that the two tend to occur together. Other conclusions remain possible. It could also be that happy people are better at forming and sustaining marriages—so that happiness leads to marriage, not necessarily vice versa.

That is, the connection could be the other way around, and the evidence—the correlation—would be exactly the same!

Or perhaps a certain sort of character—say, cheerful and kind—leads *both* to better marriages *and* to happiness. That is, marriage and happiness may have a common cause, rather than being directly connected.

Yet again, each could affect the other, in a kind of feedback loop. Maybe happy people have better marriages, which in turn make them happier, which in turn. . . . The story might well be complex.

Clearly it makes a big difference which of these stories is true. But it certainly isn't easy to tell which. This is why a good argument about causes must explain how the proposed cause could lead to the proposed effect (requirement 2 again) *and* must try to show that the proposed explanation is the *best* or most *likely* explanation of the observed correlation—requirement 3.

Many other issues involve similar questions. To return to the drug question, for example, here's another statistic. It turns out that a significant proportion of the homeless are drug users. We might conclude from this that drug use leads to homelessness. It's a plausible inference, and it suggests in turn that to address homelessness we need to crack down on drug use. On the other hand, the very same correlation could equally well suggest that homelessness leads people to use drugs, suggesting that we need to address homelessness directly, in part to reduce drug use. Probably both are true to some extent, but which is the *main* effect is a crucial question for social policy.

Or again, as I mentioned earlier, though a decline in capital punishment in the United States from 1933 to 1969 corresponds to a rise in murders, it's hard to know what to make of this. There have been vast changes in American life in this period. Cities have become crowded, weapons have become readily available, social mores and family life have changed dramatically, as have economic conditions. Any of these factors could explain the rise in murders at least as readily as the decline in executions. And why do states with the death penalty on average have higher murder rates than states that don't? Inferring from correlation to cause here is tricky at best.

DEFINITIONS

Another critical-thinking task is to clarify the very words we use in framing ethical issues. Again, the task may take a variety of forms—and usually takes work.

WHEN TERMS ARE UNCLEAR

Even some fairly basic categories are unclear in popular ethical debates. People who oppose "assisted suicide," for example, often use the term in a very different and much broader way than people who favor legalizing it. Both sides get emotional. Proponents' definitions sound positively lovely and tend to be narrowly framed. Opponents' definitions sound horrible and prominently feature disturbing cases. The proposed definitions on both sides also tend to be rhetorical, not carefully thought through.

These are solvable problems. First, when a new or specialized term is at issue, misunderstanding can be cleared away just by proposing or agreeing upon a definition. In the case of "assisted suicide," for example, the intended definition is: allowing doctors to help aware and rational people to arrange and carry out their own dying. It does *not* include allowing doctors to "unplug" people without their consent (that would be some form of "involuntary euthanasia"—another issue). There may be good reasons to object to assisted suicide so defined, but at least the parties to the argument can ensure that they are talking about the same thing.

Be precise. Don't just replace the problematic word with a synonym—it will be just as confused as the original word. Get technical if you have to.

Keep the dictionary handy—often it is a model of precision and impartiality. Just don't expect that it will resolve all your questions when issues get difficult. Dictionary definitions often just use synonyms. Dictionaries also usually give multiple definitions, so that you still have to pick and choose among them.

For some words, you just have to make the term more precise yourself. Again, explain *carefully;* use neutral, not loaded terms; and use concrete, definite terms rather than vague ones.

WHEN TERMS ARE CONTESTED

Sometimes the term in question is not merely unclear but is actually *contested*. That is, people are arguing over the term, not just confused about what it means. In this case, you cannot simply stipulate a meaning—for people are disagreeing over what the term *ought* to mean—and the dictionary, wisely staying out of moral issues, seldom does more than suggest equally inconclusive synonyms.

In this case, you must work out a careful definition yourself. The rule is: *work from the clear cases*. Here is what I mean.

Whenever a term is contested, you can distinguish three relevant sets of things. One will be those things to which the term clearly applies. Second will be those things to which the term clearly does *not* apply. In the middle will be those things whose status is unclear—including but not restricted to the things being argued over. Your job is to formulate a definition that:

1. *Includes* all the things that the term clearly fits.
2. *Excludes* all the things that the term clearly does not fit.

3. Draws the *plainest possible line* in between.

4. *Explains* why the line belongs there and not somewhere else.

In discussing the "drug" issue, for instance, we could certainly use a clear definition of the term "drug" itself. But what *is* a drug?

Drugs are substances, clearly (as opposed to institutions, or actions, or animals), and substances that we ingest (eat, breathe in, snort, or apply to various body parts). But we ingest many different substances. Which ones are "drugs"?

Clear cases of "drugs," in the current moral sense, include heroin, cocaine in its various forms, and marijuana.

Clear cases of substances that are *not* drugs include air, water, most foods, sunscreen lotions, and shampoos—though all of these substances are clearly chemicals, in a broad sense of "chemical," and all are ingested or applied to our body parts.

Unclear cases include tobacco and alcohol. Here is where the debate swirls. Is it fair, for example, to ban marijuana but allow the sale of alcohol, both of which may work on the body in similar ways and which may have at least as bad effects? Should the Food and Drug Administration be able to regulate cigarettes, on the grounds that nicotine is a drug?

Unclear in another way are substances such as aspirin, antibiotics, and vitamins and psychiatric medicines such as antidepressants and stimulants—the kinds of things we buy in "drug stores" and call "drugs" in a pharmaceutical sense. But these are *medicines,* let's say. In moral contexts the word "drug" is used more narrowly.

Is there a definition that meets the four requirements outlined here?

A "drug" has been defined—by a Presidential Commission, no less—as a substance that affects mind or body in some way. This definition meets requirement 1: it includes all the clear cases of drugs. But it is far too broad to meet requirement 2. It also includes all the clear cases of substances that are *not* drugs. (And naturally enough, it does not meet the third requirement either, since it effectively draws no line at all.) We need a more limited definition.

We also can't define a "drug" as an *illegal* substance that affects mind or body in some way. This definition might cover more or less the right set of substances, but it does not meet requirement 4. It does not explain why the line belongs where it is. After all, part of the point of trying to define "drug" in the first place might well be to decide which substances *should* be legal and which should not. Defining a "drug" as an illegal substance short-circuits this project. (Besides, if marijuana were legalized tomorrow, would it stop being a drug overnight?)

Try this:

A drug is a substance used primarily to alter the state of the mind in some specific way.

Heroin and the like obviously count. Food, air, and water don't, because even though they may have effects on the mind, the effects are not specific and are not the primary reason why we ingest them. Unclear cases we then approach with the question, is the *primary* effect *specific* and on the *mind*? Perception-distorting and mood-altering effects do seem to be what we are concerned about in the current debate about "drugs," so arguably this definition captures the kind of distinction that people really want to make.

Should we add that "drugs" are addictive? Maybe, maybe not. There are some substances that are addictive but not drugs—certain foods, perhaps. And what if a substance that alters the state of the mind in some specific way turns out to be non-addictive (as some have claimed about marijuana, for example)? Is it therefore not a drug? I think it is better to take addiction to define drug *abuse* rather than "drug" as such.

CRITICAL THINKING WITH DEFINITIONS

Definitions help us organize our thoughts, group like things with like, pick out key similarities and differences. By themselves, though, they seldom settle ethical questions.

We may look to a definition of "drug," for example, for guidance about what sorts of substances we should use or avoid and what should be legally allowed or banned. My proposed definition certainly may redraw some lines in ways that surprise or unsettle us. My proposed definition, for instance, includes antidepressants and stimulants as well as alcohol and even coffee. It doesn't follow, however, that all of these are morally problematic or should be banned as well. We'd need an *argument* to go that far.

The argument could be made—certainly for alcohol.

> Alcohol is the most widely-used drug; over 100 million Americans drink. Alcohol may cause more harm than all illegal drugs put together. One in ten drinkers—some 10 million Americans—becomes an alcoholic. (By contrast, there are fewer than 500,000 heroin addicts.) In addition, about half of all fatal car collisions, accidental drownings, and violent crimes are alcohol-related. One of the most common severe birth defects, fetal alcohol syndrome, is caused by women who drink while pregnant. And alcohol costs our economy $120 billion yearly in work, property, and medical costs. . . . We would not legalize any currently illegal drug that caused even a fraction of these problems.

This is an argument for restricting alcohol, but notice that it does not depend on alcohol's being a drug. This argument would be damning even if alcohol did *not* count as a "drug." The definition cannot do that work by itself.

On the other hand, coffee has specific effects on the mind too, may be harmful, and is clearly addictive. Still, it has nothing like the social effects of alcohol, so perhaps we would stop there. And many antidepressants and stimulants, while clearly and appropriately called "drugs" under the proposed definition, are also legal, under prescription, and have clear benefits as such.

Again, then: that a substance is a "drug" is not, by itself, a sufficient reason to object to or ban it—for otherwise we would have to object to and ban coffee and psychiatric medicines as well. The drug in question must also cause a certain degree of personal and social harm—like alcohol or cocaine.

By the same token, just because marijuana, say, *is* a drug, it doesn't follow automatically that it should be banned. Some people would argue that coffee is a better comparison to marijuana than alcohol—both have relatively mild effects, though both can be misused—and (someone might argue) the best approach might be like the Netherlands', making it available in coffeehouse-like settings where the amount used can be carefully controlled. (So perhaps the same restrictions should be extended to coffee?)

Of course, if marijuana is much more addictive than coffee, or if it really is a "gateway" to other and harder drugs, then there may be a good case for prohibition after all. It would take some good data to know better. (And by the way: is coffee a "gateway" to other stimulants? Didn't many stimulant-takers start out as coffee drinkers?) Or perhaps marijuana is most akin to certain antidepressants and stimulants—the drugstore sorts of "drugs"—medicines that are "drugs" on the proposed definition too, but call not for bans but for *control*. The point once again is just that none of these conclusions follow just from the fact that marijuana is a drug.

Nor of course are we entitled to object to or ban *only* substances that are "drugs." Tobacco, for example, may *not* be a drug according to the proposed definition (it's not clear, at least to me, whether the primary intended effect is on the mind), but it still is addictive and massively destructive (350,000 Americans die every year from it). Here we just come to recognize once again that the question of the morality or legality of substance use is more complex than the question of which substances are "drugs." Definitions contribute to clarity, but don't expect them to get you all the way home by themselves.

FOR REVIEW

1. Pick a moral debate and give an example of a specific fact that could help resolve it.

2. How would you locate a reliable source for such a fact?

QUICK REFERENCE: CRITICAL-THINKING BASICS

WHEN FACTS ARE AT ISSUE

- Clarify *what* facts are at issue.
- Do your research.
- Seek out the best sources.

WHEN INFERENCES ARE AT ISSUE

A good *generalization*:

1. Cites *specific* and *clear* examples.
2. Cites *many* examples.
3. Cites *representative* examples and gives enough *background information* to allow us to evaluate for ourselves how significant and representative the examples are.

A good *comparison:*

1. Cites as a comparison a *clear* case about which *true* claims are made.
2. Cites as a comparison a *relevantly similar* case.

A good *argument from correlation to cause*:

1. Cites *accurate* correlations.
2. *Explains* how the (proposed) cause leads to the (proposed) effect.
3. Argues that the proposed cause-effect relationship is the *best explanation* of the correlation.

WHEN DEFINITIONS ARE AT ISSUE

A good definition:

1. *Includes* all the things that the term clearly fits.
2. *Excludes* all the things that the term clearly does not fit.
3. Draws the *plainest possible line* somewhere in between.
4. *Explains* why the line belongs there and not somewhere else.

3. Pick a moral debate and give an example of a factual generalization that is relevant to it.

4. What three requirements must a reliable generalization meet?

5. Pick a moral debate and give an example of a factual comparison that is relevant to it.

6. What two requirements must such a comparison meet?

7. Pick a moral debate and give an example of a cause-and-effect inference that is relevant to it.

8. What three requirements must such a cause-and-effect inference meet?

9. Pick a moral debate and give an example of a definition that is relevant to it.

10. What requirements must such a definition meet?

EXERCISES AND NOTES

9.1 IDENTIFYING FACTS AT ISSUE

Identify at least three factual questions that are central to the following ethical debates as you understand them. That is, ask what sorts of factual claims tend to be made, or presupposed, in this debate? What facts could we find out, through the appropriate kinds of research, that would make a difference? Be specific!

- How seriously should colleges and universities take plagiarism?
- Should tax money pay for private-school vouchers?
- Should states run lotteries to help fund state budgets (e.g., for education or other good causes)?
- Should health care be considered a human right rather than a market commodity?
- Should adoption files be opened so that people separated by at-birth adoptions can later find each other?
- Does the threat of terrorist attack justify intrusive airport searches and increasing government surveillance?
- Should genetic engineering be banned?
- Should assisted suicide be permitted?

- Should a parent be encouraged or expected to stay home with preschool children?
- Should throwaway consumer goods be banned in the name of environmental protection and the needs of future generations?
- Should you stop eating meat?

Add your own favorite issues as well.

Take your time with these. Part of the lesson is that we are often far too hasty in thinking through the factual basis of our moral views. Too often we don't ask questions at all! Of course, don't multiply questions endlessly, either – at a certain point that too becomes less than serious—but take each issue carefully and give it some time. A good procedure might be to brainstorm as many questions as arise in, say, ten minutes, and then take another ten minutes to use your initial list of questions to formulate three really good ones. Then repeat for the next issue.

9.2 PURSUING THE FACTS

In Exercise 9.1 you identified three factual questions that are central to each of a number of contemporary ethical debates. The next step is to consider how you could begin to resolve these factual questions. What sources can you find? For what questions can you find reliable and reasonably objective information on the Web? Where? Will answering some of these questions require inferences? What sorts of inferences (generalization, comparison, reasoning from correlation to cause, others?) might you have to use? Which is likely to be the most successful?

The challenge is *not* to construct an argument for your favored conclusion about the whole issue. The challenge here is much more specific (and more patient!): it is simply to consider what kinds of exploration or research it would take to resolve (or, anyway, advance) the particular factual issue you've identified. You don't even have to do the actual research: just consider carefully how you *could*.

Vegetarianism, for example. You might have said that one central factual question in this debate is how readily people can live without meat. Is a vegetarian diet healthy? If this is your question, a way to find out is to consult nutritionists or nutrition textbooks. (While you're at it, you could also ask: is a *meat* diet healthy? And: what sort of diet is health*iest*?) There may be some disagreement, but with some persistence you still should be able to find a reasonably well-informed and neutral answer.

Of course this is not the same as answering the whole question. Suppose you find out that a vegetarian diet can be as healthy as or healthier than a meat diet. It would not necessarily follow that you must become a vegetarian. After all, there are other relevant values besides health. The point here is simply to ask how we might resolve the specific factual questions you've identified—not how we might resolve the whole issue. One thing at a time!

9.3 TAKE UP SOME ISSUES IN DETAIL

In Exercise 9.1 you identified three factual questions that are central to each of a number of contemporary ethical debates. In Exercise 9.2 you considered what kind of research or sources it would take to answer those questions. Now, choose a few of those questions and actually do the work: go out an answer the questions you identified as central to some of those debates, using the methods you identified as the best. Go into them in depth.

This would make a good research paper: take a very controversial moral issue and simply research its factual basis critically and open-mindedly. Make your moral conclusions secondary, if you draw any at all. See "Using Your Tools" #5 (pp. 274–278) for one example of how you might organize this work.

9.4 CLARIFYING UNCLEAR TERMS

Not all terms need clarifying—lucky for us. Still, some do. Look around at the ethical debates that currently occupy us. Ask which of them could benefit from careful attention to definition. Where is the meaning of a word or words central to the debate? What word or words are these? How could you begin to define them?

Specify a definition for *assisted suicide.* What do you think of the definition proposed in the text? Can you do better? You may need to do a little research.

Here's another example: *affirmative action.* This is a fairly specific term, and it would seem that it could be easily defined. Perhaps it can be. But we seem confused most of the time about what we mean by it. Can you formulate a good definition—or a useful set of distinctions? Try it, and then check out others' definitions. Are some that you find more reliable and usable than others?

The following terms play major roles in some current moral debates. Try to define each term. You'll need to work from the clear cases, so start by specifying what they are. Look out for possible ambiguities. Keep open the possibility that for some of these terms there are simply not enough agreed-upon clear cases to define the term successfully at all (and if not, are there other useful ways to clarify and focus the debates of which they are a part?). If you think an explicit and clear definition is possible, work it out. Sketch some sort of argument in support, and explore some of its implications in the case(s) in question as well as others.

Here are the terms.

- *Selfish,* as in the perpetual debate over whether humans are "basically just selfish" or have other motives as well. (Recall also our discussion in chapter 2.) Can you define "selfish" in some way that doesn't automatically include all human behavior (for surely we mean *something* when we say of someone that they're self-ish—don't make it true by definition) and on the other hand also does not make selfishness automatically disreputable? Once you've defined it in such a way, can you use your definition to actually *investigate* how "selfish" people really are?

• *Adultery,* as in this question recently faced by the New Hampshire Supreme Court: if a married woman has sex with another woman, is that adultery (and therefore grounds for her husband to sue for divorce)? Many dictionary definitions tend either to assume heterosexuality (that is, to define adultery for a married man, say, as sex with a woman other than his wife) or to leave the matter ambiguous (one dictionary I found even uses the phrase "sex with another" without saying another *what*). Does it matter that same-sex marriage was not legal in New Hampshire at the time?

I will not tell you what the court decided, but you might want to decide the matter yourself—argue it carefully and well—and then look up the answer the court gave.

• *Plagiarism,* as it is understood when we consider questions of academic honesty. In a broad sense, plagiarism is presenting another's work as if it is your own. A clear case is when as student downloads a paper from the Web, puts his or her name on it, and hands it in for credit. This can earn you a failing grade in the class in many American colleges and universities. Repeat offenses can get you thrown out. But when do you cross the line? What if you cut and paste a few paragraphs from an online source into the draft of your paper, thoroughly rephrase it, and cite the source in your bibliography? Would it help if you hadn't cut and pasted? What if you only somewhat rephrase it, or don't cite the source? Also, is it plagiarism to reuse your *own* work in another setting without acknowledgement? How much rephrasing or "recycling" does it take to make such an action plagiarism, as opposed to simply writing in your own voice (as we all inevitably do, after all) on the same topic (also quite natural) at different times?

• *Fairness,* as in, for example, the question of affirmative action again. What is fair? Treating people equally? Maybe, but this is a vague phrase too. In a famous simile of Abraham Lincoln's, it's hardly fair to make a runner run a foot-race hobbled by a chain and ball while others run unencumbered. Yet in some sense they are being treated "equally." No one blocks their way. They get a lane in the track just like everyone else. If this strikes you as unfair all the same, how would you specify what fairness is? An equal chance at winning? But that can't be right either, since some people do run faster than others, and that's the whole point of the race . . .

• *Natural,* in the context of environmental debates. Sometimes people argue that air and water pollution and the pollution of the land with non-biodegradable wastes (plastics, etc.) is "natural" in a larger sense because the raw materials after all came from nature ("Where else could they come from?"), as did we ourselves. Others want to argue that despoiling the earth is wrong because the materials and maybe the acts themselves are "unnatural." Is there a useful way to define "natural" in this context?

Related is the question of what constitutes "natural" foods. Since all foods come from "nature" in some ultimate sense, what makes some foods "natural" and some not natural? The absence or presence of "artificial" ingredients, maybe? OK, but what makes an ingredient "artificial"?

The last questions may sound skeptical, but they may well have answers. In any case, don't just dismiss the whole question. After all, people are trying to make some sort of distinction with this word. What distinction are they trying to make? If the word "natural" is too ambiguous to carry this kind of weight, what terms would you suggest instead?

- *Person*, especially as we try to arrive at some consistent position connecting our views on, say, abortion on one hand and the treatment of animals on the other. Very roughly, the problem is that if you define "person" broadly enough to include fetuses, then many other animals count too, which is not a welcome conclusion for many moral positions that oppose abortion but also oppose animal rights. On the other hand, to turn the very same point inside out, if you define "person" broadly enough to include other animals, then fetuses count too, which is not a welcome conclusion for many moralists who favor animal rights but tend to be pro-choice. There's also the problem that a more restrictive standard for personhood tends to exclude newborns as well as fetuses and most (though perhaps not all) other animals. And while tying personhood to being human may help draw something like the desired line, it has problems on requirement 4: why should mere species membership make such a huge difference? Surely it's not that hard to imagine nonhuman persons, even if we don't know any at present.

NOTES

Fact-finding, inference, and definition are enormous topics. Even brief guidebooks can run to hundreds of pages, and there is a wide range of texts and courses available in "informal logic" and persuasion, rhetoric, and argumentative writing. Try Lewis Vaughn's *The Power of Critical Thinking* (Oxford, third edition, 2009). A well-presented classical approach is David Kelley's *The Art of Reasoning* (Norton, many editions). A very brief introduction is my own book, *A Rulebook for Arguments* (Hackett Publishing Company, many editions)—a fine little book indeed, if I may say so myself (note that I am certainly well-informed on the subject, but not exactly unbiased!). *Rulebook* now exists in a textbook-scale treatment as well: see David Morrow and Anthony Weston, *A Workbook for Arguments: A Complete Course in Critical Thinking* (Hackett Publishing Company, 2011).

Information on hybrid cars is cited from http://www.motherearthnews .com/Alternative_Energy/2005_October_and_November/Pay-Less-at-the-Gas

-Pump-Hybrid-Revolution, accessed 10/23/06. The argument about miserable rich people comes from Nick Louth, "Wealth and Happiness Are Not the Same Thing," http://money.uk.msn.com/Investing/Insight/Special_Features/Active_Investor/article.aspx?cp-documentid=143226, accessed 10/23/06.

For an introduction to reasoning about causes, see the Vaughn book just cited or other critical-thinking texts. More difficult but also richly rewarding and provocative is Richard Nisbet and Lee Ross, *Human Inference: Strategies and Shortcomings of Social Judgment* (Prentice-Hall, 1980). Correlations among intimacy, health, and happiness are cited from Dayana Yochim, "Money = Happiness," http://www.fool.com/news/commentary/2004/commentary040120dy.htm, accessed 10/23/06.

Colin McGinn's *Moral Literacy* (Hackett/Duckworth, 1992) offers a vigorous and provocative discussion of drugs, beginning with a proposed definition: see his chapter 6. The quote about alcohol at the end of the last section comes from Mike Martin, *Everyday Morality* (Wadsworth Publishing Company, 1995), p. 149.

GUEST AUTHOR

Vance Ricks teaches in the Department of Philosophy at Guilford College in Greensboro, North Carolina, where he has also been interim director of the First Year Program, director of the Honors Program and Department Chair. He received the Ed Lowe Teaching Excellence Award in 2000. His box in this chapter, "Which Facts Are Relevant?," speaks to student questions based on his long-time use of earlier editions of this book.

Judging Like Cases Alike

Kant argues that it is the essence of a moral judgment to generalize to other cases. For my act or decision or position to be moral, it must be one that I would accept and support anyone else holding in similar cases—and one that I hold myself in similar cases. The underlying general principle is virtually a matter of pure logic: like cases should be treated alike.

In practice, though, we often make judgments about one kind of case without thinking a great deal—or thinking at all—about what our judgments imply for similar kinds of cases not before us right now. If we did think about those other cases, though, we might end up thinking differently about the one before us. This too is our responsibility. There *are* implications for similar kinds of cases, and like cases must be judged alike. The upshot is that we are called to a distinctively demanding but also quite fascinating kind of ethical thinking.

CONSISTENCY IS A CHALLENGE

Suppose I am prepared to misrepresent my car in order to sell it. It's expected, I say. Besides, the buyer can get the car checked herself. The moral question is, would I consider it equally justified for someone else to misrepresent *their* car in the same way and for the same reasons in order to sell it (say, just perchance, to *me*)? If not, then I am not judging like cases alike. As Kant would put it, I really am just "making an exception for myself"—treating others as mere means to my ends, acting like somehow I am fundamentally different from them.

In the same spirit, the psychologist Lawrence Kohlberg—you'll remember him from our brief discussion in chapter 8—spoke of "moral musical chairs." If I judge a moral situation one way from the position we occupy in it, I need to be willing to judge it the same way from the other positions too—say, in particular, from a position in which I am *dis*advantaged. "Moral musical chairs" is an imaginative method, then: a way of considering each of the different people affected and looking at the situation from their points of view. Sit in their chair for a while. A true moral act must be judgeable the same way from every position.

Would I consider it equally justified if someone else did the same thing to me? Sometimes the honest answer *could* be "yes." After all—back to the car—maybe I too would recognize that misrepresentation *is* expected, and of course it's true that I *could* get the car checked myself. In that I case I do judge like cases alike, and I have done my ethical homework (or some of it, though there may be other moral objections to misrepresenting cars). But this is probably not the norm. Normally we either don't think about it at all or would judge other people quite differently than ourselves. In that case, we have some ethical work yet to do.

"EXECUTION STOPS A BEATING HEART" Pro-life

You may have seen a bumpersticker that says EXECUTION STOPS A BEATING HEART. What does this mean?

Literally, it's just a simple true statement. Execution—capital punishment—stops a beating heart. Since stopping a beating heart—that is, killing someone—is usually a bad thing, it's a fair guess the person who put on this bumpersticker is opposed to the death penalty. But there is more going on than this.

This bumpersticker is an *argument*—in fact, a specific challenge. It's an ironic response to the anti-abortion bumper sticker, ABORTION STOPS A BEATING HEART. Essentially it argues, if you are opposed to abortion on the grounds that it's an act of killing, then you also ought to be opposed to the death penalty too, since it too is an act of killing. Many people who are pro-life on the abortion issue, however, tend to favor the death penalty. The question is: how can this be a consistent position? The implication is: perhaps you ought to reexamine your reasons for opposing abortion—or for favoring the death penalty.

This is a challenge to "judge like cases alike." It might be met in various ways, as we will see in a few pages. The first point, however, is that it must be met somehow. You may even have to rethink your views!

Note that the challenge arises the other way around too. Many people who oppose the death penalty tend to be pro-*choice* on the abortion issue. But if "stopping a beating heart" is an objection to execution, why isn't it an objection to abortion?

RESPECTING INNOCENT LIFE

Here is another example—a related bumpersticker.

> WE BRAKE FOR ANIMALS.
> WE SAVE THE WHALES AND THE BABY SEALS.
> WHY DO WE STILL TOLERATE ABORTION?   Pro-life, Anti-abortion

Good question. To spell it out: one common case for legal abortion rests on the claim that fetal human life is less important not only than nonfetal (born) human life but also less important than many other human needs, for example, the need to have a manageable family size or a chance at a career. But people who accept the case for legal abortion also often are committed to saving the whales, protecting animals, and so on. And that commitment seems to come from a very different place: from an unwillingness to subordinate other lives to human needs, at least needs such as fur coats, meat, and new drugs or household chemicals that won't harm us.

In one case innocent life seems to be a prime value; in the other it does not. How can these two commitments be consistent? Doesn't something have to give somewhere?

Nobody gets off easy here, though—this challenge too works in reverse. People who *oppose* abortion but *tolerate* the mistreatment of animals must

---

RATIONALIZATION ALERT!

Challenges to "judge like cases alike" can be irritating, downright annoying in fact. It's no fun having our consistency challenged, and it takes work to figure out just what the relevant distinctions are. And of course there's always the danger that we will not be able to find a relevant difference, so that we may even be required to change our minds!

The temptation is to dismiss the challenge—to brush it off as irrelevant or invent some excuse off the top of our heads for treating two apparently like cases in different ways—a form of rationalization, or what chapter 2 calls "offhand self-justification."

Don't do it. An honest and careful attempt to meet the challenge of consistency—acknowledging that it *is* a real challenge, and that it must be met—is what critical thinking in ethics is all about. Moral principles *are* general in nature. They do apply to other cases besides those that may be in the front of our minds. And if our reasons really are the reasons we are giving, we must be prepared either to draw similar conclusions about those other cases or to change our conclusions in the first case. As Kant emphasizes, this is what it means to live as one among equal others.

You're not obliged to change your mind instantly. It may not even be clear how to answer some of these challenges. The main thing is to keep thinking about the issues. Come back to them when you can. Raise them with others who share (and maybe others who don't share) your judgments of the cases in question. (And don't assume that *they're* so consistent either.) Some philosophers say that it's a lifelong task to work out a set of practical reasons that really do consistently apply to all "like cases." Any such reasons are going to be in constant flux as new cases come along and as we grow and learn. And that's probably a good thing too.

also consider how their commitments might be consistent. Once again, in the one case innocent life seems to be a prime value; in the other it does not. I once had a neighbor whose truck was plastered with pro-life slogans but who was also an avid deer hunter "for fun," as he put it. It didn't sound too "pro-life" to me. At the very least, he had some explaining to do.

HOW TO RESTORE CONSISTENCY

Suppose someone argues that your judgment about one case is not consistent with your judgment about another seemingly "like case." There are three possible ways in which you might respond.

- You can argue that the alleged "like cases" are not really alike. In that case you need to figure out the *morally relevant difference* between the cases and explain what difference that difference makes.
- You can change your judgment about the "like case" or cases.
- You can change your judgment about the original case or cases.

In short, you can either try to show that your judgments aren't inconsistent or change one of them.

Take again the question of abortion and capital punishment raised by the EXECUTION STOPS A BEATING HEART bumpersticker. Suppose you oppose abortion but favor capital punishment. Consider your options:

- You could try to establish a difference between the two cases and explain what difference it makes. For example, a natural response is to argue that fetuses are "innocent" but murderers are not. And innocence makes a difference because the innocent have a right to all the protection we can afford as a society. Those who have murdered, however, may forfeit the right to that protection (or some of it, anyway: they still have a right to a fair trial and humane treatment in prison). Those who murder may forfeit their own right to life, a right which all the rest of us, including fetuses on the pro-life view, still have.

Of course, this response might be debated in turn. Many people believe that it may be acceptable to kill innocents in wartime, for example. Others argue that even those who are not "innocent" still have a right to life. So there are further cases to consider. Still, probably some distinction can be maintained. Maybe the two alleged "like cases" are fairly far apart in the end.

- You could decide that, all things considered, you should change your mind and oppose capital punishment too. This is an argument made by some modern Catholic moralists who argue for a "consistent ethic of life": that if we are to be "pro-life" on some issues we need to be "pro-life" across the board.

• You could decide that, all things considered, you should change your mind and become pro-choice about abortion. The comparison of cases might show you that, in your mind, life is actually not the only or the most important value. You might conclude that your pro-life views about abortion do not reflect your most considered thinking.

There is no automatic way to decide which way to go. Trying to make the most sense of our many moral beliefs and commitments is an ongoing and hard job! You may want to try out all of the possibilities before deciding, and take some time too. Again, though, going in one of these three directions is ultimately necessary. There's nowhere else to go.

MORE EXAMPLES

We've already noted that the abortion/death penalty challenge also holds the other way around. Many people who oppose the death penalty tend to be pro-*choice* on the abortion issue. But, again, if "stopping a beating heart" is an objection to execution, why isn't it an objection to abortion?

Can *this* challenge be met? Logically there are the same three options. Perhaps pro-choice people would argue that the cases are not truly "like." Many would argue that fetuses are not fully human beings, for example—while murderers *are* fully human beings (though maybe bad ones). Or: some might conclude that capital punishment is morally acceptable too. Or: some might decide that they really ought to become pro-life on the abortion issue.

Again, there is no automatic way to decide—but thinking the question through is essential.

Another bumpersticker, remember, asks how some people can reconcile great concern for other animals with a seeming lack of concern for human fetuses, which also have a kind of life and awareness but are at risk if abortion is legal. How can there be "animal rights," say, and not fetal rights?

Once again, there may be answers. Maybe there is a relevant distinction between the two cases. Maybe it's that other animals are actually born, unlike a fetus (in fact, most animals used for food or testing are full-grown adults) and are conscious of what is happening. Or maybe you'll want to say that abortion is *not* justified when the reasons are mainly utilitarian—if solely for reasons of cost, for example—just as you might also hold that it's no excuse for testing drugs on animals merely that other forms of testing would be more expensive.

This challenge too (like most, you may be noticing) also works the other way around. Can there be fetal rights but not animal rights? If you're pro-life but not a vegetarian, I leave that question for you.

INVENTED CASES

Not all "like cases" need be *real* cases, either. The logic of invented cases is perhaps a little harder to see, but it also opens up some intriguing new possibilities. It is one of the distinctive ways that philosophers think about ethics.

THE LOGIC OF INVENTED CASES

Consider our first example again. The argument, remember, was that I cannot morally misrepresent my car in order to sell it if I would object to anyone else doing the same to me.

Now notice that it does not matter whether I am actually buying a car or not. It is enough that *if* I were buying a car I would have such objections. Here, then, you have a "like case" that is not exactly real (suppose I'm not really buying a car right now), yet it does the work that's needed. A space opens here—indeed the necessity emerges here—for what we could call "moral imagination."

If you worked on "Using Your Tools" #3, you have already encountered some striking invented cases. There was Bob's precious Bugatti (a very fancy car), in particular, sitting forlornly at the end of a railroad siding onto which Bob must divert a runaway train to save a child's life (p. 169). Peter Singer (discussed there) explicitly uses the "Judge Like Cases Alike" principle in his argument. After spelling out the Bob/Bugatti example, he writes

> If you . . . think that it was very wrong of Bob not to throw the switch that would have diverted the train and saved the child's life, then it is hard to see how you could deny that it is also very wrong not to send money to one of the [famine-relief] organizations. . . . Unless, that is, there is some morally important difference between the two situations that I have overlooked.

Again, there's no denying that the situations are *different*, indeed wildly different. Letting a train run over an innocent kid rather than sacrifice your precious vintage car certainly doesn't look the same as spending money going to restaurants or on consumer goods rather than sending it to famine relief. But the question is whether the two situations are different in some *morally relevant* way. Singer argues that they are not. As the argument proceeds, you begin to see the uncomfortable similarities. Both are cases of declining to do something that would demonstrably save a life (or many lives) in order, instead, to make life slightly more commodious for ourselves. The moralist's conclusion is that it should be troubling in both cases. The point of the invented case is just to make the logic of those troubles stand out more starkly in the real case.

You may find yourself doing the same in your own moral arguments. One of my students (**G** in the following dialogue) did so one day when a class was discussing some issues about globalization.

G: Protests caused McDonald's restaurants to pull out of many cities in India. I guess the Hindus didn't take too happily to the idea of eating sacred cows. I wonder why McDonald's didn't think of that . . .

N: I think it's outrageous. McDonald's has the right to offer a legal good for sale. People don't have to buy it if they don't want to.

G: Well, if you were a Hindu you'd probably see it a little differently.

N: I'm not a Hindu! I have no sacred cows.

G: You have certain beliefs that a restaurant could offend, don't you? What if some cannibals started a fast-food chain and opened a take-out place down the street from you. Would you have a problem with that? After all, you don't have to let human flesh if you don't want to.

N: Outrageous! I'd go down and picket the place myself.

G: Maybe you *do* have a sacred cow!

It seems to be hard for N to put himself into the Hindus' shoes—at least by imagining himself a Hindu. So G tries something else. G invents a scenario in which someone *else* does to N what McDonald's did to the Hindus, so that N can stay in his own shoes, as it were, and still imagine himself in a situation *like* theirs.

The logic stays the same. You essentially *invent* a "like case," but the point is that it is still relevantly similar (you claim) to the real-life case you are thinking about. Inconsistency can still arise, even if the allegedly "like case" may be entirely unreal. And the same options arise in response: deny the likeness, or change one of the inconsistent judgments.

THE RIGHT TO LIFE AND THE UNCONSCIOUS VIOLINIST

Here is another famous example of an argument from an invented case. On both sides of the abortion debate it is usually assumed that if the fetus has a right to life, then choosing abortion violates that right and is wrong. The philosopher Judith Thomson argued in a famous essay that this conclusion doesn't always follow. Imagine, she says, that

> You wake up in the morning and find yourself back-to-back in bed with an unconscious violinist. A famous unconscious violinist. He has been found to have a fatal kidney ailment, and the Society of Music Lovers has canvassed all the available medical records and found that you alone have the right blood type to help. They have therefore kidnapped you, and last

night the violinist's circulatory system was plugged into yours, so that your kidneys can be used to extract poisons from his blood as well as your own.

If you unplug yourself now, the Music Lovers point out, the violinist will die, and after all the violinist does have a right to life. . . . Yet surely, Thomson argues, you have the right to unplug yourself, even so. It might be *nice* to donate nine months' use of your kidneys to the violinist, but you cannot be compelled to do so.

Suppose you agree—that is, suppose you think that you have the right to unplug yourself in this case. Therefore, even if another being is dependent upon you for life support (and in Thomson's case a being who is clearly and uncontroversially a human being—and "innocent," too), and even if that being has a right to life, you believe that you may still, morally, pull the plug. It's still within your rights to refuse to go through with it.

Thomson argues that abortion in some cases, especially if you are pregnant unintentionally or against your will, is the moral equivalent of pulling the plug on the violinist. By analogy, then, in the case of abortion, Thomson concludes that the fetus's right to life does not necessarily make abortion a violation of that right. You did not ask for this other life to be hooked to yours; you are being asked to make an enormous sacrifice of your time and your body's very energies; you acknowledge that there will be a loss if you "unplug"—the dependent being will die—but your right to your own body can still take precedence. "Pulling the plug" is morally permissible, she concludes in such cases.

SO . . .?

This is a pretty wild analogy. It's not something that is actually likely to happen. But that it is a completely imaginary case, once again, does not affect the problem of inconsistency. *If* you would object to being hooked up to the violinist, real or not, then you ought to support abortion rights in at least some cases—so the argument goes. Indeed, precisely the fact that it is not likely to happen helps make Thomson's point. We would never stand for kidnapping people off the streets to provide life support for dying musicians—so, if outlawing abortion would really be analogous to *that*, we should not outlaw abortion either.

One nice feature of this analogy is that it puts males into a situation that Thomson thinks is *like* being unintentionally pregnant. (Notice that only an imaginary case is likely to do this—surely an advantage of the imaginary.) She suspects that few men, even those who are strongly anti-abortion, would agree that they have no right to unplug themselves from the violinist. But then the challenge is acute: can they then consistently be anti-abortion? What's the difference between this case and unintentional pregnancy?

As usual, the same options apply: question the likeness, or change one of the inconsistent Judgments. Some deny that being tied to the violinist really is like being unwillingly pregnant. Conservatives argue that a relevant difference between pregnancy and Thomson's case is that pregnancy is a known risk of having sex, even with contraception. In Thomson's case you're simply kidnapped off the street and involuntarily plugged to the violinist, but in the case of having sex, even with contraception, you are quite aware that pregnancy is at least possible. It's not quite so involuntary. You need to take some responsibility.

This is a fair point. Maybe the two cases aren't so "like," and we can consistently judge them differently.

On the other hand, this difference does not always hold. In some cases, at least, pregnancy *is* that involuntary. Think of pregnancy caused by rape. Though many pro-life advocates make an exception in this case, not all do. Some still insist that the fetus's right to life has priority. There, Thomson's analogy has special bite (unless, of course, those pro-life advocates agree that they must stay hooked up to the violinist for nine months too—restoring consistency in a more extreme, and frankly unlikely, way).

Thomson or her defenders might also recast the analogy to acknowledge the conservative response. Suppose it was known, for example, that the Society of Music Lovers was looking for someone to hook up to the violinist, and you went out for a walk of your own free will even knowing that there was a small probability that you might be kidnapped for this purpose off the street. (There's a non-zero probability *now*, after all, isn't there?) Maybe you even took an escort. This might be like using contraception—taking reasonable precautions—even knowing that there is a small probability that it won't work. Don't you still have a right to unplug?

Thomson would say so. After all, people can't really be obliged to stay inside all the time just because there is a small chance they might find themselves kidnapped and hooked up to the violinist if they go out. You're not responsible, even a little, as long as you take reasonable precautions. It would not be fair to ask more. This might be like saying that women can't really be obliged to refrain from sex totally until they are ready to carry through with an unintended pregnancy. Again, you're *not* responsible, even a little, as long as you take reasonable precautions—it would not be fair to ask for more.

Thomson's analogy, and others she proposes that are like it, have set off a continuing debate among philosophers, much larger than we can review here. You see the point, though: working through "like cases"—even entirely imaginary ones like hers and Singer's—is an essential part of moral thinking. It is a complicated business (no surprise), but it can also be intriguing and revealing. And sometimes necessary.

READING

"Speciesism"

COLIN McGINN

PHILOSOPHER COLIN MCGINN uses two thought-experiments— extended analogies like Thomson's—to raise questions about the offhand ways we treat other animals.

Often we look at animals as mere objects to be consumed or entertained by or experimented upon, and we justify this practice without considering what our reasons imply about "like cases." But suppose we were the *victims* of this kind of treatment rather than its perpetrators? It's not likely that we'd judge it the same way then. Or suppose the victims of it were just a little more like ourselves than other animals are now—what then? At least there would be some uneasiness about it. We'd pay some serious attention and give the victims' side a little closer look.

McGinn makes these suppositions a bit more vivid: he tells a couple of stories. Of course, these stories are made up, and so once again it may be tempting to dismiss them without thinking them through. But take care—there is a serious challenge here. Are we guilty of "speciesism"—a preference for humans over nonhumans merely on the basis of our *being* human, a difference that, according to McGinn, is not a relevant difference when issues of pain and abuse are at stake? If you are passionately convinced that it would be wrong for McGinn's vampires to suck *you* dry, why are you eating that hamburger without a second thought?

We have all seen those vampire films, creepy tales of powerful pale predators who live on human blood. Well, let me tell you a story about a particularly successful vampire species. This species is unusual among the run of vampires in that it can live equally well off human blood or orange juice.

It is also more in control of its food supply than your average vampire. In addition to producing ample supplies of orange juice, it keeps throngs of humans locked up in huge prisons so that it can get to their necks with minimum effort. The vampires raise

---

Selections from Colin McGinn, *Moral Literacy: or How to Do the Right Thing*, reprinted by permission of Hackett Publishing Company, Inc. and by permission of Gerald Duckworth & Co. Ltd. © 1992 by Colin McGinn. All rights reserved.

human infants in these prisons for the sole purpose of drinking their blood at maturity (and they have been known to do it at tenderer ages too). There is a bit of a snag, though, from the vampires' point of view, namely that you can't drink blood from the same human more than three times without that human's dying, so they are continually needing to replenish their stocks as thrice-bitten humans die off. The humans are powerless to resist because of the superhuman capacities of the vampires. When the vampires aren't dining on human blood (and the occasional glass of orange juice) they do the usual civilised things: go to the movies and the opera, make love, get married, play tennis, whatever.

They also have strict laws governing conduct within their species and are generally law-abiding and polite. They are actually not such a bad lot, generally considered, apart from this human blood business. But they don't see much of a problem about that because, after all we humans belong to a different species from them and look and act differently; anyway they have been doing it for millennia. They sometimes think it is a pity about the pain and fear the humans feel while their necks are being punctured and drained, not to mention all the death that results, but there is no point in being squeamish and sentimental about your farm animals, is there? And yes, they could live just as well on orange juice—which they actually rather enjoy at breakfast time—but it would be a little monotonous to have only that to drink: they like some variety in their diet. True, also, it would be healthier to give up human blood, as some of them are always tediously insisting, but they relish their pint of blood at dinner time and feel that life would be poorer without it. So they don't take much notice of the "juicetarians" among them, a small minority anyhow, who fitfully campaign for humane treatment for humans and even go so far as to call for complete human liberation! Why, what would become of all the humans if they were set free to roam the land? No, it is inconceivable.

I don't know about you but I find this vampire species a pretty selfish, blinkered and cruel bunch. They have got their values all wrong. If I were a powerful Martian visiting earth and found it dominated by these bloodsuckers, with the human species reduced to the status of mere blood vats, I would insist that they damn well stick to orange juice. Variety, freedom, tradition—don't give me that! Just look what you are doing to these poor humans, the pain and misery and confinement you cause them—and all because you don't fancy orange juice all the time. I mean, honestly, are you really telling me that it is morally acceptable to put that child to a slow and painful death rather than squeeze a couple of oranges? Can the difference of taste be that important to you? Human liberation! That is what I would say; and if I were one of the unlucky human victims I would plead the same case, hoping to appeal to the vampires' moral sense—of which they seem to have plenty when it comes to the welfare of their *own* species.

Here is another example, in which the human role is reversed. Imagine that there are two humanlike species, not one, either naturally evolved or created by God, rather as there are a number of monkey species. We are in the dominant position relative to the other humanlike species—call it the "shuman" species. Shumans like humans, are intelligent, sensitive, social, civilised—in fact very much on a par with humans in their level of development. However, their warlike prowess is much inferior to ours, and as a result they have been conquered and tyrannised by the "superior" species. Not content merely with enslaving them to do our dirty work, we also use them for food, as subjects of vivisection experiments and in bloodsports. Our exploitation of them gives us a higher standard of living than we would have otherwise. Their flesh is excellent when barbecued; medical science has progressed rapidly by using them instead of lower species which are biologically less like us; and it is jolly amusing to watch them running away from, and being caught by, the starved dogs we let loose on them on Saturday afternoons. Of course, the shumans complain all the time about what we humans do to them, always petitioning the government from their special reservations, trying to work up some emotional sympathy, causing trouble in the streets. We are not impressed, though, because they belong to another species from ours: we can't interbreed with them, they are completely hairless with pointy ears, and the mothers carry the babies for twelve months not nine. Admittedly we don't need to use them in this way—we already have plenty of other species to depend on, as well as the vegetable kingdom—but it can't be denied that we derive pleasure from them that we wouldn't enjoy without exploiting them as we do. So you see it is all right to ignore their interests in order to cater to ours. We don't need to *balance* their interests with ours, treating similar interests equally, since the shumans belong to a different biological group from us. The biological distinction cancels the moral commitments we would have with respect to the interests of members of our own species.

Again, I maintain that this isn't right. We are doing to them what the vampires were doing to us—trampling over the legitimate interests of another group. In essence, we are refusing to take their welfare seriously simply because they belong to a different biological species from us—*and this difference does not warrant that refusal.* There is a word for this attitude, coined about twenty years ago, namely "speciesism." It was coined on analogy with the concept of racism and sexism, and is intended to suggest that what is morally irrelevant or insignificant—species or race or sex—is being treated as if it carried decisive moral weight. The point of my two imaginary examples is to demonstrate that speciesism *as such* is a form of unacceptable discrimination. There is no good moral defence of what the vampires do to us or what we do to the shumans, and to try to base one on a mere difference of species is transparent special pleading. It is simply quite unconvincing as a justification for what looks on the surface like a naked exercise of power designed to benefit one group at the ruthless expense of another. Cruelty is cruelty is cruelty—and a mere difference of species doesn't make it right. Ditto for murder, imprisonment, and so on.

The question we must then ask, returning now to the real world, is whether our actual treatment of animals is founded on a tacit speciesism—that is, whether we would rationally condone it if it weren't for mere species differences. Do we, in other words, accord mere zoological distinctions too much weight in deciding what to do and not do to animals? Is the speciesist attitude the only thing that sustains our exploitative treatment of other species? Could we defend this treatment without reliance upon *naked species bias?*

Once this question is clearly raised, it is very hard to avoid the answer that we do rely, unacceptably, on speciesist assumptions. What tends to obscure this fact is that animals differ from us not *only* in point of what species they belong to: they differ, also, mentally, in terms of their cognitive abilities. They don't have our intellects, our brain power, our moral sense. Their minds are just not as rich and complicated as ours.

But it is easy to see that *this* difference cannot make the moral difference we tend to take for granted—unless, that is, we are prepared to set up a new and pernicious form of social discrimination: intelligenceism. Surely we don't think that mere inferiority of intelligence (by some possibly arbitrary standard) is enough to justify, say, slaughtering the intellectually inferior for food or electrically shocking them for scientific purposes. If we did believe that, we would have the freedom to do these things to human children, mentally backward adults, and senile old people. Indeed, there would be no moral objection to intentionally raising genetically engineered "simple" humans for such purposes. But being intelligent is not what gives you the right not to be abused. The reason it is wrong to cause pain to people is not that they are intelligent or members of the human species. It is that pain hurts, it is bad to suffer it, people don't like to be in pain. If you want to know whether an action is wrong, you have to look at its actual effects and ask if they are bad for the thing being acted on—not ask what *else* happens to be true of the thing. If forced confinement, say, is bad *for* an animal, then it is bad to do this *to* an animal, unless you can think of a reason why this badness is justifiable in the light of a greater good. It isn't a question of the animal's ability to do mathematics or appreciate chamber music—still less of its species per se. It is a matter of sentience, the ability to suffer.

And here we reach the nub of the issue about our moral treatment of animals. *Is* there a greater good that justifies what, considered in itself, appears to be bad? Can we argue that what is bad for the animals is overridden by what is good for us? Is it possible to defend something bad in itself by claiming that the ends justify the means? Note, now, that we are assuming that our treatment of animals would be morally wrong if it were *not* for some supposed greater good.

A clear-eyed look at the facts quickly reveals that there is no such means-end justification, at least in the vast majority of cases. The test to use here is whether you would condone a given form of treatment if it were practised on humans, thus eliminating the speciesist bias from your deliberations. You may also consider "simple" humans in order to eliminate intelligenceist bias. That is, you have to ask whether you would do to intellectually comparable humans what we regularly do to animals. I won't bother to run through the whole gamut of things we do to animals, leaving this as an exercise for the reader; once the principle has been grasped this is fairly mechanical work. But it must be clear enough already that you would not condone killing humans for food in the way we now do animals, or experimenting on humans as we now do on animals, or using them in sports as we do now, or using their skins for clothes as we do now, and so on. You wouldn't even do these things to humans who were mentally *inferior* to the animals in question. The pain, the fear, the frustration, the loss of life—these would be quite enough to deter you. And the reason for these sound moral judgments is simply that the ends do *not* justify the means. A life lost for a pleasant taste gained? Mutilation for some possibly trivial increase in knowledge? Dismemberment in the jaws of dogs for the "thrill of the chase"? Trapped and skinned for an expensive fur coat? We would never accept these calculations if humans constituted the means, so why should we suddenly change our standards when we move outside the human species? Only, it seems, because of the prejudice that declares our species sacred and other species just so much exploitable stuff. Unfair discrimination, in other words.

So what should be done, now that we have seen our treatment of other species for what it is—immorally benefiting ourselves at the expense of other animals? (Actually, it is more that we *think* we are benefiting ourselves, since a lot of what we get from them is bad for us.) We should, at the very least, do everything we can to minimise our dependence on animals, treating their interests as comparable to the interests of fellow humans in the respects relevant to the case at hand. This will mean, just for starters, stopping eating meat if you live in one of the societies in which it is perfectly possible to find other sources of food, i.e., almost everywhere on earth. Don't even think about owning a fur coat. Very few animal experiments, if any. Bloodsports—give me a break. In sum, we have to cease doing to animals what we would not in good conscience do to humans. We must make our morality consistent.

You ask: if it is so wrong, why do people do it? Good question. To answer it, a glance back at history helps. It is a sad fact about human affairs that power tends to rule, and this includes our relation to the animal world. Nor is power always, or indeed often, on the same side as justice. If A is more powerful than B, and A can get something off B which B may not want to give to A, then A is apt to take that something from B by brute force—unless A is a just and moral individual, which he very often isn't. People all too often do what they have the power to do, and to hell with morality. Whenever you have imbalances of power, and a relation of domination that serves one party not the other, then be on the look-out for the kinds of prejudice and ideology that sustain basically immoral arrangements.

Historically, two areas of intense and terrible exploitation stand out, both of which were "justified" by all manner of strange doctrines at the time: slavery and child labour. I need not review these familiar stories of human brutality and moral blindness, since they are now accepted as such, though it is easily forgotten how recently young children were put through unspeakable miseries in supposedly civilised countries like England and slavery was legally permitted in America. My point is that at the time, and for hundreds of years before, these forms of subjugation were widely taken for granted and not regarded as morally dubious. Only now, in enlightened retrospect, do we wag the finger of condemnation at our forebears and marvel at their moral insensitivity. But which of us alive now can be sure that we would have been on the side of the angels had we lived in those benighted days? The pressures of conformity and self-interest and sheer inertia are very strong. May it not now be the case that our treatment of animals, so redolent of the barbarities of slavery and child exploitation, is just one more example of brute power holding sway over natural justice—of self-interest stifling moral decency? But, as with those other cases, it is not always easy to see this when it is all around you. You tend to think it must have *some* justification, even if you can't produce one. But maybe it just doesn't.

FOR REVIEW

1. Explain "judging like cases alike."
2. How is the bumpersticker EXECUTION STOPS A BEATING HEART an *argument?*
3. When our moral stances seem inconsistent, what are the three logical ways in which we can respond?
4. Explain the first possible response with an example.
5. Explain the second possible response with an example.
6. Explain the third possible response with an example.
7. How could a purely invented case be relevant to "judging like cases alike"?
8. What is the point of Judith Thomson's violinist analogy?
9. What are Colin McGinn's two analogies to the human treatment of other animals?
10. What does McGinn conclude from his analogies?

EXERCISES AND NOTES

10.1 TAKING UP THE CHALLENGE

Working through "like cases" is a way of *thinking*. It is a way of clarifying what's morally at stake in a specific situation by comparing it with other seemingly similar cases to see what the relevant differences are—and aren't. And it is a way of working toward greater consistency and clarity in your moral views generally by comparing them with each other so as to bring out your general moral commitments.

Colin McGinn's analogies may give you much to think about: you might want to look at more of the chapter on animals in his book *Moral Literacy* (Hackett/Duckworth, 1992). Judith Thomson's violinist analogy comes from her essay

---

QUICK REFERENCE: JUDGING LIKE CASES ALIKE

PAY ATTENTION

Systematically and honestly extend your moral reasons in one kind of case to other "like cases." (Example: if you oppose abortion to protect "innocent life," then consider other cases where other kinds of innocent life are at stake.) Do you judge them similarly? If not, why not?

WHEN INCONSISTENCY ARISES

When your judgments vary between these cases, consider your options.

- You could argue that the alleged "like cases" are not really alike. In that case you need to figure out the *morally relevant difference* between the cases and explain what difference that difference makes.
- You could change your judgment about the "like case" or cases.
- You could change your judgment about the original case or cases.

CONSIDER "LIKE CASES" FOR FURTHER CHECKING

Consider hypothetical cases to sharpen and test your thinking further. (Case in point: McGinn's thought-experiment.)

RECHECK

Rethink your views, re-articulate your reasons, and try again. Remember, consistency takes time and work!

"A Defense of Abortion," widely available in recent ethics collections (a citation follows in the Notes); she also proposes a number of other striking analogies to other kinds of unintentional and involuntary pregnancy.

Go on to invent some analogies of your own to test your own or other people's moral generalizations or judgments about specific cases. Consider some issues such as responses to international terrorism, high-technology medical interventions or genetic engineering, and sexual orientation issues. Remember, of course, that your supposed "like cases" actually have to be fair analogies. The challenge is not rhetorical: instead, once again, it is to think carefully and see further than we might without the analogies. You might have to try a number of different analogies to find one that works well. If you can't find any, it might be time to rethink your initial judgment.

10.2 "SEAMLESS GARMENTS"

As chapter 3 points out, modern Catholic moral theologians are not merely "pro-life" when it comes to fetuses but argue for what they call a "seamless garment" of respect for life in all cases, which to them means being not only anti-abortion but also anti-war, anti-assisted suicide, and anti-capital punishment, and pro-environment, pro-welfare, and pro-animal. In this they differ from many Protestant pro-life activists, who tend to be pro-life on abortion but conservative on most of these other issues. If we're going to be pro-life, these moralists argue, we have to be pro-life across the board. Thus Catholic moral theology challenges those who wish to be pro-life on some issues but not on others to "judge like cases alike"—to ask if there really is a difference between those issues, and if not, to "get consistent." (See Notes for references and links.)

Of course, there are other possible responses. Perhaps some of those issues *are* relevantly different from abortion so that defending the fetus's right to life does not necessarily imply defending, for example, a poor person's right to food stamps. It is also possible to "get consistent" by giving up one's pro-life views on abortion (perhaps one could still be anti-abortion for other reasons), rather than embracing a pro-life view in other similar cases.

Once again, though, meeting the challenge takes some work. What do you say to it, at bottom? How many of us really are "pro-life" across the board? Must we be? Should we be? How could we not be? (Serious question.)

NOTES

Judith Jarvis Thomson's "A Defense of Abortion" is one of the most widely reprinted articles in recent philosophical ethics. It appears, for example, in Steven Cahn's collection *Exploring Ethics* (Oxford, 2009), where my citation can be found on pp. 168–69. Thomson also proposes a number of other striking analogies to other kinds of unintentional and involuntary pregnancy. For commentary, see Rosalind Hursthouse, *Beginning Lives* (Blackwell, 1987), pp. 181–194.

For contemporary Catholic literature on the "seamless garment" or "consistent ethic of life," see Joseph Cardinal Bernardin, *A Moral Vision of America* (Georgetown University Press, 1998). A good introduction can be found at http://www.priestsforlife.org/magisterium/bernardinwade.html. For an evangelical version of a similar argument, see Ronald Sider, *Completely Pro-Life: Building a Consistent Stance on Abortion, the Family, Nuclear Weapons, the Poor* (Wipf & Stock Publishers, 2010). Note the subtitle! On the secular side, probably the best example of an ethic that tries to follow a single principle across the board is, once again, Peter Singer's utilitarianism, laid out, for example, in his *Practical Ethics* (Cambridge University Press, 2011).

USING YOUR TOOLS #5
EXPLORING THE WELFARE QUESTION

Your challenge in this exercise is to use the tools in chapters 9 and 10 to investigate and think through a contentious moral issue in greater depth. An important and useful issue for this purpose is the question of *welfare*.

Students could undertake this project individually, with your product being a report to the class or even a major research paper. You could also work on it in groups, again with the aim of bringing a report back to your class, or perhaps some public piece of writing. Either way, this is a chance to go into it in depth. For purposes of this project, you do not need to draw final moral conclusions: you can and perhaps should leave the question at least somewhat open. You also do not need to bring in the families of moral values explicitly, except to help you determine what factual questions may be relevant (remember the box "Which Facts Are Relevant?" in chapter 9). Pay more attention to the specific definitional and factual issues posed here, as well as the challenges in the section below called "Like Cases Alike?" They're hard enough!

FACTS AND DEFINITIONS

The contemporary American debate about welfare, very roughly, is over whether public funds should be used to provide monetary support to people who are economically down and out—for help with housing and food costs and as aid to poor parents with dependent children. (Charitable support may also be a form of "welfare," but it is much less morally controversial because the funding normally is voluntary.) It can be an intensely emotional debate, on all sides, and also, not coincidentally, is shaped by many second- or third-hand beliefs. Challenge yourself to do better, using the critical thinking skills you are developing in this book.

Start with definitions. What *is* welfare? Most people in national polls oppose something called "welfare," but when asked whether they favor most of the individual federal and state programs that make it up, they overwhelmingly say yes. Opponents reduce it, sometimes, to just one or two out of the current several dozen major social-support programs, especially food stamps, or the Temporary Assistance for Needy Families (TANF) program. Among others are Unemployment Compensation, Medicaid, Supplemental Social Security for the disabled and elderly poor, housing assistance, and infant supply and nutrition programs, which are all "means-tested" (i.e., to receive benefits a person must demonstrate a certain level of financial and other need), as well as entitlement programs that are not means-tested, like the more familiar kind of Social Security, military and civil service retirement funds, Veteran's Administration medical care, Low-Income Home Energy Assistance programs, student loan programs (yup, you may be on "welfare" too), and still others. So how would *you* define "welfare"? Or rather, how *should* we define it? What is the most useful way to understand that term? What is the most useful way to understand the "welfare" programs that now exist? What do we actually need to argue about?

Get some facts. How much money are we talking about here? For which programs? How are government expenditures changing? (Increasing? Faster than cost of living?) How do they compare with government expenditures for other things (energy programs, education, highways, etc.)? Some critics argue that special corporate tax breaks ("corporate welfare," they call it) cost more money than all means-tested welfare programs put together. Are they right? How do the numbers look? (And what particular breaks do they have in mind? How are they defining "welfare" to be able to make this claim? Is this a reasonable definition?)

Welfare programs change constantly. Therefore you will also need to be sure you have the most current information. How have welfare laws and provisions changed recently? And what is their history? You or someone in your group would make a helpful contribution just by impartially exploring and reporting the history of "welfare" programs, starting way back in the ancient world. Welfare programs have changed substantially as they came under the purview of states in recent times, but some form of collective and not-always-voluntary provision for the down-and-out, though not always generous and frequently highly intrusive, has been a feature of almost all organized societies.

Who's *on* welfare—on, for starters, the most controversial means-tested type? (Look for reliable data here: this, especially, is a minefield of stereotypes, many of them distorted.) *Why* are people on welfare? How long do they tend to stay? (Once again, be very careful of the stereotypes here—talk to people to really find out.) How do poverty and homelessness relate to violence against women? To veteran status? To the impoverishment of central cities?

Look at welfare programs locally. What social-support programs are available, and to whom, in your area? When cash is involved, how much is paid? Does the amount of aid really make life liveable? (That is, how does it relate to the local cost of living? For that matter, how does it relate to *your* cost of living?) Do benefits increase with the recipients' number of children? If so, find out how much more money a parent gets per month for a second, third, or fourth child. How does it compare with the additional monthly costs of diapers, baby food, medical care, and so on? How does it compare with the stereotypes?

Also, how do you get *disqualified?* When and under what conditions does welfare end? How long do people tend to stay on it? How long *can* they? Again, look for the most up-to-date information. Local social-service workers, administrators of soup kitchens and shelters for the homeless, and human-services departments at your school should be good sources of information. For current U.S. government data, try www.census .gov/hhes/www/poverty. And finally, hardest and most important: talk to poor people themselves. If you yourself have first-hand knowledge of poverty, speak up! If you don't, you might want to find out more before being confident of any opinion (regardless of what that opinion is). If you can help out while learning besides, all the better.

I hope you see that even these quick questions both invite you to look more deeply into a variety of factual questions—there is real information, not just opinion, about most of these issues—and open up some unexpected ways of thinking and even possible creative solutions (a point to which chapters 13 and 14 return). Again, for purposes of this project, it is probably best to avoid making your report or paper into an argument for one position or another on the whole welfare question. Just concentrate on the facts, and for this part at least, make your moral conclusions more tentative.

LIKE CASES ALIKE?

To judge like cases alike when welfare is at stake is, at the very least, not to judge the question differently from different standpoints of need: that is, not to oppose it if you imagine yourself rich but favor it if you imagine yourself poor. As chapter 10 notes, Lawrence Kohlberg suggests that we imagine "moral musical chairs," which we could visualize as systematically going through all of the affected persons or roles—from (in this case) taxpayers, administrators, welfare recipients, children on welfare, and all the rest, including fairly subtly affected people, such as people who might receive more benefits or advantages if the money spent on welfare were spent on something else instead—being sure that when we finally arrive at a judgment, it is a judgment that we are willing to affirm from every "chair." Which chair or chairs we actually occupy in real life is not so important: the key moral sense is that "I could be anyone."

A more systematic way to picture something like "moral musical chairs" was worked out in the later 20th Century by the American political philosopher John Rawls and advanced in his monumental work *A Theory of Justice* (Belknap Press of Harvard University, 1971). (You may recall our brief discussion at the end of chapter 5.) Rawls asks us to imagine that we are working out a whole system of distribution of key social goods, from political and other "offices" to economic goods, from a vantage point or "contract" situation where—here is the key thing—we don't know what actual position we will occupy in the system that ultimately results. That is, to make the rules by a fully moral procedure would be as if we make the rules *before we know how the rules will actually affect us individually*. That is what makes our decision truly moral, rather than self-serving and distorted in some way. If we could be *anyone* in the system that is being created, what kind of system would we create?

After all, if being an "end in yourself" has nothing to do with your particular accomplishments (or lack thereof), or family or willpower or anything else, then it can be helpful, maybe even necessary, to put these things aside at times, at least in imagination, while thinking about moral principles. This is what Rawls calls the "Veil of Ignorance." While in certain ways the problem about ethics is that we are *too* "ignorant"—we don't know enough of the actual facts about, say, welfare programs—there is also at least one way in which perhaps we also know too much, where a little less knowledge would be helpful. On Rawls's model, which he called the "Original Position," we know all the facts, both about specific programs and about human nature generally, but there is a crucial bit of ignorance somewhere else: we don't know who we are, exactly what role we are to play, until the system is already set up. It's an elegant guarantee that our choices will not be self-serving or otherwise morally distorted.

From the point of view of moral and political theory, Rawls's great idea was that the Original Position is formally definable enough that with some use of game theory and other modern economics-like models, we can get fairly precise about what kinds of principles will result. Chapter 5 briefly outlined his conclusions: a principle of Equality in the case of political liberties, since in the political sphere any increase in one person's liberties must mean a decrease for someone else; and a principle that allows economic and other *in*equalities, since in the economic sphere one person's gain does not necessarily mean someone else's loss, but only as long as they bring the least well-off persons as far up as any arrangement can. This second idea—Rawls calls it the "Difference Principle"—is most relevant to the welfare question.

DESIGNING A SYSTEM

Exercise 1.2 proposed a Rawlsian sort of exercise: designing a company without knowing what your own status will be within it. (If you did that exercise, review your answers before proceeding.) Now let's vary it. Try designing a welfare system, in particular, without knowing what your own status will be within it. Maybe you'll be heir to some immense family fortune. Or an Iraq War veteran with posttraumatic stress syndrome, barely holding onto a job with no health coverage. Or an entrepreneur on the edge with a chance either to make it big or to end up on the streets. Or a caregiver for well-loved but very dependent children or parents or others with few resources. Or many other possible roles. How then will you set up your economic and social system in regard to the needs of the down-and-out, who might well (but then again, might well not) be you? Will you provide for them? Or not? And if so, exactly how and how far?

One Rawlsian warning. Some people, young, able, and ambitious now, might reason that although they start out with nothing, they would be likely to get rich quickly and therefore would oppose any major tax-supported system of social provision even if at first, or in what they consider unlikely cases, they might benefit from it or need it desperately. Remember, though, that in the Original Position you also don't know whether you'd end up young, able, and ambitious or, instead, quite a different kind of person—say, that partially disabled veteran who'd really just like some stability and enough support and safety net to have a chance to make a productive contribution, or a minority group member or otherwise discriminated-against person who never had the opportunity of good schools or family support in the first place. Could not justice still in some ways be served? How?

Try to define your system both as to its general philosophy (that would be the Mission Statement, so to speak, of your welfare system) and some of its specific rules (so you can tell how it would actually apply to specific cases). You might start by working out together a range of possible types of systems in this sense (philosophies plus specific rules and practices). Discuss them as a group, trying to be mindful of the veil of ignorance. Once you have envisioned a good and diverse set of possible systems, brainstorm a list of roles or "chairs" in your world: the homeless veteran, the overburdened caregiver, the overtaxed entrepreneur . . . and who else? A good way to remember that you could be any of these people in the system you set up is to plan to assign these roles randomly to individuals in your class (number them and draw numbers out of a hat or something) once you have settled on the system. First, though, return to your negotiations with your class's list of specific roles in mind: it should help to make the consequences and potential problems and issues more vivid. Then come to some group decision, if you can. Then assign actual roles and consider what you've done. Now you know who you actually are (for purpose of this exercise), and what kinds of decisions are going to come down that affect you in particular (What happens if you get sick, for instance? What happens if you end up a rich heiress—or a bag lady?). How does your proposed system look to you now?

UTILITARIANISM?

I will leave you with one other challenge from Rawls. It might be tempting to think that people creating a welfare system under a veil of ignorance, as you are trying to do, would naturally or even necessarily choose a system that sought to achieve the greatest overall social benefit or utility—that is, that they would follow a utilitarian standard. This might be a system that makes some provision for down-and-out people, but perhaps not allocating as much money or resources to this purpose as a more egalitarian system would. Society as a whole might be happier if the better-off kept more of their income even though the poor would suffer more than they might under a more generous system.

Rawls argues that for precisely this reason, people under the veil of ignorance would not use overall social utility as their standard. This is because when life prospects are at stake, we are not risk takers. It is rational, he says, to minimize the risks of really bad outcomes—say, having nothing and starving on the streets in a society with no "safety net"—rather than play the odds, even if in general the odds are very good. After all, we only get one chance at life. If we somehow experienced every different social role in turn, maybe it would make sense to choose the system with the highest total utility across all the roles: we could just tough out the less pleasant ones knowing that greater pleasures await on other go-rounds. With only one chance, though, according to Rawls, people would be most concerned to secure the best possible worst-off roles. We disvalue the really bad prospects much more than we value the marginally better ones that might be possible if some people were consigned to miserable fates.

Remember that although there are some strongly egalitarian aspects of utilitarianism, an equality of outcome is not itself a utilitarian moral principle. Even a system with radical inequalities and a great deal of seemingly unfair suffering for some people could, in principle anyway, achieve the greatest *overall* social utility. For Rawls this is utilitarianism's fatal flaw, the rationale for the Difference Principle in general, and it seems, in particular, to argue for a much more robust welfare system than a utilitarian standard might. What do you think?

To delve farther into the discussion of Rawls's theory of justice, a good starting point is once again the Ethics Update website at ethics.sandiego.edu; open the "Justice" link.

CHAPTER 11

Dialogue

As we begin to explore ethical issues with others, much of our actual day-to-day or class-to-class practice is *talking*. Judging by the usual ethical debates, though, our ways of talking about ethics could use some improvement. How can we talk more constructively with each other about ethical issues?

HOW TO HAVE A FRUITLESS DEBATE

A meets B in the cafeteria line, one thing leads to another, and a familiar kind of verbal fistfight begins.

A: Eating meat is natural! Humans have always done it. I wish all you vegetarians would get off my back. You want to go against nature.

B: Oh right, I suppose people have always lined up at McDonald's for their quarter-pounder with shake and fries.

A: Well, what do you want, to line up at some juice bar for your little organic carrot with spring water? Give me a break! Besides, you animal rights fanatics want to stop all medical research. What about the cures for so many diseases, found through experiments on animals? If it weren't for those experiments, you wouldn't even be here to bad-mouth them.

B: Why do we need all those new cosmetics and toilet bowl cleaners? That's what 99% of animal testing is about! You're just rationalizing torture.

A: I bet you don't even like pets. You're telling me I don't love my dog?

B: You think that your dog wants to live stuck in some tiny little apartment all day? You call it "love" when you pen up a dog? Talk about unnatural!!

And so it goes—a fruitless debate, but sure loud enough. This one is only slightly exaggerated from the kinds of real-life debates we have all the time. Each side aims primarily to shut the other side up, to put them down in their own eyes and the eyes of anyone who may be listening. Potentially helpful points come up, but they are immediately dropped like hot potatoes. The actual arguments don't connect.

If put-downs and "winning" are your goals, you may deliberately try to create such debates. We could even spell out some of the "rules" both sides seem to be following. One is:

- **Take All the Room You Can.** Talk *loud* and talk a lot. Fill all the space you can with *your* thoughts and opinions. Worry about your *comeback*. Restate your opinion. Restate your opinion. Restate your opinion. Use a lot of "I think that . . ." statements. After the other person is done, come right back with "Yeah, but . . ."

In this debate, neither person really listens or tries to understand what the other person is saying. They're angry; they have a lot to say on the subject; they cannot wait to jump back in with some new peeve or assertion. If one side raises a good point, the other one would not think of acknowledging it or trying to respond. Neither is willing to give an inch. Apparently the best defense instead is just to change the subject. Having a comeback is everything.

Second:

- **Separate and Polarize.** *Polarize:* that is, exaggerate differences. Emphasize what you and the other side disagree about. Define their view as simply the opposite of yours. Always assume the worst. *Stereotype* the other side ("You're just a . . ."). Use *black/white labels* ("pro-life," "pro-death"). Try to define the other side before they can define themselves. Make your stereotyped labels stick.

In this debate, it's either all medical research or none; either a quarter-pounder or carrot sticks for lunch. No space for possible agreement is explored, no shared values are acknowledged or sought. Polarizing in this way reinforces the put-downs generally: the other side is made to look silly and stupid by constant exaggeration, as if they could not be in favor of anything sensible or balanced. Again there is no attempt to understand what the other person might actually mean. Instead the worst is assumed, and then attacked and mocked.

Finally, two related further "rules":

- **Exploit All Weaknesses or Openings.** Take *potshots*. Follow "red herrings." Pounce on any small discrepancies or other difficulties; don't engage the main point. *Run down partial solutions*. If an idea is not a perfect solution, attack it as no solution at all. Protect yourself by avoiding constructive thinking or making suggestions. Always be *against* something rather than *for* something.

- **Go for the Quick Kill.** Talk in *slogans* and *sound bites*. You'll infuriate the other side and everyone will remember your brilliant pithiness. Use facts only as weapons. Only seek out the ones that support your side; deny and suppress any others. Disengage quickly once you have secured an advantage.

Demand *closure*; expect "final" answers; pull out as soon as you can claim you're "right."

In this debate, slogans and labels abound (like "you animal rights fanatics"), and all sorts of assumptions are made with no thought of checking them out to see whether they're true or not. Does B really know that A's dog is penned up all day? Does A really know what B thinks about medical research? No—they just make an assumption and blast away.

The whole debate is a series of potshots and changes of subject. Often the comeback is on a subject different from the one just being discussed. They start out talking about meat eating, then about medical research, then about pets. A's opening claim is mostly about whether eating meat is natural. B responds in a sarcastic way, though she does have an argument of sorts. Not surprisingly, A in turn responds chiefly to the sarcasm, derides what he *assumes* to be B's alternative—and then changes the subject to medical research. . . .

WELL, WHAT'S WRONG WITH THAT?

Debaters know these "rules" and use them often. For some purposes they may even be useful. For other purposes it is at least useful to know about them: they may help you fight back or avoid getting caught in such a debate in the first place.

But—obviously—these "rules" do *not* work well when we are trying to think constructively about a problem. For one thing, they are ineffective, at least at persuasion. They don't really persuade—they only dominate and silence. The "loser" in such debates goes away angry, frustrated, maybe self-blaming—and certainly not feeling understood.

Second, they don't expand or develop ideas. They give us no way of cooperatively improving an idea. Quite the contrary: since the whole aim is to gain some personal advantage from criticizing any weakness in the other side's ideas, putting forward any kind of proposal is the last thing these rules encourage. Tentativeness, hope, enough trust to take up a rough idea and brainstorm together: this is just what these "rules" *prevent*.

In short, debate in this key drives people apart; it does not promote understanding; and at bottom *it is not ethical itself.* It is not committed to listening, open-mindedness, cooperation, and careful and responsible attention to values or arguments or concepts. We need to find another way.

HOW TO HAVE A USEFUL DISCUSSION

Now imagine a dialogue on the same subject in exactly the opposite key: listening carefully, respecting the other side, hoping to learn something and perhaps even to change your own ways as a result. Not mere acceptance

("Well, whatever . . ."), which leads to no dialogue and no learning at all. No: a real discussion, even disagreement, but in a constructive key. How would the discussion go then?

Rewind the tape. A meets B in the cafeteria line, and the debate begins again.

> **A:** Eating meat is natural! Humans have always done it. I wish all you vegetarians would get off my back. You want to go against nature.

In the very first place, a good listener would notice the defensiveness in this statement. "I wish all you vegetarians would get off my back." It seems that more is at stake for A than just a disagreement about the facts. You might guess that A has felt put on the spot, or put down, for eating meat. You could easily predict, too, that A will therefore find it hard to hear and acknowledge even the best arguments against meat eating. So although B's first impulse seems to be to mock A's argument and put her down even more cleverly, this is exactly the wrong strategy. Better to deal with the anger before taking up any arguments at all.

> **B:** So someone's been on your case, eh? Sorry about that. For my part, I'm really not interested in playing guilt games, though I know it happens with subjects like this . . .

B's response in the original dialogue does raise an important point. But B should raise this point in a way that is clearer and (obviously) not sarcastic. In the original, remember, after A says that eating meat is natural, that humans have always done it, B responds:

> **B:** ~~Oh right, I suppose people have always lined up at McDonald's for their quarter-pounder with shake and fries.~~

(I will put a line through the unconstructive responses to distinguish them clearly from the alternatives that follow.)

B may be thinking that humans may *not* always have eaten meat, at least in the way we do now. Generalizations about what has "always happened" are often made in a pretty offhand way, more as a rationalization than anything else. Is this what B suspects? If so, B could make his point a lot more effectively by asking a question, for example.

> **B:** I'm not so sure that people have always eaten meat. We're not built for it, biologically: Our teeth are the munching sort, not the tearing teeth of real carnivores. At least, I doubt that humans ate so much meat as we do now. What kind of diet do you think humans evolved with?

Now consider the next exchange. In the original, A mocks B's point in turn, and then goes on to something else. Remember:

A: ~~Well, what do you want, to line up at some juice bar for your little organic carrot with spring water? Give me a break! Besides, you animal rights fanatics want to stop all medical research. What about the cures for so many diseases, found through experiments on animals? If it weren't for those experiments, you wouldn't even be here to bad-mouth them.~~

My students, analyzing this exchange, point out (1) it would be more useful for A to ask B what kind of diet he actually proposes, rather than respond to the sarcasm with more of the same; (2) A should stay on the subject (the naturalness of meat eating) rather than shift to something else; and (3) A should *ask* B what he thinks about medical research rather than assuming he's against all of it. Suppose A said:

A: I'm pretty sure our ancestors ate meat when they could get it, though you might be right that it wasn't very often. But I'm interested in what you propose instead. Eating no meat at all, ever? What about people who need to eat meat to survive in their environments, like the Eskimo? This also makes me think of the debate about using animals in medical research. Are you also opposed to that? Always?

These are good questions and once again have the effect of opening up a thoughtful discussion rather than closing the talk down into "comebacks." Notice also that A no longer assumes that B must hold the most extreme possible position. Instead, she *asks* B what he thinks—and raises the question for B himself of just how far he will go.

B in turn can respond in a more constructive way.

B: Probably many people did eat meat when they could get it. And yes, maybe some people have to. But *we* don't have to. My real point is that it's not exactly natural to eat meat like we eat meat, anyway. Not meat at every meal, and the fattiest meat at that!

A has helped B to get to his *real* point—now we are getting somewhere!

Notice that in his original response, B never answers the question about medical research: he talks only about product testing.

B: ~~Why do we need all those new cosmetics and toilet bowl cleaners? That's what 99% of animal testing is about! You're just rationalizing torture.~~

He might now be able to answer that part of A's question more thoughtfully too:

B: I'm troubled by how much pain animals are put through for even the most minimal human gain. What right do we have to do that to animals even if there is a gain for us? This relates to the question of product testing too. If some new kind of shampoo, or cosmetic, or cleaner can only be brought out if it is tested on animals, then maybe it just shouldn't be brought out. We shouldn't be causing so much suffering when we don't have to.

This last discussion is in place of B's passing remark in the original debate about "torture." No longer is it merely a passing remark. Now it opens up new aspects of the issue to explore.

Notice how shared values begin to come into view. For example, A is unlikely to think that unnecessary suffering is morally acceptable. She does not want to be responsible for imposing needless suffering on animals. This is why many people have stopped eating veal, even though they may eat other animals and use animal products. A would probably argue that in other cases the suffering isn't needless—that in some way it is necessary—or that the animals don't really suffer so much. In any case, this is now a constructive discussion, and it is beginning to sound like ethics in a more familiar sense: trying to spell out and apply shared values. It's a mutual exploration, no longer a fight.

RULES FOR CONSTRUCTIVE TALKING

Ethical dialogue *could* be like this. All it takes is some skills that are not even so difficult. None of the advice in the last few pages, I trust, has been some shocking new revelation. All of the skills, and the possibilities they open up, are familiar. We just need to learn how to put them into practice at the right times.

Earlier we spelled out "rules" for fruitless debates. We can now spell out four corresponding rules for constructive talking—your ground rules for ethical discussions.

- **Slow Down and Listen.** Speak *calmly* and listen a lot. *Avoid the automatic comeback.* If you find yourself too ready with the "Yeah, but . . .", stop and take a deep breath. Then say, "Let me see if I understand you. . . ." Watch the surprise (and appreciation). And work for better *understanding*. Ask questions, and mean them. Restate others' views to make sure you "get it"—later you can ask for the same consideration back. Expect that you have as much to learn as they do.

In the revised dialogue, instead of taking all the room they can, A and B actually show some interest in each other's views and take the time to try to understand each other. They try to put their points carefully, admit uncertainty, and identify conflict without escalating it.

- **Connect.** Seek *common ground*. Approach differences against a background of probable agreement. (Differences may emerge as interesting against this background. They certainly emerge as *bridgeable*.) Recognize complexity on the other side (and yours). Don't polarize. There are no simple "yes" and "no" positions. Keep the focus on the *main points*. You might even help other people clarify and develop their thoughts and avoid distraction.

In the revised version, A and B are not preoccupied with their differences but explore them carefully while also identifying key points of agreement. They try to "integrate values," recognizing that each side speaks for something important. It's up to us to figure out what it is.

Finally, two more related rules:

- **Welcome Openings and Opportunities.** Look for first steps and partial measures. No problem is going to be resolved all at once. Think constructively; make suggestions. Always be *for* something and not just *against* something.
- **Stay Engaged.** Think of discussion as a collaboration in search of better understanding and creative ideas. Try to speak in a careful, open-ended, and helpful way. Avoid slogans or sound bites. Treat facts as *tools*. They're probably also more ambiguous than either side makes it seem. Keep exploring and looking for them. Expect the key questions to remain *open*. There is always more learning to do; the discussion will continue.

Instead of taking potshots and seeking to disengage the moment they have an advantage, A and B now take a much more exploratory approach and don't imagine that they are going to settle things once and for all. And therefore, oddly enough, they actually get much further than the debaters for whom finding a final and "right" position, right now, is everything. Debaters lock themselves into their positions and cannot budge. Collaborators, interested in a constructive discussion and making at least *some* difference, can *move*.

And notice finally, as I have been insisting throughout, that these are *ethical* rules too. Unlike the first set of rules, these rules reflect a commitment to listening, cooperation, and careful attention to values, arguments, and concepts. They offer a way to talk about ethical issues that is itself ethical.

DIALOGUE UNDER DURESS

Dialogue sounds wonderful in theory. But what if you are talking with someone who is not interested in dialogue? Or someone who does not know how to have one, or does not trust you or the situation enough to listen or believe they will be listened to?

Don't Give Up Too Soon

Sometimes ethical discussions reduce to fruitless debates because some of the participants have no idea that there is any other way to talk—or, even if they do, they don't trust anyone else to try it.

In that case, clearly the thing to do is to try it. Create an alternative. Set alternative ground rules for discussion, such as the Common Ground Rules in the reading to follow. Anyone who thinks that debate is the only way will be pleasantly surprised—and so will you, when people who appeared to be interested only in debate turn out to prefer something else, once given a real choice. The point is that *you* may have to be the one who creates that choice— *you* may have to set the alternative ground rules, formally and explicitly or gently by example. You do not simply have to accept whatever kind of discussion you find yourself stuck in.

Even habitual complainers can be lured onto more constructive ground. To the people whose main mode of discussion seems to be constant criticism and complaining, ask, "So, what's *your* idea?" Show some interest. Carping is usually a safe strategy because carpers can avoid sticking their necks out by making positive suggestions. So make positive suggestions safer. Create a setting in which creativity and openness are rewarded and carping is not.

Resisters

Some people just *love* to argue—so much so that they do not even notice, and certainly do not respond to, invitations to dialogue. They automatically turn any discussion into a debate.

You can leave this kind of discussion. You are not obliged to keep trying dialogue forever. Usually you can pull out in a way that isn't "losing," but just refusing to play the game.

You might also challenge the debate rules. Point out what is happening, and ask your partner or the group if this is really how they want to proceed. This is uncomfortable, of course, and not subtle at all. But it may sometimes work. At least it keeps people from falling into debate as if it were the only possible way to discuss things.

Some people enter dialogue in bad faith. People may use dialogue as a means of stalling. The idea might be to talk an issue to death so that nothing really changes—an appealing option for those who like things the way they are. So you need to be sure that all parties to the dialogue enter it with some good faith. If they don't, you are again entitled to pull out.

Or stay but refuse to play along. You might still make some progress. Stallers may find it hard to keep up polarizing values and grandstanding when you are speaking carefully and in general refusing to "play debate." Try it: it can actually be fun. If you have low expectations, at least you won't be disappointed.

Some people may join a dialogue (or may have to, for example, in a classroom) but be unwilling to speak honestly and openly in it. I have seen students in discussions of homophobia or racism or other kinds of prejudice unwilling to express views they actually hold, especially if they fear seeming prejudiced. But then many useful questions never get asked, stereotypes never get addressed, and some people leave feeling oppressed by a general atmosphere of "correctness."

This can be a way of resisting dialogue too, though often well-intentioned. Some indirection might help. *You* name the stereotypes, so at least they're out on the table. Find a story or movie whose characters bring them up, so the class or group can discuss them in the third person. Encourage others to bring up views in the third person too, as in, "Someone might say that . . ." or "It's not my view, but. . . ."

Silencing

Some people go into dialogue easily and feel welcomed and rewarded. Others come into the same space disadvantaged and with well-established habits of deference and silence. The results are very uneven patterns of participation and influence.

Usually the advantaged ones, though, are blissfully unaware of this imbalance—it's just "the way things are," to them—and if it is brought up by the disadvantaged (who are generally *quite* aware of it), the reaction is typically denial and anger. So, naturally, it is seldom brought up. Things just go on as before.

Still, dialogue fails when only some members of a group do all the talking: only men in gender-mixed groups, only whites in racially mixed groups, only teachers when teachers and students are together. Phyllis Beck Kritek, a nurse-administrator experienced at "negotiating at an uneven table," gives another example:

> I once served on a statewide committee looking at maldistribution of health care services. . . . There were several Native American reservations in this state. Health care needs on these reservations were profound. Historically, these needs had been easily rendered invisible. . . . An honest effort was made to change this pattern, to invite representatives from the tribal councils to the table. They attended the first organizational meeting.
>
> The tribal councils, of course, had a well-developed model for deliberating on conflicts: requesting all parties to speak their minds on the issue one by one and uninterrupted, in a deliberative fashion; consulting the elders; seeking guidance from spirits . . .; reflection. The approach to conflict offered

by the statewide committee was open discussion and political posturing, a tug of war between competing agendas. The tribal representatives sat silently watching, saying nothing. Later one participant commented to me privately that the American Indians were sure not going to get their fair share if they didn't participate better. No one asked them to speak their mind during this time. They would only have had the opportunity to speak if they had chosen to participate in the competition for airtime. At the second meeting, they were absent.

If You Feel Silenced

When you find yourself silenced or disadvantaged, here are some suggestions.

For one thing, again, don't assume that you must play the game by the prevailing rules. Maybe the prevailing rules are the *problem*. You might try to bring up this problem directly, or you might try to subvert the rules in a less direct way. For example, if the advantage of others is sustained partly by a distinctive language or jargon, request translations. Use your own language sometimes and translate for others. As Kritek says, this at least "highlights the inequity structured into the negotiation that requires you to sit at an uneven table speaking someone else's language." Make things more complicated—you can do it.

Democratic talk needn't be the kind of "free-for-all" that Kritek describes. There are many other traditions and styles of dialogue. Native Americans often used a "talking stick," giving the holder an uninterrupted "floor," passed around to everyone in turn so that each voice could be heard and each voice had its "space." Try it. At least, if debate is not a style that you can even enter, ask for a different kind of hearing from your group. If they care to hear you out, they will agree (or at least discuss it). If they don't, then at least you know where you stand—and they will have to admit where *they* stand.

Classroom settings can be changed too. Talk to your instructor; find a way to raise the issue for the class. In a class that uses this book, call on this chapter.

When You Are Advantaged

Suppose you are one of the advantaged. Others may be feeling silenced, but not you: you might even be feeling quite expansive.

Your job first of all is to recognize the problem. Advantage is usually invisible to the advantaged because the space of dialogue does not seem constrained to *them*. It is easy to enter when you know you will be listened to and taken seriously. It is hard to imagine that others could feel any differently. "Well, why don't they just *talk*?"

But of course it is not so simple from the other side. It may help to remember those times that *you* felt intimidated from saying anything, or that no one would really listen or care anyway. Recognize now that others may feel the same way in a discussion that feels entirely open and natural to you.

Second, raise the problem with your group as a whole. Point out the unequal pattern of participation. State as directly and honestly as you can *your* interest in hearing from those who have been silent. Ask on behalf of the group (step up to leadership here) in what ways the group can change so as to lessen the barriers to participation that others may be feeling. Maybe you need a talking stick? Maybe . . .?

Once again, the challenge may be to *you* to move yourself—and to move *first*. You may have to disrupt and challenge familiar and comfortable ways (to you, anyway) and make things more difficult. It can take some courage— but remember, more constructive dialogues *are* possible, and sometimes are surprisingly easy once someone makes a move in their direction. On the other hand, there may also be dialogues that you conclude aren't possible right now. Trust must first be built in other ways, maybe; or some other kind of institutional or personal change is necessary first. Things don't get easier! But they might, slowly, get better.

READING

"Common Ground Rules"

MARY JACKSTEIT AND ADRIENNE KAUFMANN, THE COMMON GROUND NETWORK FOR LIFE AND CHOICE

THE COMMON GROUND Network for Life and Choice worked from 1993 to 2000 to bring together activists from opposing sides in the abortion conflict in the hopes of creating real dialogue, understanding each other better, and finding common ground that the two sides could build upon together, rather than frustrating each other's every move. The reading that follows comes from the group's manual *Finding Common Ground in the Abortion Conflict*, by Mary Jacksteit and Adrienne Kaufmann, published by the Common Ground Network (1601 Connecticut Avenue NW, Washington, DC, 20009) in January 1995. The "spirit of common ground," they say, is dialogue—a good in its own right as well as a precondition for actually working together to promote shared goals.

Reprinted by permission of Search for Common Ground.

The organization that sponsored the Network in turn, and produced this manual, is called Search for Common Ground (SFCG). The Common Ground Network for Life and Choice was SFCG's first project in the United States. Six projects in the United States have now been completed, with four others ongoing, as well as an impressive number of international projects, all using the same basic approach. For more information on all of these projects, as well as a downloadable version of the manual excerpted here, see www.sfcg.org/programmes.

WHAT IS THE COMMON GROUND APPROACH?

For many people the idea of searching for common ground in the abortion conflict is strange and unbelievable—even unthinkable. Some people can only imagine that you are inviting them to engage in an activity in which they will have to "compromise" their values and beliefs. Viewing the conflict as a black or white contest to see which "side" will "win," the only alternative they can envision is the creation of some shade of gray in which their values and concerns are diluted and diminished. For some, the idea of any conversation with "Them" is dismissed as an act of betrayal.

Because the very idea of "common ground" in the abortion conflict is foreign and radical to many people in this society, we are offering a variety of approaches to answering the frequently asked questions "what do you mean by common ground?" and "what is the common ground approach?"

THE SPIRIT OF COMMON GROUND IS THE SPIRIT OF DIALOGUE

The practice of dialogue lies at the heart of the common ground approach. Dialogue is different from debate. Debate is about persuading others that your views are "right" and that the views of others are "wrong." Debate tends to create winners and losers and often leads to pain and divisiveness when the subject is sensitive and people's views are as heart-felt as they tend to be on the issue of abortion.

Dialogue is a gentler, more respectful process than debate. The spirit of dialogue is to acknowledge and honor the humanity of *all* persons present regardless of their points of view. The goals of dialogue center around increasing understanding and being understood rather than persuading others and being "right."

When dialogue is attempted in a sustained and polarized conflict, a primary goal is to change the relationship between those who see each other as demonized adversaries. When an issue is explosive and relationships are already highly strained, dialogue is more likely than debate to lead to understanding and trust. A carefully constructed dialogue process can enable hard issues to be addressed without leading to bad feelings.

THE COMMON GROUND APPROACH IS A SEARCH FOR WHAT IS GENUINELY SHARED

The idea of common ground can be illustrated by two interlocking circles. Each circle represents a point of view about abortion (one circle, pro-life; the other, pro-choice). A common ground process recognizes the integrity of each circle as a complete set of concerns, beliefs, and values around this issue. A common ground process primarily focuses attention on and explores the *area of intersection*. Through the search for concerns, beliefs, and values that are *shared*, a platform of understanding is built.

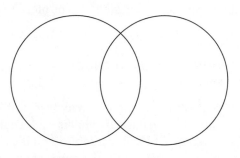

When participants stand together in the area of genuine intersection, they can also look at their *differences* with fresh eyes. The differences remain the same as before, but the perspective on these differences has changed. The angle of vision is from the common space looking out, instead of from the areas of difference where adversaries glare at one another across the submerged and unseen area of what is shared.

COMMON GROUND IS NOT COMPROMISE

Searching for common ground is not about compromising to reach a middle position but about focusing on areas of *genuinely* shared values and concerns. People are not asked to change their views on abortion or sacrifice their integrity. Participants in a common ground process seek to understand one another, not to force or pretend agreement where it does not exist.

A COMMON GROUND APPROACH ENCOURAGES LOOKING BEYOND THE LABELS AND THE STEREOTYPES

A common ground approach assumes that even in a polarized conflict, people's views fall on a continuum.

Pro-life _____|_____ *Pro-choice*

When people identify themselves as "pro-choice" or "pro-life," they are only placing themselves *somewhere* on the continuum other than the exact center.

The idea of a continuum encourages awareness of how little we can assume about another person's set of beliefs if all we know about them is that they choose one label over the other. It opens us to look for diversity on both sides, and to imagine that two given people with different labels may be as similar as two other people with the same label. It fosters curiosity about the views of the particular individuals on the "other side" encountered within a common ground approach.

A COMMON GROUND APPROACH ENCOURAGES CONNECTIVE THINKING

Debates tend to focus attention on the weaknesses of a speaker and to encourage a search for the flaws in what is said. Dialogue encourages *connective thinking* that focuses attention on the *strengths* of the speaker and encourages a search for the gems of wisdom, or pieces of truth, in what is said. Over time, the practice of connective thinking in a group can lead to the creation of a web of shared knowledge woven from the threads of truth contributed by its members. Connective thinking fosters the building of constructive relationships and the development of community because it ties together the best wisdom of each member of the group. It is an important practice in the search for common ground.

A COMMON GROUND DIALOGUE ENCOURAGES THE SHARING OF PERSONAL EXPERIENCE

A common ground dialogue usually begins with the sharing of personal experiences. Life has been experienced by each person in a unique way. Personal experiences cannot be argued about nor agreed or disagreed with. They *are*. Sharing life stories invites understanding responses from those who hear them. They are a constructive place to begin.

A COMMON GROUND DIALOGUE ENCOURAGES GENUINE QUESTIONS

Genuine questions are questions asked in a spirit of real curiosity and a sincere interest in hearing the answers. Rhetorical or leading questions are **not** genuine questions. They are questions for which we already know the answers. We usually ask them not to learn but to test or trap someone whom we view as an opponent. The posing of genuine questions and the omission of all other kinds is a trademark of common ground dialogue.

THE SEARCH FOR COMMON GROUND ACKNOWLEDGES OUR SHARED MEMBERSHIP IN THIS SOCIETY

Common ground involves acknowledging the connections that exist between people related to one another by shared community, faith, and/or citizenship. This approach can allow us to see how we are all affected by stressful and troubling circumstances in the larger social environment. It can enable participants to relate to one another as "all of us against the problems we face" rather than "part of us against the rest of us."

ANSWERS TO FREQUENTLY ASKED QUESTIONS

In this section we offer ingredients for answers to questions that are frequently asked of us or members of the Network.

WHY DO PEOPLE GET INVOLVED IN COMMON GROUND?

People have become involved in common ground activities for a variety of reasons. Prominent among those reasons are desires to promote a civil democratic society, effective problem-solving on important social issues, and peace. More specific motives frequently offered include:

- A belief that the level of confrontation over abortion is "out of hand" and destructive.
- A perception that the conflict is getting in the way of needed social change and is not helping the powerless and disadvantaged.
- The sense that the tone of the conflict is uncomfortably "out of sync" with personal systems of beliefs.
- A painful experience of division—division between people of faith, between women, between family members, between community members—and a belief in reconciliation, reconnection, and

the need for people to learn to live in community despite serious differences.

WHAT FRAME OF MIND DOES IT TAKE TO "SEARCH FOR COMMON GROUND"?

Not everyone is willing or able to join in the search for common ground at the moment they are invited to do so. Ideally, a person participating in common ground brings:

- A willingness to respect a human being who disagrees with you on the abortion issue and pledges to respect you in turn.
- An ability to listen to statements and views with which you strongly disagree without trying to convert those on the "other side" to your way of thinking and without feeling compromised by the act of listening.
- A belief in the importance of finding out what each person knows and understands about an issue.
- A desire to meet the human beings behind the stereotypes and media images.
- An openness to the unexpected, to the potential of "connecting" with an "adversary."
- A belief that conflict can be a positive opportunity for growth and understanding.
- An ability to handle skepticism and criticism from people on one's "own side" who view common ground as compromise and a dangerous way of conferring legitimacy on the "enemy."

Few people have all these qualities fully or equally developed when they enter into a common ground process. What is essential is that participants be committed to respecting the ground rules that govern the dialogue process.

WHAT SORT OF PEOPLE ARE INTERESTED IN COMMON GROUND?

- Women and men, of different ages and different backgrounds, in widely separate parts of the country.
- Catholic and Protestant Christians, Jews, people of all faiths and those who have no religious orientation.
- Committed and active advocates on the abortion issue.
- People who have a position on abortion but are not activists, and people who feel "in the middle" on this issue.

WHAT ARE PEOPLE ACTUALLY DOING?

Around the country, pro-life and pro-choice people in local communities are coming together in a number of different ways—in small informal groups, in workshops, in structured dialogues with facilitators, in retreats, in joint endeavors to solve real problems. To date, efforts to find common ground on abortion have been happening primarily at the grassroots level where people are trying to create community at a face-to-face level. This is a "bottom-up" change in the dynamics of the conflict.

HOW DO PEOPLE SEARCH FOR COMMON GROUND ON ABORTION?

- They set aside generalities and rhetoric.
- They meet and talk within a framework of ground rules based on a willingness to listen, to speak with respect, and to keep what is said confidential.
- They speak as individuals, not as representatives of advocacy organizations.
- They share personal experiences and beliefs about abortion.
- They explore areas of common concern as well as difference.
- They confront the stereotypes, perceptions, and misperceptions that people on each side hold about those on the other.
- They may organize to work on a specific project or issue of mutual concern.

READING

"Deepening Ethical Dialogue"

SPOMA JOVANOVIC

CONSTRUCTIVE DIALOGUE is a way of actually making progress on contentious issues, which is already enough to rank it as a vitally important ethical skill. But there is also much more. The attitudes that underlie dialogue—care for each other, willingness to listen and learn, an openness to the other as another center of awareness, in short as a *person*—are fundamental to ethics itself. Dialogue is a kind of representation or expression of the Ethics of the Person, with connections to the Ethics of Relationship as well. Dialogue about ethical issues then, is not just *about* ethics: it also *is* ethics itself in action.

Recognizing these connections has given rise to an aspect of Communication Studies that is often called Communicative Ethics. Spoma Jovanovic, associate professor in the Department of Communication Studies at the University of North Carolina, Greensboro, is one of the leaders of this emerging field. As she puts the central idea:

> Speaking involves far more than stringing together a series of words. . . . Speaking is [also] an *ethical act* that entails verbalizing our values, feelings, thoughts, and passions. We communicate through words, tone, and action not only our thoughts or ideas but also our ethical relationship to others. Our speech communicates our personal obligations, position of power, interest in fairness, displays of care, and ongoing expectations.

Watch as these themes unfold in the following essay, written originally for the second edition of this textbook.

DEEPENING ETHICAL DIALOGUE

Speech is a move to extend ourselves to another human being, and in doing so our talk becomes a way to *put a voice to ethics*. Put another way, we often think of speech as just an individual behavior that translates our thoughts into words. But upon closer reflection it becomes clear that because our speech is directed at another person, it is inherently value laden.

ACKNOWLEDGMENT

In fact, even to speak to another person at all is an important form of acknowledgment that we live among others who are deserving of our attention and care—as we are of theirs. Communication philosopher Michael Hyde poses a most interesting question, "What would life be like if no one acknowledged your existence?" You can imagine the isolation, fear, and anger that might mount under such conditions. Indeed, acknowledgment creates the space for others to enter our lives, and in doing so welcomes others to continue the conversation we start. As such, acknowledgment is an ethical move that oftentimes begins with a simple but earnest, "How are you?" or "Here I am!" in response to another's call.

Acknowledgment is powerful. When it is offered in positive ways, a more caring relationship between people develops. When it is offered with negative intent in some forms as sarcasm, insults, or disrespect, it has the effect of making people feel bad, unloved, and unworthy. Because we have a choice to make as we encounter friends and strangers, acknowledgment is a way to communicate our ethical posture.

FROM MONOLOGUE TO DIALOGUE

Speech is ethical when it appreciates the value of another, is spoken in a way to create new meaning, and is genuine in its expression. This special form of speech is what philosophers and communication experts refer to as *dialogue*. Following the ideas offered by Martin Buber and Emmanuel Levinas [recall chapter 5 of this book—AW], as well as the concepts taken from philosophers Mikhail Bakhtin and Hans Georg Gadamer, the theme of dialogue has over time achieved a mark of distinction in the study of communication. This is because dialogue engages another fully with a spirit of support, as contrasted to argument, which tends to encourage competitive behavior with the goal of beating the other in a reasoning game. Dialogue invites a sense of community by speaking to the other person where he or she is, as distinguished from monologue, which tends to create distance among people who are primarily concerned with their own individual agendas. Dialogue targets honest, heart-felt communication with another, with unconditional regard for his or her well-being.

Have you ever been in a classroom, for instance, when someone started talking about a difficult subject from a very personal perspective in an attempt to educate and inform others? When this happens, dialogue can follow.

Euthanasia, for instance, is a topic on which many people have a predetermined position either for or against. In a classroom discussion years ago, a student revealed that her family chose "passive euthanasia" for a loved one by not administering any more life-saving drugs. She detailed the decision-making process and the pain that accompanied both the decision and the eventual death of her father. She revealed the initial questions they considered—would it be what he wanted, would the neighbors and other relatives understand, would we be able to do it—and she detailed the lingering questions—did we do the right thing? The student offered an honest portrait of her family's situation by detailing the research they did and the tears they shared. The result was that her classmates were driven to ask more questions and eventually to understand that textbook and media discussions on the subject often miss the important human dimensions of care, agony, uncertainty, and hope that are woven into the fabric of the subject. The dialogue in the room that day transformed how many understood the controversial practice of euthanasia.

Classroom discussion in no way guarantees dialogue, however. Have you ever been in a situation when someone started talking about abortion, for instance, and soon the talking turned into heated conversation and then forceful argument? The speaker likely never even considered that there might be people in the room who had an abortion, or counseled someone not to have one, or had been close to someone who had to make a decision about keeping or terminating a pregnancy.

What typically follows when the topic of abortion becomes a depersonalized yet heated monologue is that many of the other students simply tune out what the speaker is saying. Or, if someone does respond, and the reply comes out just as forcefully as the first speaker's words, the interaction quickly becomes a competition to "win" the argument or at least to have the last say. This sets up a negative spiral of communication that disregards the possibility of deep understanding or the transformation of our views or even taking some time to think. Rather, people get locked into their positions as they experience agitation toward the others who hold different views. This kind of *polarized communication* is best recognized as the "I am right, you are wrong" form of talk.

DON'T POLARIZE—CONNECT!

The corrective to polarized communication is to encourage dialogue, often with the first move involving a question or a proposition that is open-ended. For example, someone who wanted to honestly confront the complexities of abortion might offer this opening to the conversation. "I have never known anyone who had an abortion and I know that those on both sides of the issue hold strong views. I, myself, am against it because I love children so much. Still, I know most people love children so I wonder how people who are in favor of abortion see the issue?"

Discussions of ethically controversial issues can take place with or without dialogue, but when dialogue is absent, the conversation is often full of technical arguments or settled/insistent/self-righteous moral judgments. One of the most widely witnessed case of euthanasia involved the 41-year-old Terri Schiavo of St. Petersburg, Florida. When she was 26, Terri collapsed at home, and with oxygen cut off to her brain, she fell unconscious and ten days later lapsed into a coma. Three years later she was diagnosed as being in a "persistent vegetative state." The public debate surrounding the issue came to a head in 2005 after years of legal struggles between husband Michael Schiavo and Terri's parents, Robert and Mary Schindler.

The communication in the public arena generally lined up behind either the husband or the parents. For the husband and his supporters, keeping Terri in a "vegetative state" was, just as the words suggest, cruel and not in keeping with her wishes. The parents and those who supported them proclaimed that no medical professional or other human had the moral or legal authority to take away Terri's "right to life." The way in which people took sides and labeled the situation left little room to have *any* conversation about important end-of-life definitions and issues. Instead of seeking understanding, the focus of the talk shifted to defending a position by trashing the other position, name-calling, and blaming. On March 31, 2005, Terri Schiavo was pronounced dead after her gastric feeding tube was removed in accordance with the last legal verdict.

Euthanasia is not an easy subject to discuss. And there are no guarantees that people will want to engage in a dialogue about it. However, when the euthanasia debate takes the turn toward dialogue, as it did in the classroom example described earlier, the conversation will generally surface the deep struggle we as individuals experience in wanting to preserve a loved one's dignity and at the same time exhaust all possibilities that a medical cure will be discovered to save a life that still has a beating heart. When that happens, euthanasia moves out of declarations of moral righteousness. When someone speaks from their experience to explain how and why an end-of-life decision was made or not for a family member, even listeners who have not had to face the same decision are invited to imagine something real through the words, tone, and invitation of another. The result is rarely to cast judgment. Instead, an empathetic hand is extended outward.

Sometimes that hand can be extended quite literally. Ethics is communicated not only through our words, but also in simple gestures like a celebratory pat on the back, or the enthusiastic grasp of another's hand in support, or the comfort of a touch on the shoulder. The ways we physically approach another, stand close to her, or demonstrate a recognition and appreciation of another through our head nods and eye contact convey our ethical posture. This desire to build relationships underscores the ethical imperative to put ourselves in the company of others. Philosopher Alphonso Lingis reminds us that in the end, communication is foremost an expression of this longing to be with other people.

What we say in our interactions is sometimes less important than just being there, next to someone, saying something, anything.

PUBLIC DIALOGUE

Differences among people are vast, deep, and surely inevitable. Those differences can become reasons for separating ourselves from one another or resources for working together. When we appreciate the differences, the variations among us reveal the myriad experiences, stories, successes, and failures that contribute to a rich understanding of our communal life. When people are willing to struggle together in honest, open dialogue, a collective compassion can emerge that moves conversation toward inclusion of varied views, respect for one another, and trust that our common fate in a common world will be good for all. To get there, however, requires a desire to see the value offered in another's comments.

Despite the potential for transformative outcomes that dialogue promises, experience shows that we are not always willing to struggle together through talk in cooperative ways. Sometimes, we want to hold on to our beliefs or position tightly, leaving no room for another's views. Sometimes, we feel so certain that "our" way is the best that we fiercely work to persuade others to believe the same. That can work, sometimes, when our approach is fueled by a compassionate desire that reaches the other's heart and mind. However, when the strategies we use end up backing other people into the proverbial corner—it's my way or no way—the creative spark is extinguished and along with it, any hope for meaningful dialogue. Instead, we find ourselves locked into competing positions and wondering what's wrong with those who disagree with us.

A number of models exist for encouraging dialogue about public issues. The National Issues Forum, Study Circles, Public Conversations Project, The Democracy Project, Let's Talk America, Public Dialogue Consortium, and the Search for Common Ground projects are just some of the organizations working to bring people with differing views together in order to learn from one another and make decisions about their collective future. From small groups to large gatherings, citizens generally meet to discuss a relevant topic, listen to the stories others tell about their understanding and experiences, consider options, explore choices, pursue consensus and/or public judgment, and discuss the values inherent in each position. Participants are encouraged to share their opinions, concerns, and knowledge as they listen to what others also have to say before analyzing possible next steps and taking public action. In these dialogue groups, people discuss campaign issues, the environment,

religion, community planning visions, educational reform measures, health issues, domestic and foreign policy, and even democratic cornerstones for public participation.

Whether in a group, or through one-on-one conversations, each
of us has the capacity to open ourselves up to dialogue about world
issues—ask questions, listen intently, contribute ideas, and learn
from others. You might even want to take a lesson from someone
like Fran Peavey, who traveled the world with a sign saying "American Willing to Listen," hoping to learn what mattered to people
in different countries by asking broad, open-ended questions and
then just earnestly listening. The effect was that the experience
changed her life, broadened her perspectives, and sharpened her
desire to do more to help the world.

DIALOGUE AND RECONCILIATION

It is vital to talk about our past and our hopes for the future within
a context of current conditions so that we can bear witness to the
suffering that exists in the world. Many people would rather not
see the pain and misery that occur in virtually every community
alongside the joy and success that are evident as well. But to be able
to work toward a more just world, we need to see, hear, and feel the
anguish that some people experience. We need to ask why they are
not benefiting from a community's resources. Doing so allows us
to assess how we can contribute to a collective solution. When we
choose to see the injustices in the world, talk to people who have
been wronged, and stand with those who fight for fairness and
equality, we put our ethics into action through speech and deed.

In addition to being an ally to someone or some group who
could benefit from your voice, it is vital to recognize the importance
of reconciliatory gestures to help move us through our conflicts and
pain. When Amish children in a one-room schoolhouse in Pennsylvania were taken hostage and killed by a gunman, Charles Roberts,
who then committed suicide, grief-stricken Amish families also
reached out to console Roberts's wife and children. They immediately organized a charitable fund for the family. Dozens even
attended Roberts's funeral. As we turn our passion and compassion into action, it is helpful to now and again take a step back to
survey the situation. Are there people who need to be acknowledged
for their work? Does someone deserve your apology? Can forgiv-
ing others, or ourselves, help us to repair our relationships and our
community?

From individual action to collective response, many countries around the world and cities in the United States have had to

confront difficult histories. Task forces, commissions, and state-sponsored panels have researched horrific acts of violence or tragedies with enduring effects.

In Greensboro, North Carolina, a Truth and Reconciliation Commission was established in 2004 to examine the context, causes, sequence, and consequence of the events of November 3, 1979, when five anti-Klan demonstrators were killed and ten wounded by Ku Klux Klan and Nazi party members. In the absence of any police, a nine-car caravan of white supremacists drove into town to disrupt a "Death to the Klan" march in a black public housing community. Despite film footage captured by four television crews on the scene, the Klan and Nazis involved were twice found not guilty of criminal charges by all-white juries. A third, civil trial eventually found members of the Greensboro Police Department jointly liable with Klan and Nazi members for the wrongful death of one of the victims.

Many in the Greensboro community felt that justice had not been served, and so they initiated the Greensboro Truth and Community Reconciliation Project, a democratic process to investigate and assess trial evidence, records from law enforcement departments, media coverage, and hundreds of interviews and personal statements. Seven truth commissioners, their staff, and volunteers spent two years reviewing and weighing the evidence to prepare a 529-page final report.

The commission's findings, conclusions, and recommendations were made public to prompt dialogue that could lead to much needed reconciliation among various sectors of the community. Part of that process, the commissioners hoped, would include citizens becoming more aware of the signs that problems exist in the community surrounding labor, race, poverty, oppression, privilege, and justice. Nearly one hundred religious, civic, neighborhood, and educational groups agreed to read portions of or the entire report in order to have conversations about the content. It is through those conversations that the truth commissioners expected positive changes to occur in city policies, community governance, and citizen initiatives.

Hope for a better future resides in episodes of talk and displays of action infused with an ethical sensibility to care for and understand others. This work, of taking the time to sit with another, engaging in conversation, being mindful of our speech, and sometimes even working through difficult dialogues, is not always pleasant. It is work, however, that is important and necessary to reach understanding, appreciation, and respect in a world we occupy with diverse others.

QUICK REFERENCE: ETHICAL DIALOGUE

SLOW DOWN AND LISTEN

Speak calmly and listen a lot. Avoid the automatic comeback. And work for better understanding. Ask questions, and mean them. Restate others' views to make sure you "get" it.

CONNECT

Seek common ground. Approach differences against a background of probable agreement. Recognize complexity on the other side (and yours). Don't polarize. Keep the focus on the main points.

WELCOME OPENINGS AND OPPORTUNITIES

Think constructively; make suggestions. Look for first steps and partial measures. Always be *for* something and not just *against* something.

STAY ENGAGED

Speak in a careful, open-ended, and helpful way. Avoid slogans and sound bites. Treat facts as tools. Expect the key questions to remain open.

FOR REVIEW

1. What is the opposite of "taking all the room you can" in a dialogue? Be concrete.
2. What are some specific ways to "connect" instead of separating and polarizing people and arguments?
3. What is the opposite of exploiting weaknesses and openings? Be concrete.
4. What is the opposite of going for the quick kill? Be concrete.
5. Why is dialogue an ethical task as well as a practical one?
6. How does the text recommend responding when dialogue is under duress?
7. What is the Common Ground approach to dialogue?
8. Why is the Common Ground approach not the same as compromise?
9. Contrast a monologue to a dialogue about a contentious issue such as abortion or euthanasia.
10. How can public dialogue lead to reconciliation?

EXERCISES AND NOTES

11.1 WORDS MATTER!

Practice in more constructive and ethical dialogues might well begin with some careful attention to words. For words matter! They not only communicate but also literally create and define our worlds.

Think, for example, about how we describe older people in our community. "Old," "elderly," "senior," and "mature" are considered synonyms. Yet, each of these words may be interpreted in slightly different ways. The descriptive word, "old," may generate or reinforce views that older people are frail, likely to soon die, and a burden for family members. More positive attitudes about "older adults" or "retired professionals" communicate a respect for the wisdom and wealth of experiences acquired over a lifetime. Common core values and beliefs in Asian and Native American societies translate into a deep respect for "elders" who keep culture alive, teach young people through stories, and reinforce strong family and community structures. Elders are viewed as the ones who not only know the facts surrounding traditions but also demonstrate deep and thoughtful judgment that comes from the study and practice of those traditions. (More on alternative visions of aging in chapter 15.)

It is worth noting here that our word choices are more than choosing "politically correct" language, which has acquired the connotation that "regular" people somehow have to walk on eggshells so as not to offend others. What we are discussing here is the recognition that our words indeed have an impact on others, but also shape our feelings and thoughts. In being mindful of the power of speech, and its naturally ethical nature, we will make choices to reflect our care for others.

For practice taking care with words, consider the following challenges.

- As blended families become more common, we need to find the right words to describe our new relationships. A new "stepmother" may not appreciate a term that conjures up Cinderella images of a strict old woman making her stepchildren do hard labor. "Stepbrothers" or "half-sisters" are words that define some sibling relationships, yet they also may fail to convey loving relationships that often result as two families come together as one. Consider what words and terms of endearment can best describe a blended family you know. Maybe you'll have to come up with altogether new words to communicate the quality of relationships that exist in that family.

- The abortion debate is filled with loaded language that has the ability to sidetrack conversation before it even begins. What happens when we use the term "unborn child" instead of "fetus," "product of conception," "embryo," or "baby"? What feelings do these words evoke, and how do the words condition the conversation to follow? The use of clinical or scientific terms may deflect the moral concerns, while the use of family terms will surely evoke feelings of protectiveness. Think about how our talk is affected by using words like "mother" rather than "pregnant woman." When we talk about abortion as a "procedure," we will likely focus on the medical aspects. When we talk about abortion as "murder," we evoke a very different set of values and judgments.

- Whether you are "pro-life" (against abortion) or "pro-choice" (for a woman's right to choose), draft a statement of how you feel and what more you would like to know about on this issue, but without using terms that condemn or slyly disadvantage positions different than your own. Find someone else willing to do the same and then read each other's statements. Note what conversation follows. What words triggered negative emotions for you or the other person? What words or terms invited you to ask more questions?

11.2 REWORKING DYSFUNCTIONAL DIALOGUES

Following are a number of short classroom dialogues that are also ethically dysfunctional—short exchanges that seldom rise above the level of fruitless debates. Each of them is just the opening of a discussion, but it also already presents some opportunities for new directions, for more constructive conversations. Each could be taken in many different better ways.

Read each dialogue aloud together. Then identify the places where the dialogue goes bad. What are its failures? Why does it so quickly turn fruitless?

Next, identify its missed opportunities. What are some of the places where this dialogue could have taken a more constructive turn? Are there interesting ideas that the opposed sides could explore together? Do points of possible agreement come into view? Are questions asked that could be understood as genuine questions and answered without more rhetoric?

Finally, rewrite the dialogue in a more constructive key, and read the new dialogue aloud for the whole group. Analyze the methods of dialogue you are trying to use.

One note: be watchful of the temptation to just prettify the exchanges, or to "make nice." The aim is not necessarily to agree in the end: constructive dialogue can involve very sharp disagreements. Still, try to end with at least some open question or potentially constructive possibility. On the other hand, do not just state the same disagreements in nicer ways. Try to imagine the dialogue beginning as written but then heading in different and more fruitful directions. It will help to review the rewritten dialogue in the second section of this chapter before beginning this exercise.

Poverty

M: I just passed a homeless guy holding his sign out at the intersection.

N: It's disgusting how people like that come and put themselves on display and play on your sympathies and tie up traffic too. They're just bums eating up my tax dollars.

M: Are you kidding? The problem is probably that he's *not* getting any social support because you and your right-wing friends cut them all off so you could afford bigger yachts. You call that Christian?

N: Even Jesus said that the poor will always be with us. You're ranting and raving about how terrible we are, but if you think about it, the poor in America are rich compared to even the rich in other countries. Whole families in Africa get less money in a year than one welfare mother in Chicago gets in a month.

M: Oh, right, I'd like to see you try to live on it, even for a week. As if you even know how much it is.

N: I certainly wouldn't sit around all day feeling sorry for myself. I believe in work—that's how to get ahead. God helps those who help themselves.

M: What a crazy idea of God! A really sensible God would help those who need help!

Wasteful Ways

A: The amount of waste around here is just incredible. Every time the college has a party, look at all the plastic forks and spoons and styrofoam cups—thousands and thousands of the things, and they last forever. We just throw them out. Then people go back to their gas-guzzling cars and drive two blocks that it would be healthier to walk. Not to mention that the stupid cars themselves are deliberately designed to go out of style and even stop working after a few years. Then we have to buy a new one. And already there are more cars than people in America.

B: Oh, lighten up. People choose to buy these things. It's their right—that's what America is all about. They know it will be out of style in four years. They choose to change it.

A: Then why is advertising the biggest industry in this whole country? They're spending millions of dollars to make you want this stuff. You don't object to that, you think that's just fine. . . . If I happen to have an opinion, though, but not a million dollars to spend promoting it, you get all bent out of shape.

B: People choose to watch the ads, don't they? Besides, what do you want? them all? OK, let's make a law: no ads, no new models, everyone has to the same boring old car, keep it ten years at least. . . . Give me a break!

Immigration

W: Deporting illegal aliens is easy: arrest them and send them home. You know where they are: bus stations, taco trucks, mowing your neighbor's yard. No need to round them all up at once. Just arrest one or two every day at different locations around town, and the message will get out.

Y: Right, a message of stereotyping and intolerance. "We know where the Mexicans are . . . wink, wink." Undocumented immigrants deserve better than that.

W: Oh no, you don't—I'm not playing that evasion game. Calling an illegal alien an "undocumented immigrant" is like calling a burglar an "uninvited house guest." They're not just "undocumented"—they're criminals!

Y: They may have broken a law by coming here, yes. That doesn't make them the moral equivalent of burglars. And "alien" isn't their *identity*. Many Mexican-Americans are citizens, remember, and they're all people, anyway.

V: Oh, but W has good company. The whole history of anti-immigrant fervor is a story of racism and closed-minded bias. In the 19th century there was a period of anti-Irish prejudice—Irish weren't even considered white. Before that, anti-German. Now it's anti–Central American. It's easy to stereotype and degrade the down-and-out and desperate. But unless you are Native American, your ancestors were immigrants too, and probably just about as desperate when they got off the boat.

W: I *am* a native American, dammit! I was born here. My grandparents came here legally and earned their citizenship by study and hard work. They didn't sneak in some dark night and steal a job from a real American.

Y: Sure, and how many "real Americans" are going to pick tomatoes in a hot dusty field, dawn to dusk, for minimum wage or less, no health care, constantly bullied, barely a place to live?

W: Wages may have to go up a little, I guess.

Z: A lot. And so will prices. Then I suppose the wing-nuts will start in on the unions . . .

V [to W]: So face it, gringo: you're not part of the solution, you're part of the problem.

Drugs

M: I don't get why some people are so obsessed with condemning drugs when they have never experienced the effects of drugs.

J: You mean the psychoactive type, I suppose? I mean, I don't see people wanting to ban aspirin or antibiotics, or even coffee, which is mind-altering too, if you think about it. Or tranquilizers. We're totally inconsistent, if you think about it.

M: What's wrong with a little psycho-activity? As if the "normal" kind of mind is the only kind there is. Anyhow, how can they judge something they don't know anything about?

L: Oh, good point. Like people shouldn't moralize about murder unless they have actually committed one or two. Otherwise, how would they know what it's like? And don't condemn bank robbery either, until you've picked up a few hundred thousand bucks for yourself, maybe knocked off a teller or cop or two.

M: OK, OK, but surely the experience is more relevant in the case of drugs. It's the whole point.

L: All the wrecked lives aren't "relevant"? You don't need to take drugs to see that. Maybe you need *not* to take drugs in order to see it, actually.

J: M just thinks that maybe you need to have some sort of experience of drugs to see some important part of the picture. I don't say I agree with her, but . . .

L: Yeah, and then your mind's good and ruined, and you're addicted or imbecile or dead. So you're not going to be seeing much of any picture. Or you'll be stoned out all the time, like some Indian-wannabe on peyote.

J: Indians used peyote and other hallucinogens as part of a spiritual discipline, as I understand it.

M: Did you say "wannabe" just to be politically correct?

L: Meanwhile, back in the real world, the Mafia practices offing people as a spiritual discipline, too, as I understand it.

Licensing parents?

E: Should just anyone be having kids? Look at all the bad parenting that's going on, all the child abuse, the abandonment, all the rest, and then those kids grow up and do the same thing to theirs. There ought to be a law!

F: You want the government licensing people to have kids or something? What happens when you slip up? You get jailed for getting pregnant without permission? How about the firing squad?

E: Oh come on, F, you know very well that the phrase "There ought to be a law" tends to be ironic.

G: I don't know, maybe there's something to it. After all, we do tell people who they can or can't marry. Theoretically, anyway, that's to tell people who they can and cannot have sex with and therefore have children with.

E: Conservative loons are happy to do that already, like all the gay-bashers, which I hope doesn't include you, F.

F: I'm a libertarian, thank you very much. Not the same as conservative at all, necessarily. Proudly against the government putting its fat fingers into much of anything. Most of the loons I see are on the other side. Just saying.

G: But again, at least in some people's views, it could make sense to restrict not just marriage but the right to have children to God-fearing, upstanding, heterosexual parents . . .

F: Oh my god.

E: Actually, if you look at the news reports, it's those types of families where child abuse is rampant. Like that bigamist with five wives out in Colorado or somewhere, sexually abusing everyone right and left and claiming it was his God-given right. No license for them!

F: I thought you were kidding about licenses.

E: Jesus, I was, and still am! But don't you think this is a *problem*? At least maybe there could be some mandatory child-raising classes or something, you know. How about a nutritionist every year or two? Half of all American kids are now obese, or something. Bad diets are a form of abuse too.

F: You're a left-wing loon after all! No license for you either—we don't want *you* passing on your looney genes, that's for sure . . .

Here are two more steps you might consider taking with this exercise. One is to listen in everyday life for similar dialogues—interchanges on moral subjects, or indeed any subjects—that, let's just say, could go more productively than they may be going. Talk radio will give you extreme cases, but listen in the same way to family discussions, political debates, religious dialogues, and so on. Think about why they take unconstructive turns. Again, as with the exercises here, be *specific*: that is, exactly at what point in these interchanges do you see people getting stuck or provoked and things starting to turn bad? How could you help head them in a different direction?

A next step is to try to join in those discussions at the time they are happening in the hopes of making a constructive difference. What strategies will you use? What can you achieve when you do?

11.3 LEARNING TO LISTEN

The readings for this chapter emphasize that the foundation of ethical dialogue is an openness to the other persons involved in the exchange. Here are some projects that may help you practice that openness more consciously and systematically.

- You and your friends probably agree on a lot of things—best kinds of music, important issues in society, and even ways of talking to one another. To expand your horizons, actively seek out someone who has a completely different orientation from yours and listen to what he/she has to say on these subjects. Does that change, in any way, how you feel? Do you better see (really *feel*, not just "know" in some abstract sense) that your perspective is not necessarily the "best" but only one of the possible ways of understanding?

- Spend time at a homeless shelter or assisted living facility so that you can get to know some of the people there. As you gain their trust, listen for the stories of their lives and see what values emerge in the telling. As you tell others about your experiences, notice what information you highlight and how that carries with it certain values as well. Do the two sets of values coincide? What differences emerge?

- Identify someone with whom you have a relationship who would benefit from your heartfelt listening and set up time to do just that. It may be helpful to set aside 30 minutes for the other person to do most, if not all, of the talking. At the end, consider what you learned about this person you didn't know before, and examine your own feelings at stepping back into the role of listener.

- Identify a situation where you have a different perspective than the one being discussed, and, staying true to ethical speech that considers fully the other person (or people), put forth your best attempt at explaining your position and understanding the other position. What happens? Analyze what you might do differently next time.

- Attend a public meeting (city council, county commissioners, school board) and pay attention to the ways in which the elected or appointed officials listen (or don't listen) to one another and the public. Notice, too, if you can tell what values are being communicated in the words, tone, and focus of their talk. What recommendations could you make to improve the quality of ethical discussion?

NOTES

I am grateful to Professor Spoma Jovanovic not only for her contribution to this chapter but for her consistent engagement with this whole text, which has enriched not only this edition but the project as a whole. In addition to her essay reprinted here, I owe Exercises 11.1 and 11.3 very largely to her, as well as the last three paragraphs of these notes.

Two helpful practical book on ethics and dialogue are Roger Fisher and William Ury's classic book *Getting to Yes* (Penguin, 1983) and Tom Rusk, *The Power of Ethical Persuasion* (Penguin, 1994). Rusk "applies the ethical principles of respect, understanding, caring, and fairness . . . to high-stakes conversations often threatened by strong emotions and defensive reactions." Many of Rusk's themes parallel this chapter's, though his focus is chiefly on one-on-one conversations about professional or personal matters, rather than larger conversations about moral issues.

For a practical introduction to the emerging field of "invitational rhetoric"—an explicitly ethical and constructive approach to public argumentation—see Sonja K. Foss and Karen A. Foss's text *Inviting Transformation* (third edition, Waveland Press, 2011).

This chapter's box on dialogue under duress draws upon an intriguing book by Phyllis Beck Kritek, *Negotiating at an Uneven Table: Developing Moral Courage in Resolving Our Conflicts* (Jossey-Bass, 2nd ed., 2002). The story about Native Americans comes from her p. 36, the advice about "using your own language" from p. 279. There is much other useful advice.

For more on communication ethics and dialogue, see William Neher and Paul Sandin's introductory textbook *Communicating Ethically* (Allyn and Bacon, 2007), and Josina Makau and Ronald Arnett's *Communication Ethics in an Age of Diversity* (University of Illinois, 1997). Sharon Bracci and Clifford Christians's *Moral Engagement in Public Life: Theorists for Contemporary Ethics* (Peter Lang, 2002) details the assumptions and prescriptions of twelve philosophers on moral reflection and practice from a uniquely communicative perspective.

To read the Greensboro Truth and Reconciliation Commission's Final Report or Executive Summary (discussed in Professor Jovanovic's essay), see www.greensborotrc.org. For more information on the project that initiated the commission, see www.gtcrp.org. A practical account of twenty-one truth commissions from all over the world is offered in *Unspeakable Truths: Facing the Challenge of Truth Commissions* (Routledge, 2002) by Priscilla B. Hayner.

To access the many free guides and reference materials available about community dialogue projects, see the websites for the organizations listed in this chapter:

- The National Issues Forum, www.nifi.org
- Study Circles, www.studycircles.org
- Public Conversations Project, www.publicconversations.org
- The Democracy Project, www.aascu.org/programs/adp
- Public Dialogue Consortium, www.publicdialogue.org
- Search for Common Ground, www.sfcg.org
- National Coalition Building Institute, www.ncbi.org

CHAPTER 12

When Values Clash

One of the aims of ethics is to help us make progress when values clash. Mindful dialogue can help, and you can take more care with facts and inferences and look for "like cases" and carefully spell out the values at stake. Still, even so, deep conflicts will arise. What then?

RIGHT VERSUS RIGHT

Here is a starting point. Consider that in nearly every serious moral conflict, each side has a point. Each side speaks for something worth considering. *Each side is right about something.*

On one level, this statement is totally obvious. In fact, it is the reason we have such deep-seated conflicts in the first place. Each side fastens onto one or a few relevant values and makes it the whole story. They're right: the values for which they speak *are* relevant, indeed maybe even essential. It's just that there are quite likely others that are also relevant and maybe essential too. Like the proverbial blind men and the elephant, we each come to the debate tightly grasping our one small part of the beast, certain that we have the whole truth—and of course our part *is* true enough. But it is probably not the only true part.

In popular moral debate, though, the loudest advocates almost always act as if only one side can be right, that only one side—their own, of course—has a monopoly on truth and the other side is just misguided or blind. On most major moral issues, there are usually supposed to be just two, clearly distinct and opposite, positions. "Pro-life" sets itself up against "pro-choice" and vice versa. On animal rights, assisted suicide, abortion, and a host of other issues, it's always just "yes or no." Almost no other options even get discussed. No ambiguity, no gray areas, no middle ground.

Yet the minute we step back from the heat of debate, we can readily see that both sides could be right in their ways. Most moral conflicts are real, not just mistakes by one side or the other about what really matters. There is genuine good (and/or right, and/or virtue, and/or care) on *both* sides—on *all* sides. There are compelling reasons to promote assisted suicide and affirmative action and abortion rights and animal rights—*and* there are other compelling reasons to resist them. That's life. "Only dogmatism," wrote the pragmatic social philosopher John Dewey,

> can suppose that serious moral conflict is between something clearly bad and something known to be good, and that uncertainty lies wholly in the will of the one choosing. Most conflicts of importance are conflicts between things which are or have been satisfying, not between good and evil.

Again—they are choices between one good thing and another. Not "right versus wrong" but "right versus *right*." We need to start by honoring that fact.

WHAT IS EACH SIDE RIGHT ABOUT?

If moral conflicts pose choices between one good thing and another, then instead of approaching the opposing views looking for their weak points (according to us), we need to start the other way around. Look for their strong points. Ask not which side is right, but what *each* side is right *about*. Even moral arguments that make absolutely no sense to you do make sense to others who are every bit as intelligent and well-intentioned as you. Surely there is *something* in them. Figure out what it is.

Yes, the question of "wrong" can also be raised. Each side, including our own, is likely wrong about something too. Still, the first and vital step is to seek out the *positive* on the other side. In fact, our side and the other side are often two ways of looking at the same thing. What's weak or incomplete (in that sense "wrong") about our own views is often a strong point of (something "right" about) others'—and vice versa. We might as well look at it constructively!

Take, for example, the debate about assisted suicide. Should doctors be able to assist certain people to enable their own dying—at least, people who are approaching death or total disability and probably in great pain? One side says yes: suicide may be the only way in which some people can finally escape their unrelenting pain; and besides, we are free individuals entitled to make that choice. Others say no: allowing and perhaps encouraging doctors to kill, or even just to assist in death, takes a step toward devaluing life, and who knows where it will lead. Life is precious even in pain.

This is a difficult matter, for sure. But it is difficult precisely because both sides have valid points. Freedom from pain matters, and autonomy matters, and also respect for life matters. We do have a problem here. But the problem is not really that we disagree about basic values. We agree all too well, about *many!*

The same goes for ethical theories. Utilitarians are surely right to stress that one good reason in favor of assisted suicide is the relief of pain. The prevention or relief of pointless suffering is a good thing. Listen to the stories of some of the people who want and need help to die, and your heart goes out to them. They have little to look forward to but unrelenting and debilitating pain. Let them go!

But there are other values in play too. Kant, for example, proposes a striking way to think about suicide. "If [we] kill [ourselves] in order to escape from painful circumstances," he wrote, "we use a person [ourselves] merely as a means to maintain a tolerable condition to the conclusion of life." Once life offers us no more pleasure, we conclude that our life has no more value. But this move, so very natural if you think just in terms of pleasures and pains, is for Kant to overlook a whole dimension of value. Our lives, he argues, matter *in themselves,* not just as a means to something else, even of our own. We must respect our *own* lives just as we must respect the lives of others around us.

Character matters too in the face of suffering and death. We can respond with courage, humility, resoluteness—virtues. We are called to care and responsiveness in the face of others' suffering as well. When we begin to realize that people sometimes choose suicide out of a pain that is not so much physical as emotional (from bereavement, abandonment, sense of uselessness—in short, from the loss of community and relatedness), we realize that other and more life-affirming responses are also possible.

Each family of values has a contribution to make. We're not necessarily stalemated if we can't choose between them—that's only if you assume that we must finally go with just one. But we don't. Each highlights certain values left to the side by the others. They're *all* right in their ways. Each has at least some pieces of the puzzle.

Naturally, this does not make the problem easier. Still, we end up with a complex situation—many sorts of values that we are trying to live up to together—which is already very different than a *fight*. Not a collision between polarized points of view, but instead a shared challenge to take up together.

IS CONFLICT THE NORM?

For some people ethics seems to be *only* about the conflict of values. Mention the word "ethics" itself and we may immediately think of moral controversies: abortion, affirmative action, animals, assisted suicide . . . and that's just the A's.

But conflict stands out partly because we expect and look for it. We are told constantly that we live in a conflictual society. Some media thrive on opposition and anger. Adversarial argument is the foundation of our court system. Even the TV news now features opinionated and loud arguments.

Even so, I would argue that conflict is really more like a special case, not the whole story of ethics, or even the main story most of the time. Many moral values have very friendly relations. Think of the four main families of moral values. Each is a big tent. Aristotle and Confucius endorse very similar virtues. Philosophers as diverse as Kant and the Pope converge in their reverence for persons. Each family may be viewed as an inclusive group—an extended family, we might say, with room for relations from many times and places.

Of course, the families themselves differ, at least in theory. In practice, though, many times the different families agree on practical conclusions. It's not surprising that what serves happiness, for example, also tends to be considered virtuous, caring, and so on. Even when the families do not entirely agree, you could read the differences not so much as oppositional as complementary: that is, they simply speak for different but important aspects of problematic situations.

Specific moral values differ all over the map, actually. Just think of how differently various cultures have treated sex, or our obligations to the poor, or who raises the children. But again, difference about these things does not automatically equal *conflict*. Sometimes our differences are just fascinating. They may even be a kind of cultural resource: looking at other cultures' ways may give us more new angles on our own. And often, even when we do feel dissonance between specific values, we can at least treat it as an invitation to keep thinking and exploring, not somehow as a demand to immediately nail down "our" single answer.

Of course there are, sometimes, clashes of values: direct oppositions, either within ourselves or between ourselves and others, that seem to require immediate attention. But how many must really be settled, once and for all, right now? What if we looked for complementarity or common ground even then—and also took our time?

INTEGRATING VALUES

Probably the chief reason we hesitate to acknowledge that "Both (or, all) sides are right" is that we're afraid that then we'll be unable to do or decide anything. If both sides are right, what can we *do*? How can we possibly resolve the question and move ahead? Wouldn't we just be stuck?

In fact, there are many ways of going on from the acknowledgment that both (or all) sides have a point. People who deal regularly with conflict resolution usually insist that only such an acknowledgment makes it *possible* to go on constructively. Moreover, most of the conflict resolvers' methods are familiar. All of them are so eminently sensible that nothing in this section will be a surprise—though I hope it will be an inspiration. The task is to put them to use in ethics.

METHODS

Specifically, the task is to *integrate* the values at stake. We need to try to answer to all of the important values at stake, to try to honor what is right in each of them, rather than just one or a few.

This is a lot less mysterious than it may sound. In fact, we do something of the sort constantly in nonmoral matters. We can distinguish three progressively more ambitious integrative methods.

One simple method is *compromise*. Suppose that for a trip my partner wants to go to the beach and I want to go to the mountains. We could just battle it out, or flip a coin, and end up doing one or the other. That's how it usually goes—a "win/lose" battle. Better would be to at least split the difference. Maybe this trip the beach, next trip the mountains. Or maybe we could do a little of each this time. Though compromising is sometimes treated as disgraceful or weak willed, here it seems to be quite the opposite: a clear-headed acknowledgment of the diversity of values at stake, no big deal, and an attempt to answer at least partly to both of them.

Another method, better still, is to work from *compatible values*. Suppose that my partner and I try to figure out *why* we want to go to the beach or the mountains. Maybe it turns out that she wants to be able to swim and sun-bathe and I want to be able to hike. These goals are not incompatible at all. There are some great lakes in the mountains and some great hiking trails at the beach. Both of us could have exactly what we want, at the same time. Why are we arguing?

Or suppose tonight my daughter and I are at home, and she wants quiet and I want to listen to music. It would be a little crazy for us both to insist that only our desire is "right" and fight it out until one of us gets just what we want, putting down the other in the process. Why not just have music for a while and then quiet? Some of both. Or we can just work in different rooms. Or I could just get a pair of earphones, in which case we could both have exactly what we want. Here we move beyond mere compromise to a truly "win/win" solution. It may turn out that our competing desires aren't incompatible at all.

Finally, sometimes when we really look into the values on the "other" side, it turns out that some of them are not merely compatible but are in fact the very same values we hold ourselves. Though we tend to focus on our disagreements, our background agreements may be far more important. We can work from *common ground*. For example, in the trip question, my partner and I agree from the start that we want to spend our free time outside—in nature. It may be that the exact location matters much less than simply being outside together, and being physically active. Suppose that we started our negotiation there. Basically, we're on the same page. We're in it together. Only the details need to be worked out.

CASE IN POINT

You may already glimpse many ways to apply these integrative strategies in ethics too. Here too, actually, they are no more than applied common sense.

Take the assisted suicide debate again. As soon as we shift focus and look for integrative possibilities, the "conflict" looks very different. For one thing, there is extensive shared moral ground. Though it is almost completely invisible if we view it as a battle, one of the most obvious things about the whole issue is that both sides agree that life is ordinarily a very precious thing, and *also* it is a very bad thing to suffer such pain that death seems appealing by comparison.

Well then, we need to ask, what can be done about *that?* What about developing super-powerful painkillers? What about removing the barriers that still block some dying people from using massive amounts of morphine or other painkillers that would be addictive or otherwise harmful if used by healthy people? Right away we have some common strategies.

And what about those people whose pain is so intense, even with medical help, and hope so remote, that it seems hard to deny that death can be a considered and humane choice? Your heart goes out to them, and I for one know that in their situation I might well wish the same thing.

My experience in many discussions of this issue over the years is that many people on both sides would be willing to accept a policy that allowed assisted suicide in such cases, but under tightly controlled conditions—that is, a compromise. Several independent doctors would have to concur; waiting periods could be required; double- and triple-checks would be necessary to be sure patients were not just temporarily depressed; communities and governments would need to be sure that people in pain always have alternatives— but *then,* given all this, if a person resolutely seeks to die, it is time to respect their wishes.

It may be possible, in short, to legalize assisted suicide in a limited way that both acknowledges the seriousness of taking life and its social dangers, while also recognizing that, sometimes at least, it can be a humane and proper choice. You might be interested to know that just this kind of solution has been adopted in the state of Oregon (and reaffirmed by the voters), with results that, while still controversial, at least aren't an epidemic of suicides. About forty to fifty people per year have secured permission to request assisted suicide in recent years.

More exploration might help us see other possibilities and overlooked complexities. Actually, for example, pain isn't always the main issue. Surveys suggest that people who seek assisted suicide often feel helpless, useless, and abandoned. Some of my students found a website that included biographies of the people that Dr. Jack Kevorkian—the famous (some say infamous) freelance crusader for assisted suicide—had helped to die. Though it was a pro-Kevorkian website, in reading people's stories we began to realize that Kevorkian became a last resort for many people because they were not only in pain but also lacked any kind of family or social support. In some cases their spouses or children were driven away by their very condition—and in at least one case this very absence meant in turn that the affected person could not take strong painkillers, since he had no one to look after him when he was partly "knocked out."

Neither side would say that in this kind of case the right "answer" is death. The real answer is to create communities of care such that people are not abandoned in this way. Relationship-centered values come to the fore. That's a challenge to all of *us*, too, not just to stand by and judge the morality of certain kinds of suicide, but to keep people from the kinds of losses that drive them to such desperation in the first place. Once again, a constructive and *shared* response.

"FOCUS ON INTERESTS, NOT POSITIONS"

You've seen fine wood furniture whose pieces are fitted together with interlocked wedge-shaped cuts, like a dove's tail, that fit together to form a tight joint. Carpenters call this "dovetailing." Roger Fisher and William Ury, in their influential book *Getting to Yes*, invite us to take dovetailing as a metaphor for another integrative possibility when values conflict. We may be able to fit seemingly opposite values together in a like way.

The key, they say, is to separate what they call "positions" from "interests." Your position is what you say you want—which is often, truth be told, a rhetorical or political exaggeration, quite separate from your actual *interests*, which are your carefully considered needs. Fisher and Ury observe that although our positions often conflict head-on, our underlying interests may be much more compatible. Enter the integrative thinker. . . .

Here is a classic political example. From the Six-Day War of 1967 until Israel and Egypt sat down to negotiate after their next war in 1977, the Sinai Peninsula was a central and seemingly irresolvable issue between them. Egyptian territory, it had been captured by Israel and occupied as a buffer zone. Egyptian tanks right on the border had put hostilities on a hair-trigger in 1967, and Israel did not want to be so vulnerable again. Egypt, for its part, naturally wanted its territory back. Both sides insisted on their firmly opposed positions and the fundamental and quite legitimate principles (self-defense, historical right) behind them.

Their *interests,* however, were not so opposite. Neither side wanted another war, for one thing. On that point even these (then) deeply antagonistic states had something fundamental in common. And this was a remarkably useful fact, it turned out—though such basic common interests are often easy to overlook precisely because they *are* so basic. Moreover, even about Sinai their goals were rather different—not exactly opposite. Egypt wanted sovereignty: they wanted the land back. Israel wanted security: some kind of buffer zone. Do you see any way forward?

The eventual solution: Sinai was returned to Egypt, but *demilitarized.* Egypt got the land back *and* Israel got security. And the solution has held. Egypt and Israel have been at peace ever since.

In ethics too, we know that "positions" often collide head-on. For decades, for example, moral and political pressure mounted to stop whale hunting, while whalers, from the shipowners to the crews, resisted. No surprise— their livelihood was at stake. Others were resolutely opposed to the whalers. Members of Greenpeace began to motor out in small boats in the open ocean to place themselves between the harpooners and the whales. Radical moral challenges were being raised, animals were dying, species were threatened. Things were intense.

Yet about a decade ago a transformation occurred. Shipowners began to realize that they could make far more money taking people out to *watch* whales than they could by killing them. Things started to look rather different. The very people who were the industry's resolute enemies could become, well, *customers* of a successor industry, and an industry that did not endanger its own resource, to boot. Sea-people's livelihoods turned out to be compatible, after all, with a new attitude toward the great sea mammals. It was not long before the old whaling ports were becoming whale-*watching* ports, and we were discovering that even the most hostile whales (and why wouldn't they be hostile after three centuries of being hunted without mercy?) can be astonishingly affectionate and curious. People are even out there making music with them. A benign (and from a business point of view, profitable) fascination with whales is blossoming all around the world (though whaling, and the struggle against it, still go on as well).

Did the whalers change their minds about whales too? Some did, I'm sure, once they were freed to look at whales another way. But some did not. They may still look at whales as a source of jobs and income. Yet even so, there turns out to be a better way than killing them—and a way that makes peace with the whales' defenders as well. Former whalers themselves now campaign against the whale-killing that continues. It's bad for business! And a variety of different interests are served—including the whales' own.

WHEN TO HOLD FIRM

Integrative methods do have their limits. "Each side is right about some-thing," I have claimed. But there are surely exceptions. Mightn't some issues really come down to "right versus wrong"? And don't we want to hold firm to the "right" there?

How to Tell?

Sometimes it is easy to tell when a viewpoint really can't claim any valid-ity. Seething hatred, needless injury, random violence—these things have no defense.

In real, deep moral disagreements, things are not so clear. How can we tell whether we face another view that does speak for something impor-tant, even if at the moment we can't see it—or a view that really *is* just plain wrong?

There are some ways. In the first place, keep in mind the basic families of values: the rights of the person, the happiness of society, the essential virtues, care and community. If major violations of these *central* values are proposed without a genuine reason of equal seriousness proposed in justification, warning flags should go up. This may not be a situation for compromise or any other kind of accommodation.

Of course, basic values can conflict—that is what creates the toughest moral problems in the first place. To serve fairness, the general happiness sometimes may need to be curtailed, and vice versa. But these are conflicts *between* basic values, not between basic values and less basic ones. To vio-late rights for the sake of appearances, or to abandon caring obligations because they got a little more expensive than we expected, is not a valid com-promise but more like a betrayal.

Also: listen to the people. Normally there are serious people of good will on the other side, people who are reasonable and well-intentioned, informed and careful. If you can find such people, you have a good sign that they do indeed speak for something important. If you can't, more warning flags.

Of course, to do this you really have to *listen*. Remember that merely dis-agreeing with you does not make a viewpoint invalid or a person "uninformed" or "unreasonable." (That would argue in a tight little circle, wouldn't it: I'm right—because anyone who disagrees with me is uninformed and unreason-able—and I know they're uninformed and unreasonable because they disagree with me!) It's hard but not impossible: it just takes some honesty and humility on your part. Take your time.

In fact, even when we really are confronted with an evil viewpoint, it is still essential to listen to its advocates. Not because we agree with them, but to ask why the evil is so attractive. For example, fanaticism may sometimes arise out of a profound sense of insecurity. Hatred against "outside" groups may arise out of a deep sense of exclusion and disempowerment. And this too, before it settles on some scapegoat, could be a perfectly valid feeling. Just repressing the advocates of such evils leaves the attraction of the evil itself untouched. It may even become more attractive. Even here, then—even when we can genuinely speak of right versus wrong—we need to try to listen, to try to figure out the other side rather than just condemning it outright. That's ethical too!

Drawing the Line in Real Life

Knowing where to draw the line is probably easier in practice than it sounds in theory. Many of the most difficult moral conflicts occur within groups or between people who are in other ways in regular contact and already respectful of each other. Here the other side's intelligence and good intentions are not in question. And, of course, it's easier to listen to them.

For example, many politically liberal secular groups make common cause with Catholics in a wide range of "pro-life" issues, from welfare and children's rights to environmental causes. The same sides tend to divide sharply over a few issues, especially abortion. Here, though, channels of respect and communication have been easier to keep open. Neither side can demonize the other—they know each other too well!

Day to day, meanwhile, the people we argue and negotiate with—constantly—are our family, and friends, and colleagues, whose intelligence and good intentions are not in question either. Here especially the polarized language of "right" and "wrong" is not helpful. Keep a more open mind. There are certainly times to refuse any kind of integrative thinking, but they are the exception—not the rule.

BIG DECISIONS

Sometimes conflicting values go to the core of a community's very identity. A religious congregation may be trying to decide whether or not to bless same-sex marriages. A town or city may be trying to decide how to defend its shrinking open space while being fair to landowners and keeping housing affordable. Are we willing to use extreme measures—what many would call torture—on suspected terrorists? And could we *please* work out some sort of settlement, finally, on abortion, and avoid a similar thirty-year battle over stem-cell research?

These are big decisions. The stakes are high, everyone in the community or nation, or maybe even the world is potentially affected, and the consequences are lasting. Thus the stakes are high also for integrative decision making. In everyday integrative thinking, a certain amount of horse-trading is fine: that is how legislatures pass budgets and co-workers in an office get along. But for larger and community-shaping decisions, integrative thinking must *draw explicitly and centrally on basic and broadly shared values*. It takes more time—and patience.

TAKING DEMOCRACY SERIOUSLY

Democracy is one of our key values. But democracy means much more than making decisions by majority vote. It means working by persuasion, open discussion, and consensus building around basic shared values. Again, *broad* majorities must be *settled* in their direction, not only to make a "big" ethical decision stick, but also to make such a decision ethical in the first place.

True, a temporarily ascendant side may suppress the opposition and force a decision. Prohibition is one example. Temperance moralizing had always had a place in America, especially on the frontiers, right alongside a lot of hard drinking. Activists would enter saloons, singing, praying, and urging saloon keepers to stop selling alcohol—a striking precursor to modern sit-ins and other protests on both ends of the political spectrum. But all of this remained on the moral fringes. With World War I, though, the government needed to divert grain from alcohol production to ethanol, saving gas for the war effort, and it became possible, just for a moment, for the Anti-Saloon League to play on anti-German sentiment (German immigrants were the stereotypical beer drinkers) and push the 18th Amendment through state legislatures. A major though now mostly forgotten impetus was also the early feminist movement, which blamed alcohol, logically enough, for the abuse and abandonment of women and children by drunken husbands.

Prohibition actually succeeded, in the sense that it reduced alcohol consumption sharply in many areas. The problem was that it had few roots in broadly shared and durable values, and what roots it did have, like social justice concerns for women and children, were readily swept aside by the pushback.

Its moment passed almost immediately. Already by the mid-1920s, normalcy returned. Prohibition was widely mocked, then ignored, and soon repealed—but not before it helped fuel the rise of the Mob and undercut the moral authority of future prohibitions that might be better founded.

Likewise, some commentators suggest that the *Roe v. Wade* decision short-circuited a larger discussion that was moving toward a more sustainable resolution on the abortion issue. It's hard to imagine now, but in the early 1970s momentum was building for liberalizing the then very strict abortion laws. Conservatives actually tended to favor legalizing abortion as a means of population control. Many churches were acknowledging that abortion could be a moral choice under some circumstances. The law was lagging behind, yes, but it was still a shock when the 1973 Supreme Court declared abortion a constitutionally protected privacy right in the first trimester of pregnancy.

Roe has been controversial ever since, both as an exercise of judicial power and as an assertion of the priority of privacy rights over other rights and/or other relevant values. But what might have been? What if we had been able to work the abortion question out in a less polarized and gradual way? The last thirty-odd years might have been different. Even now some such movements are happening. The Supreme Court spent much of the 1980s and 1990s hedging: a variety of restrictions, such as waiting periods, parental notification, and so on, have been allowed by the Court, while others have been rejected. Middle ground may be reemerging, but it is such slow and difficult work!

By contrast, consider the way in which the nation moved in response to the civil rights movement. It too evoked intense opposition at first. But here the appeal to shared values, basic human rights, was also evident and clear. It was the genius of the civil rights movement's leadership to put the challenge in just those terms. Think of Martin Luther King Jr.'s constant appeals to the Declaration of Independence, the Bill of Rights, and the Bible. Demonstrations also galvanized moral responses. When people were harassed, beaten, even murdered for trying to *vote*—when the whole world saw fire hoses turned on black children peacefully demonstrating for basic rights—we knew what we had to do. In five years we had a Voting Rights Act and an end to de facto school segregation. Although racial equity remains a difficult and ongoing struggle, there is no question about the basic commitments. Now we can't even imagine that basic civil rights were ever controversial.

"SHAREABLE TERMS" AGAIN

In response to sectarian religious dogmatism, chapter 3 insisted on *finding shareable terms*. The point here is the same, only broader. Common values do exist—they are in fact the norm. They can be drawn upon strategically for integrative decision making at many levels, from family trip destinations to demilitarizing the Sinai. But in the big decisions, they need to be especially clear and settled, and drawn upon explicitly and repeatedly.

And contrariwise, if you *can't* draw on such basic shared values, then it might be the better part of valor to reconsider a little. Certainly no group should try to make the community as a whole take on its particular or unique moral stances—even if that group strongly believes that its stance is the only right one—without a real give-and-take in which their views too are open to question, and without a broad consensus emerging as a result. Maybe it will, maybe it won't . . . but in any case the shared values must come first.

Even dogmatists might see the wisdom of this if they consider how many other dogmatists are out there who have just as fervent beliefs as they do but in different or opposite directions. Each side likes to demonize the extremists of the other—"Do you want *them* making the law?" No. But most of us don't want *you* making the law either. You are welcome to try to persuade the rest of us—using good arguments, of course—but you need to listen too, and then we decide together. If we are ready! Otherwise, let's honor democracy—let's celebrate our shared communities whatever they are—and, well, keep talking.

READING

> ## "Can We Talk? Understanding the 'Other Side' in the Animal Rights Debates"
>
> ### ROGER GOTTLIEB
>
> **ROGER GOTTLIEB** is a professor of philosophy at Worcester Polytechnic Institute and writes widely on political philosophy, environmentalism, ethics, religion, spirituality, the Holocaust, and disability. One of his recent books is *Engaging Voices*, a series of dialogues exploring some of today's ecological issues and challenges with special attention to how we relate to each other and to others who differ from us, sometimes radically, in coming to terms with those issues. To what degree do both our differences and our difficulties in dealing with them—and in really hearing the "other sides"—stem from our own deep-lying uncertainties and fears, blocking not only constructive dialogue but the possibilities for making progress together, in more open-ended and integrated ways?
>
> The following excerpt has been abridged [by AW] from a much longer essay by Gottlieb of the same title, originally intended to be part of *Engaging Voices*. Gottlieb writes as an unapologetic animal rights sympathizer working, all the same, to come to terms with the real concerns—not just the surface arguments—of the "other sides." Watch as he makes use of all of the integrative tools offered in this chapter. You also might want to revisit the two readings in chapter 1 on the same topic.

When you order a delicious Veal Parmesan at a fancy Italian restaurant you are consuming the flesh of a living being who had been confined in a cage so small that it could barely move, always in the dark so that its flesh would be pale, without any company (which it needs, being a social animal), and, to preserve the delicacy of its taste, never fed the solid food it requires.

Clearly there are all sorts of cultural reasons to keep eating that Veal Parmesan. It has been a delicacy for a very long time. It tastes great. People earn a living raising, cooking, and serving it. If you lean in the animal rights direction, as I do, it might seem pretty easy to dismiss all such defenses of veal by pointing out that slavery was culturally supported and that people made money off of the Holocaust. But this quick dismissal does not work when you are talking to someone who remembers how his family really enjoyed his grandmother's cooking—whose heart opens in the memory of everyone sighing with pleasure around the dining room table; or who is paying for his son's alternative medical treatments for debilitating asthma by working in at Ricci's Italian Paradise. . . .

Yet it *is* very hard to defend the way veal calves are raised without saying flat out that the pain of animals is morally meaningless. This position says that we can cut down trees, dig holes in the ground, hammer brass—and in exactly the same way that we can do what we want to any animal that is not human. . . . People are the center of all things and the beings out on the periphery do not count for very much. Yet, interestingly, even people who believe this sort of thing typically do not believe it *completely*; and it is that lack of completeness which leaves an opening for the other side. For example: a good number of the veal parmesan eaters (or servers) doubtless have their own special, favorite pets that they would not dream of treating the way veal calves are treated: animals whose welfare, happiness and pleasure count for something. The fundamental inconsistency here—that the pain of our pets matters but that of our dinner does not—creates a deep logical hole that is very hard to climb out of.

So when we look at veal—and indeed meat eating generally—what we have is a deeply entrenched social practice which is, when examined, pretty much without any moral justification. Whether or not this moral indefensibility extends to every other use of animals, such as hunting buffalo a thousand years ago, or to the Inuit peoples in the Arctic Circle who pursue seals now, or even to individual hunters with waterproof camouflage jackets and long distance rifle scopes taking a bead on some moose, is really beside the point. Right now, we are talking about mass produced animals who end up in shrink wrapped packages at the local supermarket.

What can the veal eater say in response? Not much, which is why his or her response is generally laughter, contempt, ignoring the truth, not looking at films of factory farms and slaughterhouses, saying "that's just the way we do things around here," and repeating "it tastes good," as if that were sufficient *reason* to keep eating it. One usually gets a lot of attitude, but very little argument.

So if the cheerful meat eater does not want to engage seriously with an animal rights advocate's claims that July 4th barbecues are like Nazi death camps, what are we to do?

Well, and initially this might seem to be beside the point, we can start by recognizing that the moral failure of modern meat eating is not the end of the story. For if the modern meat eater is doing something morally wrong every time she whips out her Visa card to pay for prime rib, she is surely not the only one who commits moral wrongs. . . . Indeed every animal rights activist, including the ones who believe that our mass consumption of animals is a kind of Holocaust, lives in a way that harms animals. Such activists drive their cars and plug into the power grid, thus contributing to the global warming that is eradicating countless species. Even a fully vegan diet involves large-scale agriculture that displaces animals. And when their children are sick, they do not reject "out of principle" medicines that have been developed through testing on animals. . . .

[T]here may be some comfort for both sides to be found in what is probably for most readers an unexpected source: the vegetarian perspective of Rabbi Abraham Isaac Kook, who at his death in 1935 was the chief rabbi of pre-state Israel. As an esteemed leader of Orthodox Jewry, Kook functioned in a community in which meat eating—and lots of it—was the accepted rule. There was no way he could simply demand vegetarianism from his followers: the ruling would not have been understood, and certainly not followed. But Kook was not about to issue such a simple, absolute rule. In fact, he argued that biblical history showed that humans, though ultimately headed for a non-meat diet, simply were not capable of it yet. In Genesis God initially gives Adam and Eve only vegetable food to eat; after the "sinful generation" of Noah, however, God told them they could eat flesh "after all the desire of your soul." At the same time, however, as Kook pointed out, there are many biblical rules which restrict what and how we eat: we are not allowed to boil the kid in its mother's milk, or take the mother bird along with the eggs, or eat blood. There are foods that are forbidden. Thus the way we eat is a matter in which God's commands operate. It is morally significant and demands that we limit ourselves. These rules, said Kook, indicate that humans are involved in a very long process of moral development. This process starts with some restrictions on what we can do to animals. It will end up in an ideal of respect and care, including a refusal to use animals for food. We are not capable of the end point yet, but we are on the way to it.

One does not have to be an Orthodox Jew, or a religious believer of any kind, to appreciate the force of this position. One need only see that a partial improvement is better than no improvement at all, even in the realm of morality. And that the practical truth of any moral claim . . . is only as powerful as the level of moral development of the people we are talking to. No matter how right a moral claim is, if humanity is not ready to take in its truth, it will have no social consequence. Like so much else in life, the effectiveness of a moral truth depends on where we are historically and socially. . . .

How can we make all this at least a little better? This question has some resonance in the real world. For somehow there has been agreement on legal restrictions in some countries on how you can raise veal, and in other matters relating to animals as well. If these new laws are not enough for the moral vegetarian, I completely understand. But moral life is often, perhaps typically, not a case of "enough." It usually is, at best, a case of getting a "little bit better."

Here's another context: Your child has been born with Cystic Fibrosis, a generally fatal genetic condition in which a missing enzyme leads to lung and digestive problems. While CF used to spell a quite early death for everyone, recent research has now enabled many to live into their 30s and 40s.

If it is your child, doomed to a life of frequent lung infections, rounds of seemingly endless coughing, near constant chest physical therapy to clear the distinctly thick and immovable CF mucous, do you care how many lab animals have to die to find a cure, or even something that will enable your child to have a somewhat longer, somewhat more tolerable, life? In forty years the median survival age for CF has gone from 10 to 37. *That's* what you're counting, not the number of mice that were used up to develop treatments, and potentially a cure, for your child. . . .

Here we have what looks like a clear choice: allow a child to suffer and die young, or do what needs to be done for the human at the expense of animals. If you are that parent—or the child himself—do you think you will put much stock in accounts of animal suffering?

Once again of course the Animal Rights defender can simply say that there is no reason to prefer the human to the animal. And questions of degree and scope can also be raised. How many animals would you sacrifice for a cure? A million? A hundred million? A hundred billion? And for what disease?—for one that afflicts some 300,000 in the U.S. like CF? For one that afflicts 300? Or 3? Is there no limit at all? . . .

Perhaps once again the only approach with a reasonable chance of success is to try to make things a little better. First, stop all the stupid, wasteful, even insane animal experiments: the ones that drip cosmetics into rabbits' eyes until they go blind; or that smash monkey's heads into walls to see if having heads smashed into a wall will injure the brain; or that test how long it takes to make animals crazy by randomly subjecting them to electrical shocks.

As for the CF experiments? Well, even if they are wrong, perhaps we could agree to talk about them later. Just as it would be an improvement, even if not necessarily good enough, to improve the living conditions of veal calves, so there is a lot that can be done to limit or eliminate animal experiments *before* we get around to stopping the research aimed at curing lethal illnesses.

In a moral life we are often faced with difficult choices. Sometimes these are really false choices, and we should make sure we know who or what has said "Choose between A and B." Maybe there is a C that would work out for us all—like preventive health measures to clean up the environment so fewer people get cancer from pollution, or teaching people to have better health habits so lifestyle diseases diminish. But at times, and sadly, there are cases when no way out of the painful alternatives is possible. "People are born to trouble," said Job, "as the sparks fly upwards." "Life," said the Buddha, "is suffering." We will have pain in this life, and so will everyone else, and no amount of moral goodness will ever take that away. Even the animal rights defender cares more for his own child than his own pet; or would be more upset if he ran over a neighbor's child than if he ran over a neighbor's dog. Just as the "I can do anything to animals I want" types might have pets they cherish, animal rights supporters still privilege people. That is one reason this issue of animal experiments is both very difficult and a place where agreement across real differences might be reached. . . .

Another argument often used in favor of eating animals is that animals themselves kill and eat other animals. So why shouldn't we? To be honest, this is a concern it is often hard for me to take seriously. Yet I have heard it so many times from students and from people at my public lectures that my inability to see its force must signal a real lack in me.

. . . We are, say some hunters (at least the ones who want to talk about it), getting back into nature, experiencing the wilderness as our forbears did, tracking and killing in a primordial struggle that bonds us with the circle of life the way humans used to before we were made weak and decadent by civilization. There is a mystic connection between hunter and animal which all those who buy packaged hot dogs can never understand. And those of you who criticize hunting as a brutal celebration of death do not comprehend the respect, the love even, that passes between hunter and prey.

But if people truly want to experience the primordial struggle between hunter and prey, well then let them actually have that experience. Let them walk to wherever they are going to hunt, using weapons and wearing clothes they have made themselves. Let their total consumption of meat be dependent on the hunt and the hunt alone. No more $200 boots and toasty down parkas. No going out for steak afterwards, or driving to the national forest for deer season. When today's hunters want to do try it this way, they will at least be more honest. I still might wonder why they can't commune with a living being without killing it; or have a bean salad and soy yogurt for dinner instead of venison. Perhaps they could connect to animals by tracking them, taking pictures, or writing poems. But until they make the real sacrifices needed to "get back to the primordial" their stated desire seems a little insincere. . . .

As attractive as a moral position seems initially, if you cannot live by it, it does not amount to much. By that I do not mean perfection. I am not suggesting that if we cannot love our neighbors as ourselves we should totally abandon the religions which tell us to; or that if we do not always take other people's rights seriously we should abolish the *Declaration of Independence*. I do mean that if we put forward a moral position which seems to require a certain amount of responsibility, and we are not willing to even try to live up to that responsibility in our own lives, we should not pretend it is really a something we believe in. It is pretty clear that our hunters will not live like Native Americans of a thousand years ago; and that the person who wants to live "like nature" will also want his or her own life and property protected by a moral code and a good police force.

Thus my arguments, I am convinced, win. But so what? Is that the best we can hope for in a moral conversation? Could it be that there is something more important than my own knee-jerk rejection of moral stands I do not like?

I think there is. And here is part of it. Any widely held belief— even one that is inconsistent, poorly informed, or just dead wrong— almost always has some connection of vital importance to the people who hold it. If we truly are to understand one another, to develop our moral life through connected conversation with other viewpoints, and to create a moral community *together*, we must try to find out what it is that binds people to positions we completely reject.

At this point some people will point to revolutions or activist social protest movements and say *that* is how we should respond to moral evil, not by trying to find out what is vital and authentic in it. We do not need to "understand" Nazis, wife-beaters, racists, or colonialists—we just need to confront and defeat them. Indeed that may be the case in some situations, though it might certainly be argued that often a lot of unnecessary antagonism, self-righteous condemnation of other people, and outright violence slows things down or leads to a continuation of violence in the end. Maybe feminism in the U.S. would be further advanced now if the movement in the 1970s and 80s had showed more compassion for men, for example. Perhaps violent revolutions tend to create violent post-colonial governments. Maybe nonviolence—political and emotional—is a more effective, long-term answer to the problems of profound injustice. And maybe it is not.

In any case right now what I am concerned with is the process of *moral* life, sustaining a moral community, and trying to hear and be heard by people who may think very differently than we do. Here the goal is understanding and connection, not victory and correctness.

The hunters, and those who would think nature teaches us to act without moral limits, are both expressing, however indirectly, a yearning to find some source of value, meaning, and connection that is beyond the human. . . . In nature there is vitality, honesty, strength, and acceptance of fate. In nature the only masks are part of an evolutionary strategy, like the butterflies whose markings make them look poisonous when they are not. In nature there is no waste, and everything fits, and everybody's death is someone else's life—or at least so it may seem to those of us trapped by television, roads, bureaucratic regulations, the tax code, and email. . . .

If this speculation about the deeper motivations of people whose attitudes towards animals I reject are true, then there is a basis for some kind of communication. Even, perhaps for some kind of commonality and solidarity. For I too seek some wisdom and inspiration in the realm of nature, and I too admire the clarity and integrity of animals. If I can see what is beautiful in what other people think and want, as well as what is wrong, I will have upped my chances at finding allies, and at least will have learned to be a little less angry, superior, and self-righteous. . . . And maybe I and the people whom I am so sure are wrong can join together on things we both support, like protecting wilderness. Better they should hunt and join Sierra Club to help protect the forest and the animals in it, than be so alienated from all the soft-hearted and morally superior environmentalists like me that they ignore everything but the next kill.

QUICK REFERENCE: WHEN VALUES CLASH

WHEN TRULY OPPOSITE VALUES CONFLICT, AT LEAST SPLIT
THE DIFFERENCE

Both (all) sides can be, and often are, partly right. Even when we have trouble seeing what the other side is about, splitting the difference affirms and sustains the shared moral community. Here each side gets half, anyway, of what it wants.

FOCUS ON INTERESTS, NOT POSITIONS

Different values may still be compatible. Look beyond contending positions to try to *dovetail* the underlying interests: the core values. Often there are ways to satisfy both at the same time. Here each side can get more than half of what it wants—and again, shared community is served too.

WORK FROM COMMON GROUND

When disagreements are framed by deeper shared values, work from those shared values toward jointly agreeable resolutions. Each side might even get *all* of what it *really* wants. Rather than defining ourselves by our disagreements, let us highlight our commonalities.

BIG DECISIONS

When the ethical decision involved has especially high stakes and major consequences, take special care to act from broadly shared and carefully articulated values.

FOR REVIEW

1. How does John Dewey characterize most moral conflicts?
2. What does this chapter advocate instead of asking which side is right?
3. How could "both sides be right" in the assisted suicide debate?
4. According to this chapter, are conflicting values the norm? Explain.
5. What is the concept of "integrating values"?
6. What are three specific methods for integrating values?
7. What is "dovetailing" values? Give an example.

8. Those big decisions—what special standards come into play?

9. According to the text, why did Prohibition fail? What's the relevance of that failure now?

10. How does Roger Gottlieb suggest that we can make progress in the animal rights debates?

EXERCISES AND NOTES

12.1 FOR DISCUSSION

Why are we so ready to think that moral issues must be matters of "right versus wrong"? Why do we polarize values? Take some time with this question: the answers are not obvious at all, and there are many levels on which you might address it.

Here is another way into these questions. Many differences of moral values don't bother us at all—or at least, most of us. We're more apt to just find them fascinating, like differences in speech or sexual customs. Still, very serious values may be involved here. We don't generally announce anymore that the work ethic, say, is "right" and any other way is wrong—yet work is one of the central projects of our lives. Chivalry is an ethic too—rooted in the medieval practices that also give us romantic love—but, again, we are not prone to moralize. A certain chivalry may be nice in a lover, but people may as well prefer to do without. Why do we seldom worry or argue about "conflicts" of values in cases like these? Why do we not insist that these differences be morally sorted out too?

Quite apart from what you may think about the morality of abortion, do you think that a Supreme Court decision such as *Roe v. Wade* was the best procedure for resolving the question? What would have been a better one? Why? Apply your answer to emerging contemporary issues.

12.2 PRACTICING INTEGRATIVE THINKING: LESS CONTENTIOUS ISSUES

Integrative methods need a *lot* of practice in ethics. It is useful to begin, though, with issues where they are at least a little more familiar: with certain non-ethical issues, or at least value issues that are not so hotly debated. These may be troublesome issues too, in the sense that they bring important values into conflict and readily produce polarized advocacy groups and debate. Still, they are generally understood to be open to intelligent discussion and even reasonable resolution. Certainly in most non-ethical cases it is less tempting to insist that only one or a few of the contending values are right and the others wrong, or that there is no other possible outcome beyond the total victory of one side. The point of this exercise is to remember the skills that are required to approach issues in that constructive way.

Here are some questions that might qualify:

- Should students who have moral reservations about dissection be allowed to opt out?
- Should health insurance pay for alternative medicine (e.g., massage, acupuncture)?
- Is driving a right, or a privilege? (Should we expect more driver responsibility than we currently do?)
- Should children's TV watching be limited?
- Should tax money pay for private-school vouchers?
- How can public schools approach controversial subjects such as creationism or sex education?
- How serious an offense to academic integrity is plagiarism?

For your practice, ask first what are the values that are competing here. What is each side speaking for that is important? Take some time with these questions—don't just name one value on each side. You know from chapter 4 that the real story is likely to be more complex.

Now bring your integrative methods to bear. Are there ways to "split the difference" in these debates? What ways? Can the relevant values be dovetailed? Is there common ground to be found? What new options then open up? As Roger Gottlieb might ask, Can We Talk about them? What does it look like when we do?

12.3 PRACTICING INTEGRATIVE THINKING: CONTENTIOUS ETHICAL ISSUES

Now turn to more contentious ethical issues and apply the same integrative skills to them. Pick some of the following questions to work on (or others of your choice):

- Is health care a right, or a privilege? (or something else?)
- Should we allow the testing of new drugs and other products on animals?
- Should hate speech be banned?
- Should pornography be banned?
- Are better-off people and countries obliged to do more to address world hunger?

- In an age of fears of terrorism, how far should individual rights be compromised for the sake of greater security?

I still recommend putting off the hottest-button issues, such as abortion, until you have had a lot of practice with others. (If you can't wait, go to chapter 14 and read the section called "Reframing the Abortion Debate.")

For clarity's sake, start by identifying your position on each question (if you have one—but a definite opinion is not required, and indeed is not especially wise if you don't know much about an issue). Now consider the opposite position—the other side or sides—or, if you're not sure of your own, just consider the main contending views. Ask yourself what the other side(s), or each side, is right about—not wrong, but *right*. Where do you actually *agree* with them? What are their strongest and most important points?

It pays to go slowly here. Remember that integrative thinking begins with the acknowledgment that all sides very likely speak for something worth considering. This is already a hard habit to change, given the ways we usually debate ethical issues. When we get into contentious ethical issues, just the mere possibility that the other side has some points may be hard to acknowledge. Of course you don't agree with their conclusions—or most of them—but it's almost certain that you can still find common ground, or at least compatible interests. In fact, probably you even share *most* of the other side's values, though you may give them somewhat different weights or rankings.

So what are those shared or compatible values? Take your time, be careful, and try to put them in a fair way. For example, suppose you are thinking about capital punishment. Shared or compatible values might include:

- *Life* (both sides insist that life is precious, which is why murder is considered by both so heinous a crime, why the pro side thinks murderers deserve death, and also why the anti side thinks that execution only doubles the crime)
- *Appropriate punishment* (since both sides condemn murder, both propose "ultimate punishments": execution or life in prison)
- *Deterrence* (preventing future murders)
- *Fairness* (convictions must be fair; the execution of innocent people and racially tainted verdicts are wrong)

Can you come up with a similar list of shared or compatible values for the contentious issues suggested above?

Please note: the task is not just to *describe* the other side's view. It's tempting to answer by just summarizing what you think they think. "They think this; they think that." That's helpful too, but the task here is to go much further. What do they think *that you think too*? What do you actually think they're *right* about? Go beyond "I think . . ." and "They think . . ." to "*We* think. . . ."

If you're in a group setting, a variation of this exercise is to make a list together of all of the relevant values that both (all) sides in some debate share. Usually you can come up with a very long list! That in itself should be surprising—and inspiring.

12.4 INTEGRATIVE BUMPER STICKERS

Visit some parking lots and write down the bumper stickers on ethical issues you see. Look for a wide range, including the ones that infuriate you.

Now pay attention to the ways in which positions are misrepresented and common ground—shared values—is obscured. Look at the manipulative language, the appeals to authority, the insistence on finality and completely conclusive judgments. Of course, there is a limit to what can be said in a bumper sticker. But how often do we fall into "bumper sticker thinking" even when we could actually say something constructive?

Now take some of the issues that turn up in your survey and try to write *integrative alternative bumper stickers*. Is there a way to say something pithy that brings us together rather than divides us, that clarifies or connects rather than misrepresents and polarizes?

You will discover a great deal of pro-choice and pro-life sloganizing, for example. **God hates abortion**, they say. **Abortion stops a beating heart**. On the other side, **If you're against abortion, don't have one**. So it was an inspiration one day to see **Every child a wanted child**. Think of that: instead of trashing the other side for the evils of their ways, here is an appeal to the kind of value that unites us. It doesn't insist on one "side" over the other; it reminds us of what we should all aim for in the end. Every child a wanted child—which means: women have both the right and the responsibility to regulate pregnancy. Every child a wanted child—which means: when pregnancy occurs, we need to do everything we can to be sure the potential child is "wanted"—that is, that the family can sustain the pregnancy and the child. The whole issue appears in a different light—and as a collective responsibility, an invitation to try to better the world.

Another one I'd like to see: instead of the current **It's a child, not a choice**, how about **It's a child *and* a choice**? Here's one I actually saw recently: **Pro-choice before conception, pro-life after**. I realize that this is meant to be pro-life, the way the debate is now framed, and even a little nasty. But doesn't it have bigger possibilities?

NOTES

John Dewey is quoted from "The Construction of Good," chapter 10 of his book *The Quest for Certainty*, widely reprinted, for example, in James Gouinlock, *The Moral Writings of John Dewey* (Hafner-Macmillan, 1976), chapter 5, where the quotation can be found on p. 154. The general theme of integrating values is thoroughly Deweyan, as Gouinlock's collection makes clear. A previous and (somewhat) more theoretical work of my own on this theme is *Toward Better Problems* (Temple University Press, 1992).

Roger Fisher and William Ury's book *Getting to Yes* (Penguin, many editions) is essential practical reading on integrating values: see especially chapters 2 and 3. On compromise, a careful philosophical treatment is Martin Benjamin's *Splitting the Difference* (University Press of Kansas, 1990). Benjamin systematically contests the various arguments that ethical philosophers have offered (or might offer—the arguments are seldom fully spelled out) against taking compromise seriously as an ethical method.

USING YOUR TOOLS #6
CAN WE TALK . . . ABOUT MARRIAGE?

BY MARTIN FOWLER

You have just received a traditional-looking wedding invitation on heavy card stock in cursive script rarely used for any other kind of announcement. It states: *"Together with their parents, Julia Smith and Melinda Jones request the honor of your presence at their marriage on Sunday. . . ."* You pause and read the invitation again. You're thrilled because Julia is your dear friend. Perhaps you're shocked because your dear friend Julia never told you about her fiancée or that she is lesbian. Maybe you wonder (or worry) about who else received this invitation. Whether Julia is your ex-girlfriend, sister, teacher, or pastor, how you respond to the RSVP is not only a personal decision, but an *ethical* issue.

Both those for and against legalizing same-sex marriage usually agree that legal matrimony is terribly important. (Though not always; some think that government has no proper business declaring which relationships are "legitimate" and which are not.) This is in itself a remarkable piece of common ground, almost always unnoticed in the midst of the uproar: both sides value marriage. Moreover, in the event, almost everyone feels pretty much the same about the actual ceremony. I've attended plenty of same-sex weddings, and what's remarkable in practice is how unremarkably guests already know how to act at a wedding. While you witness the ceremony, it looks and feels so normal that you could wonder what all the fuss is about. Still, people's conflicts about the meaning of marriage don't vanish because you throw rice and confetti at them. Resolving a conflict may demand time, creativity, and patience. The guest sitting next to you may privately think that two people of the same gender can never be truly married, even if the couple call themselves spouses, their religion blesses it, the government declares it legal, and everyone approves. This guest is only there to be silently supportive but has voted against legalizing same-sex marriage.

So: your challenge for this exercise is to *plan a wedding*.

Couples sometimes make their own vows, but they typically rely upon some civil protocol or religious liturgy. There is the first question: *what would the wedding vows for a same-sex couple look like?* Would it be the same as one for a man and woman, only with different pronouns? If it would be different, how and why? (Does some notice even need to be taken of the existence of controversy? What kind of notice? Defiance? Sadness? Or something else?)

Next, *design wedding invitations*. Put your graphics expertise to work. Decide how you will announce this event to others. Who will receive invitations and who most certainly will not? Would you have brides' maids for both women and "best man" for each groom?

Then, *share your wedding plan* with a same-sex couple and an opposite-sex couple and see what they think of it. Use their questions, comments, and objections to modify and improve the wedding plans.

If you really don't think you could plan a wedding, plan a banquet for after the wedding. Write some speeches for friends and family who will toast the couple. Who gets to come to the banquet and who does not? Does the menu differ for two women vs. two guys? Where would they hold the event? Will it be catered or will friends and family cook a meal for the couple? Then share your banquet plan with a same-sex couple and an opposite-sex couple and see what they think of it. Incorporate their questions, comments, and objections to modify and improve the speeches and the event.

And a last question. A couple may get cold feet and decide at the last minute to postpone or cancel their wedding and banquet. Perhaps one or both of them cannot handle family or social controversy about same-sex marriage. How then will you inform guests about this and what it means?

DIALOGUE

Here are some guidelines for starting and sustaining a discussion about same-sex marriage:

1. How people treat each other when they dialogue matters more than the content of what they say. So, don't assume that people you talk with are heterosexual unless they say so. If you talk with someone in a same-sex relationship, don't start by declaring what you think such a relationship is or must be. Have the courtesy to ask his or her view about what same-sex marriage means. Keep in mind that the meaning of "marriage" depends on where you and your disputant reside (something we may overlook if the argument occurs online). Suppose you live someplace where the relationship is recognized as a marriage, civil union, or domestic partnership. Maybe your disputant (if they disagree) lives someplace where same-sex marriage is not recognized or is prohibited. That will make a difference. Likewise, if you think of same-sex marriage strictly as a religious commitment, but your opponent thinks of it as a civil right, you may talk past each other without realizing it when you discuss same-sex marriage. First allow each other to carefully articulate what you mean by "marriage."

2. Listen carefully and with genuine (if grudging) respect for the person who disagrees with you so that you hear and understand the reasons for their disagreement before you speak. Don't start the dialogue with *"How on earth could you possibly believe . . ."* or by calling your opponent a bigot. Be brave enough to admit that you could—just possibly, out somewhere at the very limits of imagination—be wrong about same-sex marriage. It's no defeat to acknowledge objections from a different perspective or to be persuaded by better reasons than your own. You may not feel much like thanking the person who enlightens you, but do it anyway.

3. As your dialogue develops, someone may introduce a position that neither of you had considered. Two people may have a relationship as emotionally meaningful, deep, and committed as marriage, but the word "marriage" simply misrepresents what the two people mean to each other or to their family and community. You need a different word or concept. For example, loyal friendship has been described with all the devotion and self-sacrifice usually associated with marriage. Two people come to understand each other, put up with each other's flaws, and help each other to grow, even when they fight. Two lives can be bound together in many ways, including (many different kinds of) marriage. In fact, if your dialogue is a success, it might count as such a relationship! In any event, be honest and clear about what you think, but only after you consider that the truth may be bigger and more diverse than your opening set of pro and con arguments.

4. After working for years with attorneys, I'm never satisfied with my arguments for a position until I can argue for the contrary *better* than my opponents. If that's too competitive for your temperament, consider that reasoning and dialogue are also cooperative, even when (or especially when) people are in conflict. That's because how opponents treat each other shapes their future relationship, regardless of who "wins" the argument. It can keep open or forever close the possibility for further discussion.

5. Finally, don't overlook the obvious. Someone may object vehemently to a particular same-sex marriage because they are absolutely certain that the couple just aren't right for each other. ☺

A real wedding story may help you plan. On March 15, 1986, Clyde Zuber and I had a Holy Union ceremony at the Metropolitan Community Church of Dallas. No government recognized same-sex marriage. We couldn't legally call it a "marriage ceremony." I wanted to invite only a few people, but Clyde printed and distributed invitations to all his co-workers, friends, family, and former classmates at a conservative Bible college. We had no idea how these invitees would respond. The former classmates stopped talking to him. However, our parents, friends, and Clyde's co-workers attended. His sister asked the date and time for our rehearsal dinner. We confessed that we didn't plan one. She was so angry with us that she made the dinner arrangements herself. In our defense, there is still no magazine called "Groom" with wedding tips for guys. Our friends sprayed "just married" in shaving cream on our rear windshield. As we drove home, people honked and waved to congratulate us, though, at stop lights, some had deer-in-the-headlight looks on their faces when they saw two guys in tuxes.

After that great beginning, my husband and I tried to join a different church, closer to where we lived. It was much more conservative. They handed us a leaflet entitled "Belong Where You Live" featuring footprints leading to a church. Still, the pastor and deacon were eventually unnerved by us sitting in their pews as a gay couple. They tried to return our collection plate offering and begged us to l leave. Next Sunday, we sat on the curb across from the front of the church where we read the Bible during the service. We did so each Sunday morning for months.

The congregation began entering the church through the back door. They were confident about excluding us, but we stubbornly remained as part of their lives, just as they were part of ours. Some wanted to welcome us; others wanted to chase us away. We neither went into the church nor left it. Belonging where we lived was not easy. We didn't try to convince them to accept us. It was no protest or vigil. It wasn't pouting. It was definitely more than loitering, but not any less than that. We were hanging out in our neighborhood. We belonged where we lived, so that's where we parked our butts. We didn't have much dialogue unless you count our silent vigil and their silent refusal to speak as clear communication of a sort.

In 2004, Clyde and I were legally married to each other in Canada where he could visit me if I were hospitalized and would be entitled to the same government benefits as any spouse. If I divorce him, I must wait a year before it is granted. (If you can legally divorce someone, does that imply that the marriage was legal?) Back in the United States, none of those rights are recognized. In some countries, it could get us killed. You can see our 1986 ceremony on line at http://www.zuberfowler.com/christian/cenbef.html and our 2004 civil ceremony at http://www.zuberfowler.com/2004nw/04before.html. —MF

WHEN VALUES CLASH

How would you identify and help to resolve a clash of values when people deal with same-sex marriage? Here are some places to look:

1. The family and community may object to the relationship counting as a marriage because marriage alters the legal and social responsibilities and obligations of the couple's family and community as well as the responsibilities and obligations of the couple themselves. What changes do they fear or find objectionable? Start with the simplest: no one gets to choose whether they become an in-law, do they? What are some ways that same-sex marriage can strengthen families and communities instead of threatening these groups?

2. When society extends a political franchise such as citizenship or the right to vote, that affects the status of those who had thought of their right as a privilege. When you think of how same-sex couples have invisibly endured conventional weddings as public declarations that only love between a man and a woman deserves public celebration, it's hard to sympathize with the majority's loss of special privileges. It looks like sulking. But it is a loss, for something has been "taken away." Dialogue is needed about what is really lost or gained for all parties.

3. We can look up the definition of "marriage" in the dictionary, but what marriage means to people is more complex. For example, as the box "Which Facts Are Relevant?" in chapter 9 notes, marriage has both religious and civil meanings. A religious

community or institution may bless, endorse, or sanction a relationship as marriage, or it may prohibit or simply refuse to recognize such a relationship as valid. Likewise, a government or agency may acknowledge or legitimate a relationship as marriage within a jurisdiction. Or it may refuse to extend recognition, or may constitutionally define marriage so as to exclude same-sex relationships. The religious and political tracks on how to define or deal with same-sex marriage are separate but they may merge or collide at times.

4. When my husband and I returned from Canada to the United States after our civil ceremony, American government officials could have behaved as though we had stepped out of a dream or cartoon upon entering American reality. However, as more states legalize same-sex marriage, that American reality is becoming more of a crazy quilt in which a person can be married in one state, but unmarried when they cross state lines.

   Most countries can legalize or prohibit same-sex marriage entirely by national policy. The United States has handled this state-by-state. If only half the states in America recognize such marriages, and the federal government has no national policy, this would be analogous to free states vs. slave states before the Civil War. Yet not every battle between jurisdictions is a clash of values. The clash here seems to be the state's right to declare which relationships are legitimate vs. citizens' right to live within a social framework of consistent and predictable laws, rules, and expectations. Think of ways in which both rights can be properly acknowledged.

5. It helps to remember basic human needs. Keep some perspective. On July 22, 2011, Anders Behring Breivik, after killing people in Oslo with a car bomb, opened fire at a summer camp on the island of Otøya, killing 69 attendees, mostly teenagers. This massacre was a horrible event. A married lesbian couple, who lived nearby, Hege Dalen and Toril Hansen, were having dinner when they heard gun shots and jumped into their small boat to cross the lake and see what was going on. They grabbed as many teenagers as they could from the water, pulled them into their small boat, and brought them to safety on the other side of the lake while their boat was under fire. They saved forty teens after going back to the island four times. The couple did not seek or receive much publicity in the United States. In life's crises, committed relationships of all sorts can matter very much to the community and to the well-being of children.

   Breivik claimed that he was crusading to protect Norway against religious and ethnic incursions. There is no meaningful clash of values about massacres, but some cannot tolerate clashing values without resorting to violence and brutality. That's why the hard work of sustained dialogue as a response to conflict and disagreement matters so much. The alternative is not necessarily bloodshed, but a barren public space where people care more about how they define other people's relationships than they do about recognizing and supporting people in the rights and responsibilities of marriage. Silence and screaming need to be replaced by dialogue and trust. That humanizes public space. It's humanized when we come together to mourn and reaffirm the value of life. It's also humanized, I submit, as we gather to support and celebrate two people declaring their commitment to each other.

CHAPTER 13

Creative Problem Solving

Many times, confronting an ethical problem, we feel stuck. Only a few options come to mind, and none of them are very appealing. Indeed, one of our most immediate associations with the word "moral" seems to be the word "dilemma": moral *dilemmas.* We are supposed to have two and only two choices—or anyway only a few—and often neither choice is much good. We can only pick the "lesser of two evils." But, hey, that's life. Or so we're told.

Is it? In all seriousness: is it? How many alleged "dilemmas" are actually only what logicians call *"false* dilemmas"? How many times, when we seem stuck, do we just need a little more imagination? For one thing, mightn't there be some ready ways of multiplying options: of simply thinking up other possibilities, options we might not have considered?

THE NEED FOR INVENTIVENESS IN ETHICS

The psychologist Lawrence Kohlberg, briefly introduced in chapter 8, conducted his research on moral reasoning by confronting children with a series of moral dilemmas such as this one, famously known as the "Heinz dilemma":

> A woman was near death from cancer. One drug might save her, a form of radium that a druggist in the same town had discovered. The druggist was charging $2000, ten times what the drug cost him to make. The sick woman's husband, Heinz, went to everyone he knew to borrow the money, but he could only get together about half of what it cost. He told the druggist that his wife was dying and asked him to sell it cheaper or let him pay later. But the druggist said "no." The husband got desperate and broke into the man's store to steal the drug for his wife. Should the husband have done that? Why?

It is all too easy to agree with Kohlberg's assumption that Heinz really has but two choices: either to steal the drug or to watch his wife die. But mightn't there be other options too? If we look at such problems with fresh eyes, might we even see possibilities in them that we can barely imagine now—maybe even new ways of approaching ethics itself? How far might a few creative problem-solving skills take us?

I ask my students to re-approach the Heinz dilemma with the problem-solving tools you will pick up in this chapter. Can they imagine any other options for Heinz? Yes they can . . .

Maybe Heinz could offer the druggist something besides money. Maybe he's a good piano tuner, or a skilled gardener, or a chemist himself. Why not trade his skills for the drug?

Or again, is this drug actually scientifically tested? Apparently not yet. In that case, maybe the druggist should pay "Ms. Heinz" for, in effect, volunteering in a drug test.

Why is the druggist so inflexible, anyway? Possibly he needs the money to promote or keep on developing his drug. But in that case Heinz could argue that a spectacular cure would be the best promotion of all. Maybe his wife should get it free! Or Heinz could buy half the drug with the money he can raise, and then—if it works—ask for the rest to complete the demonstration.

Also, Heinz and his wife don't live in a vacuum. What about public aid? Where are their family, friends, community? Think of the appeals you see in hardware stores and community groceries, complete with photos, a town rallying to buy an afflicted kid a bone marrow transplant, another chance at life. Just this summer my little hometown on the Wisconsin prairie raised $35,000 to buy a young man an artificial leg. Two thousand dollars is not exactly a lot of money anymore.

So Heinz—and his wife, and the rest of us too—*do* have a few more options, don't they? And how many other problems might be similar? How will we know, without re-approaching them with some creative skills in our toolbox?

Notice too: many of these suggestions do much more than merely bring forward some dramatic and unexpected practical options for Heinz and his wife—which is already a lot. They also invite us to think very differently about ethics itself. Just asking what Heinz should do overlooks the question of what *we* can do—and sometimes that is a lot more. Suppose our job, in the end, is not so much to judge this alleged dilemma as to figure out how we can help?

A full-scale ethical resolution, for one thing, also challenges us to think about how we can prevent such dilemmas from even coming up in the first place. American health care reform continues to be controversial in the 2010s, but one of its widely-shared premises is that it is morally unacceptable to leave millions of Americans susceptible to such impossible choices. Inevitably it is partly a political question. We need to work out better systems, better policies, more of a safety net. Here too we can and must take some responsibility for making the world a better place—not just judging someone else's (say, Heinz's) response to the world as it is.

CREATIVE EXPLORATIONS

We now begin a survey of specific methods for creative problem solving in ethics. First up are a number of modest types of *exploratory* thinking. Modest, yes—but don't underestimate them on that account. Slowly but surely they can open up unsuspected new ethical possibilities, and meantime they help prepare the ground for the more dramatic methods to come.

GET A FULLER PICTURE

First find out as much as you can about the specific situation that presents itself as an ethical problem.

Suppose someone put this question to you:

Terri Schiavo was on life support for 15 years, diagnosed as in a "persistent vegetative state" by most doctors. Was it ethical to remove her feeding tube and allow her to die?

You should answer, "Isn't there more to the story?" This too-brief sketch gives us no idea of Schiavo's actual situation: how she ended up on life support with such brain damage, what her family situation is, if there is any hope of recovery, and what her own wishes might have been in this situation. It is a bit like the Heinz case and other Kohlberg dilemmas: a short and starkly presented description, stripped down, with details resolutely left out. In fact in the original Kohlberg research, respondents were specifically discouraged from asking for more information, and their moral rankings were downgraded if they persisted. Yet it is precisely in the details that we may find unsuspected possibilities in such problems that on the surface just seem "stuck."

You'll remember that the reading from Spome Jovanovic in chapter 11 offered more detail on this case. Spelling it out further, we begin to get enough detail to get a sense of where there might be room to move.

Terri Schiavo suffered severe brain damage from oxygen deprivation after cardiac arrest, leaving her on life support for 15 years in a condition diagnosed as an irreversible "persistent vegetative state" (PVS) by most doctors. Her husband, Michael, began efforts to remove her feeding tube and let her die, reporting that Terri had said several times that she would not want to be kept alive in such a state. Terri had made no formal declaration of her end-of-life wishes, though, and her parents disputed her husband's report. The diagnosis of PVS was also disputed by her parents and a few doctors, and became the center of court battles and political debates. In the meantime Michael became engaged to another woman, fathering two children with her, but was unable or unwilling to end his marriage to Terri. He also won a large malpractice award, partly to be devoted to continuing to take care of Terri, but soon afterwards seems to have lost all hope for her. Her parents continuously sued to recover custody and declared that they wished to keep Terri alive almost regardless of what her wishes might have been. . .

The added detail makes the case stickier, yes—even gruesome. On the other hand, the very same detail opens up new possibilities that would not even have been on the horizon before. There's the point: we can already get much more creative than we could with just the first bare description.

If Schiavo had been kept alive, for example, various new therapies for PVS or near-PVS conditions might have been tried on her. If she recovered, wonderful, but even if not, testing new therapies might still "serve the cause of life," as some of her defenders were so eager to do. There would have been a better reason to keep her going.

The fuller description brings husband and parents into the picture too, which complicates things but again opens up new angles. My students insist, for instance, that Michael Schiavo needed to be able to move on. Fifteen years wedded to someone who cannot respond to you in any way is enough.

Terri's parents, though, seem to have taken a pretty extreme position too. So maybe what Terri really needed was a freshly appointed, and hopefully somewhat impartial, legal guardian. We have worked out ways of appointing relatively impartial mediators, even in very contentious cases. Why not extend them?

Finally, the fuller description also tells us that the case really turned on lack of clarity about Terri Schiavo's end-of-life wishes. Surely then, we should promote living wills: ways that people can declare their end-of-life wishes while still in full possession of their faculties. Apparently many people did fill out living wills after the Schiavo controversy hit the news—but we'd do well to make it an expected thing. An ounce of prevention . . . well, you know.

WATCH FOR SUGGESTIVE FACTS

Suggestive facts are those that open up whole new ways of approaching a problem. Keep an eye peeled especially for them.

It turns out that air conditioning is necessary in cars partly because roads heat up so much in the summer sun. How unfortunate, we might say! How badly planned! Reframe such little facts as suggestive, however, and you could be off and running. Couldn't we make roads that are less heat-absorbent? Why not use different, less absorbent materials? Paint the roads white to make them more reflective (and more visible at night). Or couldn't we figure out something else to do with the heat besides just letting it radiate back into cars? Install pipes in the roads and pipe through water to warm it up for home heating or wash water? Generate electricity?

A few years ago I looked up the number of deaths caused by guns every year in America. The answer is about thirty thousand. This is a vastly disheartening number, in my view, but I already knew it was something like that. What surprised me was another figure that showed up along the way. Nearly half of these deaths are *suicides*. (Did you know that?)

This one number put the whole debate in a different light for me. True, the old argument is still there: the availability of guns makes impulsive killing easier, whether you kill yourself or someone else. But impulsive suicide is less likely than impulsive homicide: the inhibitions are greater, or maybe it's that we are just less likely to get murderously angry with ourselves.

I'm still leery about guns. But the fact that fifteen thousand people a year deliberately kill themselves with guns surely suggests a need not so much for gun control as for suicide-prevention programs. And since suicide prevention must ultimately mean giving people compelling reasons to live, what it really means is finding ways to make life more exciting and rewarding for everyone. I was led to a very new way of thinking about the whole issue. Notice also that *this* project, unlike the continuing debates about gun control, both works from common ground (chapter 12) and starts from a compelling moral vision (chapter 15).

GET HELP

Other people naturally have different perspectives and different experiences than you do. They can also help bounce ideas around, sparking a new one or making a rough idea better. Seek out friends who are willing to think in an exploratory spirit with you—and be such a friend to others.

Here is a short creative dialogue about the Heinz dilemma.

A: It's funny that we aren't told what "Ms. Heinz" herself wants her husband to do in this dilemma. I wonder what she thinks.

B: I don't—I have enough trouble figuring out what *I* think.

C: She could be quite ready to die. Heinz could be the one grasping for straws, desperate to do something, anything, like stealing the drug.

A: And landing himself in jail, where he's not going to do her much good either. She'd be better off trying to steal it herself!

C: You know, what if "Ms. Heinz" *did* steal the drug? She has less to lose, that's for sure.

B: That's brilliant—jail will do wonders for her health.

A: Actually it just might! Did you know that jails have to provide medical care for inmates? That might just be her ticket to the drug!

This is a brief but productive exchange. We catch sight of several new ideas. And it works for a very specific reason. A and C are consciously exploring, working toward some new possibilities together. Their sentences start with phrases like "I wonder . . ." and "What if . . .?" They bring in new knowledge. They prompt each other's thinking along. Even in this very short exchange we get three or four new ideas and perspectives, ending with a really unique one: that "Ms. Heinz" could deliberately get herself arrested so that she'd have a legal right to the drug. Now there's some real creativity!

But B is a foot dragger. He seems to think that his job is only to judge or to react to the others' ideas, rather than add to them or develop or deepen them or even to offer an alternative. Reactions like B's could derail such a conversation. But notice the spirit in which the others take them here. They keep right on thinking in a more open-ended way, while making a few bows toward B along the way, and even take his last remark in an unintendedly suggestive light. B helped out in spite of himself!

BRAINSTORMING

Though we speak loosely of "brainstorming" for any attempt at creative thinking, the idea has a specific origin. Advertising executive Alex Osborne invented it (in 1939!) as a deliberate process to facilitate creativity in groups. The key rule is to *defer criticism*. Welcome all new ideas without immediately focusing on the likely difficulties and problems. Give new ideas, still barely hatched, enough space to develop and link up with others, to pass around the room, to provoke other ideas in turn.

The other guidelines for formal brainstorming work are:

- *Hitch-hike on others' ideas.* Improve the last idea; or spark off it.

- *Wild ideas are OK.* No taboos; let the creative "juice" flow.

- *State ideas briefly, like telegrams.* This keeps the process flowing. You can always come back to expand the best ideas later.

- *Aim for quantity, not quality.* If you stop to try to develop the first good idea you have, you'll miss even better ideas that may come along after you've really gotten going.

COMPARE AND CONTRAST

Do you know that there are some societies that will not tolerate leaving even a single person homeless? That many countries have both fewer restrictions on alcohol and dramatically fewer drunk-driving deaths? That for certain tribal peoples in North America no decision was settled until the people had heard from the animals?

Even the wildest (to us) arrangements have probably been normal for some group of people somewhere and sometime. Probably even now. Did they learn anything from this? Couldn't we—from them?

Well, of course. We are not the only people to think long and hard about life-and-death decisions, or marriage, or punishment, or justice. All sorts of people have been thinking about ethical problems for a long time. All sorts of answers have been tried.

Another method for creative problem solving in ethics then, is simply to explore some of those other answers: that is, to explore other approaches to the same problems, at other times and places. Find out how quite different people and societies have dealt with these issues. You do not have to agree with them. Nor is it the point to instantly produce workable solutions. The point *is* to free up our thinking: to look at our problems from new directions, once again, to widen our sense of possibility.

You may discover that certain problems that seem utterly stuck to us may not be problems at all for other people or at other times. Abortion, for example, one of America's most divisive and painful, and seemingly fundamental social conflicts over the past thirty years, is barely an issue in many other countries, and historically was not much of an issue even here. (It may feel that the abortion debate has been going on forever, but that is only because most of us aren't that old—and because we haven't really gotten anywhere.) Just by itself this background may not suggest any solutions, of course, but it does give us a sense of possibility and movement. Things aren't necessarily as stuck as they look.

Or take the much-fought-over issue of marriage. In Australia many couples live together in so-called "de facto" marriages: they seem to do about as well as the more official kind. The French have created civil contracts for same-sex couples, with the unexpected result that an even larger number of opposite-sex couples also opted for them. Some conservatives are now promoting a new and stricter kind of marriage themselves. Different arrangements are possible. Instead of struggling over the definition of one kind of marriage, maybe we should, well—diversify?

Comparing and contrasting may take some research. You need to look for contrasting views and approaches: that is, contrasting both to our own and to each other. Find the practical details, too. How do the French civil contracts work? How *do* other countries handle alcohol? How do native peoples manage to listen to the wolves and even the rivers and stones? How can it be that very potent hallucinogens are widely used but not addictive in intact indigenous cultures? Really, *how?* The detail alone is often fascinating; the practical lessons are sometimes vital; and above all we may come back to our own problems with an entirely new set of ideas.

CREATIVE PROVOCATIONS

Creative ethical thinkers also attempt some rather more dramatic kinds of exploration—methods of mental *provocation* as well. These are also, as it happens, the favorites of most creativity experts. Maybe they'll be yours as well.

INVITE EXOTIC ASSOCIATIONS

For better or worse, we are creatures of habit. If we always had to think things through from the beginning, we'd barely be able to get out of bed in the morning. But mental habits can also become mental ruts. We can get so stuck in certain ways of thinking that we barely are aware of them at all—so it's especially hard to realize that there may be entirely new possibilities right next door, so to speak, but invisible to us still. And therefore the task of creative thinking is to wake us up to them—even abruptly, as sometimes it may have to be.

Already in the last section you have been watching for suggestive facts and drawing on your friends for their different experiences and ideas. They can be sources of unfiltered and unfamiliar ideas. By way of a full-scale method, you can now take the same process much further.

Try this: generate a set of prompts or "provocations" in a random way, and then free-associate from there. That is, invite—even force—*exotic associations.*

For such "provocations," your source can literally be anything: a dictionary, an overheard conversation, some images from your house or a book, a mystery, a magazine. If you're using words, it's best to have a source with a varied and rich vocabulary—a good classic writer, maybe—but in a pinch you can even take words or images from billboards along the freeway, or by turning on the car radio for two seconds, as I sometimes do if I am using this method while driving. Or look around the room you are in, right now (or out the window, or try to remember last night's dreams. . .).

The aim is simply to produce as truly different and varied a set of new ideas as you can. Now you really have a new, unfiltered stimulus for your thinking—from outside whatever "box" you are currently in. Right away something fresh. Then put it together with the problem you are thinking about. Don't censor, edit, judge. Give each association, however crazy it may seem, some time. What new possibilities, what new ways of thinking, might it suggest?

Take the problem of litter—of thrown-out cans and bottles for instance. We're used to hearing all about our responsibility to use trash cans, to recycle. Well, it's true, we should. But is that it? Nothing more to say? Could we think further and more creatively about this problem that is so familiar it's boring?

Let us try some exotic associations. Looking around, just past my desk, I see my houseplants. Alright then: could the image of a houseplant (that's random, eh?) suggest some new associations, different ways of thinking about discarded cans and bottles?

Now I free-associate . . . hmm . . . Well, houseplants do make the room more beautiful. So maybe . . . we could start making cans and bottles that are the same? Art made with "junk" can be wonderful; but we could imagine something more systematic, like juice containers made of different-colored plastic that can be joined Lego-style into kids' play structures, or (who knows?) stained-glass windows. Paper wrappers that could be used for origami?

Plants are also food—one way or another nearly everything we eat comes from plants. Well then: what if we associate edibility with can and bottle litter? Any usable ideas there?

How about . . . um, edible cans and bottles?

It sounds crazy at first—new ideas quite likely will. Some of them no doubt *are* crazy. But this one has some promise. Picture it: you could eat your food, then eat the wrapper to top it off. Drink your coffee and then down the cup too. Actually, we do this very thing already with some foods: think of tacos, or pita-wraps, or, for heaven's sake, ice cream cones. So edible food "wraps" are not even that unfamiliar. Couldn't we extend the idea?

Maybe there's something to this exotic-association method after all?

Plants . . . gardens? Bottles and cans in the garden . . . ? This may provoke yet another idea: bottles and cans as *fertilizer*? At least we could make cans and bottles so that they biodegrade really fast, couldn't we?

Keep going. . . . Suppose we add some fertilizer and grass seeds, or wildflower seeds or something, and then, rather than discouraging "litter," encourage it instead. Don't stick those cans and bottles in the boring old bins; just throw them onto some bare ground, thank you. Or into your garden. Cans of tomato juice could have tomato seeds in them, apple juice bottles could contain apple seeds. . . .

We could go further with this, but you see the point. Even with a couple of seemingly unpromising associations, we are now thinking *way* out of the box about the litter issue. No more guilt-tripping about recycling—just eat the stuff. There's creativity for you!

NO FILTERS

How to pick useful provocations? The key point is, you can't select them in advance according to your hunches about what would be most relevant or

helpful. That is exactly what you are trying to *find out* in the first place. No—
just try some different prompts and see what comes of them.

A good rule is: stick with any prompt, no matter how unpromising it
seems, for at least three minutes (and use a timer: three minutes may be
longer than you think). You won't know what you can get from it until you
try.

Trust the process. Don't try to edit or filter or prejudge it—just give yourself over to it. Free-associating on the Heinz dilemma, for instance, I turned
to the dictionary for random words, and the first word I found was "oboe."
"Oboe?" I said to myself. "You've got to be kidding!" Then I thought, well,
an oboe is a musical instrument; an oboe-like instrument is used to charm
cobras in India; maybe Heinz could somehow charm the druggist?

How? Well, I'm not sure, but it seems worthwhile for Heinz at least to
talk to the druggist some more. We shouldn't assume the druggist is a completely boxed-in automaton, any more than Heinz is, or you or me.

Or again: people play oboes—it is a skill—people have skills—Heinz has
skills . . . From here it might occur to us that Heinz could barter other things
besides money for the drug.

The next word I found was "leaf." Leaf: "Turn over a new leaf"? "Read
leaves"? (Hmm—foretelling the future, as people used to do with tea leaves?
How do we know that this drug is any good . . .?) Use leaves instead of drugs?
(Are there herbal remedies . . .?)

If you absolutely must shape your prompts, seek out the wildest ones
you can find. Oboes, leaves, OK, but what about *really* wild provocations, like
going to the Moon, or lassoing a dinosaur, or the year 5000 CE. Skydiving?
The circus? (Try them.)

ᴚƎɅƎᴚƧⱯ⅃Ƨ AND EXAGGERATIONS

Another way to provoke your thinking out of the usual boxes is to deliberately
reverse certain features of the problem. Take for example the issue of animal
dissection in schools: should students with objections be excused from animal dissection? Should animals be used in this way in the first place? Now
think of the elements of this possibly problematic situation: students, curriculum, teachers, the specimen animal, and so on. Perhaps these could be
interestingly switched around. What if . . . I don't know . . . maybe students
dissect the teacher? Come to think of it (which is really what we're doing,
isn't it—helping ourselves to come to think of new things?), what if the specimen animal dissects *you?*

The moralist in you may be shocked, and you may want to quickly disavow
any morally questionable or otherwise gross sorts of options. But again, don't.
Obviously we are not going to actually dissect a teacher or ourselves—but
couldn't this thought, taken as a provocation, open up some other interesting
ideas, just around the corner?

One interesting new question is: how much can we learn from looking carefully at our own or one anothers' bodies—maybe about blood flow, or muscles and leverage? Think of how exercise machines are designed to isolate muscle groups. Truly, we could learn anatomy by paying attention to our own living bodies. And notice: studying our own bodies, live, would mean that we wouldn't need to use animals at all. Or we could study animals themselves *live,* rather than dead. Now there's a practical and fresh idea!

Yet another way to go to extremes is to *exaggerate* some aspect of the problem before you. Take some feature of it and make it as extreme, as overdone as you can. Then stand back and see what new ideas or perspectives it might provoke.

How do you exaggerate dissection? What I visualize is somehow literally going inside the animal. Not merely by methodically disassembling its remains with a knife in a lab but actually jumping inside its body.

Wild, eh? Impossible, of course. But hold on . . . couldn't we once again move from this "crazy" idea to something more workable? How about computer simulation? In fact, doesn't the computer open up all sorts of nifty possibilities, like shrinking yourself down to the size of a cell and touring a living body through the veins (or lymphatic system, or bile ducts, or . . .) or tracking changes in the body over time or in different activities (sleep, exercise, sex, alarm . . .)?

Along these lines, here's my suggestive fact for the day: already in use are jellybean-sized "camera pills" that can pass through the stomach and intestines scanning for tumors or infections. Next up are even smaller and remote-controlled versions that can also collect cell samples and administer medication. Soon enough we should be able to send them through the blood as well.

So really, in the long run, we might not even need computer simulations: we can tour our own bodies *in fact.* We need only expand the use of "camera pills" from diagnosis into the schools. We can explore our very own bodies as living laboratories. Students can explore one another's stomachs, bad knees, you name it, from the inside. Kids will love this! And who would need dissection then?

THE "INTERMEDIATE IMPOSSIBLE"

Finally, here is my own favorite method: what the problem-solving guru Edward DeBono calls the "intermediate impossible." Imagine what would be an *ideal* solution to your problem. Then, once you've imagined such an outcome, however "unrealistic" it might be (or seem), you can work your way back to a more realistic idea. In short, make your very first imaginative step a really big one. It's easier to tone it down later than to ramp up a timid little half-step idea into something bigger.

Take, for example, the question of assisted suicide. Usually we just ask: should it be legalized or not? Neither way is very "ideal." But now try the intermediate impossible. What would be a *radically better* solution to the underlying problem? Immortality wouldn't hurt, of course. Apart from that, though, a radically better solution might be for people to be able to choose death in some way that is not so secretive, passive, and (at least in some people's eyes) shameful. So one "perfect" solution might be a *heroic* death, like carrying out some sort of "suicide mission"—in space, underseas, in places where those who want to survive can't go—or (more likely) volunteering to test a new drug or medical procedure. Not that this could be made a requirement: but the idea does, immediately, give us something dramatic and new to work with. Ideas begin to flow.

Once you practice the intermediate impossible, you will quickly discover that in many cases we do not really know what a "perfect" solution to our problem would be. We complain a great deal, we believe things are bad, yet often we have not really begun to imagine—to consider carefully—what we want instead. Maybe when we actually arrive at an idea of what we want, we'll discover that it is not so different from what "the other side" wants. Or not so different from what we've got already.

Do we really want to say, for example, that no one should ever want to die—that no one *could* ever want to die so much that they should be helped to do so? Is that really the "ideal" answer? Contrariwise, if we agree that some people could justly choose death, then what counts as an "ideal" death? These are not easy questions, and it is natural to wonder whether we are so confused about assisted suicide in general partly because we are so confused about them.

"WHAT IF . . .?" ETHICAL THINKING

Creative thinking can provoke us to stretch and rearrange ideas and even values in search of new perspectives and possibilities. It may not only open up new practical options but also give our ethical thinking itself more depth and resiliency. Ultimately our moral views may be stronger for having really considered them from a wide range of different points of view and "what ifs." Besides, who knows, sometimes we may even change our minds!

Take the question of meat-eating. Vegetarians question whether we should eat meat at all. By way of self-provocation, perhaps we could *exaggerate* in the other direction.

What if . . . we eat nothing but meat?

Some native peoples do: traditional Inuit, for example (Eskimo), who live so far north that nothing really grows. Fish, seals, and whales form their entire diet. What shall we say of them? Should they move? But moving would destroy their culture—other values would suffer more. Importing non-meat foods would also damage the culture, making them economically dependent. It may be better to conclude that for them, at least, eating meat is acceptable. They have no real alternatives.

The other side of this thought, though, is that meat may be much more questionable when there *are* alternatives. And almost all of the rest of us do have alternatives. So perhaps "ethical eating" is different depending on where one lives?

Reversal? Meat as we know it comes from animals. So

What if . . . meat does not come from animals?

At first the idea seems crazy. But keep thinking. . . . Scientists can now take a single cell from an animal body and create tissue cultures—test tubes of animal tissue, but without bodies or brains—on which to test drugs. Might they do the same for meat—that is, to grow animal muscle tissue without body or brain? It would be a way of having meat without animals, and therefore without animal suffering. And apparently it is technically possible *now*.

This may or may not be a good idea. (If it strikes you as ghoulish, a good question would be, why does it *not* strike you as ghoulish to eat the flesh of an actual animal?) In any case, the point is, it's an idea. We're out of the box now for sure!

Another reversal. Here some "normal" feature of a situation is turned exactly on its head. We eat animals, so . . .

What if . . . animals eat us?

A few animals do eat us—or would if they could. It seems to strike some people as "only fair" that therefore we eat them. The problem is that the animals who eat us are not the animals we eat, like cows and chickens, who tend to be friendly and who in nature mostly eat plants or insects. We don't even favor animals who typically eat other animals (except for fish). So maybe it is acceptable to eat animals, but not the ones we currently eat? Crocodile, anyone? Vulture?

Or maybe the idea is that if we are to eat animals, we need to allow ourselves to be eaten in return in some way? After death, many of the Plains Indians tribes put out corpses in special places where the wolves and the vultures would pick the bones clean. Is that the idea—some appropriate ceremonial return of our own flesh to the flesh of the living world? How might we do something of the sort now?

Vegetarians sometimes complain that the lives and deaths of the animals we eat are normally completely out of view. Children often are shocked to discover what meat actually is when they finally put two and two together. So . . .

> *What if . . . the lives and deaths of the animals we eat were completely* in *view?*

That is, what if the "facts of meat" were not hidden? What if we did not try to disguise the costs to animals with cute ads about fish leaping into tuna cans and chickens living it up in factory farms? Perhaps people might even be expected to kill some of the animals they themselves eat. This is not impossible: hunters, for example, do it all the time. But it does change the picture. It makes us think about meat eating in another way—and that, once again, is the point.

QUICK REFERENCE: CREATIVE PROBLEM SOLVING IN ETHICS

In dealing with any ethical problem or issue, use creative methods to widen the range of options you consider and to deepen your sense of the issue and the values involved.

- Get a fuller picture. Find out as much as you can about the specific situation; look to the details to suggest new ideas.
- Watch for suggestive facts.
- Get help. Find people to brainstorm difficult issues with you.
- Compare and contrast. Explore how the same problem is treated in other places and times.
- Invite exotic associations. Seek unfiltered "provocations" in random words, analogies, or images; free-associate from there.
- Reverse or exaggerate key features of the problem.
- The intermediate impossible: start with "ideal" solutions and work toward realism.

FOR REVIEW

1. What are some creative options in the Heinz dilemma?
2. What is the point of seeking a fuller picture of an ethical problem? Who needs more details?
3. What is an example of a "suggestive fact"?
4. What is the key rule for brainstorming? Why?
5. "Compare and contrast"—what could be creative about that?
6. How can you "invite exotic associations"?
7. Illustrate "reversal."
8. Illustrate "exaggeration."
9. Illustrate the "intermediate impossible."
10. Illustrate "what if?" moral thinking.

EXERCISES AND NOTES

13.1 PROBLEM-SOLVING WARM-UPS

The methods introduced here are useful across the board, not just in ethics. Though the aim is to use them in ethics, you might begin by practicing more broadly. Try some "novel function practice," for example. Most of us have been asked, in some game or quiz book, how many new and different uses we can think of for some everyday object, like a brick. What can you do with a brick, besides build houses? Well, a brick can be a paperweight or a doorstop. You can make bookcases out of bricks and wood. Are there more creative uses? Suppose you tape on a return-postage-guaranteed junk mail reply form and drop it in a mailbox—a good way to protest junk mail. Suppose you leave it in your yard until you want to go fishing, and then lift it up to collect the worms underneath. (This suggestion is courtesy of one of my students. Brick as "worm-generator," he called it.)

So find some other everyday object and practice. What can you do with a . . . cheap ballpoint pen (besides write)? . . . a piece of paper? . . . a rotten apple? . . . a bad joke? Can you think of ten ways (or if that's easy, twenty) to get water out of a glass without moving the glass or damaging it? (Evaporate it? Soak paper towels or sponges in the water? Suck it out with a straw? And where do you get a straw, right now? How about the casing of that cheap ballpoint pen?) Or: suppose an elephant (or python, or pack of cats, or . . .) has escaped in your neighborhood. Figure out five (or ten, or . . .) ways it can be recaptured.

Now pick some specific practical problems in your experience—you could start with your school or region—and challenge yourself to add to (let's say, double or triple) the number of options usually considered (if any). Don't evaluate them yet—just aim to diversify options. Here are some sample problems to get you started.

- Waste (styrofoam cups, lights left on all the time, recyclables in the trash, overuse of paper . . .)
- Too much television
- Bad cell-phone etiquette (loud public conversations as if no one else were present)
- Sports teams that have to travel increasingly long distances to find suitable competition
- Parent-teen relations (they don't have to be so conflicted, surely—and they aren't, in some families and some other cultures: what could we do differently, better?)
- "Empty nest syndrome" (you eighteen-year-old college students may not be thinking about it, but I bet your parents are)
- Lack of affordable child care for working families with young children
- Lack of inexpensive travel options (for college students, and for everyone)
- Poor diets (predictably leading to health problems, missed work . . . and unhappiness in general)
- Rising waters and changed rainfall patterns (usually toward more intense, if fewer, storms) due to climate change. Think of cities on the edge of seas and rivers—New Orleans is only one of the more visible. What is to be done?

13.2 CREATIVE PROBLEM SOLVING IN ETHICS

Now consider more familiar moral issues, and treat them exactly the same way. Use the option-multiplying methods just as you did with the practical problems in the last exercise. Again, don't evaluate them yet—just aim to diversify options. Challenge yourself to double or triple the number of options usually considered. Here are some possible issues.

- Irresponsible driving: for example, speeding, poor attention, uninsured or underinsured driving, poor car maintenance, and so on. In handling a car we have immense potential to harm or take others' lives. How can we take this responsibility more seriously?

- Marriage. With a 40%+ divorce rate, marriage is not working very well in general. There are plenty of issues besides the gender of the participants (if that is a problem at all), such as lack of relationship skills, lack of supportive extended families or communities, many people's resistance to asking for help or counseling, economic and other stressors, including the need to care for aged parents, etc.

- Plagiarism: presenting someone else's work (especially writing) as if it were your own. Colleges and universities are increasingly aware of this issue— just as the Internet makes it much easier to do. How else can this issue be approached besides more suspicion and stricter punishments?

- Gun control. Surely there are a few options besides "yes" and "no." (Even the degree of gun control we have now is more complex than that.) What might you think up? Get some data here, for example on gun use in other countries as well as how guns are or aren't legally regulated elsewhere. What can we learn from other countries' practices—either to copy, or avoid, or adapt?

- Drug abuse. We say that drugs offer an escape from school, or work, or just life itself. But this leads to other questions. Why do so many people need such an escape in the first place? And what can we do about school, or work, or life itself so that such an escape is less tempting?

- Medical testing on animals. There's no other way to test drugs? Really? And do we need them—all of them, that much—anyway?

- Sweatshops. We know that our clothes and other consumer goods are sometimes made by unjustly exploited workers in other, desperate parts of the world (and sometimes right here at home)—though often we don't wish to know (or can't find out) more details. What can be done to respond to this problem?

- What might the elderly do with their time? Could society be restructured to respond better to their needs? What new kinds of places could they find? How about a system of adoptive grandparents, as some of my students have suggested? And what other opportunities might aging represent?

- We have a minimum wage—currently $7.25 per hour by federal law, higher in a few states. Some economists argue that this is a bad thing. If there are people who might wish to work for less, and employers who might hire them, is it right to prohibit this voluntary transaction (which to some degree happens anyway)? Others deny that any such transaction is truly "voluntary": people are desperate and are being exploited without the benefit of social protection. Can you think of any other approaches to this issue? While you're at it, consider that there are also people who get paid tens of thousands of dollars per hour, if you break their salary and bonus packages out down to an hourly rate. Is there a moral case for a *maximum* wage as well? Or—again—can you think of other and better approaches to this whole issue?

- Some standard objections to welfare programs are fairly specific and not so hard to fix once you seriously try to think creatively. For example, many people are offended because they think food stamps can be used to buy morally disapproved items like cigarettes and alcohol (which is not true, exactly—but they can be used to buy other things and therefore free up a little cash for such things). Supposing that this is a widespread problem (Is it? Find out from reputable sources), is it so hard to resolve?

- What happens when personal ethics conflict with organizational practices: say, in business or the military or government? How could such conflicts be handled better? Are there new and creative ways to deal with the problem of "whistle-blowing"—and the kinds of problems that lead to the need for whistle-blowing in the first place?

- Rich countries try to help less well-off countries when natural disasters strike (earthquakes, hurricanes, etc.). What about also helping to overcome the underlying causes of poverty itself? Meanwhile, aren't there some ways in which *we* need *their* help? What would a system of truly *mutual* aid look like?

- We are consuming food, energy, and other natural resources at unsustainable rates, and what kind of world we will pass on to our descendants is becoming increasingly uncertain as a result. What to do?

13.3 ANOTHER FAMOUS DILEMMA

This chapter began with the Heinz dilemma, a case that philosophers have found so difficult that it became a classic example of an ethical dilemma. Here is another—we could probably even say *the* other—famous modern moral dilemma. The French philosopher Jean-Paul Sartre described a young man in occupied Paris during World War II who came to him for advice.

> His father was on bad terms with his mother, and, moreover, was inclined to be a collaborationist [that is, he cooperated with the Nazis]; his older brother had been killed in the German offensive of 1940, and the young man, with somewhat immature but generous feelings, wanted to avenge him. His mother lived alone with him, very much upset by the half-treason of her husband and the death of her elder son; the boy was her only consolation.
>
> The boy was faced with the choice of leaving for England and joining the Free French forces—that is, leaving his mother behind—or remaining with his mother and helping her to carry on. He was fully aware that the woman lived only for him and that his going off—and perhaps his death—would plunge her into despair. He was also aware that every act that he did for his mother's sake was a sure thing, in the sense that it was helping her to carry on, whereas every effort he made toward going off and fighting was an uncertain move which might run aground and prove completely useless. . . . He was faced with two very different kinds of action: one concrete, immediate,

but concerning only one individual; the other concerned an incomparably vaster group, a national collectivity, but for that very reason was dubious, and might be interrupted en route.

Imagine that this young man came to you for some help in this situation. Do you see any options for him? Take your time, and use the methods in this chapter.

NOTES

"False dilemma" is a classic fallacy in informal logic that is usefully discussed and illustrated in many informal logic textbooks, such as Howard Kahane's *Logic and Contemporary Rhetoric* (Wadsworth Publishing Company, many editions). Moral philosophers who might want a bit more about my treatment of the Heinz dilemma as a false dilemma should consult appendix 1 at the end of this book.

There is a huge literature on creative problem solving, but most of it addresses non-moral issues and contexts, such as management and design. For a range of approaches to problem solving broadly conceived, see Edward DeBono, *Serious Creativity* (HarperCollins, 1992) and *Lateral Thinking* (Harper, 1970); Barry Nalebuff and Ian Ayres, *Why Not? How to Use Everyday Ingenuity to Solve Problems Big and Small* (Harvard Business School Press, 2003); Charlie and Maria Girsch, *Inventivity* (Creativity Central, 1999); and Marvin Levine, *Effective Problem-Solving* (Prentice-Hall, 2nd edition, 1993). On proactive thinking, Stephen Covey's *The Seven Habits of Highly Effective People* (Simon and Schuster, 1990) is classic. Two books of my own specifically on the subject are *Creative Problem-Solving in Ethics* (Oxford, 2006), which mostly covers the same ground as this and the next chapter, and its sister, *Creativity for Critical Thinkers* (also Oxford, 2006), which you might find a helpful complement.

For an introduction to "What if . . .?" thinking (DeBono calls it PO thinking, for POssible or hyPOthesis) and the specific methods outlined here, see his *Serious Creativity* (HarperCollins, 1992), especially pp. 163–176. On the origins of brainstorming, see Alex Osborne's *Applied Imagination: Principles and Procedures of Creative Problem-Solving* (Creative Education Foundation, 1993).

Another useful way of organizing (and remembering) the creative-thinking methods introduced here, as well as some others, is the SCAMPER mnemonic: see http://people.bethel.edu/~shenkel/PhysicalActivities/CreativeMovement/CreativeThinking/Scamper.html.

The extended description of the Schiavo case is based on the account at http://en.wikipedia.org/wiki/Terri_Schiavo_case, accessed 10/5/12. One of the great strengths of Wikipedia is the extended and open discussion of the evidence in contentious cases such as this (for a sample, go to the "Talk" page and then to "Archives"). I have learned from it myself since the first edition of this book.

Jean-Paul Sartre is cited from his *Existentialism and Human Emotions* (Philosophical Library, 1957), pp. 24–25.

CHAPTER 14

Reframing Problems

We come next to a set of creative strategies that work at a deeper level. It's one thing to solve a problem more or less in the terms in which it is presented. A wider-ranging kind of creativity invites us to rethink and possibly to transform the problem itself in fundamental ways.

OPENING UP A PROBLEM

Just back from study in Bolivia, a student told me one day that the practice among the young Bolivian males he knew was to go to a prostitute for their sexual initiation. He was disturbed by this, and since he knew that I write ethics books, he wanted my opinion.

I suppose he expected moral outrage. And I'm sure that moral outrage is appropriate, especially from the point of view of a society struggling to value women as full partners and equals. The problem, once again, is that the insistence on making such judgments pretty much closes down the discussion. Nothing else is explored; we think we've said everything that needs to be said.

In fact we'd only begun. My student and I ended up in a long conversation. It turned out that when he had expressed his surprise and confusion to his Bolivian friends, they became curious about how sexual initiation works in America. Do *we* have a better way? My student was not at all sure. How do we teach young people about sex, anyway? Locker-room conversations? Movies? Pornography? How ethical is that?

Notice how the question shifts here. We don't have much say over Bolivian men, but we can make a difference to what we ourselves do. So how might *we* do better? Seriously: this is a real question. Never mind the Bolivians—right here at home is where we might be able to make some creative moral progress. That is a complex question, an ongoing struggle, a much more open but also vital question.

ATTENTION SHIFTS

Ethical problems can be pressing and painful. They may compel our full attention. Often some kind of crisis brings them to us. But crisis management is not the only mode in which we can or should engage them. At some point we also need to step back far enough to be able to ask how we got into this crisis in the first place, and what can be done about *that*. We can begin to *reframe problems.*

We debate whether doctors should be able or obliged to help people die. But how did doctors—and now increasingly hospitals and their lawyers—get in this position of power? Is this arrangement a good idea? What might some better alternatives look like?

Likewise, the Heinz dilemma poses a compelling question that seems to require a yes-or-no, one-or-the-other sort of answer—while all around and before and beside it are a number of other, more intriguing and also more unsettling questions to ask, and other directions our thinking might go. Answering "the" original question is important, for sure, but that's only a beginning. Oughtn't we be asking about the design of the whole health care payment system as well? Why does the sick woman have no insurance? Why can't public assistance help her? If either insurance or public assistance were real options, Heinz's dilemma would not even come up.

And what are the causes of this illness, anyway? The American Cancer Society estimates that 80 percent of all cancers are environmentally caused. So perhaps we have here a workplace issue or a diet issue, or polluted air or water? How could we leave all of this alone, as if the whole problem were just Heinz's, or rather his wife's?

Indeed this may be the best response of all to the original Heinz problem: that there is *no* good solution to the problem as it stands—and therefore the best thing we can do is to try to prevent such dilemmas from even coming up at all. The best strategy is to "look upstream," to head it off next time, or to try to transform it into something more easily manageable. These in turn may well require structural change, rethinking and trying to reconstruct and indeed reframe larger social arrangements: insurance, public provision, how medicine itself is organized, workplace safety or environmental protection. No simple answers—but good work to do.

It is true that large families of moral values also seem to come into conflict here. This is why the Heinz dilemma is widely used by moral theorists to illustrate the difference between a consequence-oriented moral theory like utilitarianism, which might support stealing the drug, and a theory of personal rights, which is often supposed to favor the druggist. But this needn't be the end of the matter either. If we care so deeply about both consequences and rights, oughtn't we try to redesign our institutions *in general* so that these two families of values conflict less often or less viciously? How hard would that be? Reconciling rights and utility is arguably one of the aims of modern systems of public provision. So perhaps it is time to begin to work out new ways as well....

READING

"Strategic Questioning"

FRAN PEAVEY

> **"FRAN PEAVEY** is an inventive, resolute and funny woman whose life is an adventure in progressive social change," reads the first line of Fran's biography on the back of her third book, from which this excerpt is taken. She worked to clean up the Ganges, did stand-up comedy on nuclear weapons as a member of the Atomic Comics, and developed Strategic Questioning as a major part of the social change work she did in the world.

Strategic questioning is the skill of asking the questions that will make a difference.* It is a powerful and exciting tool for social and personal change. I have found it a significant service to any issue because it helps local strategies for change emerge.

Strategic questioning involves a special type of question and a special type of listening. Anyone can use strategic questions in their work and in their personal lives to liberate friends, coworkers, and political allies and adversaries to create a path for change.

Strategic questioning is a process that may change the listener as well as the person being questioned. When we open ourselves to another point of view, our own ideas will have to shift to take into account new information, new possibilities, and new strategies for resolving problems.

What would our world be like if every time we were listening to a gripe session, someone would ask, "I wonder what we can do to change that situation?" then listened carefully for the answers to emerge, and then helped that group to begin to work for change? What would it be like for you to do that in your work,

---

* I didn't invent the words "strategic questioning," although I thought I did. I had been using the term for four years when a few years ago, while doing some research, I came upon a small book about teaching called *Strategic Questioning* written by Ronald T. Hyman, a close friend of a college professor of mine. So I must have heard the words twenty-five years ago and the word seeds got planted way back there in my mind; then when I needed them they came blossoming up. Thank you, Ronald T. Hyman.

From Fran Peavey, *By Life's Grace* (New Society Publishers, 1993), pp. 87–93.

family, or social context? Your attention and context might shift from a passive to an active one. You could become a creator, rather than a receiver, of solutions. This shift in perspective is one of the key things that people need in our world just now. And the skill of asking strategic questions is a powerful contribution to making such a shift.

Were you ever taught how to ask questions? Were you ever encouraged to ask questions where the answers are not already known? Have you ever been taught about asking questions that will really make a difference? Most of us who were brought up in traditional families or in a traditional education system were not. Traditional schooling was based on asking questions to which the answers were already known: How many wives did Henry VIII have? What color is that car? What is four times five? We learned that questions have finite and "correct" answers, and that there is usually one answer for each question. The wrong answer is punished with a bad grade. The landscape of learning was divided into "right" and "wrong."

This may be a convenient way of running schools and testing people's capacity for memory in examinations but it has not been a very empowering learning process for students, or a good preparation for the questions that come up in life.

Shaping a strategic question involves seven key features:

1. A STRATEGIC QUESTION CREATES MOTION

Most of the traditional questions that we've been taught to ask are static. Strategic questions ask, How can we move? They create movement. They are dynamic rather than allowing a situation to stay stuck.

Often the way a conversation is structured creates resistance to movement. The martial art t'ai chi teaches a lot of wisdom about meeting resistance. It says that when you meet an obstacle, you only make it more firm by pushing directly on it. If you meet an object coming at you with resistance, it is not very useful at all. T'ai chi says that if you meet and move with the energy of the obstacle coming at you, taking the energy from the other, then motion in a new direction emerges. Both parties end up in a different place than where they started, and the relationship between them is changed.

This same shift in a new direction happens when you ask a strategic question. As an example, suppose Sally is working on where she will live, and perhaps she has heard of some good real estate bargains in Sydney, and she's a bit stuck on what she should do next. I could say to her, "Why don't you just move to Sydney?" This question might be provocative, but is not very helpful. Really it's a suggestion pretending to be a question. For my own reasons I think she should move to Sydney. Perhaps I am projecting into the question my own wish to move to Sydney. Whatever my reasons I'm leading her because I am asking a manipulative question, and it is likely that the more I pressure Sally, the less likely she is to consider the Sydney option.

A more strategic question would be to ask Sally, "What type of place would you like to move to?" or "What places come to mind when you think of living happily?" or "What is the meaning of this move in your life?" Sally is then encouraged to talk about the qualities she wants from her new home, to set new goals. You can then work with her to achieve these goals.

Asking questions that are *dynamic* can help people explore how they can move on an issue. On my first working trip to India with the Friends of the Ganges project, I asked the local people, "What would you like to do to help clean up the river?" Now, you might ask, "How did I know they wanted to clean up the river?" Well, I wanted to ask a question that assumed motion on this issue. I assumed that people are always wanting to do more appropriate behavior. I further assumed that they wanted to move from their state of powerlessness regarding what to do about the pollution in the Ganges. Many interesting ideas emerged when I used that question—some of which we have implemented.

When we are stuck on a problem, what keeps us from acting for change is either a lack of information, or that we have been wounded in our sense of personal power on an issue, or that no system is in place that enables us to move the issue forward. In our stuckness, we don't see how to make the motion. When I ask a question like, "What would you like to do to help clean up the river?" I open up a door for the local people to move beyond their grief, guilt, and powerlessness about the pollution to active dreaming and creating of their own contributions.

2. A STRATEGIC QUESTION CREATES OPTIONS

If I asked Sally, "Why don't you move to Sydney?" I have asked a question that is dynamic only in one direction (Sydney). It very much limits the options she is challenged to think about. A more powerful strategic question opens the options up. "Where would you like to live?" or "What are the three or four places that you feel connected to?" These are much more helpful questions to ask her at this time. Sally might have been so busy thinking about the real estate bargains in Sydney that she has lost a sense of all the other possibilities and her real goals.

A strategic questioner would help Sally look at the many options equally. Supposing Sally says she could move to Byron Bay or Sydney. It's not up to me to say to myself, "I think Sydney is the best, and I should encourage her down that path." If you're being ethical about it, then you could best help Sally sort out her own direction by questioning all the options evenhandedly, with the same enthusiasm and interest in discussing both Sydney and Byron Bay. Not only that, but you could help by asking if any more options occur to her during the questioning time (Twin Falls, Idaho...or New Plymouth, New Zealand). Out of these questions, a new option may emerge.

It is particularly important for a strategic questioner not to focus on only two options. We are so accustomed to binary thinking, whether it's either Sydney or Byron Bay...that Brisbane cannot emerge as a viable alternative. Usually when someone is only considering two options, they simply have not done the creative thinking to look at all the possibilities. People are usually comfortable when they have two options and think they can make a choice at that level. This "choice" is part of the delusion of control. And since two alternatives are already more complex than one, people stop thinking. Though the world is far more complex and exciting than any two options would indicate, having two options creates the idea that a choice, however limited, is being made.

I have a friend whose daughter got into some trouble and ran away. My friend was fortunate in that she knew which train her daughter was probably leaving on in a few hours' time. She was trying to decide whether to just let the daughter get on the train and run away, or to go to the train and insist that she come home. I talked it over with her, and we worked on these options for a while, and then I asked, "What else could you do to help your daughter with her conflicts?" She thought and then a new idea came up. She could run away *with* her daughter, and take the twelve hours on the train to help her sort things out. Now, because my friend was scared and afraid for her daughter, she had been unable to think of this fine option until the door was opened through the question. It was the kind of option that she might have thought of when all her anxious feelings had subsided.

3. A STRATEGIC QUESTION DIGS DEEPER

Questions can be like a lever you use to pry open the stuck lid on a paint can. And there are long-lever questions and short-lever questions. If I have just a short lever, we can only just crack open that lid on the can. But if we have a longer lever, or a more dynamic question, we can open that can up much wider and really stir things up.

Some people approach problems with their heads just like a closed paint can. If the right question is applied, and it digs deep enough, then we can stir up all the creative solutions to that problem. We can chip away a lot of the crusty sediment that is trapping the lid on that person's head. A question can be a stirrer. It can lead to synthesis, motion, and energy.

4. A STRATEGIC QUESTION AVOIDS "WHY"

When I asked Sally, "Why don't you move to Sydney?" it was a question that focused on why she doesn't do it, rather than creating a more active and forward motion on the issue. Most "why" questions are like that. They force you to defend an existing decision or rationalize the present. "Why" questions also have the effect of creating resistance to change.

The openness of a particular question is obvious at the gross extremes, but becomes far more subtle and subjective as you deepen your understanding of the skills of strategic questioning. For example, can you feel the difference between asking, "Why don't you work on poverty?" and, "What keeps you from working on poverty?" Sometimes a "Why" question is very powerful as you focus on values, and meaning. But in general it is a short-lever question.

5. A STRATEGIC QUESTION AVOIDS "YES OR NO" ANSWERS

Again, these type of questions ("Have you considered...") don't really encourage people to dig deeper into their issues. A question answered with a "yes" or "no" reply almost always leaves the person being asked in an uncreative and passive state. A strategic questioner rephrases their queries to avoid the dead end of a "yes" or "no" reply. It can make a huge difference to the communication taking place.

I heard of a student who was very intrigued by the ideas behind strategic questioning. He realized that he hardly ever spoke a question to his wife without getting simply a "yes" or "no" in reply. A week after the class on strategic questioning, he reported that the technique had completely changed his home life! He had gone home and told his wife about these special types of questions, and they agreed to avoid asking a question that had a "yes" or "no" answer for a week. He reported they had never talked so much in their lives!

6. A STRATEGIC QUESTION IS EMPOWERING

A strategic question creates the confidence that motion can actually happen, and this is certainly empowering. When I asked people in India, "What would you like to do to clean your river?" it assumes that they have a part in that picture of healing. It even expresses a confidence in the person being questioned that they have a contribution to designing the cleaning-up process.

One of my favorite questions is, "What would it take for you to change on this issue?" This question lets the other person create the path for change. Imagine an environmental protester going to a lumber mill owner and asking, "What would it take for you to stop cutting down the old-growth trees?" This question is an invitation to the mill owner to cocreate options for the future of his business *with* the community. The owner might tell the questioner the obstacles he faces in making changes to his business, and maybe they can work together to satisfy some of their mutual needs so that the old-growth trees can be preserved. The planning that comes out of asking such a strategic question may not exactly resemble what either party wanted in the beginning, but a new reality is born out of the dialogue and could well work to achieve both the protester's and the mill owner's goals.

Empowerment is the opposite of manipulation. When you use strategic questioning, rather than putting ideas into a person's head, you are actually allowing that person to take what's already in their head and work with it.

7. A STRATEGIC QUESTION ASKS THE UNASKABLE QUESTIONS

For every individual, group, or society, some questions are taboo. And because those questions are taboo they wield tremendous power. A strategic question is often one of these "unaskable" questions. And it usually is unaskable because it challenges the values and assumptions that the whole issue rests upon.

I like the fairy tale about the emperor who walked in a parade without any clothes on because he had been tricked by some unscrupulous weavers into thinking he was wearing a magnificent costume. It was a child that asked the unaskable question, "Why doesn't the emperor have any clothes on?" If that child had been a political activist, she might have asked other unaskable questions, such as, "Why do we need an emperor?" or "How can we get a wiser government?"

In the early 1980s, one of the unaskable questions for me was, "What shall we do if a nuclear bomb is dropped?" You couldn't answer that without facing our overwhelming capacity for destruction, and the senselessness of it. That question allowed many of us to move beyond terror and denial, and work politically to keep that destruction from happening.

Some other unaskable questions might be: for the seriously ill person, "Do you want to live or die?" For those involved in sexual politics: "Is gender a myth?" For the workaholic: "What do you do for joy?" For the tree activist: "How should we make building materials?" Or for the politician: "What do you like about the other party's platform?" or "How could both parties work together more closely?"

Questioning values is a strategic task of our times. This questioning is important because it is the values behind highly politicized issues that have usually gotten us into the trouble in the first place. We need to look at a value, a habit, an institutional pattern, and ask, "How is this value functioning in my own life?" "In what ways do these values work for and against the common good?" "Are these values pro-survival (pro-life) or anti-life?" If you can ask the unaskable in a nonpartisan way, not to embarrass someone but to probe for more suitable answers for the future, then it can be a tremendous service to anyone with an issue on which she or he is "stuck."

THREE METHODS

Here are three specific methods for reframing problems in ethics.

THINK PREVENTION

We understand the logic of prevention when it comes to health. Everyone knows that it's better to take vitamins and exercise than to wait until you get sick and then have to deal with the illness. We don't always act on this knowledge, for a variety of reasons, but we do know it.

In ethics the strategy could be the same: look before or behind a problem as it is usually presented. Don't just take "the" problem for granted. Instead, consider whether it even needs to come up in the first place. Ask whether a few changes a few steps back can change everything about "the" problem here and now, or perhaps even keep it from coming up at all.

For example, we are consumed by the question of whether killing murderers is right or wrong. But the best answer may lie in a different direction entirely. Why not refocus at least part of our energies toward reducing the number of murders in the first place? After all, we do understand something about what drives people to kill other people. Everything from emotional and social stresses (unemployment, for example) to the easy availability of weapons makes a difference. And not just to murder, of course. A great many other goods would also be served if weapons were less readily available, if employment were higher and more reliable, and if people were enabled to deal with conflicts and anger in more constructive ways.

Of course, reframing the problem in this way doesn't answer the moral question of capital punishment itself. The point is that problems like this may not *have* "solutions"—at any rate, no solutions a tenth as good as trying to head the problem off, so to speak, at the pass. Sometimes prevention is not only the best medicine, it is the *only* medicine. Of course we will not eliminate all murders, and therefore we will still have a moral question about capital punishment. But we do not need to spend so much energy on that question and so very little energy where it could do so much more good.

Or take "the drug problem." It's a large and puzzling issue. By way of response, though, we are usually invited to consider only tougher law enforcement or drug resistance training. Sometimes "the" drug problem is even reduced to the question of how to get dealers off the streets. Longer jail terms, mandatory sentencing, more police.

Once again, we need to ask: what is the bigger challenge? Are there ways to rethink and shift "the" problem itself? Why, in particular, are so many people tempted by drugs in the first place? What combination of social pressures, hopelessness, the wish to experiment, and so on, are at play, perhaps on the part of different people and with respect to different drugs?

Surely part of the allure of drugs is that they offer some excitement in the midst of an otherwise uninteresting life. Then one bottom-line reconstructive question is: are there less lethal ways to make life interesting? Yes, obviously. Well, what ways? What can we do to make life so interesting that people are no longer tempted to escape through drugs?

Now *there's* a fine question—what Fran Peavey would call an empowering strategic question: no longer punitive, widely engaging, open-ended, more promising for all of us. Here too, of course, the old questions remain—but they are no longer the only questions. A new sense of freedom opens up, and maybe of hope as well. Surely were *all* interested in exciting lives!

PAPER OR PLASTIC?

The quandary of the modern grocery check-out is "paper or plastic?" It *is*, in part, an ethical question: a question of our impact on the Earth and on future human generations. It's also a debatable question. Even some ecologists advise using plastic bags because they can be used longer and take less and cleaner energy to produce. Plastic bags save trees. On the other hand, thousands of tons of nonbiodegradable plastic wastes are an environmental disaster too. Which is the lesser of two evils?

We could get creative with that question, for sure. Maybe we could invent lighter bags, or perfect biodegradable ones, or...

But why must we pick one or the other "evil"? Suppose that we step back a little and reframe the problem itself. Why do we need to use disposable bags, of *either* kind, in the first place? Surely the best answer is to *reuse* bags: cloth bags, super-strong paper bags, backpacks, and so on. We do not need to choose the lesser of two evils. Pick *no* evils. Try to change the problem instead.

The best answer to the littering question, in short, is to avoid creating the potential litter in the first place. My Chinese students tell me that it is common in China for people to carry around their own chopsticks, rather than requiring new ones every time they eat out. Japanese carry around their own cups. Why couldn't we?

The story goes that when Henry Ford was setting up the first assembly lines to build the Model T, his suppliers got very specific requests about how to build the boxes in which they sent their bolts or cushions. A certain kind of wood had to be used, cut to certain sizes, with holes drilled just in certain places. Puzzled, but anxious for Ford's business, they complied. It turned out that once the boxes were unpacked at the assembly line, they were taken apart and used for the Model T's floorboards. They were already cut and drilled in just the right ways!

In short, Ford took two problems—getting rid of unwanted boxes and procuring floorboards—and turned them into one solution. Reuse was planned into the very design of things. We could do the same. Rather than raising the question of recycling only after a thing has been used, we ought to raise it before the thing is even made. Imagine selling food in containers that you could then use as plates and glasses (or just *eat* too), or milk or juice containers that you could refill at the store, or automotive frames that can be updated in pieces rather than junked as a whole. Or...? Some thinkers now call this "precycling": it is still, sadly enough, a cutting-edge idea.

Environmentalists argue that there are good alternatives to *most* of our environmentally destructive practices. Air conditioners are massive energy hogs—but there are other ways to beat the heat, like building houses open to the breezes, or partly buried and thus insulated and cooled by the Earth itself. The supposed problem might also be reframed. Maybe we should just get used to the heat again? How about just taking siestas rather than insisting on working all day in wool suits? Once again the results might be better all around.

REVISIT OUTLYING PARTS OF THE PROBLEM

In a well-known riddle, a truck stands before a highway overpass, half an inch too high to get under. How to get through? Most people focus on somehow raising the bridge. But the answer is not to raise the bridge. It is to lower the truck—readily done just by letting some air out of the tires.

Confronting an obstacle, we're tempted to charge right into it, tackle it head-on. If there are major hurdles, we prepare to jump them. But a straight line is not always the best way between two points. What about running *around* the hurdles, using a side door, finding another way? This is what Edward DeBono calls "lateral thinking." I prefer a more descriptive label: *revisiting outlying parts of the problem.*

The method is this. Systematically survey all the parts of a problem, not just the one or two that currently fill the screen. Highlight and reconsider each part of the problem. Each can be deliberately varied and questioned. New possibilities will come up. It may well be that some other aspect of a problematic situation, pushed into the background at the moment, offers us a way to go forward, while the current routes seem blocked.

Emmanuel Evans ran a department store during the 1940s and 1950s in my city, Durham, North Carolina. The store had an attached sit-down cafeteria. Segregation-era laws forbade the seating of black people in such eating establishments. Black people had to stand, get their food, and go outside to eat. Evans was unwilling to treat his black customers in this way. But what to do? The direct approach—seating black people in defiance of the law—would quickly end with fines and jail (remember, this was before the civil rights movement and the era of mass civil disobedience). Closing the cafeteria served no one's interests either.

So the direct approach was blocked. What about an indirect approach? Mightn't the problem yield to an approach from another angle? Think about it...

Naturally we first imagine changing things for the black customers. But suppose things could be changed for the *white* customers instead? Couldn't white people (also) *stand*? Evans finally realized that he could just remove *all* the tables, so that no one was seated. Which is what he did. No law was broken, but a powerful statement was made. His cafeteria became the first desegregated eating place in town. And Evans, by the way, later became one of Durham's best-loved mayors.

Environmentally too there are many examples of "lowering the truck," shifting the action to readily solved problems rather than beating our heads against immovable obstacles. Rather than building ever more electrical generating capacity, for example, it is usually far easier and quicker, as well as far less expensive, for power companies to promote conservation. Some even give away high-efficiency lightbulbs. Instead of building more reservoirs and sewage systems, cities can promote water conservation. Low-flush toilets reduce water usage and sewage flow by an astonishing 80 percent. Native plants that don't require watering at all reduce lawn water needs by, well, 100 percent...

LOOK FOR OPPORTUNITIES IN THE PROBLEM

A third and still more dramatic way of reframing problems is to take the problem before us not as a difficulty to be overcome or gotten rid of but as an actual *opportunity* to be welcomed. Believe it or not: instead of trying to get rid of "the problem," we can ask instead how we can make *use* of it—and not, or not just, as a "problem," but as a resource, as a solution already, if we can just find the right problem for it or reframe the one in front of us.

The method itself is, once again, very simple. Take any problem. Seek out the very core of the difficulty. Identify it, state it clearly. Then ask yourself: can I think of any way in which this "problem" might actually be *welcomed*? Are there opportunities in it? For what?

Power plants produce, among other things, heat. Big plants build huge cooling towers and locate where they can discharge large volumes of hot water. The heat, in short, is considered a problem—a waste. And so it becomes. But then again...isn't heat often just what we want? Why consider it "waste" at all? Couldn't it be used for something? Suppose for instance that we piped the hot water or steam into homes for heat. In fact this is already done in Scandinavia, where they speak of "co-generation." The power plant becomes a heating plant as well. Viewed ecologically, the co-generated heat is not an inconvenience and a burden, to be dumped as cheaply as possible into the environment, but a *resource*.

Go to any old-age home and you will find people desperate for something constructive to do. There are some organized games and other activities, but the feeling is simply that time is being filled. Professionals are even trained and hired to find ways to keep the occupants busy—disguising what we normally assume to be the simple fact that really there *is* "nothing for them to do."

I am sure, after the last chapter, that you can readily think of some creative responses in the usual problem-solving mode. Creating or adapting computer games for older people? (A rather large market, you'd think.) Or how about more crafts? And these are fine ideas. They are also still entirely in the mode of solving the problem as it stands: filling up old people's time. A seriously creative approach would be to ask what their unfilled time is an opportunity for. Is it really a problem, at all, we'd want to ask—or, once again, more like a *resource*?

Ask the question in this way, as radical as it may sound, and everything looks different. *Of course* it is a resource! Obviously most older folks aren't going to be blazing wilderness trails or hanging telephone lines or sheet rock or something. Surely, though, there are many ways that they can contribute. Here we have skilled, experienced, patient people, anxious for some constructive work…why should it be hard to hook their abilities up with community needs?

Nursing homes could be connected with public libraries, and the occupants take over cataloging and book care. It's good, careful, and quiet work— plus they'd have all the books and videos they want close at hand. Older people could take over or create community historical museums. In almost all tribal and traditional communities, the elders are the custodians of the community's history. They carry the memories and instruct the young. Why are we letting both the elders and the history slip away?

Even better, we know that many young parents are desperate for good-quality daycare. Once again buildings are built, sometimes right next to the nursing home, where staff are once again trained and hired, this time to find ways to keep the children busy and maybe even teach them something. Hopefully not just watching TV. But why not bring the very young and the very old *together* in a setting in which both can help each other? The old can tell their stories to the very people who above all love stories. And the young can help tend to the needs of the old, learning something of life cycles and of service in the process.

In traditional societies, the older generations are also the natural custodians not just of the past but also of the *future*. Freed from the immediate pressures of survival, reproduction, and work, having lived long enough to glimpse the grander flow of time, older people can take a longer view of things. Perhaps a little forgetfulness also helps. (Could memory loss even be an *advantage* in certain ways?) The old are the ones, freed up precisely by the changes that age brings, who can become society's greatest visionaries! A colleague of mine is hard at work creating councils of elders who take vision-ary thinking as their project, indeed their responsibility. He's creating a new kind of retirement community as well—as natural homes for such councils. A core group of elders would live in such places and regularly host wider groups, of all ages, for facilitated visioning. Elder communities as creative incubators of the future—a beautiful and unexpected vision. We'll return to it in the next chapter.

Reframing problems in this way does take some imaginative work. Usu-ally it will not be obvious at first what the seeming problem could possibly be an opportunity for (except for pulling your hair out). Often it will seem silly even to ask. Patience, patience...Just ask anyway: "Even so, even so, what *could* it be an opportunity for?" Use the tools from previous chapters to help generate some concrete ideas. Stick with it. Don't be blinded just because a situation is *labeled* a "problem" (or "dilemma"). There will still be possibilities in it. The essential step is your willingness to look for them—your expecta-tion that maybe, just maybe, there might be something to be found.

REFRAMING THE ABORTION DEBATE

Let us now use these tools for reframing problems to re-approach the most painful and seemingly "stuck" debate we have: the abortion debate. I am sure that what I will say about it will not please everyone. Parts may even displease everyone, which may or may not be a good sign, but I hope you'll at least agree that the abortion issue—even the abortion issue!—has some quite unexpected possibilities once we approach it with some of the tools in this chapter.

THE SPACE FOR INTEGRATING VALUES

Sometimes I divide my students into pro-life and pro-choice groups. Each group looks at case studies of unintended pregnancy and is asked to guess what they *and the other group* will say about them. Pro-life groups assume that the pro-choice side will more or less automatically opt for abortion when the going gets tough. They are surprised to discover that the pro-choice groups consider abortion only a last resort. Similarly, pro-choice groups assume that the pro-life group will be against abortion no matter what. But they're not: they make exceptions too. The commentator Roger Rosenblatt reports something similar:

> Pro-choice advocates are often surprised to hear themselves speak of the immorality of taking a life. Pro-life people are surprised to hear themselves defend individual rights, especially women's rights.

In truth, every one of us is pro-life. Life is what makes love, and community, and beauty, and everything else possible. Those acts associated with creating and preserving and honoring life—sex, childbirth, nurturing a baby, caring for the sick, mourning the dead—are among the deepest and most profound of life's experiences.

Every one of us is *also* pro-choice. Freedom, self-determination, the right to control what happens in and to our own bodies—these are basic values too. In politics, in the stores, in "lifestyle"—choice is everything. Some people even think that seat belts and speed limits are unjustified limits on physical freedom, but these are trivial restrictions compared to pregnancy and childbirth.

Rosenblatt argues that there is therefore a broad and persistent middle ground on the question: something like "permit but discourage." For the last twenty-five years, while the abortion debate raged all around us, the U.S. population consistently has divided into about a fifth strongly anti-abortion, a quarter strongly in favor of abortion rights, and the remaining 55 percent or so against abortion personally, most of the time, but also in favor of allowing it as a limited legal right. Almost 60 percent continue to support the *Roe v. Wade* framework.

Likewise, the most common view I find among my students, too, is that "I probably wouldn't choose abortion myself, but I think the choice should be there for others." This would probably be classified as a "pro-choice" view, as the usual categories go—but those categories may hide more than they reveal. There's middle ground here—*between* the usual views. *Both* sides acknowledge that abortion can be a painful and tragic, but also (sometimes) necessary, choice.

In fact, then, despite the painful and persistent debate between two single-minded sides, most people recognize that abortion choices pit two genuine values against each other in a case where both of them count. Both of them are right in their way. How to put them together is still a (hard) question, but at least we can find here a kind of shared starting point. It might help to remember that there already is a large network of people devoted to working from common ground, or at least compatible values, in this very debate: The Common Ground Network for Life and Choice—again, Life *and* Choice—devoted to dialogue and working from a common agenda. You've seen some of their materials in chapter 11. They were not much in the news, but they worked away for ten years, and their umbrella organization—Search for Common Ground—has expanded to other conflicts too.

STRATEGIC QUESTIONS: PREVENTION

Common agenda: did I say that? Anyone immersed in the current debate may have trouble even beginning to imagine what such a thing might look like. But in fact common concerns emerge immediately and even obviously once we reframe the problem in the way just suggested. Rosenblatt again says:

Both sides might be surprised to learn how similar are their visions of a society that makes abortion less necessary through sex education, help for unwanted babies, programs to shore up disintegrating families and moral values, and other forms of constructive community action.

No one thinks that abortion, by itself, is a good thing. This is why the term "pro-abortion" is unfair: the pro-choice view is really only that abortion is sometimes the least bad option. The natural next questions are how we can prevent situations with such bad options from even arising. As Julie Polter writes in *Sojourners,* a social justice–oriented Christian journal, "If pro-life people know that one abortion is too many and many pro-choice people can at least agree that there surely shouldn't be as many abortions as there are, shouldn't we do what we can in the scope of that common territory?"

We could start by asking how to reduce the demand for abortions themselves. Is there any realistic way to reduce the number of unwanted pregnancies and to keep those unintended pregnancies that do occur from being unwanted?

More than half of all women who seek abortion were not using contraception when they got pregnant. Why? We need to find out. Lack of access? Lack of education? Violence? These things can be changed. Changing them might not even be controversial.

And what about the other half, women who used contraception and still got pregnant? Again we need to find out why. Poor or difficult-to-use methods? Resistance from spouses and lovers? These things too can be changed. With a fraction of the energy and intensity put into the present abortion debate, they *could* be changed.

When the welfare laws were up for revision in 1996, conservatives proposed to deny assistance to children born of mothers under 18, or currently on welfare, or whose paternity hadn't been established. Many of these limits are now law. But a remarkable thing happened along the way. Nearly all major organizations on *both sides* of the abortion issue campaigned against the bill— including the National Right to Life Committee, Planned Parenthood, the U.S. Catholic Conference, and the National Organization for Women (NOW). Both sides feared that the results would be to coerce abortions among poor women. Both sides made the connections back to economic conditions. Pro-choice and pro-life organizations even *jointly designed* a comprehensive child-support reform plan. Common ground emerged in the face of a common threat. Maybe next time we shouldn't wait.

STRATEGIC QUESTIONS: SURPRISES

But of course there will still, sometimes, be unintended pregnancies. What about when prevention fails? Why does abortion sometimes become so desperate a need? Why does a child, or another child, or a child at the "wrong" time sometimes promise only disaster for a mother or family?

Some on the pro-life side answer: the real problem is that we think we can have everything. We want to control every aspect of our lives. Maybe we ought to be more humble in the face of life's mysteries. When we speak of "unintended" pregnancy, for example, we set it up from the start as a failure of control and therefore a problem, a potential disaster. Some people propose to speak of "surprise" pregnancy instead. A "surprise" is not necessarily a disaster—it can also be a kind of gift, an opportunity.

But *still*, "surprises" can be unpleasant. More must be said. Why is the surprise sometimes unwelcome? A "strategic question" might be, How can we make these particular surprises more welcome, more bearable?

Part of the problem is that women still confront inflexible expectations about career tracks, work schedules, and schooling, coupled with lower pay in general, poor-quality or super-expensive child care, distant extended families (not much help), and all the rest. Though a few in the pro-life movement may believe that women should not aspire to careers, most pro-lifers agree with nearly everyone else that careers ought at least to be one option for women. Women have a right to seek that kind of life—and to have a sex life too. But then the trap closes: How to have a baby when it would mean two or three years out of school or part-time at work, long-term financial costs, and permanent emotional commitments elsewhere?

This is a fixable problem. We need more flexible expectations and alternative work and schooling patterns that do not punish or impede women (and men) who also choose major family responsibilities. Most European countries are far ahead of the United States in this area. It's not so hard to work out the details.

Equal pay for women is, or ought to be, one goal. Shared child-raising has everything to recommend it. At the very least, fathers should be expected to support their children financially (at present, even with greatly expanded enforcement, only a third contribute anything at all). Paid parental leaves are the norm in Europe. My students, working on this problem in a creative mode, have suggested still other ideas, such as a system of "adoptive grandparents." What do you think?

The same goes for schools. One of my ethics classes was discussing the abortion issue with our college chaplain. He remarked that in his decade or so at the college he had seen only three or four students carry pregnancies to term and stay in school too. A (male) student then said

> I'm pro-life, but I can't blame a fellow student for getting an abortion when the choice is between the abortion and finishing college. Your whole future is at stake. I think the real question is: why should she be put in that position?

Why indeed. So the question to us is, what can *we* change—teachers, students, chaplains—so that fewer women are put in this position in the future? Class schedules, assignments, how financial aid is calculated? How hard would that be?

And adoption? Far more could be done to make it more workable, from settling the vexed question of adoptees' access to biological-parent records to genuinely supporting women who choose to go through pregnancy and then choose adoption: that is, supporting them economically, emotionally, and especially socially. Deep-seated sexual norms and expectations have regularly been stood on their heads in the last half-century: the "shame" of bearing and "giving up" an unintended child would hardly be the biggest. How much would it really take?

ACKNOWLEDGMENT AND RECONCILIATION

Sometimes, though—still—there will be losses, indeed tragic losses, no matter what is chosen or how you look at it. Different lives and life choices are at stake, all of them precious, and they cannot all be lived out. Most people, even most pro-lifers, for instance, accept abortion in cases of rape or when the mother's own life is at stake, though the fetus and potential baby is no less innocent for all that.

The most obvious loss, of course, is the physical life of the fetus, the child-to-be. The loss of a pregnancy to miscarriage is acknowledged all around as a serious loss. Why not the same in abortion? The usual response is that sometimes the other stakes—the life prospects of the pregnant woman or also those around her—are also great, though less visible. Often, surely, this is true. In practice, though, we have trouble holding both kinds of stakes, or potential losses, in mind at the same time. Tragic choices trouble us—we do like to see the world in blacks and whites—and so there is a tendency (on *both* sides) to discount or even deny the losses on the "other" side.

But why? Mightn't this kind of denial even be part of the problem? Trying another tack, suppose that we consider how to make the loss of the fetus— the loss of a potential life—both more visible and at the same time possibly more bearable.

Japanese Buddhists have developed a kind of memorial ritual, even sometimes a kind of apology, for aborted as well as miscarried fetuses (also, strikingly, for animals deliberately killed in the course of drug experiments). Mizuko Kuyo, it is called. It is a way of facing rather than denying the consequences—underscoring the seriousness of the choice, which is surely good from the point of view of all sides—but also reaching some kind of closure, making it possible to go on. Loss can be acknowledged without shutting down the hard choices required. Those facing such a choice can have a better way to get a grip on just what is at stake. Those who have made such choices can have a better way to make peace with them.

It seems wise to me. What could similar rituals look like with us? Wouldn't it be a worthwhile project to develop our own forms of remembrance and reconciliation, while also acknowledging that sometimes, at least, the choice must remain with the pregnant woman and those close to her? A delicate task, yes, especially in the present atmosphere of intense moralism and blame, private tragedies made public, and wounds again and again rubbed raw. But there is also a glimmer of an unexpected possibility of healing here. Another place for some good reframing and reconstruction!

QUICK REFERENCE: WAYS TO REFRAME PROBLEMS

OPEN UP THE QUESTION
Ask open-ended or "strategic" questions—of others and also of yourself. How did we get into a situation in which this sort of thing (whatever it is) emerges as a problem? Are there other ways it could be viewed? How can we dig deeper and create more options? What keeps us from moving toward effective solutions?

THINK PREVENTION
How can this problem be headed off before it even comes up?

REVISIT OUTLYING ASPECTS OF THE PROBLEM
Mentally vary *all* the changeable aspects of a problematic situation, not just the ones right now in the spotlight. See what new ideas are provoked.

LOOK FOR THE OPPORTUNITIES IN THE PROBLEM
Could the very situation that seems to be such an ethical problem actually be an ethical opportunity if viewed in the right way? An opportunity for what?

FOR REVIEW

1. What is the aim of opening up a problem?
2. What further ways does this chapter suggest to rethink the Heinz dilemma?
3. What is "strategic questioning"?
4. Give two examples of strategic questions.
5. Illustrate preventive thinking.
6. How can we think preventively about the drug problem?
7. "Revisit outlying parts of the problem"—what does this mean?

8. How can an ethical problem be taken as an opportunity?

9. How can preventive thinking help us reframe the abortion debate?

10. What might Japanese Buddhist practice have to offer the abortion debate?

EXERCISES AND NOTES

14.1 PRACTICE REFRAMING PROBLEMS

Consider again a list of practical problems in your experience—you'll remember the list from Exercise 13.1. There you practiced multiplying options, finding creative ways to solve these problems as they are usually understood. Now go farther: try to *reframe* these problems. Use Peavey's "strategic questioning." What things need to be changed so that the present problem does not come up, or comes up in a more manageable way than it does now? How might changing the problem in some of these ways be preferable to leaving the problem as it stands and trying to solve it as such?

Here is the list again:

- Waste (styrofoam cups, lights left on all the time, recyclables in the trash, overuse of paper, etc.)
- Too much television
- Bad cell-phone etiquette (loud public conversations as if no one else is present)
- Sports teams that have to travel increasingly long distances to find suitable competition
- Parent-teen relations
- "Empty nest syndrome"
- Lack of affordable child care for working families with young children
- Lack of inexpensive travel options (for college students, and for everyone)
- Poor diets (predictably leading to health problems, missed work…and unhappiness in general)
- Rising waters and changed rainfall patterns (usually toward more intense, if fewer, storms) due to climate change. Think of cities on the edge of seas and rivers—New Orleans is only one of the more visible. What is to be done?

Preventive options might sometimes seem easy. If the problem is crowded roads, for example, we could prevent it by building more roads. But again, think more creatively. Look deeper. We can't keep building roads forever: they have massive social and economic costs, and they tend to create even more demand. Are there deeper ways to reframe the whole problem? Could you think of the problem not as lack of enough roads but of *too many cars*? Or is there a way we could reduce the amount of required travel itself? For example, could we not begin to relocate work and shopping closer to home, so people need to drive less in the first place? There's a preventive strategy that is also creative, and it offers a vision of a better life for all of us.

Use your other tools from this chapter as well. Revisit outlying aspects of the problems. Look for opportunities even in what seem to be irresolvable disasters.

14.2 PRACTICE REFRAMING MORAL PROBLEMS

Now pose the same kinds of questions about moral problems. Treat them exactly the same way. Here are some the items from the list in Exercise 13.2.

- Irresponsible driving: for example, speeding, poor attention, uninsured or underinsured driving, poor car maintenance, and so on. In handling a car we have immense potential to harm or end others' lives. Could we reframe this whole issue?

- Marriage. With a 40%+ divorce rate, marriage is not working very well in general. There are plenty of issues besides the gender of the participants (if that is a problem at all), such as lack of relationship skills, lack of supportive extended families or communities, many people's resistance to asking for help or counseling, economic and other stressors, including the need to care for aged parents, etc.

- Plagiarism: presenting someone else's work (especially, writing) as if it were your own. Colleges and universities are increasingly aware of this issue—just as the Internet makes it much easier to do. How else can this issue be approached besides more suspicion and stricter punishments? For example, is there a way to head it off before it even arises?

- Gun control. What are the roots of the problems about guns, anyway? Is controlling the gun itself actually the best solution? What other factors might we address?

- Drug abuse. We say that drugs offer an escape from school, or work, or just life itself. But this leads to other questions. Why do so many people need such an escape in the first place? And what can we do about school, or work, or life itself so that such an escape is less tempting? Aren't there less lethal ways to make life more joyful and interesting?

- Medical testing on animals. There's no other way to test drugs? Really? And do we need them—all of them, that much—anyway?

- Sweatshops. We know that our clothes and other consumer goods are some-times made by unjustly exploited workers in other, desperate parts of the world (and sometimes right here at home)—though often we don't wish to know (or can't find out) more details. What can be done to respond to this problem?

- What might the elderly do with their time? Could society be restructured to better respond to their needs? What new kinds of places could they find? How about a system of adoptive grandparents, as some of my students have suggested? What other opportunities might aging represent?

- We have a minimum wage—currently $7.25 per hour by federal law, higher in a few states. Some economists argue that this is a bad thing. If there are people who might wish to work for less, and employers who might hire them, is it right to prohibit this voluntary transaction (which to some degree happens anyway)? Others deny that no such transaction is truly "voluntary." Can you think of any other approaches to this issue? Remember that we also question whether there might be a moral case for a maximum wage as well. Again, can you think of other and better approaches to this issue?

- What happens when personal ethics conflict with organizational practices: say, in business or the military or government? How could such conflicts be handled better? Are there new and creative ways to deal with the problem of "whistle-blowing"—and the kinds of problems that lead to the need for whistle-blowing in the first place?

- Rich countries try to help less well-off countries when natural disasters strike (earthquakes, hurricanes, etc.). What about also helping to overcome the underlying causes of poverty itself? Meanwhile, aren't there some ways in which we need their help? What would a system of truly mutual aid look like?

- We are consuming food, energy, and other natural resources at unsustain-able rates, and what kind of world we will pass on to our descendants is becoming increasingly uncertain as a result. What to do?

14.3 FULL CREATIVITY CHALLENGES

Here are some further moral problems on which to use your full set of creativ-ity tools—that is, from both chapters 13 and 14, multiplying options as well as reframing problems. Give them some serious time and thought. I think you'll be surprised and pleased by how far you can go with them.

- Defenders of the death penalty say that murderers forfeit their own right to life, that execution is the only really "proportionate" penalty for murder, and that the threat of execution deters would-be murderers from commit-ting the act. Opponents argue that if cold-blooded killing is wrong, it is wrong when the state does it too, when the blood's even colder; that life in prison is at least as appropriate a penalty; and that the threat of execution does not deter real murderers. American states that use the death penalty do not, on average, have lower murder rates than states that don't; some actually have higher rates, though it could be argued that they would have had higher rates anyway. Hard to know. How else could you think of this whole issue?

- The average age of first sexual intercourse is under 16 years for American teens, the lowest age of any major industrialized countries. It seems a bit young. (Is it? Why?) Meanwhile the United States also has a much higher teen pregnancy rate than most other industrialized nations and a vastly higher STD rate—in part because we do such a bad job at sex education. (Sure, you can teach abstinence, but the majority of young people who nonetheless choose to be "sexually active" consequently don't get decent information on contraception, STD prevention, or, for that matter, sexual relationships in general.) Any ways to change our angle here? (Hint: why does "sexually active" have to mean exactly *one* form of sexual activity? Isn't that just a bit, well, unimaginative?)

- Another drug issue: the "performance-enhancing drugs" used, and abused, by some athletes. High school and even younger athletes risk their health for an unnatural edge; meanwhile on a global scale, the World Anti-Doping Agency (great name, huh?) polices competitions such as the Olympics. Other competitors want to stay drug-free but to compete on a level playing field. Any other ways to approach all of this?

- People who disagree profoundly with important political and social decisions need some way to register their disagreement visibly and to attempt to sway others to their point of view—in short, to protest. But what is the best form for such protest? Too many of the current forms of protest are so obviously pushed into invisibility or irrelevance that the protestors become embittered and cynical—or turn to violence. (Witness the fringes of the anti-abortion and anti-logging movements, just for two examples.) See if you can imagine healthier and more productive forms of protest. What would be two steps toward making them workable?

- Especially in rough economic times, large numbers of people fall into poverty and need some kind of help, at least for a short time. On the other hand, dependency and abuse are worries in the welfare system as we have known it. How else might welfare systems be organized?

Hint: Compare welfare systems around the world. One thing we might learn from Norway is that what's really important is not the sheer amount of money spent on social welfare, but *what* it's spent on. It's not spent on so-called "handouts" to people who have already fallen into poverty. Norway spends it on social-support measures that are intended to prevent poverty (as exclusion, disempowerment) from even arising in the first place. Good medical care for all, good education, good transportation and housing. As one writer describes the system: the approach "is not an individualistic, Band-Aid approach, but rather a universal, preventive one, a policy consistent with a value system based on care and absolute security." Notice that such a system has immense advantages not just for those who would otherwise be poor, but for everyone. Medical care for *all*; education... (If you did "Using Your Tools" #5, you might want to review your answer here.)

- We also struggle with how to respond, person to person, to people asking for money in the streets. We want to help, we say, but have also learned to wonder what the money is really going for. Some of us give a dollar any- way—how can you turn away? Others make it a policy to refuse. Couldn't there be some rather different ways of meeting the situation? (Hint: what if what's given isn't money?)

14.4 WHY WAIT FOR PROBLEMS?

A further step. Look around for institutions or practices that are *not* currently ethical problems, and consider how you might creatively improve them in eth- ical directions. For example, we have Mother's Day, Father's Day, and increas- ingly Grandparents' Day, but mostly as occasions for sending a card or maybe a shopping trip. Why not ask, How can we better celebrate each other—more fully, more meaningfully, more consistently? (Fun question, eh? Also, by the way, what about *Children's* Day? Cat Day? School or State Day? Who and what else are we not celebrating enough?)

Or again: might we soon need to develop a new set of expectations for e-mail, cell phones, and so on, so that we are not constantly "on call," expected to respond just as fast as the messages arrive, and also, too often, only half attentive to wherever we actually are and whomever we are actually with? Better start now... (And a hint: must an "etiquette" of this sort, if that is what it will be, be merely a set of *constraints*?)

Variation: look for places where ethics has been notably successful, and then ask whether the same successes can be generalized to other areas. Find solutions first, so to speak, and then search for suitable problems. Chapter 1 spoke of solidarity, for example, as when families or neighborhoods shave their own heads to support someone who has lost their hair to chemotherapy. We have the general idea. But are there other and still more powerful ways, both practical and symbolic, to show solidarity with those fighting cancer or similar diseases? With the dying? With children, with soldiers? With each other, day to day? With the Earth?

While you're at it, why not invent some new ethical practices out of the blue? Create something *completely new!*

NOTES

Parts of this chapter closely follow chapter 4 of my book *Creative Problem-Solving in Ethics* (Oxford, 2007).

For general background on reframing problems, see the works of Edward DeBono cited in chapter 13. Also widely discussed is the idea of "proactive thinking": looking ahead to potential problems and working now to head them off later—as opposed to "*reactive* thinking," which waits until they arrive as full-blown problems and then struggles to find some response. See Stephen Covey, *The Seven Habits of Highly Effective People* (Simon and Schuster, 1990), Habit 1. Covey subtitles his book *Restoring the Character Ethic*. Proactive thinking for him is a moral *virtue*!

Philosophers who want more argument for the importance of reframing problems might consult my book *Toward Better Problems* (Temple University Press, 1992), where it is mostly called "reconstructive thinking," using John Dewey's term. The classical source is Dewey's *Reconstruction in Philosophy* (Beacon Press, 1948). See also Caroline Whitbeck's article "Ethics as Design: Doing Justice to Moral Problems," *Hastings Center Report* 26 (1996): 9–16.

Roger Rosenblatt is quoted from "How to End the Abortion War," in his book *Life Itself: Abortion in the American Mind* (Vintage, 1993).

For data on abortion attitudes I draw on an online article, "Most Americans Back Legal Abortion Under Certain Circumstances", *Angus-Reid Public Opinion* reports, June 26, 2012: see http://www.angus-reid.com/polls/45391/most-americans-back-legal-abortion-under-certain-circumstances/. Julie Polter is quoted from her article "Women and Children First: Developing a Common Agenda to Make Abortion Rare," *Sojourners,* May–June 1995. On Mizuko Kuyo, see William R. LaFleur, *Liquid Life: Abortion and Buddhism in Japan* (Princeton University Press, 1992) and the "Ethics Updates" website at http://ethics.sandiego.edu/Applied/Abortion/index.asp.

USING YOUR TOOLS #7
REFRAMING BIOETHICAL ISSUES
OR, WHERE ETHICS MEETS POLITICS

Bioethics is a field of "applied ethics" that addresses ethical issues that arise specifically within the practice of medicine, health care, and the biological sciences. Since the 1970s bioethics has become a major focus of many philosophers as well as of hospitals and policy makers. Most hospitals now have Ethics Committees and even ethicists with beepers on call. Training in ethics is expected of most doctors and other medical decision makers. Politically, one of the biggest debates of recent years has been over the health care system and some of the moral values that bear on it, such as social justice and personal autonomy, as well as health itself.

If you are a student in an ethics class, you may very well encounter bioethical problems in your other course materials. Possibly you are even a student in a class specifically devoted to them. In any case, we need to have a look. This "Using Your Tools" exercise invites you to bring your reframing strategies to bioethical issues in particular.

This exercise has another aim as well: to bring into focus the political decisions and practices that shape many ethical issues, bioethical issues very much included. I don't just meant the obvious politics of the health care reform debate. There are also many other and often unnoticed "background" political decisions and practices that frame the ethical problems that come up front and center. We make choices, as a political community, about how much and how far the government regulates, or doesn't regulate, medical care. We decide, through our representatives, how much tax money we as a community will spend to provide (some kinds of) medical care to (some) people—or to research cures, or to support preventive programs, or to train doctors. Or not. We also decide, by setting up and sustaining a legal system that applies to the practice of medicine, among other things, what kinds of legal rights patients (and families, doctors, pharmacists, insurance companies, etc.) are granted.

All of these choices, and many more, shape the practice of medicine. They therefore give rise to various kinds of ethical issues that might not arise, or would arise differently, if we made different political choices. Of course, to decide some of these issues we'd probably need a whole political philosophy. I do not mean that you must do so for this UYT exercise! The key point here is just to recognize that there *are* such political choices in the background of the bioethical problems that we face. This in turn gives us, at the very least, more creative room to move. We *reframe* ethical issues, remember, when we look behind and around such problems to see if there are ways to rearrange their causes so that they come up in different and more manageable forms, or maybe (ideally) don't come up at all. It is a way of recognizing that we have more options than just tackling the immediate problem head-on. Indeed, sometimes the only decent options are political.

THE HEINZ DILEMMA ONE MORE TIME

One good illustration is the discussion of the Heinz dilemma in the last two chapters. It seems at first (we said) that this problem requires a yes-or-no, one-or-the-other sort of answer that applies only to Heinz and people in similarly desperate straits. Once we considered that dilemma with a wider lens, however, we began to see that it is "framed" by a number of institutional and community arrangements and expectations that could themselves be different. Even though the Heinz dilemma as it stands may be useful as a way of highlighting the differences between utilitarian and rights-based ethical theories, it may also be misleading as an example of a real ethical problem, especially if we insist in leaving it just as it stands. Remember: the whole point of reframing is to *change* the problem!

For this UYT I am going to ask you to begin by spelling out some of the background social and political choices that you think are involved in certain standard bioethical problems. You could do this in quite a basic and even bold way. For example, in the Heinz case, one thing we can say right away is that such a dilemma can arise in the first place only in a system in which health care is a commodity—that is, something to be purchased—rather than a right, and in which individuals may or may not be able to make the purchase (or buy insurance to help cover the costs). You could therefore predict that the ability or inability to pay will be a major ethical issue, in a way that it would not be an issue in a system in which medical care, or at least basic life-saving drugs, were provided to people as a matter of right.

Of course, it is possible that a commodity system for medicine (like life-saving drugs) is, after all, the best possible system, or that such a system is mandated by the proper understanding of freedom and property rights (such as doctors' and pharmacists' and inventors' rights and freedoms). This is certainly an arguable moral and political position. But it is not the only possible position—and one of the arguments against it is precisely that it can end up putting many people into situations like Heinz's, which also seem unjust and morally disturbing. It is at least a question.

Moreover, even if we aren't going to settle the answer anytime soon, the question at least opens up some new kinds of responses to dilemmas like Heinz's. For example, one might be publically funded "catastrophic" medical insurance—not necessarily a full system of medical care as a right, but some of kind of supplemental aid to people in truly desperate straits. After all, it might be argued, we already have a system in which access to life-saving drugs (and other kinds of care) *is* taken to be a right for some groups. Senior citizens get Medicare, for example. Veterans get free medical care at VA Hospitals for service-related medical problems. These are choices we have made as a political community. Veterans have put their lives on the line for us, for our country: it seems the most elementary principle of justice, and the least we can do, to provide for the treatment of the injuries they sustained in the line of service. This is not controversial, as far as I know, across the entire political spectrum.

As noted in the sample dialogue in the section on brainstorming in chapter 13, we've even made the choice as a political community that inmates in prisons should get free medical care, presumably because otherwise imprisonment might unjustly become a death sentence. We've taken on the responsibility of caring for them by depriving them of the freedom to do it themselves. This too seems a pretty elemental requirement of justice.

In short, there seems to be some room to reconsider things here. Social backup in desperate or deserving cases is not unheard of. In many developed countries, in fact, it is the norm across the board. It is at least an option—at least a starting point for some creative rethinking.

The Heinz dilemma and others are sometimes classified as "lifeboat cases," meaning a kind of case that presents very stark choices, usually life and death, and in which it is not clear that there are any good choices at all. The model is an overloaded lifeboat in the open ocean, close to sinking unless some of its occupants go overboard—voluntarily or not. What to do? How to decide? Some philosophers specialize in such cases—at least, again, for teaching purposes: they are supposed to make certain principles very salient. Others argue that at such extremes, ethics simply cannot apply.

It's perhaps more important to note, though, that "lifeboat" cases are themselves products of certain specific social and political choices: how to regulate passenger ships, or not, for one thing. One reason that more than 1,500 people died when the *Titanic* hit an iceberg and sank in 1912 was that the ship had far fewer spaces on its lifeboats than it had passengers. It did comply with the law at the time—but the law was, it turned out, far too lax (partly at the behest of the passenger lines themselves). This was changed after the disaster: laws were passed to require enough lifeboats for everyone on board such ships.

Again: a political choice. The aim was not to "solve" lifeboat cases: of course such laws won't help if somehow you are already stuck in a sinking ship without enough lifeboats. The aim was to try to prevent such cases from even coming up. That's the point of reframing. We are not obliged just to accept such choices as some puzzle-poser, or even life itself, puts them to us. We can revisit outlying aspects of the problem, think prevention—and give ourselves more room to move in our ethical problem solving. How many other "lifeboat cases" might be best approached in this way?

ANOTHER HARD CHOICE

Here is another schematic example of a common type of bioethical problem.

> A is the victim of a traffic accident, now lying unconscious in the ICU and wholly dependent on life support. Short-term survival is likely with help, but brain damage is probable and even the return of consciousness is uncertain. A's family is traumatized but may be willing to accept her death. What should be done?

We may ask what A's doctors, or A's family, or A herself if she could participate, should decide to do. We may ask what Mill or Kant would advise, what the Ethics of the Person or of Relationship suggest or allow or require, and so on. Notice, though, that once again there is a range of "framing" questions that are harder to see, but also crucial.

Why did this accident happen, for instance? Why is there often more money for intensive care units in hospitals than for erecting stoplights and fixing potholes so that people like A are less likely to make the acquaintance of the ICU in the first place? Why are cars so unsafe that people are so often badly injured? And why do people sometimes drive so unsafely—and fail to use seat belts that might readily prevent such injuries?

These questions again open up larger and unexpected possibilities. They are not going to help A very much—but they may represent a much more powerful ethical response to A's *type* of situation. Suppose for instance that A is the tenth accident victim seen this week. One good question surely is: is there some special cause for so many accidents? Such questions are seldom raised within the hospital itself. It is not the hospitals' business, we may say—it is hard enough just to care for the victims. Reframing the problem, though, surely we could argue that it *is* hospitals' responsibility at least to pay attention to such patterns. One reason is that hospitals are in an especially good position—indeed, a unique position—to collect the relevant data. Hospitals already follow local trends in mortality and morbidity: it should not be too hard to get a little more specific.

These questions have political consequences in turn (which is one reason why they often don't). Maybe what the city really needs is a concerted effort to up seat-belt use. Or maybe traffic flows should be redesigned at some especially treacherous intersections. If we wanted to address these issues, or the ever-present pothole question, we'd have to do it through City Council or the State Highway Department—agencies of the same governments that also fund the hospitals. Maybe funds need to be reallocated.

Unavoidably these are political questions, and again likely to be controversial. There are major constituencies for all sides—victims' support groups, traffic engineers, public health officials. Still, in the hospital case, to put more money into Emergency Room staff when a few more traffic lights would, say, halve the accident rate is not only cost-ineffective but also, arguably, ethically problematic. At least the issue should be *raised*...in the name, once again, of at least giving ourselves more options.

RESPECT FOR PERSONS

Conservative critics point out that in a system in which major medical decisions are made, in effect, by bureaucrats and lawyers, patients and their families are disempowered: they can't make such choices for themselves. This is one traditional argument for a market for medical services and goods. People can choose their own priorities and act on them so far as they have the means.

Notice that this argument is not somehow for better bureaucratic processes, as if a better committee process or different criteria for rationing health care (should choices sometimes come to that) would be the right kind of solution. Maybe such changes would produce better results in particular cases, yes, but the larger point is that a system in which such choices are made by government policy or hospital committees staffed by lawyers and administrators—even when the choices are usually good ones—still violates the rights of the person, of individual patients, to make such major choices for themselves. Conservatives critique and resist a *system* in which bioethical questions are framed for others, besides the patient, to decide in the first place. It's not up to us—it should be up to *them*.

A more libertarian side of this argument might go on to reframe the question of assisted suicide, for example, as a question of how patients got into a situation where they have to depend on someone else's approval to end their own lives. If suicide is a right—perhaps even an instance one of our most fundamental of rights, the right to conduct one's life as one chooses so long as it does not impinge others' rights to do the same—then presumably one also has the right to contract with others to make that right real if one cannot end one's life by oneself. We need to rearrange our legal system accordingly.

You may or may not agree with this kind of critique, but the philosophical point it makes is, once again, a deep and valid one. Again, the very ways in which we decide, as a community, to set up our medical system profoundly shape the kinds of ethical issues that will come up within it. It can even create whole new categories of ethical issues that didn't exist before—and that we might well be better off without. Since it is a political choice to create a system that ends up framing bioethical questions in this way, it may also be that our best response is not to answer them as they stand but to *change the system*. Once again, we may not need to simply solve "the" problem as presented. "The" problem as presented may itself *be* the problem!

On the other hand, it's a serious moral criticism of a pay-for-service medical system that it only works for the (vanishingly) few who can pay their medical expenses out of pocket or afford their choice of insurance plans. Most people, even those with reasonably good insurance, still have to cede a major decision-making role to insurance companies and their committee of accountants and lawyers to make major medical decisions. For most of us, in other words, a "free market" in medicine does not really empower us to make our own choices instead of "bureaucrats," but instead empowers a different set of bureaucrats, and probably a less visible and accountable set of decision makers at that. At least with government policies we all have a voice in affecting or changing—not so for insurance companies. In a market system health care is still "rationed," one might argue, just not by the government.

These are not easy questions, obviously, but they are after all what come up. It is no good not facing them!

GETTING TO THE QUESTION

You see that it takes some work to recognize and conceptualize the political "frames" implicit in bioethical questions, and to see where reframing them might lead. The windup to this UYT is a little longer than some of the others for this reason. It takes more work than usual just to get the question in focus.

Of course there are good reasons for ethics courses to give much of their attention to individual medical decisions, like what to do with A. Many students in those classes are heading into medical careers. They will be making such decisions some day—and individual medical decisions, case by case, not the political decisions that shape the system. Still, though, doctors also have a role to play in larger community decisions about health-related rules and practices, such as hospital record keeping and major health threats in the community. Doctors are regularly called upon, as doctors, to contribute to the political debate as well. They—*you*, someday soon, perhaps—need to be able to think on *both* levels.

Then too, many ethics students, even in bioethics courses, are not heading into medical careers but are philosophy students or other interested people—all future citizens and community members who also should be looking at the whole problem with creative as well as ethically and politically sensitive eyes.

Political dimensions are not easy to see. We are not trained, in general, to see the deeper, background forces that shape such choices: and indeed they *are* harder to discern. The desperate cases, like Heinz's or the lifeboat situations, catch our attention, and all we can or want to do is deal with what is right in front of us. Still, this is the challenge of reframing problems and asking "strategic questions" in general: to begin to see that we are not as stuck as it may seem. Indirect routes may be wiser. That is why we are practicing this skill.

Another factor, these days, is that we tend to avoid political discussions because so often they degenerate into fruitless shouting matches, manipulated by pressure groups that are sometimes more interested in prolonging and intensifying confrontation than in constructive dialogue or problem solving. It's true enough, alas. An extraordinary number of hopes and (it seems, especially) fears come into play in medical issues, and sometimes so dominate our thinking that, in effect, we stop thinking. A single phrase, for example— Sarah Palin's "death panels," a 2009 allegation against the health care reform bill then being proposed by President Obama—pressed so many buttons that it alone thoroughly derailed the debate. PoliticFact.com called it the "Lie of the Year." Actually, there is nothing remotely like involuntary euthanasia in the bill, and the one very modest provision that turned out to be Palin's concern, a proposal that physicians be reimbursed for time spent counseling patients about end-of-life options, which was endorsed by all major physicians' groups and many patient-advocacy groups, including conservative ones, partly as a means of *empowering* patients, was removed in the uproar just to try to calm things down. Still, that one phrase tainted the whole legislation and turned countless public meetings into shouting matches. Even many Republicans objected—but by then the damage was done.

I don't mean that "ObamaCare" was, or is, necessarily a good idea—that is another discussion. I *do* mean that we should be able to have more thoughtful and fact-based debates on such matters. Our politics is, indeed, in some ways, in a shambles. But repairing it is also, as chapters 11 and 12 suggest, part of the task of ethics too: to embody and promote more constructive and more *ethical* ways of working things out together. The conclusion is certainly not that ethics should avoid the political dimension. It is the opposite: that we need to get more thoroughly and effectively engaged.

YOUR CHALLENGE

Now, at long last, you should be ready to take up the challenge of this UYT. You may be working alone, or with other students. Either way, follow these steps.

1. Choose or find some cases in bioethics that interest you. Maybe you are a student in a bioethics or ethics class already looking at such cases, in which case your instructor or textbook will probably give you such cases. If not, or for additional resources, try some of these links (or do your own Web search with keywords such as "medical ethics cases").

   http://www.mhhe.com/biosci/genbio/olc_linkedcontent/bioethics_cases/ Bioethics cases studies from McGraw-Hill (accessed 9/10/11).

   http://www.scu.edu/ethics/practicing/focusareas/cases.cfm?fam=HEALTH
   and
   http://www.scu.edu/ethics/publications/submitted/cirone/medical-ethics.html Materials from the Markkula Center for Applied Ethics at Santa Clara University (both accessed 9/10/11).

   http://www.ascensionhealth.org/index.php?option=com_content&view=article&id=4 9&Itemid=173

   Resources for Catholic health care ministries: excellent cases and outlines of relevant ethical principles (accessed 9/10/11).

   http://sciencecases.lib.buffalo.edu/cs/collection/The National Center for case Study Teaching in Science; search for medical ethics cases (accessed 9/10/11).

   There are also a variety of medical ethics casebooks in print, such as John Freeman and Kevin McDonnell's *Tough Choices: Cases in Medical Ethics* (Oxford, 2000).

   Again, these are only a few of many options. You might also want to survey your classmates and acquaintances for other and probably more personal examples.

2. Begin your analysis by identifying the problem and the core values involved. You can frame the alternatives in the usual way—staying within the usual range of options (like

what should Heinz do? or, should the plug be pulled on A?). Later you can come back and add to your answers here as you begin to see more aspects of the problem and values involved.

3. Now try to identify some of the "framing" choices that have led to this problem coming up in this way in the first place (like the fact that life-saving drugs are often treated as market commodities in our system, or the likelihood that A's accident had correctable causes). Use the discussions in this UYT as a first model.

4. Finally, highlight some of the ways that your answers to #3 may open up some new kinds of room to move, some new creative options (like alternative systems for providing life-saving drugs, or building a campaign to increase seat-belt usage as a way of making A's life and death a positive legacy). Try for practically achievable options, at least for a start. As you present and discuss them, try to keep the core *shared* values in full view so as to keep the discussion inclusive and constructive.

VARIATIONS

Finally, here a few further or different directions you might take with this UYT.

- You could after all directly tackle the more sweeping question of the organization of medicine and health systems as a whole. Should we perhaps reform the whole medical system, for example on the model of the VA or other countries' "single-payer" medical systems? (And please do not think that the public debate of the last few years, or anything at all that you may have heard on television, is necessarily *any* true indication of how such systems function or their track records: this will take some careful research.) Conversely, is the solution perhaps something much more libertarian? Or, yet again, are there other options still: for example, a publicly funded but much more local system of primary care, neighborhood, and workplace clinics with health care providers who do not necessarily have to go to school for ten years just to provide first aid and public health training? (Remember: there are usually many more than just two options....)

- Many of the arguments in the recent and current health care debate are explicitly ethical arguments. Look at some of the speeches by supporters and opponents of "ObamaCare"—the thoughtful ones, anyway—as well as the more ethical and carefully considered ethical and philosophical statements on both (all) sides of the issue. Understand the ethics!

- RU-486 (Mifepristone) is a drug developed in the 1980s as an abortifacient (a drug that causes abortion) in early pregnancy and also as an emergency contraceptive. It was also, as you might expect, very controversial. The French drugmaker, Roussel-Uclaf, came under immense pressure from anti-abortion activists and in late 1988 decided to withdraw the drug from the market. The French Health Minister at the time, Claude Évin, responded by ordering Roussel-Uclaf to distribute Mifepristone in the interests of public health and explained his order in these words: "I could not permit the abortion debate to deprive women of a product that represents medical progress. *From the moment Government approval for the drug was granted, RU-486 became the moral property of women, not just the property of a drug company.*" [See Ulmann, André (2000). "The development of Mifepristone: A pharmaceutical drama in three acts." *Journal of the American Medical Womens Association* 55 (3 Suppl): 117–20, online at http://www.ncbi.nlm.nih.gov/pubmed/10846319, accessed 9/10/11.]

    The subsequent history of Mifepristone is fascinating and complex (currently it is available in most countries, but under heavy medical control—another political choice:

see http://en.wikipedia.org/wiki/Mifepristone, accessed 9/10/11). The question I would propose to you here, however, has to do with the French Health Minister's argument. In his view, there are conditions under which a drug (and in this case, notice, not exactly a life-saving one) become the "moral property" of potential users, not of the company that produces it. Can you elaborate the ethical values that underlie this kind of claim? (That is, what is the best case you can make for it?) Also, what kind of ethics might draw the opposite conclusion? Again, try to answer carefully and thoughtfully, and in a way that furthers constructive discourse rather than inflames passions.

- Can you see the same potential for reframing other (that is, non-medical) kinds of ethical issues along similar lines? After all, political choices frame many aspects of our collective life besides medical ones. Consider business ethics, or environmental ethics, or any other ethical domain of your choice. Are there analogous ways to *reframe* other issues and cases—and open up new possibilities as well?

CHAPTER 15

Moral Vision

Making an ethical contribution is not merely a matter of issuing moral judgments or just reacting to ethical problems that come along. It may ask for
more than creatively resolving or even reframing problems as well. *Vision* is
vital in ethics too.

WORKING FROM A VISION

August 28, 1963. Under a nearly cloudless sky, more than a quarter of a million people gathered near the Lincoln Memorial in Washington for a rally to
forward the cause of civil rights, and in particular to insist that the Kennedy
administration's civil rights bill, bottled up in congressional committees by
Southern opponents, be brought out of committee and passed.

The idea of such a march was itself visionary. By far the largest march
on Washington ever held (more than ten times larger than the next largest,
which turns out to have been a Ku Klux Klan rally in 1925), it brought together
a wide range of previously unconnected groups, both black and white—a fifth
of the marchers were white—and a range of black groups that were often
at odds. Though the police and the administration feared that violence might
occur, all was peaceful. There were speakers from nearly every segment of
society—labor leaders, clergy, actors, folksingers like Bob Dylan and Joan
Baez. It was a watershed day for many more who listened on the radio, or
perhaps were not even born in 1963 but who still look back to that day as a
turning point. And chiefly what we remember is one speech: Martin Luther
King, Jr.'s "I Have a Dream."

WE NEED DREAMS

Now here is a remarkable thing. When King walked up to the microphone
at the Lincoln Memorial, he did not have that whole speech prepared. Only
the first part was written (in fact, it was handed out in advance), a somewhat formal recitation of Negro injustice and suffering and an exhortation
to carry on the struggle for equal rights with "dignity and discipline." He

intended that to be the whole speech—it was all that fit within his allotted time.

He finished the prepared speech. He was about to sit down. But the story goes that the gospel singer Mahalia Jackson called out, "Tell them about your dream, Martin! Tell them about the dream!" Other listeners shouted encouragement too. And so King launched into an impassioned improvisation that made an already good speech into one of the most moving and powerful speeches of the 20th century.

Obviously King was an extraordinarily adaptable speaker. He was a preacher, of course, experienced in the cadences that make the end of his speech so memorable. He knew how to weave the Bible into his preaching, holding many verses in memory. Likewise he could draw upon the great rhetoric of America's founding documents. He began by echoing Lincoln's Gettysburg Address and ended by citing the Declaration of Independence.

Yet for our purposes another point stands out. It is what Mahalia Jackson asked for: the Dream. King had only barely mentioned it, but she wanted more. The reaction to the speech afterward—continuing to this day—shows that she was not alone in wanting more. What she asked for was a *positive moral vision:* a vision framed not simply as a set of complaints but in terms of ideals and hopes. An explicit and open invitation to a wary nation to join in the spirit that the march had already embodied. And that is what King then—on the spot—offered: the Dream.

> I have a dream that one day on the red hills of Georgia the sons of former slaves and the sons of former slave owners will be able to sit down together at the table of brotherhood.
>
> I have a dream that one day even the state of Mississippi, a state sweltering with the heat of injustice, sweltering with the heat of oppression, will be transformed into an oasis of freedom and justice.
>
> I have a dream that my four little children will one day live in a nation where they will not be judged by the color of their skin but by the content of their character. I have a dream today.
>
> I have a dream that one day, down in Alabama, with its vicious racists, with its governor having his lips dripping with the words of interposition and nullification; one day right there in Alabama, little black boys and black girls will be able to join hands with little white boys and white girls as sisters and brothers. I have a dream today.

Now that King's speech is so famous, this imagery of a "dream" has gotten rather, well, dreamy, and people invoke it for any kind of unrealistic fantasy. But King's Dream is much more focused and modest. In fact it is only a vivid description of what ethics itself asks of us. Community with all others without prejudice. Children, and everyone, judged by who they are and not by external characteristics. King just paints the picture in a way that brings tears to our eyes and makes us all want it too.

VISION AS MORAL PULL

Sometimes moral values operate by *pushing* us, somewhat unwillingly or at least unexpectedly, toward some sort of moral minimum, morally getting by. But pushes are generally not so welcome or so motivating. No one likes to be nagged or constantly reminded of their failings, however necessary it sometimes is.

A moral *pull* is also possible. It captivates us, it rouses the heart and the mind: we move not wearily or out of accommodation but out of real inspiration. This is what I mean by *moral vision:* the capacity to do just what King did—paint a picture of a morally better world in a way that deeply engages and attracts us. It is to draw us toward something grand and lovely.

Of course the civil rights movement was against things: discrimination, disenfranchisement, the routine terrorization of whole populations. It took on deeply entrenched, hateful, often violent resistance. But it never defined itself in predominantly negative terms. What it opposed was not the fundamental point. Always the language, the imagery, even the demonstrations and legal briefs and political platforms, were framed in terms of ideals and hopes. And this is why King's speech is the iconic speech.

It could have been argued—in fact it *was* argued, all the time, by the "realists"—that dreaming was a luxury. But who would remember King's great speech today if he had put all the same points negatively? Suppose he'd said it this way:

> I have a *nightmare* that one day on the red hills of Georgia the sons of former slaves and the sons of former slave owners will *never* be able to sit down together at the table of brotherhood.
>
> I have a *nightmare* that...the state of Mississippi, a state sweltering with the heat of injustice, sweltering with the heat of oppression, will *never* be transformed into an oasis of freedom and justice....

You get the picture. These are exactly the same points, in a way, only the moral tone is reversed. Here racial equality is presented only as a way to stay slightly ahead of moral disaster. The feeling is aversive, unwelcome. We may go forward, but unhappily, always looking backward in fear and pain. King, by contrast, invites us to something wonderful. That is the vision, and that is what compelled people and spoke so powerfully to the moment. King showed us a future that we want to run forward to greet.

SHAREABLE TERMS

Notice also how consistently King appeals to shared terms and common values. At the time, the civil rights movement was regarded by many conservatives as anti-American, and therefore, in the Cold War categories of the time, "Communist." Indeed King was called a Communist many times, was harassed and constantly watched by J. Edgar Hoover's FBI, and was constantly criticized by mainstream politicians and clergymen for moving too fast and asking too much. Yet his appeals are always to the most fundamental American values, and beyond them to biblical values and precepts that will be recognizable and compelling to nearly all his hearers. He's asking for very little, and for what we all recognize to be every American's birthright.

The march itself came at a moment of great tension and uncertainty. King makes this point early on:

> It would be fatal for the nation to overlook the urgency of the moment. This sweltering summer of the Negro's legitimate discontent will not pass until there is an invigorating autumn of freedom and equality.... Those who hope that the Negro needed to blow off steam and will now be content will have a rude awakening if the nation returns to business as usual.

These are strong words. They could even be taken as a threat. Yet King's aim was very different. He wanted to call black people and their white allies to continue the struggle with "dignity and discipline" and indeed peace and love. It was an invitation for more allies. Literally in the very shadow of Lincoln, King spoke of the Emancipation Proclamation as a kind of "promissory note" that the nation had not yet paid. Yet he fully expects that it *will* be paid, and freely and gladly too, once Americans recognize the moral need. That is the Dream, and that is what people so needed to hear: a dream of genuine equality, a better way for everyone.

> Five score years ago, a great American...signed the Emancipation Proclamation. This momentous decree came as a great beacon light of hope to millions of Negro slaves who had been seared in the flames of withering injustice. It came as a joyous daybreak to end the long night of their captivity.
>
> But one hundred years later, the Negro still is not free.... One hundred years later, the Negro is still languishing in the corners of American society and finds himself an exile in his own land.
>
> In a sense we have come to our nation's capital to cash a check. When the architects of our republic wrote the magnificent words of the Constitution and the Declaration of Independence, they were signing a promissory note to which every American was to fall heir. This note was a promise that all men, yes, black men as well as white men, would be guaranteed the unalienable rights of life, liberty, and the pursuit of happiness.
>
> ...Instead of honoring this sacred obligation, America has given the Negro people a bad check, a check which has come back marked "insufficient funds." But we refuse to believe that the bank of justice is bankrupt.... We have...come to this hallowed spot to remind America of the fierce urgency

of now.... Now is the time to make real the promises of democracy. Now is the time to rise from the dark and desolate valley of segregation to the sunlit path of racial justice.... Now is the time to make justice a reality for all of God's children.

King's whole strategy was to call America to recognize in this struggle its own deepest ideals. Here in Washington he speaks from a "hallowed spot," he says. Justice appeals to all of us as equally "God's children." How could the bank of America's moral promise be out of funds? The founding documents of this country, still loved by her black citizens despite her manifold injustices, offer everyone basic and unalienable rights. The dream of racial equality itself, King says,

is deeply rooted in the American dream. I have a dream that one day this nation will rise up and live out the true meaning of its creed: 'We hold these truths to be self-evident: that all men are created equal.'

And so his appeal is to *all* of us, together. Racial equality is not simply about black people: it is about what sort of society we create and sustain together.

The marvelous new militancy which has engulfed the Negro community must not lead us to distrust of all white people, for many of our white brothers, as evidenced by their presence here today, have come to realize that their destiny is tied up with our destiny and their freedom is inextricably bound to our freedom. We cannot walk alone.

In fact, then, contrary to the accusations, it was King and not his accusers who was quintessentially American—and that was the very source of the civil rights movement's power.

WHOLE VISIONS

Vision looks ahead to an ideal state or possibility. To be realistic, though—to really make a difference—that ideal must be in some way attainable. It is not enough to imagine changing one feature of the world, or making a specific moral choice, as if it were independent of everything else. Our visions of better moral choices need to be imagined *inclusively:* they must speak to multiple values and to our practical situation as a whole.

Our vision must be a *whole* vision. The task is to integrate one set of moral values and moral actions with a larger encompassing set of values and actions so that the whole is compelling and lovely and grand. People must be able to see a way to realize them in their own lives and society. And our visions in turn become stronger by being linked to other values and families of values.

Suppose you are very concerned about animal rights. It is certainly important to argue with people about how much animals feel and understand and how our basic families of values—say, the value of persons or utilitarianism—might have to be extended to at least some of them.

Fair enough, so far. But it's not far enough. We need something more: a sense for how these arguments relate to others. For one thing, it may be hard to see how animal rights can apply in our own lives. Many people think that they literally cannot live without meat. They need some idea of how to cook and eat differently. Meanwhile, we may also have a sense—quite justified too—that the animal question opens the door to many others: that taking animals seriously will soon require us to rethink all sorts of other things, not just our attitudes toward food but also our attitudes toward ourselves, toward the natural world as a whole, and maybe even some of our religious beliefs.

So...open up some of these other questions too. Shall we after all rethink that supposedly sharp line between humans and the rest of the world? How *do* our values and even perceptions and maybe even our theology change when we do so?

It's not necessarily that we are averse to looking at these other questions too. We know that there is much to learn! The point is just that we need some help. "Dreaming" a different relation to animals is not enough. Now comes the work of giving it substance, looking at the bigger picture.

ENVIRONMENTAL VISIONS

In the popular impression, environmentalists are the very model of nay-sayers. Opposed to this, worried sick over that, ill-disposed by reflex to almost any human impact on nature. The Voice of Doom. We may listen and adjust, yes, but unhappily and with a constant sense of worry. Mightn't we conclude that what environmentalism really needs is—a vision?

THE VISION

Certainly there is much to worry about. Yet worry is not at all the whole story. The story is really, at bottom, about *love:* love for the Earth, love for Creation, love for the more-than-human wonders that surround us.

And dreams? We know very well what the dreams are. The eco-theologian Thomas Berry even wrote a book explicitly in this key: he called it *The Dream of the Earth*. So cannot we take our cue from Martin Luther King and highlight our dreams more brightly than our fears? Why are we so hesitant about this love?

Try it:

> We have a dream that our own children and our children's children will again be able to freely drink the waters of rushing streams and breathe deep in the morning air and see the glittering stars at night.

We have a dream that we will at last learn to treasure the purple mountain majesties and the great wild creatures of this land—and give them the space that they require to flourish in their own ways.

We have a dream that the children of loggers and the children of tree-huggers will one day work together in a vibrant forest from which they can take what they need without taking its vibrancy.

This is not just stating the obvious: it is *changing the key*. Here, finally, environmentalism clearly and emphatically is presented as *for* something, not just *against* things. Just as King did, it pulls us toward something and doesn't just push. Again: what truly motivates and inspires is a picture of what the world might be instead.

A WHOLE VISION

Once again we must also go further. One of the persistent difficulties with environmentalism is that it has not always been so visibly integrated with other values. Critics continue to argue that nature is a "special interest": that it doesn't really fit with our other values, or with most people's values, and indeed that it is at odds with more central values that most of us hold, such as a good standard of living and a healthy economy. Some years back a memorable newsmagazine headline—it happened to be about the stand-off between timber interests and defenders of the endangered spotted owls in the Pacific Northwest—read "Owl Versus Man." That stark image of opposing interests struck a nerve. We need to know how environmental values *fit in*.

For one thing, we need a vision of a healthy nature that is not only compatible with a healthy economy but also crucial to it. Even in purely economic terms, most environmental measures are actually more profitable in the long run than one-shot exploitation, which enriches a few investors but leaves the community poorer, indeed often wrecked and displaced. (Think of clear-cutting forests, or rainforest burning: what remains is *nothing*.) Economies further into solar and wind power turn out to have fuller employment and healthier populations than those more invested in oil and nuclear power.

Of course we need to cut and use some trees. But what we really need is a *sustainable* timber industry, using wood in a more intensive, craft-based way, rather than shipping massive amounts of raw wood abroad or pulping it for plywood, as the timber corporations do at present. Imagine forest communities once again developing furniture shops and speciality woodcrafts—living *with* the forests rather than "off" the forests until they're gone. The wood stays at home, and every tree, every log, invites a great deal more labor than it takes merely to cut it down and ship it out. That kind of logging, unlike the present practice, would have a future: better for loggers *and* the forests.

Besides, environmental ethics argues here that we are working with far too narrow a picture of human values. We do value comfortable living, of course, but we also value many other things, like keeping awe and respect alive in response to nature—say, endangered owls and the old-growth forests that are their only homes—or just having natural and wild places to go to see the stars and rediscover the tanagers and the turtles. These are genuine values too. Indeed, we are speaking of the whole encompassing Earth, the air, and the water, and the living communities of land and sea which all of us, *and* all of our children and our children's children, *and* all of the other creatures, depend upon. These are hardly "special" interests—they are universal, common, basic interests, which literally ground all others. Here a whole vision brings us back to basics—the "big picture" indeed!

In that sense, titles like "Owl Versus Man" sell "Man"—humans—terribly short. Our interests, our values, are not just economic. The unifying vision is one that is better for us *and* nature—for us as *part* of nature. Tensions no doubt remain—as in any family, short-term interests sometimes pull apart—but the idea that "we" live irrevocably at odds with "nature" is really part of the problem. It's time to look first for the commonalities—the ways in which the "web of life" is *one*.

TOWARD A CELEBRATORY ENVIRONMENTALISM

Now about those creativity skills…they too may have a role to play as we both paint the visionary "big picture" and also push it further.

Creative environmental thinking is bubbling up already. As established religions are coming to the forefront of environmentalism, for example, they bring new and unexpected associations to the table. People are founding "eco-steries" on the model of the medieval world's monasteries, places where nature is honored and preserved "for the long haul" and for its own sake. Meanwhile, NASA is experimenting with "Living Arks," realizing that entire living communities must go into space if long missions are to be possible at all. While philosophers labor over an ethic of respect for other animals, other people are developing new forms of life that actively embody such a respect—some of them absolutely new and fascinating, like musicians creating new musical forms with orcas. They actually go out and *jam*. What next?

To truly establish a visionary turn in environmentalism, we might add our own forms of environmental creativity. Here's one: suppose that we imagine a *celebratory* environmentalism? Suppose, for instance, that we begin to create new environmental holidays. Festivals, maybe, for bird migrations and eclipses. Already at New Year's many people all across the country venture out, before dawn, to count birds for the Audubon Society. Why not take this much further? Imagine weeks of preparation by eager schoolchildren learning to identify birds. Imagine the hopefulness of the observers that a rare bird might come their way, like amateur astronomers hoping to discover a comet. Imagine "Star Nights" on which all lights everywhere are turned out, even in the blazing cities, timed to coincide with meteor showers, eclipses, occlusions. Ralph Waldo Emerson once said, "If the stars came out only one night in a thousand years, how people would believe and adore, and preserve from generation to generation, remembrance of the miracle they'd been shown." For us the miracle is there every dark and clear night—we just need a little help to see it.

The word "holiday" itself, by the way, comes from "holy day," a time when we remember what really matters. Who wouldn't want a few new ones? And when we come to the Earth as a holy place, in love and joy rather than in fear and ignorance, treasuring and preserving it isn't even a question.

We can take a new look at the old holidays too. Many of these are rooted in natural cycles as well. Winter Solstice, the moment when the long descent of the cold and the dark finally ends, the days stop shortening, the sun begins its ascent anew. It is the rebirth of the year: and of course at the moment of greatest darkness we celebrate with lights, on Christmas trees and in menorahs (Hanukah) and kinaras (Kwaanza). Spring brings the Vernal Equinox: Earth itself is, well, resurrected, bursting into new life. Ancient "Samhain," midway between Fall Equinox and Winter Solstice, became All Saints Day— its eve, All Hallows Eve, which we now call Halloween: the death festival, as the leaves fall and the darkness descends. No light without dark, no life without death. Why not? Really, why not?

READING

From What Are Old People For?

BILL THOMAS

RECENTLY I saw a flyer in a store for a skin cream that announces "Miraculous results!": that is, it turned out, a skin that "doesn't reveal your age." (This is called its "philosophy," which is why I noticed it in the first place.) Ordinarily I'd probably not have thought much of it, other than to wonder idly about my own skin, maybe—not that I much mind "looking my age," anyway. Because I'd just been reading Bill Thomas's book *What Are Old People For?*, though, I found myself thinking in a completely different way. I knew Thomas's ideas belonged in this chapter on moral vision.

Bill Thomas is a geriatrician and activist on issues of aging and nursing-home reform. Early on, as a doctor at nurs-

ing homes, he encountered first-hand the profound loneliness of his patients. At first he had no resources for dealing
with it, and pushed it aside, as so many do, as an inevitable
aspect of aging. But it struck him repeatedly and forcefully,
and finally set him off on long journey both for major reform
in the design and administration of old-age homes (he's more
or less against them...or rather, for a totally different model)
and, even more fundamentally, in the social status of the aged
and aging.

Take that seemingly small matter of the "miracle cream,"
for example. "What would it be like," Thomas asks, "to live in a
society that adored wrinkles?"

> The idea may seem laughable at first, but for millennia,
> living to a ripe old age was an exceptional achievement
> and recognized as such by society.... What if the war in
> wrinkles were replaced by a crazy new wave of wrinkle-
> promoting ingenuity? Any desire to intentionally age
> one's face seems bizarre to those reared in a youth-dom-
> inated culture. It upsets unspoken assumptions about
> aging. However, imagine, if just for a moment, that we
> lived in a world that embraced the arrival of [what Mari-
> lyn Monroe once called] a face with character.... Such a
> society would swoon over wrinkled actors, artists, and
> models.... Spas and retreats would promise "You'll look
> ten years older in just two weeks." It really would be a
> different world.

Must aging be a disaster, a decline and fading away? What
if it were instead deeply treasured and revered? The coming of
wisdom, even blurring of the lines between ancestors and the
living as one moves close to ancestor-hood oneself... mightn't
such a thing even be eagerly anticipated? And then we may ask
a key "strategic question": what would it take to create a culture
that honored age in this way? For one thing, rather than build
itself so wholly around the young and their demands and needs,
it would have to be a culture that asked first how to accommodate
the needs of older people, starting with technologies more user-
friendly for them. Poor eyesight would not be a problem if signs
and print were bigger. The old would be expected to live at the
centers of life rather than exiled to the irrelevant peripheries. We'd
look forward to *pro*-tirement rather than re-tirement: that is, the
graduation to greater rather than lesser tasks. Maybe you couldn't
even *begin* certain kinds of work until you were, say, seventy-five.

And what kind of work might that be? Is it possible that
it is even work that elders are already doing—and arguably
have always done—but today has been made mostly invisible,

not recognized or honored by our society, and systematically pushed to the edges and disabled as a result?

Here, in short, is an invitation to a radical new vision of aging as a whole. You can find in Thomas's work all of the aspects of moral vision pointed out in this chapter. He certainly offers a *positive* vision: he even calls it "Eldertopia." It is an *inclusive* vision—it is for all of us, not just the (presently) aged (for in due time, with luck, all of us will get there). And it is a *whole* vision, in the sense that he asks us to re-envision an entire set of interrelated factors and changes that together will transform the culture and life for all of us, the old and the not-yet old. He even has the audacity to subtitle his book *How Elders Will Save the World.*

The pages reprinted here are from the very end of Thomas's book. In the pages that precede them, Thomas argues—among many other things—that old age is not just a form of declining adulthood. It is *different* from adulthood, just as adulthood is different from childhood. "There is something vital and true to be grasped within the distinctively human experience of growing old." Other cultures have known it: Thomas uses chapter 13's tool, "Compare and Contrast," to ask us to consider tribal cultures, for example, who literally initiate their elders into *post-adulthood*—the most profound honor the tribe gives. Thomas also relates speaking to an Alaskan tribal member who even considers Alzheimer's dementia (memory loss) not as a tragedy but as a *gift.* She said, he reports, "that when an elder living with dementia made reference to seeing and speaking with long-dead relatives, it was taken as proof that the elder had been gifted with the ability to have one foot in this world and one foot in the spirit world." I have heard others emphasize that elders across traditional Native American cultures are considered to be wise partly *because* they are no longer preoccupied with the day to day details of life (a little short-term memory loss helps here) but correspondingly more clearly remember the deeper and longer-held things, the tribal memories and the bigger pictures. A vital role too—and one that today's culture, arguably, suffers for lacking.

Thomas points out that the generation now hitting the leading edge of "post-adulthood" is the 60s generation. More than any generation in history, he says, "they have demonstrated an eagerness to challenge and even overturn long-established beliefs. There is little to suggest that the role of the quiet, uncomplaining grandparent will appeal to them." But, he continues, *"what they are missing—what we are all missing—is a vision of elderhood with its own claim to greatness"* (my emphasis). Might we find such a vision here?

The relationships that have powered human cultural advancement for tens of thousands of years are a complex set of intergenerational interactions. Taken together, they form the engine that has shaped us, served us, blunted our worst tendencies, and magnified our best. Given the terrible might of modern industrial society, we need this engine more than ever before. The cult of adulthood is insistent in its claims that old age is irrelevant and possibly on the edge of its own extinction (given sufficient progress in pharmaceutical laboratories). Though few actually believe that old age can be vanquished, it is easy to wish that it were so. Many find refuge in treasured illusions about traditional aging. In truth, the old way of growing old was never as good as we like to remember it being and is especially ill suited to the society in which we live today. We really have no choice but to look ahead. The times demand that we create a new elderhood—one that fits the way we live now. We need this new elderhood not only for ourselves (we all deserve a better, richer, more meaningful old age) but for people of all ages.

Public discourse, however, operates from very different assumptions. Within its realm, longevity is imagined to be of concern solely to the aged, those who care for them, and those who pay for that care. We are constantly reminded of how expensive this is, and like the miser who feels he may have been cheated, we expect a precise accounting of what has been paid and what has been delivered. Former Colorado governor Richard Lamm begins his essay "The Moral Imperative of Limiting Elderly Health Entitlements" by noting that "one of the great challenges in America's future is to retire the baby boomers without bankrupting the country or unduly burdening future generations.... Age could well be as divisive in the next forty years as race and sex have been for the last forty years."

Given the sums involved and the potentially devastating consequences of mismanagement, much of this concern is warranted. What is missing from the debate, however, is a proper accounting of what elderhood can contribute to society. This side of the ledger is given scant attention by those who can see only the wealth and vigor of adults and the potentially ruinous burden imposed by the aged. Lamm goes on to point out that, regardless of how it may make us feel, decisions will have to be made: "We are a compassionate society and can afford a lot, but we cannot afford everything. No publicly financed health system can ignore the law of diminishing returns.... It is necessary to find, among the myriad of things we can do, what practically in a budget we ought to do."

The worldview that former governor Lamm represents places old age outside the pale of productive, contributing adults. They are expensive accessories and, while we may be a "compassionate society," there is a limit to what *we* can do for *them*. I am arguing for a very different conception of elders and elderhood—one that places them (and their needs) within rather than outside the central purposes of our society. What we need is a holistic perspective that appreciates and respects the contributions that people of all ages have made and are now making to the pursuit of happiness and our collective well-being. It should not come as a surprise that our language lacks a word that describes the interdependence that joins young and old. Instead, we have "entitlements" and "cross-generational wealth transfers." The wisdom of living in a multigenerational social structure is ancient, undeniable, and deserving of a word of its own. I like *Eldertopia:*

> **Eldertopia** *noun* A community that improves the quality of life for people of all ages by strengthening and improving the means by which (1) the community protects, sustains, and nurtures its elders, and (2) the elders contribute to the well-being and foresight of the community. An Eldertopia that is blessed with a large number of older people is acknowledged to be "elder-rich" and uses this human capital to the advantage of all.

Our longevity exists, has meaning, and creates value because it provides human beings with a mechanism for improving the lives of people *of all ages.* That mechanism is a pattern of reciprocal relationships that unite the generations. Far from being society's expensive leftovers, elders and the elderhood they inhabit are crucial to the well-being of all.

This assessment highlights the flaws inherent in the accounting systems of the "old-age welfare state." Conventional practice tabulates to the penny the money spent serving the elderly, even as it ignores the vital contributions that our longevity makes to society as a whole. We need a new and much more realistic set of accounting books.

Fortunately, Eldertopia can lead us to a deeper and far more accurate understanding of how longevity completes us. For a start it can shed light on the complex and easily overlooked intergenerational transfers that are essential to people of all ages. The idea of the "greedy geezer" is the product of a society that counts only what the young pay to the old. Becoming more conscious of the contributions that elders make to the young is a good first step in correcting the bias against the old. Fully developed, this more balanced approach can document in black and white why our longevity is a solid investment.

MAPPING ELDERTOPIA

Eldertopia supposes that human communities rely heavily on reciprocal altruism and calls for a detailed accounting of all sides of these exchanges. In its most basic form, such a chart of accounts would include answers to the following questions:

- In what ways and to what extent do elders receive support from adults?
- In what ways do elders contribute ongoing assistance to the adults of the community?
- How are we to recognize and properly value the gentling and acculturation of children by elders?
- In what ways and to what extent do we acknowledge the ongoing assistance and affection given to elders by the children in their lives?

Some of these contributions can be reduced to numerical terms; others cannot. The current public debate surrounding aging and its entitlements is distorted by the nearly exclusive emphasis that is placed on the financial cost of publicly funded programs and the pitiful lack of attention that is paid to the more qualitative elements of the ongoing exchange between young and old.

In order for any exchange to be fair and just, both parties must fully understand the value of what is being given and received. Alarmist rhetoric of the "plague of locusts" variety becomes shrill precisely because it fails to acknowledge the value of what elders have done, do now, and will continue to contribute to the young. Public officials and academic experts have surprisingly little to say on the subject of how the aged help sustain their families and communities. Studies of volunteerism have lauded the work that senescents and elders do within faith-based and community organizations, and a few studies have even attempted to put a price tag on those contributions. Far greater, though, is the commitment that the aged make to the people they love. Most people suppose that adults support their aged parents with material resources (and many do), but taken as a whole, the elders of our society give more to their children and their children's families than they receive from them.

Perhaps the most endangered and least appreciated element of the ancient exchange between young and old is the gentling and acculturation of children by elders. Historically, this has taken place exclusively within the family and kinship group. Life in modern society has, of course, disrupted many of these arrangements. Children are increasingly confined to and molded by large, professionally run educational institutions. Elders are segregated, by choice and by fiat, within their own age-specific institutions, facilities, and housing developments. The result is a generation of young unlike any before it, a generation that is growing to maturity without the guiding hand of elders and elderhood. This arrangement penalizes elders as well. Many must live and die without knowing the tender embrace of the very young in their daily lives.

A full accounting of these exchanges, even one that lacked precise values, would alter public policy and reshape public opinion. The material aspect of such an exchange—goods and services—is the easiest to document and can usually be tallied in dollars and cents. But we must also make the informal and private dimensions of the exchange known, and give them their due. Eldertopia is, at its most fundamental level, a path to a new consciousness of age and aging. It sets aside incomplete ideas about dependency and decline and presents instead the dynamic image of an active and ongoing exchange between the generations. Taken seriously, it can help us document the staggering value contained within the global age boom. It can change how we live together. Consider the following Eldertopian possibilities.

Elders Giving Warmth   Elders have always made important contributions to the young of their families and communities. For thousands of years, relationships created between young and old have made life better for both groups. In Eldertopia, all school construction and remodeling projects would include housing and community services for elders. The idea of isolating one group from the other would be seen as the ridiculous waste that it is. Those who sought to provide care and services for the elders would take care to integrate their offerings with the routines and needs of the young. In Eldertopia the wall that separates young and old would have to come down.

Elders Receiving Warmth   The myth of independence has led millions of elders to prefer living alone to any form of communal life. This is in spite of the fact that old age, like childbirth, was never meant to be confronted alone. The Meals on Wheels program is intended to improve life for elders living at home by delivering meals to their homes. Because of the expense involved, some programs have turned to weekly deliveries of frozen food instead of daily deliveries of hot meals. Of course, the daily delivery of meals offers much more than food. It also provides what one elder calls "a face at the door." In the future, daily meal deliveries will be difficult to sustain unless there is a community-wide awareness of the value of bringing human warmth into elders' lives. In Eldertopia, community leaders would acknowledge that elders cannot live on frozen food alone.

Elders Giving Wisdom   Many traditional societies maintain mechanisms whereby the wisdom of elders can be communicated to the leaders of the day. Elder councils, for example, provide a balancing perspective that considers the long-term consequences of any proposed action. Too often in our society, the perspective of elderhood is reduced to just one of many competing interest groups. Eldertopia encourages the formation of elder councils that meet regularly and offer their views on the challenges and opportunities facing the community. The topics addressed might well include matters that the conventional political system would rather sweep under the rug. The media can and should cover the elder council and its deliberations. In Eldertopia, the community as a whole would no longer be deaf to the voices of it elders.

Elders Receiving the Benefits of Technology   Advances in technology have done much to improve the well-being of older people, but so much more could be done. There is a tremendous potential for using ordinary off-the-shelf technology to help elders do more themselves, expand their potential to live independently and in dignity, and maintain vital connections to their community and people they love. We can and should embrace a smart technology that fuses an accurate understanding of the challenges of old age with the best tools that our industrial society has to offer. Eldertopia would ensure that the elders had access to technology capable of aiding the pursuit of the best elderhood possible.

Elderhood's Commitment to Stewardship   Elders have long been critical of the adult's desire to get, have, and take all that he or she is capable of getting, having, and taking. The consequences of such avarice can be found in our dirty air and water and the mass extinction of species that is currently in progress. Elders have long spoken for Earth, its living creatures, and the children who are yet to be born. They have not always prevailed, nor should they, but a society that marginalizes elders and the value of their lived experience endangers us all because it removes their concerns from our thoughts. There is much to be done if we are to repair the damage that has been done to the living world that sustains us. Eldertopia would have an Elder Environmental Conservation Corps that would tackle projects that would strengthen the health and vitality of the natural world. In Eldertopia, nature would have an influential new ally.

Elders Receiving Well-Being from Nature   There is a dawning awareness that nature should be an important part of any setting intended to improve health or assist in healing. Eventually, the inclusion of nature in plans for these environments will seem as essential and ordinary as planning for doors and windows. In Elder-topia, the community would organize itself to see that the healing effect that comes with a connection to nature is made available to every elder.

Eldertopia is a useful concept because we can use it to improve the well-being of all members of society. It makes explicit the ancient patterns of exchange between the young and the old. We all benefit when these connections are strengthened and enriched, just as we all suffer when they are ignored or trampled. The most elder-rich period of human history is upon us. How we regard and make use of this windfall of elders will define the world in which we live. Eldertopia restores aging to longevity and returns the aged to a worthy elderhood. Even more than that, it restores elderhood to its rightful place in the human life cycle. In this way, it creates the possibility of a better life for us all.

NEW DIRECTIONS

The word *Eldertopia* is tinged with impossibility. Sophisticated adults, after all, feel that they have outgrown utopias—left them behind on their journey into the future. We should not be so hasty. The utopian ideal has long served to reveal the gap between what is and what ought to be. At its best, it is distilled imagination placed into the service of everyday life. Utopias have the power to change how we think about our times and our selves. Eldertopia is nota-ble because it offers not the violent disruption of revolution but a patient, gentle return to an evolutionary process that began long ago and that is already deep in our bones. Because it is founded on millennia of human experience, Eldertopia requires neither federal legislation nor a court order in order to come to life. In fact, we can begin creating Eldertopia today.

Marcel Proust observed, "The real voyage of discovery consists not in seeking new landscapes but in having new eyes." This is the challenge of Eldertopia. How can we convert ordinary situations and daily decisions into extraordinary opportunities to explore a new way of seeing, thinking, and acting? How do we bring the complex web of interdependencies that define a healthy community out into the open? How can we cope with the grinding efficiency of the cult of adulthood, which is, increasingly, putting the true nature of our longevity beyond our reach?

This alienation is not inevitable. Not a day, not a moment passes when we do not have the opportunity to move our society toward the ideals of Eldertopia. The importance of this idea grows with the gathering power of adulthood and the distortions that come of living in a world run by and for adults. There is a limit to how long we can continue to discount and dismiss the guiding intelligence of elders and elderhood. How does society acknowledge the bilateral nature of the community's relationship with its elders? How do our decisions and priorities enlarge or diminish our ability to sustain this exchange? Does the item you are hearing about at a meeting, reading about in the newspaper, or discussing within your family aid in the rebirth of elderhood, or does it simply extend the power of adults and adulthood?

Consider the following situations according to how well or poorly they bring forth the possibility of Eldertopia:

- A local nursing home is requesting approval for an addition to its existing facility. This move simply strengthens the grip that the old-age archipelago has over the aged and offers the community little or nothing in return. **Rating: Poor**

- A local senior center announces that it is hosting a "brown bag" evaluation of local elders' prescribed medication regimens. A licensed pharmacist tours local communities, helping elders avoid the perils of polypharmacy and drug interactions. The elders who attend save money by eliminating unnecessary medications and reduce their exposure to unpleasant medication side effects. **Rating: Good**

- A coalition of organizations serving the young and the old creates a summer camp that accommodates and integrates the needs of older people (including people currently confined to nursing homes) and local children. Such an intergenerational summer camp strengthens the community by enriching the bond between young and old. **Rating: Excellent**

Does the change actively recognize that elders are a vital resource in the community and that the community is, in fact, elder-rich? How is that richness integrated into innovation?

- Nursing homes lobby for increased funding for the services they provide, and the dollars needed to fund the increase are taken from programs that provide home- and community-based services. This outcome reflects the political strength of an industry rather than the preferences of community elders. It fails us because it slows the move away from institutional long-term care. **Rating: Poor**

- A local school initiates a program that connects elders with latchkey children. A participating elder makes regular daily phone contact with a child and provides a reliable source of interest and concern. This reduces loneliness among both groups and teaches children about the meaning and worth of elderhood. **Rating: Good**

- A newspaper article announces the creation of a local chapter of the Elder Environmental Conservation Corps. The Corps recruits members and organizes projects with a special emphasis on bringing the young and old together. The Corps also reaches out to those who have been removed from the community by taking an active role in the "greening" of local long-term care environments. This work provides visible proof of the value of stewardship and creates opportunities for the young to share the company of the old. **Rating: Excellent**

To what degree does the project or service demonstrate a commitment to improving the quality of life for people of all ages? Healthy communities rely heavily on the virtues of reciprocal altruism; we can guide social change by favoring innovations that foster reciprocity and by discouraging changes that rely solely on the movement of material resources from one group to another.

- A local agency seeks funding to extend its Meals on Wheels service area. It supports its request by emphasizing the number of people who will be served and the number of meals that will be prepared and delivered. **Rating: Poor**

- The request is revised. This time the funding is justified both in terms of the number of people served and a promised increase in participation by volunteers of all ages. The desired outcome is evaluated in terms of a combined measure of service delivered and growth of the volunteer effort. **Rating: Good**

- Another revision is submitted. This time the envisioned outcomes include the number of meals delivered, diversity in the age and background of volunteers, the variety of efforts contributed, and the impact of an outreach effort to communicate Eldertopian ideas to elders, volunteers, and community members in the new service area. **Rating: Excellent**

The need for human warmth touches people of all ages. Eldertopia is dedicated to creating human warmth for young and old alike. In fact, it leverages the ancient virtues that have held the generations together for millennia. In our families, in our jobs, in our thoughts and conversations, we can dedicate ourselves to the creation of a community with greater warmth for everyone. Human warmth is associated with optimism, trust, and generosity. How does what we do create or destroy human warmth?

- The local Area Agency on Aging announces the creation of a geriatric case management system for frail elders living in the community. This worthy goal is presented solely in terms of cost control and the arm's-length delivery of professional services. **Rating: Poor**
- A group of community and faith-based organizations begins to teach its members how to advocate for people they care about. This unites young and old and enables people to demonstrate their commitment to the elders in their lives in an effective new way. **Rating: Good**
- A United Way agency announces its intention to evaluate all requests for funding in terms of the precepts of Eldertopia. This does not mean that it will fund only "services for the elderly." In fact, it is just the opposite. The United Way will back efforts that can demonstrate how they intend to improve the quality of life for people of all ages by strengthening and improving the means by which (1) the community protects, sustains, and nurtures its elders and (2) the elders contribute to the well-being and foresight of the community. **Rating: Excellent**

How can our mastery of tools and technologies be used in support of elders and elderhood? Smart technology acknowledges the human dimension of the tools we use and is conscious of how those tools shape the communities in which we live.

- A local senior center installs Internet-ready computers for use by the elderly. **Rating: Poor**
- The school district arranges for elders to use the school's equipment and staff for computer technology education. **Rating: Good**

- Senior centers match children with elders so that each can teach the other about computers and the uses of the Internet. Simultaneously, elders are encouraged to go to schools to learn and share computer skills. Children and elders act as both teachers and students as time and circumstances dictate. Eldertopia cultivates a growing awareness of the bilateral nature of the exchange between generations—each gives, each receives. The key variable is enlarging the bilateral exchange of skills and abilities. The temptation to pigeonhole either group according to stereotyped attitudes is resisted. **Rating: Excellent**

In what ways does society acknowledge the importance of nature and contact with the living world?

- A nursing home establishes a pet visitation program. While it is better than doing nothing, this type of intervention medicalizes the joys we associate with the human-animal bond. **Rating: Poor**
- Local gardening clubs (whose members are mostly older) actively recruit school children into their ranks. **Rating: Good**
- Your local Elder Environmental Conservation Corps announces its first meeting. You and your grandchildren decide to attend and mark the date on your calendars. **Rating: Excellent**

One of the advantages of a concept like Eldertopia is that it weaves a concern for our elders together with the interests and desires of people of all ages. In the context of Eldertopia, groups that support children, refugees, women, education, entrepreneurship, and ecology can all find reasons to be enthused about bringing elders into their own work.

This idea of bringing elders into the work of various groups provides a powerful opportunity to spread the concept of Eldertopia and leverage the power of social change across a wide range of community agencies and organizations. A similar strategy was employed with respect to public art in the city of San Francisco. In the 1990s, a small group of people were intent on seeing a wider array of art become available to the public outside of museums. Though their funds were limited, they saw value in sharing their ideals with many other stakeholders, including architects, developers, neighborhood associations, and community groups. The result is that many of these other entities included public art in their own projects and initiatives. The impact ultimately went far beyond anything they could have done on their own.

QUICK REFERENCE: WORKING FROM A VISION

WORK FROM A VISION

Aim for more than a collection of criticisms and negative moral judgments. What truly motivates and inspires is a picture of what the world might be instead. Paint a picture of a morally better world in a way that deeply engages and attracts. Speak the dream.

WORK FROM A SHAREABLE VISION

Draw on shared values. Speak to everyone—to the best aspirations in us all.

WORK FROM A WHOLE VISION

Paint the big picture. Make the dream practical—show "how to get there from here." Integrate it with other values and even other dreams. Make the whole hang together!

PRACTICE RADICAL IMAGINATION

Things do not have to be the way they are right now. Even basic things can change, sometimes quite fast. Ask *how* (not whether) they could be different. Push yourself to find a path. Imagine not just two steps down that path, but all the way. Why not?

 FOR REVIEW

1. What is "moral vision"?
2. How is Martin Luther King, Jr.'s "I Have a Dream" speech an example of moral vision?
3. In what ways does King's vision draw upon "shareable terms"?
4. What is a "whole vision"?
5. Why is whole vision necessary?
6. Does environmentalism need a vision? What vision?
7. Does environmentalism need a *whole* vision? What whole vision?
8. What is "celebratory environmentalism"?

9. How does Bill Thomas exercise moral vision in his proposal for "Eldertopia"?

10. According to Thomas, what *are* old people for?

EXERCISES AND NOTES

15.1 REFRAMING MORAL POSITIONS AS VISIONS

We do not always put moral positions as visions. Environmentalism was the text's case in point, but there are many others. But, as the text argues, things may look very different if we did.

Take this as a challenge. Take prominent moral positions on issues that interest you, and reframe them as visions. Do this for your own positions, for sure—and just as important, try to do it for moral positions to which you are indifferent or opposed. Remember, it's not just a matter of stating the position or of stating it fairly and accurately. These are important skills in their own right, but you've already practiced them in previous chapters. The challenge here is to find the vision, the "dream." Do a little research if you need to. Are some of these dreams already articulated? Why don't we hear more of them?

Can you do this for both sides (all sides) in the abortion debate, for example? Look also at the different positions on capital punishment, sexuality, gay marriage, business ethics, welfare, and any other issue that interests and engages you.

15.2 REFRAMING VISIONS AS WHOLE VISIONS

Use this exercise as a follow-up to the last one. You have now laid out some of the visions that lie behind current moral contentions. Now try to develop them as *whole* visions. That is, don't leave them just "dreamy." Make them as integrated with other values and as practical as you can.

Abortion, for example. Here again both sides' positions can be better expressed as visions, in fact as complex whole visions. Again, I leave it to you to spell out the "dreams"—just notice that they are *big* dreams. They are not simply about abortion. Passionate defenders of "life," say, would hardly rest content if *Roe v. Wade* were merely overturned. There are a host of other things to do: strengthen the family, enhance prenatal and postnatal care, speak to the hypersexualization of everything teenaged. Work it out.

Use your other ethical tools as well. For example, as you become more detailed, be alert for ways in which different dreams intersect and overlap. Passionate *defenders* of abortion rights, for example, would hardly rest content if *Roe* were merely secured either. Once again there are a host of other things to do, such as . . . strengthen the family, enable adequate prenatal and postnatal care, and speak to the hypersexualization of everything teenaged, as well as promote equal access to child care, family leave policies, and rethinking the relations between the sexes in general. Common ground here looks extensive. Of course disagreements remain, even fundamental ones. But again: the "big pictures" are not pure and simple opposites. Whole visions complexify, overlap, draw us back into connection and interdependence, make it possible for us to go forward together.

Your challenge, then, is to take up this same sort of *whole* visioning for some of the other issues that interest and engage you. Gay rights? Business ethics? What about that slogan, "If you want peace, work for justice"? What about the work ethic? Chapter 7 hints that perhaps the work ethic is evolving into something new. But what? What is the vision? How much further might the vision go?

15.3 PRACTICING RADICAL IMAGINATION

If things really do not have to be the way they are at the moment, then whenever we confront something morally problematic or even just morally neutral, we can always ask: how else could this be? What seems to be a "given" can be reapproached as a *question*—and, often, a fairly radical question. Quite seriously and practically, we can ask: why? And the natural follow-up is: How could it be different?

Bill Thomas rethinks aging *radically* in the selection from *What Are Old People for?* Again, it's not just a matter of making slightly nicer nursing homes or a few more programs at the Senior Center. *Everything* changes. The possibility of a different kind of *culture* comes into view. Take a deep breath and sit up straight. This is not for the faint of heart.

Yet it is worth a try—worth at least knowing what vision on this scale might actually feel like. Can you imagine other such changes, then, in other areas of life?

Of course this is easier said than done. Remember, though: chapters 13 and 14 already have offered you a range of creative-thinking tools. Your task now is just to push them further. Invite *really* exotic associations. Exaggerate once, and then do it again. And again. Revisit *many* outlying aspects of the original problem. *Seriously* look for opportunities in the problems. If it is possible to see even dementia as an opportunity (of course it also needs another name, like "timeless vision"), then where are the limits?

In 2003, worldwide demonstrations against the pending military action in Iraq were organized on the Internet in the space of a week. The result was the largest mass action in the history of the planet. This already is an amazing and suggestive fact, regardless of what you think about the war itself. But suppose it were only the beginning? How much further could we extrapolate? What if we now used the Internet to build ongoing worldwide organizations based on direct contact between people, rather than always mediated by nation-states? Suppose we even built a whole new representative structure out of this—with representatives' "districts" being virtual rather than geographical, say, including people already in contact with each other all over the globe? If state and land don't have to be geographically distinct, we could also begin to visualize a totally new approach to, say, ongoing struggles between two peoples claiming the same land.

Doctors Without Borders brings not just medicine but also moral succor, or at least visibility, to oppressed communities around the world. Great, but why stop there? Already there are Students Without Borders, linking students around the world to promote travel, cross-cultural understanding, and academic freedom. Now how about, say, Electricians Without Borders, or Librarians Without Borders, or Musicians Without Borders, or Democrats Without Borders, or, who knows, even Ethical Philosophers Without Borders? Election Monitors Without Borders? (Notice that this is actually already happening: think of the post-Presidential career of Jimmy Carter). Likewise—Elders Without Borders? Imagineers Without Borders?

NOTES

Martin Luther King, Jr.'s "I Have a Dream" speech is widely available on the Web and in historical collections. On the end of the speech as an inspired improvisation, see http://usinfo.state.gov/usa/infousa/facts/democrac/38 .htm.

Thomas Berry's *The Dream of the Earth* is out in a second edition from Sierra Club Books, 2006. *Time*'s "Owl Versus Man" cover appeared on June 25, 1990. A thorough study concluding that environmentalism and economic welfare are *not* at odds—that, in fact, they go together—is Stephen Meyer, *Environmentalism and Economic Prosperity* (MIT Project on Environmental Politics and Policy, 1992).

I cite Bill Thomas's *What Are Old People For?* (VanderWyk and Burnham, 2004) from pp. 10, 31, 59, and 283–84—but I recommend the whole book, of course. For a quick introduction to his thinking from the man himself, watch Thomas's TED talk at http://tedxtalks.ted.com/video/TEDxSF-Bill-Thomas-Elderhood-Ri.

By way of training the more radical side of the imagination, try my brief handbook, *How to Re-Imagine the World* (New Society Publishers, 2007), from which I borrow at the end of Exercise 15.3. On environmental visions, including some well off the usual scales, try my *Mobilizing the Green Imagination: An Exuberant Manifesto* (New Society Publishers, 2012).

IV

CHALLENGES

CHAPTER 16

Response-ability

"Realists" will tell you that ethics is nice for classrooms or Sunday mornings but not practical in the world as it is. And as for actually changing the world—"get over it!" But this book tells a different story. Ethics as pictured here is *essentially* practical, and possibilities for making ethical change, even dramatic ethical change, lie all around us. Recognizing those possibilities and effectively taking them up is also an ethical skill. Methods for change-making—and concepts, inspirations, stories—should be part of your ethical toolbox as well.

We can start right at home: with the question of changing *ourselves*. Rethinking and perhaps remaking our own habits and practices. Here is a kind of change you very definitely *can* make—never mind the rest of the world for a moment—with an excellent chance of real success. Changing yourself may even be a precondition for being able to make changes in the larger world beyond.

SELF-POSSESSION

Self-possession means the capacity to choose for yourself who you will be and what you will do. And *truly* choosing: that is, thinking and choosing in a way that is relatively free from the familiar social pressures that are questionably ethical, such as the pressure to conform, and from old habits that may seem the most natural things in the world but still need rethinking. John Sullivan, remember, speaks of self-possession as "response-ability": the capacity to choose one's responses, or, more specifically, the capacity to observe one's own habits of responsiveness and then to rethink them and change them as necessary.

Sullivan points out that response-ability must be *cultivated*. It is not a natural thing. Too many forces push the other way. People are often afraid to step even a quarter inch out of line, even when no one else would notice. Unhelpful habits can be immensely restricting too. We try to force ourselves into impossible body types or take up habits we know are self-destructive, because, well, others around us are doing so. TV ad campaigns create overnight fads, and ads in general fuel the persistent craving for more *stuff.* Two years later we wonder what got into us. The same is sometimes true for political passions, going to war, seizing on a career, even getting married. Sometimes we are very far from freedom.

Experiments even suggest that people will readily accept a completely mad system just because someone in authority expects it of them. You may have heard of experiments conducted by social psychologist Stanley Milgram in the early 1960s. Prompted by the trial of Nazi war criminals, Milgram wrote,

> I set up a simple experiment...to test how much pain an ordinary citizen would inflict on another person simply because he was ordered to by an experimental scientist. Stark authority was pitted against the subjects' [participants'] strongest moral imperatives against hurting others, and, with the subjects' [participants'] ears ringing with the screams of the victims, authority won more often than not.

What Milgram described as the "extreme willingness of adults to go to almost any lengths on the command of an authority"—in this case, simply an actor wearing a white lab coat—is deeply disturbing. Some subjects woke up as a result of the experience—a few even wrote to Milgram later to thank him for showing them the need for moral backbone—but most apparently did not, and of course, even when people had regrets later, their original acts still stood.

The problem is not merely that lacking response-ability makes us susceptible to bad influences. After all, in the same way we're also susceptible, presumably, to good influences. Lack of response-ability can also make of our selves a resentful wasteland. Spending our lives feeling (and *being*) manipulated and weak does not make for self-respect or creativity or joy. It leads to anger that can easily be manipulated back against others, or even against ourselves. We need another way.

CULTIVATING RESPONSE-ABILITY

So how do we make our thoughts—our *selves*—a little more our own, and therefore also make our acts more self-possessed and free?

Of course it is partly a matter of willpower, determination, even of a kind of courage. Commitment and persistence are essential. We have to be willing to take on self-possession as a project, stop simply "going along," and sometimes take a harder path.

But will by itself is not enough. In fact, it's hardly even a start. What we really need are *methods,* strategies: ways of creating an alternative momentum for ourselves. Some of these methods may seem obvious— some *are* obvious, but need to be pointed out anyway—while others may surprise you.

First: give yourself some space to think. Literally. Regularly seek out quiet places to be safe and alone, set aside time that is not rushed or distracted. It is for good reason that the world's religious traditions embrace the practice of spiritual retreat. Give yourself the chance to catch your breath, to get a little distance, to take stock of things on your own terms.

Second: rearrange your inputs. Carefully list the pressures that tend to pull you in the way you really want to go, and then consider how you might rearrange your life so that more of these pressures are present, and/or fewer counterpressures. To use your school time productively, hang around productive places like libraries and studios and gyms. If you want to reduce your alcohol use, don't spend your time in bars or with drinkers. Find yourself attractive alternative activities and friends. In general, don't set up your life so you constantly have to battle temptations and swim against the current. In all seriousness: find yourself a different river! Avoid manipulators: the incessant and insistent voice of the commercial media, for example, and ads or films that are regularly using ever more extreme imagery to catch your attention.

Keep at it. You will not free your mind overnight. Also, take manageable steps. This may mean starting small. It may take time to find your moral voice and the courage of your convictions. One thing will lead to the next. Get in the habit of going your own way about small but important things to you—avoiding sexist or racist humor might be one good place to start—so that when bigger things come along, you have had some practice. You may also find, once you step out on your own in any way, that people will begin to look to you for leadership. Even small things make a difference.

Get informed. Identify the facts and resources you will need, and go find them. I have seen many students decide to go meat-free, for instance, with the best of intentions and goodwill, only to discover after a month that they cannot, so to speak, live on bread alone. Of course not! Yet an informed vegetarian diet can be easy and extremely healthy, and fellow vegetarians (and cookbooks, grocery stores, restaurants, clubs, etc.) can now be found nearly everywhere.

Remember your critical thinking skills. The point is not to embrace some new dogma and thereafter define yourself by it. Ultimately that isn't response-able either: you make yourself unable to respond in any way but one. Thinking more deeply means recognizing complexity and ambiguity and the changing face of many issues. Expect—and invite and celebrate—growth and change.

SEXUAL CHOICES

Sexual self-possession is a case in point. Sex is an unmatched source of pleasure and celebration, an essential element of happiness for many people.

As such it is already, also, of central moral value. Though the term "sexual ethics" seems to suggest to some people a kind of killjoy fuddy-duddyism, ethics has a few more notes to play than that.

SEX AND MORAL VALUES

We get crude, maybe, if we reduce sex to nothing but the immediate pleasure or release of tension. But there is much more to sex than this, even in purely hedonistic terms. Sex involves the many pleasures of companionship and mutual appreciation, of touching and simple physical togetherness, of wonder and gracefulness and humor too. The needs it fulfills are not just passing and physical but go to the very core of our beings. Nothing crude about that.

Other families of moral values also immediately come into play. Sex can be seen as the desire to unite with another person, to go beyond the limits of our own being and solitude. In this way we can view sex as a fitting completion of our natures, both as animals and as social and spiritual beings. Sex is part of what brings us into caring and community. It transmutes physical desire into loyalty, sharing, family, love.

Cautions and limits therefore arise against this very background of moral complexity—out of the very nature of sex itself. They aren't arbitrary moral impositions from somewhere else. One familiar guideline comes straight from the first family of values: sexual love should respond to a *whole person*— body *and* soul, as it were, together. Sexual acts are physical, in part, usually: but sex is nonetheless a relation between persons, and thus has the power to put us and keep us deeply in touch with the reality of another person, inexhaustible and "infinite," as Levinas would say; an end in themselves, as Kant puts it, not as a mere means to pleasure.

Sex also offers a radical kind of trust, which calls for trustworthiness in return. We give of our bodies, which can be treasured and honored, or hurt or infected or unwillingly impregnated; and of our feelings, which can be shared and deepened, or betrayed or manipulated. Thus we are called to take care with the gift of another's trust. In a situation of such profound vulnerability, irresponsibility—carelessness, deception, coercion—is the complementary vice.

A second guideline, then, is that sexual love should sustain connection, relationship, and trust. It is no accident that we speak of *making* love. Questions of attachment and love are unavoidable. Sex so understood is part of the central dynamics of our lives: part of marriages, families, and communities, part of the joint work of a household and child-raising, part of life partnerships that go far beyond what happens in bed. And so, our moral traditions suggest, moral sex—or "good sex," if you like—needs to attend to the whole network of relationships that come to be at stake. It should sustain and deepen them, not undermine or weaken or pull them apart.

Younger people may have a more exploratory sexual attitude. Though moralists take varied views of this, a basic and common-ground imperative is this: at least, *communicate*. Sex itself, the very acts, are deeply communicative—far beyond words. But ethics would also have us attend to "communication" in the more ordinary sense, even to just plain talking. Generally speaking, young lovers and especially first-time lovers can *not* assume that there is just one sort of thing that sex could be or that what's happening is understood the same way by both parties. *Ask,* talk, keep talking...you will find yourself with a deeper and more fulfilling sex life as well as a deeper and more ethical relationship generally.

"PERVERSION"

To "pervert" something, according to *Webster's*, is to "turn it aside from its proper use or nature." We can pervert justice; we can pervert sport—what about sex? "Can you deflect sexual desire," philosopher Colin McGinn asks, "from its true or proper course?" It's a vexed and loaded question, of course. Yet McGinn's answer is *yes.*

"To make sense of this," he begins, "we obviously need some concept of what the 'proper use or nature' of human sexual desire is." Here is his proposal.

> From a purely biological perspective, the human sex drive has as its primary object sexual activity of a kind that would lead to conception if it occurred in the right circumstances.... But of course there is more to sexual desire than this purely biological function; it also has an emotional or personal side. Sex makes us relate in certain ways to other persons *as persons;* it is connected in all sorts of respects to our nature as social beings. I would like to suggest that the proper nature of sex, from a psychological point of view, involves a desire for another person as a sentient and physical entity: it is a complex passion aimed at another person conceived as possessing a sensual nature.

Think the object of sex in this way, and it turns out that we can readily define what "perversion" could mean:

> That sensual nature is the proper object of sexual attraction—a living body capable of sexual feelings and desires. If sexual desire becomes detached from such an object, it can be said to have been perverted from its proper course.

So sex with objects is perverse, obviously, because they are not living and have no "sensual nature" of their own at all. Sex with animals is another example, where responding to and being responded to as a "whole sensual nature" is not possible.

Sex with other humans can be perverted too, by this definition. Here too, sexual desires can be "detached from the whole sensual nature" of the other person.

> I think we generally appreciate that certain elements in [the structure of our sexual desires] shouldn't be allowed to take on a life of their own, squeezing out the rest. The focus must remain on the other person as a complete sensual being, and not shift to something that lies to the side of the person, or is a mere part of him, or is quite impersonal.

"Sexual tunnel-vision," then, is the essence of sexual "perversion" according to McGinn. Perversion is a failure (or inability?) to respond to another person as a *person*—thus a failure of respect as well.

The term "pervert" is still sometimes thrown—not necessarily in polite company—at people whose sexual orientation is bisexual or homosexual. Even as studies suggest that up to 10 percent or more of the population may be primarily homosexual (and more bisexual), there is a vast well of uneasiness, condemnation, and hostility toward anyone perceived to be "perverse" in this way. But notice that, on McGinn's analysis, the term does not apply. Homosexual desire can respond to the "whole sensual nature" of a person just as can heterosexual desire. Likewise, and even more important for our purposes here, both homosexual *and* heterosexual desire may *fail* to respond in this way—may become "tunnel-visioned," fixated, or objectified. There is nothing in homosexual love *as such* that makes it necessarily objectified, any more than in heterosexual love. Neither orientation has a monopoly on objectification—or true love.

Sexual "tunnel-vision," in short, is "perverse" wherever it occurs. Addiction to pornography or hitting on someone only to "score" are perverse whether gay or straight. On McGinn's account, sexual perversion simply has nothing to do with sexual orientation. It has everything to do with sexual *ethics*.

SEXUAL RESPONSE-ABILITY

Another moral guideline for sex arises directly out of the discussion of response-ability in the first part of this chapter. *Sexual choices should be response-able.*

Of course you have heard all too often about sexual responsibility: keeping yourself safe from unwanted pregnancy and STDs, and so on. Note well: the theme here is different. To be response-*able*, remember, means that you come to recognize that we can choose how we respond to anything—and that there is always more than one way to respond. Response-*ability* means embracing the freedom to choose: the real, deep freedom to shape the world you will live in. Freedom of mind is as vital in sexual choices as anywhere else.

I do not have to remind you that sexual pressure in our society is intense. Young children, especially girls, are molded by social ideals of beauty—that is, more or less, sexual attractiveness—practically from birth. Teen anorexia and other kinds of self-starvation to fit the current hyper-thin ideal body types; all-consuming attention to the details of clothing and makeup, for females, and rigid gender roles for males; and much more—you know the story. As sexual maturity arrives, the dance around sexual acts themselves begins. Your whole life may seem to turn on whether a certain person likes you this afternoon, and what you do with him or her. And all of this can continue, in one form or another, practically throughout a life.

Sexual pressures arise in relationships as well. My students, especially women, report regularly feeling pressured into having sex. Others feel pressure from a more subtle source: their own past acts. Having had a sexual relationship that they later regret, they may feel permanently marked by it, as if, to use the religious metaphor, they have "fallen" in a way that can't be redeemed, and they may as well continue to follow the same path.

Sullivan's ethic of response-ability invites you to another way of thinking. All of these pressures are just that: pressures. They are not necessities. You are not on an irresistibly slippery slope with only one place to end up— at the bottom. There are always other ways to respond, whatever other people expect and whatever your past responses have been. We can always, as it were, repossess ourselves.

Build the personal strength, then, not necessarily to say no, but to find out and then express what you really want to say yes to. Or maybe you will find yourself in the end saying neither no *or* yes but something that is truer and more specific to you, now. Why reduce sexual communication to monosyllables?

READING

From Being Sexual...and Celibate

KEITH CLARK

HOW WE ENGAGE in sexual activity is a choice, or rather an ongoing series of choices, but it is not the only kind of sexual response-ability to which we are called. Prior to these choices in turn is the choice to engage in sexual activity itself in the first place.

Other choices are possible. Abstinence—anyway, from sexual intercourse until marriage—is widely promoted by many

From Keith Clark, *Being Sexual...and Celibate* (Ave Maria Press, 1986), chapters 2 and 3.

religious conservatives. A more radical choice is to abstain from sexual activity entirely: a life of *celibacy*, a choice that, however radical it may seem, has always been expected of its priests by the Catholic Church. In this selection, Father Keith Clark, a Capuchin Franciscan monk, seminary administrator, and author, portrays the celibate life from the inside. "Part of the reason celibacy seems so irrelevant to many people," he writes, is that "the connection between celibacy and sexuality is almost completely ignored." Read on as he connects them.

Much of the discussion of human sexuality seems to center around the biological and bio-psychological level, and comparisons are made between what humans experience and what is true of the higher forms of animals. A lot of what I have heard and read relegates consideration of the personal/spiritual level to the domain of philosophers and theologians. The implication seems to be that anything said about sexuality beyond the biological and bio-psychological cannot be verified by empirical research, and has little value. Sociology claims to add to the discussion of human sexuality by researching human sexual behavior and the verifiable consequences of behavioral patterns in a given culture. Anthropology compares the sexual practices of various cultures. But human sexuality, like that of the higher forms of animal life, is thought by many to have been completely covered in its objective aspects when the biological and bio-psychological levels are studied.

I think I have experienced something sexual which is not merely biological or bio-psychological and which does not stem from the fact that I am a Christian and a Catholic. I am spiritual even if I have no interest in religion. I have experienced connecting with other human beings in ways which I cannot explain solely by my biological urges and bio-psychological drives.

Even the sexuality of the higher forms of animals is not totally explained by their biology and bio-psychology. There is something else operative in their sexual lives: the level of need. And the meaning of animal sexuality is determined by the need which is met by the animals' instinctively moderated sexual activity. Meeting the need is achieved, not through the having and the operation of the animal biology and bio-psychology, but by the instinctively moderated behavior.

In human sexuality there is also a third level of need which gives meaning to human sexual activity. But that need cannot be ascertained simply by observing human sexual behavior, because human sexual behavior, while instinctively motivated, is not *regulated* by instinct. It is regulated by the spiritual and personal capacities of insight and freedom.

With insight we human beings can see that the species needs more human beings. The need for the species to continue gives meaning to human sexuality.

But there is another human need which gives meaning to human sexuality. It is the need for intimacy with other human beings. It is the deepest personal need we have, and it is a spiritual need. We long to come together with other human beings so that our spirits touch and our personalities fuse without being lost in each other. In intimacy the expanse which separates us from every other human being is bridged, and the separateness, the insufficiency, the neediness which we inherit from our birth is temporarily alleviated. . . .

Some people accept the gratification of urges and drives as sufficient meaning. I do not. Even animals are instinctively directed in their sexual activity to achieve more than that. My interpretation of what I have heard from married couples suggests that human sexual activity achieves its highest meaning when both the need for the species to be propagated and the need for intimacy are intended and pursued. Sexual activity which intends and pursues neither need ranks among humanity's most disappointing and devastating experiences.

I don't believe that married couples who love each other are supposed to enter into sexual activity encumbered with weighty thoughts and lofty ambitions. I presume sex is fun! It's a way for people who are permanently committed to each other to play, to enjoy each other, and to further their intimate relationship. Such play and fun has meaning, not because the partners' heads are full of ideas about "meaning" and "communication" and "self-disclosure," but because they have an intimate, committed relationship.

Sexual activity which is not more than the gratification of urges and drives is frequently portrayed as fun and fulfilling. But conversations I have had over the years with those who engaged in sexual activity in such a way have convinced me that genital sexual activity and romantic behavior of themselves will eventually disappoint, not because they are bad, but because they are not enough.

I have chosen a celibate life for myself, and my intent in my own sexuality does not include having a child of my own. I must find other ways to be generative. But my need for intimacy is as great as anyone else's. And intimacy is just as much a part of my sexuality as it is part of a married person's. Having decided not to marry and have children does not make my view of human sexuality that of an outsider.

"Human sexuality is about intimacy, period!" Jerry said one night. I told him I thought he had a point, but that he was overstating it. We argued and discussed the matter for several hours that night and on many other evenings. Eventually he convinced me. Human sexuality IS about intimacy. Not only about intimacy, but always about intimacy. Intimacy is possible for me because I was born a *sexual person*. Both words are important—"sexual" and "person."...

In the presence of those with whom I have an intimate relationship, I feel invited to *be* myself and to *reveal* myself. I have a sense that they feel the same with me. When we can be ourselves and reveal ourselves to each other, something grows between us....

For me, romantic pursuits are those activities which stimulate our sexual emotions for another and are designed—consciously or unconsciously—to evoke a similar emotional response from another. Although romance can distort our perception of one another, it can also lead us to a sense of safety and relatedness with one another which will allow us to eventually be ourselves and reveal ourselves to one another. If we do, intimacy can arise from the romantic pursuits. Romance is not intimacy, but it can lead us to behave in ways which will allow intimacy to arise. What is important is that we recognize with our insight and pursue with our free choice those behaviors which will bring us together without anyone being dominated, manipulated, mutilated or changed.

A good friend, a perpetually professed woman religious for about ten years, told me very matter-of-factly one evening that she was quite sure that she would be seeking a dispensation from her religious vows. I was shocked. In fact, I said to her, "You're kidding!" and took another bite of the Chinese food we were sharing. Then I looked at her expression, set my fork on the plate, and said to myself more than to her, "No, you're not kidding."

She told me of a man who had been instantly able to invite her out of herself like no one else had ever been able to do. She was both popular and respected within her community, a potential leader because she was intelligent, witty, personable and sympathetic. As the evening together continued, she told me of her own sense of isolation within her community. She was becoming very aware of her great need for intimacy, for connectedness. Randy entered her life and invited from her a response no other person had ever invited; and she responded. She found she could be open with him—completely open. "He loves all of me," she said with feeling too great and too real to be dismissed.

Within three months she had taken a leave of absence from her community and had moved in with Randy. During the course of those three months we spoke several times, and she appeared to me to be completely infatuated with Randy. Over those months she had told several of her sisters in the community of her decision, and saw the pain and sadness in each of their faces. But she regarded leaving as something she had to do. Being with Randy had awakened in her feelings and responses which she had never had before. She attributed to Randy the ability to make her feel what she felt. And she therefore attributed to him the response she gave him. "He makes me feel so free, so loveable, so able to be myself."

She cried with almost every one of her sisters whom she told about her decision to leave. At first, with real pain and disappointment and eventually with some deep anger, she asked why it was only when she was leaving that her sisters seemed to reach out to her. "Now that it's too late they are willing to get close," she said to herself in my hearing.

I tried arguing with the stories she told herself. But I lost every argument. I remain convinced that she found Randy "the right one," the one who stimulated her romantic sexual emotions and she became fascinated and then infatuated with him. These emotions led her to behave in ways which allowed intimacy to begin to arise in her life. She told her sisters one by one, and the revelation of herself to them and their response gave her the first taste of intimacy she had experienced with them. And she resented them for being too late.

By the time she left, she was in fact experiencing intimacy with a lot of people. She chose behaviors with Randy which were romantic as well as intimate; romance had awakened in her the inclination for behaviors which allowed intimacy to arise. Intimacy had come into her life on the wings of romance, and she really couldn't imagine that she could experience intimacy without romance.

Randy is a Catholic who was free to marry my friend. My friend said he loved all of her. But he didn't love her commitment to a way of life which precluded her marrying him. In their coming together a very significant part of my friend was obliterated. That having taken place, I imagine that their life together will be as happy as any other life. I assume that genuine intimacy will continue to grow between them. I don't know what happens to the realization in my friend that part of her is gone. She chose to have it be gone; I can't argue with her for that. But she did so by telling herself the story: "He loves all of me." I do argue with that.

The stories I tell myself about romance and intimacy come from my experience of being in love. I too have been loved by a woman who felt as romantically inclined toward me as I did toward her. I too told my brothers in the Order of my feelings for her. And they marvelled, feared, laughed and cried with me. I too thought seriously about romantically pursuing this woman. I didn't think at first of marrying her, just behaving toward her in ways which would continue the stimulation of my romantic feelings and perhaps encourage her romantic feelings for me. Ten years later she is still the woman I would want to marry. Her romantic feelings for me were never acted out. I never received from her any "mixed messages" which suggested that she wanted me to leave the Order and marry her. Nor did I give her any such messages. Today we talk about our relationship over the years, and she says to those who occasionally ask her why she never married me, "I love him too much to try to take him away from his commitment." She loves all of me. The intimacy we share is as great as any I have experienced in my life. It is an intimacy arrived at without romantic activity. Her love is one of the greatest gifts of my life.

READING

From Real Live Nude Girl

CAROL QUEEN

WRITER AND ORGANIZER CAROL QUEEN tells us on her website that

> [m]y focus, whether writing, speaking, consulting, or providing erotic entertainment, is to empower and inspire others to discover their own unique sexual profile—we have to remove the stigma from sex before we can make it fabulous. I have had to struggle to find the place and permission to express my own sexuality, and I am committed to facilitating others as they do the same. Until we honor the full spectrum of consensual erotic desire, none of us will be truly free to pursue our own.

You can read Queen's essay as the polar opposite of Clark's, and in many ways her vision is indeed far from his celibate ideal. But then again...Queen celebrates sexual expression in many forms, yes, but she too questions what is "normal" sexually, as

From Carol Queen, *Real Live Nude Girl* (Cleis Press, 2002), pp. ix–xxiv.

if one form of sexual expression were really the only form possible, and in speaking frankly of sexual experience she is also morally specific and demanding. Do not *both* writers actually put sexual expression in the mode of response-ability?

Consider how you might (re?)read Queen's title, too: as the insistence that there is after all a *real live person* in the sexual picture. What follows?

I believe that most of us want enough sexual knowledge to let us feel comfortable and competent. (If we don't want this for ourselves, it is a quality we want in our partners.) I believe most people want sex to be good, not problematic, dangerous, or bad. They want (though often they are nowhere near able to articulate wanting) a sex-positive world: a world in which sex enhances human connection and sexual possibilities can be explored without shame.

Hearing the words "sex-positive" made me realize I'd grown up in a fundamentally sex-negative world. Even the so-called sexual revolution hadn't knocked out the old guns: religious morality, legal sanctions, threadbare sex education or none at all, the "war between the sexes." Erotophobia fed on itself, generation after generation, continually reproducing conditions of fear, shame, and danger. This has not truly changed. Even the generation which fought for sexual liberation has mostly retrenched, refusing to stand up and fight for good sex education for its own children.

It may sound odd to make the claim that U.S. culture is erotophobic. We live, after all, in a society that splices sex into practically everything: music, movies, commercials, the Internet, cable TV.... But sexual variety is not in fact so mainstreamed, and neither is the notion that everyone deserves the sex life that is the expression of their own unique set of desires, as long as it can be had consensually. The people bouncing up and down on adult cable are not fat, old, or in any way ordinary-looking. They're not queer—at least, the script doesn't portray them that way. They're not disabled. And on the info and opinion shows, most sexual discussion is not especially deep. Eroticized images are great for keeping us distracted, and they're pretty good at getting us to spend money. But shows that risk exploring sexual subjects are preceded by a warning: "May be offensive to some viewers." Instead of the message that sex is of very nearly universal interest and deserves the best efforts of our culture-makers, we get spam.

We're sexually schizophrenic. We don't want kids to have good, clear, pleasure-based information. We want, if we're grown-ups, to have access to sexual materials, but we won't fight for them, and often we can't tell if they're any good when we get them. We won't insist our elected representatives stand up for this material, so for the most part they don't, even when they're big consumers of it themselves. Sex drives us, and it is cannily marketed to do so, and most of us get enough sexual titillation and entertainment that we can easily ignore the question of sexual rights. Anyway, why would we involve ourselves in someone else's personal issues? Sex is supposed to be private....

...[T]he culture is lousy with sexual secrets and people who have been punished for them. My parents lived their pain around sex in airless silence, though their pain around everything else was easy enough to see. I was eighteen before my mother admitted to me she had been married twice (imagine that as a source of shame!), twenty-seven before she told me she had a history of incest. She had only told my father a few years before he died. He lived for thirty years with a woman who took no pleasure in sex; for most of those years he had no way of knowing why. I knew, before I knew what sex was, that something was wrong with them, very wrong. Today I know what was broken, and I know it never had half a chance to heal.

Gays and lesbians are incorrect when they say straight people have it easy. Sometimes straight people lack the very language to name the pain they feel when the culture thwarts their desires, even cuts off their access to desire itself. Did it ever occur to my parents to try to get help with their broken sex life? Did it seem "normal" to them—men wanting sex, women resisting? Did they even understand they each had a sexuality, much less that they had choices around how they would manage their sexualities over the course of their lives? My friend Will Roscoe once told me his theory of homophobia: Straight people, he said, are jealous of us, because we have a sexual orientation and they don't. In our sexual otherness, we have to learn to talk about sex; it defines us in a way it doesn't define heterosexuals, and in the process of becoming a community, we learn comfort with the language.

Many of us do, anyway. Not all of us escape the closet, the self-hatred, the too-tight clothes of Normalcy that fit us so poorly. But no one can tell me that the life of a hidden queer is unhappier than the pain I saw in my father. No one can tell me that heterosexual privilege did my mother a damned bit of good.

I saw in my parents' example, and I learned from the gay movement, how crucial to happiness sexual honesty is. When I realized that my fantasies hid a sexual profile much more complicated than I admitted to, I knew I hadn't yet done justice to Harvey Milk's directive to "Come out!" I started by moving to San Francisco, where every kind of queer has fled to escape restrictive homes.

There my world no longer seemed split so neatly into Us and Them. I learned in the gay and lesbian communities a way to understand and politicize sexual identity: The idea of "sexual minority" lends itself to looking at other secret or embattled or oppressed ways of living in the desire-and-gender-coded body. But when gayness proved unable to contain all my desire, I learned to translate "Gay Is Good" to "Sex Is Good," and that is a badge virtually all of us could learn to wear.

It is clear to me today that the pain and failure at the heart of my parents' sexual relationship does not mean less—or more—than the pain and oppression the gay-rights movement works to alleviate; that even below the hatred and small-mindedness that power homophobic and all manner of censorious impulses, there is distress and pain about sex that, were it healed, might wither the roots of the poisonous tree. Erotophobia and xenophobia work together to empower every sort of despisal, including many of those at the heart of the "war between the sexes." Given this, I wish to speak to a vast and varied audience.

More than any academic credential that provides both an overview and a screen of depersonalizing ivory-tower smoke, my experience living in many different sexual realms sources my qualification to speak up now. Too often we hear talk about sex that never seems to come from anyone's first-person experience; how much easier to discuss *other people's* real and imagined sexual experiences and shortcomings. We lack, more than any other things, an atmosphere in which each of us might tell the stories of her or his experience and be heard by an audience who did not presume it appropriate to immediately hit the switch of excoriation or analysis. While we lack this in any sort of public arena, too many of us also lack it in private, in the silent circles of our marriages and significant-otherhoods, which should be the first places adults practice the skill of tolerance. And in our families, within which most of us failed to learn that our desires are our own, failed to have our growth in them respected, too many of us find our sexuality undermined and learn from this the habits of secrecy and blame....

For a while I believed what others told me: that men and women were erotically incompatible; that males got what they wanted out of sex while women did not; that it was my partners' incompetence that kept me from having orgasms during sex with them. Men and women were seemingly separate species, and only gradually did it dawn on me that the legacy of my parents' and my culture's sexual silence resided in my own body, not just in mismatched sexual couplings: I did not know how I could be pleased, and so how could anyone be expected to know how to please me? By now it seems that I can trust my own experience more than anyone else's version of love and sex, but in those days I had practically no experience on which to draw. Most of the sex I had had was not very impressive. It seemed as likely that clumsy, selfish male sexuality was to blame for this state as any other thing.

But in retrospect I realize I didn't have enough information. I couldn't even make myself have an orgasm until I snitched my parents' vibrator (and, bless them, they never asked for it back—it must not have been missed). It shouldn't have been surprising that my partners couldn't "make" me have an orgasm, either. When my lovers asked me what I wanted in bed, I said, "Oh, everything you do feels wonderful," even when it didn't. I failed them as thoroughly as they failed me—partly because, as a young woman, I'd gotten too little access to good sex information and even less access to anything that would encourage me to take my own sexual needs seriously. Of course, my adolescent male partners hadn't had much access to useful information, either.

I think now that much of the sexual resentment I see troubling women and men derives directly from our having been hormone-ridden, largely ignorant teenaged animals struggling to learn to make love while burdened with the weight of acculturated shame and crippling gender roles. My prescription for change—that children and adolescents be freely given permission and correct, wide-ranging sex information—seems farther away in this decade than it did when I was a teen. Child abuse is heinous—but why do I hear no outcry about the abuse that lies at the heart of sexual silence, of inculcated shame?

...Each of us can stop cowering at the notion that we might be different. Of course we are—we all are....While there's more to life than sex (I guess), sex is a good place to start this project of listening to our own voices. *Sex-positive,* a term that's coming into cultural awareness, isn't a dippy love-child celebration of orgone—it's a simple yet radical affirmation that we each grow our own passions on a different medium, that instead of having two or three or even half a dozen sexual orientations, we should be thinking in terms of millions. "Sex-positive" respects each of our unique sexual profiles, even as we acknowledge that some of us have been damaged by a culture that tries to eradicate sexual difference and possibility....

...Once I decided most of what my culture had told me about sex was wrong, I set out on a prolonged walk on the wild side, and by now I've walked into more secret places than I ever knew existed.

They are wild and spirit-filled gardens, indeed.

EATING

Food is certainly a less sexy topic than, well, sex. But choices we make about food are at least as significant for ourselves, for others, and even more for the world. Eating is a practice that also begs for ethical thinking.

MORAL VEGETARIANISM

First of all, unavoidably, there is the question of animals. From the first chapter of this book, you'll remember, the exercises and sometimes the text raised the question of animals and suggested that at the very least our use of animals for food, however habitual and traditional, needs serious thinking. Our diets are literally full of the bodies of other living creatures. But animals *suffer*, massively, in the run-up to our plates. Many are tightly confined, against all of their natural instincts, often for their entire short lives. Every element of their environment is manipulated to produce the most meat (or eggs, or milk) in the shortest time. And they come to their deaths knowing what is happening—in slaughterhouses with hundreds of others, the smell and sounds of death always in the air, often with other animals killed right in front of their eyes.

You may know how veal is produced. At birth, male calves are immediately separated from their mothers. They are tightly penned to prevent them from developing their muscles (it toughens the meat). They are restricted to a liquid diet when all their urges tell them to begin chewing grass. That diet among other things deprives them of iron (which would also develop muscle and color the meat) so that they become so desperate for it that they may spend hours gnawing on the bars of their pens or any nails in sight. Then they are slaughtered, at four months or less—unless they have died already, as 10–15 percent regularly do, from the sheer stress and frustration of their lives.

Many people have given up veal out of outrage at this way of treating calves. Yet animal advocates argue that veal production is only slightly more horrible than what is done routinely with all the familiar meat animals. Commercially raised chickens may spend their whole lives in cages too small for them even to turn around, much less spread their wings or fly, or in huge sheds holding tens of thousands of birds, so large that all social structure breaks down and the birds have to be "debeaked" (have their beaks cut off) so that they do not kill each other in their fury and confusion. When egg production in a multiple-thousand bird unit falls off too much, the whole bunch is just shipped off for killing. Americans currently consume about five *billion* chickens per year.

Utilitarians, not surprisingly, have therefore taken the lead in arguing for moral vegetarianism. Pain is pain, suffering is suffering, and if animal suffering counts at all, then even the roughest calculus requires major changes. But the other families of moral values have their say too. Some animals suffer knowingly, as "subjects of a life," and so the values and rights of persons arguably also apply. When we don't live in relations of community and care with other animals, or when we cut ourselves off from them emotionally to avoid recognizing their suffering, we also do violence to ourselves and deepen the oppression of all life, as Alice Walker suggests. A caring community must make some bows toward other creatures, even though it may not follow that they have as strong a claim as we do.

The arguments on the other side have a harder time of it, frankly, at least in my view. It's no longer very plausible to argue that animals don't suffer at all. More common is the claim that they don't suffer as much, or suffer differently. But these admissions already have ethical implications. Surely we should still reduce what suffering we can. Making such trade-offs, even if they are often in our own favor, is very different from dismissing the whole subject from the beginning.

Likewise, though rights arguments may not apply to all animals, they may apply to some: pigs, cows, maybe chickens, maybe not fish. But few non-vegetarians make these kinds of distinctions. What I usually hear is the argument that vegetarianism is simply not healthy or not practical. Even standard grocery stores carry a wide range of meat-free options, though, and if anything it's meat that isn't healthy: the two leading killers in America, cancer and heart disease, are both linked directly to high-meat diets. Vegans—people who eat neither meat nor dairy products—have the highest life expectancy of any Americans. And, vegetarians report, their meals taste just as delightful and varied—if not more—than the traditional meat meals.

Meat or not, then—it is a *choice*. When it comes to food we need to have some idea of what we are doing, morally speaking, and why. And there are compelling reasons to at least reconsider a kind of diet most people still take for granted.

VEGETARIANISM 101

I am a vegetarian myself, but I am not arguing here that you should become one too. My point, again, is only that whatever we eat is a choice, and that there are moral reasons as well as other kinds of reasons, to think it through seriously. If you do make the choice to give up meat, though, you need to know what you are doing! Here is the briefest of guides to a nonmeat diet.

For one thing, a vegetarian is not someone who simply eats vegetables. Actually, the term "vegetarian" does not refer to vegetables at all: it traces back to the Latin word *vegetus*, meaning "whole, sound, fresh, lively." Vegetarians do not eat the flesh of other creatures, but we certainly enjoy food in all of its fabulous variety! Good eating for us is vital to a "whole, sound, fresh, and lively" way of life. But like any healthy and enjoyable diet, it takes planning.

I can't say this strongly enough: *don't just drop meat out of your diet and expect that everything else can stay the same.* Instead, replace the usual meat entrée with a nonmeat entrée—or do away with the "entrée" format entirely and prepare a different *kind* of meal. In any case, carefully plan to include adequate proteins. Here are some specific meal-planning suggestions.

Pasta and sauces: There are many interesting and even exotic varieties of pasta available. In the sauce, replace any meat with marinated artichokes or olives. Add a little tofu or textured vegetable protein (TVP) to the sauce for more texture and protein. Vegans can use a soy cheese. Variations: tomato, pesto, or cheese sauces (e.g., rarebit, fondue) over bread or baked potatoes; pizza of all sorts; spinach lasagna.

Beans and rice: Beans and rice are an inexpensive full-protein combination, which is why so many different cuisines are built upon them. Think Mexican here. In many Cajun-spiced dishes the beans can mainly carry the dish. My own household is big on bean-rice soups (nice thick hot soups for cold winter evenings; add a loaf of fresh bread and a salad and you have an unmatchable meal).

Ethnic foods: Middle Eastern food is great for vegetarians: falafel, hummus (chickpeas and tahini), baba ganouj (eggplant sauce), tabbouli (wheat bulghur salad), stuffed grape leaves, and so on. All of this can be served cold: wonderful summer fare. For an oriental meal, stir-fry vegetables (broccoli, onions, bamboo shoots, etc.) with soy or teriyaki sauces, and serve over brown or wild rice. Nuts or tofu give you protein. From India come great meatless curries and dals (lentil soups). From Mexico, try quesadillas: beans, salsa, cilantro, tomatoes, cheese perhaps, and anything else you want (my children like okra, a friend includes sweet potatoes), all layered together inside a tortilla shell and pan-fried five minutes or so each side.

Also consider nutloafs, tofu and tempeh products (there are many varieties of tofu and tempeh burgers, as well as beanburgers), vegetable soups (e.g., gazpacho), and all the other delightful things you might do, like garnishing salads with flowers or making fresh bread. Our household Thanksgiving tradition is nutmeat brioche (an egg bread with a spicy nut-wine-cheese filling), sweet-potato soup, artichoke salad, fresh rosemary bread, and lots of pies (and singing).

For some cookbooks and other resources, see the Notes for this chapter.

THE ECOLOGY OF FOOD

The strongest arguments *for* eating meat may come from another direction—and invite other forms of mindfulness (too). Though meat production is typically an ecological disaster, the typical vegetarian diet is not so ecologically benign either. As Ted Kerasote argues (remember chapter I), many small animals of the fields die when grains are harvested. Vegetables and fruit are sensitive to growing season and are often shipped cross-country in trucks, which pollutes and increases the demand for fossil fuels—the same fuels that are often used to produce fertilizers and power the farmers' tractors. Kerasote argues that shooting and eating a local elk is more ecological than eating vegetarian. Hunting and eating wild animals, he argues, is part of living close to the land, and ecologically it is most efficient.

Of course, this is no defense of eating hamburger that may also have been shipped halfway across the continent from a slaughterhouse that pollutes the local rivers and brings you meat from cows that were fed grain produced in the same harvests just mentioned. Wild fare will also vary depending on where you live. Around where I live, it probably means eating squirrels. Or maybe roadkill.

Kerasote also reminds us of the Buddhist argument that all food suffers—not just animals. All things have souls, they say, and life pretty much *is* a round of suffering. But Buddhists certainly do not go on to conclude from this jolly thought that we should therefore be completely heedless of our effects upon animals—as if, since suffering is inevitable, it doesn't really matter how much suffering we cause. Their view, by contrast, is that since suffering is inevitable, we must be as careful as we can be *all the time.*

So vegetarianism is not the only ethical option. The question is too complex for that. The key thing, I believe, is not necessarily to follow Kerasote's conclusions—you'll remember that he himself struggles with the question and has eaten differently at different times and places—but rather to take on a similar mindfulness. To pay attention, or, again, to think response-ably. We have obligations to ourselves and other people, *and* to the animals, *and* to the Earth; and how all of these balance out, case to case, isn't so clear. Nonetheless our task is to try.

More religiously, we might view eating as a form of communion with the Earth. It's the literal truth: we eat the very Earth itself—its plants, its other beings, and its water, air, soil, even rocks (salt). We must not continue to act as if our food were just another industrial product like flyswatters or something (not that even flyswatters don't come from the Earth too, in the end, but...), or plastic food is what we'll end up with. In some ways we're close already.

Many writers and activists argue for renewed attention to the sources of our foods, as much as possible staying with organic, local, and seasonal foods. *Organic* foods mean foods raised without chemical pesticides, herbicides, or fertilizers. Instead the health of the soil is maintained by recycling food and animal wastes and by good maintenance. The soil, earth, is regarded as a living thing itself, and treated with respect and love.

Local foods are those grown as close to you as possible: in any case not shipped across the whole continent or even flown around the world as is so often the case now (tomatoes from California, kiwis from New Zealand—the energy costs and pollution consequences of getting them to us are spectacular, and they are often of much poorer quality because they must be picked unripe). Our local farmers' market only admits growers who farm within fifty miles of the market. Know where your food comes from, support those in your own community who love not just any land but *this* land, your place too.

Seasonal eating is one consequence: when you eat what the local farmers are harvesting at the time, it varies over the year. It's one way of coming back into tune with the land, and natural food advocates argue in addition that it's simply healthier too. Local foods at each season give you what you need to deal with the seasonal changes: high-starch root vegetables in late fall and winter, for example, as we pull back a bit into ourselves; exuberant light greens in the spring, as both we and the world burst back into life. "Health" means, in part, being in tune with the world. Why wouldn't the daily "communion" of food be *essential* to that process?

SLOW FOOD AND NO FOOD

At the other extreme from a response-able sort of thoughtfulness about eating is, I'm sorry to say, *fast food*. Even the name gives it away. Completely homogenized, completely disconnected from anything local or seasonal, replete with styrofoam or other immensely wasteful and usually nonbiodegradable packaging—well, let's just say it might be something you want to reconsider. Just saying.

There's a final point too: the *fast* part. Food slapped together and then gulped at the same speed. It's not even pleasurable, really; it's just a way of keeping fuelled, like a fast gas station. Well, if we were just cars, it might make sense, but....

There are alternatives. We are, once again, response-able. In particular, a growing "slow food" movement already claims tens of thousands of members in one hundred countries, devoted to biodiversity issues, new types of food growing, and recovering the sheer pleasures of eating—by consciously eating *slow*. Worth a try?

The sheer amount of eating is also an issue. We seem to train ourselves, courtesy of the ads and the restaurants, to eat vastly more than we need, which is one reason why weight is such a problem in this country. Worldwide there are now more overweight people than there are people starving, an astonishing enough fact in itself even before we add that there are huge numbers of both. Some vast proportion of American children are overweight, a product of couch potatoism, TV and computer games, poor food choices, and sheer overeating. Binge eating and binge self-starvation are both epidemic. Indeed, it is possible to be both overweight *and* malnourished (in the sense of lacking vital nutrients)—and increasing numbers of Americans are both.

Once again, the point is simply that there are other choices—choices that ethics surely asks us to think about. *What* we eat, *how* we eat, *when* we eat, how *much* we eat—all of these may need more response-ability.

In fact, even *whether* to eat is a choice. Many people, both traditionally and today, periodically fast: that is, stop eating entirely for some period. And they don't do this out of some kind of masochism. The point is not to take pleasure out of life. It's more getting the pleasure, or the mindfulness, or both, back *into* life: to sharpen the senses, to cleanse both body and mind, to make us appreciate food when we do eat it.

Once again, fasting is not something to undertake without knowing what you are doing! There are long traditions and practices for fasting, many of them originally rooted in the great religions. Here in this chapter, it's at least a useful reminder about response-ability. Once you realize that fasting is an option—that even eating when we are truly hungry is a *choice*, and not a choice that everyone always makes—you have opened up some space for freedom. Feeling a strong desire for anything (say food or, for that matter, sex) is not somehow the end of the matter. Desire only poses a *question*. How you answer it, about sex, or food, or anything else, always remains up to you.

FOR REVIEW

1. What is "self-possession"?
2. Why does response-ability need cultivating?
3. What are some ways to cultivate it?
4. Why is ethics relevant to sexual matters?
5. According to Colin McGinn, what is sexual "perversion"? Why?
6. What does sexual response-ability imply?
7. According to Keith Clark, how is it possible to be both sexual and celibate?
8. According to Carol Queen, what does a "sex-positive" world require?
9. What is the utilitarian argument against eating meat?
10. What are some other questions of response-ability in regard to eating?

EXERCISES AND NOTES

16.1 MORE RESPONSE-ABILITY

This chapter raises the question of response-ability in sexual choices and in eating. It turns out that ethics has more to say about both of them than we sometimes think, and that the space for choice is also much greater than we are usually told. But these are certainly not the only areas of life in which the challenge of response-ability comes up. You might now ask: are there other areas where similar ethical questions come up for you—that is, specific questions of personal response-ability and freedom?

One often identified by my students is racist or sexist humor. Prejudiced joking can become habitual for individuals or in groups. It sometimes gets further and persists longer than more overt prejudice because it can excuse itself as "just in fun"—not exactly an honest excuse, though, since the jokers know very well not to share the "fun" with those who are being mocked. But you do not have to play this game, and you can do more than abstain from it yourself. *Visibly* abstain from it, first of all—change the subject in a deliberately awkward way, maybe; or explicitly discuss it with your group; or find more deft ways to make change, maybe by making fun of the prejudiced joking itself. Or find different friends.

Are there other kinds or expressions of prejudice you might also work on? You might find Peggy McIntosh's classic short essay on "white privilege" useful here: it is available on the Web in several places, such as http://www.nymbp. org/reference/WhitePrivilege.pdf.

Health is an issue: building healthy habits, from eating decently to getting enough exercise to avoiding substance abuse. Again, if you are tempted to unhealthy behaviors, analyze causes and try some changes. Though the major effect of most bad health habits is on yourself, others are most definitely involved too, and when it comes to substance abuse issues in particular, the effects on others—on those you love and on those who love you, as well as on random unlucky strangers who deserve better—can be just as lethal as to you.

Finally: one of the ways in which my students are very definitely not free is that they feel compelled to get a job and start their career right after college. They know they're supposed to "use their degree" (and get a degree that they can "use"), settle down, have a nice place to live and a nice car and maybe get married and start a family…Meanwhile, so much more is possible! Nothing is stopping them—or you—from building Habitat for Humanity houses in New Orleans or trails in the High Sierras or bumming around Europe or the South Pacific, or joining the Peace Corps, or starting a downtown artist collective and making free art or music festivals, or you name it.

Imagine that your college education has been offered to you free, on one condition: that afterward, for five years, say, you are required to find an imaginative and adventurous way to better the world. You are expressly *forbidden* to get a standard job or "settle down." Work out some ideas about what your alternative work/life could be. Then find three actual, existing job openings or programs that are actually hiring or looking for people to do such work—conceivably someone just like you. Make contact with at least one. *Now* you have some options, eh?

16.2 SEX AT ANTIOCH COLLEGE

Sexual pressure and coercion, up to and including date rape, is widespread on college campuses. Most colleges now offer some warnings about sexual miscommunication and coercion at least as part of standard orientation presentations. Some administrations have formalized policies for dealing with allegations of sexual coercion.

A few have gone further. At Antioch College, in Yellow Springs, Ohio, the entire community—students, faculty, administration, and staff—formulated and tested a policy meant to deal with, and prevent, "sexual offenses" such as this.

The statement begins with values:

> Antioch College has made a strong commitment to the issue of respect, including respect for each individual's personal and sexual boundaries. Sexual offenses are dehumanizing. They are not just a violation of the individual, but of the Antioch community.

Sex must be *consensual*, the policy insists. That is, participants must "willingly and verbally agree to engage in specific sexual behavior." Participants need to share enough common understanding to be able to request consent and to clearly consent or not, and also must not be so intoxicated or threatened that consent or the request for it is meaningless. Moreover, and crucially, "silence and/or non-communication *must never be interpreted as consent.*"

Consent, moreover, is understood to be an *ongoing process* in any sexual interaction. The most controversial part of the policy was this:

> Verbal consent should be obtained with each new level of physical and/or sexual behavior in any given interaction, regardless of who initiates it. Asking "Do you want to have sex with me?" is not enough. The request for consent must be specific to each act.

Certainly Antioch's is not the only way that a college community might address issues of sexual communication. It may seem awkward and stiff—but is it better to leave all the crucial things unsaid? And it raises useful questions. Does sex at Antioch sound exciting? If fully mutual sex with explicit consent at each stage does *not* sound "sexy," why not? What does it say about *us* (about what we assume sex *must* be like) if we can't imagine sex like that?

Is there even a way to make the requirement of consent at each stage into a kind of *opportunity* (remembering chapter 14)? One of my students wrote, in response to these questions: "Actually, I think whispering to someone, communicating, and asking permission to do fun things is pretty cool."

Consider the pros and cons of such a policy for your own school. How would it change or not change sexual interactions for you and your fellow students?

How would you write such a policy for your own school? Should your class try it? Can men and women in your very own class actually communicate about these things? Why or why not? If communication breaks down, where do you think it breaks down, and why?

16.3 RESPONSE-ABILITY AT WORK

Consider the question of response-ability and basic ethical values in a little more depth, specifically on the issue of *work*.

Work is what most of us spend most of our lives doing. Forty hours a week (now on average somewhat higher, for those who have work at all), for forty or so years, with occasional vacations: this is what most of us get to do with what the poet Mary Oliver calls "our one wild and precious life." Indeed, work is not only what we *do* but often what we say we *are*. I *am* a teacher, I *am* a carpenter. It's not just a shorthand way of telling what our jobs are. Work is also how we identify and value ourselves, and expect others to do the same.

Before even the question of what work we might choose then, there is the question of our attitude toward work itself. At the same time that we say that our work is what we *are*, after all, our culture also often invites us to consider work something that is only a necessary evil, something just to be tolerated and endured, putting in our time, until vacation comes, or retirement, and we finally can *live*. But this is not the only attitude we might have. Indeed, when you consider that work is after all what we spend the greatest portion of our time and energies doing, it seems a great loss to suppose that work itself cannot be the activity that makes us feel most alive and most real.

This is a question of response-ability as well. We choose our work, after all. We could try to choose differently: more consciously seeking work (and to prepare for such work, for example by choice of major in college) that is a satisfying self-expression—and promoting a society that itself is devoted to offering and supporting that kind of work, and not merely labor or (at an all too common extreme) drudgery just to get by.

Many moralists make this kind of point. Pope John Paul II, for one, in a 1981 encyclical on the subject of work called *Laborem Exercens*, pointed out that the Bible's first model of work—right away on the first page, in fact—is God's creation of the universe. Human work, in his view, should be modeled on God's. It too should be free and creative, as befits a being made "in the image of God."

You can embrace this kind of aspiration even if you are not a Catholic, or even a believer in God. Karl Marx, for example, makes a very similar point in his critique of capitalism: he claims that capitalism reduces the worker to mere objects and slaves of the machine, while work can and should be affirmative, expressive, and satisfying. Pope John Paul II's early training was in Marxist philosophy, so the parallels are perhaps not surprising, though the starting points are very different. John Paul ended, however, by turning the tables on Marx and arguing that Communist systems, in practice, did no better to emancipate workers. The Pope, writing during the Cold War, condemned the prevailing doctrine on both sides as mere "economism": reducing work to activity that meets the demands of the economy, rather than arranging the economy to meet the basic human and expressive needs of the worker. Valuing the *person*. We all must do better, he said.

These are large issues, obviously, but you can make practical and personal use of them all the same. If the moral task is, as we might put it, making a *life* rather than just making a living, then at the very least we need to be more conscious of work as a choice, and indeed one of the most important choices we make in our lives. What do you think we can hope for from work? What do you think we *should* (be able to) hope for from work?

Sometimes I ask my students what it is that they really want to do in life. Usually, at least for the near future, it is some form of adventure: learning to skydive or sailing across the ocean, or traveling around other parts of the world. Often too it involves some forms of learning: going to vet school, or learning Portuguese, or Swahili, or wilderness medicine, or oil painting. When I ask them if they are going to do any of these things, however, the light goes out of their eyes and they reply, well, no, I am going to law school or getting a job at an ad agency. And of course there is nothing wrong with those lines of work. Both the law and the ad business can be adventurous too, for the right person. But for a great many students these choices are made simply because they think they have no real alternatives. Meanwhile, though, I seldom see those same students actively investigating the possibilities for being able to do what they really, in their heart of hearts, want to do—not even to the point of doing a few simple Web searches or putting together a possible plan to test for feasibility.

Therefore, for one project, I suggest that you try. Consider the question, anyway, how you might make your choice of life-work more response-able to yourself.

Work as Contribution

Ethics also asks us to consider what kinds of contribution to the world our work makes—what values our work sustains and promotes in the larger society. A great many jobs do so—of course. Think of the many helping professions, for example: medicine, teaching, the ministry, firefighters, and the police. There's scientific research, exploration, and the arts. Farming—it feeds us all. Crafts are crucial, from construction to manufacturing to all the forms of repair and maintenance that keep everything looking good and running well. Many forms of unpaid work also make essential contributions: parenting, for example, and, as Bill Thomas reminds us, grandparenting too.

Yet not every line of work, or every way of working at jobs such as those just mentioned, contributes to the betterment of self and others or to meeting legitimate expectations. It is possible to run afoul of ethics here as well—one reason to pay better attention. When people are cheated or disenfranchised or hurt in deeper ways; when the land or water or air are poisoned, even if the poisoners cannot be held legally responsible; when the financial system is manipulated to yield massive profits for the manipulators but ruin for many others and an over-all sapping of the system as whole—these and other types of work (for these are forms of work, too) are not moral and ought to be challenged.

I do not mean that we need to be able to anticipate every effect of work that we do. There are always unintended consequences and uncertainties. Maybe a skilled surgeon will end up saving the life of a person who goes on to become a serial killer. We can't know all the details—at some point we must just hope for the best. But it is certainly clear that it is better to be a surgeon, regardless, than to be a serial killer. We need to ask, then, about the moral consequences of dif-ferent lines of work, and be sure that we are choosing work that serves a moral standard—or at the very least does not violate it.

This leads in turn to questions about one's personal response-ability for potential harms (and goods!) done by your organization or business as a whole. Ethical tradition is fairly resolute in insisting that a person is not freed of moral obligations simply because they are part of a larger whole and may be operating under orders from superiors in that whole. Even the military, where command structures are enormously powerful and where obedience can easily become a life-or-death necessity, still holds soldiers responsible for immoral or illegal actions even if they are "only following orders." It is a tempting excuse to make when an organization or business for which you work is doing the same, but it is no better an excuse (actually, arguably, a much worse one: there's less urgency) than in the military. And while it is also certainly important to rec-ognize that loyalty (to co-workers, to the enterprise, to the mission) is a good thing, loyalty too cannot excuse immoral conduct. It would be better to head in the other direction: to work from within, calling on *others'* loyalties—again, to co-workers, to the moral aspects of the enterprise's mission, to the values of the larger society—to try to call the enterprise back to moral basics.

More Questions

Here are some further questions about ethics and work—yours to explore.

How *hard* should you work? We inherit an idea of the "Work Ethic" that tells us, basically, that we should work our hearts out. But where is the Work Ethic today? These days we have a word for people who work their hearts out: "workaholics." We do not necessarily admire them. Are there moral limits, then, to work?

On the other hand, work is serious business. If you have steered yourself into a kind of work that both satisfies yourself and serves the world in an impor-tant way, what then are the limits? And is the expectation of *hard* work more an expectation for yourself, or for others? How far are others entitled to ask this of you? Is this a moral question?

What makes a moral workplace? That is, what sorts of relationships between co-workers and between workers and their superiors and owners or administra-tors are more (or less) moral? What does "moral management" look like—and how can all parties contribute? Are there structural features of business and management settings that make moral relationships more difficult to achieve and sustain? What can be done about them? Likewise, are there structural features of business and management settings that make moral relationships easier to achieve and sustain? How can they be enhanced?

More generally, what does the ethical centrality of work require of others: of employers, most notably, and of society as a whole? If people *are* going to work their hearts out, or just work well and honestly, what do those for whom they work owe them in return, if anything beyond a decent paycheck? There was a time when a loyal and hard-working employee could more or less count on stable, permanent, decently paid employment in return. Today, many commentators conclude, that "social contract" is in tatters. Whole companies are bought out, moved, bankrupted, or downsized, seemingly at the drop of a hat. Pension funds are regularly raided, or their investments devalued, leaving a lifetime's promise of a comfortable retirement in shambles. In general, workers no longer trust employers to hold up their end of the bargain. Employers themselves have vanished into faceless bureaucracies and distant financial rein-holders. One talks not to the boss but to the "Human Resources Department." What, if anything, can or should be done about this?

Finally, what can or should be done about the similar situation on the community level? A city, say, has a long and close relationship with a particular business or type of business. The business has supported the city through taxes and other philanthropies, and likewise has been supported by the city through preferential treatment and provision of services. Then at some point the owners close up the plant and move overseas where labor is cheaper and there are fewer regulations overall. Events like these can devastate whole communities as well as the workers themselves. Capital can move, but most workers cannot—nor, obviously, can a city. What should be done about such events? Can it be argued that it is a requirement of justice that workers—who after all *are*, literally, the "company," in terms of its personnel—have some voice in such matters? What kind of voice could it be? And what about the city?

NOTES

Stanley Milgram is cited from his article "The Perils of Obedience," an article abridged and adapted from his book *Obedience to Authority* that originally appeared in *Harper's Magazine*, December 1973, http://harpers.org/archive/1973/12/0021874. On the ethics and the aftermaths of the experiment itself, see the provocative discussion under "Milgram Experiment" at http://en.wikipedia.org/wiki/Milgram_experiment, accessed 9/25/11.

On the inner work of freedom and self-possession, two useful and accessible works are *This Book Is Not Required: An Emotional and Intellectual Survival Manual for Students,* by Terri L. Anderson, John Gunderson, Inge Bell, Bernard

McGrane (SAGE, 2010), and John Sullivan's *Living Large,* of which you got a taste in chapter 7.

On "perversion," Colin McGinn is cited from his essay "Sex," in *Moral Literacy* (Duckworth/Hackett, 1992), pp. 60–64. For a sampling of what philosophers say about sex, see Robert Baker, Kathleen Winninger, and Frederick Elliston's collection *Philosophy and Sex* (Prometheus, 3rd edition, 1998) and Sallie Tisdale's personal and deeply philosophical *Talk Dirty to Me: An Intimate Philosophy of Sex* (Anchor, 1995). See also the Internet Encyclopedia of Philosophy's entry for "Philosophy of sexuality," by Alan Soble, at http://www.iep.utm.edu/sexualit/. An intense book on male identity and the devaluation of the female is John Stoltenberg's collection of essays, *Refusing to Be a Man* (Routledge, 2000). One especially relevant essay invites men to consider a range of erotic possibilities available beyond, as he puts it, "a macho definition of maleness."

A comprehensive and contemporary philosophical anthology on ethics and animals is Susan Armstrong's *The Animal Ethics Reader* (2nd edition, Routledge, 2008). For a broad overview of the discussion, though now somewhat dated, try the "Ethics Updates" website, http://ethics.sandiego.edu under "Animal Rights." For more information on meat-free menu planning, vitamins, and vegetarianism and children, start with the Vegetarian Resource Group's website at http://www.vrg.org. For vegan resources (eating no animal products at all, i.e., no dairy either), see http://www.americanvegan.org. On other food issues, see Eric Schlosser, *Fast Food Nation* (Harper Perennial, 2002); http://www.slowfoodusa.org on the "Slow Food" movement; Norman Wirzba, ed., *The Essential Agrarian Reader: The Future of Culture, Community, and the Land* (Shoemaker and Hoard, 2004); and Wendell Berry's classic, *The Unsettling of America* (Sierra Club, 1996).

Pope John Paul II's encyclical *Laborem Exercens* can be found at http://www.vatican.va/holy_father/john_paul_ii/encyclicals/documents/hf_jp-ii_enc_14091981_laborem-exercens_en.html. A measured survey of the history and cultural expectations about work is Joanne Ciulla's *The Working Life* (Times Books, 2000). For a collection of essays on various aspects of work and ethics mostly from individual points of view, try Joanne Ciulla, Clancy Martin, and Robert Solomon's *Honest Work* (Oxford University Press, 2010).

USING YOUR TOOLS #8

PERSONAL ETHICAL MISSION STATEMENTS

BY NIM BATCHELOR

Imagine a deathbed scene where a dying man recounts all the ways that he wishes he had lived his life differently. He regrets that he failed to give his most important values their proper priority and that he did not build or live a life in accordance with his most important values. As the saying goes, not many people's dying wish is that they had watched more TV.

Similarly, we are all familiar with stories about people who have survived a serious brush with death. Often these people respond by undertaking a serious re-evaluation of their lives, which sometimes leads them to initiate radical changes. We also see this kind of "value panic" in the phenomenon called a "midlife crisis." In all of these cases we see a life in which relatively trivial concerns have somehow managed to be been taken too seriously or in which that person's important values have been subordinated or neglected. The good news, of course, is that if you are reading this right now, it is not too late for you to take steps to avoid living a life that you might later come to regret. You are still "response-able."

This exercise asks you to write a Personal Ethical Mission Statement. You can do this in many ways—I will suggest some alternative forms below—but however you do it, a personal mission statement typically lays out and explains a set of values, principles, and commitments that are central to the life that you hope to live. Since you actually want to be able to live by it, your statement should be internally consistent (that is, not contradict itself or posit incompatible standards), somewhat comprehensive (celebrating the best of your past, anticipating future challenges), and it should give some indication of how you might prioritize the central values it brings up. Your statement should acknowledge and reflect the fact that your ethical life will involve engagements with a diverse array of people in a variety of circumstances. Take it as an opportunity for you to give your comprehensive ethical life vision a more concrete form.

Most people who write personal mission statements find that they can be a vital tool that can help you keep your priorities and core values in place when you face important decisions in your life. However, this fact should not lead you to develop writer's block. Remember, this is only your first personal mission statement. Since your values and commitments will evolve over time, you will need to re-write your mission statement every so often. This project is an invitation to think seriously about your values and your priorities and to initiate a practice that will help you construct a life that you can—at any moment—reflect upon without regret and embrace as a life well lived.

RESOURCES AND OPTIONS

The most well known guide to writing a personal mission statement can be found on pages 96–144 of Stephen Covey's best-selling book, *The Seven Habits of Highly Effective People (Free Press, 1989)*. Christopher Gergen and Gregg Vanourek offer a similar project in their book *Life Entrepreneurs* (Jossey-Bass, 2008). If you don't have access to these books or if you are more digitally inclined, you might want to work through the "mission statement builders" that you can find on the websites that are associated with these books:

http://www.franklincovey.com/msb/
http://www.lifeentrepreneurs.com/

You could also stimulate your thinking about these matters by writing a "This I Believe" essay. Back in the 1950s, Edward R. Murrow hosted a radio show that featured essays written by prominent personalities. Recently, National Public Radio revived this project and their efforts have greatly enhanced the collection of inspiring and insightful essays. If you want to try your hand at this, you should begin by listening to some of the online readings. Then read the "writers guide" (all of this can be found at: http://thisibelieve .org/). My only advice here would be that since you are doing this to enhance your personal mission statement, you will probably want to focus your essay on an ethical dimension of your life.

Your exploration of your core values might also be deepened by thinking about how you might respond to an "ethical life-story interview." Begin by collecting a series of ethical episodes or vignettes from your life. These "critical events," or "episodes," or "scenes" should be selected because they were particularly influential in shaping your ethical character or in teaching you a particularly influential value. This exercise was inspired primarily by Dan P. McAdams' instruments, "Guided Autobiography" and "Life Story Interview," which you can find at the Foley Center for the Study of Lives (http:// www.sesp.northwestern.edu/foley/instruments/).

Here is a list of questions that might help you remember some of these key moments from your ethical life:

- What are some of your earliest ethical memories?
- What ethical realizations have you had that others find insightful?
- What are some of your ethical high moments? These will likely be moments of personal pride.
- What are some of your ethical low moments? These will likely be moments of personal shame.
- When did you stand by your principles? What did you learn from this?
- When did you abandon your principles? What did you learn from this?
- Morally, who do you admire or seek to emulate and what underlying values are revealed by that choice?
- Morally, who do you find repugnant and what underlying values are revealed by that fact?
- To what have you donated your time, energy, or money?
- What are some of the most important moral lessons that you learned from your parents?
- What conflicts have you had that have had a lasting influence over you?

- Are there any important turning points in your ethical life story?
- What events contributed most to your ethical growth?
- How have your religious or spiritual experiences influenced your moral development?
- What losses or traumatic experiences have you suffered and how have they influenced your moral development?
- What are the underlying values that guide your political affiliations?

This self-interview alone will probably raise a number of additional considerations that you might want to include in your personal mission statement. However, if you want to pursue it a bit further still, try to imagine your life as a novel. It has a setting, a cast of characters, and while it likely does not have a single coherent plot, it surely has a handful of main motifs. And notice this: YOU have the honor of being both the main character AND the author of this novel. As the author of your life, your goal is to develop or craft a future that realistically emerges out of your actual past. Of course, it would be unrealistic to propose an instant character transformation, gradual changes happen all the time. Furthermore, while no one can escape their past, we are all "response-able," and thus we are free to choose many aspects of our future. Your mission—your story—could, after all, if you choose, be a story of growth and *change*.

CHAPTER 17

Making a Difference

THE POWER OF ONE

The Nobel Peace Prize for 2004 went to Kenyan Wangari Maathai for promoting sustainable economic and cultural development in Kenya and in Africa. The "Green Belt Movement" that she founded thirty years ago has mobilized tens of thousands of poor women to plant more than thirty million trees. She has been violently assaulted—once beaten unconscious by the police, served years in jail for demanding fair elections and equal rights for women, almost single-handedly saved a major Nairobi park from pillage by cronies of the corrupt former president, run for Kenyan president, was later elected to Parliament (with 98 percent of the vote), and has been assistant minister in the Ministry of Environment, Natural Resources and Wildlife ever since. She's also, by all accounts, a lovely and generous person.

Nelson Mandela was awarded the Nobel Peace Prize in 1993 along with F. W. De Klerk, the South African president who set in motion the end of apartheid in that country. Mandela spent his life fighting apartheid and the governments that enforced it; spent twenty-seven years in prison, often in solitary confinement or at hard labor, for that fight; and came out of prison not seething with hatred for the lost years but just as anxious as when he was imprisoned to create—in his famous words from the dock as his imprisonment was about to begin—"a democratic and free society in which all persons live together in harmony and with equal opportunities." In 1994, as blacks attained the right to vote for the first time, the previously banned African National Congress swept to power and Mandela became the first black president of South Africa. He too, by all accounts, has an almost saintly way.

Chapter 3 has already spoken of Mandela's colleague, the Anglican bishop Desmond Tutu, himself the winner of the Nobel Peace Prize in 1984, while still in the midst of the struggle against apartheid. Everything still teetered on the brink. Descent into civil war and the bloodiest of revenge taking were universally expected. Tutu became the prime mover behind the Truth and Reconciliation process that, astonishingly, brought former killers together with families of victims all over the country. Mandela managed to make his own person and story, known to every South African, into a kind of parable of reconciliation and coexistence. South Africa's transformation, inspired by these remarkable figures, remains one of the most amazing moral success stories of the 20th century.

MUHAMMAD YUNUS: "THE GOOD BANKER"

The Nobel Peace Prize for 2006 went to Muhammad Yunus, a Bangladeshi banker, inventor, and tireless promoter of "micro-credit" through the now-famous Grameen Bank. Beginning by lending small amounts of money out of his own pocket to destitute village craftspeople, mostly women, Yunus discovered that such loans were enough to free the craftspeople from middlemen and make them canny and effective entrepreneurs. Scaffolded by support groups but with no collateral requirement and no repayment date, his loans are still repaid at a higher rate than many banks can boast—out of, basically, *gratitude*.

Yunus started out as a professional economist, teaching "elegant theories of economics" (as he puts it) in the newly independent Bangladesh while massive numbers of people were dying of hunger in the streets. The famine of 1974, which killed a million and a half Bangladeshis, changed his life. "Why did people who worked twelve hours a day, seven days a week, not have enough food to eat? I decided that the poor themselves would be my teachers. I began to study them and question them on their lives."

He began to work with farmers and set up farmers' cooperatives. But it soon became apparent that the truly destitute, the landless rural poor, needed some more dramatic kind of help. Alan Jolis's article "The Good Banker" explains:

> One day, interviewing a woman who made bamboo stools, [Yunus] learnt that, because she had no capital of her own, she had to borrow the equivalent of [30 cents] to buy raw bamboo for each stool made. After repaying the middleman, she kept only a [2 cent] profit margin. With the help of his graduate students, he discovered 42 other villagers in the same predicament.
>
> "Their poverty was not a personal problem due to laziness or lack of intelligence, but a structural one: lack of capital. The existing system made it certain that the poor could not save a penny and could not invest in bettering themselves. Some money-lenders set interest rates as high as 10 per cent a month, some 10 per cent a week. So, no matter how hard these people worked, they would never raise themselves above subsistence level. What was needed was to link their work to capital to allow them to amass an economic cushion and earn a ready income."

And so the idea of credit for the landless was born. Yunus's first approach was to reach into his pocket and lend each of the 42 women the equivalent of [about $40]. He set no interest rate and no repayment date: "I didn't think of myself as a banker, but as the liberator of 42 families."

Immediately, Yunus saw the impracticality of carrying on in this way, and tried to interest banks in institutionalising his gesture by lending to the poorest, with no collateral. Bankers laughed at him, insisting that the poor are not "creditworthy." Yunus answered, "How do you know they are not creditworthy, if you've never tried? Perhaps it is the banks that are not people-worthy?"

He went on to create his own lending system, at first run by his own students; he then finally convinced the central bank to take it on and later incorporated Grameen to go it alone. Grameen Bank is now the largest rural bank in Bangladesh, with millions of borrowers. It also has spinoffs the world over, including more than five hundred community banks in the United States alone.

ORDINARY PEOPLE

The list of Nobel Peace Prize winners is an inspiring list all around. Martin Luther King Jr.; Lech Walesa, the Polish dockworker who became central to the Solidarity movement in Poland under the last years of Communism and eventually became president of Poland. The Dalai Lama; Mother Theresa. Betty Williams and Mairead Corrigan, cofounders of the Northern Ireland Peace Movement.

Of course these world changers are now highly honored. Some are household names around the world. They serve in governments, run organizations. People listen when they speak.

But they did not start that way. Most of them started in ordinary places. Maathai just planted a few trees in her backyard, and got to thinking. No one supported or believed her in the early years—not even her then husband (who in fact quickly divorced her). Walesa was a shipyard worker, a common electrician. Fired for organizing a memorial to some assassinated workers, he scaled a wall to rejoin the next strike...and one thing led to the next. Williams and Corrigan met when an Irish Republican Army getaway car was hit by British gunfire and veered out of control, killing three children. Corrigan, a Catholic, was the children's aunt; Williams, also Catholic but with Protestant and Jewish roots, just happened to be walking by. One a secretary, the other a receptionist; both ordinary mothers with small children themselves. Two days later, they led ten thousand Protestant and Catholic women, marching together, at the dead children's funeral. That march was disrupted by Catholic hardliners for being "dupes of the British." So they held another, and this time thirty-five thousand people came. A peace movement was born.

These people didn't make change alone, of course. Walesa cofounded an organization literally called "Solidarity"—the very name announced that change only comes when many people stand together. Sometimes, recognizing the crucial role of organizations, the Nobel Peace Prize is awarded to organizations directly. Yet more common is that, even when an organization is honored, so are the individuals who created and sustained it in turn. In 1997 the prize was co-awarded to Jody Williams and the organization she helped create, the International Campaign to Ban Landmines, for their work banning and clearing anti-personnel mines. The 2006 prize went jointly to Muhammad Yunus and his Grameen Bank.

Right in my community and among people I know personally, there are artists who use "Art Walks" to revitalize their neighborhoods, both economically and personally; specialists in socially responsible investments; schoolteachers who spend their own money to buy poor students textbooks or take them on trips when neither the school nor the parents can pay; and the creator of a new organization to promote long-term adaptive thinking about climate change.

At my university, colleagues are helping to rebuild New Orleans and take students to Central America over spring break to build homes with Habitat for Humanity. They advise and staff local social services and health organizations and prison ministries. Students organize for Sexual Assault Awareness and to bring locally grown and organic food into the university cafeterias, supporting local growers and introducing fellow students to totally new ways to eat. The chaplain's office invites students every year to nominate people from their hometowns who have made a difference. "Hometown Heroes," they're called. The winners, five a year, are invited to campus, speak to classes, and are honored at a convocation. Regularly the winners are family members—father, grandmother, sibling—reminding us among other things that among "the powers of one" is *inspiration*. This year one of the winners was the nominator's father, a police officer who has run the torch for Special Olympics for twenty years and has become chair of the International Torch Run Council. Another student's mother is a breast cancer survivor who made herself into an advocate for other cancer sufferers and for more research, earlier detection, and better treatments. Several created local projects to support people in some of the poorest countries on the planet, such as Haiti. Another was among the liberators of the Woebbelin concentration camp at the end of World War II who has, ever since, annually revisited the spot and has dedicated his life to understanding the genocide and to the theme of "Never Again."

Again: these are ordinary people, ordinary friends, and family, and neighbors. In fact, I am sure that most readers of this book have already taken part in the kind of work just outlined, or at least know someone who is doing it, right here and now. The challenge and invitation now, maybe, is to step up to more of a leadership role. But the opportunity and the role models are already here—often enough, right there in front of us.

READING

From On the Rez

IAN FRAZIER

IAN FRAZIER'S *ON THE REZ* chronicles the modern life of the Plains Indians, especially the Oglala Sioux. This excerpt describes a deed of SuAnne Big Crow, the most admired Oglala basketball player of all time, which Frazier calls "one of the coolest and bravest deeds I have ever heard of."

The setting is a racially charged 1988 high school basketball game in Lead, South Dakota, where SuAnne's team from the Pine Ridge reservation are the visitors. The host gym, as often happens, "is dense with hostility...."

SuAnne was a full member of the team by then. She was a freshman, fourteen years old. Getting ready in the locker room, the Pine Ridge girls could hear the din from the fans. They were yelling fake-Indian war cries, a "woo-woo-woo" sound. The usual plan for the pre-game warm-up was for the visiting team to run onto the court in a line, take a lap or two around the floor, shoot some baskets, and then go to their bench at courtside. After that, the home team would come out and do the same, and then the game would begin. Usually the Thorpes lined up for their entry more or less according to height, which meant that senior Doni De Cory, one of the tallest, went first. As the team waited in the hallway leading from the locker room, the heckling got louder. The Lead fans were yelling epithets like "squaw" and "gut-eater." Some were waving food stamps, a reference to the reservation's receiving federal aid. Others yelled, "Where's the cheese?"—the joke being that if Indi-

From Ian Frazier, *On the Rez* (Farrar, Straus, and Giroux, 2000), pp. 208–213. Used by permission of Farrar, Straus, and Giroux.

ans were lining up, it must be to get commodity cheese. The Lead high school band had joined in, with fake-Indian drumming and a fake-Indian tune. Doni De Cory looked out the door and told her teammates. "I can't handle this." SuAnne quickly offered to go first in her place. She was so eager that Doni became suspicious. "Don't embarrass us," Doni told her. SuAnne said "I won't. I won't embarrass you." Doni gave her the ball, and SuAnne stood first in line.

She came running onto the court dribbling the basketball, with her teammates running behind. On the court, the noise was deafeningly loud. SuAnne went right down the middle; but instead of running a full lap, she suddenly stopped when she got to center court. Her teammates were taken by surprise, and some bumped into one another. Coach Zimiga at the rear of the line did not know why they had stopped. SuAnne turned to Doni De Cory and tossed her the ball. Then she stepped into the jump-ball circle at center court, in front of the Lead fans. She unbuttoned her warm-up jacket, took it off, draped it over her shoulders, and began to do the Lakota shawl dance. SuAnne knew all the traditional dances—she had competed in many powwows as a little girl—and the dance she chose is a young woman's dance, graceful and modest and show-offy all at the same time. "I couldn't believe it—she was powwowin', like, 'get down!'" Doni De Cory recalled. "And then she started to sing." SuAnne began to sing in Lakota, swaying back and forth in the jump-ball circle, doing the shawl dance, using her warm-up jacket for a shawl. The crowd went completely silent. "All that stuff the Lead fans were yelling—it was like she *reversed* it somehow," a teammate said. In the sudden quiet, all you could hear was her Lakota song. SuAnne stood up, dropped her jacket, took the ball from Doni De Cory, and ran a lap around the court dribbling expertly and fast. The fans began to cheer and applaud. She sprinted to the basket, went up in the air, and laid the ball through the hoop, with the fans cheering loudly now. Of course, Pine Ridge went on to win the game.

[Frazier inserts here a short history of Lead. The name, it turns out, refers not to lead, the metal, but rather to the miners' term for a gold-bearing deposit, in this case what became a $10 billion gold mine in land that was dispossessed from the Sioux in the midst of the Indian wars of the 1870s. It took a hundred years for the U.S. Supreme Court to affirm the Sioux (Lakota) people's right to at least minimal compensation for the theft of their land—a tiny fraction of what the land yielded in gold, which now sits in a bank account unused, because the Sioux no longer want minimal compensation for the land but want back at least

some small portion of the actual land itself. Everyone on the reservation, and in Lead, knows this story. —AW]

Inescapably, this history is present when an Oglala team goes to Lead to play a basketball game. It may even explain why the fans in Lead were so mean: fear that you might perhaps be in the wrong can make you ornerier sometimes. In all the accounts of this land grab and its aftermath, and among the many greedy and driven men who had a part, I cannot find evidence of a single act as elegant, as generous, or as transcendent as SuAnne's dance at center court in the gym at Lead.

For the Oglala, what SuAnne did that day almost immediately took on the stature of myth. People from Pine Ridge who witnessed it still describe it in terms of awe and disbelief. Amazement swept through the younger kids when they heard. "I was, like, '*What* did she just do?'" recalled her cousin Angie Big Crow, an eighth-grader at the time. All over the reservation, people told and retold the story of SuAnne at Lead. Any time the subject of SuAnne came up when I was talking to people on Pine Ridge, I would always ask if they had heard about what she did at Lead, and always the answer was a smile and a nod—"Yeah, I was there," or "Yeah, I heard about that." To the unnumbered big and small slights of local racism which the Oglala have known all their lives, SuAnne's exploit made an emphatic reply.

Back in the days when Lakota war parties still fought battles against other tribes and the Army, no deed of war was more honored than the act of counting coup. To count coup means to touch an armed enemy in full possession of his powers with a special stick called a coup stick, or with the hand. The touch is not a blow, and only serves to indicate how close to the enemy you came. As an act of bravery, counting coup was regarded as greater than killing an enemy in single combat, greater than taking a scalp or horses or any prize. Counting coup was an act of almost abstract courage, of pure playfulness taken to the most daring extreme. Very likely, to do it and survive brought an exhilaration to which nothing could compare. In an ancient sense which her Oglala kin could recognize, SuAnne counted coup on the fans of Lead.

And yet this coup was an act not of war but of peace. SuAnne's coup strike was an offering, an invitation. It took the hecklers at the best interpretation, as if their silly mocking chants were meant only in goodwill. It showed that their fake Indian songs were just that—fake—and that the real thing was better, as real things usually are. We Lakota have been dancing like this for centuries, the dance said; we've been doing the shawl dance since long before you came, before you got on the boat in Glasgow or Bremerhaven, before you stole this land, and we're still doing it today; and isn't it pretty, when you see how it's supposed to be done? Because finally what SuAnne proposed was to invite us—us onlookers in the stands, which is the non-Lakota rest of this country—to dance, too. She was in the Lead gym to play, and she invited us all to play. The symbol she used to include us was the warm-up jacket. Everyone in America has a warm-up jacket. I've got one, probably so do you, so did (no doubt) many of the fans at Lead. By using the warm-up jacket as a shawl in her impromptu shawl dance, she made Lakota relatives of us all.

"It was funny," Doni De Cory said, "but after that game the relationship between Lead and us was tremendous. When we played Lead again, the games were really good, and we got to know some of the girls on the team. Later, when we went to a tournament and Lead was there, we were hanging out with the Lead girls and eating pizza with them. We got to know some of their parents, too. What SuAnne did made a lasting impression and changed the whole situation with us and Lead. We found out there are some really good people in Lead."

BECOMING A CHANGE-MAKER

How can we become change-makers ourselves? Here are some guidelines.

FIND YOUR OWN WAY

There is no one single way to make ethical change. Very varied people are change-makers: housewives and office workers, tribal elders, dockyard electricians, yoga students, college professors. Even bankers, of all things, like Muhammad Yunus.

There are *many* ways—probably as many ways as there are different individuals. Play to your strengths. You may not be witness to a society-changing event, or arrive on the scene just as some new need opens up that you might fill. But don't assume you haven't, either—for *noticing* the need, noticing the possibilities opening up, is part of the creative and perceptive challenge. Again, find ways that work for you.

KEEP AT IT

Persistence pays off. Few substantial ethical changes come easily or quickly. Many of the changes cited here—in fact, nearly all of them—are still being contested, still being achieved. Some Nobel Peace Prize winners spent years or even decades in jail, endured risks, struggled against prejudice and ill will and just plain inertia for much of their lives. They found joy in it still—and it was the right thing to do, in their view—but there is no denying the difficulty and the danger. Be ready.

Don't expect that you will always know what difference you are making or have made. The ways of the world can be subtle and circuitous. Have some faith. Here is one instructive story, described by Paul Rogat Loeb in his collection *The Impossible Will Take a Little While.*

> In the early 1960s, a friend of mine named Lisa took two of her kids to a Washington, DC vigil in front of the White House protesting nuclear testing. The demonstration was small, a hundred women at most. Rain poured down. The women felt frustrated and powerless. A few years later, the movement against testing had grown dramatically, and Lisa attended a major march. Benjamin Spock, the famous baby doctor, spoke. He described how he'd come to take a stand, which because of his stature had already influenced thousands, and would reach far more when he challenged the Vietnam War. Spock talked briefly about the issues, then mentioned that when he was in DC a few years earlier he saw a small group of women huddled, with their kids, in the rain. It was Lisa's group. "I thought if those women were out there," he said, "their cause must be really important."

And that was enough to set him down the path. Lisa might never have known that she and a few others helped change the course of history, yet she did.

We honor Rosa Parks for sparking the fateful bus boycott in Montgomery, Alabama, that helped bring down the segregated South. She refused to leave her seat when it was demanded by a white man. It doesn't detract from her courage and her accomplishment to know that her arrest, and the boycott that followed, was carefully planned and prepared. And who, Loeb asks, got *her* started? It turns out that she was prompted to attend her first NAACP meeting by her husband, who was already involved. And who got *him* involved? Loeb concludes: "Even in a seemingly losing cause, one person may unknowingly inspire another, and that person yet a third, who could go on to change the world."

So be careful not to judge yourself or someone else a failure, or ineffective, just because you, or they, maybe did not have the immediate effect intended. Be careful not to suppose that the only worthwhile ends of action are quick and clear "results." Do what is right and don't worry too much about it. You never know what pathways you may be starting for yourself or someone else.

AIM HIGH

A third guideline: always remember that much more is possible than we usually imagine. People and situations always have hidden possibilities. Beware of the self-satisfied "realism" that looks at the world as it is (or anyway *seems,* on some interpretations) and imagines that the world as it is is the only world possible. Remember your vision!

Muhammad Yunus again:

> Poverty covers people in a thick crust and makes the poor appear stupid and without initiative. Yet if you give them credit, they will slowly come back to life. Even those who seemingly have no conceptual thought, no ability to think of yesterday or tomorrow, are in fact quite intelligent and expert at the art of survival. Credit is the key that unlocks their humanity.

In short, he imagines that everyone has the ingenuity to lift themselves out of poverty. We just aren't going to *see* that ingenuity until it is given the chance to show itself.

Likewise, Mandela and Tutu actually imagined that South Africans could forgive the apartheid regime for the decades of oppression it fostered, and go on together. It certainly didn't look that way at the time—yet they were right. Vaclav Havel and Lech Walesa actually imagined that a few playwrights or ordinary workers, standing up in their lonely way for the right thing, could bring down authoritarian governments that had the whole might of the Soviet superpower behind them. These were not exactly "realistic" hopes. Nonetheless, these things came to pass. Maybe what's "realistic" is a little more fluid than we think.

Considering how far we've already come toward questioning our use of animals for food, it is entirely possible that in twenty years most people will no longer eat meat at all. Perhaps instead of executing anyone, we will expect those sentenced to death to choose self-sacrifices of some sort (drug tests? suicide missions?) that offer a kind of redemption or restitution for the life they have taken. Perhaps...who knows?

So don't be deterred by the "realists" who look at the present situation and see no hope. "Realism" may only be an excuse for resignation or lack of imagination. They may actually be right: maybe there really isn't any hope in the present situation. Your response might be that therefore we need to *change the situation.*

USE YOUR CREATIVITY

A fourth guideline: use your creativity. General thinking skills can get pushed to the side when we think of ethics primarily as a mode of personal response. Yes, ethics is in part an affair of the heart. But other skills come into play as well—and sometimes creativity is the most crucial.

Bo Lozoff, cofounder along with his wife Sita of the Human Kindness Foundation, was living in a yoga ashram—a secluded and intensive religious community—when he noticed with a certain shock (as it happened, visiting a relative in jail) that their life was not so different from the life of a prisoner. Both are very highly constrained and lack many worldly comforts. But their life was *liberating*. How interesting, he thought. And just possibly a creative provocation.... He went on to create the "Prison-Ashram Project" to enable prisoners to treat their prisons as ashrams: that is, to make use of the very isolation and "deprivation" and silence that can make prison so awful as, instead, occasions for spiritual growth. He reframed the entire experience and institution of prison.

Among the many recognitions Lozoff has received for this work is an award for "Creative Altruism" from the Institute for Noetic Sciences. Creative. Altruism. Those two words are not often put together. But why not? As we've seen already in chapters 13 and 14, creativity has as much to offer ethics as it has to offer anywhere else—maybe even more.

STAY OPEN TO COMPLEXITY

It can be tempting to picture ethical change-makers as single-minded, even fanatical, and to think that we must make ourselves the same in order to succeed. When I say that you need to find your own way, persist, and have confidence that dramatic change is possible, it may seem that these guidelines too suggest a kind of dogged self-confidence or even moral self-righteousness.

But the stories we have told actually have a different moral. The change-makers we have featured are firm in certain ways, but not in a narrow-minded or self-righteous way. Muhammad Yunus is devoted to eradicating poverty (completely!), but his means are maximally flexible and creative. SuAnne Big Crow made change just by dancing and singing, inviting a hostile crowd to look again. Nelson Mandela was always committed to equality for black South Africans but never to suppression of white South Africans. Mandela's long imprisonment, in fact, actually made him *more* open and tolerant.

If anyone in these stories is morally self-righteous or dogmatic, it is the defenders of the status quo. They're the ones a little too comfortable with how things are—too threatened, maybe, by the thought of change to see the change-makers clearly. They're the ones who will not understand your motives and will make all sorts of stereotypical assumptions—such as, most basically, that you're the fanatic. Don't fall into that stereotype! Part of your strength, in fact, is that you are (can be) much more flexible. You're more apt to build alliances, find an unexpectedly innovative alternative, to bring together a variety of values into some more balanced picture.

On the other hand, advocating for ethical change can put you out in edgy and controversial territory. Many of those we celebrate—even many of those Nobel winners, for example—worked for changes that at the time seemed politically and even ethically questionable to most people: civil rights, artistic and political freedom under Communism, tree hugging, religious diversity.

So again: in ongoing and unsettled struggles, avoid stereotyping any of the advocates involved as fanatics, even the ones you don't like. And avoid sliding toward narrow- and single-mindedness yourself. Think one more time of our debates over guns, or abortion, or the ethical claims of other animals. Sometimes, I am sure, some of the people involved really are fanatics. But that is no reason to make ourselves fanatical in response, or to respond to others only in a dismissive or single-minded way. Expect to find common ground; stay open to complexity in your own stance and to complementarity in others'.

· THERE IS NO WAY TO ETHICS; ETHICS *IS* THE WAY

Our last guideline is a Gandhian saying you may have heard: "There is no way to peace; peace is the way." This puzzles people. Isn't peace a goal that we are struggling for, someday to achieve down the road? Not exactly, says Gandhi. We certainly work for a world in which everyone has well-developed and nonviolent habits of living with and working out conflicts. Yes. Right here and now, though, *we* at least can develop our own nonviolent habits of living with and working out conflicts, including our conflicts with those who themselves are prone to violence. Peace is how we relate to each other *right now*.

Exactly the same is true in ethics proper. There is no way to ethics; ethics *is* the way. We can certainly work for a world in which everyone has well-developed ethical habits and a full ethical toolbox. Yes. But right here and now *we*, at least, can develop our own ethical habits, including ways to deal ethically with those who themselves have only a few ethical tools, or none at all. Ethics is how we relate to each other *right now*.

Here's another of Gandhi's sayings you may have heard or seen on a bumper sticker:

> YOU MUST BE THE CHANGE YOU WISH TO SEE IN THE WORLD

In the first place, this means: actually *do* something. Promote the change you wish to see in the world. Advocate a serious environmental ethic, for example, in part by actually living it.

This much is obvious. The deeper meaning is more intriguing and difficult. Acting in the name of ethics, even as we strive to bring that ideal into reality, we cannot and must not act in ways that are unethical or violate that ideal. Do not imagine that you can achieve peace with your neighbors by killing some of them. You may attain the façade of peace, but hatred and pain will be at its foundation still and will poison the so-called peace in time. Do not imagine that legally imposing your ethics on other people somehow makes the world right. Maybe sometimes we will conclude that it is necessary, but the true ethical change only follows when you, or they, bring others around by force of example, by word and deed, by *being* a full-fleshed ethics in action.

An environmentalist friend of mine says: People will not live in harmony with nature until we also come to live in harmony with *each other*. Therefore it does not effectively promote long-term environmentalist goals to create sustained conflict among people: politically, in local communities, wherever. No: our way of moving toward an ecological future must itself be ecological. It must seek connection, mutuality, interdependence, synergy—right now, and in every move we make toward a more ecological world. Even when we must set ourselves into opposition to others, do not let it become total opposition. Hug trees *and* hug people! she concludes. Let us live our own lives in ways that so manifest a love for Creation in all its forms that other people, feeling themselves already included in that love, are drawn to change their lives too.

Maybe this sounds way too sentimental or idealistic for us? Gandhi, though, would not regard it as sentimental or idealistic at all. It's just *practical*...

THIS MEANS YOU!

Most users of this book will be students and probably young. People like you, you might be thinking, seldom have the connections or the power to make major ethical changes.

Sometimes it's true. Sometimes making change does take powers you don't yet have. But only sometimes. Remember that some of the change-makers featured in this very chapter are just like you, or even younger. SuAnne Big Crow, for instance, was only fourteen, a high school freshman.

Moreover, sometimes it's precisely the fact that you *are* young people or students that gives you a kind of power that other, older people don't have. For one thing, simply being a student gives you a natural solidarity with other students everywhere. You can organize *as students* across campuses, across the country, even across the world. This is especially true when the ethical issues around which you organize show up on campus—and across campuses—in distinctive ways. Students around the country stand in the forefront of organizing against sweatshops, for example, because their universities are among the prime customers for products made in sweatshops: clothes stamped with university logos. Students have a good bit of leverage at their own institutions, and universities, being large single-order custom-ers, have a good bit of leverage over suppliers. Very specific changes can therefore be demanded. This is why national organizations like Students Against Sweatshops are naturals, and have been very effective in recent years.

In Eastern Europe in the 1990s, hundreds of thousands of students and young people took to the streets to protest, and soon enough to replace, authoritarian governments no longer propped up by the Soviet Union: in Czechoslovakia and East Germany and Bulgaria and Romania, and in the former Yugoslavia, and then again in the separate republics into which Yugo-slavia dissolved, especially Serbia, where students resisted the authoritarian Milosovic regime and eventually helped oust him as well. It's happening again in Egypt as I write in the spring of 2011. Not that it was easy. Whole universities were closed down. Activists were harassed and sometimes "dis-appeared." The entrenched political leadership stalled or sympathized (with-out changing anything) or just lied through their teeth. But the students persisted. They took their universities back, or started "Free Universities" of their own. They continued to take to the streets—and increasingly to the air-waves and the Internet. Older people had all the power, or so it seemed—but the young had the chutzpah and the computer savvy to catch the attention of the world.

Nearly all of this was accomplished peacefully. Here too the students' powerlessness—in the usual terms—was crucial to their success. You've seen the famous photo of the unknown young man in China's Tiananmen Square, during the mass protests of the summer of 1989, single-handedly holding off a line of tanks simply by standing in front of them. Those tanks could have crushed him in seconds. But he had—and used—a moral power rooted precisely in his extreme vulnerability. And he didn't stop there, either. Apparently he also yelled at them, "Why are you here? You have caused nothing but misery!" and later climbed up onto the turret of the lead tank to speak to the soldiers—young people, after all, like himself—inside.

Hundreds of students at Tiananmen went on a hunger strike to advance their demands, prompting the national leadership itself to come to the Square and plead with them not to starve themselves to death. ("We were young once too," they said.) The students also invoked a long-standing Chinese archetype of the selfless intellectual who speaks truth to power. And although the Tiananmen protests ultimately were suppressed, the after-effects continue even now, both in Chinese and world politics and in the imagina-tions of change-makers everywhere. *Time* magazine subsequently named that anonymous young tank-stopper one of the one hundred most influential peo-ple of the entire 20th century.

Young people stand among the most prominent ethical change-makers in the United States as well. The Freedom Riders, for example, young black and white people together, rode interstate buses into the segregated South in the summer of 1961 to test a Supreme Court decision outlawing racial segregation in interstate transportation facilities—and to visibly model a new respect and cooperation across racial lines. They were imprisoned, beaten, harassed. But when one group could no longer take the violence, student organizers brought in others. They kept coming. By the end of that summer the Interstate Commerce Commission was enforcing and extending the Supreme Court decision, and the civil rights movement had been galvanized. Campaigns for voter registration and desegregation of restaurants, hotels, and workplaces were underway as well—again often spearheaded by young people. One of the many leaders of this action was John Lewis, soon to chair the Student Non-Violent Coordinating Committee and later a long-time U.S. congressperson from Atlanta and one of the leaders of the Congressional Black Caucus.

Young people continue to take the lead in certain areas—again drawing precisely on their youthfulness, inventiveness, and natural openheartedness and solidarity. For example, you may have seen "Invisible Children," an MTV-style film by three students from the University of Southern California who went to Africa with a camera bought on e-Bay to see what was happening and ended up encountering the massively displaced and orphaned children of Northern Uganda. It's a film, a website—and a movement to help rebuild schools and create teacher exchanges and volunteer opportunities for everyone to help. Twenty-somethings have started get-out-the-vote campaigns based on music, like Rock the Vote, and even general disaffection, like the League of Young Voters (also known as the League of Pissed-Off Voters), founded by William Upski Wimsatt—a college dropout and phenomenal journalist and organizer.

Students are taking a major lead in environmental action. Every school has its student Sierra Clubs and environmental coalitions. Look on the Web (e.g., www.broweryouthawards.org) for biographies of young people who have stood up and stood out for environmental action: organizing to promote green buildings on their campuses or loggerhead turtle preservation or campaigns to reduce campus paper use to help save old growth forests or creating relay races thirty-six miles up salmon streams, paralleling the run of the salmon themselves. Many are still in high school—in fact, some started still earlier. Shadia Wood began at the age of *seven* to lobby New York State lawmakers to fund toxic waste site cleanups, doing everything from appointing herself national spokesperson on the issue to setting up a lemonade stand on the steps of the Capitol and donating her $16 in earnings to the cause. The media loved it—and Shadia stood by the governor's side five years later when he signed the Superfund reauthorization.

I'd like to leave you with one more especially inspiring example. At age 23, Julia Butterfly Hill spent two years living mostly alone 200 feet up in an ancient redwood tree, Luna, trying to keep it from being cut down. Her book *The Story of Luna* is an account of how she ended up in Luna and how it felt, day to day, often enough full of despair and doubt as she worked the cell phone, weathered storms of all sorts, and tried to make a human connection with the loggers and the lumber company executives.

It was not exactly what she planned to do with her life. Starting as what she describes as a "somewhat aimless regular teenager," she suffered a traffic accident that forced a slow recovery and eventually led her to a cross-country road trip with friends. Almost by chance, along the California coast, she encountered a grove of magnificent and ancient redwood trees—and fell in love.

> At first [the trees] seemed like normal trees, but as I leaned my head back as far as I could, I looked far up into the air. I couldn't even see their crowns....Their trunks were so large that ten individuals holding hands would barely wrap around them. Some of the trees were hollow, scorched away by lightning strikes, yet they still stood. These trees' ancestors witnessed the dinosaur days. Wrapped in the fog and the moisture they need to grow, these ancient giants stood primordial, eternal. My feet sank into rich earth with each step. I knew I was walking on years and years of compounded history.

She soon learned that groves like these were rapidly being destroyed by lumber company clear-cutting. She resolved to help stop the cutting. But the defenders of the trees were desperate. Everything had been tried and had failed. Tree-sitting was their last resort. If a tree-sitter's tree is cut, the sitter dies with it. It has happened—though, supposedly, by accident. Like the Chinese tank-stopper, they put their own lives on the line:

> "I have no other way to stop what is happening" is basically what a tree-sitter is saying. "I have no other way to make people aware of what is at stake. I've followed the rules, but everything I've been told to do is failing. So it is my responsibility to give this one last shot, to put my body where my beliefs are."

So up she went, for what she thought would be a two- or three-week stint. It turned out to be more than two years, on a tiny, leaky, rickety platform, before her feet touched the ground again. She endured two winters, weeklong El Niño storms, helicopter harassment, sieges by company security guards, repeated close calls as the loggers took down the trees around her, and the tremendous sorrow it all brought. Yet there was unassailable joy too, as she finds an unexpected and deep intimacy with Luna and with the whole ridge where she stands. She climbs to the very top—250 feet high, in her bare feet.

> I made it to her lightning-hardened pinnacle, the most magical spot I'd ever visited. Luna is the tallest tree at the top of the ridge. Perched above everything and peering down, I felt as if I were standing on nothing at all, even though this massive, solid tree rose underneath me. I held on with my legs and reached my hands into the heavens. My feet could feel the power of the Earth coming through Luna, while my hands felt the power of the sky....
> No way could I allow Luna to be cut! Ever!

Speaking of famous photos, there is also a picture of that moment, with Julia at the very top of the tree, exultant—and a banner she unfurled, far below, saying "Respect Your Elders!," meaning Luna herself.

And she succeeded in the end. After long negotiation, she was able to save Luna and at least a small surrounding grove (and Luna still stands, though damaged by an unknown chainsaw attacker in 2000). Through an almost equally long and sometimes comical struggle, she also succeeded in being recognized as an actual person by at least some of the loggers. Through her Circle of Life Foundation, Julia Butterfly Hill serves now as a spokesperson for the interdependence of all life and for the power of every individual as well as every community to make a real difference in the world. "The question," she says, "is not 'Can you make a difference?' You already do make a difference. It's just a matter of what kind of difference you want to make."

COMMUNITIES MAKING CHANGE

A *community* is a group of people united by common interests and concerns. People who live in the same neighborhood or city, or even region, form one kind of community. Other times the people involved may live widely spread around a region or even the world, as when we speak of "the business community," "the community of scholars," "the black community," and so on. Communities of all sorts can be essential agents of ethical change.

LOCALITIES

First of all, we are inevitably in community with those right around us. We share schools and roads, political and cultural life, and of course the air, water, and land. Much community action is local in this sense. We have marches to raise money to aid soup kitchens or preserve open space. Local "preservation communities" try to protect local heritage, from buildings to watersheds. There's downtown revitalization work: for when inner cities are cut off and impoverished, the whole community is affected, and the walls of fear and denial begin to rise. "Communities in the Schools" programs aim to keep kids in school through adult mentoring. Recent graduates, also part of the school "community," stick with their schools to bring younger kids along. The Community-Supported Agriculture movement aims to preserve rural open space, water quality, small farms and the culture that goes with them: people buy the produce directly, know where it comes from, sometimes work the farms themselves—it's not called *Community*-Supported Agriculture for nothing.

Specific localities bring with them specific issues. Progressive communities in New Orleans are trying to rebuild an entire city in an ecologically sustainable and just way. Community organizations right in the West Virginia coal fields have risen up to demand an end to the coal companies' practice of creating huge toxic sludge ponds near or even right above town, infiltrating ground water and threatening floods, challenging as well the massive dynamiting of whole mountaintops that creates such toxic by-products in the first place. Individuals help: recently the grandfather of a child attending elementary school directly below a three-billion-ton sludge pond walked hundreds of miles from the capital of West Virginia, near the coalfields, to Washington, DC, holding press conferences and other events all along his walk. Once upon a time, he was a sludge pond builder. One purpose of his walk was specifically to move his own town's school. But never far from the surface was the crying need to organize his community and all such communities—often poorly educated, disempowered, discouraged people, traditionally beholden to the coal companies and with no sense of any real options—to take control of their lives and communities and find new ways.

One night last spring three crosses were burned in several parks in my city. This was perceived, immediately and widely, as an assault on all of us: on everyone committed to even the most minimal ideal of racial justice and respectful coexistence. And I am proud to say that the community responded. Hundreds of people came the very same night at the burning sites to "reject the hate." A week later a mass meeting drew thousands from the city to condemn the burnings and to build better ways to go on together. Musical groups, religious leaders, mayors and state representatives and police chiefs and even the state attorney general turned out.

Of course the hate still exists—no one is so naïve as to think that it doesn't. But the actual effect of the burnings, thanks to immediate and effective community response, was to reinvite serious commitments from across the community to continuing to improve race relations. And in Greensboro, North Carolina, just down the road, as Spoma Jovanovic describes in chapter 11 of this book, a citizens' commission has just finished a three-year project of hearing testimony and drawing conclusions about a 1979 incident, modeling their work after the Truth and Reconciliation Commissions set up in South Africa at the end of apartheid.

ORGANIZATIONS

Churches, synagogues, and mosques can also be ethical change-making communities. They are organized primarily around religious commitments and beliefs, of course, but many of these commitments and beliefs are in turn ethical. They are meant to be acted upon in the world. Historically it was the black churches that nurtured the civil rights movement. Lately nearly all of the established religions, from the most liberal to the most fundamentalist, are getting into environmental issues.

Businesses also support ethical causes and make ethical changes themselves. When the world finals for the Special Olympics—sporting events for mentally handicapped people—came to my area a few years back, local businesses moved quickly from just giving money to the Olympics to (also) hiring mentally handicapped people in special programs. That is, they not only gave charity but also made long-term changes in their own practices to expand opportunity and justice for mentally handicapped people. Other businesses are moving from just donating money to environmental causes to (also) reducing their own pollution. Some offset their pollution by investing in an equivalent amount of clean energy production or in mitigation projects such as tree plantings to absorb the CO_2 produced. Whole Foods Corporation, for example, already buys enough wind-power credits to offset all of its electricity use.

Then there are voluntary organizations of so many sorts that a quick Web search turns up over three hundred such organizations just in my own city, Durham, North Carolina. Some of these are more service-oriented than change-making—Hospice, the Humane Society, Meals on Wheels—but some of these are change-makers too, and meantime there are many others primarily about change. Just a bare sampling: Boat People SOS (action for the Vietnamese expatriate community); the Empowerment Project (democratizing access to media); Child Abuse and Family Violence Prevention; Fair Housing Advocacy; Fighting Blindness; Guardian Ad Litem programs (advocacy and human rights work); Mothers Against Drunk Driving; Justice for Animals; groups to limit kids' exposure to TV; Peace Action; the Hunger Network; StandUp for Kids (helping homeless and street kids); Americorps Youth Mentoring; Student Action with Farmworkers; Student Literacy Coalition; Stop Hunger Now; the Rails-to-Trails Conservancy; Keep America Beautiful; urban gardening organizations ("working together to create green areas of neighborhood pride and enjoyment"); the Center for Economic Justice; the World Library Partnership ("advocates for sustainable, community-based libraries in developing areas of the world"); the World Wildlife Fund...and finally the alphabet runs out. This is just in one medium-sized city, remember. There are still other change-oriented organizations that didn't make the list, for whatever reason: political organizations, neighborhood-specific organizations, the co-ops, less formal groups...

TWO ORGANIZATIONS FOR DIRECT ACTION

You may have heard of the group Doctors Without Borders.

> Doctors Without Borders/Médecins Sans Frontières (MSF) is an inde-
> pendent international medical humanitarian organization that delivers
> emergency aid to people affected by armed conflict, epidemics, natural or
> man-made disasters, or exclusion from health care in more than 70 coun-
> tries....In emergencies and their aftermath, MSF provides health care,
> rehabilitates and runs hospitals and clinics, performs surgery, battles epi-
> demics, carries out vaccination campaigns, operates feeding centers for mal-
> nourished children, and offers mental health care.

A line featured on their website is simple and eloquent: "There is so little
care available that the only ethical position is to take action" (Jean Hevre
Bradol). They too have been awarded a Nobel Peace Prize—as a whole
organization.

MSF also is committed to what they call "witness." They do not simply
deal with the medical need and suffering they see on the ground. They also
aim to make it visible to others as a way of making change.

> MSF unites direct medical care with a commitment to speaking out against
> the causes of suffering and the obstacles to providing effective assistance.
> MSF volunteers raise the concerns of their patients with governments, the
> United Nations, other international bodies, the general public, and the
> media. In a wide range of circumstances, MSF volunteers have spoken out
> against violations of international humanitarian law they have witnessed—
> from Chechnya to Sudan.

This tradition of "witness" is carried on by other change-oriented organizations, such as the environmental direct-action group Greenpeace. Rex
Wyler, cofounder of Greenpeace International, was interviewed on this
theme in 2006:

> The Quaker idea of bearing witness is that when we witness an event, espe-
> cially when we witness injustice, we become an agent of change. If you
> see injustice and you understand it as injustice, you almost can't help but
> become an agent of change—even if all you do is talk about it or point it out
> or shine the light of day on it.

So "shine the light of day" is part of what Greenpeace did:

> One of our innovations was to actively engage the electronic media and
> produce images that we knew and felt strongly would move through that

media. For example, most people—when they thought of whaling at that time in the late '60s, early '70s—would have had a 19th-century version in their mind's eye: little men going up against Leviathan, throwing spears out of boats. That was the image that people had of whaling from all the woodcuts and artwork of the *Moby-Dick* era. No one had ever seen a whale being dragged up on the stern of a factory ship, making it look like a little fish.

Greenpeace began sending dramatic and gruesome images around the world of what an industrialized whale hunt actually looks like. Everyone became a witness, and it was no longer possible just to turn away. Activists also began putting themselves in small boats on the high seas between harpooners' guns and whales, as well as chaining themselves to chemical discharge pipes to protect rivers and sailing or hiking into nuclear test zones to put their own bodies in the way of bomb tests.

There is also a deeper aspect of "witness": making unethical acts visible in a new way to the perpetrators themselves. Often we think that in the face of unethical actions our only or best response must be force: actually stopping the actions. Quakers and others committed to nonviolence, by contrast, argue that simply stopping such an action does nothing to address the ethical failures that brought it about in the first place. In fact it may worsen some of them, locking the perpetrators into a new self-perception as victims. Ultimately the perpetrators themselves must be changed, and (the idea goes) this change can be set off if the perpetrators are made to see themselves through someone else's eyes. They cannot any longer act so anonymously or habitually, or respond automatically as they would if they were physically or otherwise threatened or attacked.

In this respect Rex Wyler isn't quite right to say, "No one had ever seen a whale being dragged up on the stern of a factory ship." The *whalers* saw it all the time. On the Quaker theory, though, they hadn't quite *seen* it—that is, fully looked at it, understood it, rather than simply accepting it or not thinking about it—until they had to see it through someone else's eyes. Just watching, then—just "witness"—can be a powerful force for ethical change.

Both groups lobby in the traditional way too. Greenpeace advocates much stronger environmental protection, permanent weapons test bans, and of course an end to whaling and other assaults on the seas and sea creatures. And MSF again:

Based on its field experience, MSF is addressing obstacles preventing people in the developing world from obtaining affordable, effective treatments for diseases such as HIV/AIDS, malaria, and tuberculosis.... MSF

is advocating to lower drug prices, stimulate research and development
of new treatments, and overcome trade and other barriers to accessing
treatments. . . .

GOVERNMENT

Communities also make change through the basic functions of local governments, school boards, planning commissions, and the like. Vital matters are
decided here: how well your community preserves open space, how fairly
it deals with different neighborhoods or different groups' concerns, what
is taught in the schools, what kind of public transportation is supported,
whether you will act as a community on pressing issues of the day, from
problems with voting machines to global warming—all of these issues are
decided in local meetings in which any citizen can take part.

When zoning changes are requested or new building proposals are being
advanced, my city has open hearings, at first specific to different parts of
the city, where anyone can come, hear, and discuss the proposals. Eventually
there is also a vote—of whoever happens to show up. The results go to the
City Planning Commission—on a nonbinding basis, but they do make a difference. I have seen one or two knowledgeable and concerned citizens stop
an ill-conceived project in its tracks—and I have also seen the lawyers for that
project publicly thank the community gadflies, by name, at a later meeting,
for making them improve their projects.

Likewise, school boards struggle with curricular issues: sex education, evolution and creation, and the like. Of course these can be frustrating struggles
on all sides. The deeper point, though, is that community discussion of such
questions is entirely appropriate in a democratic society, and school board meetings are a good place for it. We ought to be glad we live in a society in which
there are places for such discussions. Maybe we even ought to join them!

Cities and other localities even act on the global stage. In the absence of
U.S. federal action on global warming, for example, state governors and even
mayors of cities publicly committed their states or cities to meeting international greenhouse-gas emission standards. In the political arena, there are
many national and international political discussions and communities as
well: the political parties, both the old standards and small and new ones;
human rights action groups such as Amnesty International; and national
lobbying groups on a vast range of issues. Just enter the phrase "National
Coalition for..." as a Web search, and in the blank you get everything from
"Literacy" and "Anti-Deportation Campaigns" to Cancer Survivors, Haitian
Health, the Promotion of History, Marine Conservation, Homeless Veterans,
Life, Sexual Freedom, Dialogue and Deliberation... and on and on and on.

JOINING A CHANGE-MAKING COMMUNITY

This chapter began with guidelines for working to make a difference on your own. When organizations or communities or movements are involved, the task may be easier. You're in it with others, and the organization or movement already exists and is (let's hope!) in motion. Your job is to *get involved*.

FIND A PLACE

First: explore what is actually happening. It might be helpful to start by asking what change-making communities are you already part of, though perhaps you have not yet thought of them quite that way. Where is change already underway in your neighborhood or city your business or work? If you belong to a religious congregation, for example, what kinds of social or community work is it already involved with? Is more help needed? Is there potential to broaden the work (perhaps, as your special contribution)?

In general, think about what issue or issues you should take up, and who is doing the kind of work you want to join. Obviously the answer will vary with your interests and abilities and location. You'll want to explore specific issues: look for organizations working on those issues in particular. You'll also want to explore what's happening in your communities in general. This is often a larger and less well-defined realm. Your first question might well be: what *are* the issues that most deeply affect this community? Then find out who is pursuing them. Who is doing things? What things? Where are the openings?

We've just looked at a wide range of communities that are making change. You might just note in addition that a wide range of approaches are involved. Some kinds of change are immediate and direct, like responding to an emergency or making a drastic change in policy. Others are slower and work more in the background, like trying to keep more kids in school (preventing a whole range of more difficult problems down the road) or preserving locally owned media (enabling more diverse and locally empowered discussion of *other* issues). Likewise different kinds of change may call for very different strategies, sometimes even on the same issue. Direct-action strategies coexist readily with longer-term structural change goals. Again, your task is to find a good fit for you: for your resources, your skills, and what you see as the most pressing demands of the moment. Others will do other things, and there is no lack of things to do. Find a place!

SHOW UP

Next, show up. Meet the people, join the organization or recommit yourself to it if you're already a member, start going to meetings. See what needs to be done. This may take some time. Go and listen for a bit to see what is happening, then commit yourself to some part of the work, maybe small at first. See what grows on you.

If your interests run toward local governance, show up for public meetings: City Council, School Board, community responses to crises or opportunities that arise. If you are a student, check out your student government, and also committees and other institutional planning and organizing that involves students along with faculty and administrators. Do you know when and where your local student government association meets? The meetings must be open to all, so you do not have to ask to come, or be invited, though you may have to ask ahead of time to be on the agenda. To speak persuasively when you seek to get on the agenda, of course, you also must have something to say. Seek something within the student government association's power to grant, and something that will be good for at least a number of your fellow students. Refine your understanding of the issues, and of what can be done at the point where you are intervening.

The same is true for local government meetings. They are usually held "in the sunshine," which means they are required by law to be open to the public, although again, you usually have to request in advance to be on the agenda to speak. In addition to usual, regular meetings of government entities, most cities and towns in the United States are required to hold hearings on important decisions to be made by that entity.

Make yourself visible at these meetings—and then make yourself heard. In most organizations, new people with ideas and energy are always very welcome. Speak up! In the case of local governmental decision making, the actual deciders are your elected officials, but a great deal of influence is still simply a matter of ordinary people showing up. Sometimes that's literally all it takes: officials often judge public opinion on a matter by how many people come to the relevant meetings. (A great line from Woody Allen: "Eighty percent of success is just showing up.") Actually say something besides, and you magnify the effect. Not only come and speak, but speak *well*, and you'll pretty quickly be approached to run for office yourself. And why not?

Also, watch who else shows up. You will probably encounter the same cross-section of civic-minded people at a variety of public and organizational venues. Introduce yourself, see what is happening, who they represent and who stands behind them. Make yourself one of them!

BRING YOUR WHOLE TOOLBOX

Once you've jumped in, the key thing is to *bring along your ethical toolbox*— all of it. To make yourself a voice for ethics within your organization or community, as well as articulating its ethical commitments to others, draw on Part II of this book. To "think out of the box" on issues where other people might not even realize that there *is* a "box," reframe problems and ask strategic questions, bring in your critical thinking skills, mindful speech, moral vision—all skills from Part III. Dialogue skills will be essential (chapter 11). And so on. Keep all your skills sharp and ready for use.

Be strategic. Some situations call for pressure on elected officials; others call for independent organizing. And some of course for both. To help the homeless, for example, we need better municipal provision of shelters (work for local governments, ideally partly backed by state and federal support), as well as enhanced private shelters (here in North Carolina, anyway, mostly sponsored by religious coalitions), *and* more serious public efforts to address the causes of homelessness in turn (economic squeezes, mental health issues...). As with many issues, this suggests work on a variety of fronts.

Ask yourself (and others) where real movement is possible, and where you can make the most change with the most efficient effort. On campus, for example, directly battling students' addiction to fast foods and throw away containers, say, by offering more classes on nutrition or by multiplying recycling bins, may be a difficult task. Suppose instead you work with the food service to change the cafeteria offerings, or with local take-out restaurants to use only biodegradable containers? Here you could have a big and quick impact. Trying to change state-wide Department of Education policy on sex education, say, can take enormous energy to gain mere inches, if that. While such efforts are important as a way of keeping up public dialogue on the basic issues, it might be more helpful, especially to the young people actually affected, to create new independent resources for and with the community, such as some of my own students have done by launching websites for local teens both to help them toward sexual "response-ability" and also to connect them with local resources for information, birth control, and counseling. Or again, on national or international issues, Greenpeace's strategy of "witnessing" and exposing whaling to the world did not directly address lawmakers or the International Whaling Commission, yet the impact on policy was very powerful. Multiple strategies can easily coexist too, of course.

Get creative. Alongside the familiar kinds of work on homelessness, for example, there are truly amazing initiatives underway. The Homeless World Cup organizes annual international street soccer tournaments with teams made up of homeless people. Another project facilitates and trains homeless people to mount *opera,* of all things—no kidding—and places them in arts organizations and as performers. ("With Streetwise Opera I not only exist, I *live,*" says one formerly homeless participant.) Why not?

DON'T POLARIZE—CONNECT

One danger in making change in community is that communities can exclude others, or indeed, all too often, set themselves up in opposition to others. You have tools in your toolbox to avoid this kind of polarization too: dialogic, collaborative, and integrative approaches. Use them!

As chapters 11 and 12 suggest, deep and long-lasting change requires us to hear everyone's voice, especially those often left out or made invisible.

So ask: is everyone included? What other people or groups or institutions in your (local, geographical) community may have a stake in addressing and resolving the problem or issue? Work for collective solutions, and nurture the process of framing them together.

It's true, local disagreements are one reason we often seek nonlocal communities in the first place. In almost any geographic community of any size, we find important differences in people's values and concerns. We find disagreement, disparity, inequality, and different life experiences, all of which result in people who are all members of the same (local) "community" who may take very different positions on community issues. And they are probably people who not only don't think like us, but who also don't look, eat, sound, play, or work like us either.

So prejudice rears its head....Still, we need to notice these kinds of prejudices and work to end them. Deliberately meet and form friendships with people who are different from you. Figure out what are their issues of concern and embrace them. Remember that there are very likely common interests underlying even seemingly directly opposed "positions." Expect to find them, then; welcome them; work to dig them out. We have already noted some surprising confluences of interests: pro-life and pro-choice movements, for instance, joining forces to promote better economic support for unexpectedly pregnant women; evangelical and conservative church groups joining the environmental movement in the name of "Creation Care"; and so on. Not only do we not have to live in a world of opposition and polarization: we'll get much further together.

Remember also that the boundaries of "community" are more fluid than we sometimes think. This chapter has spoken of "community" solely in human terms. Often, though, more-than-human communities may also be at stake. On most environmental issues, as Aldo Leopold urges, the "community" includes also other animals, the plants and trees, and the land itself. Global threats require a response on behalf of the whole community of life, with the interests of all living things in mind. Australian environmental activists have created "Councils of All Beings," one framework in which we can begin to find our way back to dialogue beyond the realm of the merely human. Plains Indians peoples, in tribal council, would appoint spokespeople for the wolves and the buffalo, and even the mountains and rivers. Sometimes, the shamans said, they even consulted them directly. Remember that Lakota saying: they too are "our relations."

FOR REVIEW

1. For what was Muhammed Yunnus awarded the Nobel Peace Prize?
2. In what sense did SuAnne Big Crow "count coup"?

3. Outline the guidelines this chapter suggests for becoming a change-maker.

4. Why do single-minded people sometimes make less effective ethical change-makers?

5. Explain: "There is no way to ethics; ethics *is* the way."

6. How can powerlessness, for example in students, also sometimes be a source of change-making strength?

7. Give examples of two different kinds of communities making ethical change.

8. What are two ways that "witness" can lead to ethical change?

9. Outline the guidelines this chapter suggests for making ethical change in community.

10. According to the text, what is one pitfall in making ethical change in community? How do we avoid it?

EXERCISES AND NOTES

17.1 FOR REFLECTION

Recently I learned that philosophers are among those people entitled to nominate a person for the Nobel Peace Prize. In fact I learned this from a colleague who says that it is one of his life's ambitions to come to know and work with a suitable nominee. He's still young. But put yourself in his position. Who would *you* nominate? (You don't actually have to know the person.) Why? What traits would you look for?

Why do you think we are sometimes so pessimistic about the possibility of making real change? It's not as though real change hasn't happened. In fact it is happening all around us right now. Twenty-five years ago Communism ruled the East, and South Africa was on the brink of a massive racial bloodbath. We could not have imagined even something now as basic as recycling bins in everyone's basement or the rise of environmental consciousness in general.

Radical change happens. But suddenly then the new status quo seems to define the limits of possibility in turn, and we can't imagine even the same degree of change happening *again,* in the same or some other direction. Why not? Can you figure out the psychology of this rather limiting kind of "realism"? Do you see any useful ways to help ourselves and others avoid it?

17.2 SEEK CHANGE-MAKERS

Find people in your community or among your circle of friends and connections who are ethical change-makers. Again, they needn't be high profile. A lot of moral action goes on way below the radar, by people who don't think of themselves as special. Think again of my university's "Hometown Heroes," for example. Who are *your* change-making heroes? Perhaps there are even some in your class, right now.

Cast your nets widely. People who are energetic and visible advocates for certain moral positions are good candidates, but they are by no means the only ones. Look also for people who are making a creative difference, or bringing more people into moral action, or are in any of a hundred ways "being the change they wish to see in the world." Once you've identified some ethical change-makers, invite them to speak to your class or group. Talk with them. What are they doing? Why and how do they do it? What motivates them? It will be an honor for them and an earful, I hope, for you.

17.3 JOIN THE WORK

Ultimately, of course, the task is to become an ethical change-maker yourself. Commit yourself as an individual or a group (your class? why not?) to some project of ethical change. Use your work with this book to frame your project. Expect it to be a learning experience, about basic values as well as the nitty-gritty of getting action moving. Work toward and work *at* dialogue. Get your facts straight. Speak and act mindfully. Use your creativity and vision. There is no lack of possibilities right around you. Identify a doable project—something you can at least initiate—and get to work.

Note that this work is somewhat different than "service" or "service learning" as usually conceived. Service is *helping*: dealing with immediate need by offering aid and succor. Change-making more likely addresses the causes of need themselves or promotes changes that offer all of us opportunities for ethical transformation and better understanding. (More on this in "Using Your Tools" #9.)

Defining these projects is hard, and finding some that get seriously underway in the space of an academic term is even harder. This is itself usefully educational. Consider a multiterm project that a teacher's classes (or school or department) could sustain over a number of years. A single class could at least get the ball rolling. My own students, lately, have initiated such projects as making our own school more connected and responsive on issues of race—both working to make race issues more prominent and consistent in the curriculum and forging links between the university and communities of color right in our own region. Another group instituted biweekly meals at all of the university's cafeterias with all locally grown, seasonal, and organic food, educating students, staff, and food service personnel about alternative agriculture and diets and creating ongoing connections between the university and local suppliers. A colleague's class is partnering with students at other and very different institutions to jointly further the work of Greensboro's Truth and Reconciliation Commission (introduced in chapter 11) from the student side. Another group has just constructed a website for local teens to get them sex-education information they were being denied in their own schools, along with local resources and help designed to promote sexual response-ability, up to and including abstinence. Now they are handing the site off to local high-schoolers themselves.

So many possibilities. More projects are afoot. I would be honored to hear about yours. Good luck!

NOTES

At http://almaz.com/nobel/peace/peace.html you can find a listing of all the recipients of the Nobel Peace Prize, along with short biographies and useful links. I might add to the discussion in the text that it is sometimes the intention of the Nobel Peace Prize committee to lift up certain people or organizations precisely so that they can be heard, or even to protect them, to make them too visible for governments to suppress or for others to hurt. Again, then: however extraordinary the work they may be doing, often they are ordinary people who have simply stepped up to a need or a responsibility. Here the prize serves the struggle.

Alan Jolis's essay on Muhammad Yunus, "The Good Banker," comes from *The Independent on Sunday Supplement* (London), May 5, 1996, and can be found online, along with much other useful information, at http://www.grameen-info.org.

Paul Rogat Loeb is cited from the introduction to his collection *The Impossible Will Take a Little While* (Basic Books, 2004), pp. 6–7. On Bo Lozoff's work, see http://humankindness.org. Julia Butterfly Hill's book *The Legacy of Luna* (Harper San Francisco, 2000) is excerpted from pp. 7, 24, and 123. For updates on Luna and on Julia Hill's current work, see www.circleoflife.org.

I cite the Doctors Without Borders website at http://www.doctorswithout borders.org, accessed 11/12/06. Greenpeacer Rex Wyler is interviewed by Micah Toub in "Man Overboard," accessed 11/12/06 at http://www.thismagazine .ca/issues/2005/07/qa_manoverboard.php. You can check out the Homeless World Cup ("Kick Off Poverty") at http://www.homelessworldcup.org. On opera with the homeless ("Giving the Homeless a Voice"), see http://www .streetwiseopera.org.

On change-making in communities, two inspiring sources are Frances Moore Lappe, *Democracy's Edge: Choosing to Save Our Country by Bringing Democracy to Life* (Jossey-Bass, 2005) and Laurent Parks Daloz *et al.*, *Common Fire: Leading Lives of Commitment in a Complex World* (Beacon, 1996). For an introduction to the Councils of All Beings, see http://www.rainforestinfo.org.au/deep-eco/coab.htm.

Beth Raps was instrumental in shaping this chapter's themes and approaches, based upon her many years' experience in community organizing and change-work, and many of her words are here as well.

The Future of Ethics

We have been speaking very positively about ethics in the course of our survey of families and values and skills for ethical practice. That's natural enough. This is, after all, a textbook *in* ethics. It remains, though, to survey some of the possible weaknesses and pitfalls of ethics: that is, some doubts about ethics itself. In the spirit of reframing problems, we may also take these very doubts to be challenges and opportunities as well. Our look at the future of ethics then closes with a look at the ethics of the future.

THREE DOUBTS ABOUT ETHICS

IS ETHICS TOO INDECISIVE?

Moral values are by nature not empirical or readily verifiable matters. Generally they are much less definite, matters of interpretation and aspiration. This is one reason why we are tempted to base them on some kind of explicit authority, God for example, but then naturally enough people's religious beliefs also vary. Variety, vagueness, and untestability seem to come with the territory.

On one popular image of ethics then, ethical values are too indefinite to help us sort out real problems—to allow for rational public discussion and timely decision making. The real result is more like confusion, controversy, and uncertainty. Meantime, though, we *do* need to make decisions, both personally and collectively. The result has been the rise of alternative standards and systems for decision making, especially in political and collective matters where the risks and costs of prolonged and indeterminate debate can be very high.

Science, for example, seems to offer much clearer methods for reaching conclusions, and methods that all sides accept from the start. Naturally people are therefore tempted to dismiss ethics in favor of just relying on science to make the necessary decisions—especially because science often claims to be "value-free." Why engage in endless and fruitless debates when we can just run tests?

Or again, for many decisions on the governmental level, policy makers have increasingly turned to cost-benefit analysis and other economic methods of decision making. We need to make the most economical or "efficient" choices, after all—achieving the greatest gain for the least cost—and the discipline of economics offers an unmatched set of tools for determining efficiency. For example, it is seldom efficient to eliminate all pollution from a power plant or factory: the cost of eliminating the last units (the "marginal cost") may be astronomical compared to the costs of removing the rest, and the "opportunity costs" (the value of the other possibilities that become unavailable when we choose to use our resources in a particular way) may be too high. It's a fair criticism that ethics tends to miss even such basic points as this, instead issuing in simplistic and all-or-nothing declarations. We assume that if pollution is bad, for instance, then it ought to be eliminated entirely, rather than recognizing that eliminating the last vestiges is a very different question, from a resource point of view at least, than reducing most of the rest.

If nothing else, then, ethics' critics sometimes say, let us just be practical. Let us decide using the hard facts in front of us. Vague and indecideable worries—say, about long-term consequences or "subjective" effects on moral persons or communities—should be noted, perhaps, but then mostly put to the side. If it seems that ethics inevitably complicates decision making—so much that we may never be able to make any decision at all—then a practical response must be more hard-headed. It may seem that political decision making does better to steer clear of anything but the most basic ethics. If that.

The promise, in short, is some kind of relatively "value-free" decision making: a way of settling key questions that simply doesn't require getting into the gridlock of moral values at all. If it really is possible, then *who needs ethics?*

IS ETHICS TOO DEFENSIVE?

In some circles, ethics has a bad name for another reason as well: it tends to reduce to kind of defensive moralizing. The worry is that moral values often reflect inherited prejudices and habits that are given undue weight and respect just because they are traditional.

No doubt we're always a little tempted to mistake our customs and prejudices for deeper truths and eternal values. But ethics, according to this challenge, doesn't resist. Instead it may actually make matters worse, allowing us to dress up our customs and prejudices in weightier terms (i.e., moral terms, "good" and "right," and the like) and therefore making them harder to change or even question. The result, say the critics, is that ethics tends to be behind the times, at the very least, and what is worse, sometimes ethics reinforces such backward-looking values at moments when we especially ought to be looking forward.

Ethics was not notably out in front in the civil rights struggle, for example, or in questioning the prevailing doctrines of total nuclear war or the morality of capitalism. The figures who spearheaded those movements were mostly religious—Martin Luther King, for example, and more recently the American Catholic Bishops on the economy—though as a whole, religion too, probably even more often, also tends to reflect social norms rather than challenge them. King's famous "Letter from a Birmingham Jail," for example, was actually addressed to a group of his fellow clergymen, who had expressed reservations about King's push for civil rights. Disturbing as it may be, there were ethical as well as Biblical arguments in favor of slavery, too.

Of course, there is nothing necessarily wrong with defending certain traditional or customary values. On the contrary: some such values we *should* defend. And of course there may also be a moral case for capitalism and even, alas, for war. But some values, some practices and customs and norms, should *not* be defended, and many should be more vigorously questioned. Moreover, new practices and possibilities—from animal rights to human cloning to gay marriage—are also arising that may make some people uneasy, morally or personally or otherwise, and here too we need some careful critical and constructive thinking.

Is ethics up to this task? The critics and doubters are not sure. Ethics seems more prone instead, according to them, to backslide into rationalizing. Sometimes old prejudices and habits are so familiar and seem so *right* that we mistake them for moral intuitions, for values that just *have* to be some kind of moral truths so that we eagerly grasp the first moral-sounding rationalizations that arise. Sometimes too, it is tempting to mistake unease by itself for a moral argument, or to invoke it indirectly with some irrelevant, red-herring argument and then just stop, relieved to be able to turn away. Sometimes, indeed, raising questions (pro *or* con) on matters such as these is branded as immoral itself. You know (say the critics) that ethics is too defensive then!

Freud argued that people are good at rationalizing across the board. It's not just ethics' fault. Still, we would like ethics to have a more critical edge—in the name of the very values it stands for. Can it?

IS ETHICS TOO INDIVIDUALISTIC?

Here is a third problem. "Using Your Tools" #7 points out that we miss something striking and fundamental when we look at cases like the Heinz dilemma and ask only what Heinz should do, leaving aside questions like what the rest of us should do, or why a society would let people get into that desperate a situation in the first place.

Or take the problem of homelessness. Individual acts of kindness and comfort are at one end of the continuum. They are fine and admirable as far as they go. On the community level, there is also a need for better facilities for homeless people—that too is a visible moral project, and often undertaken, to their great credit, by religious or other charities or municipal governments. At the same time, however, there are much larger, society-wide types of actions that typically do not come into ethical focus, or any other kind of focus either. We might work to create or sustain better jobs for people who might otherwise be jobless. On the state or national level, we could work to end homelessness itself, by addressing its root causes, such as companies relocating their factories to foreign countries, and the lack of a social and economic "safety net" here at home.

Even moral "service," as laudable as it is, runs the danger of accepting profoundly problematic social structures and reducing ethics to individual band-aiding and commiseration. Not that band-aids are bad—people are wounded, for sure, in soul as well as body, and they need to be treated and healed, held and supported. But we must also ask why so many are wounded in the first place, and what we can do about *that*—even though those questions are much less comfortable.

We honor Martin Luther King for inspiring the Civil Rights struggle but tend to keep him safely historical when we can. It is much less widely known or celebrated that he was also a sharp critic of the war in Vietnam, of war in general, of economic inequality, and of what he saw as U.S. cultural imperialism around the world. "True compassion," King once said, "is more than flinging a coin to a beggar; it comes to see that an edifice which produces beggars needs restructuring." Ethics, unfortunately, too often stops with the coin fling.

Of course there are also many worthwhile individual moral questions. Ethics should probably have something to say about the Heinz dilemma as it is usually posed. But there are other questions to be asked, and sometimes just as important, if not more important—and also deeply concerned with moral values and consequences. Sometimes we need, as chapter 14 put it, to reframe moral problems instead.

Ethics has trouble with questions like these. The problem is partly that we Americans, at least, have little experience thinking on the social level. We do tend (for complex and interesting reasons beyond the scope of this book) to want to leave many collective matters to individual and charitable initiative rather than to social and economic reform. Among the moral frameworks, moreover, *rights* loom especially large for us: indeed, politically at least, it sometimes seems that there are no other relevant moral values at all, or at least that rights must have an absolute priority. There are after all the immortal words of Jefferson: "We hold these truths to be self-evident...that all men...are endowed by their Creator with inalienable rights..." However *nice* a more generous social structure might be, we might say, it cannot be *right* if it requires imposing on or limiting individual rights—freedom of action, for example, or even the right to most of our income.

Here ethics almost seems to insist that an individualistic perspective is the only possible ethical one. Other times it is at least assumed implicitly: nothing else comes up. If so, though, how can ethics meet the kind of challenge King poses? Can ethics also incorporate a social and structural perspective?

ETHICS IS INESCAPABLE

Can we reaffirm ethics against these doubts? I believe that we can. But we must choose our ground carefully. I do not want to argue, for one thing, that ethics is so much more decisive than the critics who worry about indecisiveness say. Maybe ethics *is* often uncertain and untestable. But maybe that isn't such a bad thing. It does not follow, in any case, that we should strive to make decisions in "value-free" ways instead, for example, by scientific or economic or other "practical" standards. The reason is that we *can't*.

There simply is no such thing as "value-free" decision making. Instead, all decision making—indeed, one could argue, all action—is value-*laden* (as it's often put). Indeed, any time we choose to do one thing rather than another, or anything at all rather than nothing, we are acting on certain values and leaving others to the side. When the needs and legitimate expectations of others as well as ourselves are at stake, the values involved are ethical by definition. The only question is how explicit and deliberate we are going to be about them.

ETHICS AND SCIENCE

It is true that ethics partly depends upon and responds to science. Ethics on its own is not going to discover how to prolong the life of cancer sufferers, or create alternatives to dissection in classrooms, or discern the pattern of climate change. Ethics can and should respond to what science discovers.

On a deeper level, though, *science* responds to *ethics*. Scientists *choose* what issues and questions to concern themselves with, and what methods they will use (or not use). And these choices depend on values. In this sense, science is not "value-free" at all. It is because we *value* human health and life that we research lifesaving and life-prolonging therapies. It is because we *value* the relief of suffering all around that we are interested in alternatives to dissection and ways to mitigate climate change.

A more subtle point is that even our choices of scientific method are shaped by ethics. For example, we could probably find out a lot more— certainly a lot more reliably and quickly—by doing painful and dangerous medical experiments directly on humans, whether they liked it or not. But that would violate the most basic respect for persons. We don't do it. We have elaborate safeguards to prevent even going anywhere near doing it.

Or again, we no longer study whales, for example, by killing them and studying their bodies. Now we are more apt to try to learn about them by establishing relationships. Some jazz musicians, for instance, have taken to jamming with orcas. All of this is just as much science as the old science, but it reflects quite different values—and reveals to us a different set of possibilities. The world opens up in different ways.

Science does not render ethics somehow dispensable. A science that was truly "value-free" would actually be monstrous. Ethics gives science its very shape.

ETHICS AND ECONOMICS

It is true that we need to make the most economical or "efficient" choices—achieving the greatest benefit for the least cost—once our goals are set. The discipline of economics offers an unmatched set of tools for determining efficiency. And yes, the need for economically sophisticated judgments (say, about marginal costs) has not always been so obvious to ethical thinkers.

But here's the key point: economic analysis comes into play *once our goals are set*—once we decide what *is* a benefit and what *is* a cost. Those choices themselves, however, are ethical choices. Economics, then, is no more "value-free" than science. On the contrary: it presupposes values from the start. Costs and benefits are, well, values!

One effect of a broadened assisted suicide policy, for example, may be that more people will choose to end their lives on their own terms. Is this a cost, or a benefit? To some, it reflects a proper respect for rights, and a way of avoiding pointless suffering. For others, it cheapens life. We have to choose which of these effects we are going to value, and which way. These are ethical choices.

The same goes for policy choices. One effect of a new highway, for example, may be that more people more quickly can leave the city. Again: is this a cost, or a benefit? Obviously some city dwellers will prefer it. Others will prefer that they stay where they are. Meanwhile the land outside the city is more heavily burdened. Once again, we have to choose which effects we are going to value, which way, and how much.

It is true that "positive" economics tries to avoid these choices by using market prices to quantify values, just counting every market choice as equal. How much are people willing to pay for the new road, and for the gas and other costs associated with using it? (Or for assisted suicide?) How much are others willing to pay to preserve the land and the quiet that the road might destroy? (Or to stop assisted suicide?) In principle we can simply compare prices. But the problem, of course, is that these supposedly value-free measures just reflect unacknowledged or taken-for-granted values and assumptions, such as what people are willing (and able) to spend money for is a good reflection of what things really matter. That is another ethical stance, and not the only possible one. It's doubtful, besides. Americans spend ten times as much every year on home pizza delivery as we spend on the Environmental Protection Agency, but I certainly hope that this does not reflect our considered moral values.

Ethics' claim is not that this kind of economics is a mistake. The claim instead is that this kind of economics is an *ethics*: that is, a particular set of ethical commitments. In fact, you already know what family it belongs to: it is a form of applied utilitarianism. Its underlying ethical goal is to maximize preference satisfaction, which is supposed to be a more quantifiable measure of the good than the old moral notions of well-being or happiness. Nonetheless, utilitarianism represents but one family of moral values among others—and only one expression of the Ethics of Happiness at that.

Market prices do reflect people's preferences and choices, which certainly does recommend them as one ethical measure among others. On the other hand, they are also distorted in a variety of ways: by radical inequalities of wealth, for one thing. They are also restricted to humans alone, and human values in turn are reduced pretty much to those desires we (are said to) express by what we buy. One could even argue, as Aldo Leopold did, that our very *problem* is that we look at everything economically. Ethics today—beyond utilitarianism, anyway, though it certainly also has its points—could be thought of as precisely a challenge to purely economic or commercial measures of value. Certainly it is a challenge to the assumption that economic values can simply replace ethical ones in ethical decision making!

THE USES OF INDECISIVENESS

You'll not be surprised, then, if I also assert that "just being practical" is not somehow "value-free" either, but also, like the parallel arguments in science and economics, actually depends on underlying commitments that are simply not being recognized as ethical themselves.

Sticking to the "hard facts" typically means impatiently dismissing any but the most concrete and immediate considerations. This kind of dismissal, however, tends to favor the most vocal and assertive voices in a debate, who can point to demonstrable and concrete effects *now*. And it is true that sometimes matters are urgent and such voices, or at least effects, ought to prevail. Other times, though, they shouldn't. All too often it happens that the benefits of some new policy or technology—nuclear power, say, or genetic engineering, or cloning—are evident sooner than the costs, which may be indirect, unexpected, and emerge slowly. But in that case, vaguer and less assertive worries are very much to the point.

Care and caution are ethical principles too, as is a sense of justice toward the future, and they may be served by going slow—even if it seems less "practical." In the long run, indeed, things are more likely the other way around. It is certainly not "practical" to let impatience and heedlessness saddle us with a range of far more intractable problems down the road.

But what then? Must we leave ethics so indecisive? I may surprise you when I answer that yes, to some extent, we should. I would argue that the very uncertainty of ethics, its perpetual debate and controversy, is also an absolutely crucial reminder that although we do have to make decisions from time to time, the underlying ethical questions still remain *open*. Any proper decision method will revisit them the next time, and may even decide differently then. Here too we need to stay open to ethical learning.

I might even say that the task of ethics, in part, is to make it *harder* to decide certain things. Ethics' task is at least to remind us that many things that matter to us morally—many things that relate to our needs and legitimate expectations—are not so concrete and do tend to get pushed out of the picture by the more insistent, loud, sometimes commercial values that dominate our society, by the values that suit the dominant and the powerful and the impatient. Resistance, here—a different vision—is part of what ethics is *for*.

Finally, though, it does not follow that we cannot make decisions at all. Really we are speaking here of issues on the edge, some of the most controversial or contentious ones, where values really are not clear. Premature resolution may be worse than confusion. Though these do tend to be the most visible cases, I have suggested throughout this book that they are not in fact the norm. Chapter 12, for example, holds that most of the time moral values are fairly clear and point in fairly definite and commonly agreeable directions. For various reasons we have become, of late, a culture that focuses more on the conflicts and disagreements. It pays to remember the bigger, less conflicted picture.

TURNING CRITICAL

Another complaint about ethics is that it can too readily provide a kind of cover for customs and prejudices that ought to be challenged and rethought rather than rationalized. Here, ironically, ethics stands accused of being *too* definite, certainly too rigid and "behind the times"—not critical or self-critical enough.

The first thing to say by way of response, as I've hinted already, is that sometimes the defense of certain values is exactly what we should want. We *need* a practice that insists upon the basic ethical values this book has identified: values of the person, of happiness, of virtue, and of relationship. Ethics itself exists because the needs and legitimate expectations of others, as well often enough as our own, are often forgotten or devalued and dismissed when they should not be. We *should* insist upon these things, even when it complicates rather than simplifies matters, or sounds "conservative," or raises inconvenient obstacles. If a "conservative" is someone who sticks up for the ethical basics, then we all should be conservatives, whatever our politics.

The problem of rationalization is another matter. Human beings seem to rationalize by nature, about all kinds of things and in any available way, so it is no surprise—and no unique objection—that ethical rationalization happens as well. Naturally too, rationalizing is easiest in the direction of the traditional views. Since they are widely shared and unquestioned by many people already, just hinting at the traditional values is often taken to be enough of an argument all by itself, and we may feel that we can turn away without doing much more thinking than that.

Still, neither of these tendencies, troubling and all too human as they may be, is distinctively a problem with ethics. Ethics just needs to be watchful here, as we need to be watchful everywhere, and persist in critical thinking.

It might help to distinguish core moral values from outlying and more specific values. Core values, again, are those basic to the families, and these we should, and pretty much do, all hold dear. Outlying values are those that may be without a family, or graft themselves onto a family but come to us from more particular historical settings, not necessarily applicable elsewhere or anymore, or from particular interest groups or perspectives. Civility, for example, is a core value in the ethics of relationship, but particular forms of etiquette and social custom are usually very culturally specific and don't carry much moral weight. Reckless driving really is a moral affront. Breast-feeding in public, arguably, is not. It's not impossible to tell the difference, but it does take some thinking.

ETHICS IN A RADICAL VOICE

There's more to say to the charge of defensiveness, however—and a more essential point about the possibilities for ethics generally. Ethics has at times been anything *but* traditionalist or conservative. It has instead challenged traditional views and prejudices, deeply and persistently, to the point that the powers that be often resist and mistrust ethics itself.

Consider again the issue of other animals. Certainly the whole question is ripe for rationalization and dismissal. It happens constantly. Still, the striking fact is that ethics has lately and insistently been in the lead in raising the question of animals and working out alternative ethical systems in which animals are recognized and taken seriously as moral subjects. The conclusions may be unbelievable, to some, but the arguments are hard to resist, on grounds of consistency if nothing else.

If suffering is a morally bad thing, for instance, as utilitarianism insists, then it is not at all clear why animal suffering, however different it might be from ours, does not count morally as well. Simply because they are not human? This retort is now widely rejected as "species-ist," remember, and utilitarians have taken the lead in pro-animal agitation. Likewise, defenders of animal rights take their lead from the ethics of respect, arguing that many animals, at least, have the same *kind* (not necessarily degree) of sense of self and forms of self-consciousness that mandate respect for humans. One can argue as well for taking animals seriously from the standpoint of relationship.

Working it all out is difficult. The point, however, is that here, far from being traditional or allowing the usual hand waving to waft the usual rationalizations over some pretty thin logical ice, ethics is persistently forcing us to face new questions and to consider some serious change. Whatever you may think of their arguments, it has been ethical philosophers from the very core of the ethical tradition, such as the utilitarian Peter Singer and the rights theorist Tom Regan, who have propelled huge social changes in the treatment of animals in recent decades. Think again, also, of the reading from Colin McGinn in chapter 10. It's the *culture* that's "defensive" here, not ethics!

I would argue that the same is true across a variety of issues today. Ethics *is* contesting some of the major and taken-for-granted features of our society. The work of John Rawls and others on the concept of justice has immensely influenced social welfare policies. Environmental ethics has given ethical voice to the environmental movement, and again, like animal rights arguments, appeals to core ethical values, like community and relationship, that may call us to new ethical recognitions on the basis of consistency, if nothing else. Think, for instance, of Leopold's extension of the moral concept of the community to include the land. Or again, as we have seen, Pope John Paul II consistently challenged capitalist economies as well as communist ones to take the person more seriously. His arguments were both religious and moral, and not terribly popular with the powers that be anywhere. In the midst of the economic turmoil of the early 80s, the American Catholic Bishops, astonishingly enough, followed suit by rolling out an emphatic moral argument against capitalism itself.

I conclude that ethics has many sides. Think of it, here, more as a way of opening questions than necessarily of closing or answering them. Clearly ethics *can* serve, at times, to reinforce, justly or not, prevailing prejudices and customs. But its tendency, and certainly its potential, seems at least as much to be the opposite: to be disruptive, to unsettle certain habits and practices no matter how widely accepted. To raise questions, and not accept easy or familiar answers.

The powers that be, I'd say, would rather that people be cynical than ethical—that is, to believe that ethics is pointless and useless, and instead just to go along with the demands of convenience or power or profit of the moment. History suggests that when people take moral values seriously, they start wanting to change things. That should *recommend* ethics—anyway to *us*!

INDIVIDUALISM *AND* BEYOND

Speaking for myself, the doubt that concerns me most is the last one: ethics' tendency to take an individualistic view of things, often to the point of not even noticing, and certainly not highlighting, the larger social or structural factors that shape so many moral "dilemmas" in the first place.

There is no denying that ethics has this character. I have even been told, more than once, by other ethical philosophers, that ethics by definition is about individual choices and that the project of reframing problematic ethical situations against a social background, addressing the sources of the problem rather than "the" problem as usually framed, is either "evasive" (as it's sometimes put) or at least (more politely) "misses the point of ethics." These comments seem to imply that a social perspective is just *something else*—politics, maybe—which, I guess, ethics "proper" can just ignore.

My response at this point is that we should not be interested in being "proper"—if that's what being "proper" really means. There is certainly great value in the individual questions, for sure. Much of the time we *are* addressing individual problems, and in any case, whatever sorry or re-frameable set of circumstances led to them, we must figure out what is ethically the best thing to do. But if that is all that ethics is or can be, then we must also go beyond it. Often, as I have been arguing, reframing ethical problems—the long and sometimes uncomfortable way around—is the only way to make genuine progress on them.

I am not willing to leave matters here, though. In fact, I argue, we need a systematically social and critical perspective within ethics itself—as *part* of ethics itself. Why cede ethics as such to the narrower perspective alone? Remember, one last time, that at the very beginning of this book we defined ethics as taking care for the needs and legitimate expectations of others as well as yourself. This definition does not require that we only take such care as individuals for other individuals. It does not even imply that our only needs are individual, either, or that we have legitimate expectations only from or for other individuals. Indeed it might well be argued that we also have needs and legitimate expectations for a political and social community that takes care not to put people in impossible binds—that takes care that fundamental social arrangements do not put basic ethical values into stark conflict in the way that some of our favorite ethical dilemmas seem, alas, almost to welcome.

Please note: this is not somehow a case for "liberalism," exactly, either. It is true that liberals are more inclined to think in social terms, and to regard existing social systems as more open to reform, less "given" or changeable. Liberals are more apt to challenge capitalism or expand the ethical franchise beyond the human species. But conservatives—that is, in the political sense—are also keenly tuned to the social or political framing of many issues. As "Using Your Tools" #7 noted, for example, conservative critics point out that a system in which major medical decisions are made, in effect, by bureaucrats and lawyers is also a system that is likely to seriously disempower patients and their families. Those conservatives favor social reform too: leaving medicine more to the market, which empowers people, on their view, in fundamental ways, and thus respects moral rights in a way that a government-managed system cannot. Conservatives critique and resist a *system* in which bioethical questions are framed for others, besides the patient, to decide in the first place.

For both sides in the health care debate, then, the very ways in which we decide, as a community, to set up our medical system and payment mechanisms profoundly shape the kinds of ethical issues that will come up within it. It can even create whole new categories of ethical issues that didn't exist before—and that we might well be better off without. Since it is a political choice to create a system that ends up framing bioethical questions in this way, it may also be that our best response is not to answer them as they stand but to *change the system*. Once again, we may not need to simply solve "the" problem as presented.

There is no reason that ethics cannot ask these questions. Ethics can ask them, and arguably *should*. It's up to us. Just don't argue that ethics cannot somehow ask them at all simply because we may have been slow to do so in the past, or find them unfamiliar or unsettling today. Again, it's up to us. Ethics is an ongoing and *living* practice that you now can take response-ability for as well. Maybe 21st century ethics hasn't seen anything yet.

READING

"Design for a New World"

WILLIAM McDONOUGH

ETHICS SEEMS REMOTE from questions about how buildings are constructed, the kinds of materials that go into everyday products, or how the industrial system functions as a whole. Yet for architect William McDonough, design questions are crucially ethical—and ethics now requires an entirely new approach to design across the board.

McDonough is a visionary architect and designer, and author, along with Michael Braungart, of the influential book *Cradle to Cradle: Remaking How We Make Things* (North Point Press, 2002). He is a frequent panelist and speaker around the world and winner of three U.S. Presidential awards: the Presidential Award for Sustainable Development (1996), the National Design Award (2004), and the Presidential Green Chemistry

> Challenge Award (2003). *Time* magazine recognized him as a "Hero for the Planet" in 1999, stating that "his utopianism is grounded in a unified philosophy that—in demonstrable and practical ways—is changing the design of the world."

One of the great leaders of the United States, Thomas Jefferson, saw himself primarily as a designer. This is evident from his tombstone, which he designed, and on which we can read three things: *"Thomas Jefferson, author of the Declaration of American Independence, author of the Statute of Virginia for Religious Freedom, and Father of the University of Virginia."* These were the three things Jefferson thought were worth mentioning on his tombstone. He did not record his various activities—that he had been President of the United States, minister to France, an architect. He recorded only what he had left behind for future generations: his creative legacy to the world, his lasting contributions to prosperity. Consider looking at the world as a series of design assignments. How would we present the design assignment of the Declaration of Independence? Perhaps it could be framed like this: please prepare a document that provides us with the concept of "life, liberty and the pursuit of happiness free from remote tyranny." That would be the retroactive design assignment of the Declaration of Independence.

In Mr. Jefferson's case, "remote tyranny" referred to the King of England, George III: someone who ruled from a distant place, who was not sensitive to local needs and circumstance. Now, seven generations later, I believe we need to look at the concept of many Declarations of Interdependence, because we realize that some of the remote tyranny future generations will suffer—is us. Right now, we—as a culture—are imposing what I call intergenerational remote tyranny. I would like to focus on this tyrannizing effect from a design perspective and consider how we can design it out.

Thomas Jefferson clearly understood the idea of intergenerational remote tyranny. In 1789, he wrote a letter to James Madison, which I paraphrase here:

> The earth belongs to the living. No man may by natural right oblige the lands he owns or occupies to debts greater than those that may be paid during his own lifetime. Because if he could, then the world would belong to the dead and not to the living.

In *Silent Spring*, Rachel Carson stated that the founding fathers who wrote the Bill of Rights—despite their intellectual gifts and foresight—could not have imagined that corporations, governments, and individuals would poison children downstream. They did not protect us from this kind of tyranny in the Bill of Rights because they could not even conceive of such a problem. We have to remember that Jefferson and Madison were living in a world that was effectively solar-powered. Their homes, the original grounds of the University of Virginia, were built with local materials: local clay, local fuel sources, solar-driven fuel sources. These people inhabited a world of natural energy flows. At that time, you could look out to the West and see a vast expanse of natural resources. Petrochemicals had not yet been invented. Yet Jefferson's phrase "The earth belongs to the living" is a powerful commentary on the tyrannies we are now seeing due to poor design. . . .

Jefferson's design legacy still provides for us, his seventh generation, and it continues to offer profound benefits even as the world changes around us. To see the legacy he brought to the Bill of Rights more clearly, we have to consider what it promulgated over time and imagine what it might promulgate in the future.

Jefferson wrote, "No man may by natural right. . . ." "Natural rights" had become a fundamental concept for Jefferson, and he expanded on it often. In *The Rights of Nature,* Roderick Nash pointed out that the concept of rights has been expanding since the Magna Carta gave rights to white noble English males in 1215. In 1776, the Declaration of Independence gave rights to white American landowning males. In 1864, we had the Emancipation Proclamation. In 1922, female suffrage. In 1964, the Civil Rights Voting Act. And then, in 1973, the Endangered Species Act: the first time in our history that human beings took responsibility for giving other living species the right to exist. We acknowledged the rights of nature itself. From our perspective, "natural rights" has now expanded to include the rights of nature itself.

If we project this pattern out, it is clear that our next discourse must be about endangered ecosystems, because we are finally realizing our interdependent connection to the natural world, and it won't be enough that there's a snail here or a condor there. We now understand that we are all connected to the web of life. Our understanding of rights and responsibilities must expand to include the rights and responsibilities of all living things. . . .

We used to be able to throw things away. Remember that? Things went "away." Where is "away" now? "Away" is here. "Away" is someone's backyard. There is no place to go from here. We now see that we inhabit a smaller and smaller planet. "Away" has become very close indeed.

In this context, we must again ask ourselves, "What is natural?" and, "What are our intentions as evidenced by our designs?" Early in the 1830s, Ralph Waldo Emerson went to Europe on a sailboat and returned on a steamship. Let me abstract this for effect: He went over on a solar-powered recyclable craft operated by craftpersons practicing ancient arts in the open air. He returned in a steel rust bucket putting oil on the water and smoke in the sky, operated by people working in the dark shoveling fossil fuels into the mouths of boilers. We are still designing steamships. Most buildings we design are essentially steamships. On any given day, the sun is shining and we're inside with the lights on causing the production of nuclear isotopes, carbon dioxide, nitrous oxides, and sulfur dioxide. Every time you find yourself in a building illuminated by electric light when the sun is shining, you should think, "I am in a steamship. I am in the dark." We need a new design....

I would like to posit the design principles for the Next Industrial Revolution, and I would also like to describe a new design assignment. But first, let me describe the retroactive design assignment of the First Industrial Revolution: Would you design a system of production and a system of commerce that

- produces billions of pounds of highly toxic hazardous material and puts them in your soil, your air, and your water every year?
- measures prosperity by how much of your natural capital you can dig up, burn, deplete, throw into holes in the ground and into the rivers and otherwise destroy?
- measures productivity by how few people are working?
- measures progress by how many smokestacks you have?
- requires thousands of complex regulations to keep you from killing each other too quickly?
- produces a few things so highly dangerous and toxic they will require future generations to maintain constant vigilance while living in terror?

That is the retroactive design assignment of the First Industrial Revolution. Is this an ethical assignment?...We have now reached the point where we can agree that this is not a design assignment we wish to accept in our time, and it is certainly not one we want to pass on to our children. It is time to look again at the horizon with delight and anticipation, with a new responsibility and a new design legacy in mind.

Let's design a system for what I call the Next Industrial Revolution that

- introduces no hazardous material into the soil, the air, and the water every year
- measures prosperity by how much natural capital and how much solar income we can accrue in productive and fecund ways
- measures productivity by how many people are being gainfully and meaningfully employed
- measures progress by how many buildings have no smokestacks, no dangerous effluents, and no pipes
- does not require regulations to stop us from killing one another too quickly
- produces nothing that will require future generations to maintain vigilance and live in terror...

I have developed some principles that we use in our work:

I) *Waste Equals Food.* In nature, there is no such thing as waste, so the first thing we must do is eliminate the concept of waste. I am not saying we need to minimize waste; I am saying we need to eliminate the entire concept of waste....

We talk about recycling, but most of us don't recycle in the full sense of the word; we often do what Michael Braungart and I call "downcycling"—we reduce the quality of a material until its value is practically nonexistent. In other words, we slow its journey to the landfill. For example, when a high quality plastic like PET is "recycled" it may be mixed with other plastics to produce a hybrid of much lower quality, which is then used to make park benches. The original elevated quality can never be retrieved. So what we call recycling is still working with a *Cradle-to-Grave* life cycle.

Michael Braungart points out that the *Cradle-to-Grave* mentality is definitely Northern European. In Sweden, if you throw a banana peel on the ground it is going to be there a long time, because nothing rots quickly. Northern Europeans tended to bury everything. Western culture, then, tends to bury unwanted things. Consequently, our culture developed products in terms of a *Cradle-to-Grave* life cycle concept; once you finish with something you bury it because you don't want to look at it. In the abstract, one might say it's too bad the First Industrial Revolution didn't begin in a place like Mali. As Dr. Braungart notes, if you go to "primitive" places today, you might see a lot of aluminum cans lying on the ground outside a fence and think the people there are inconsiderate and slovenly. But those people once drank out of clay cups or gourds, and when they finished, they would simply toss the vessel over the fence and the goats, ants, or beetles would take it away. Its organic materials would nourish other organisms and go back to the soil. So these people are still doing what they've been doing forever; modern production just hasn't provided them with an intelligent design for a container that turns back into dirt....

Plastic bottles could easily be redesigned so that they don't contain questionable substances and could safely replenish the soil. Right now they may contain antimony, catalytic residues, UV stabilizers, plasticizers, and antioxidants. What happens when the people in Mali throw that over the fence? Why not design a bottle so that when you finish with it you toss it into the compost or it biodegrades by the roadside, or it can be used as fuel for needy people to cook with? It should be safe fuel. If a clothing manufacturer wants to make clothing out of it, it should not contain potentially toxic substances. Plastic bottles were not originally designed to become clothing; they were designed to hold liquids. We have a fundamental design problem. We need to design things so they go into the biological or the technical cycle, safely, *Cradle-to-Cradle*.

2) *Use Current Solar Income.* Nature does not mine the past; it does not borrow from the future. It operates on current income. Most of us can't pursue our professional lives working out of capital reserves. We have to work with current income, and so should our designs.

I think we're going to resolve the energy problem, because we have current solar income. Energy from the sun is the only income the planet has (except for meteorites); all our other materials are already here. If you're in business, you understand that you must work from current income, not savings. Because we have that income from the sun, I think it won't be long before we find elegant solutions to the energy situation.

The University of Virginia's School of Architecture is about to build a building addition project designed to be a net energy exporter, a structure that produces more energy than it consumes. Why would we want to make a building that produces more energy than it needs? The reason is that *sustainability* may just be a shibboleth—the magic word that lets us into the temple of hope. A lot of people use the term *sustainability* as if it's going to save us. But sustainability as it's presently defined may be only the edge between destruction and restoration. Why would we want to simply sustain where we are now? We're in a depletive mode. We need to actually design things that are restorative. Think about the high-tech designs you see around you: airplanes, computers, space age stores. Imagine how much farther we can go, how wonderfully ambitious we can really be.

What is one of the best designs we know of for inspiration? How about a tree? How about a design that can accrue solar income, is fecund, produces habitat for all sorts of living things including people, provides fuel, food, and micro-climate, distills and transpires water, sequesters carbon, and makes oxygen? How many things do you know that do that? How many things have humans designed that make oxygen?

Why not make a building that produces oxygen? Why not make a building that produces energy? We're not very bright or ambitious designers if we can't even emulate a tree, which nature has put right there in front of us as an obvious model. Just compare a tree to most rooms. Right now, I'm in a room that sucks electrical energy from a grid, I'm responsible for the production of nuclear isotopes simply by turning on a light switch, and I'm probably breathing all sorts of chemical experiments I don't even realize I am undertaking. Compared to a tree, this is obviously primitive design. If I'm going to be a sophisticated designer, I had better start thinking more about trees—about buildings that produce more energy than they need and purify their water, and I had better start thinking about designing buildings and sites that absorb water quickly and release it slowly in a pure form like healthy soil. A building could be a restorative thing, a thing that is more fecund than destructive....

Let's get creative and start redesigning a new kind of prosperity for ourselves, but let's make sure this prosperity includes everyone else, including our seventh generation to come. Design for all of our prosperity, not just your own prosperity. We can start by eliminating our destruction masquerading as consumption, and begin to enjoy the search for our rightful and responsible place in the natural world. Get prosperous. Get very prosperous, because then people will want to imitate you. But honor that thing in yourself, that creativity in your spirit and your place that is really the sacred trust for all generations. We need to design a system of production and consumption and a system of commerce that will allow everyone life, liberty, and the pursuit of happiness in their own place, free from remote tyranny—the remote tyranny that is us and our bad design.

FOR REVIEW

1. Why are some people tempted to seek a "value-free" alternative to ethics?

2. Why do some people worry that ethics is too defensive?

3. Why do some people worry that ethics is too individualistic?

4. Why not decide ethical questions using cost-benefit analysis or other forms of economics, rather than introduce all the uncertainty and debate that seem to come with ethics?

5. How does the text argue that it might be the very point of ethics to be indecisive at times?

6. How does the text argue that ethics is not "too defensive"?

7. Where does the text leave the question of individualism in the end?

8. What does William McDonough mean by "intergenerational remote tyranny"?

9. What are McDonough's new design principles? Explain.

10. Why must we go beyond sustainability, according to McDonough?

EXERCISES AND NOTES

18.1 MORE DOUBTS ABOUT ETHICS?

The first part of this chapter raises three doubts about ethics today. Do you have others?

Is ethics possibly too often tied to religion, in your view—or not tied to religion enough? Is it, perhaps, too demanding in general—or not demanding enough? What else?

When I say farewell to my ethics students at the end of a college term, I sometimes ask them what they expected ethics to be about when they began the course. All too often, what they say is—to put it baldly—that they expected a lot of stuffed-shirt moralizing about sex, especially, and maybe alcohol abuse, or plagiarism, or a few other personal malfeasances that parents and older people and college administrators tend to be concerned about. They were surprised to find themselves in a course with such an open-ended and often social view of ethics and more concerned with critical and creative rethinking than with judgment. I am grateful, of course, but I also am worried for ethics, if that narrow view of it is the one most people hold.

You're at the end of this book now, so your view too is, I hope, much broader. But there are still questions. That stuffed-shirt moralizing remains common. Perhaps it would he helpful to reverse the lens a little and ask why moralists *are* sometimes so preoccupied with sex, anyway. This is an easy question to make fun of, or have fun with (remember, as chapter 1 noted, that George Bernard Shaw once reduced morality itself to "the suspicion that other people are not legally married"), but—also—take it seriously. Peter Singer argues that driving a car actually poses more serious moral questions than sex—other people's lives and bodies are more at stake and can be more seriously harmed—yet moralists hardly pay attention to driving at all. Why the difference? And then there's Mary Eberstadt—remember "Using Your Tools" #1—who claims that we no longer pay *enough* moral attention to sex. What do you think?

Whatever doubts you harbor about ethics, finally, you might ask whether the problem actually is inherent in ethics itself, or with the way it is taken up in our society and times. Is ethics' individualism, for instance, due to something about ethics itself, or our society? How about the defensiveness?

18.2 ETHICS AND THE LAW

The second part of this chapter argues that "ethics is inescapable": that science and economics and "practicality" do not offer an alternative, "value-free" way of making decisions, but are essentially ethics themselves, and depend on ethical assumptions that might justly be questioned. There is no escaping thinking in ethical ways.

Here, though, is another argument that is sometimes made. Maybe we can avoid ethics by simply taking it upon ourselves to follow the *law*. Isn't it enough to just respect the law, without getting into ethical quandaries and indefiniteness? For a time this was an argument widely heard in the business world: the law is definite; it sets rules that require a certain degree of self-limitation and at least minimal social responsibility, very like moral rules; and when it is unclear, there are the courts to figure it out. Once again, then, who needs ethics?

Consider this question yourself, using the arguments of this chapter as a model. Some questions you might ask are: is following the law *enough* for ethics? (Give examples to back up your answer.) How do we determine what laws to pass in the first place, especially when they concern ethically difficult matters? If a law is based on ethical commitments that are controversial, is the ethics then settled (or just irrelevant)? And couldn't a law itself be immoral? Aren't we back then to having to evaluate the law itself morally? Relate your answer to the arguments in chapter 3 about "Thinking for Yourself," as well.

18.3 DESIGN FOR A NEW WORLD, CONTINUED

William McDonough asks us to think about the ethics of design somewhat literally at times: how to build far greener houses and material products. In writing of Jefferson's design for our form of government, though, he goes much farther: one can also think about design in terms of social and political practices and institutions. Jefferson clearly believed that the political and ethical imperative to prevent tyranny required the careful crafting of a system of government that was *structurally* disinclined or even unable to tyrannize its people—unlike the British system the new Americans were resisting, which had clearly failed in that regard, at least with respect to the colonies. (He also declared in famous words that a rebellion every twenty years or so mightn't be a bad idea—it keeps the rulers honest.)

Beautiful words in a document will not by themselves keep people free and equal: it takes a suitably structured political system. Likewise, ethical ideas about caring for nature will not by themselves produce a cleaner world for ourselves and our descendants. Once again, it takes a structural redesign. This is ethics in action!

Here is a challenge for you: think of the design of yet other features of our world in the same way. *The way things are* is only the way people have made them, right now and right here. They could be otherwise. Maybe...should be.

Social practices, for example. Bloggers often complain about the incivility, unintelligence, and all too often sheer hate that shows up in online discussion forums and other such public sites. Yet such sites do serve a vital social function, and *could* even be a place where genuinely constructive social and political discussion takes place. Every once in a while I actually do stumble across a truly intelligent, perceptive, and respectful online dialogue, and my faith in the possibility of the medium is restored. Usually it is sorely tested.

This is a design problem too, isn't it? How might we (re)design the structure of such online forums such that, instead of quickly descending to the lowest common denominator, they move in the other direction? To adapt what McDonough says about Jefferson, how can we craft a system of online interaction that is *structurally* "self-ethicizing" or self-civilizing? What would it take? Having to sign your name (as some sites now require)? Some kind of ongoing rating system, such that rants and other unhelpful entries quickly drop down into unread regions of the site? Or what?

Get creative. It's an interesting problem. Work out a good design, by the way, and it might also be generalized to other kinds of structured ethical dialogues—remembering chapters 11 and 12 as well.

Could there be self-ethicizing sports? Games are "designs" too—maybe it is time to do some redesigning. In Ultimate Frisbee, for one example, there are no referees. You'd think the result would be a free-for-all. Instead, the game becomes a much more cooperative endeavor, and when violations seem to occur, play stops entirely and both teams gather to discuss the question and decide what to do. It sounds impossible, but it works: removing the authority figure results in *everyone* taking responsibility for the rules. Could this model be generalized beyond games as well?

Could there even be designs for self-ethicizing *governments*? McDonough suggests that Jefferson's design legacy might now have to be augmented to deal with contemporary society's destruction of nature. What might it take? Representatives of future generations in Congress? Spokespeople for endangered species or mountains or rivers? (It's not impossible: some indigenous tribes actually appoint people to "speak for wolf" and such...and besides, we're inventive creatures, right? So, let us invent... something new.)

What else needs some serious ethical redesign?

NOTES

On the Web, some sites concerned with newly emerging ethical issues are

> http://www.newethics.com/en/
> http://blog.practicalethics.ox.ac.uk/
> http://myplace.frontier.com/~lestershepard/index.html

These are all quite different, but all open up edgy and also potentially fruitful new possibilities.

For more on William McDonough and his work, see http://www.mcdonough .com/writings/new_design.htm, and listen his TED talk at http://www.ted. com/talks/william_mcdonough_on_cradle_to_cradle_design.html, in which he asks "what our buildings and products would look like if designers took into account 'all children, all species, for all time'." What a great question!

USING YOUR TOOLS #9
ETHICAL CHANGE PROJECTS

Many of the later parts of this book encourage you to think in bigger than usual ways about what kinds of difference ethics—and you—can make. Chapter 14, "Reframing Problems and chapter 15, "Moral Vision," both give you some tools to think beyond the kinds of alternatives usually considered and to look forward in a more visionary way as a means of circumventing blocked issues and debates in the present. Chapter 17, "Making a Difference," invites you to think about how to carry some of the new ideas you generate into actual practice. And chapter 18, The Future of Ethics," ends by posing the challenge as a design issue, bringing specific tools and models to bear.

For this final exercise, I challenge you to put all of these pieces together: to devise for yourself, or with your class, or organization, or group, some adventurous and ambitious ethical change project, and begin to carry it into action.

More specifically, here are some features of the sorts of projects you could aim to undertake for ethical change work growing out of your engagement with this book.

1. AN ETHICAL CHANGE PROJECT IS EXPLICITLY MOTIVATED BY MORAL VALUES.

Justice, fairness, community, character; these and other moral values invite us to consider how we might make the world better. Your projects should be motivated by (some of) these; and you should be explicit—forthright, clear, and detailed—about your moral starting points.

Moral commitments do not have to be contentious ones. In fact, for the widest reach, we should appeal to common interests and avoid polarized moral "positions" that unnecessarily exclude values on the other side(s). Acknowledge values widely; find constructive ways to go forward together.

2. AN ETHICAL CHANGE PROJECT USES AVAILABLE MEANS TO MAKE BIG AND SYNERGISTIC CHANGES.

"Available means" means things within your power. But remember, as chapter 17 argued, your power may be greater than you think. As members of a university community, for example, you have some influence over that community's choices. As students you also have some natural links with students other places and even around the world (there's a world-change organization, remember, called "Students Without Borders"). Starting from such existing connections and communities is wise: think about where *you* already have some leverage.

"Synergistic changes" mean changes that achieve many connected and mutually-supportive goals at once. For instance, getting more seasonal and local foods into university dining halls would do many things at once: offer students a healthier diet, make us all more aware of the seasons and of what's happening on the land right here, greatly reduce transport costs (both in monetary terms and in terms of costs to the environment for fuel, air pollution, etc.), support local growers (so that the university begins to do more for the local community), and anticipate a "greener" economy in which radical localism may be necessary.

3. AN ETHICAL CHANGE PROJECT IS CONCERNED, AT LEAST IN PART, WITH STRUCTURAL CHANGES.

By "structural" change I mean changes in the practices and institutions that underlie and often generate familiar moral problems—the kinds of changes urged upon ethics by chapter 14, UYT #7 and discussed again in chapter 18. Again, it is not enough to band-aid a problem, even if people are injured (to extend the metaphor) and need band-aids among other things. Martin Luther King again: "an edifice which produces beggars [itself] needs restructuring"—not just nicer and better-staffed homeless shelters. A production system that turns ever more of the natural world into trash needs more than better recycling programs. What *does* it need? Ah, that is now your question.

4. AN ETHICAL CHANGE PROJECT REQUIRES DIALOGUE, CONSULTATION, AND COLLABORATION WITH STAKEHOLDERS.

"Stakeholders" are affected or concerned people and communities both within and beyond your group or action community: people with a *stake* in the situation, and correspondingly, very likely, also a lot to offer as far as collaboration, expertise, and energy toward improving the situation.

It is crucial that the ethical involvement not be just one-way, as sometimes happens in "service" work. There is nothing wrong, of course, with service work!—but much *more* is possible. Change projects are not a matter of helping others out of pity or from an ethically secure position ourselves. Thus in the case of the homeless, for example, whatever is done needs to be done *with* them rather than just *for* them. This is not only a means to a far more effective project, with far more buy-in from others: it is also *ethical*, plain and simple, in the sense that it is premised on a fundamental equality and respect between all of the people involved.

5. AN ETHICAL CHANGE PROJECT IS MAXIMALLY CREATIVE AND VISIONARY.

Far wilder and more wonderful projects are possible than we usually think. It's only that some training and some methods are necessary to engage serious creativity. Exaggerate and extrapolate starting-point ideas; learn to invite exotic associations; always ask "what's the next step?" before settling down on some halfway-creative idea...remember, one last time, chapters 13 and 14.

This book has offered a very wide range of possible examples, from projects that my own students have carried out over the years to all manner of inventive projects envisioned and carried out by others. Now, though, the ball really is entirely in your hands. You must find your own way forward. Take your toolbox—all of it, but especially these most ambitious parts—and go out and use it. Good luck!

APPENDIX **1**

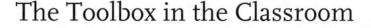

The Toolbox in the Classroom

The approach to ethics in this textbook poses unique challenges as well as opportunities. This Appendix begins with some commentary speaking to general philosophical issues—concerns addressed here because they are much more likely to come up for fellow teachers than students—and continues chapter by chapter with notes on some of my own uses of this material, sometimes with other pedagogically or philosophically oriented notes. I hope they will be of some use to teachers, especially to those who may be coming to this material for the first time. Let me add that I would very much appreciate hearing any of your suggestions and exercises or projects that prove useful with this text, or any other reactions that you or your students may have—please e-mail me at weston@elon.edu.

GENERAL ISSUES

PRAGMATISM

Many philosophers prefer to concentrate on ethics' unique intellectual challenges—on theory-building and conceptual analysis—following a model of ethics essentially laid down by the English philosopher Henry Sidgwick in the late 19th century. In my view, though, while this essentially professional model of ethics may be appropriate in upper-level classes mostly for majors or where some specialization is useful and appropriate, it is not the best approach in lower-level, introductory, general-curriculum ethics courses, in which very few if any students intend to become specialists in ethics. It seems to me that we are missing an opportunity to offer them (and perhaps, ourselves) a much more useful and engaged model of ethics.

Students in such classes, like most people, come to ethics to learn how to live. This is a far broader matter—not merely or mainly an intellectual challenge, but a challenge to the imagination and to the heart too, and to ourselves as effective moral citizens. It may be that by concentrating on certain intellectual challenges unique to ethics, we have slighted the practical skills that are vital to ethics but not unique to it. So part of the aim of this book is to rejoin ethics to life skills—to put ethics into what I see as its rightful place.

This approach to ethics traces back to the American pragmatists, John Dewey in particular, and has affinities as well with a number of pragmatist, feminist, and other critical views of ethics that are now developing in the midst of the current and vast philosophical debate about the very foundations of ethics. But I don't defend my starting points in this book itself—though it's been difficult to resist!—nor critique the usual ones. A textbook is not the place for methodological debates (and of course it's not exactly as though traditional textbooks spend their time laying out and defending their presuppositions either, do they?). Interested or provoked readers might consult my book *Toward Better Problems* (Temple University Press, 1992) for a development and defense of some of my assumptions. A useful overview of Dewey's approach can be found in James Gouinlock's collection *The Moral Writings of John Dewey* (Prometheus, 1994).

Just a few basic points here. Pragmatism shifts emphasis away from moral *judgment*. This is often almost incomprehensible to moral philosophers as well as many everyday moralists, for whom the very point of ethics is to judge actions: to deliver ethical verdicts. Ethical problems on the traditional view are a kind of puzzle that needs to be solved. But pragmatism points in another and surely appealing direction. The real point of ethics is to actually improve the world: to apply intelligence in a constructive way in what Dewey called "problematic situations," and to let the results feed back to revise our practice and theories as needed.

For pragmatism, then, ethics is essentially practical, not merely (or perhaps at all) in the familiar sense that it issues in practical judgments, but in the sense that it takes up practical problems of value from a reconstructive, and even what Dewey called an "experimental," point of view. Ethics is also essentially *social*. For example, for the philosophical tradition, "the" question of assisted suicide calls for judgment of what a dying person can justly ask— nothing to do with *us*, apparently—while for pragmatism a better question is how we—society in general, or a sick or dying person's community, and even I personally—can respond to that person's situation.

Ethical values are diverse and plural; ethical practice therefore also requires a variety of tools. Theories are only one such tool (a useful way of expressing or connecting the families of values) but are also apt to get out of hand (don't we know) and claim the whole show for themselves. Again, ethics *also* needs critical thinking; it needs expressive and creative skills; and it calls upon the abilities to connect and stay connected with others and to create and sustain community, moral vision, and inspiration.

It's a striking thing, though, that despite the current challenges to "ethics as usual," it remains virtually impossible to teach practical ethics without plowing the same old theoretical furrows. There are vanishingly few textbooks, and no others, I believe, from major publishers, that systematically present ethics in a pragmatic key. My main aim, then, has just been to write such a book—to make it possible to teach ethics on the view laid out in this book's Preface: as a collection of practical skills that enable us to make a constructive difference in problematic ethical situations. Practical pragmatism, so to speak. That is task enough for one book.

Finally, though, I do admit that I hope that *A 21st Century Ethical Toolbox* will be read as a contribution—albeit oblique—to the philosophical debate about the foundations of ethics too. Every approach to ethics must be judged partly by how it looks in action: by what kinds of tools it brings back to practice, by how constructively and invitingly it enables us to contribute to improving our common life. Could not each then be judged partly by what kinds of introductory texts and courses it makes possible—by what an introduction to ethics *that* way leaves students able to *do?* A good pragmatic maxim is that proof is partly in the pudding. I am proud to offer this book as one relevant kind of pudding.

COURSE DESIGN USING THIS BOOK

The book is designed to serve as the chief or sole textbook in an ethics course, though it can be supplemented in a variety of ways too, and could well serve as a supplement itself. Some may wish to supplement it with a standard text, like a collection of readings from traditional ethical theories, or a collection of more professional articles on "applied" themes, or a text that combines both. Others may supplement it in quite different ways: say, with books that go into depth on a single issue raised here more briefly. Some colleagues have used it successfully with Peter Singer's *Animal Liberation*; others have used Ram Dass and Paul Gorman's *How Can I Help?* or Colin McGinn's brisk little essay *Moral Literacy*, which takes provocative positions on a number of the issues discussed here. (I draw upon McGinn several times myself, you'll recall.) Others couple it with popular and provocative books such as Daniel Quinn's *Ishmael*. I have also used this book as the first of several main texts in mid- or upper-level practical ethics courses such as Environmental Ethics and Ethics and Decision Making.

I usually assign one chapter per class (I have 100-minute classes twice a week). This schedule presupposes, of course, that students read and understand the chapters mostly on their own. In class I may spend five or ten minutes reviewing the chapter, just to remind students of the main points, but I rely on the students to raise questions or issues if there are sticking points in the chapters. (Some colleagues have students do this by email or on an online class discussion board. In the old days I just used 3 x 5 cards available at the beginning of class each day: students could ask questions or about points of unclarity in the day's reading; I organized these at a later short break and responded to them right then.)

Class meetings themselves are almost entirely application and practice, always with a good bit of variety. Some narratives of in-class applications and practice, chapter-by-chapter, follow below.

Please note that there are often substantive new points in the "Exercises and Notes" and "Using Your Tools" sections. I assign them right along with the text sections, even if the exercises aren't always used as writing projects or classwork.

Earlier editions' reviewers reported that they taught through the chapters of this book in a variety of different orders. I have rearranged the order myself in each new edition. The third edition moves the chapter on dialogue to Part III, for example: it seems more logical to put it with other skills for ethical practice. Some subsections do unfold in order—chapters 4 through 8, for instance, and 13 through 15. Still, for the most part, the chapters remain largely independent and non-sequential. You can use them in a variety of orders. Many of my colleagues use the dialogue chapter near the beginning of their classes, for example, to help set ground rules for class discussions. I should report that in my own current teaching I actually use the chapters entirely out of order too. My class begins with a skeleton of skills and topics—chapters 1, 2, 4, 9, 13, 14, 15, and 17—to help student groups frame and launch their own ethical-change projects (see "Using Your Tools" #9); then we return to the rest as the projects get underway.

GRADING

Over the years I have graded my course in a variety of ways. Half of the grade has sometimes depended on journals—student notebooks with notes and their own thoughts (that's a crucial part) on all the chapters and class discussions. Group work, attendance, and service work made up the rest. Other times I have graded mainly on short weekly papers, mostly assignments directly from the Exercises that conclude each chapter. I say more about paper assignments in the next section.

Currently I keep tabs on students' reading with short weekly quizzes. I use the review questions at the end of each chapter as quiz questions at the beginning of each class day. For some variation and challenge, I also recycle some questions from earlier chapters as we move through the book, and add some bonus questions that can only be answered by a student who has gone above and beyond the reading to, say, look up some references. I couple quiz grades with attendance and participation grades, regular short writing assignments or options, contributions (written and other) to the service or project work of the class, and maybe some final writing.

PAPER ASSIGNMENTS USING THIS BOOK

For short writing assignments I offer the exercises that conclude each chapter. They ask for a variety of kinds of responses: for self-reflections, for critiques or extensions of the ideas in the text, or other and quite different projects. All aim to give students a strong start and some good support, drawing on the material in the chapter in focused ways.

I am no longer much inclined to assign freestanding writing of any length, like the usual term paper. It's certainly true that writing such papers may be one way in which students can display some of the skills they are learning. But papers are not the only way, and often may well not be the best way. I'm more inclined toward practical projects, actually trying to make a difference. Exercise 17.3 briefly outlines some of the projects we have attempted. This kind of work can be coupled with writing—one of my requirements with all of these projects, in fact, is that students produce an explicit and detailed ethical rationale, posting it online, for example, if they put up a website. But these pieces are not academic papers in the usual sense. They are usually written by groups rather than individuals; they are public rather than addressed solely to me, part of larger projects with multiple stakeholders who will also weigh in; and the usual academic voice is often out of place, if not inappropriate. This kind of writing is certainly rigorous and demanding in its own way, and is also, in my view, much better preparation for the collaborative and community-oriented ethical work students are likely to undertake in their lives after university, or even outside classes while still students.

When I do assign longer academic papers, I emphasize that a wide variety of writing styles are possible. Too often we, and correspondingly our students, assume that only papers in an argumentative style are appropriate in philosophy. Once again, certainly it is an important thing to train students to write in this style. It asks a vital kind of rigor and clear thinking, and is one style of contributing to public debate. Yet, just as certainly, it is not the only kind of effective and appropriate writing. Much of the writing in this book—to take models very close at hand—is (quite on purpose) in very different styles. Right away in chapter 1, for example, Alice Walker's "Am I Blue?" and the excerpt by Ted Kerasote offer contrasting models both to each other and to the usual "paper." Bertrand Russell's "The Harm That Good Men Do" is another nice model, despite or maybe because of its irony (chapter 6). Think also of Aldo Leopold's "The Land Ethic" (chapter 8); Colin McGinn's "Speciesism" (chapter 10); and the pieces from Rayna Rapp (chapter 4) and William McDonough (chapter 18). There is clarity and rigorous thinking here too—among other appeals. Students often find it useful to compare and contrast some of these essays specifically with attention to aims and writing strategies. Then they are in a much better position to appreciate the expectations for the writing they will be doing themselves.

As to the mechanics—especially but not exclusively for the usual sorts of academic papers—some of my other books offer some guidance. *A Rulebook for Arguments* offers rules for argumentative papers of any sort. The last chapter of *A Practical Companion to Ethics* includes a box on writing papers in ethics, specifically asking students to start planning their paper by asking what is their aim with it. Explore an issue? Get some problem "unstuck"? Make a case? Take a stand? Each aim suggests a quite different kind of paper. Know where you are going! There are also many other fine resources for paper writing in philosophy generally, such as Anthony Graybosch *et al.*, *The Philosophy Student Writer's Manual* (Prentice-Hall, 2nd edition, 2003).

TOOLBOX BY CHAPTER

CHAPTER 1: "ETHICS AS A LEARNING EXPERIENCE"

My strategy in most of the chapters is to focus on one or a few practical topics, so that the "applications" stay somewhat consistent through the chapter. Chapter 1's readings thus focus on the question of our relation to other animals. Students typically have a great deal to say. There will be vegetarians and vegans in the class, alongside others who grew up hunting. There will be many others vaguely aware of moral questions about meat but unaccustomed to (or uncomfortable with) giving them any serious thought. Most of the meat–eaters in my classes at this stage cannot even imagine living without it—despite the fact that right there in the same room there are other students who do. Many of the vegetarians, correspondingly, have little direct experience of other animals other than pets. The hunters often know the actual animals much better. It makes for interesting interactions all around.

The aim, of course, is not to close down the question, as if there is only one simple right answer. It is to wake up to them as *questions*. (Sometimes I bring in guest speakers, on these or other issues; I find this a useful point to review with them in advance.) Of course there is also a vast literature on the issue of ethics and animals. For a start, there is the "Ethics Updates" website, http://ethics.sandiego.edu, under "Animal Rights."

The definition of ethics in this chapter is slightly revised from previous editions and discussed more at length. Previously I defined ethics as a *concern* with the basic needs and legitimate expectations of others as well as our own. Some reviewers found this too subjective a way of putting it, as if it implied that ethics depends on a feeling of being "concerned." I meant something else: "concern" in the sense simply that basic needs and legitimate expectations are what ethics is *about* (as in, maybe, "this letter concerns Alphonso"—whether or not Alphonso is concerned by it). However, it's certainly a fair point that this way of speaking seemed too ambiguous for such a central definition.

I have tried to correct this impression while retaining the thrust of the original definition. Ethics, I now say, *takes care* for basic needs ... etc. I realize that this too could sound subjective. I hope, however, that the three-way analysis of "taking care" suggested in the text clarifies in what sense we may "take care": everything from "looking into" to "being conscientious about" to "sustaining and furthering." In this way ethics *is* emphatically defined in terms of modes of engagement then, but these are mostly public and behavioral, as it were, not mostly internal or "subjective." And wider-ranging.

Another reviewer objected that my definition applies problematically to Divine Command theories of ethics, which, he argues, can be quite "antihumanist"—therefore presumably not concerned with basic needs and legitimate expectations of either (human) others or our own—but still, surely, ethical. This raises difficult substantive issues. I am inclined to say, dogmatically, that: (i) It is not clear how to get the proper denotation for any definition of "ethics" without *some* reference to something like human needs and expectations. Widening the definition to something like just "systematic thinking about what we should do"—the traditional view, I guess—makes it far too broad. (ii) The traditional response, that ethics concerns those values that *override* all others, is the wrong way around. What values are overriding, if any, is an open question. (My own view, for what it is worth, is that *no* values are overriding by nature or definition, though often moral values do in fact carry greater weight.) We'd like to hope that those values traditionally considered ethical are overriding, but that hope of course is no argument. When arguments are offered at all, unfortunately, they seem to me to be question-begging or hand-waving. If we defined ethics in terms of overriding values, we might end up with an empty set. (iii) An inhuman Divine Command system of values is of course "overriding" in its own terms (and only in such terms), but I would argue that it is also not ethical. This is partly because, as chapters 2 and 3 argue, ethics does require thinking for yourself. But one may still end up choosing other-than-ethically. Kierkegaard characterized such choices at the extreme, remember, as "the teleological *suspension* of the ethical." Obviously, though, as I say, these are difficult issues!

CHAPTER 2: "ETHICS-AVOIDANCE DISORDERS"

As soon as my class gets underway, I assign one or a few students each day to bring in a short article or something else that we can look at together that involves some sort of ethical issue. These have ranged from on-campus debates to current Supreme Court cases to surprising or disturbing international political or technological developments, and occasionally even a cat, a piece of trash, or an art object. We begin class by looking at these—a kind of warm-up. Right away I stress that our aim is not to judge the issue or in any other way close it down. Instead, our aim is to explore it in as open-ended and intelligent a way as we can: to see it more deeply, to see possibilities in it that might not have been evident at first or to participants, even to consider if there is some useful intervention or contribution we might make.

This procedure continues through the term, but I like to introduce it in conjunction with chapter 2. Dogmatism, dismissal, "flip" relativism—none of them work in the face of this kind of exploration. Yet this exploration is fascinating, inviting, and a way of talking and thinking about ethics that students will rarely have encountered before. Ultimately, I believe, this is the best pedagogical answer to the various ethics-avoidance "disorders": to exemplify, together, an alternative—to begin to experience provocative, intelligent, *exciting* ethical thinking. Thus "Using Your Tools" #1, for one thing.

Generally I do not tackle any of the "disorders" head-on in class. Here, as in general, I hope that the text is enough already. We don't want to drive people into defensiveness. And we don't need to. It is striking, for example, that although the spectre of relativism seems to loom extremely large for some ethics instructors—and, it seems, just about all ethics textbook writers—it vanishes into thin air the minute a real issue comes on the scene. (Nobody says things like: "Oh well, maybe executing innocent convicts is right for Texans.") Despite the veneer of relativism, most of us come with strong moral opinions. Dogmatism is the much more real danger.

Students do express relativistic sentiments from time to time (like "Who am I to say?"). Still, I think that philosophers read too much of a theory— Relativism with a capital-R—into them. Maybe when students say things like "Who am I to say?" they are just trying to give others some space—and asking for space themselves, in a context where they are unsure of themselves. After all, college is a time of change and experiment for many people: things are in flux; they justly want room to move. Maybe they want some freedom from the moral deliverances of others, time to work things out for themselves. This is not unreasonable—and it has nothing to do with the philosophical debate about relativism. I don't think it is wise to take a few relativistic-sounding expressions as on the way to relativism, as it were, and then try to lay out the whole capital-R theory and defeat it. It may actually *make* students relativists, for one thing—if they're persuaded by this that philosophical relativism is the only way to defend the personal space they genuinely do need—and then it *will* be a problem.

Besides, even if they really are (philosophical) relativists from the beginning, it strikes me as unwise pedagogy to think that we must begin a course by "defeating" something students are supposed to believe so strongly. Wiser and more effective would be to take them where they are and build from there. How inviting is ethics likely to be if it sets itself up from the start as a furious (and, to be honest, somewhat desperate) assault upon their convictions? Show them instead, by example, how much careful thinking and constructive engagement is possible in ethics after all.

So my practice is to just tolerate the occasional "Who is to say?" rhetoric without wheeling out the heavy artillery. I just point out that we do in fact have more to think about and say. I send the harder-core relativists to the box at the end of this chapter. We get a lot more space for the real work of ethics.

CHAPTER 3: "ETHICS AND RELIGION"

Modern philosophical ethics tends to avoid religious themes and terms. However wise this may be as an expression of secular pluralism, it does make it much harder to speak to many of our students, whose ethical frames of reference are often insistently religious and sometimes sectarian. I think we need to take them more seriously. The aim of this chapter is to suggest a path toward the sort of ethics familiar to philosophers that lies *through* religion rather than opposed to it.

Actually reading the Bible can be a fascinating project in an open college classroom. A few examples are suggested in the text. Another I find useful is the story of Judah and Tamar in Genesis 38. Sometimes I hand out a copy of that chapter and we read it right in class. It is a wild tale of sudden unexplained death, betrayal, seduction and adultery, which concludes with the pardon and full acceptance of the female adulterer (Tamar) and no question even being raised about the male adulterer (Judah). In fact, Tamar is specifically listed as one of the ancestors of King David and therefore of Jesus Himself. Judah founds one of the twelve tribes of Israel and later gives his name to Judaism itself. So the story seems to go rather light on adultery and seduction, to say the least. It is also complicated by certain sexual customs practiced by the Hebrews of the time, in particular the expectation that if a husband dies, it is the obligation of his next youngest brother to impregnate his widow—in particular, to sire a son—who counts as the dead man's son for the sake of inheritance. (Recently I learned that something like this "levirate marriage" is still practiced in Iraq; there are a lot of widows.)

In this story, Onan, the second son, does in fact follow his dead brother (killed by God for an unspecified reason) to the widow's bed but deliberately does not get her pregnant. God kills him too, for a reason that seems unclear.

Was it that he disobeyed his father? Was it his selfishness—for if his dead brother had no heirs then the father's property would pass to Onan and *his* descendants? Or something else? It is not so clear. Yet this story, like the story of Sodom, was made the basis for a very strong prohibition in the Christian tradition. I challenge the students to figure out what exactly, on this view, was the sin of Onan (they find it most intriguing) and then to ask whether the actual story can be made to bear such weight.

Often I invite in our college chaplain for a dialogue on these matters with me and the class. Most college chaplains deal with a religiously diverse community: they have to be ecumenical. In most places they also have to make their peace with the prevailing secularism. All of this is fascinating to explore with them.

Exercise 18.2 is also applicable to this chapter if instructors wish to highlight this chapter's general points about the necessity of Thinking for Yourself in nonreligious contexts as well (see also chapter 2 of my *A Practical Companion to Ethics*, "Beyond Authority.")

CHAPTER 4: "TAKING VALUES SERIOUSLY"

For this chapter I take current issues out of newspapers, bring in children's story books, bring the Bible back, invite in people who practice Taekwondo, or weekly fasts, or Civil War reenactments (there are some in your class) or, well, whatever I can find. Whatever I put in front of them, I ask my students to try to understand and uncover the values at stake and spell them out just as the chapter does. For example, if a value like "responsibility" comes up, ask *whose* responsibility, and for *what?*

Sometimes I organize this kind of work by dividing the class or group into small groups, each of which is asked to identify one value at stake in the situation (practice, issue, or whatever) and write a description of it, in a few words, on the board (use one section of the board for each issue) or on a flip chart—in, say, three minutes (the first one is easy).

Then each issue passes to the next group (number the groups and issues: issue 1 now goes to group 2, etc.), with the same assignment and, say, five minutes. Repeat for as much time as you have, allowing a few more minutes each time around if needed.

My students generally do not believe that more than two or three values can be drawn out of such issues. They are surprised when the groups are still going strong on the fourth or fifth round. Questions arise about how distinct are certain expressions of value. Sometimes in later rounds a number of values from the same family also come out together: it's striking to see connections between quite different issues emerge. By the end, you have a board full of different values all drawn out of situations that we usually just quickly pass over. Next time we ask more of ourselves.

CHAPTERS 5–8: FAMILIES OF MORAL VALUES

For these chapters I arrange for brief classroom visits by some of the figures we read: Kant, Russell, Lao Tzu, or others (they can be contacted at your local costume store or theater department). A student or a colleague can usually be induced to interview them (i.e., me usually) talk-show style. I try to personify them, in short—that way their thought becomes far more vivid.

Compared to the usual treatment of theory in ethics texts, these chapters go light. A *family* is much broader than a *theory*. Families are much more loosely related; they are more like a style of thinking and certain characteristic preoccupations than anything tight or systematic. This treatment reflects my own and my department's teaching practice, in which the traditional ethical theories and the usual forms of contention about them are introduced, at least in the usual elaborate ways, only in the *second* ethics course. For instructors who wish to do more theory in the first course, though, supplementation is natural and easy. There are dozens of theory-oriented collections to choose from. Theodore Denise *et al.*, *Great Traditions in Ethics* (Wadsworth, many editions), presents a number of traditional theorists, along with some less traditional contemporary and ancient figures, in their own words with helpful arrangement and commentary. Wanda Torres Gregory and Donna Giancola's *World Ethics* (Wadsworth, 2003) is another helpful and wider-ranging collection.

I try to pick two or three specific issues that we can explore from the point of view of each of these families of values: whatever issues are pressing or intriguing for me and the students at the time. We address them first as we take up chapter 4; then we revisit them with each ensuing chapter. Issues around race and racial prejudice work well for this purpose; animal issues are excellent and provocative. Often I also try the question of drugs.

The families of values are first introduced in chapter 4 and then elaborated in chapters 5–8. Sharon Hartline's essay, following these notes, suggests an exercise to invite students to really inhabit these distinctions—very useful when we come to the end of Part II. For my own favorite approach, see Exercise 8.4.

Utilitarianism has many intriguing ins and outs. Some of these are broached in the exercises, such as the infamous "Experience Machine" (if pleasure is really the sole good, then is it not equally good whether the causes are real or not?), and possibly radical implications for our treatment of other animals. Peter Singer's little book *Practical Ethics*, as my Notes indicate, is an excellent source on a variety of questions here: his views are much more subtle than the public debate over them might suggest. There are also well-known questions about rule–versus act–utilitarianism, and less well-known questions about utilitarianism's sometimes bizarre implications for population policy and the future. This is a good opportunity to give students a taste of how theory might work in ethics, for instructors who might want to head that way. The latter part of "Using Your Tools" #5 is relevant to the debate between utilitarian and justice perspectives (Rawls, especially), for instructors who may wish to use it in Part II.

CHAPTER 8: "THE ETHICS OF RELATIONSHIP"

One of the key questions in this chapter is what the true boundaries of the moral community are. It is worth remembering that for most of human history, not even all human beings were included in the moral community. As Leopold points out, for Odysseus the slave girls in his own household were just property, to be disposed of as he saw fit. Even in the Greek Golden Age, the city-states enslaved captured soldiers from other Greek cities and considered everyone else barbarians without any moral standing at all. The European conquerors of the Americas saw the native people as animals, sexual objects, circus attractions, slaves, and finally just impediments—certainly not as fellow human beings. Only slowly did the moral categories develop that enabled people to see all other humans as part of a moral community—and we are certainly not all the way there even yet. So are we entitled to be so sure that now we've finally gotten it right? What about other animals—some or all? How about artificial intelligence, for that matter? What about even mountains and rivers, or the encompassing Earth itself?

On the next few pages is a simulation exercise that is a provocative follow-up. To use it, I have students read the introduction and then divide themselves (or I assign them) into groups corresponding to the five possible responses outlined. Each group prepares and presents its case, after which we can try in discussion to reach some sort of consensus. My classes often end up roughly in the middle. When they're done, I ask them how their proposed Olamian ethic compares to the way we've treated our own Earth. Likely it will be much more ecologically minded and respectful. This is an interesting result already. It's a little as if (as one of my students put it) Olam offers us a "second chance"—a chance to do right what we did so wrong on Earth. But then: why couldn't we begin to do better, right here on the real Earth, and right now?

There is a further twist. Olam actually *is* Earth! ("Olam," is Hebrew for "world.") Every animal on or feature of Olam is actually an animal on or feature of Earth (whales, octopi, chimps, bacteria, "Gaia" herself). Sometimes when we do this exercise I play whale songs in the background—they sound truly alien indeed—so at this point in the discussion I reveal what they really are. Even the abruptness of the human species's arrival on Olam is mirrored, more or less, by our very short tenure on Earth.

Now we ask: what does it mean that the class has settled on an ethic for Olam that is so radically out of joint with the kind of ethic we have lived by on our own planet, which actually *is* Olam except for a few details? Does the question of our relation to Earth now seem a little different? How?

OLAM, 2274 CE

Imagine you are the crew of a starship, crash-landed on a planet called Olam. You have no way to leave for a *long* time. You quickly discover that most of Olam is quite temperate, and there are many suitable places for human habitation or other use (mining, agriculture, etc.), though of course all of them are currently occupied by Olamian ecosystems and species.

Olam has an enormous number of species. The exact number or even its order of magnitude cannot be guessed even by your best scientists. Tiny single-celled beings make up the bulk of its inhabitants, as measured by biomass. These beings live just about everywhere, from high in the atmosphere to the intestines of some of the animals to deep in some rocks. Next most common are the beetlelike species, of which there are several million different species at least. Other species range from the microscopic (1 Millimeter or less, like the single-celled beings just mentioned) through the enormous (there are several huge four-legged land species, up to 3 meters high and 7 meters long, and sea creatures up to 30 meters long).

There are intelligent species on Olam too. Among them are sea organisms of different sorts, like a tenacled blobby creature with complex feelings (it changes colors with different emotions) and a seemingly high capacity for problem solving. Some of our scientists have established contact with several species of large finned sea creatures with brains up to six times the size of human brains. They produce complex sound patterns, and it appears that some of these "songs" (100 million "bytes" in length—about like *The Odyessy*—sung in half an hour) are transmitted all the way around the planet through the oceans. Your scientists have held "jam sessions" with these animals using electric guitars and microphones lowered into the Olamian oceans. However, you have not been able to master their language, nor they yours—if indeed there *is* any way you might translate their "songs" at all.

There are two- and four-legged social species that show advanced social behaviors (fidelity, care, complex interaction patterns). Some of your crew members, perhaps out of homesickness, have adopted them as pets. (Actually, many of your survey crews have adopted Olamian "pets," everything from some flying and swimming creatures to large predators to snaky reptile-like tubular creatures. It all seems to work out quite well.) There are some vaguely humanoid animals that have a rudimentary language and also very tight social groupings. These creatures seem to be too disturbingly similar to humans to be made into pets, or perhaps they wouldn't tolerate it, but they have been fairly friendly and are certainly smart.

There are also vast communities of smaller organisms, sometimes containing millions of individual members, which appear to work together as a single unit. Indeed your scientists disagree about which is the real "organism":

the individual insectlike creatures or their whole "hives." At any rate, it appears that on Olam intelligence can exist on several levels at once. Some scientists even speculate that *all* life on Olam works together as a single unit, maintaining the optimal atmospheric and other conditions for life itself.

Again, this is only a small sampling of Olamian species. Some of these species consume each other for food. Many other species eat the plants, trees, or even the rocks. Humans could survive and thrive on a diet of either Olamian plants, animals, or both. Certain Olamian animals could also live on humans.

As you take stock of your situation, ask yourselves how you should relate to Olam. Are there moral limits to what you should do here? Should you take into account only your own good, or do the goods of some of Olam's species or ecosystems, or perhaps the planet itself also have a claim on you? As you continue to talk, suppose you find yourselves divided into five basic views:

A: Might makes right. We should take and use anything and everything on Olam. No moral considerations apply. Tough luck to the other species; lucky for us they're here to use. God probably planned it this way from the start so they'd all be here when we crash-landed.

B: Only we humans count morally—morality only came to Olam with us, as it were—but we need to take a little care not to ruin the planet for ourselves and our children. So we need to keep our consumption and exploitation somewhat within bounds, but of course only where necessary to serve our own future happiness. It also wouldn't hurt to try to understand Olam a little better. If it's anything like Earth, it's an incredibly complex place with a lot of hidden surprises.

C: We do need to take some care for Olam and its species in their own right. Maybe we're the most important species here but the other species have some valid claims too. They are ancient, beautiful, mysterious: this planet is bigger than us, even though—now that we're here—we're at the moral center.

D: We are only one species among all the others. Rightly understood, all species are at their own "centers." Nothing special about us—or rather, something special about *all*. Thus, we should seek to become part of Olam's larger community of life. We should seek to establish only limited colonies, and only where we will cause the least harm. We should also try harder to make contact with the intelligent life-forms on Olam.

E: We have no right to be here at all. We are alien invaders in a world that is complete without us and does not want us. We should write a statement explaining what we are doing, in case anyone ever finds the wreckage of our starship, and then commit mass suicide (of course in an ecologically responsible way).

Question: Which view strikes you as the most reasonable? Why? How would you defend your view against the others?

CHAPTER 9: "CRITICAL THINKING"

The themes of this chapter are familiar to most teaching philosophers, though not so often considered in ethics courses. There is time only to touch on a few main points: chiefly, that taking some care to identify and seek out the relevant facts is a key to intelligent ethical thinking. A handout of sample ethical arguments, drawn from the newspaper or widely available critical-thinking texts, is useful to analyze inferences. Any of the exercises can easily take up a whole class period: sometimes I allow several days for this practice. If students work in groups, some of this work can be initiated in the first session, carried on in between, and presented to start off the next.

CHAPTER 10: "JUDGING LIKE CASES ALIKE"

Most ethical philosophers agree that we must "judge like cases alike," but this requirement cashes out in different ways. For many contemporary philosophers, it means arriving at universal principles that can be tested by application and defended against or adapted in the face of possible counter-examples (allegedly "like cases" where the proposed principle seems to yield the wrong result). This Sidgwickian approach still so dominates ethics in England and America that many philosophers simply identify it with moral reasoning as such.

Lately there has been criticism, most markedly from philosophers who want to recover a case-based approach, which starts with those cases about which there are clear and accepted conclusions and then explores their analogies—similarities or differences—with confusing or contested cases. On this way of thinking, universal principles seldom come up or get us very far. This is "casuistry," a far older approach, long a strength of Catholic moral theology, with Jewish and Islamic parallels too. For a fascinating history of casuistry, see Albert Jonsen and Stephen Toulmin's *The Abuse of Casuistry: A History of Moral Reasoning* (University of California Press, 1988). For an impressive and accessible example of casuistry in practice, see Hugo Adam Bedau's *Making Mortal Choices: Three Exercises in Moral Casuistry* (Oxford, 1997). In this chapter I have tried to present the requirement to "judge like cases alike" in a way that is compatible with both standard and casuistical approaches.

Physically playing something like "moral musical chairs" is a revealing and fun exercise. I try to create scenarios in which students actually, visibly, switch roles (that is, move between chairs), or set it up in a Rawlsian way, as suggested in "Using Your Tools" #5, so that they don't know until the dust settles which role they will actually occupy.

In the reading, Colin McGinn asks us to imagine a species of vampire doing to us essentially what we do to other animals we use for food. You could elaborate this into a sort of simulation. Suppose that some species of alien has taken over the Earth and are preparing to factory-farm humans for meat and use us to test drugs and other products. Could we—and how could we—persuade them to stop? Just such a scenario has been the premise of science-fiction movies from time to time: for example, "Z," a TV miniseries from the 1980s. In all of the science-fiction versions of which I am aware, though, the aliens lose in the end, usually through some fluke, as in "War of the Worlds," the original of this theme, where they fall victim to the common cold. Beware of the Hollywood cliché that humans will somehow win out in the end—and of the Wild West version in which we finally just fight them off. No: for us only moral arguments will do.

Suppose that the human race has one last appeal before the aliens' plan is put into effect. As it turns out, by some unexpected but strangely appropriate twist of fate, *this class* must convince them to stop. We are the defense team for the whole human race. Teams of students should prepare arguments that can be presented to the aliens (also role-played by students from the class) in a grand hearing. This exercise works especially well if animals also show up. (Perhaps as a surprise, a group or two can prepare outside the classroom and just appear, in costume perhaps, on Judgment Day.) The animals need not be anti-human—though you can understand why they might be—but they should make sure that humans judge like cases alike. If the humans really want the aliens to take human suffering seriously as a moral counterargument to their plan, for example, humans obviously need to clean up their own act as well. Or is there some way to show that humans are distinct from the other animals in ways that make them more akin to the aliens—so that, maybe, the aliens really should eat animals too, or instead?

CHAPTER 11: "DIALOGUE"

We practice identifying loaded language in various statements, perhaps first in statements students disagree with, and then in more congenial statements, including their own (I videotape some discussions on controversial topics for this and other purposes). Most textbooks in informal logic cover "loaded language" and offer exercises to practice identifying and avoiding it. The habit of analyzing ethical arguments on their merits and putting them fairly, even if we don't agree with them, comes as a shock to many students, but for precisely that reason it is crucial.

Then we work to extend the same kind of care to dialogue. I try to use difficult and real dialogues as starting points for discussion or reenactment. One example of an intense, often angry or despairing, but also (in the end) constructive dialogue on an enormously difficult problem—race relations—is Lee Mun Wah's film "The Color of Fear" (Stir Fry Productions, www.stirfryseminars.com). The topic is a useful one to raise with students anyway, but the film also appeals as a model of dialogue under the most trying conditions.

Early on in my class I make it an assignment for every student to learn every other student's name (me too, obviously). Sharon Hartline offers a concrete way to do this in her essay to follow. My colleague John Sullivan asks his students to bow to one another, after a long look right into their eyes, all in silence. These practices sometimes subtly or dramatically change how we then relate. This is ethics too!

The box at the end of this chapter speaks about "silencing." I ask students to recall some occasions in their own experience when dialogue failed. Consider why it failed, I ask. Recall the various kinds of nonparticipation, resistance, advantage, and disadvantage outlined in that box. Were any of these factors at play? What could have been done about them? What could be done about them next time? If you're very brave, consider your own class or group in this regard. Who typically speaks and who doesn't? Why? Consider having a day when only certain people can speak: only people who have not spoken before; or only women (say, on the subject of abortion); or only those who admit to being confused about the whole topic; or...? What changes? Or try a "talking stick." Again: what changes?

In Exercise 11.2, students are often tempted to simply rewrite the disagreements in a way that preserves the disagreement but merely makes it "nice." My students, at least, are too easily satisfied if tensions are kept submerged or politely sidestepped. But it's not enough if people just don't insult each other any more. No: they need to confront those tensions, but in a constructive way. I also ask students to be especially alert to missed opportunities in these little exchanges: to questions that could be taken as real questions, for example, and not just as mere rhetorical battering rams (even if that's how they were intended). I try to highlight any movement toward creative thinking. For more dialogues to work on, I sometimes videotape some talk shows on current issues and pick some excerpts short enough to view a number of times and then rework.

CHAPTER 12: "WHEN VALUES CLASH"

In presenting ethical theories in Part II, I try to leave space for many nontheoretical approaches to conflicts of values as well. Nothing there is meant to suggest that every moral value must have a family or that thinking through issues from the point of view of family-associated theories is the only way we can think.

Integrative methods will be fairly unfamiliar to many moralists and philosophers, at least in the context of ethical debates. They're quite familiar, though, in our everyday lives. I used to feel some temptation to spend some class time justifying them. I don't anymore, and I don't recommend it. The justifications were more for myself, I finally concluded—or colleagues I imagined looking over my shoulder. Few students have this kind of resistance. Indeed it's the other way around. They resist *theory*.

Since the culture does not support them, though, at least in ethics, integrative skills may be hard to put into practice. Thus I always spend some good time on the exercises, 12.3 especially. Though this exercise sounds easy, in my experience it is very hard for most students to pull off, even when it is assigned in advance, and even after we've practiced with 12.2. Typically students end up, despite the instructions, describing moral debates in an "I think…" / "They think…" kind of way. It takes some work to get to "We think…."

Note that many of these strategies are useful on the practical level even if you wholeheartedly subscribe to a theoretical approach. A fuller toolbox of conflict-resolution skills is still helpful. Fisher and Ury, for example, make no claims about the disutility of theory: they only elaborate another and very powerful—but often overlooked—set of tools in addition.

On the next page is a survey on abortion attitudes used by the Common Ground Network for Life and Choice. I have the class fill it out before I assign this chapter, since (I hope) reading this chapter might affect how they answer it. I use an op-scan type answer sheet (no names) so that the results can be automatically tabulated and graphed.

To tabulate the results, I divide the answer sheets into three groups—Pro-Life, Pro-Choice, and Uncertain (using Question 26)—and then calculate the average answer for each question for each group.

Now the class can compare the averages (it helps to have them displayed graphically and juxtaposed with each other). We take it that differences of 1.0 or less between the averages are not significant differences. Differences of more than 1.0 show some serious divergence. How many of the twenty-five questions actually show a significant difference between Pro-Life and Pro-Choice groups?

Network organizers find that there is generally much less difference than we are led to believe—and that's among *activists* on the issue. Using this survey over a number of years, I have seldom had a class differ significantly on more than five or six questions, usually the same ones. And it is not merely that our agreements are more numerous than our disagreements. We can also use those agreements as starting points for "common ground" problem-solving: that is, for integrating values. We can look at the questions on which we agree. Number 3, perhaps: that reducing the number of abortions is a worthwhile goal? Or: Number 2? What would that suggest? Number 7? Then start working on alternatives! Number 8? Once again we have an agenda—quite likely a shared agenda.

Network organizers sometimes use this survey to open their dialogue sessions and ask people to answer it twice: once for themselves, and once giving the answers they think the "other side" would give. It emerges that both sides think the other side is much more extreme than they really are. Once again it's a useful basis for reframing the problem in the way proposed in this chapter. This usually leads to quite a bit of surprise and discussion too.

ABORTION ATTITUDES: SURVEY

Please answer each of the following questions on a scale of 1–5, where 1 means strongly agree and 5 means strongly disagree.

1. Economic constraints make it very difficult for some women to carry their pregnancies to term or to imagine being able to raise their children.
2. Adoption can be a positive choice for structuring family life.
3. Reducing the number of abortions is a worthwhile goal.
4. Abortion is an appropriate method of birth control.
5. To preserve their independence and freedom women sometimes need to have abortions.
6. There are acceptable alternatives to abortion currently available.
7. Alternatives to abortion should be encouraged.
8. In order to reduce the number of abortions, it is important to improve the economic status of women.
9. It is inevitable that some of society's problems can only be solved by using violent means.
10. Recreational sex without relational commitment is acceptable.
11. Women and men are equal in rights, value, and human dignity.
12. Motherhood is one desirable full-time career for women.
13. The future of children ought to be a major concern of U.S. public and private policy.
14. Women and men are equally capable and both should be encouraged to take part in public decision-making roles.
15. Spirituality is an important dimension of being human.
16. Abortion is an acceptable option for terminating a pregnancy.
17. The natural order of things dictates that males are the dominant gender in societal structures.
18. Belonging to an organized religious group is an important aspect of full human development.
19. In most circumstances a collaborative decision-making process is preferable to having one clearly designated authority figure.
20. We cannot always live up to our ideals, because the world of everyday circumstances makes this impossible.
21. Fidelity to one sexual partner is preferable to multiple sexual relationships.
22. Abortion is a violent procedure for terminating a pregnancy.
23. I feel certain about when human life begins.
24. It is very difficult to establish a law or rule that can be applied universally and justly in all circumstances.
25. Marriage is the proper context for sexual intercourse.
26. Are you: 1 Pro-Life, 2 Pro-Choice, 3 Uncertain

CHAPTERS 13 AND 14: CREATIVE THINKING IN ETHICS

Creative thinking tools are less familiar to many ethical philosophers too, but I hope the text makes their usefulness clear. These tools certainly tend to be among the most engaging to students as well.

I begin by organizing into three- to five-person problem-solving teams. Each team's first challenge is to devise a team name or slogan ("Brainstorm-ers"; "We eat problems for breakfast"; etc.). This is fun, it builds group spirit, and it opens up the kind of mutual appreciation and whimsy helpful to cre-ative thinking generally. Then we move on to "novel function practice" and other warm-ups. The first exercises in both chapters (13.1 and 14.1) start on purpose with non-ethical problems. We might spend half a class or more on them before shifting to moral problems. Note that exactly the same tools apply in exactly the same way. Then we move into 13.2 and 14.2. A follow-up writing exercise is to ask students to come up on their own with a completely new idea on one of these or other ethical topics.

It can be a challenge to make sure the students actually use the tech-niques. Sometimes they can be only halfhearted and thus never get the full effect. When we discuss ideas together in the end, I require students not only to report their results but also report what method they used to get them—what was their specific random prompt, for example—and how it worked.

On the level of commentary, I want to add a bit more about my treatment of the Heinz dilemma in these chapters, as this goes to the very heart of how creativity relates to ethics as traditionally conceived. Ethical philosophers typically consider the Kohlberg dilemmas to be useful illustrations of the divergences and conflicts among major ethical theories, especially between utilitarian and deontological theories. And of course if that is your interest in the dilemmas, you can alter them in various ways to close off the possibility of other alternatives. I have even seen ethics textbooks in which students aren't considered to have understood an issue until they identify "the" dilemma that is supposed to lie at the root of it.

The problem, of course, is that this just begs the question: it makes ethical problems dilemmas by fiat. It simply *builds in* the assumption that dilemmas are, after all, what we typically face. But are they? How can we know, with-out creatively seeking alternatives? This requires different attitudes from the start, as I have tried to show; and I hope it is also evident from these chapters that many alleged dilemmas actually can be resolved or at least constructively reframed. The supposed dilemma between utilitarianism and deontological ethics itself has come in for some question, even theoretically; but even if these theories do conflict, one *could* construe their conflict as another prac-tical creative challenge—to so design social institutions that these different sets of values seldom or only harmlessly conflict in practice. That an entire approach to ethics should instead be built around the supposedly fundamen-tal conflict is not obviously the best response. Surely, at the very least, such an approach is not entitled to claim with no further ado that it alone constitutes "ethics" itself.

Professor David Schmidtz tells a striking story that makes a similar point about another standard case in "dilemma ethics," the so-called Trolley Problem:

> A trolley is rolling down a track on its way to killing five people. If you switch to another track on which there is only one person, you will save five and kill one.

Schmidtz writes:

> When I presented the Trolley case and asked audiences whether they would switch tracks, most would say, "There has to be another way!" On a trip to Kazakhstan, I presented the case to an audience of twenty-one professors from nine post-Soviet republics, and they said the same thing. I responded as I always did, saying, "Please, stay on topic. I'm trying to illustrate a point here. To see the point, you need to decide what to do when there is no other way." When I said this to my class of post-Soviet professors, though, they responded in a way no audience of mine ever had. They spoke briefly among themselves in Russian, then two of them quietly said (as others nodded, every one of them looking me straight in the eye), "Yes, we understand. We have heard this before. All our lives we were told the few must be sacrificed for the sake of many. We were told there is no other way. What we were told was a lie. There was always another way."
>
> They were right. The real world does not stipulate that there is no other way. We are not to sacrifice one person for the sake of another. If we find ourselves seemingly called upon to sacrifice the few for the sake of the many, *justice is about finding another way.* (David Schmidtz and Elizabeth Willott, editors, *Environmental Ethics: What Really Matters, What Really Works* [Oxford University Press, 2011], p. xxii. My emphasis–AW)

Certainly from a pragmatic point of view, but even from Schmidtz's more moralized perspective, the task in such cases is not to simply accept whatever situations the world supposedly throws up to us, as if they themselves did not already reflect debatable ideas about ethics and ethical problems, but to seriously question and rethink the nature and presuppositions of the supposed problems themselves. One central task of ethics may be to prevent certain kinds of problems from even coming up in the first place. The challenge here to "ethics as usual" is quite deep.

Sometimes my students try to cook up dilemmas that really do allow no other options. That's a useful discussion too, I guess, but for the most part it is worth trying to set up the dynamics in the opposite direction. See if they can cook up situations that *look* like complete traps but really have dramatic new options. I offer some exercises to this effect in my book *Creative Problem-Solving in Ethics*, chapter 3.

CHAPTER 15: "MORAL VISION"

Spend good time on all the exercises. They are not easy, but they are also usually very welcome, changing the key from so much moral debate and discussion now. Note that "Using Your Tools" #7, on reframing bioethical issues, could also profitably be put off until after chapter 15, so that moral vision can be called upon too. What would the *ideal* health care system look like? How often do we ask questions like that? How far might a whole, shareable vision go?

CHAPTER 16: "RESPONSE-ABILITY"

Students all know about sexual "responsibility": it means using contraception and protecting themselves from STDs, right? The more dramatic themes in this chapter are apt to get them thinking: the possibility of choosing not to have sex at all, ever (Clark's position); the possibility that gender itself is significantly a social construction (Queen's suggestion); the sharp but intriguing contrast between the two (Queen calls herself "sex-positive": does this mean that Clark is "sex-negative"?). Practitioners of celibacy make intriguing class speakers (hint: try for people close to your students' age); or anyway advocates of abstinence (hint: try to look at it as a spiritual issue but not one of religious dogma—it's too easy to dismiss if seen as only a sectarian or public-health argument).

On the food question, I often try bring in some vegetarian food (which is really just plain old food, of course, without meat, but it helps to bring in less familiar and "alternative" foods: hummus, tofu, etc.). We may cook right in class. Sometimes my university's health program sponsors a vegetarian cafeteria in conjunction with health classes—we take a field trip. Or we go to the local farmers' market. Students might look into fasting—food abstinence, as it were. (And by the way, is there any connection between the food and the sex topics? Back to "Using Your Tools" #1...).

CHAPTERS 17 AND 18: CLOSING CHALLENGES

The chief aim of chapter 17 is inspiration, advice, and empowerment. Students may wish to follow up some of the references, looking at the biographies or websites of people and communities and organizations making a difference—especially in unexpected ways, and ideally close to home. Meanwhile I try to bring in some local change-makers as speakers.

To go all the way, I invite my class in turn to collectively undertake some kind of change project of their own—that is the challenge of "Using Your Tools" #9. They will need all their tools from this book. They also need time to frame their project and put it into action, which creates a bit of a bind at the beginning of the class: it's as if you need to do everything at once. As I have mentioned, I start with only a skeleton of the book—chapters 1, 2, 4, 9,

13, 14, 15, and 17—to help students frame and launch their own projects. We work through the rest as the projects get underway. Larger classes sometimes launch several projects, ideally closely related, side by side.

If not something quite so ambitious, I have found it immensely rewarding to at least set up class service projects, starting as soon as we can in the term. We go into the local shelters for the homeless, for example—meeting as a class in the shelters sometimes, and always talking and working with the guests, including major joint projects, like rebuilding a whole shelter's bed-frames—and my students consistently report that that experience is among the most significant aspects of the course for them. Some say it changes their lives. This kind of service is not hard to arrange—quite the contrary, most service organizations are dying for help, are more than happy to help coordinate a hefty group of volunteers, and often take public education to be part of their mission.

I've tried to highlight some pitfalls in this, though: chiefly that service can easily become a sort of unilateral do-goodism. It can be too easy to put into familiar categories and therefore never becomes as unsettling and reciprocal as it can be at its best. Lately, therefore, I have been pushing my classes into less unilateral situations, such as studying jointly (versus tutoring) with students at disadvantaged schools. If we do go into shelters or other more familiar helping situations, I try also to arrange to have the students go individually or in very small groups. Without someone familiar to fall back upon, they attend better and more readily take the steps to connect with people very different from themselves. And of course, sometimes our students themselves are from the shelters, or know that kind of life all too well. I have to strive to be alert to the range of experiences right among my students.

This work, I find, is always a bit of a whirlwind ride, but it is also always immensely invigorating, and the projects become great learning experiences for me as well as the students. And of course the students end up with the most vital message of all: that they can change the world! Best of luck to you and to them, and once again, I would love to hear of the work that you and they undertake.

APPENDIX 2

Experiential Teaching in Ethics

SHARON HARTLINE

On my office door at Radford University hangs a poster that I received from an art major last year. This poster was his response to an assignment that involves advertising an ethics class to the students at our university. I asked students, "How do you sell ethics?" In this poster, the student drew two pundits who are literally "taking sides." Their faces are strained because they are yelling at each other across the paper. Between them appears the face of a young man. His chin is on his fist, the corners of his mouth are drawn down, and he looks out at the audience with a bored expression on his face. The caption reads, "Ethics: Where do you stand?"

What I love about this poster is that it is NOT an advertisement for ethics. It does not sell ethics, but rather it is a striking representation about what is wrong with ethics. It addresses the way in which ethical issues are often discussed in our society. It visually represents how ethics boils down to what Weston calls "polarized debates" where pundits line up on opposite sides of a page about abortion or stem-cell research and attempt to outdo their opponent or rehash the same debate we heard about last year. Quite frankly, it can get tedious and boring.

Similar limitations continue in many ethics classrooms. Many university courses focus on the Western philosophical tradition and show how these theories can be applied to ethical issues. Often, the rights theorists position themselves on one side of the page and the virtue theorists line up on the other; the Kantians locate themselves on the right side of the page and utilitarians stand on the left.

Is it important to cover different theoretical frameworks in class? I think so. Theories help us understand the social discourse about ethical issues and provide students with the tools to organize and evaluate personal and social issues. What becomes problematic is when this approach serves as the main (or only!) focus of the classroom. This focus can conceal the fact that there may be other ways to consider ethical issues that do not result in polarization.

Another problem lies in the methods that are used to teach in this fashion. If ethics is construed as debate, then how do teachers transmit knowledge and teach other constructive skills? Some of my students have studied ethics in high school or at community colleges before they enroll in my class. When I ask them about how those classes were taught, they tell me that their teachers lectured. Sometimes, teachers set up debates—the "pros" on one side of the room and the "cons" on the other. Some teachers required students to pick a position with which they disagreed and then argue for that viewpoint.

There is a lot to be said for these techniques. Lecturing is a straightforward method of transferring information to students. Sometimes, it may even be necessary! Who really understands Kant's ethical philosophy when they read the original text for the first time? It's very useful to know how to think critically and be able to debate ideas. But is that it? Is this the best we can do? Are there other topics that are required for people to become ethically competent? Do we need other teaching methods? Can we improve our ethics classrooms? I think we can.

THE ACTIVE CLASSROOM: CONTENT AND METHOD

Weston's text makes it very clear that we can alter the content of ethics classes. We can incorporate material that attempts to move beyond the polarization that characterizes so many ethical debates and, for example, discuss how we can change ethical problems themselves. The focus is on "us" because ethical issues seldom arise in isolation from other people, and therefore, one person can seldom solve such issues by herself. Weston's text incorporates creative thinking, problem shifting, prevention, and opportunism in order to help students, individually and collectively, think and act beyond polarization.

Weston's text not only suggests changes to the content of ethics classes, but also implies a radical departure from traditional teaching methods used in ethics classrooms. His work shifts our attention to the kinds of skills one needs to enact ethics when they leave the classroom. No longer is ethical competency about retaining knowledge and acquiring rhetorical skills, but now morally mature people must actually know how to have fruitful discussion with people who hold differing viewpoints, how to resolve real conflicts and issues they will face in the workplace and community, how to uncover and critique the assumptions that inform social institutions, and how to unleash their creativity when they really need it.

Suddenly the classroom looks a lot different. Students practice skills and discover their capabilities as well as make mistakes. Teachers employ student-centered learning techniques like experiential learning techniques. These changes don't only come from teachers, for students are also responsible for the operations of the classroom. Students can request activities or develop their own to use for presentation materials.

So how does one go about developing techniques that give students (and teachers!) the opportunity to learn by practicing together and learning through group activities in the classroom? Now you may be thinking, "Oh no! She's going to talk about group work." Teachers may also be thinking, "I've tried group work, but students don't really do that much with it." Students may also be thinking "It's such a waste of time! And I always end up doing the work for everyone else in the group." Both of these outcomes can occur when group activities are used in the classroom. But there are also ways to structure group work, as well as quite different kinds of engaged classrooms, that sustain and even intensify everyone's focus on the real content.

THE EXPERIENTIAL LEARNING CYCLE: A TOOL FOR TEACHERS AND STUDENT PRESENTERS

While lecturing is useful, not everyone learns best by sitting and listening to someone else speak. We are multidimensional beings who inhabit bodies, rely on senses, recall memories, and make associations that help us process information. We learn through discussions, through visual cues, and through physical activities and personal experiences. People learn in all sorts of ways.

So how can we address these various modes of learning and still teach the content of courses? I've used the experiential learning cycle (ELC) to help me incorporate a variety of activities into the classroom. The ELC outlines the learning process and presents a structure for setting up activities in the classroom so that the learning process can take place. It relies on the idea that in order to learn we have to have an experience and then reflect on it. There are different models of the ELC. I use a four-stage method, presented in David Kolb's *Experiential Learning* (Prentice Hall, 1984). This model allows me to focus on different cognitive processes that help clarify the concepts in my classes. But there are other models out there. See Kolb's *Experiential Learning Theory Bibliography 1971–2001* (McBer and Co., 2001). Find one that works for you.

As one would expect, the first stage of the ELC begins with the *experience or activity*. The trick is that the activities or experiences have to be carefully planned. Below I share with you a couple of the activities that I use. But you can use readings, labs, videos, games, puzzles, and meditation—just to name a few.

The second stage of the experiential learning cycle involves *reflection*. Here reflection usually means individual reflection upon the experience or activity. This is the stage where I hold individual students accountable for their learning by requiring them to write down their reflections about the material or relate their response to an activity. For part of their grade, students have to convince me that they REALLY participated in the exercise by at least sharing their reflections on the activity.

The third stage of the experiential learning process involves *generalization*, whereby participants are asked to abstract from their concrete experience. One can do this as an individual exercise, but I often do this in groups. I find that because students have written something down from the reflection phase, they are more likely to participate in the group discussion and contribute to the process of generalizing.

The fourth stage of the experiential learning process involves *transfer or application*. At this stage I try to begin with issues that students really care about and interest them. Then I may move on to other issues that I think are important for them to consider.

Here's what I've learned by using the ELC to plan my classes. If I am going to use an activity, the goal has to be clear and specific. I also have to make sure we apply what students learned during the activity and reflection, preferably to something they cared about or find interesting. This isn't easy. It takes time and effort. Sometimes, even I consider just lecturing—it's actually much easier. Yet, it doesn't meet all my goals in the classroom. Something else I've learned is that I have to require verbal and/or written feedback from the individual and groups. Inertia is a fact of human life; we all feel it sometime during our life. So I have to find ways to respond to it in the classroom. A student once said to me, "I couldn't fall asleep in here if I wanted to!" I took it as a compliment.

The last thing I learned was that I can use experiential learning IN my classroom. In many universities "experiential learning" is the label that covers activities that take place beyond the bounds of the classroom through programs like internships and service learning projects. But you don't have to leave the classroom to participate in experiential learning.

EXPERIENTIAL LEARNING IN THE CLASSROOM

So how does one put this cycle into practice? The best way for me to answer that question is to elaborate several exercises that I have developed while using this text. The first activity, the Ethics Advertisement, is fairly simple and relies mainly on facilitation skills and a few leading questions on the part of the presenter. The second activity, the Moral Values Exercise, is a rather complex exercise. You need to bring different materials with you, and there are many parts to the exercise.

ETHICS ADVERTISEMENT

The first exercise is called the Ethics Advertisement. This is a wonderful exercise to do the first week of class. Also, with a few minor changes this exercise can be used in any class. I use it when I teach other philosophy courses as well.

Experience/Activity

At the end of a class, I give students a sheet of newsprint and tell them that they have to advertise the class to the students at our university. They can use any medium—collage, drawing, painting, etc....I suggest that in order to do this exercise they have to figure out two things. First, they have to answer the question, "What is ethics?" Second, they have to figure out how to sell it! "How do you sell ethics?"

When they arrive for the next class, I ask them to hang their posters at eye-level on the walls and remind them to put their names on the front. I then ask students to participate in an "art show." I tell them that one can view art in two different ways. One can view art like the person who trots through a museum, quickly glancing from side to side with a puzzled expression on his or her face. Or one can view art like a student who has the audio-tour in hand, holds a pencil and pad in the other, and misses a lunch date because she or he is engrossed in the artwork. I ask them to approximate the latter person's mode of viewing. I ask them to take notes on topics, verbs, names, and other ideas that they learn from the posters.

Reflection

When they are finished viewing, I ask them to get into groups. Once in groups, the students pick a scribe to take notes on the information they gleaned about topics, verbs, and names as well as their individual reflections about the posters. (I collect the "scribes' report" at the end of class.) I ask them to come together as a class, and we put the groups' ideas up on the board.

Generalization

After we've listed their responses on the scribes' report, I ask them "What is ethics?" At this point, someone inevitably states a standard definition of ethics—the study of moral standards/principles or the study of the standards or principles of moral conduct. (A few posters always include such a definition.) Then we explore that definition. What is a standard? What is a principle? What terms on the board refer to standards? What does one do with standards? If we move beyond that definition, what else can we say about ethics generally? Here are some of the ideas we often discuss:

1. Why study ethics? How does this "study" of ethics help us in our day-to-day lives? Ethics allows us to explore moral problems that we have to deal with on a daily basis. Here I talk about the distinction between ethical theory

and applied ethics. Theory can help us make sense of complicated issues like the issues presented on the posters.

2. People often point out that this definition is abstract. The real goal of ethics is to help us live our lives well. We usually talk about happiness at this point. Also, we discuss the ways we are already always in relationships that presuppose ethics—from the respect we grant a waiter to the trust we have of the drivers on the other side of the road. Someone inevitably brings up the fact that if we didn't have this trust we would never leave our homes! I read Judith Boss's quote, "Ethics is like air; it is pretty much invisible. In fact, for many centuries, people did not realize that such a substance as air even existed. So too we often fail to recognize the existence of ethics or morality until someone fails to heed it." [See *Ethics for Life: An Interdisciplinary and Multicultural Introduction* (Mayfield Publishing, 1998).]

3. "There are only two answers to ethical issues." I use this comment and talk about the polarization of ethical issues presented as decisions about right and wrong, pro and con, good and bad, or appropriate and inappropriate. We talk about whether this is the only way to discuss ethical issues. Sometimes we will get into discussions of compromise or prevention as other viable approaches. I ask the students if these problems can be viewed as opportunities for learning or development. Many are skeptical or reject the idea that one can approach polarized issues in any other way.

Transfer/Application

Next we take some of the ideas we discussed and apply them to topics that are presented on the posters—abortion, death penalty, premarital sex, underage drinking, and discrimination, among others. We discuss how standards are used to make moral judgments about these topics. I guide the discussion in order to bring out the point that people's convictions about standards are what create polarization with respect to the issues at hand. I also suggest that ethics isn't just about those polarized issues. I ask them for ethical issues that don't have to do with these polarized topics. They talk about relationships with partners, raising children, and even caring for pets. We talk about what it means to live one's life well and what it means to be a good person. Students often say that moral standards aren't enough. Emotions and kindness count. At this point, I talk about the Good Life and the unit on Greek philosophy, and we are ready to move into a closer study of ethics.

THE MORAL VALUES EXERCISE

I specifically call the Moral Values Exercise an "exercise." I used to call it a game, but eyes rolled when I said that. So now it is an "exercise." Remember delivery is important in gaining the attention of your audience.

Experience/Activity

When students enter the room, I put a card on each person's back with a specific moral value printed on it (e.g., responsibility, right to life, well-being, etc.). I also hand them a 3 × 5 index card. When everyone is assembled, I tell them that we'll be doing an exercise called the Moral Values Exercise, and that during the exercise they will receive clues regarding their moral value. I tell them that by the end of class each student will have to guess what moral value is on his or her back and what kind of value it is.

Then we review the operating definition of a moral value (that which gives voice to our needs and legitimate expectations that we have of ourselves and others) and we revisit the families of values and their definitions (the boxes in chapter 6 and at the head of each chapter in the rest of Part II). Note that the structure of this exercise is flexible. You can highlight different categories of values. For example, you may wish to highlight the values of justice as a separate category.

Next, I describe the rules of the exercise. Here are the rules:

1. Find a partner.
2. Each person looks at the card on his or her partner's back and gives the other person clues regarding their moral value. "Good clues" tell what needs or legitimate expectations that moral value gives voice to. "Good clues" should not state the moral value or what kind of value it is.
3. Write down the clues on the 3 × 5 card. You will need them later.
4. When you are cued, find a new partner and repeat the process.

I have students do three or four rounds with different partners. I give each pair about one to two minutes to give each other a clue. I check in with them and if many of them still need a clue, we do one or two more rounds. At this point, students sometimes ask me what they should do if they know what their value is. I ask them to continue to collect clues.

Reflection

Next I ask students to work by themselves and fill out a worksheet with some reflection questions. I ask them to do four things: write down their three best clues, guess what their moral value is, tell what family (kind) of moral value it is, and explain what they learned about their individual moral value through this exercise. On the walls around the classroom I put up cards with the titles of the families of moral values written on them. After students have completed the worksheet, I ask each student to go to the area by the card that indicates the type of moral value on his or her back. After groups form around each of these cards, I have each group stand up and show their backs

to the class. Many students are in the correct group. If a student has not identified their type of moral value correctly, I ask a student to direct them to the
correct family and then explain why that value belongs to that family. This is
one way to incorporate "student teaching" into the exercise.

Generalization

This stage, in which students are asked to abstract from their concrete experience, relies heavily on the facilitation skills of the teacher. When I facilitate
during this stage, I start with getting them to verbalize their responses to the
last question on the handout—what did you learn about your moral value?
Then through questions and discussion, I get them to generalize further.
Here are some examples of their statements and ideas for facilitation of the
subsequent discussion.

> a. *"Our moral values were in the rights category, and they were easy ones."*
> *"We use this language all the time."*

[Facilitation questions: is that the case in all cultures? Are there other values
that take precedence in our culture?]

> b. *"Our parents use virtue language, and we resist it!"*

[Facilitation questions and responses: do certain groups rely on certain kinds
of language and use certain types of values? We discuss which people tend
to use which kinds of values. For example, economists/teens often discuss
goods; religious leaders/parents often address virtues; lawyers/disenfran-
chised groups often speak of rights.]

> c. *"Everyone gave me the same clue."* *"People have very different expecta-
> tions regarding this moral value."*

[Facilitation questions or responses: why do we agree (or disagree) on the
meaning of this value? Is this a group phenomenon, e.g., parents, children,
professionals? Is this true of our culture? Is it true of other cultures?]

> d. *"I didn't know what I was because people don't know what this value
> means."*

This comment was actually made about nonmaleficence in a nursing class.

[Facilitation questions or responses: what does the principle of no harm
mean, and will it mean the same thing to your clients/patients? Will you
have to explain your intentions as you hurt them? I remind them that all
health care professionals cause pain to their patients sometime. In addition,

we discuss the difference between knowing terminology and understanding an ethical principle.]

I also used this comment as a "teachable moment" about accountability. (Nonmaleficence was discussed in their reading the week before we did this exercise.) Students recognize that in our classroom if they aren't prepared, they let their classmates down. In addition, I use this as a bridge to the next stage because it brings us to the issue of recognizing and using principles. This is related to application, the final stage.

Transfer/Application

For this stage of the Moral Values Exercise, I use case studies or scenarios. When I use this with nursing students, I give them cases in medical or professional ethics. I ask students to identify the major moral values that define the case. I also ask them to explain what they would do if they were the professional in the case, and why they would choose that approach. Students get to practice identification, definition, and application of values to a specific situation that they care about. After all, they may find themselves in a similar situation one day.

Here is what I observe: most students are very good at identifying the moral values of the persons with whom they identify. But many have difficulty identifying moral values of people with whom they do not identify or about whom they have negative judgments. One of the major tasks that I have is getting them to be objective, that is, to see the perspectives of all parties involved in the situation. They also bring up concerns about the conflicts of the values that they see operating in case studies. These concerns propel us toward chapters 5–8 about different families of values, chapter 11 about ethical dialogue, and chapter 12 about how we can resolve conflicts among moral values.

These are, of course, only two examples of how one can use the ELC to develop a class that requires student preparation and participation and allows students to learn thinking and communication skills by using these skills. Remember that there are many types of materials already available to use. For example, you can show a short film, design meaningful questions for reflection and generalization, and find a text or scenario to which students can apply their conclusions. The possibilities are endless and the outcomes rewarding!

CREATING A TEMPORARY COMMUNITY

I want to leave you with a few suggestions for creating an active classroom in which experiential learning techniques can succeed. I have found that experiential learning exercises work best in classes that become *temporary communities.* Respect and beneficence are two main components of communities, for they create an atmosphere in which people feel valued and are willing to participate. When people respect each other, they take each other seriously. They listen to each other's ideas. In addition, beneficence motivates people to help each other so that they provide constructive criticism and nurture initial thoughts of their classmates. In turn, students facilitate discussion by tracking the implications of others' ideas. So how can we promote these values and activities in the classroom?

1. NAMES, NAMES, NAMES!

I find it quite ironic that in ethics classes where we discuss respect for individuals, a student can remain "The Woman in the Second Row, Third Seat" or "You there" for the entire semester! Teachers and students don't always know the names of other people in the classroom. Knowing these names fosters respect, assists with discussion, and helps to create the Active Classroom.

I often start my semester with a name game. I ask students to rise and get into a circle. I then give these directions. The first person, whoever begins the exercise, says his or her name. The second person says the first person's name and his or her own name. The third person states the first person's name, the second person's name, and his or her own name. The game continues until each person in the circle has had his or her turn. I always go last and say everyone's names. This game often requires that students ask for other students' help (some forget the names) and that students offer this help. At the very beginning of class, it sets up the kind of reciprocity that is required in communities and in the Active Classroom.

2. EVERYONE'S RESPONSIBLE

It's everyone's responsibility to create an Active Classroom. Traditionally, students are not responsible for how the class operates, except when they are required to make presentations. In the Active Classroom, everyone contributes to the pace, flow, and content of the class to some extent. One problem is overcoming inertia. Inertia is a fact of life with which we all struggle. We're all busy and we get tired. I try to find ways to make all the members of the class accountable for the class. I often require students to hand in individual or group writing to account for their reflections during the class period. In addition, I know my students' names, and they know it. I can call on them at any moment. Students don't always find that a comfortable position, but they tell me that it keeps them on their toes.

In order for students to be responsible and effect change in the classroom, they must be given the opportunity. Thus, I use a variety of feedback mechanisms. One is called the "minute card" that was suggested to me by

Bethany Bodo. It's no surprise that she is the director of Academic Assessment at Radford University! At the end of class I give students a slip of paper with the following items printed on it.

1. What concept do you feel is the most important one you learned regarding this topic?
2. What one concept is unclear to you?
3. What is one question you have about this topic that you would like to have answered?
4. Think of one real-world situation in which a concept from this topic is demonstrated.

I collect these papers, and I use them to review and to inquire about what we need to revisit and how we should do that. I use another feedback form on which I ask students to evaluate their performance and my performance. I ask them to give suggestions for changes and improvements of the course. I also ask them to explain how these changes will assist their learning process. This last item requires that they reflect on learning and how they learn. There are many ways to collect feedback, but all of them require students to take responsibility to some degree for their learning and how the class operates.

3. DIALOGUE!

Presenters need to remember that the attention span of a person can only be pushed so far. If you use lecture, break it up with shorter activities. I often begin with a summary of ideas and then have students break into groups and then finish the class with discussion and lecture. I also have students write questions down during class, and we work our way through the material. Inevitably, if I address a question in writing, verbal questions follow, and before you know it we're talking about the material. If all else fails I ask students to think of a concrete experience in their lives. People can usually talk about themselves and these experiences can be used to illuminate the material.

4. MAKE MISTAKES, PLEASE!

Very few people get anything "right" the first time. It takes time to experiment with and perfect new methods. If a teacher or presenter is comfortable making mistakes as he or she tries new techniques, it gives other people permission to express themselves and take risks. If you're not making any mistakes, you're not challenging yourself, and you're not learning.

Patricia Ryan Madson, founder of the Stanford Improvisors, discusses how she requires her acting students to make "at least one ego-crushing mistake per class to get used to the experience." In her chapter, "Make Mistakes, Please!" she describes the "Circus Bow."

> This is how circus clowns deal with a slip in their routines. Instead of shrinking and berating himself silently with "Oh, no, I really blew it!" the clown turns to the crowd on one side and takes a magnificent bow with his hands extended and his arms high in the air, proclaiming "Ta-dah!" as if he had just pulled off a master stunt. [See Madson's *Improv Wisdom: Don't Prepare, Just Show Up* (Bell Tower, 2005).]

I have started doing the Clown Bow in my classes when I stumble over words or get confused on a point. I find that it helps to create an atmosphere in which it is acceptable to make mistakes. This doesn't mean that one does not prepare or pay attention to details. This does mean that if an exercise does not go according to plan, it is all right to admit that and try another avenue. I find that this atmosphere helps students feel comfortable sharing their views.

CONCLUSION

I invite you to experiment with experiential learning techniques and wish you much success. If you would like to share or discuss an experiential exercise that you use in your ethics classes, I would enjoy hearing from you. Contact me at shartlin@radford.edu.

GUEST AUTHOR

Sharon E. Hartline is Professor in the Department of Philosophy and Religious Studies at Radford University, where she has also chaired the Peace Studies program. Her research interests include ethics, professional ethics, and Buddhism. She works extensively with health and human service programs at Radford University and serves on ethics committees in the New River Valley area in Virginia. She is actively working to promote responsible development in Blacksburg, Virginia, where she currently lives.

INDEX